Interpreting
Canada's Past

Fifth Edition

Interpreting Canada's Past

A Post-Confederation Reader

EDITED BY

Michel Ducharme

Damien-Claude Bélanger

J.M. Bumsted

OXFORD

UNIVERSITY PRESS

OXFORD

UNIVERSITY PRESS

Oxford University Press is a department of the University of Oxford.
It furthers the University's objective of excellence in research, scholarship,
and education by publishing worldwide. Oxford is a registered trade mark of
Oxford University Press in the UK and in certain other countries.

Published in Canada by
Oxford University Press
8 Sampson Mews, Suite 204,
Don Mills, Ontario M3C 0H5 Canada

www.oupcanada.com

Library and Archives Canada Cataloguing in Publication

Interpreting Canada's past : a post-confederation reader / edited by
Michel Ducharme, Damien-Claude Bélanger, and J.M. Bumsted. -- Fifth edition.

Includes bibliographical references and index.
ISBN 978-0-19-902026-3 (paperback)

1. Canada--History. 2. Canada--History--Sources. I. Ducharme,
Michel, 1975-, editor II. Bélanger, Damien-Claude, 1976-, editor
III. Bumsted, J. M., 1938-, editor

FC170.I57 2016   971   C2016-902882-8

Oxford University Press is committed to our environment.
This book is printed on Forest Stewardship Council® certified paper
and comes from responsible sources.

Printed and bound in the United States of America

1 2 3 4 — 20 19 18 17

Contents

Six ❧ Environmental History and the Canadian North   181

Seven ❧ Anti-Asian Hostility   214

Eight ❧ Dealing with Hunger and War   249

Nine ❧ The Rise of the Welfare State   283

Ten ❧ Cold War Canada   319

Eleven ❧ The Quiet Revolution   355

Twelve ❧ Immigration and Multiculturalism   393

Preface

As with the fourth edition of *Interpreting Canada's Past,* it remains our intention to provide students of Canadian history with a collection of primary and secondary sources, a collection that represents the material historians use daily. Paying attention to current scholarship is essential, and bearing in mind the not-so-current interpretations of a particular theme is likewise part of the historian's job. The privilege of setting aside the work of historians and encountering voices from the eras under examination is another perk not usually available to students in lecture courses. We wanted once again to give those using the reader an opportunity to see how our understanding of the past is built upon evidence, carefully sifted and handled, and how sometimes these bits of evidence can lead historians to offer conclusions that prompt still more questions.

This reader has been conceived not as a replacement but rather as a complement to lectures and textbook chapters. It focuses on specific issues that may or may not have been discussed at length in class. The topics covered in this edition are varied and demonstrate the breadth of questions, approaches, methodologies, and primary sources inspiring Canadian historians, though we have chosen to privilege social issues, as the general trends in Canadian political and economic history are likely to be covered in lectures or other textbooks.

As with the previous editions, the emphasis is again on interpretation. The primary documents have been chosen so that students will take those first steps toward generating the kind of questions that are useful even outside the discipline of history: What does this document mean? Why did its creator want to express the ideas it contains? How reliable is it? What does it tell us about change? The historical interpretation selections have been simplified in this edition, with the assumption that students can dig deeper into each article or excerpt, dealing less in terms of who-did-what-when, but discovering more in terms of connections with the primary sources and the overall theme of each section. On the basis of user comments and classroom experience, we have retained the more popular selections and added ones that are entirely new, while also altering our lists of topics.

We thank the staff at Oxford, along with Len Kuffert and Jack Bumsted, for their vision for the readers and commitment through the previous editions. We also wish to thank Sean Graham, Aaron Boyes, and Gisèle Dubeau for their assistance.

Michel Ducharme, University of British Columbia

Damien-Claude Bélanger, University of Ottawa

Introduction to Primary and Secondary Sources

The work of historians is to understand the past or, to be more precise, to understand the lives of people who lived in the past. Just like undergraduate students working on their essays, MA students working on their theses, or PhD students working on their dissertations, professional historians have to design manageable research projects. In order to do so, they first select a topic and then focus their attention on historical questions that have not already been answered. Once they have decided which questions deserve exploration, they start looking for information to answer them. The first challenge they face is that their objects of study (i.e., the past) does not exist anymore. While the past has shaped the present, the present is different from the past.

In order to make sense of the past, historians have to use whatever evidence or testimonies they can find. They call this evidence, produced by the societies they are studying, primary sources or documents. It is by finding primary sources, analyzing them, and comparing them that historians can answer their research questions; they can find out how people lived in the past, establish causal relationships between facts and events, and develop their own interpretations about past societies. Depending on the objects of their inquiries, historians use different kinds of primary sources. Written documents are the most commonly used. Some of these written documents have been created by public institutions such as governments and courts of justice. Others have been produced by individuals or groups of individuals for a public audience: for instance, political treatises, pamphlets, brochures, newspapers, and books such as novels, travel guides, or cookbooks. Other sources are private, created by individuals and private institutions and not intended for public consumption. Internal documents from specific institutions such as voluntary associations, religious institutions, and charitable organizations are among these sources. Personal correspondence, journals, and diaries are also private, even if some have been made public over time. While many of these primary sources can be consulted in their original format, some have been reproduced on microfilms, republished, or digitized. Depending of the nature of these sources, historians can access them in archives (public or private), in libraries, or online. Although most historians base their research on written documents, some use alternative primary sources such as artistic works (paintings, photographs, and cartoons, for instance) or even architecture and landscapes. Others focus on material culture such as old coins, clothing, and other artefacts. And last, historians can also use oral sources. These sources are especially useful to study societies with strong oral traditions such as Indigenous societies, or to think about more contemporary issues. What is important to remember is that all these sources are valid and valuable. The challenge for historians is to find the right sources to examine their own questions and to compare and confront those sources.

Regardless of the type of sources, historians need to analyze them carefully. They need to know exactly what these sources can and cannot tell them, as historians do not want to make unsubstantiated claims. In order to determine the limitations of their sources, historians must first question the documents themselves: What are the origins of these sources? Where are they coming from? Who created them? When were they created? Why were they created? Are they authentic? Once they have answered these questions, then historians can analyze their content: What do they say? What do they not say? What are their underlying assumptions? Lastly, historians can analyze these sources by putting them into dialogue, comparing them, and establishing how they relate to each other.

Once historians have collected all the primary sources they need (or that they can find), analyzed them, and compared them, then they can answer their questions and develop their own interpretations of the past. Their interpretations are embodied in what is known as secondary sources. These secondary sources, produced by historians, may take the form of monographs (books answering one question), book chapters, and journal articles, among other things. Historians use secondary sources for different reasons. They can use them to contextualize their topic, complement their own information, or situate their work within the overall historical production.

As readers will notice, we have included in this collection a wide variety of primary sources: from official documents to personal recollections, from transcription of speeches, interviews, and radio broadcasts to cookbooks, photographs, and political cartoons. All these sources include information that historians can use to understand the past. These sources have been paired to historical interpretations that offer an overview of the different questions asked by historians as well as the different approaches used to answer them. By reading these sources together, students will better understand the work of Canadian historians.

Chapter 1

Debating Confederation

READINGS

Primary Documents

Historical Interpretations

INTRODUCTION

Historians of Canada have devoted much attention to explaining how Canada's four original provinces were brought together. The partnership was not an equal one, nor was it a harmonious arrangement in the beginning, given the variety of backgrounds and interests represented (even then) among the new partners. Debate over how the new provinces were to co-operate continued after the deal was made. Some, like the wary Nova Scotians, who were the first to raise the possibility of leaving the federation, valued their roles as more autonomous members in a "family" of imperial outposts and were afraid of becoming "sub-species" within the larger Dominion. Their provincial Assembly debated the possibility of repealing the British North America Act and leaving Confederation—a threat that was not issued idly and did not go away for almost a generation. Despite Nova Scotians' discontent with their new status, the new federation could not pause to address such internal tensions. These tensions arose at least partly because Canada was a nation created by politicians and was not held together by one language, one religion, or a unifying experience like a successful revolution against colonial rule. Canada entered a phase of "adolescence" with the added pressure of growing up next to a boisterous and dynamic neighbour. Within its first decade, the young federation expanded, taking control of the vast North-West Territories, from which Manitoba was carved in 1870. British Columbia joined in 1871, and Prince Edward Island in 1873. The result answered the prayers of expansionists, who viewed these additions as Canada's destiny, and set off a wave of speculation as to what Canada would do with all this land. Our selections here reflect this contentious period, first with the Nova Scotia debate over nullifying the Confederation pact, and then with a hymn of praise to British Columbia. In the former case, Attorney General Wilkins speaks of the "rival and discordant interests" that Confederation cannot reconcile, while lauding the ingenuity and perfection of the British parliamentary system. In the latter, Lt.-Col. Coffin tells us that the metal mining potential of British Columbia is its greatest asset. Or is it coal? No, wait, timber's the thing! No, the ocean! But finding out how the new province was to prove its worth would probably have to wait until the much-anticipated Canadian Pacific Railway was finished. In our first selection from a historian, Forrest Pass addresses the same sort of question, but with a great deal more hindsight. Parliamentarians asked: Was British Columbia going to be Canada's western window on the world, or was acquiring it going to be an expensive folly? The debates over these "competing conceptions of Canada" and concerns about how newly acquired territory would benefit the new nation reveal how unsettled public and elite opinions were at the time. Peter Russell's comprehensive discussion of provincial rights outlines how Canada moved away from Prime Minister Macdonald's ideal of a more unified system toward one in which the provinces became more comfortable asserting their needs and desires. Though Macdonald was a masterful acquirer of land, the newer provinces were especially successful at acquiring a greater measure of control over their own fates.

QUESTIONS FOR CONSIDERATION

1. Why does Wilkins mention the United States and its constitution?
2. Why did Coffin consider it important to report on British Columbia's prospects, even though the province had already joined Confederation?
3. We now recognize that Canada has distinct regions with differing interests. Why might this have been a difficult admission for some Canadians to make immediately after Confederation?
4. If you were debating the British Columbia Terms of Union, would you have sympathized with the "commercialists" or the "agrarians"? Why?
5. Quebec played an extraordinary role in the struggle over provincial autonomy during the first few decades after Confederation. What impact did it have?

SUGGESTIONS FOR FURTHER READING

Forrest Duncan Pass, "Pacific Dominion: British Columbia and the Making of Canadian Nationalism, 1858–1958," PhD Dissertation (History), University of Western Ontario, 2009.

Kenneth G. Pryke, *Nova Scotia and Confederation 1864–74* (Toronto: University of Toronto Press, 1979).

Paul Romney, *Getting It Wrong: How Canadians Forgot Their Past and Imperilled Confederation* (Toronto: University of Toronto Press, 1999).

A.I. Silver, *The French-Canadian Idea of Confederation, 1864–1900* (Toronto: University of Toronto Press, 1997).

Garth Stevenson, *Ex Uno Plures: Federal–Provincial Relations in Canada, 1867–1896* (Montreal and Kingston: McGill-Queen's University Press, 1993).

Robert Vipond, *Liberty and Community: Canadian Federalism and the Failure of the Constitution* (Albany: State University of New York Press, 1991).

Primary Documents

1 From Martin Isaac Wilkins, "Attorney General's Speech," Nova Scotia, House of Assembly, *Debates on the Resolutions Relative to Repeal of the "British North American Act" in the House of Assembly of Nova Scotia, 1868* (Halifax: Nova Scotia House of Assembly, 1868), 3–16.

Debate on the Repeal Resolutions
Monday, Feb 10
HON. ATT. GENERAL'S SPEECH.

Hon. ATTORNEY GENERAL addressed the House as follows—[. . .] I am about to lay before the members of the House, before the people of this country, and probably before the people of England, the facts of one of the most important political cases that ever arose in the Colonies, and in order to do so satisfactorily I shall endeavour to show the true condition in which this country was placed before certain political changes took place in its constitution. I shall endeavour in the first place to show that Nova Scotia was a well governed and law respecting, a contented and a happy country. She was well governed because her institutions were moulded in miniature on the model of the British constitution, which is the finest political system by which any nation was ever governed—a system calculated to maintain order and harmony among all orders of people—a system under which obedience to law and the necessary result of obedience to law, liberty, have been better maintained than in any other country; for, sir, however paradoxical it may seem, it is a literal truth that the highest degree of freedom consists in obedience to law. It is obedience to law which preserves to me my rights and liberties, my property and my life; and therefore, however inconsistent it may seem, it is actually true that the highest degree of liberty consists in obedience to law; and that country which possesses institutions calculated to produce that result, must be the happiest nation on earth. Now the constitution of Nova Scotia was based upon the principles of the British Constitution—those principles which best suit the genius of the people. Its whole condition was different from those of any other country on the Continent of America, and the constitution which was granted to the people of this province by King George II, and which had been enlarged and greatly improved by his successors on the throne of England, was a well working constitution. It was as much like the British constitution as it was possible to make things which are different in their nature. [. . .]

When we compare our constitution in Nova Scotia with that of the Great Republic, the contrast must be favourable to this province. We admire the people of that country, we have sincerely sympathised with them in their recent distress and troubles. We feel towards them all the emotions of fraternal affection, but we do not approve of their constitution. We consider that their institutions are possessed of two fatal defects—the one is democracy, the second Confederation. We consider that having our little constitution moulded upon the monarchial institutions of England makes it infinitely superior to that of the United States, although the latter is a master work of human hands, and the finest piece of composition ever prepared by men for political purposes. It was manufactured by men who were really statesmen—by men who loved their country—by men who had been educated in an English school—by men who had sense enough to perceive the beauties of the British constitution—by men who endeavoured with the utmost imaginable pains and skill to apply the principle of the British constitution to a democratic system and form of government; but the people of the United States were unfortunate, after having separated from England in 1783, in the political system which they instituted. Had they combined in a legislative union— had they incorporated all the States into one Legislature, having one set of laws and revenues, they would undoubtedly, at this time, be the greatest nation upon the earth. They certainly would not have been second to any other; but, unfortunately, they chose Confederation, and that Confederation has resulted as every Confederation must result, for it is impossible so to adjust the rival and discordant interests of different countries under a Confederation as to maintain permanent harmony. It is not in the nature of things that they should continue as separate and individual countries, having separate legislatures and individualities, without

clashing with one another at some time or other. We have seen, notwithstanding the skill with which that famous constitution of the United States was made—notwithstanding the intelligence of that people, that great evils have made their appearance already. The Confederation was broken, an internecine civil war deluged their land with blood, and they expended in three years more than probably three times the amount of the national debt of England, in money, and the destruction of their property; and sir, at this moment there is no man on earth who is able to say what is to be the result of the political affairs of that great country. An earthquake is growing under their feet, and no man can tell when and where the volcano is to burst, bringing with it destruction and ruin. I make these observations with the greatest possible regret, for I believe that every man in Nova Scotia wishes well to the people of the United States, although the people of this province have no desire to be connected with them. They are too wise, too sensible to desire for a moment to part with their own well-working public institutions, and enter into Union with the States.

I shall now turn your attention to another Confederation—the Confederation of Canada—and contrast it with the United States, and show you that if it be not desirable to enter into the Union with the United States, Confederation with Canada is absolutely hateful and detestable to the people of this country. We object to a union with the American States, because we disapprove of *Democracy* and *Confederation*, but there is a worse political combination, that is *Oligarchy* and *Confederation*. If we dislike the constitution of the United States we are bound to hate and detest the constitution which the Confederation Act has prepared for the people of those fine colonies. If we were to join the United States, Nova Scotia would possess all the freedom that every State of the Union possesses. We would have the choice of our own Governors, of our Senators, of our Legislators; we would have the power of self-taxation and self-government in the highest degree; but what would be our position if we suffered ourselves to be dragged into this hateful union with Canada, where would Nova Scotia's freedom be? Before the British America Act was imposed upon us Nova Scotia was as free as the air. How could the people of this country be taxed? There was no power to tax them except this House, their own servants, whom they commissioned to tax them. Is that the state of things now? Have we any power over the taxation of this country? Does not the Act in question confer upon Canada the fullest power of taxing all the property of Nova Scotia at their arbitrary will? What is our control over that Legislature? We have but a paltry voice of 19 members in the popular branch, but a single one in the other. We have, therefore, to protect the rights of this country from spoliation, only 19 members out of 253. If we should continue in Confederation we should not be governed by the people, as is the case in the United States, but by a little knot of Executive Councillors in Canada. Therefore we have no disposition to unite with the one or the other—neither with the United States nor with Canada; and, sir, if we were driven to the necessity of making a choice between the two calamities, we would be bound to choose the least, and that would be, to join the United States of America, and participate in their liberty and prosperity rather than submit to the tyranny of Canada. We would have to prefer the democratic tyranny of the one country to the oligarchical tyranny of the other, and there would be no difficulty in making a choice; but thank Heaven we are not called upon to choose between them. We have a constitution of our own, and that belongs to the people of Nova Scotia; and I am going to show you that the constitution they enjoy is their own property—that the Parliament of England had no power to take it away from them—that the British America

Act is entirely unconstitutional—that Nova Scotia has never been legally confederated with Canada—and it rests with her to say whether she will ever be so or not.

Before I come to look to the constitution of this country, I must make a few remarks with regard to England. We intend to send to the mother country certain gentlemen authorized to present to the Queen our humble address, praying Her Majesty to relieve us from this Confederation with Canada. We go in the most perfect confidence that our prayer will be heard. We know to whom we are going to appeal. We are not placed in the condition that the old thirteen colonies were in under old King George III. We have a very different person to deal with in Queen Victoria. We have to approach ministers very different from those of the last century. We have no stubborn King like George III; we have no prejudices of the royal mind to counteract; we have not the infatuation of his ministers to meet. We have the greatest princess that ever adorned a human throne—a most virtuous Queen, who, when she accepted the sceptre, took the oath that she would rule the country according to the laws, customs and statutes of the realm. She has most nobly fulfilled her obligations, and, in answer to the prayers of her own church, "she has been endued most plenteously with heavenly gifts." In her person she is an example of every virtue; her obedience to the laws exalts her above all monarchs.—Her personal virtues are brighter than all the gems which adorn her Imperial diadem. It is to a Queen like this that the people appeal. Have the people no right to present themselves before their Sovereign Queen? Has not this ever been the most loyal portion of her dominions? Did not our forefathers flee from their country because they would not participate in rebellion? Did they not leave their property for their king's sake? I have seen a resolution passed by the Legislature of Nova Scotia at the time the thirteen colonies rebelled actually petitioning the King to impose taxes upon the Province to assist the Empire in its extremity. From that time to this the people of Nova Scotia have been the most loyal that ever dwelt in any part of Her Majesty's dominions. They will have confidence in presenting themselves before the Queen, and asking to be restored—to what? To anything that they have no right to demand? Simply to get their own. Can any man suppose for a moment that they will be rejected by a Sovereign like ours? We need be under no apprehension. We are pursuing the proper course to obtain a legitimate end, and there is no power on earth that can prevent the people from being restored to their rights but downright tyranny, and that we cannot expect from the hands of the Queen and her Government. Do not let the loyalty of Nova Scotia be suspected. Has any one a right to suspect it? Look at the injuries done to this Province within the last six months. See their liberties taken away, see them taxed by a foreign and alien Legislature; see their property taken from them,—all their customs handed over to others, collected by strangers before their very eyes. See stamp duties and tea duties imposed upon them. Those very acts which forced the old thirteen colonies to rebellion have been imposed upon Nova Scotia with the same extraordinary fatuity. And yet have the people rebelled? I have heard of no movement of agitation on the part of the people beyond the simple burning in effigy of one of the delegates. [. . .]

Now, having made these preliminary remarks, I shall turn your attention to the history of our Constitution. I have heard men assert that we have no valid constitution—that it is made up of despatches. I have been at the pains of examining into this question, and can show you that Nova Scotia has had a chartered constitution, an irrevocable constitution—one that no power on earth can take away except by force or violence. Neither the Queen nor Parliament of England has any right to touch or abrogate that constitution. [. . .] In 1747 [Nova Scotia] came into the hands of George II,

and he, being desirous of having it settled by English subjects, promised the people of England who would undertake the settlement of the country that he would give them the British Constitution in miniature. Accordingly he ordered a patent to be drawn up, with the Great Seal—a Seal larger than the crown of a hat—for Lord Cornwallis, by which he granted to the people of Nova Scotia the constitution they were to possess. I shall call your attention briefly to the words of that part of the patent which refers to the establishment of a Legislative Assembly in the Province. He established by this patent a Governor in the place of King, a Council in the place of Lords, and a House of Assembly in the place of Commons, and made the constitution of the colony as nearly like that of Great Britain as he could. "And we do hereby (this patent is dated 6th May, 1747,) give and grant unto you (Edward Cornwallis) full power and authority, with the advice and Consent of our said Council, from time to time, as need shall require, to summon and call general assemblies of the freeholders and planters within your jurisdiction according to the usage of the rest of our plantations in America, and that you, the said Edward Cornwallis, with the advice and consent of our House of Assembly or the major part of it, shall have full power and authority to make and ordain (here is power given to the Legislature) laws, statutes and ordinances for the public peace, and welfare, and good government of our said Province and of the people and inhabitants thereof, and such measures as shall tend to the benefit of us and our successors, which said laws and ordinances are not to be repugnant, but as nearly agreeable as possible to the statutes of this our said Kingdom of England."

This solemn deed and covenant cannot be repudiated. [. . .] The King having given the charter in question, had no power to make laws. Wherever a country is conquered, the conqueror to whom it is ceded has the power to do as he or she pleases in its management. He may, if he chooses, allow the inhabitants of that country to make their own laws, or put them all to death, or he may send them a code of laws made by himself, and allow his Governors to execute them within the country. But if he confers upon the country any privileges, the deed is obligatory upon himself and heirs, and he cannot annul it, he is bound to submit to it. It is just the same with an individual, as soon as he signs a deed for a piece of land to his neighbour, neither he nor his heirs can afterwards dispute that seal. The day the King signed that deed and appended the seal to the commission of the Governor, he conceded the power to make laws. Both his Attorney and Solicitor Generals tell him, we have looked at Lord Cornwallis' patent, and you have not the power to make such laws. No law can be binding upon the people of Nova Scotia except such as are passed in accordance with that charter. [. . .]

Now, Mr. Speaker, I shall endeavour to bring this argument to a close by inviting the attention of the House, and of the people of England to whom I am speaking at this moment, to the great importance of Nova Scotia to the British Empire. This is a subject which has never been well considered. The old colonies are the most valuable portions of the earth—by the stubbornness of a British King and the stupidity of his Ministers they were lost to the Empire; and that dismemberment was the most serious that ever befell the British nation. Lord Chatham actually died protesting against it. Nova Scotia stands on the front of the American continent just as England does in that of Europe. She possesses great mineral wealth, the source of England's greatness. Her coal and iron, with the energy of her people, have brought the mother country to her present high condition. We possess the same advantages—we too are almost an island. If Nova Scotia were lost to England she might bid adieu to New Brunswick, to Prince Edward Island, and to Newfoundland. These four Maritime Provinces together have a territory similarly situated to the British Isles, and are capable of sustaining a population equal to theirs. Now Great Britain has been to Nova Scotia a very affectionate parent. She has been most kind to us, but we sometimes hear the statesmen of England grumbling a little about the expense incurred in defending these colonies. I must confess I cannot see what that expense is. Great Britain is a maritime nation and a military power. She must have the best navies on the ocean and one of the strongest armies in the field. Where could she maintain her troops and navy more economically than in these Colonies. The climate is a very healthy one; the statistics show that mortality here is less than in any other part of the world. The people of England would never consent to a standing army remaining in their own country. Therefore the scattering of the troops through the colonies has been a kind of necessity. Therefore, so far from those colonies costing England anything they are little or no expense to her. She was always a kind mother although not a wise one at times. When she adopted her trade policy in 1848 she left these colonies entirely unprotected; she left the trade of Nova Scotia to be managed by people who knew nothing about it. She had up to that time managed our trade herself; she withdrew her fostering care and left us to walk alone. We have managed to live very happy and contentedly, but she did not act wisely towards these colonies. Since 1848 no less than six millions of people have left England, Ireland and Scotland; where have they gone to? They have gone directly past us into the United States. If England had been a judicious foster mother she would have diverted the emigration into these colonies. If she had encouraged the commercial advantages of Nova Scotia and the agricultural capabilities of Canada we would now be a strong nation instead of having only four millions of souls in our midst. We would have a population of nine or ten millions, and instead of being afraid of invasion the people of the United States would be pleased to think during their internecine war that such was the peaceful character and orderly disposition of Her Majesty's Colonies in America that there was no danger to be apprehended from them.

I believe there is no time that a parent knows the value of the child he loves until he hears the cold earth falling upon the coffin, and the sad words, "earth to earth, ashes to ashes, dust to dust." Let England transfer this little province to the United States, and she will, after a few years' time, wake up to the loss she has sustained. If the people of the United States succeed in restoring the union, in healing the differences between the North and the South, and in concentrating their tremendous energies, she must become one of the greatest powers of the world. She is now a great naval power, but give her the harbour of Halifax,—which in her hands could be made just as impregnable as Gibraltar. Give her the coal, iron, and fisheries of Nova Scotia, and her power will be largely increased, and millions of people will pour into this country. The fisheries alone of these provinces would be to the United States a nursery for a million or a million and a half of seamen. How long would England then boast of her maritime supremacy? When the Americans had only a few miserable ships they brought more disgrace upon the British flag than any other nation ever succeeded in doing. What would they be if, when challenged to the test by Great Britain, they had possession of the Colonies in addition to their ordinary strength? Suppose in the order of things France, another great naval power, should combine her energies with those of the United States, against England, in what position would the mother country be? How could she contend with such maritime nations as these? Therefore the loss of these Colonies might lead to the degradation of England, and instead of standing at the head of nations she might be lowered to the condition of a secondary state, if indeed she were not converted into a province of France.

I shall now very briefly call the attention of the House to the resolutions before it. They develop the arguments on which we ask for a repeal of the Union. The first clause contends that the Legislative Assembly of Nova Scotia had no power to change the constitution; they had none except what was given them in the charter. Parliament had no power over this country—it never had any. This country belonged to the Queen of England, and our Assembly had no constitutional right to consent to or make the slightest alteration in the constitution under which they were elected to make laws. That is the position which we take, and I would like to see the British constitutional authorities examine this subject, for I am convinced they will acknowledge that I am correct. The second resolution is to the effect that the only authority which the Delegates had was derived from the Assembly, who had no power to give any such authority at all. Even this authority, however, they disregarded. Their authority simply extended to the negotiation of the terms of a Federal union between all the British North American Colonies. They had no power to select three provinces and confederate them, and therefore in that respect they did not act up to their authority. Then, sir, their delegation was not legally constituted. [. . .] No constituent assembly was constituted—it could make no constitution, or do any act until all the delegates were present. [. . .]

The sixth resolution states that no change can be made without an appeal to the people. Here is a self-evident proposition. The constitution belongs to whom? To the House of Assembly? No. To the Legislative Council? No. It is the property of the people of Nova Scotia—every man, woman and child are the owners, and it cannot be taken away from them without their consent. Even the arbitrary monarchies of Europe admit that principle. When Napoleon seized upon the Empire what did he do? At all events he went through the ceremony of sending around the ballot box, and asking the people whether they were willing to change their constitution. The other day two States of Italy, Nice and Savoy, were transferred after the Austrian campaign, and what was done? Did one king sit down and cede the country to the other? No; the people were called upon to decide whether they were prepared to accept the change of constitution or not. No constitution can be lawfully and constitutionally taken away without consulting the people who own the constitution. This is a self-evident proposition—just as evident as the fact that no man can have his farm taken away from him without his consent.

These resolutions go on to argue that the people of Nova Scotia were never consulted until the 18th September, 1867, after the British North America Act had passed the Parliament, and the Queen had given it force by her proclamation. They were then for the first time asked whether they were willing to accept the change of constitution. Then did the people answer emphatically that they would have nothing to do with it. These resolutions state that the preamble of the Imperial Statute is false, and I believe that when the Quebec scheme went home no such words were in it. But no sooner did the crown officers cast their eyes over it than they, knowing the constitutional course in all such matters, perceived that it was impossible for the Imperial Government to legislate upon the question without the consent or request of the people of these colonies. Accordingly they added the preamble declaring that "whereas the people of Canada, Nova Scotia and New Brunswick desire to be federally united, &c." That statute could not have been placed before the Imperial Parliament unless it had these words in it, for it

would be unconstitutional unless the people of these colonies had testified their assent to it. Therefore the preamble being false, the statute is unconstitutional and falls to the ground.

The resolutions go on to say that the people were not only not consulted, but that they were purposely and designedly prevented from being consulted. Is not that a true statement? What did the House of Assembly who recently sat upon these benches, with no great credit to them, do in the month of March last? When it was moved that the people of Nova Scotia had a right to be consulted at the polls, whether they would consent to be confederated or not, that resolution was negatived by 32 against 16 representatives of the people. Whose servants were these 32 persons? The servants of the Executive Council; they ignored the authority of the people, and said that the constitution of Nova Scotia belonged to Dr Tupper and a few others. Then I think we have asserted strictly in accordance with the fact that the people of Nova Scotia were systematically and perseveringly kept from passing upon the subject of confederation. We have also stated with truth that the last election turned entirely upon confederation. I have heard men venture to assert that other issues entered into that election, but men who say this will state anything. No man living before or during the election, can venture to deny the fact that confederation was the great question which excited the people from one end of the province to the other. [. . .]

We shall pass these resolutions and we may, if necessary, add one or two more; and when we have done so, it is the design of the Government and House to send Delegates to England as soon as we can, to submit to the Queen a humble Address, embracing the substance of these resolutions; and I have much pleasure in announcing, so far as I am able to judge, my belief and conviction that the Delegation cannot possibly fail of success.

2   From Lieutenant-Colonel Coffin, "Our New Provinces: British Columbia," *The Canadian Monthly and National Review* 3, 5 (May 1873) (Toronto: Adam, Stevenson, 1873), 361–72.

Mr. Langevin's Report, as Minister of Public Works, is an exception to the general wearisomeness of blue books. Divested of its externals it rises, as read, in the opinion of the reader. As being the result of five weeks of laborious and well directed enquiry, it is most creditable—terse, yet not dry; compendious, replete, suggestive. It comes too, most opportunely, when the popular mind in Canada craves for information on the subject of British Columbia, and it comes *ex cathedra*. We know that, if we can rely upon anything, we can rely upon this, for the writer has achieved a reputation for truthfulness and discrimination, and from the position he occupies is, therefore, doubly trustworthy. [. . .]

We shall have occasion, by and by, to revert to this leading feature in Mr. Langevin's picture, but among the accessories we may note, first, the agreeable climate of Vancouver Island, which resembles that of England without its humidity; where the summer is dry and warm, the autumn bright and balmy, the winter and spring open, though wet; where, in seasons exceptionally severe, ice forms to the thickness of a penny piece, but where, in compensation, gooseberry buds open in February, early plants burgeon in March, and strawberries bloom in the middle of April. The littoral, both of the Island and of the mainland—British Columbia proper—partakes of these characteristics, but the interior of both is mountainous and highly picturesque, intersected by valleys, deep and fertile, by elevated and extensive plateaux, where in winter the snow does not impede travelling, and the pasture is such—a species known as bunch grass—that animals thrive well at all seasons.
[. . .]

These conditions of climate operate exuberantly on a soil whereon flourishes, in great abundance, the Douglas pine, rising often to 150 and 175 feet, without knot or branch; and turns out logs which would make the mouth of an Ottawa lumberman water—say 80 feet long by 6 in diameter—and yet, by the side of this sylvan giant, and other noble forest trees, common to Canada, do not disdain to grow cabbages, carrots, turnips and potatoes, equal to any in the Dominion; and even at a level of 2,700 feet above the sea, on the plateaux before adverted to, were seen fields of wheat, oats and barley, which, aided by an ingenious system of artificial irrigation, presented the finest possible appearance, proclaiming, as it is prettily put, "in their mute language, that those who believed that Columbia was a land of mountains, unfit for cultivation and destined to prove a source of expense to Confederation, had made a great mistake."

[. . .]

But the hidden riches of this picturesque country far exceed those which meet the eye. In the bowels of the earth, in the waters under the earth, on the rocky shores of the inland seas, in the beds of rivers, nature has been prodigal of gifts. Gold and silver, copper and coal, crop out, geologically, all over the country. Near the town of Hope, on the Fraser River, Mr. Langevin saw specimens of silver of such richness as to justify the construction of extensive works, including a road from Hope to the mine itself; and there is every reason to believe that the silver region extends through the range of mountains in which this mine is situated. Of the copper little is said, but Governor Douglas, in a report communicated to the Colonial Office, dated August 27, 1852, stated that he had "procured a rich specimen of copper ore found in a distant part of Vancouver Island," and manifestations of the existence of this metal have reproduced themselves since; but when gold can be had for the trouble of picking it up, but little of research will be vouchsafed to the inferior metals. The auriferous regions extend over the whole Province, from the United States frontier to the 53rd degree of north latitude. For a width of from one to two hundred miles gold is found, but specially in the beds of the great rivers, the Fraser and the Thomson, the Peace and the Ominica, and in the rivers and creeks flowing into them. The *detritus*, borne down by freshets, had created banks and bars, which on the subsidence of the water were found to abound with gold. The precious metal was literally to be had for the "picking of it up". The wonder was how it should have remained so long undiscovered, for the Indian, now as keen and as greedy as the white man in his quest for gold, must for ages have passed it by unnoticed. [. . .]

Happily for the country, the days of surface diggings, of washings and scrapings, of easy gains and wicked waste, have passed away, and have been succeeded by systematic mining and the employment of capital, scientific skill, and steady labour. Mr. Langevin speaks cheeringly of the prospects of mines at the extremity of the Cariboo road: "At a depth of from 100 to 150 feet under ground, and with shafts communicating with galleries, each more than 200 feet long, is the 'Lane & Kurtz' mine, owned by an American company with a capital of $500,000, which, though stopped for a time by subterranean inundation, is expected yet to reward great sacrifices by a rich harvest of gold." The Columbian Blue Book for 1870 gives the yield of gold for the year from the mines of Cariboo, Silionet, Columbia, Gale and Lytton, at $1,333,745, without counting the quantity of gold carried out of the country in private hands.

The golden shower which immortalized Dame gave, at first, but a doubtful reputation to British Columbia. In either case less of greed, and far less of guilt, might have accomplished better things. For a mining population will, of itself, never make a country; the gold which is not squandered in waste and wassail, is carried out of it.

We find by authentic returns, that from 1862 to Sept. 1871, gold to the extent of $16,650,036 has been shipped from British Columbia by banks, registered and known, to which amount should be added at least $5,000,000 carried out of the country by miners themselves. This outflow might be arrested, and utilized *in transitu*, as suggested by Mr. Langevin, by the re-establishment of a mint, the machinery for which, originally imported by the Government of Columbia, is carefully preserved. The constructors of our Canadian Pacific Railway will, no doubt, direct it in the direction of our eastern enterprises, manufactures and products. [. . .]

But the great promise of the future of British Columbia lies deep seated in its coal measures. Coal has been found, of excellent quality, to lie on Vancouver's Island and on the main. In 1859 coal was obtained outcropping in Coal Harbour of Burrard's inlet, and was critically used on board of H.M. ship *Plumper*, with most favourable results. Coal abounds all over the north end of Vancouver Island. It has been found of good quality a little way to the northward of Fort Rupert. But the present chief source of supply, the most practical and the most convenient, is Nanaimo. This place is 75 miles north of the capital, Victoria, on the Gulf of Georgia. The harbour is good, and there is no difficulty in making it. The coal is found handy to the ships' side. It is highly bituminous and well suited to the manufacture of gas. For economic purposes it is most valuable, resembling in quality the varieties of coal produced in the central coal fields of England, and it has been remarked at Nanaimo that the deeper the workings have been carried the better the quality becomes. For domestic consumption and for use in factories, it is thought to be equal to that brought from the Welsh mines. It is considered to be better steam coal than that of Newcastle. The English ships of war stationed at Esquimault are all supplied with it. It can be laid down alongside the ship at from $5 to $6 per ton.

It is sold at San Francisco at from $12 to $15 per ton, where English coal costs from $20 to $35. [. . .]

Anthracite coal has been found in the interior of Columbia, on the River Nicolas, 160 miles from the sea, of a very superior quality to that produced on the coast, although this mineral exists on Queen Charlotte's Island in vast quantities, and is considered to be equal, for smelting purposes, to the Pennsylvanian anthracite; but the price should be reduced below $10 per ton at the mouth of the pit, to make it marketable. This commodity has already attracted the attention of capitalists. Mr. Langevin speaks of one company which had expended $80,000, which, from distance of markets, cost of labour and a depleted purse, had been compelled to abandon both mines and capital. These enterprising individuals have probably been ahead of the times, but the day cannot now be far distant when this traffic must revive, and the real difficulty will be to supply the wants of the immense and increasing steam-fleets, military and commercial, which frequent the coasts of Eastern Asia, and throng the Pacific seaboard from Cape Flattery to Cape Horn. There can be no doubt but that the heavy import duty imposed by the American tariff on Canadian coal prejudices grievously the trade between British Columbia and its nearest market, San Francisco. Though we are satisfied that the American consumer is the greater sufferer, though he pays us our price for our commodity, and thus, "to gain his private ends," taxes himself to boot; still, it is beyond question that, were the duty removed, we should sell two tons where we now sell one, and it is only to be the more deplored that the Canadian House of Commons, in the session of 1870, should by precipitate action, and showing its hand too soon, have played the game of foreign manipulators, and by emasculating the Washington Treaty, have deprived the Dominion of "free coal," which had been freely tendered by the American High Commissioner as a pendant to "free fish". [. . .]

But the real treasury of British Columbia is in the ocean—the untold and immeasurable wealth of its fisheries. The waters of the Gulf of Georgia are alive with fish, proper for the food of man, while the Northern Pacific abounds in the *cetaceae* and other deep sea species known to commerce. The whale, the "right whale" of Scoresby, the whale of train-oil and whalebone, the porpoise and the dog-fish, all oil-producing, have given birth to enterprises which, though still in their infancy, present an infancy full of promise. In 1871 three whaling expeditions were in successful operation. The most prominent was the "British Columbia Whaling Company". They had already secured 20,000 gallons of oil and expected 10,000 more. The value of this oil is 37 cts. per gallon. In England it is worth £35 per ton of 252 gals., or about 2s. 9d. per gallon. Dog-fish oil, worth 55 cents the gallon in California, is produced in large and increasing quantities; it is stated that the catch exceeds, in importance, that of the whale. In 1870, 50,000 gallons were rendered, and at that time this branch of commerce was steadily improving. These oils, under the operation of the Treaty of Washington, will find at San Francisco not only a ready market but an increased demand. The price may or may not increase, but the demand will be doubled. [. . .]

The Gulf of Georgia swarms with salmon, cod, (the true cod,) herring and houlican, each in its season, with halibut, sturgeon, smelt, haddock and sardines. The salmon begin to enter the river in March, species after species following each other in regular succession. The spring or silver salmon is the first and the most valuable arrival. They vary from 4 to 25 lbs. in weight, and have been known to reach 75 lbs. These fish, instinct-driven, force their way in myriads up the Fraser river and its tributaries to the distance of a thousand miles from the sea, and at times, exhausted by their labour, are stranded in such numbers as to heap the shores with their remains and poison the air with their exhalations. [. . .]

Then we have the houlican, the Indian name given to a small fish, about the size of a sprat, which produces oil of superior quality and delicate flavour, to which is ascribed all the sanative virtues of cod-liver oil, free from its nauseousness. So oily is its nature that, when dried, the fish may be lighted and will burn like a candle. Our great navigator, Cook, who, by the way, while giving a name to Cape Flattery ignored the existence of the Straits of Fuca, eat houlican at Nootka Sound. He calls them "sardines," and lauds highly the quality both of the fish and of the oil. The houlican swarm in millions. By means of a rude apparatus the full of a canoe may be taken in two hours. If these fish are sardines (the flavour is pronounced to be delicious), and can, like others of their class, be preserved in tins, we have here a most lucrative article of commerce.

[. . .]

Providence has been bountiful to the hardy Norsemen in either hemisphere. The riches of the sea redress the rigour of clime. The hardy fisherman of Newfoundland, contending with the tempest and a winter of intense severity, supplies the Catholic markets of France and Spain, Portugal and the Brazils; the West Indies share in the dispensation; but the produce of the Grand Bank will not stand a voyage round Cape Horn. It must be salted until it loses all savour or it perishes. Within the Tropics, the fish, parti-coloured and picturesque in aspect, will not bear curing, and would hardly be worth it if it did. The Southern Pacific, therefore, looks to its Northern waters and to Vancouver Island for the same stores and supplies which the Atlantic and Mediterranean derive from Newfoundland. Both islands, so diverse in climate, lie in the same latitude. The Line 49° bisects each. Both islands,—the one the glory and the other the hope of this Dominion,—command and minister to one great need of the Catholic world; and beyond all peradventure the fisheries of British Columbia, rightly cultivated, will create a market, unrivalled, producing more of wealth than the gold mines of Ominica and Cariboo, and a wealth still more inappreciable in a vigorous growth of stalwart native seamen.

[. . .]

We have thus far touched but superficially on the great staple of the country, the great staple indeed of this continent, which, disappearing rapidly elsewhere, abounds throughout British Columbia. It is stated that the supply of timber from British Columbia has been barely tapped, hardly enough to make any impression upon these vast forests. The white pine and the yellow pine, and that most valuable species of all, the Douglas pine, are universally found on the sea coast and up to the Cascade range of mountains. Cedar and hemlock attain an enormous growth; oak, pine, poplar and maple are chiefly used for fuel. The river and the inlets of the sea coast afford unbounded water power and immense facilities for the development of a trade which must command the markets both of the Pacific sea coast and of the Eastern Ocean. [. . .] It would be difficult to follow Mr. Langevin through the diversity of subjects which crowd a report at once exhaustive and instructive, but the number and the character of the population, and the social status of British Columbia, demand observation. The exotic population of British Columbia, the whites and the Chinese, increased by a long-drawn process of immigration, does not exceed 15,000. It must be kept in mind that this country, the existence of which was doubted by Cook in 1778, which was only explored superficially by Vancouver in 1792, was practically unknown to civilization until 1857, and then became first known to the crews of a small British exploring squadron. The previous knowledge of the Hudson's Bay Company was limited to the quantity and quality of its peltries, and their policy ignored all further knowledge. The country was, in fact, from remoteness, inaccessible, while other countries, nearer and as attractive, were, moreover, easier of access. [. . .] In 1857, contemporaneous with the surveys, came the rush for gold. This discovery brought down an avalanche, which on its subsidence left a rough *moraine*; but amid the wreck remained a very large amount of building material. The work of reconstruction dates from the advent of Confederation. In the interval the country has become known and is appreciated, and the completion of the Canadian Pacific Railway will find it populous and make it wealthy. Among the relics of the wreck were left men of education and ability, of settled habits and social standing in the land from whence they came. They have given an impulse to intellectual progress, and united with the families of officials in civil life, and of officers of the British army and navy, constituting a society which embellishes and refines, and which, for elegance and geniality, is unsurpassed in any part of this Dominion. We have had, recently, in Ottawa, in the Grand Columbian Ball, an entertainment second to none ever seen in the metropolis—an evidence of the princely spirit which presides among those who represent the social element of British Columbia.

But the scarcity of labour is a great drawback to the enjoyments of society and the wants of life. So long as the white man can get $5 a day, and the Chinaman and Indian $3.50, at the gold mines, they can hardly be expected to delve for coal, or dig in gardens, at a lower figure. Seeing, too, that the female population is, in number, less than one half of the male, it will easily be understood that the ministering angel is angelic in its dispensations. They are few and far between. Female "help" is almost unattainable, and the simple-minded man who soars above sentiment, whose tastes take a practical turn, would starve were it not for the intervention of the opportune Chinaman.

Of this class of the population Mr. Langevin speaks very favourably. The Chinese are pronounced to be thrifty, clean, docile and industrious, not popular with the whites, because they work cheaper, and are a living antidote to "strikes"; saving of what they make and careful of what they spend, but still consumers. They travel "first class" on steamers and stages, take their meals with others and pay for them, cook well, and make good domestic servants. We trust that under British rule they will increase and multiply and replenish the land, to the discomfiture of a generation of cooks who spoil our victuals, and of laundresses who destroy our clothes. Let the Chinaman feel that he is safe and respected; that upon British soil he becomes a British subject, with the rights, privileges and aspirations of a British subject, and we shall secure a valuable class of settlers, an invaluable aid in the construction of our great public works, and at some future day, possibly, a successor not unworthy of Mr. Pope in the Bureau of Agriculture.

The Indian problem admits of a solution more honourable to humanity in British Columbia than has been achieved in other parts of this continent. The Indian population does not exceed 35,000 souls, decreasing annually from causes almost beyond human control or cure, but not from want of food. In the Plains, the progress of civilization is fatal alike to the Indian and to the buffalo; the destruction of the one entails the destruction of the other, but the tribes which inhabit British Columbia, both the coast tribes and the tribes of the interior, are, to a great extent, supported on fish, and the supply is inexhaustible. They are all imbued with a profound respect for the British name and character. They are not averse to labour. With a strong passion for acquiring property they combine a mania for squandering it; a love of wealth and generosity of disposition, however morbid, are ductile elements of character. They form communities, and live in permanent dwellings, crowded and filthy, and rife with disease, and yet they give ear to the voice of reason and religion, and have greatly amended their ways under the teaching of missionaries, both Catholic and Protestant. The Catholic establishments "though small and restricted as to means, have been productive of very satisfactory results." They are conducted on the principle of "schools industrial and agricultural; where ten children are lodged, boarded and clothed, where they acquire regular habits of order and discipline, and a taste and liking for work, receiving elementary instruction at the same time." Their exertions among adults have also been eminently successful, but the system above devised is the true groundwork of permanent improvement.

[. . .] Thus speaks Chief Justice Begbie of these tribes, a witness beyond peradventure: "The Indian admires and desires to acquire our stores of knowledge and our means of wealth. He appreciates our comforts, of clothes and food, and dwellings. But his inborn capacity for enduring hardship, the very qualities which render him useful as a hunter and a pioneer, make him tire of steady industry and less influenced by the results. Accordingly, after years of cultivation, he constantly relapses, for a time at least, into the painted savage, and goes hunting, and fishing, or starving, for relaxation."

The Indian of the interior is not the nomadic horseman of the plains, whose vagrant habits and plundering propensities, like those of the Arab, are probably ineradicable. The tribes of the North have something of the Yorkshireman about them. They have an eye to the main chance, are good judges of horseflesh, breed horses for sale, obtain employment in "packing" or forwarding goods and merchandise, and as "common carriers" are perfectly trustworthy. [. . .]

These Indian tribes lean with implicit faith on the honour, truthfulness and superior knowledge of "King George's men". In their simple way they plead for protection and guidance. May the people of our great Dominion discharge this most sacred duty constantly and well. Provide tenderly for the guardianship and management of these children of the wilderness. Look upon them as wards in the Chancery of Heaven, as the greatest national trust that could be confided to the hands of men. Watch over them, instruct them, and guide them, improve and elevate them in the scale of humanity, and be assured that, as you do your duty by these helpless ones, so will God toward you.

But to enjoy as well as to admire, we must find a way. To work out the great future of British Columbia, material as well as moral, to apply its wealth, to develop its resources, we must surmount inaccessibility and remove distance. We must conquer time and space, and this has been the great object of Mr. Langevin's mission. [. . .]

The Canadian Pacific Railway Company had become a "fixed fact" in public opinion and in law, long before Mr. Langevin illustrated the subject by his experiences, but the terminus of the road, on the Pacific coast, second only to the construction of the road itself, had not yet been decided upon. It is impossible to overestimate the importance of this decision, and a recent event, the award of the Emperor of Germany on the San Juan arbitration, has added to its cogency. Upon this point—the dominating idea of the whole report—Mr. Langevin has evidently bestowed grave thought, and expresses himself with becoming caution. He deals with the subject generally, both in a military and commercial aspect. He discusses the passes through the Rocky Mountains; he details, with great fairness, the claims of the different harbours of our West to outvie the olden glories of Alexandria and Venice in the East. [. . .]

Finally, we thank Mr. Langevin very heartily for his excellent report, faulty alone in externals. Had it been even *relié en rouge* it would have circulated better. He has brought out, in strong relief, the wealth and resources of British Columbia. He holds up to light that gem of the Pacific, Vancouver Island—a diamond, uncut but of the first water, and destined to be the brightest jewel in the diadem of this Dominion.

Historical Interpretations

3   From Forrest D. Pass, "Agrarian Commonwealth or Entrepôt of the Orient? Competing Conceptions of Canada and the BC Terms of Union Debate of 1871," *Journal of the Canadian Historical Association* 17, 1 (2006): 25–53. Reprinted with permission.

"All hail Columbia! not least though last." So the Rev. Aeneas McDonell Dawson opened his 1871 ode, "British Columbia Becomes a Province of the Canadian Confederation." Over 61 lines, the Ottawa Roman Catholic priest—and brother of the well-known surveyor and expansionist, Simon James Dawson—extolled British Columbia's resources and, more importantly, the position its acquisition would soon give the fledgling Dominion of Canada.[1] Dawson was not alone in waxing poetic on the riches that Canada would accrue through its annexation of British Columbia. For Dominion Day 1869, a verse in the Belleville, Ontario *Daily Intelligencer* eagerly anticipated the extension of the Dominion's borders to the Pacific, "where the stormless waves have no angry crest / As they wash our barques to the gorgeous East."[2] Two years later, the *Intelligencer*, the organ of North Hastings MP and Conservative cabinet minister Mackenzie Bowell, supported unequivocally the Terms of Union admitting British Columbia to Confederation.[3] The transcontinental railway promised as one of the Terms of Union would, the paper predicted in an editorial of 1 April 1871, "be certain to become the great artery for [the] great traffic" between China and Liverpool.[4] In extolling the value of Asiatic commerce, Dawson and the *Intelligencer* positioned themselves firmly on one side of the fierce debate over the admission of British Columbia, a debate which provides an intriguing insight into the competing conceptions of the new Canadian nation that prevailed in the years immediately following 1867.

Historians have explained satisfactorily the motivations of British Columbians in seeking federation with Canada, but the eastern Canadian parliamentary and press discussion of British Columbia's entry into Confederation has received considerably less scholarly attention.[5] The authors of the national surveys have presented the Terms of Union as a "Made-in-BC" solution to local economic problems, a solution eagerly endorsed by an expansionist parliament.[6]

Though these historians have downplayed the significance of the debate, the proposed Terms of Union sharply divided the Canadian parliament and press. Even if, as Ormsby suggests, Canadians believed in a manifest destiny they disagreed on whether this destiny included British Columbia: the Pacific colony's admission to the union was a considerably more divisive question for Canadian parliamentarians and journalists than the purchase of Rupert's Land two years earlier, the *Manitoba Act* the previous year, or the Prince Edward Island Terms of Union two years later. Both government and opposition commentators recognized the British Columbia debate as one of the keenest fought battles in Canada's short parliamentary history.[7] The financial cost of the Terms, and of the promised railway in particular, figured prominently in the discussion, as Ormsby correctly noted. "It wouldn't pay Canada to take many British Columbias at this price," the Orangeville, Ontario *Sun* opined, and most opponents of the Terms were inclined to agree.[8] However, it is simplistic to characterize the debate as merely a conflict between government patriotism and opposition parsimony. Rather, the debate on the Terms was so contentious because it enflamed a pre-existing ideological conflict over the source of Canada's future prosperity. For those, generally opposition Liberals or Reformers, whose conception of Canada was inspired by the agrarian ideal, distant, barren, and sparsely settled British Columbia was an expensive and unnecessary liability, and its population failed to conform to their ideal of the upstanding yeoman-citizen. On the other side were those, including Rev. Dawson and the staff of the Belleville *Intelligencer*, who saw Canada's future prosperity in its emergence as a nexus of international commerce. British Columbia, already rich in mineral wealth, was well situated to control the trade of the Pacific, and the construction of a Canadian Pacific railway would make Canada the entrepôt between Europe and the Orient. The division I posit between the commercial and agrarian camps was not perfect. Commercialist Conservatives were certainly concerned about agriculture and frequently sought to reassure the opposition that parts of British Columbia were indeed arable. For their part, Liberal agrarians asserted, often formulaically, their commitment to the eventual consummation of a transcontinental union and even to the desirability of expanding trade with Asia. Party allegiance certainly informed the final division on the Terms, but we should not dismiss partisanship as a mere antipathy between the "ins" and the "outs". Rather, the parties that emerged in the decade after Confederation were themselves products of competing conceptions of Canada's economic and political future. Ben Forster in particular has emphasized the importance of the tariff question, which divided farming and business interests, in defining the political landscape of the 1870s.[9] That the debate on the Terms of Union was so acrimonious, especially when compared to the relative bi-partisanship that had typified discussions of other expansionist legislation, suggests an important role for the agrarian-commercial dichotomy generally,

and the British Columbia debate specifically, in defining Canada's early two-party system. Considering the Terms of Union debate as a contest between two competing conceptions of Canada's ideal economic foundation accounts for the debate's contentiousness.

[. . .]

The debate on the British Columbia resolutions concerned not only the political future of a far-off colony, it also served as an opportunity for Canadians to discuss once again the nature and future of their "new nationality".

The circumstances and provisions of the British Columbia Terms of Union are well known to most students of British Columbian and Canadian history. In the years following the union of British Columbia and Vancouver Island in 1866, rival factions emerged favouring either federation with Canada or annexation to the United States as a means of alleviating the depopulation and economic recession that followed the Cariboo gold rush. Meanwhile in Canada, Prime Minister Macdonald lobbied the Colonial Office to replace British Columbia's anti-Confederationist Governor, Frederick Seymour, with someone more favourable to union.[10] After Seymour's sudden death at Bella Coola in June of 1869, the Colonial Office complied with Macdonald's request and dispatched Anthony Musgrave, the Governor of Newfoundland, to Victoria. Frustrated with the divisions among the colony's pro-Confederationists, Musgrave presented draft terms, as a motion of the Government, to the colony's unicameral legislature during the winter of 1870.[11] Upon the legislature's ratification, with some minor modifications, of the Governor's proposed Terms, a delegation of three under the de facto leadership of the colony's Commissioner of Lands and Works, Joseph Trutch, travelled to Ottawa to negotiate with the Dominion government. Macdonald's Quebec lieutenant and fellow leader of the great coalition, Sir George-Etienne Cartier, acted for the Dominion, famously offering the British Columbians a transcontinental railway when only a wagon road had been requested. The revised Terms, ratified by the colonial legislature in January 1871, included a per capita subsidy for the maintenance of the provincial government; representation in Parliament by six members and three senators; and, most importantly and controversially, a promise to commence construction of a transcontinental railway within two years, for completion within ten.[12] Trutch then returned to Ottawa, where British Columbia's political future now lay in the hands of Canada's parliamentarians.

Cartier introduced the address to the Queen embodying the British Columbia Terms of Union in the House of Commons on 28 March 1871.[13] For the governing party, the admission of British Columbia was simply the culmination of the road to nationhood embarked upon at Charlottetown in 1864. Cartier reminded the House that the former Colonial Secretary, Sir Edward Bulwer Lytton, had predicted as early as 1858 that the colonies of British North America would one day form a united empire from the Atlantic to the Pacific, and he marvelled at the speed with which Lytton's prediction had been accomplished. The progress of the Dominion evoked favourable comparisons with the American experience: expansion to the Pacific had taken the Americans six decades, Cartier remarked, but Canada had accomplished it in less than ten years, indeed in less than five.[14] Canada's development ought to mirror or even overtake that of the United States, for it was the new Dominion's duty and destiny to establish a British empire in North America.[15] If a transcontinental empire was the "ulterior object" of Confederation, as Postmaster General Alexander Campbell suggested on introducing the Terms of Union in the Senate on 3 April 1871, certainly the admission of British Columbia was integral to the success of the project.[16]

The supporters of the Terms of Union looked beyond expansion to the Pacific. Cartier's speech only briefly alluded to the purpose for which Canada should acquire a Pacific seaboard. English history, he suggested, demonstrated the "splendid position" that could be achieved through maritime power, and access to the Pacific was critical "if ever this Dominion was to be a powerful nation in the future."[17] In conversation with the British Columbia delegates, Cartier had expressed his belief that Quebec, as a manufacturing centre, and British Columbia, as the inlet for the Pacific trade, would become the most important sections of the Dominion, and his Montreal organ, *La Minerve*, was quick to develop the theme of maritime commercial power.[18]

[. . .]

Conservative MPs and newspapers from Ontario also looked forward to Canada's emergence as the world's leading commercial power. The member for Russell County, Dr James Alexander Grant, spoke in terms very similar to *La Minerve*. Like the nations of classical antiquity and more recent commercial centres, British Columbia was destined to become the new centre of Asian trade. When he considered the geography of the Strait of Georgia basin, Grant saw a series of harbours "set apart by a special Providence as a depot for the shipping of the East, and as an entrance to the great highway of all nations across the British American continent."[19] The national prosperity that Oriental trade would bring was worth the price the British Columbians demanded. Equally enthused was Alexander Morris. The Inland Revenue minister and member for Lanark South had been among the earliest proponents of transcontinental Confederation. His 1858 lecture on "The Hudson's Bay and Pacific Territories" foresaw the emergence of a "Great Britannic Empire of the North" that would become the thoroughfare for the trade of China and Japan.[20]

For some years Maritimers had eagerly anticipated that the trade of the Orient flowing into British North America through British Columbia would flow out through

Halifax and Saint John.[21] Cartier had predicted that the merchant communities of the lower provinces would make common cause with the British Columbians, and indeed many Maritime MPs and newspapers came out in favour of the British Columbia resolutions.[22] The member for the City of Saint John, former New Brunswick premier Sir Samuel Leonard Tilley, spoke to the commercial benefits for eastern Canadian ports. He argued that, unlike a railway that ended at the eastern foothills of the Rocky Mountains, as some in the opposition proposed, an interoceanic line would capture not only local but also through traffic, and this trade could only benefit the terminal cities of the St Lawrence and the Atlantic seaboard.[23] [. . .] Maritime newspapers sympathetic to the federal ministry also saw the Canadian national destiny in global terms. "We have entered upon an era of great public works," predicted the Halifax *Daily Reporter*, "all tending to give British North America its true position in the British Empire as the great central link uniting the three Islands that constitute the 'Motherland' with those great dependencies of India, Australasia and New Zealand and forming the great highway over which traffic and travel to and from these dependencies shall pass by the shortest and speediest route."[24]

[. . .]

Cartier himself linked the admission of British Columbia with the national aspirations of French Canada in a speech at a banquet for Joseph Trutch.[25] One Anglophone paper melded *La Minerve*'s French-Canadian interpretation with the British imperialist view. According to the *Ottawa Times*, the railway was a significant imperial concern, insofar as it would strengthen Great Britain's military and commercial position in the Pacific. However, in recounting Cartier's speech at Trutch's banquet, the paper deemed it noteworthy that the opening of a western route to Asia would be the work of a "lineal descendant" of Jacques Cartier, who had also sought "Oriental splendour" up the St Lawrence.[26]

In the centuries-old quest for the Northwest Passage, the commercialists found common ground for French and English Canadians.

La Minerve's appeals to see the admission of British Columbia as the culmination of a long history of Canadian progress were not, of course, shared by all French-Canadian commentators. A rival Montreal paper, *Le Franc-Parleur*, argued that in considering only the commercial side of the Terms, the government would increase the national debt and thus compromise Canada's future.[27] In the House of Commons, the most vocal French Canadian opponent of the Terms of Union was Henri-Gustave Joly de Lotbinière, ironically the man Wilfrid Laurier would later appoint as British Columbia's Lieutenant Governor. Ever fond of illustrating his contentions with the fables of Lafontaine, Joly compared the Canadian expansionists with the frog who, aspiring to be as large as an ox, inhaled air until he exploded.[28] He ridiculed in particular the notion that Canada might become a highway to Asia. "It was very fortunate," he observed sarcastically, "[that] the Pacific made a boundary to the land to be annexed, although it was true [that] China and Japan were beyond, and perhaps the Pacific might yet be made a Canadian sea."[29]

Joly was joined by English Canadians in dismissing the notion of a Canadian empire built on commerce. The Toronto *Globe* acknowledged that Canadians were interested in Eastern trade and were therefore willing to offer prudent and economical inducements to British Columbia.[30] Others in the English-Canadian opposition were less charitable. For Montreal Centre MP Thomas Workman, the notion that merchants would send Oriental goods over the Pacific Railway was ridiculous because long distance travel by rail would damage fragile items.[31] William Miller might profess that Canadian expansionism had goals more just and more noble than mere self-aggrandizement, but both Thomas Workman and Ontario Senator William McMaster saw in the resolutions and the speeches of their proponents a "spread-eagleism" more characteristic of American than Canadian nationalism.[32] [. . .] In Loyalist Ontario, no comment against a policy could be so damning as the suggestion that it reeked of Americanism.

Opponents of the Terms argued that the ministry's American precedents were not apt because British Columbia and the American West were at different stages of development. Senator David Wark of New Brunswick observed that there was already a substantial population and a rich economy in California before the Americans contemplated a railway.[33] To the opposition, British Columbia lacked a critical feature necessary for nation-building, namely the presence of, or even the potential to attract, a significant and permanent population. The mining colony's population was composed largely of transient sojourners, who rarely stayed long in one location and felt no compunction against quitting British Columbia when the mines ceased to be profitable. For Canadians, as for others, mining was a valuable pursuit insofar as it garnered attention for new fields for colonization, but it was not in itself a viable economic foundation for a new nation.[34] A railway intended to carry through-traffic was a purely speculative venture and no more a suitable basis for national stability than gold mining. Agriculture alone was the basis for lasting prosperity. The Canada the opposition envisioned was a nation of thrifty yeoman farmers, with a fiscally prudent legislature constituted strictly upon the principle of representation by population to protect them from the excesses of corrupt ministers and monopolistic corporations. [. . .]

The alleged agricultural sterility of British Columbia underpinned much of the opposition to the Terms of Union, and the proponents of the resolutions worked vigorously to refute it. Although the commercialists had presented the British American West as a "passage to India," they also subscribed to the second great myth of the west,

the myth of the "Garden of the World."[35] Lacking personal experience of the colony, politicians on both sides of the floor drew on anecdotal and published sources for their information about the colony's productivity. On the basis of Trutch's reports, Alexander Morris stated that British Columbia encompassed almost as much agricultural land as Ontario.[36] Others sidestepped the issue of British Columbia's fertility to emphasize its other resources. Cartier himself in introducing the resolutions suggested that the land offered to the railway company would be "not merely agricultural land, but mineral land," and *Le Journal des Trois-Rivières* noted the colony's mineral and timber wealth, citing Trutch as its source.[37] [. . .] Senator James Ferrier of Quebec drew attention to the colony's mines and fisheries, while William Miller, acknowledging the "uneven ground," spoke of rich supplies of coal and timber, as well as the prospect of a thriving trade in fish between British Columbia and Catholic South America.[38] In addition to its strategic importance for the Pacific trade, the commercialists saw in British Columbia the resources necessary for diverse economic pursuits, including agriculture.

For the opposition, however, the lack of agriculture loomed large. In addition to trade statistics printed in the sessional papers, opponents of the Terms drew, albeit selectively, on the reports of Canadians who had first-hand knowledge of the far west. David Christie related to the Senate his recent personal conversation with Malcolm Cameron, the Sarnia politician and newspaperman who had visited the Pacific colonies in 1862. Cameron's initial reports from British Columbia to eastern newspapers had been favourable, emphasizing the colony's mineral wealth and dismissing Canadians who had returned home prematurely and now denigrated British Columbia's resources as "not worthy sons of the men who made Canada."[39] Indeed, like the Macdonald-Cartier government six years later, Cameron predicted in an

1865 speech that political unification of British North America would make Canada the great commercial emporium of the world.[40] However, as Christie emphasized, Cameron had been only lukewarm in his assessment of the colony's agricultural potential. [. . .]

To the opponents of the Terms of Union, the government's suggestions that British Columbia would attract settlers, and consequently that sales of land in the province could finance railway construction, were absurd. "If you could not derive a revenue from the fertile lands [of Ontario and Quebec], how could you expect to do so from this miserable region of the West?" inquired Senator Benjamin Seymour. Timothy Warren Anglin, member for Gloucester County, New Brunswick, made much the same point, asking why settlers who would not take lands in Ontario would choose to settle in a "sea of mountains" where "it would be difficult to find those vast tracts of fertile country spoken of by Hon. Members opposite."[41] In Anglin's view, perpetual landslides and avalanches would frustrate efforts to construct railways and farms in British Columbia's "sterile mountains" and gloomy canyons.[42] For Quebec nationalists Antoine-Aimé Dorion and Luc Letellier de St Just, the money necessary to build "a railway in a barren and mountainous country" would be better spent to improve transportation networks in the proven agricultural districts of the St Lawrence Basin.[43] Without an agricultural base, critics of the Terms of Union feared British Columbia would never enjoy significant population growth.

The small size of the present and projected population of British Columbia was a significant concern for opponents of the Terms. The resolutions estimated British Columbia's population at 60 000 for the purposes of determining its per capita subsidy and parliamentary representation, and, accordingly, granted the province six members in the House of Commons. However, if British Columbia did have a population of 60 000, even by the most generous estimates only one-quarter of that population was white, the rest comprising Aboriginal peoples and Chinese.[44] The British Columbia government was most concerned about the population estimate as it affected the subsidy.[45] The Canadian press and Parliament, however, were most concerned about the apparent violation of the principle of representation by population. To Ontarians in particular, the constitutional violation, which followed a dangerous precedent established by the *Manitoba Act* the previous year, threatened to reignite sectional hostility.[46] The Goderich *Huron Signal* calculated that British Columbia would have one member of parliament for every 2000 white citizens, while Ontario had but one member for every 20 000 citizens.[47] In his memoirs, Richard Cartwright, the member for Lennox, speculated that in admitting British Columbia the ministry had sought to compensate for projected electoral losses in the east with new, safely Conservative seats in the far west.[48] In Parliament, member after member rose to challenge the representation formula.[49] [. . .]

For the opposition, permanent landed settlement, almost certainly agricultural, was the only basis for political participation. In their view, agriculture determined not only the size but also the moral quality of a population.[50] Governor Musgrave himself gave the opposition ample evidence that the nature of British Columbia's economy indeed produced moral degradation. "The white inhabitants," Musgrave had written to Governor General Young, "are chiefly male adults of wasteful and expensive habits," and the Canadian opposition seized upon this characterization.[51] A people so un-Canadian in their morality were only fit for an un-Canadian form of government. Senator Sanborn thought it humiliating that "a country like [Canada], enjoying responsible Government and representative institutions for many years—with a superior system of colleges and schools, with a territory and resources in a high stage of development," should have terms dictated to it by a despotism such as British Columbia.[52] For those opponents of the Terms who did accept the principle of extending the Dominion's boundaries to the Pacific, the American model of territorial administration was preferable, both economically and politically, to the admission of full provinces in the west. Inexpensive to administer and represented only by a non-voting delegate, territories were only admitted to statehood when they reached a certain population threshold and a concomitant level of infrastructure development and political maturity.[53]

If the opposition saw the white population as degraded by their economic circumstances, they were even more indignant at the suggestion that Aboriginal peoples be included in the population for the purpose of calculating subsidies and parliamentary representation. This was further evidence of the government's intention to undermine representation by population; why else, the opponents wondered, should British Columbia's Indians be included in the population estimates if Ontario's were not?[54] Musgrave acknowledged that the population included "a large number of Indians," but he also noted that they were consumers.[55] If one accepted his contention that contribution to revenue was an appropriate basis for representation, and if the Aboriginal population participated in a taxable market economy, then there was, ironically enough, no contradiction in including Aboriginal peoples in the representation formula. The opposition, however, mocked the government's presentation of the Aboriginal population. Senator Christie suggested instead that the Indians in question were "perfectly worthless," and, according to Arthur Harvey's *Statistical Account of British Columbia*, contributed nothing to the labour force.[56] The most damning assessment of British

Columbia's racial composition came, however, from the Halifax *Morning Chronicle*, which warned that "the 'fellow countrymen' we would meet at the end of the [Pacific railway] would be mostly Digger Indians and 'Heathen Chinees'."[57] While the prospect of having "heathen Chinees" as compatriots was probably offensive enough to white Canadian sensibilities, the American term "Digger Indian" connoted all that was undesirable about the indigenous peoples of the Pacific Slope.[58] Lazy, dirty, and simian to the settler's eye, the Digger Indians of California were seen as the lowest, most degraded form of humanity, much lower in the hierarchy of races than the First Nations to the east of the continental divide.[59] In California, the degradation of the Digger Indian justified expansion and dispossession. For Canadian opponents of the British Columbia Terms of Union, the presence of degraded western Aboriginal peoples, combined with the lax mores of the settler population and the sterility of the soil to present British Columbia as quintessentially un-Canadian space.

[. . .] Increasing the size of the union could only increase the scope for government patronage, and indeed the opposition contended that this had been the cynical aim of Confederation in the first place. "Injurious as has been the effect of Confederation to the best interests of this province," opined the *Canadian Gleaner*, "it has yielded rich fruits to Cartier and his colleagues. It has enriched and aggrandized them in every way. They look for greater results from this admission of British Columbia."[60] After all, the paper predicted, the Pacific Railway would provide considerably more opportunities for corruption than the Intercolonial Railway, a remarkably prescient observation considering the scandal that would sweep the government from office two years later. [. . .]

The opposition was particularly concerned that the principal beneficiaries of the government's new railway patronage would be large private interests. Fear of corporate capitalism had been a strong feature of pre-Confederation reform ideology, as Allan Greer has demonstrated, and the prospect of a privately constructed but state-subsidized transcontinental railway rejuvenated these concerns.[61] Where the proponents of the union and of the railway saw the fulfillment of the dream of the Northwest Passage, the opposition remembered a previous gamble on the value of Pacific trade, the South Sea Bubble of 1720, in which rampant speculation had ruined many an investor.[62] Now the investor that faced ruin was the State. Numerous politicians and newspapers feared that cost overruns in the construction of the Pacific railway would drive the Dominion to bankruptcy. Aside from the ministers who would profit from patronage, the only beneficiaries of the railway speculation would be large capitalists, who would receive substantial land grants to finance the project. The government presented the proposed land grants as a means of financing railway construction without spending public funds, but the opposition saw it as a massive giveaway of public property to private interests. [. . .] The anti-corporate sentiment that inspired opposition to the railway scheme, also led the leader of the opposition to dismiss the economic attractions of British Columbia. "The gold mines have certainly proved remunerative," granted Alexander Mackenzie, "but they are carried on by large companies," so presumably little of the wealth they produced went to the ordinary miner.[63] The virtuous Ontario yeoman who settled in British Columbia, unable to draw a living from the land, could only hope to become the degraded wage slave of a mining conglomerate.

The opposition's arguments failed ultimately to influence the will of Parliament. The division in the Commons was 91 in favour (56.9 per cent) to 69 opposed, while in the Senate the resolutions were passed by a slightly larger margin of 36 (63.2 per cent) to 21. [. . .]

The commercialists' conception of Canada carried the day, and British Columbia was admitted to Confederation with the hope that the barques of "the gorgeous East" would soon ply the province's harbours and the transhipment of their wares would enrich the entire nation. [. . .]

The parliamentary and press debates on the British Columbia Terms of Union were about much more than the future of British Columbia. For the government and its supporters, swift extension of the Dominion's boundaries to the Pacific promised to make the new country the centre of international commerce, with the Canadian Pacific Railway cutting thousands of miles off the voyage between Asian and European ports. For the opposition, however, the extravagant promises made to secure the admission of a barren, under-populated colony threatened Canada's future as a nation of virtuous, self-governing yeoman farmers. Thus, Canadian politicians used the proposed admission of British Columbia as an opportunity to rearticulate their visions of Canada's future, and in its ideological underpinnings the Terms of Union debate represents a continuity from earlier discussions on British North American union, and a foreshadowing of discussions yet to come. This analysis of the Terms of Union discussions suggests we must expand our definition of what constitutes the "Confederation Debates" to include the parliamentary discussions about the admission of the latecomer provinces, for it is in the significances Canadians attached to territorial expansion that their aspirations and anxieties concerning their new nation were most evident. Pitting the opposition's conception of Canada as an agrarian commonwealth against the government's dream of becoming the entrepôt of the Orient, the debate on the admission of British Columbia clearly demonstrated that, in the first years of Confederation, a longstanding conflict over Canada's character and future remained unresolved.

NOTES

1. Aeneas McDonell Dawson, "British Columbia Becomes a Province of the Canadian Confederation," in his *The North-west Territories and British Columbia* (Ottawa: C.W. Mitchell, 1881), 218; Doug Owram, *Promise of Eden: The Canadian Expansionist Movement and the Idea of the West, 1856–1900* (Toronto: University of Toronto Press, 1980), 39.

2. "Land of the Maple Leaf," *Daily Intelligencer* (Belleville) (3 July 1869), 4, col. 1.

3. P.B. Waite, "Sir Mackenzie Bowell," *Dictionary of Canadian Biography*, www.biographi.ca/EN/ShowBio.asp?BioId=41353.htm, (viewed 16 January 2007).

4. "Admission of British Columbia," *Daily Intelligencer* (1 April 1871), 2, col. 2–3.

5. Margaret Ormsby, *British Columbia: A History* (Toronto: Macmillan, 1958), 245–9, 257; Jean Barman, *The West Beyond the West* (Toronto: University of Toronto Press, 1996), 96; Patricia Roy and John Herd Thompson, *British Columbia: Land of Promises* (Don Mills: Oxford University Press, 2005), 49–50.

6. Arthur Lower, *Colony to Nation: A History of Canada*, 4th rev. edn (Don Mills: Longmans, 1964), 361; W.L. Morton, *The Kingdom of Canada: A General History from Earliest Times*, 2nd edn (Toronto: McClelland & Stewart, 1969), 338; Desmond Morton, *A Short History of Canada*, 5th edn (Toronto: McClelland & Stewart, 2001), 104–5.

7. Alexander Morris to Sir John A. Macdonald, 1 April 1871, cited in Donald Grant Creighton, *John A. Macdonald*, vol. 2 (Toronto: Macmillan, 1955), 105; "The British Columbia Resolutions," *Perth Courier* (7 April 1871), 2, col. 3.

8. "The Resolutions to Admit British Columbia . . . ," *Sun* (Orangeville) (6 April 1871), 2, col. 1.

9. Ben Forster, *A Conjunction of Interests: Business, Politics, and Tariffs, 1825–1879* (Toronto: University of Toronto Press, 1986), 147–64.

10. Public Record Office (hereafter PRO), CO 537, Colonial Office Secret Supplementary Correspondence, 1832–1922, /100, no. 204, John A. Macdonald to Sir John Young, 23 May 1869.

11. PRO, CO 60, British Columbia, Original Correspondence, 1858–1871, /38, no. 11, Anthony Musgrave to Sir John Young, 20 February 1870.

12. *Terms of Union, 1871* (Victoria, BC: Queen's Printer, 1981).

13. Macdonald was in Washington as part of the British delegation negotiating a new fisheries treaty with the Americans. The absence of references in his papers suggests that he had little involvement in the British Columbia debate.

14. Canada. House of Commons, *Debates of the House of Commons, 1871* (Ottawa: Queen's Printer, 1871), 663.

15. See, for example, the speeches of Col. John Hamilton Gray, Hector-Louis Langevin, and William Miller. Canada. House of Commons, *Debates, 1871*, 692, 700; Canada. Senate, *Debates, 1871*, 179.

16. Canada. Senate, *Debates, 1871*, 151–2.

17. Canada. House of Commons, *Debates, 1871*, 663.

18. Quoted in John Sebastian Helmcken, Dorothy Blakey Smith, ed., *The Reminiscences of Doctor John Sebastian Helmcken* (Vancouver: University of British Columbia Press, 1975), 358; "La Colombie et le chemin du Pacifique," *La Minerve* (Montreal) (29 March 1871), 2, col. 2–5.

19. Canada. House of Commons, *Debates, 1871*, 675.

20. Alexander Morris, *Nova Britannia: or Our New Canadian Dominion Foreshadowed* (Toronto: Hunter, Rose and Co., 1884), 88.

21. T.T. Vernon Smith, *The Pacific Railway, and the Claims of Saint John, New Brunswick, to Be the Atlantic Terminus Read before the Mechanics' Institute of Saint John, February 7, 1859* (Saint John: W.L. Avery, 1859), 19–20, 28–9.

22. Quoted in Helmcken, *Reminiscences*, 358.

23. Canada. House of Commons, *Debates, 1871*, 668, 671.

24. "Marching On," *Daily Reporter and Times* (Halifax) (1 April 1871), 2, col. 1.

25. *British Columbia and the Pacific Railway, Complimentary Dinner to the Hon. Mr. Trutch, Surveyor-General of British Columbia, Given at the Russell House, Ottawa, on Monday, 10th April, 1871* (Montreal: Gazette, 1871), 4.

26. "'The Star of Empire Glitters in the West,'" *Times* (Ottawa) (13 April 1871), 2, col. 1–2.

27. Adolphe Ouimet, "La Colombie Anglaise et le chemin de fer du Pacifique," *Le Franc-Parleur* (Montreal) (6 April 1871), 314–16.

28. Canada. House of Commons, *Debates, 1871*, 696; Janet Azjenstat, et al., eds, *Canada's Founding Debates* (Toronto: Stoddart, 1999), 138–9; "British Columbia," *Owen Sound Advertiser* (6 April 1871), 2, col. 2; "An Outrageous Proposition," *Norfolk Reformer* (Simcoe) (6 April 1871), 2, col. 1; "The Dominion Parliament," *Weekly Dispatch* (St Thomas) (6 Apr 1871), 2, col. 1–2.

29. Canada. House of Commons, *Debates, 1871*, 696.

30. "The British Columbia Resolutions," *Globe* (Toronto) (30 March 1871), 2, col. 1.

31. Canada. House of Commons, *Debates, 1871*, 723.

32. Canada. House of Commons, *Debates, 1871*, 723; Canada. Senate, *Debates, 1871*, 247.

33. Canada. Senate, *Debates, 1871*, 224.

34. "An English Gentleman . . . ," *Globe* (Toronto) (5 September 1865), 2, col. 2–3.

35. John Logan Allen, *Passage through the Garden: Lewis and Clark and the Image of the American Northwest* (Urbana, IL: University of Illinois Press, 1975); Henry Nash Smith, *Virgin Land: The American West as Symbol and Myth*, Reissue edn (Cambridge: Harvard University Press, 1978); Doug Owram, *Promise of Eden*.

36. Canada. House of Commons, *Debates, 1871*, 714.

37. Canada. House of Commons, *Debates, 1871*, 662; "Parmi les mesures . . . ," *Le Journal des Trois-Rivières* (17 April 1871), 2, col. 2.

38. Canada. Senate, *Debates, 1871*, 172–3, 227.

39. Quoted in "Hon. M. Cameron on British Columbia," *Globe* (Toronto) (14 November 1862), 2, col. 2.

40. Malcolm Cameron, *Lecture Delivered by the Hon. Malcolm Cameron to the Young Men's Mutual Improvement Association, the Lord Bishop of the Diocese in the Chair* (Montreal: G.E. Desbarats, 1865), 21.

41. Canada. House of Commons, *Debates, 1871*, 718, 720.

42. This characterization of British Columbia's geography does not appear in the official record of the Commons debate but it does appear in at least one press account of Anglin's speech. See "The Dominion Parliament," *Weekly Dispatch* (St Thomas) (4 April 1871), 2, col. 1–2.

43. Canada. Senate, *Debates, 1871*, 165; Canada. House of Commons, *Debates, 1871*, 729.

44. Several estimates of the white population were posited, ranging from 10 000 to 17 000. Canada. House of Commons, *Debates, 1871*, 665, 696, 718,729.

45. Helmcken, *Reminiscences*, 348–9; British Columbia Archives, GR-0441, Premier's Papers, Box 4, File 4, Item 579/96, Alexander Begg to Premier John Herbert Turner, 26 October 1896.

46. "A Hundred Million Dollars, and a Hundred Million More," *Huron Signal* (Goderich) (6 April 1871), 2, col. 1.

47. Richard J. Cartwright, *Reminiscences* (Toronto: W. Briggs, 1912), 94.

48. Canada. House of Commons, *Debates, 1871*, 666, 672, 680, 698, 702, 727; Canada. Senate, *Debates, 1871*, 164, 250, 257.

49. PRO, CO 60, /38, no. 20, Musgrave to Granville, 23 February 1870.

50. Adele Perry, *On the Edge of Empire: Gender, Race, and the Making of British Columbia, 1849–1871* (Toronto: University of Toronto Press, 2001), 3–19.

51. PRO, CO 60, /38, no. 11, Musgrave to Young, 20 February 1870.

52. Canada. Senate, *Debates, 1871*, 184.

53. Canada. House of Commons, *Debates, 1871*, 666; Canada. Senate, *Debates, 1871*, 251–2.

54. Canada. House of Commons, *Debates, 1871*, 672, 698.

55. PRO, CO 60, /38, no. 11, Musgrave to Young, 20 February 1870.

56. Canada. Senate, *Debates, 1871*, 252; Arthur Harvey, *Statistical Account of British Columbia* (Ottawa: G.E. Desbarats, 1867), 9.

57. "British Columbia," *Morning Chronicle* (Halifax) (3 April 1871), 2, col. 1.

58. Allan Lönnberg, "The Digger Indian Stereo-type in California," *Journal of California and Great Basin Anthropology* 3, 2 (1981): 215–6.

59. Ibid., 219; William Penn Adair, "The Indian Territory in 1878," *Chronicles of Oklahoma* 4, 3 (1926): 258–9.

60. "The Admission of British Columbia," *Canadian Gleaner* (Huntingdon) (6 April 1871), 2, col. 5–6.

61. Allan Greer, "Historical Roots of Canadian Democracy," *Journal of Canadian Studies* 34, 1 (Spring 1999): 18–22.

62. Canada. Senate, *Debates, 1871*, 166.

63. Canada. House of Commons, *Debates, 1871*, 672.

4   From Peter H. Russell, "Provincial Rights," *Constitutional Odyssey: Can Canadians Become a Sovereign People?* (Toronto: University of Toronto Press, 2004), 34–52. Reprinted with permission of the publisher.

The great conceit of constitution-makers is to believe that the words they put in the constitution can with certainty and precision control a country's future. The great conceit of those who apply a written constitution is to believe that their interpretation captures perfectly the founders' intentions. Those who write constitutions are rarely single-minded in their long-term aspirations. They harbour conflicting hopes and fears about the constitution's evolution. The language of the constitution is inescapably general and latent with ambiguous possibilities. Written constitutions can establish the broad grooves in which a nation-state develops. But what happens within those grooves—the constitutional tilt favoured by history—is determined not by the constitutional text but by the political forces and events that shape the country's subsequent history.

Canada's constitutional development in the decades immediately following Confederation is a monument to the truth of these propositions. Although a majority of the Fathers of Confederation favoured a highly centralized federation, it soon became apparent that their aspirations would not be fulfilled. Instead, the most effective constitutional force in the new federation was the provincial rights movement. Far from moving toward a unitary state, Canada, by the end of the nineteenth century, had become a thoroughly federal country.

One might have expected the stiffest challenge to Macdonald's centralism to have come from Nova Scotia or Quebec. Nova Scotians, as we have seen, voted against Confederation in the provincial and federal elections of 1867. Immediately following Confederation a significant secessionist movement was developing in the province.[1] In 1868 Joseph Howe led a delegation to London seeking a repeal of the union. Nova Scotian opposition to Confederation, however, was not based on a desire for stronger provincial powers. In the

end, Nova Scotian separatism was quelled by persuading Howe to join the federal cabinet and by offering Nova Scotia better terms, not through a constitutional amendment but by bringing its debt allowance into line with New Brunswick's.

From the very beginning, the Province of Quebec, in the words of A.I. Silver, "was seen as the geographical and political expression of the French-Canadian nationality, as a French-Catholic province and the French-Canadian homeland."[2] It was not just the *rouge* opponents of Confederation who championed the cause of provincial autonomy and resisted federal interference in provincial affairs. The *Bleus* had promoted Confederation in Quebec largely on the grounds that it would give the French majority in Quebec exclusive control over matters basic to their culture. A *bleu* paper in 1872, for example, claimed that "as Conservatives we must be in favour of provincial rights and against centralization."[3]

It was not Quebec but Ontario that spearheaded the provincial rights movement. Ontario would seem the least likely province to play this role. After all, support for Confederation had been stronger in Ontario than in any other province. With the largest and fastest-growing population, Ontario was expected to be able to dominate national politics. Why at this formative stage in the federation's history should its provincial government be in the vanguard of the provincial rights movement?

The answer is to be found in the pattern of partisan politics that developed soon after Confederation and has endured ever since. Even before Confederation, the Great Coalition of Conservatives and Reformers had broken up. The first federal government after Confederation was headed by the Conservative leader John A. Macdonald. As Ontario Reformers and Quebec Liberals began to organize a competing national party, they naturally took up the provincial cause. In the words of Christopher Armstrong, "If Macdonald's Conservatives were the party of centralism, then its opponents would become the party of localism and provincialism, recruiting the anti-Confederates of the Maritimes to the Reform cause."[4]

The Conservatives dominated the first 30 years of federal politics, holding office in Ottawa for all but four of those years. During that same period the Liberals were having their greatest success at the provincial level. Nowhere was this more true than in Ontario, where Oliver Mowat's Liberals won six successive elections between 1875 and 1896. While Mowat found Liberal allies in other provincial capitals, notably Quebec's Honoré Mercier, he was in office the longest and built the strongest record of provincial rights advocacy. Mowat's championing of this cause is remarkable in that he began his professional career as a junior in John A. Macdonald's law office, was a Father of Confederation, and had moved the Quebec Resolutions setting forth the division of powers between the two levels of government.[5]

The pattern of politics in which one party dominates at the federal level while its main opposition gathers strength in the provincial capitals has been repeated several times in Canadian history. For a long stretch of the twentieth century the Liberals dominated the federal scene while the Conservatives and other opposition parties won in the provinces. The reverse has been developing since the Mulroney Conservatives came to power in Ottawa in 1984. The fact that the largest national parties have gone through long periods in which their experience in government has been concentrated at the provincial level has done much to make provincial rights a cause that transcends partisan politics.

Although this phenomenon is one that stems from the fluctuating fortunes of partisan politics, it is closely tied to the Canadian system of parliamentary government. Responsible government tends to concentrate power in the hands of the prime minister and the cabinet. After Confederation it soon became apparent that this concentration of power would occur in the provincial capitals as well as in Ottawa. In Canada, provincial premiers emerged as the strongest political opponents to the federal prime minister. State governors in the United States, hemmed in by an elaborate system of checks and balances, are political pygmies compared with provincial premiers who perform as political giants on the national stage. Canadians, without any conscious design, found their liberal check and balance not *within* the national or provincial capitals but in the rivalry and tensions *between* those capitals.

The success of the provincial rights movement cannot be attributed to weak governments at the national level in Canada's formative years. Quite to the contrary, federal administrations presided over by John A. Macdonald, who was prime minister of Canada for 19 of the country's first 24 years, were strong nation-building governments not at all shy about asserting federal power. Under Macdonald's leadership, Canada's "manifest destiny" of becoming a continental nation-state was quickly fulfilled. In 1869 the Hudson's Bay Company's territories covering the prairies and the far north were purchased and added to Canada. A year later, following military suppression of the Métis led by Louis Riel, the Province of Manitoba was carved out of the North-West Territories. In 1871 Canada was extended to the Pacific, when British Columbia became a province on terms agreeable to its colonial government. Prince Edward Island became the seventh province, agreeing to join Confederation in 1873. To this expanding national territory Macdonald's Conservatives applied a National Policy, completing the transcontinental rail link, erecting tariff walls to protect manufacturing, and stimulating immigration to populate the west and provide a market for the protected industries.[6]

Important as the achievements of Macdonald's governments were in building the material conditions of nationhood, they contributed little to a Canadian sense of political community. Nor did they translate into constitutional gains for the federal government. The Conservatives' economic nationalism, as Reg Whitaker has observed, relied "on elites and on their exclusively economic motives."[7] It did not have much emotional appeal at the mass level. Government in far-away Ottawa had difficulty competing with provincial governments for the allegiance of citizens in the new provinces. During these years it was the provinces, not Ottawa, that seized and held the initiative in constitutional politics.

The first objective of the provincial rights movement was to resist and overcome a hierarchical version of Canadian federalism in which the provinces were to be treated as a subordinate or junior level of government. An early focal point of resistance was the office of provincial lieutenant governor. From a Macdonald centralist perspective, the lieutenant governors were essentially agents of the federal government in provincial capitals. In the 1870s, however, Ontario, under Mowat's leadership, began to insist that lieutenant governors had full Crown powers in matters of provincial jurisdiction and that they exercised these powers on the advice of provincial ministers. [. . .] Implicit in the provincial claim was an assertion of the provinces' constitutional equality with the federal government.

No element of the Constitution was potentially more threatening to provincial autonomy than the federal powers of reservation and disallowance. These powers derived from an imperial rather than a federal structure. Under the reservation power, the lieutenant governor of a province could refuse to sign a bill that had passed through the provincial legislature and could reserve it for consideration by the federal cabinet. If, within a year, the lieutenant governor was not instructed to give royal assent, the bill would die. Disallowance was simply a veto power under which the federal government could render null and void any provincial law within a year of its passage by the provincial legislature. These federal powers mirrored powers of reservation and disallowance over federal legislation that the imperial government retained and that were also written into the BNA Act.[8] The only difference was that the British government had two years rather than one to decide whether to block Canadian legislation.

The powers of reservation and disallowance are classic examples of how a shift in political sentiment and principle can render formal legal powers unusable. Well before Confederation, the British government had greatly reduced the use of its imperial powers of control over the British North American legislatures. Soon after Confederation these powers fell into desuetude. In the first decade a few Canadian bills were reserved, but royal assent was always granted and there were no reservations after 1878. Only one Canadian act was disallowed, in 1873, and the act in question was clearly unconstitutional.[9] At imperial conferences in the late 1920s declarations were made that these imperial powers would never be used and that steps would be taken to remove them from Canada's Constitution. Although the latter step was never taken, no one really cares that the powers remain formally in the Constitution because there is a clear political understanding—a constitutional convention—on both the British and Canadian sides that the powers are completely inoperative.[10] This convention of desuetude was established because use of the imperial powers was incompatible with the principle of Canadian self-government, a principle which, at least in matters of domestic policy, was so firmly in place by the 1870s that breach of it would have had the gravest political consequences.

A similar process occurred with respect to the federal government's powers of reservation and disallowance. Over time, the principle of provincial autonomy—self-government in those areas constitutionally assigned to the provincial legislatures—became so strongly held in the Canadian political system that the federal powers of reservation and disallowance, though remaining in the Constitution, became politically unusable. This did not happen all at once. It occurred only because the idea that the provinces are not subordinate to but coordinate with the federal government became the politically dominant conception of Canadian federalism.

At first federal governments—not only Macdonald's but the Liberals too when they were in power in the 1870s—made extensive use of the powers of reservation and disallowance.[11] Macdonald's first administration withheld assent on 16 of 24 provincial bills reserved by lieutenant governors. Between 1867 and 1896, 65 provincial acts were disallowed by the federal government. Although the powers continued to be used, they came under increasing attack from the provinces, and from no province more than Ontario. Even when, as was most often the case, the rationale for using these powers was the federal government's view that the legislation was outside the province's jurisdiction, provincial rights advocates were inclined to argue that questions concerning the division of powers should be settled in the courts, not by the federal cabinet. When the Macdonald government in 1881 disallowed Ontario's Rivers and Streams Act primarily to protect the interests of a prominent Conservative, Mowat decided to fight back. He promptly had the legislation re-enacted. After being disallowed and re-enacted three more times, the legislation was allowed to stand. The courts had the final say when the Judicial Committee of the Privy Council upheld the provincial law in 1884.[12]

Abolition of the federal disallowance power topped the list of constitutional proposals emanating from the Interprovincial Conference of 1887. The conference was called by Honoré Mercier, premier of Quebec, who had come to power largely on the strength of Quebec's resentment of the use of federal power in the hanging of Louis Riel. Macdonald and the Conservative premiers of British Columbia and Prince Edward Island declined Mercier's invitation. Delegates from the Liberal governments of the four original provinces and from Manitoba's Conservative administration, "angered by repeated disallowances of their railway legislation,"[13] met for a week under Mowat's chairmanship behind closed doors. The 22 resolutions that they unanimously endorsed amounted to a frontal attack on the centralist conception of Confederation. Besides calling for the abolition of federal disallowance and an increase in federal subsidies, the conference proposed that half of the federal Senate be chosen by the provinces. Once these proposals had been approved by the provincial legislatures, they were to be submitted to London for enactment as constitutional amendments by the imperial Parliament.

In the end, nothing concrete came of these proposals. Only the lower houses of New Brunswick and Nova Scotia sent them on to London. The imperial authorities refused to act without having heard from the federal government or the other provinces.[14] Nonetheless, the 1887 conference is a significant landmark in Canada's constitutional politics, for it clearly demonstrated that the constitutional initiative had passed to the provinces. Strong centralist voices could still be heard, not least John A. Macdonald's, but the centralist view was losing its ascendancy in both French and English Canada.

During the first 30 years of Confederation, the provinces made their most tangible constitutional gains not through the process of formal constitutional amendment but through litigation in the courts. Their judicial victories were achieved in London before the Judicial Committee of the Privy Council. The Supreme Court of Canada had been created by the federal Parliament in 1875, but it was supreme in name only. Although the Liberal government which had sponsored the Supreme Court Act aimed at making the court Canada's highest tribunal, the Conservative opposition and the Colonial Office were able to thwart this objective.[15] The right of appeal to the highest court in the British Empire, the Judicial Committee of the Privy Council, was retained in Canada until 1949.

Retaining the Judicial Committee as Canada's highest court had significant consequences for the development of the Canadian Constitution. [. . .]

It did not take long for the English law lords who manned the Judicial Committee of the Privy Council to reverse the Supreme Court's approach to the Constitution. By the 1880s a steady stream of constitutional cases was being taken on appeal to London. The fact that so many constitutional questions were coming before the courts gives the lie to the pretension of the Fathers of Confederation to have settled all questions of jurisdiction. [. . .]

Between 1880 and 1896 the Judicial Committee decided 18 cases involving 20 issues relating to the division of powers. Fifteen of these issues (75 per cent) it decided in favour of the provinces. What is even more important, as Murray Greenwood has observed, is that in these decisions the committee reversed "every major centralist doctrine of the [Supreme] Court."[16] [. . .]

The theory espoused by the Judicial Committee of the Privy Council is often called the theory of "classical federalism".[17] There can be no doubt that Macdonald and many of Canada's constitutional founders did not think of the country they were building as a classic federation. Some of the Fathers of Confederation, however, especially Quebec leaders like Cartier and Taché, were apprehensive of the centralist view and hoped that the provinces would be autonomous in the areas of law making reserved for them. The Quebec supporters of Confederation realized they could not retain their political support if they portrayed Confederation publicly in centralist terms. The political coalition that put Confederation together never came to a clear and explicit accord on federal theory.[18] What the Judicial Committee did was to give official legal sanction to a theory of federalism congenial to those who, at the time of Confederation and afterwards, could not accept centralism.

The impact of the Judicial Committee's constitutional decisions demonstrates a fundamental feature of constitutional development which is still, at most, only dimly understood by the Canadian public. In countries with written constitutions stipulating the powers of government and the rights of citizens, and in which the constitution is taken seriously, judges will play an important role in enforcing the constitution. The process through which judges play that role is called "judicial review." In performing the function of judicial review, judges review the acts of the executive and legislature and rule null and void those that do not conform with the constitution. Through these determinations, especially those of the highest court, the meaning of the constitution's general terms is fleshed out. This process of judicial review has been so important in the United States that it is said that "the constitution is what the judges say it is."[19]

The Fathers of Confederation did not discuss judicial review. Although some of them were aware of the important role the Supreme Court was playing in the United States, they did not see that there would be an immediate need for a Canadian Supreme Court.[20] Their constitutionalism was much more British than American, and hence more attuned to an unwritten constitution. They were accustomed to having the Judicial Committee of the Privy Council, as the highest imperial court, review colonial laws for their conformity with imperial law. Since the Canadian Constitution took the form of an act of the imperial Parliament, it was logical that this mechanism of imperial judicial control would apply to the BNA Act. For enforcing the rules of federalism internally, within Canada, it is evident that the Fathers of Confederation looked more to the federal executive using its powers of reservation and disallowance than to the judiciary. Also, it was to the federal executive, not the judiciary, that the BNA Act directed minorities to appeal if they believed a province had infringed their constitutional right to denominational schools.[21]

Federal government enforcement of the Constitution made sense, of course, so long as Canadian federalism was viewed primarily as a hierarchical, quasi-imperial structure in which the provinces were a junior level of government. From this perspective, the objective of constitutional enforcement was to keep the provinces from exceeding their powers. John A. Macdonald never contemplated that Canadian courts would find federal laws unconstitutional.[22] Once however, the hierarchical view of federalism began to be eclipsed by the theory of classical federalism and dual sovereignty, it was much more logical for a judicial tribunal independent of both levels of government to exercise the primary responsibility for applying the Constitution. [. . .]

The success of the provincial rights movement did not mean that in terms either of governmental power or of citizens' allegiance the provincial political realm had come to surpass the federal. Laurier, after all, was a national leader whose government would pursue important initiatives in domestic and international politics. Indeed, Laurier and other Quebec leaders, by supporting the rights of French Catholics outside Quebec, were encouraging Quebecers, in the words of A.I. Silver, to look beyond "the still-special home of Quebec" and see that "all Canada should yet be a country for French-Canadians."[23] Since the 1890s there have been shifts back and forth in the balance of power between the two levels of government, but there has always been a balance; neither level has been able to dominate the other. Canada's citizens have been thoroughly schizophrenic in their loyalties, maintaining strong associations with their provincial governments as well as the federal government. In this sense Canada, despite the ambiguities and contradictions in its Constitution, became, as Donald Smiley put it, "in the most elemental way a federal country."[24]

One measure of how ingrained the balanced view of federalism has become is the fate of those imperial powers of reservation and disallowance which the federal government held over the provinces. They are still in the Constitution, but they are simply not used any more. Disallowance has not been used since 1943. The last time a lieutenant governor reserved a provincial bill was 1961, and then his action was totally repudiated by the federal prime minister, John Diefenbaker, as violating the basic principles of Canadian federalism.[25] When the Parti Québécois came to power in Quebec in the 1970s and enacted Bill 101, the Charter of the French Language, the Trudeau government in Ottawa, which bitterly opposed this legislation, did not ever indicate that it would disallow it. [. . .] By the 1980s political parties and leaders of all persuasions, like Laurier and the Liberals a century earlier, would not protect minority rights at the cost of violating provincial rights.

The sovereignty at issue in the struggle for provincial rights was not the sovereignty of the people but the sovereignty of governments and legislatures. The sovereignty claimed and won for provincial legislatures and governments within their allotted sphere of jurisdiction was primarily a top-down kind of sovereignty.[26] Canadian constitutional politics continued to be highly elitist, with federal and provincial leaders contending against each other in intergovernmental meetings and the courts. Still, traces of a more democratic constitutionalism were beginning to appear in the rhetoric, if not the reality, of the constitutional process. [. . .]

Out of this rhetoric and the political success of its authors was born the myth of Confederation as a compact entered into by sovereign provincial communities. According to the compact theory, the provinces as the founding, constituent units of the federation retained the right to alter the terms of their original union.[27] This was the theory promulgated by Honoré Mercier and the other provincial premiers who attended the 1887 Interprovincial Conference: "the conference represented all of the original parties to the compact of 1864, and the partners should now assess the state of their joint enterprise."[28] Not surprisingly, the theory found its most articulate spokesmen in Quebec, where the notion of the province as a founding community could be infused with a sense of ethnic nationalism.

What is meant in referring to the compact theory as a "myth" is that its validity depends not on its historical accuracy but on its capacity to serve as a set of "beliefs and notions that men hold, that they live by or live for."[29] Confederation, as we have seen, did involve a two-stage agreement, first between English- and French-Canadian politicians and then between Canadian and Maritime politicians. Leading participants in the agreement, including John A. Macdonald and George-Etienne Cartier, as well as some of the imperial authorities, frequently referred to the Quebec Resolutions as a treaty or pact. But it is not clear that when they used this terminology they had the same thing in mind. It is most unlikely that when John A. Macdonald talked of a treaty he meant that the parties to the agreement exercised and retained sovereign political authority.

From a strictly legal point of view, the founding colonies in 1867, as colonies, did not have sovereign powers to retain. They did not formally sign or give legal authority to the Constitution. Further, given the elitist quality of the process and the failure, indeed the disinclination, to seek a clear popular mandate for the Confederation deal, it is a total fabrication to maintain that the peoples of the founding provinces had covenanted together to produce the Canadian federal union. This fabrication flies in the face of the top-down process whereby new provinces

were added—especially the two provinces carved out of the North-West Territories in 1905. As Arthur Lower observed, "there was not the slightest vestige of a 'compact' in the Acts of Parliament that created the provinces of Alberta and Saskatchewan in 1905."[30]

Nor was the compact theory strictly followed in constitutional practice. If the Canadian Constitution was a compact or treaty among the provinces, then no changes should have been made to it without the consent of all the provinces. Formally constitutional changes, as amendments to the BNA Act, were enacted by the British Parliament, but that body would act only on a request from Canada. During the period that the compact theory was gathering force, however, several amendments were made to the BNA Act at the request of the federal government and Parliament without consulting the provinces or seeking their consent. While none of these amendments directly affected the powers of the provinces, two of them related to the structure of the federation: one empowered the federal Parliament to create new provinces and the other provided for the representation of territories in the federal Parliament.[31] Prior to the 1907 amendment,[32] which revised the subsidies paid to the provinces, Laurier did hold a federal–provincial conference and eight of the nine provinces (British Columbia held out for better terms) agreed to the federal proposal. But the provinces were not consulted on the 1915 amendment that redefined the divisions of the Senate, forming a new section out of the four western provinces.[33]

Even though the compact theory was not consistently observed in the constitutional amendment process, it had become a powerful constitutional ideal by the turn of the century. Provincial rights and the compact theory had, as Ramsay Cook put it, "attained a position close to motherhood in the scale of Canadian political values. It would be difficult to find a prominent politician who was not willing to pay lip-service to the principle of provincial rights and its theoretical underpinning, the compact theory."[34] As a constitutional doctrine, the compact theory may have contained ambiguities and lacked precision, but its strength as a political value in Canada meant that the Canadian political community that was forming would be complex and deeply pluralist. Canada would take its place in the world as an interventionist state and its nationwide activities would take on increasing significance in the lives of its citizens, but the provinces would nonetheless endure as strong constituent elements of the Canadian community.

The ambiguities of the compact theory were intensified by the co-existence of two competing versions of the compact: a compact of founding provinces and a compact of founding peoples.[35] The latter contended that Canada was founded on the basis of a covenant between English Canadians and French Canadiens. In the final analysis, the making of Canada in 1867 was "the free association of two peoples, enjoying equal rights in all matters."[36] These were the words of Henri Bourassa, the theory's most eloquent spokesman and founder of the great Montreal newspaper *Le Devoir* in 1910. Again, the significance of this theory in Canada's constitutional politics rests not on its historical accuracy but on its potency as a political myth. It is easy to show that neither in law nor in politics was the BNA Act a formal agreement between the French and English people of British North America. Nonetheless, that constitutional settlement depended, as we have seen, on English- and French-Canadian leaders agreeing to a federal structure with a province in which the French Canadians would remain a majority. For many English Canadians, assent to this agreement was only grudgingly given; for French Canadians it represented liberation from Lord Durham's scheme to assimilate them into a unicultural English political community, the triumph of their cultural survival—and, indeed for many, of national survival. The expectations on the French side flowing from that agreement gave rise to the theory that Confederation was based on a compact between two founding peoples.[37]

As originally espoused by Bourassa and other French Canadians, the two founding peoples theory was applied to all of Canada. Indeed, it was advanced as the theoretical underpinning for a pan-Canadian nationalism that viewed all Canada in dualist terms. Its exponents defended the rights of the French minorities outside Quebec and of the English minority in Quebec. In this sense, it may have provided "moral support for minimizing the consequences of the compact of provinces" and of provincial rights.[38] At the same time, this dualist view of Canada always retained a special place for the province of Quebec. As the homeland of one of the founding peoples, it had the right to be secure against intrusions into its culture by the general government answerable to an English-speaking majority.

Lurking within these rival compact theories were deep-seated differences on the nature of Canada as a political community. The idea that Quebec has a special place in Confederation as the only province in which one of the founding peoples forms the majority would collide with the doctrine of provincial equality. More fundamentally, the idea of a Canada based on the English and the French as its two founding peoples would be challenged at the end of the twentieth century by Canadians who were neither British nor French in their cultural background and by the Aboriginal peoples.

So long as Canadians were not interested in taking custody of their Constitution into their own hands, this conflict over the nature of Canada as a political community was of no great political importance. It was bound, however, to become salient once that condition changed. The time arrived in 1926, when the Balfour Declaration declared Canada and the other self-governing dominions to be "autonomous Communities" within the British Commonwealth.[39] Canada's political leaders then faced the challenge of arranging for Canada to become constitutionally self-governing.

NOTES

1. W.P.M. Kennedy, *The Constitution of Canada, 1534–1937: An Introduction to Its Development, Law and Culture*, 2nd edn (London: Oxford University Press, 1938), 318–20.
2. A.I. Silver, *The French-Canadian Idea of Confederation, 1864–1900* (Toronto: University of Toronto Press, 1982), 111.
3. Ibid., 121.
4. Christopher Armstrong, *The Politics of Federalism: Ontario's Relations with the Federal Government, 1867–1942* (Toronto: University of Toronto Press, 1981), 14.
5. A. Margaret Evans, *Sir Oliver Mowat* (Toronto: University of Toronto Press for The Ontario Historical Studies Series, 1992).
6. Craig Brown, "The Nationalism of the National Policy," in Peter H. Russell, ed., *Nationalism in Canada* (Toronto: McGraw-Hill, 1966), 155–63.
7. Reginald Whitaker, "Democracy and the Canadian Constitution," in Keith Banting and Richard Simeon, eds, *And No One Cheered: Federalism, Democracy and the Constitutional Act* (Toronto: Methuen, 1983), 250.
8. Sections 55–7.
9. R.M. Dawson, *Government of Canada* (Toronto: University of Toronto Press, 1947), 142.
10. Peter W. Hogg, *Constitutional Law of Canada*, 2nd edn (Toronto: Carswell, 1985), 38.
11. Gerard V. LaForest, *Disallowance and Reservation of Provincial Legislation* (Ottawa: Department of Justice, 1965).
12. Paul Romney, *Mr. Attorney: The Attorney General for Ontario in Court, Cabinet and Legislature, 1791–1899* (Toronto: University of Toronto Press, 1986), 255–6.
13. Armstrong, *Politics of Federalism*, 29.
14. See Paul Gérin-Lajoie, *Constitutional Amendment in Canada* (Toronto: University of Toronto Press, 1950), 142–3.
15. Frank MacKinnon, "The Establishment of the Supreme Court of Canada," *Canadian Historical Review* 27 (1946): 258–74.
16. F. Murray Greenwood, "Lord Watson, Institutional Self-Interest and the Decentralization of Canadian Federalism in the 1890's," *University of British Columbia Law Review* 9 (1974): 267.
17. K.C. Wheare, *Federal Government*, 4th edn (London: Oxford University Press, 1963).
18. P.B. Waite, *Life and Times of Confederation, 1864–1867: Politics, Newspapers, and the Union of British North America*, 2nd edn (Toronto: University of Toronto Press, 1962), chap. 8.
19. A.T. Mason and W.M. Beaney, *American Constitutional Law* (Englewood Cliffs, NJ: Prentice-Hall, 1959), 3.
20. Jennifer Smith, "The Origins of Judicial Review in Canada," *Canadian Journal of Political Science* 16 (1983): 115–34.
21. Section 93(4).
22. Peter H. Russell, *The Supreme Court of Canada as a Bilingual and Bicultural Institution* (Ottawa: Queen's Printer, 1969), chap. 1.
23. Silver, *French-Canadian Idea of Confederation*, 243
24. D.V. Smiley, *Canada in Question: Federalism in the Eighties*, 3rd edn (Toronto: McGraw-Hill Ryerson, 1980), 1.
25. See Edwin Black, *Divided Loyalties: Canadian Concepts of Federalism* (Montreal and London: McGill-Queen's University Press 1975), 132–5.
26. Whitaker, "Democracy and the Canadian Constitution."
27. Ramsay Cook, *Provincial Autonomy, Minority Rights and the Compact Theory, 1867–1921* (Ottawa: Queen's Printer, 1969).
28. Black, *Divided Loyalties*, 154.
29. R.M. MacIver in *The Web of Government* (New York: Macmillan, 1947), 4.
30. Arthur R.M. Lower, *Colony to Nation: A History of Canada*, 4th edn (Toronto: Longmans, 1964), 432.
31. Guy Favreau, *The Amendment of the Constitution of Canada* (Ottawa: Queen's Printer, 1965).
32. The British North America Act of 1907.
33. The British North America Act of 1915.
34. Cook, *Provincial Autonomy*, 44.
35. Filippo Sabetti, "The Historical Context of Constitutional Change in Canada," *Law and Contemporary Problems* 45 (1982): 11–32.
36. Quoted ibid., 21.
37. Daniel J. Elazar, "Constitution-making: The Pre-eminently Political Act," in Keith G. Banting and Richard Simeon, eds, *Redesigning the State: The Politics of Constitutional Change in Industrial Nations* (Toronto: University of Toronto Press, 1985), 245–6.
38. Sabetti, "Historical Context of Constitutional Changes in Canada," 20.
39. Dawson, *Government of Canada*, 63.

Chapter 2
Establishing a New Order

READINGS

Primary Documents

Historical Interpretations

INTRODUCTION

As Chapter 1 indicated, Confederation did not bring harmony or homogeneity to the former British North American colonies. Yet, the young Dominion had to exert authority over a huge land base and a variety of people, many of whom, especially in the North-West, had little experience as citizens in the European or colonial sense. This was also the age of railways and of restless capitalists envisioning cities where others saw only wilderness. Developers were eager to build quickly, but they also wanted to project a sense of decorum and civility, and conquering the wilderness would be easier if the process could be rendered more predictable. They fondly wished that before long Canada would gain status as a young lion of the Empire, an Empire that was not yet ready, as Prime Minister Macdonald would find out, to allow Canada a free hand in its dealings with other nations. Still, there was more than enough for the

Canadian government to do at home as it experienced first-hand the difficulties of managing a kind of "internal empire." Each new province added to the federation held the promise of new resources for Canada, but this rapid expansion also meant further expenditure to maintain control over the newly added land and those living on it. Dominion also meant the informal process of defining who (or what) represented order, and ensuring that the legal and moral standards of faraway places like Montreal or London were at least loosely adhered to on the frontier. This resulted in treaties with Aboriginal peoples and the establishment of institutions and infrastructure, most famously the North West Mounted Police (NWMP) and the transcontinental railway. The abrupt changes brought about as these arms of the state reached into the lives of long-time residents are what concern us most here. The first primary source sets out the composition of the well-known mounted police force, but also gives us a distilled version of the laws that were considered most important for the territory. The new force accompanied federal government officials whose job was to conclude treaties with various First Nations in the territories. We have also included parts of Treaty Six, one of the "numbered" treaties that lumped First Nations living in particular geographical areas together for the purposes of negotiation and administration. The treaty shows what was expected of the Aboriginal signatories, and what they could expect in return. It makes few, if any, allowances for Aboriginal conceptions of possession, as the treaty expected that the First Nations involved would make way for the inevitable. The secondary sources both deal with the impact of treaties and the more formalized relationships created by the treaties. Keith Smith's contribution shows how the federal government, churches, and police forces controlled the movements of Aboriginal people and their relationships with settlers so that a liberal order could take hold in the West. Sarah Carter addresses the state's responses to polygamy in Aboriginal communities, noting that condemnation of the practice allowed authorities to reach deep into the family unit to reconfigure (or at least attempt to reconfigure) the lives of individuals.

QUESTIONS FOR CONSIDERATION

1. Considering the various provisions in the act establishing the NWMP, what sort of vision did the Canadian government have for the West?
2. Why do you think Treaty Six was between Queen Victoria and the First Nations named in the treaty?
3. What seemed to be the purpose of exerting all the effort to "civilize" Canada's newest territory?
4. Smith describes the Department of Indian Affairs's dealings with the churches. Why did these two parties sometimes have their differences?
5. Why did the department care that some bands included families that had more than one wife?

SUGGESTIONS FOR FURTHER READING

Sarah Carter, *The Importance of Being Monogamous: Marriage and Nation Building in Western Canada to 1915* (Edmonton: University of Alberta Press, 2008).

———, *Lost Harvests: Prairie Indian Reserve, Farmers and Government Policy* (Montreal and Kingston: McGill-Queen's University Press, 1990).

James Daschuk, *Clearing the Plains: Disease, Politics of Starvation, and the Loss of Aboriginal Life* (Regina: University of Regina Press, 2013).

Olive Patricia Dickason, *Canada's First Nations: A History of Founding Peoples from the Earliest Times*, 3rd edn (Toronto: Oxford University Press, 2002).

Cole Harris, *Making Native Space: Colonialism, Resistance, and Reserves in British Columbia* (Vancouver: UBC Press, 2003).

John Sutton Lutz, *Makúk: A New History of Aboriginal–White Relations* (Vancouver: UBC Press, 2009).

J.R. Miller, *Compact, Contract, Covenant: Aboriginal Treaty-Making in Canada* (Toronto: University of Toronto Press, 2009).

————, *Shingwauk's Vision: A History of Native Residential Schools* (Toronto: University of Toronto Press, 1996).

John S. Milloy, *A National Crime: The Canadian Government and the Residential School System* (Winnipeg: University of Manitoba Press, 1999).

Arthur J. Ray, Jim Miller, and Frank Tough, *Bounty and Benevolence: A Documentary History of Saskatchewan Treaties* (Montreal and Kingston: McGill-Queen's University Press, 2000).

Jill St Germain, *Indian Treaty-Making Policy in the United States and Canada, 1867–1877* (Toronto: University of Toronto Press, 2001).

Primary Documents

1 From "An Act Respecting the Administration of Justice, and for the Establishment of a Police Force in the North West Territories" (1873) *Acts of the Parliament of the Dominion of Canada . . . first session of the second Parliament, begun and holden at Ottawa, on the fifth day of March, and closed by prorogation on the thirteenth day of August, 1873* (Ottawa: B. Chamberlin, 1873), 110–18.

CHAP. 35.

An Act respecting the Administration of Justice, and for the establishment of a Police Force in the North West Territories.
[Assented to 23rd May, 1873.]
HER MAJESTY, by and with the advice and consent of the Senate and House of Commons of Canada, enacts as follows:—

1. The Governor may from time to time appoint, by commission under the Great Seal, one or more fit and proper person or persons to be and act as a Stipendiary Magistrate or Stipendiary Magistrates within the North West Territories, who shall reside at such place or places as may be ordered by the Governor in Council; and the Governor in Council shall assign to any such Stipendiary Magistrate a yearly salary not exceeding three thousand dollars, together with his actual travelling expenses.

2. Every Stipendiary Magistrate shall hold office during pleasure; and shall exercise within the North West Territories, or within such limited portion of the same as may be prescribed by the Governor in Council, the magisterial, judicial and other functions appertaining to any Justice of the Peace, or any two Justices of the Peace, under any laws or Ordinances which may from time to time be in force in the North West Territories.

3. Any Stipendiary Magistrate shall further have power to hear and determine, in a summary way and without the intervention of a jury, any charge against any person or persons for any of the following offences alleged to have been committed within the North West Territories, as follows:—

1. Simple larceny, larceny from the person, embezzlement, or obtaining money or property by false pretences, or feloniously receiving stolen property, in any case in which the value of the whole property, alleged to have been stolen, embezzled, obtained or received, does not, in the judgment of such Stipendiary Magistrate, exceed one hundred dollars; or

2. Having attempted to commit larceny from the person or simple larceny; or

3. With having committed an aggravated assault, by unlawfully and maliciously inflicting upon any other person, either with or without a weapon or instrument, any grievous bodily harm, or by unlawfully and maliciously cutting, stabbing or wounding any other person; or

4. With having committed an assault upon any female whatever, or upon any male child whose age does not, in the opinion of the magistrate, exceed fourteen years, such assault, if upon a female, not amounting, in his opinion, to an assault with intent to commit a rape; or

5. Having assaulted, obstructed, molested or hindered any Stipendiary Magistrate, Justice of the Peace, Commissioner or Superintendent of Police, a policeman, constable or bailiff, or Officer of Customs or Excise, or other officer, in the lawful performance of his duty, or with intent to prevent the performance thereof;

And upon any conviction by such Stipendiary Magistrate, the person so convicted may be sentenced to such punishment as he thinks fit, by imprisonment for any period less than two years in any gaol or place of confinement, with or without hard labour, and with or without solitary confinement, or by fine, or by such imprisonment and fine.

4. The Chief Justice or any Judge of the Court of Queen's Bench of the Province of Manitoba, or any two Stipendiary Magistrates sitting together as a Court, shall have power and authority to hear and determine within the North West Territories, in a summary way and without the intervention of any Grand or Petty Jury, any charge against any person or persons for offences alleged to have been committed within the North West Territories, and the maximum punishment for which does not exceed seven years imprisonment; and such Court shall be a Court of record; and if imprisonment in a penitentiary be awarded in any such case, the Court may cause the convict to be conveyed to the penitentiary in the Province of Manitoba; and he shall undergo such punishment therein as if convicted in the Province of Manitoba.

5. Any Justice of the Peace, or any Stipendiary Magistrate or any Judge of the Court of Queen's Bench of the Province of Manitoba, shall have power and authority to commit and cause to be conveyed to gaol in the Province of Manitoba, for trial by the said Court of Queen's Bench according to the laws of criminal procedure in force in the said Province, any person or persons at any time charged with the commission of any offence against any of the laws or Ordinances in force in the North West Territories, punishable by death or imprisonment in the penitentiary: and the Court of Queen's Bench and any Judge thereof, shall have power and authority to try any person arraigned before the said Court on any such charge; and the jury laws and laws of criminal procedure of the said Province shall apply to any such trial; except that the punishment to be awarded, upon conviction of any such person, shall be according to

the laws in force in the North West Territories: and the sentence may be carried into effect in a penitentiary or other place of confinement in the said Province, as if the same were in the North West Territories.

[. . .]

7. Where it is impossible or inconvenient, in the absence or remoteness of any gaol or other place of confinement, to carry out any sentence of imprisonment, any Justice of the Peace or Stipendiary Magistrate, or any two Stipendiary Magistrates sitting together as aforesaid, or any Judge of the Court of Queen's Bench of Manitoba, may, according to their several powers and jurisdictions hereinbefore given, sentence such person so convicted before him or them, and sentenced, as aforesaid, to such imprisonment, to be placed and kept in the custody of the Police of the North West Territories, with or without hard labour,—the nature and extent of which shall be determined by the Justice of the Peace or Stipendiary Magistrate or Stipendiary Magistrates, or Judge, by or before whom such person was convicted.

8. The Governor in Council may cause to be erected in any part or parts of the North West Territories any building or buildings, or enclosure or enclosures, for the purposes of the gaol or lock-up, for the confinement of prisoners charged with the commission of any offence, or sentenced to any punishment therein; and confinement or imprisonment therein shall be held lawful and valid.

9. Whenever in any Act of the Parliament of Canada in force in the North West Territories, any officer is designated for carrying on any duty therein mentioned, and there shall be no such officer in the North West Territories, the Lieutenant Governor in Council may order by what other person or officer such duty shall be performed; and anything done by such person or officer, under such order, shall be valid and legal in the premises: or if it be in any such Act ordered that any document or thing shall be transmitted to any officer, Court, territorial division or place, and there shall be in the said North West Territories no such officer, Court or territorial division or place, then the Lieutenant Governor in Council may order to what officer, Court or place such transmission shall be made, or may dispense with the transmission thereof.

Mounted Police Force

10. The Governor in Council may constitute a Police Force in and for the North West Territories, and the Governor may from time to time, as may be found necessary, appoint by commission, a Commissioner of Police, and one or more Superintendents of Police, together with a Paymaster, Surgeon and Veterinary Surgeon, each of whom shall hold office during pleasure.

[. . .]

12. The Governor in Council may, from time to time, authorize the Commissioner of Police to appoint, by warrant under his hand, such number of Constables and Sub-Constables as he may think proper, not exceeding in the whole three hundred men; and such number thereof shall be mounted as the Governor in Council may at any time direct.

13. No person shall be appointed to the Police Force unless he be of a sound constitution, able to ride, active and able-bodied, of good character, and between the ages of eighteen and forty years; nor unless he be able to read and write either the English or French language.

[. . .]

15. The Commissioner and every Superintendent of Police shall be *ex-officio* a Justice of the Peace; and every constable and sub-constable of the Force shall be a constable in and for the whole of the North West Territories; and may execute the office in any part thereof, and in Manitoba

in the cases hereinbefore mentioned and provided for.

[. . .]

17. The Governor in Council may, from and out of any of the lands of the Dominion in the Province of Manitoba or in the North West Territories, make a free grant not exceeding one hundred and sixty acres, to any constable or sub-constable of the said force, who, at the expiration of three years of continuous service in the said Force, shall be certified by the Commissioner of Police to have conducted himself satisfactorily, and to have efficiently and ably performed the duties of his office during the said term of three years.

[. . .]

19. It shall be the duty of the Force—
   1. To perform all duties which now are or shall be hereafter assigned to constables in relation to the preservation of the peace, the prevention of crime, and of offences against the laws and Ordinances in force in the North West Territories, and the apprehension of criminals and offenders, and others who may be lawfully taken into custody;
   2. To attend upon any Judge, Stipendiary Magistrate or Justice of the Peace, when thereunto specially required, and, subject to the orders of the Commissioner or Superintendent, to execute all warrants and perform all duties and services in relation thereto, which may, under this Act or the laws and Ordinances in force in the North West Territories, lawfully be performed by constables;
   3. To perform all duties which may be lawfully performed by constables in relation to the escort and conveyance of convicts and other prisoners or lunatics, to or from any Courts, places of punishment or confinement, asylums or other places,—

And for these purposes, and in the performance of all the duties assigned to them by or under the authority of this Act, they shall have all the powers, authority, protection and privileges which any constable now has or shall hereafter by law have.

20. The Governor in Council may, from time to time, make rules and regulations for any of the following purposes, viz:—To regulate the number of the Force, not exceeding in the whole the number of three hundred men as hereinbefore provided; to prescribe the number of men who shall be mounted on horseback; to regulate and prescribe the clothing, arms, training and discipline of the Police Force; to regulate and prescribe the duties and authorities of the Commissioner and Superintendents of the Force, and the several places at or near which the same, or the Force or any portions thereof may from time to time be stationed; and generally all and every such matters and things for the good government, discipline and guidance of the Force as are not inconsistent with this Act: and such rules and regulations may impose penalties, not exceeding in any case thirty days' pay of the offenders, for any contravention thereof, and may direct that such penalty when incurred may be deducted from the offender's pay: they may determine what officer shall have power to declare such penalty incurred, and to impose the same; and they shall have force as if enacted by law.

[. . .]

22. Any member of the Force may be suspended from his charge or dismissed by the Commissioner or by any Superintendent to whom the Commissioner shall have delegated the power to do so; and any Superintendent may be suspended from office by the Commissioner until the pleasure of the governor in Council shall be known; and every such suspension or dismissal shall take effect from the time it shall be made known either orally or in writing to the party suspended or dismissed.

23. Any Superintendent or any member of the Force suspended or dismissed shall forthwith deliver up to the Commissioner

or to a Superintendent or to any constable authorized to receive the same, his clothing, arms, accoutrements and all property of the Crown in his possession as a member of the Force or used for police purposes; or in case of his refusing or neglecting so to do, shall incur a penalty of fifty dollars.

24. Whenever the Commissioner shall deem it advisable to make or cause to be made any special enquiry into the conduct of any Superintendent or of any member of the Police Force, or into any complaint against any of them, he, or the Superintendent whom he may appoint for that purpose, may examine any person on oath or affirmation on any matters relative to such enquiry, and may administer such oath or affirmation.

    [. . .]

28. The Governor in Council may also from time to time regulate and prescribe the amounts to be paid, for the purchase of horses, vehicles, harness, saddlery, clothing, arms and accoutrements, or articles necessary for the said Force: and also the expenses of travelling, and of rations or of boarding or billeting the force and of forage for the horses.

29. The Governor in Council may make regulations for the quartering, billeting and cantoning of the Force, or any portions or detachments thereof; and for the furnishing of boats, carriages, vehicles of transport, horses and other conveyances for their transport and use, and for giving adequate compensation therefor; and may, by such regulations, impose fines not exceeding two hundred dollars for breach of any regulation aforesaid, or for refusing to billet any of the said Force, or to furnish transport as herein mentioned. But no such regulations shall authorize the quartering or billeting of any of the Force in any nunnery or convent of any Religious Order of females.

30. All sums of money required to defray any expense authorized by this Act may be paid out of the Consolidated Revenue Fund of Canada.

    [. . .]

32. All regulations or Orders in Council made under this Act shall be published in the Canada *Gazette*, and shall, thereupon have the force of law from the date of their publication, or from, such later date as may be therein appointed for their coming into force; and a copy of any such regulations purporting to be printed by the Queen's Printer shall be *prima facie* evidence thereof.

33. The Department of Justice shall have the control and management of the Police Force and of all matters connected therewith; but the Governor in Council may, at any time order that the same shall be transferred to any other Department of the Civil Service of Canada, and the same shall accordingly, by such order, be so transferred to and be under the control and management of such other Department.

34. The Commissioner and every Superintendent of Police, shall be *ex-officio* a Justice of the Peace, within the Province of Manitoba; and the constables and sub-constables of the Police Force shall also have and exercise within the Province of Manitoba, all the powers and authority, rights and privileges by law appertaining to constables under the laws of the Dominion, for the purpose of carrying the same into effect.

35. The Governor in Council may from time to time enter into arrangements with the Government of the Province of Manitoba for the use or employment of the Police Force, in aiding the administration of justice in that Province and in carrying into effect the laws of the Legislature thereof; and may, in any such arrangement, agree and determine the amount of money which shall be paid by the Province of Manitoba in respect of any such services of the said Police Force.

2
"Articles of a Treaty made and concluded near Carlton . . . " (Treaty No. 6, 1876), in Canada, *Indian Treaties and Surrenders from 1680 to 1890 in Two Volumes*, Vol. 2 (Ottawa: Brown Chamberlin [Queen's Printer], 1891), 35–43.

ARTICLES OF A TREATY made and concluded near Carlton on the 23rd day of August and on the 28th day of said month respectively, and near Fort Pitt on the 9th day of September, in the year of Our Lord one thousand eight hundred and seventy six, between Her Most Gracious Majesty the Queen of Great Britain and Ireland, by Her Commissioners, the Honourable Alexander Morris, Lieutenant Governor of the Province of Manitoba and the North-West Territories, and the Honourable James McKay, and the Honourable William Joseph Christie, of the one part, and the Plain and Wood Cree and the other Tribes of Indians, inhabitants of the country within the limits hereinafter defined and described by their Chiefs, chosen and named as hereinafter mentioned, of the other part.

Whereas the Indians inhabiting the said country have, pursuant to an appointment made by the said Commissioners, been convened at meetings at Fort Carlton, Fort Pitt and Battle River, to deliberate upon certain matters of interest to Her Most Gracious Majesty, of the one part, and the said Indians of the other.

And whereas the said Indians have been notified and informed by Her Majesty's said Commissioners that it is the desire of Her Majesty to open up for settlement, immigration and such other purposes as to Her Majesty may seem meet, a tract of country bounded and described as hereinafter mentioned, and to obtain the consent thereto of Her Indian subjects inhabiting the said tract, and to make a treaty and arrange with them, so that there may be peace and good will between them and Her Majesty, and that they may know and be assured of what allowance they are to count upon and receive from Her Majesty's bounty and benevolence.

And whereas the Indians of the said tract, duly convened in council, as aforesaid, and being requested by Her Majesty's said Commissioners to name certain Chiefs and Headmen, who should be authorized on their behalf to conduct such negotiations and sign any treaty to be founded thereon, and to become responsible to Her Majesty for their faithful performance by their respective Bands of such obligations as shall be assumed by them, the said Indians have thereupon named for that purpose, that is to say, representing the Indians who make the treaty at Carlton, the several Chiefs and Councillors who have subscribed hereto, and representing the Indians who make the treaty at Fort Pitt, the several Chiefs and Councillors who have subscribed hereto.

And thereupon, in open council, the different Bands having presented their Chiefs to the said Commissioners as the Chiefs and Headmen, for the purposes aforesaid, of the respective Bands of Indians inhabiting the said district hereinafter described.

And whereas, the said Commissioners then and there received and acknowledged the persons so presented as Chiefs and Headmen, for the purposes aforesaid, of the respective Bands of Indians inhabiting the said district hereinafter described.

And whereas, the said Commissioners have proceeded to negotiate a treaty with the said Indians, and the same has been finally agreed upon and concluded, as follows, that is to say:—

The Plain and Wood Cree Tribes of Indians, and all other the Indians inhabiting the district hereinafter described and defined, do hereby cede, release, surrender and yield up to the Government of the Dominion of Canada, for Her Majesty the Queen and Her successors forever, all their rights, titles and privileges, whatsoever, to the lands included within the following limits, that is to say:

Commencing at the mouth of the river emptying into the north-west angle of Cumberland Lake; thence westerly up the said river to its source; thence on a straight line in a westerly direction to the head of Green Lake; thence northerly to the elbow in the Beaver River; thence down the said river northerly to a point twenty miles from the said elbow; thence in a westerly direction, keeping on a line generally parallel with the said Beaver River (above the elbow), and about twenty miles distant therefrom, to the source of the said river; thence northerly to the northeasterly point of the south shore of Red Deer Lake, continuing westerly along the said shore to the western limit thereof; and thence due west to the Athabasca River; thence up the said river, against the stream, to the Jaspar House, in the Rocky Mountains; thence on a course south-eastwardly, following the easterly range of the mountains, to the source of the main branch of the Red Deer River; thence down the said river, with the stream, to the junction therewith of the outlet of the river, being the outlet of the Buffalo Lake; thence due east twenty miles; thence on a straight line south-eastwardly to the mouth of the said Red Deer River on the south branch of the Saskatchewan River; thence eastwardly and northwardly, following on the boundaries of the tracts conceded by the several treaties numbered four and five to the place of beginning.

And also, all their rights, titles and privileges whatsoever to all other lands wherever situated in the North-West Territories, or in any other Province or portion of Her Majesty's Dominions, situated and being within the Dominion of Canada.

The tract comprised within the lines above described embracing an area of 121,000 square miles, be the same more or less.

To have and to hold the same to Her Majesty the Queen and Her successors forever.

And Her Majesty the Queen hereby agrees and undertakes to lay aside reserves for farming lands, due respect being had to lands at present cultivated by the said Indians, and other reserves for the benefit of the said Indians, to be administered and dealt with for them by Her Majesty's Government of the Dominion of Canada; provided, all such reserves shall not exceed in all one square mile for each family of five, or in that proportion for larger or smaller families, in manner following, that is to say: that the Chief Superintendent of Indian Affairs shall depute and send a suitable person to determine and set apart the reserves for each band, after consulting with the Indians thereof as to the locality which may be found to be most suitable for them.

Provided, however, that Her Majesty reserves the right to deal with any settlers within the bounds of any lands reserved for any Band as She shall deem fit, and also that the aforesaid reserves of land, or any interest therein, may be sold or otherwise disposed of by Her Majesty's Government for the use and benefit of the said Indians entitled thereto, with their consent first had and obtained; and with a view to show the satisfaction of Her Majesty with the behaviour and good conduct of Her Indians, She hereby, through Her Commissioners, makes them a present of twelve dollars for each man, woman and child belonging to the Bands here represented, in extinguishment of all claims heretofore preferred.

And further, Her Majesty agrees to maintain schools for instruction in such reserves hereby made as to Her Government of the Dominion of Canada may seem advisable, whenever the Indians of the reserve shall desire it.

Her Majesty further agrees with Her said Indians that within the boundary of Indian reserves, until otherwise determined by Her Government of the Dominion of Canada, no intoxicating liquor shall be allowed to be introduced or sold, and all laws now in force, or hereafter to be enacted, to preserve Her Indian subjects inhabiting the reserves or living elsewhere within Her North-West Territories from the evil influence of the use of intoxicating liquor, shall be strictly enforced.

Her Majesty further agrees with Her said Indians that they, the said Indians, shall have right to pursue their avocations of hunting and fishing throughout the tract surrendered as hereinbefore described, subject to such regulations as may from time to time be made by Her Government of Her Dominion of Canada, and saving and excepting such tracts as may from time to time be required or taken up for settlement, mining, lumbering or other purposes by Her said Government of the Dominion of Canada, or by any of the subjects thereof duly authorized therefor by the said Government.

It is further agreed between Her Majesty and Her said Indians, that such sections of the reserves above indicated as may at any time be required for public works or buildings, of what nature soever, may be appropriated for that purpose by Her Majesty's Government of the Dominion of Canada, due compensation being made for the value of any improvements thereon.

And further, that Her Majesty's Commissioners shall, as soon as possible after the execution of this treaty, cause to be taken an accurate census of all the Indians inhabiting the tract above described, distributing them in families, and shall, in every year ensuing the date hereof, at some period in each year, to be duly notified to the Indians, and at a place or places to be appointed for that purpose within the territory ceded, pay to each Indian person the sum of $5 per head yearly.

It is further agreed between Her Majesty and the said Indians, that the sum of $15 per annum shall be yearly and every year expended by Her Majesty in the purchase of ammunition, and twine for nets, for the use of the said Indians, in manner following, that is to say: In the reasonable discretion, as regards the distribution thereof among the Indians inhabiting the several reserves, or otherwise, included herein, of Her Majesty's Indian Agent having the supervision of this treaty.

It is further agreed between Her Majesty and the said Indians, that the following articles shall be supplied to any Band of the said Indians who are now cultivating the soil, or who shall hereafter commence to cultivate the land, that is to say: Four hoes for every family actually cultivating; also, two spades per family as aforesaid; one plough for every three families, as aforesaid; one harrow for every three families, as aforesaid; two scythes and one whetstone, and two hay forks and two reaping hooks, for every family as aforesaid, and also two axes; and also one cross-cut saw, one hand-saw, one pit-saw, the necessary files, one grindstone and one auger for each Band; and also for each Chief for the use of his Band, one chest of ordinary carpenter's tools; also, for each Band, enough of wheat, barley, potatoes and oats to plant the land actually broken up for cultivation by such Band; also for each Band four oxen, one bull and six cows; also, one boar and two sows, and one hand-mill when any Band shall raise sufficient grain therefor. All the aforesaid articles to be given once for all for the encouragement of the practice of agriculture among the Indians.

It is further agreed between Her Majesty and the said Indians, that each Chief, duly recognised as such, shall receive an annual salary of twenty-five dollars per annum; and each subordinate officer, not exceeding four for each Band, shall receive fifteen dollars per annum; and each such Chief and subordinate officer, as aforesaid, shall also receive once every three years, a suitable suit of clothing, and each Chief shall receive, in recognition of the closing of the treaty, a suitable flag and medal, and also as soon as convenient, one horse, harness and waggon.

That in the event hereafter of the Indians comprised within this treaty being overtaken by any pestilence, or by a general famine, the Queen, on being satisfied and certified thereof by Her Indian Agent or Agents, will grant to the Indians assistance of such character and to such extent as Her Chief Superintendent of Indian Affairs shall deem necessary and sufficient to relieve the Indians from the Calamity that shall have befallen them.

That during the next three years, after two or more of the reserves hereby agreed to be set apart to the Indians shall have been agreed upon and surveyed, there shall be granted to the Indians included under the Chiefs adhering to the treaty at Carlton, each spring, the sum of one thousand dollars, to be expended for them by Her Majesty's Indian Agents, in the purchase of provisions for the use of such of the Band as are actually settled on the reserves and are engaged in cultivating the soil, to assist them in such cultivation.

That a medicine chest shall be kept at the house of each Indian Agent for the use and benefit of the Indians at the direction of such agent.

That with regard to the Indians included under the Chiefs adhering to the treaty at Fort Pitt, and to those under Chiefs within the treaty limits who may hereafter give their adhesion thereto (exclusively, however, of the Indians of the Carlton region), there shall, during three years, after two or more reserves shall have been agreed upon and surveyed be distributed each spring among the Bands cultivating the soil on such reserves by Her Majesty's Chief Indian Agent for this treaty, in his discretion, a sum not exceeding one thousand dollars, in the purchase of provisions for the use of such members of the Band as are actually settled on the reserve and engaged in the cultivation of the soil, to assist and encourage them in such cultivation.

That in lieu of waggons, if they desire it and declare their option to that effect, there shall be given to each of the Chiefs adhering hereto at Fort Pitt or elsewhere hereafter (exclusively of those in the Carlton district), in recognition of this treaty, as soon as the same can be conveniently transported, two carts with iron bushings and tires.

And the undersigned Chiefs on their own behalf and on behalf of all other Indians inhabiting the tract within ceded, do hereby solemnly promise and engage to strictly observe this treaty, and also to conduct and behave themselves as good and loyal subjects of Her Majesty the Queen.

They promise and engage that they will in all respects obey and abide by the law, and they will maintain peace and good order between each other, and also between themselves and other tribes of Indians, and between themselves and others of Her Majesty's subjects, whether Indians or whites, now inhabiting or hereafter to inhabit any part of the said ceded tracts, and that they will not molest the person or property of any inhabitant of such ceded tracts, or the property of Her Majesty the Queen, or interfere with or trouble any person passing or travelling through the said tracts, or any part thereof, and that they will aid and assist the officers of Her Majesty in bringing to justice and punishment any Indian offending against the stipulations of this treaty, or infringing the laws in force in the country so ceded.

IN WITNESS WHEREOF, Her Majesty's said Commissioners and the said Indian Chiefs have hereunto subscribed and set their hands at or near Fort Carlton, on the days and year aforesaid, and near Fort Pitt on the day above aforesaid.

Signed by the Chiefs within named in presence of the following witnesses, the same having been first read and explained by Peter Erasmus, Peter Ballendine and the Rev. John McKay.

ALF. JACKES, *M.D.*
JAS. WALKER, *N.W.M.P.*
J.H. McILLREE, *N.W.M.P.*
PIERRE LEVAILLER, his X mark
ISADORE DUMOND, his X mark
JEAN DUMOND, his X mark
F. GINGRAS,
J.B. MITCHELL, *Staff Constable N.W.M.P.*

[other witnesses and councillors . . .]

ALEXANDER MORRIS, *L.G.N.W.T.*
JAMES McKAY, *Indian Commissioner.*
W.J. CHRISTIE   *do*

MIS-TO-WA-SIS, his X mark
AH-TUK-UK-KOOP, his X mark

Head Chiefs of the Carlton Indians

PEE-YAHN-KAH-NICHK-OO-SIT,
  his X mark
AH-YAH-TUS-KUM-IK-IM-AM,
  his X mark
KEE-TOO-WA-HAW,
  his X mark
CHA-KAS-TA-PAY-SIN,
  his X mark
JOHN SMITH, his X mark
JAMES SMITH, his X mark
CHIP-EE-WAYAN, his X mark

Chiefs

Historical Interpretations

3 From Keith D. Smith, "Churches, Police Forces, and the Department of Indian Affairs," in *Liberalism, Surveillance, and Resistance: Indigenous Communities in Western Canada* (Edmonton: Athabasca University Press, 2009), 51–91. Reprinted with permission.

The precise techniques applied by liberal Canadian institutions to "de-Indianize" Indigenous populations were neither uniform nor consistent across time or geography. Rather, the specifics were a fluid array of disciplinary techniques that were constantly adjusted to meet local conditions. Increased pressure on land as the result of an influx of non-Indigenous settlers, localized resistance to a particularly offensive policy or official, stubborn refusal to readily accept the dogma of the newcomers, or the need to explain previous policy failures might necessitate an adjustment in strategy or a change in tactics. Liberalism, as it was applied to Indigenous people in western Canada, was creative and adaptable. The feature common to all of these shifting schemes that ranged from education in various forms to military force and from legislation to morally reprehensible actions that had no basis in law, was that they were informed and reinforced by surveillance. Surveillance was the primary means of normalization. On "Indian reserves," as in the other disciplinary institutions, the smallest details of activity were supervised and recorded. In this way normalization was disseminated through day-to-day activity and secured through relentless monitoring.

The importance of surveillance was well understood by those concerned with "civilizing Indians" in the late nineteenth century.

When, in 1875, well-known Anglican lay missionary and founder of the Metlakatla settlement, William Duncan, offered his suggestions on policy that should be followed in the new province of British Columbia, he wrote under the leading head, "surveillance," "[t]his I conceive to be the proper starting point for commencing a right policy in Indian affairs; for without surveillance no satisfactory relationship can ever exist between the Government and the Indians."[1] Hayter Reed, Indian Commissioner for the North-West Territories, spoke more specifically when he told all agents under him that "closer supervision would ensure better results" in agricultural pursuits.[2]

The surveillance of Indigenous people in western Canada was primarily the responsibility of the DIA [Department of Indian Affairs] and it is the DIA that gets most of the attention in this study. Additionally, though, there were many other groups and individuals engaged in scrutinizing Indigenous people. While their tactics may have varied and their specific objectives may have differed, there was considerable collaboration between and within groups watching, judging, and set on reforming Indigenous people. Additionally, these groups and individuals were actively involved in observing the activities of each other. Policemen watched DIA employees, missionaries watched policemen, DIA employees watched missionaries, farmers watched policemen, and individuals within each of these groups observed and judged their colleagues.

MISSIONARY SURVEILLANCE AND SURVEILLANCE OF MISSIONARIES

Protestants and Catholics watched each other carefully and jealously guarded any advances they made into First Nations communities.[3] This jealousy extended not only to the building of churches and schools, but also to the provision of on-reserve health services.[4] The *Calgary Herald* declared, "something should be done to prevent the agents of the denominations from interfering with each other's labors" in "their efforts to elevate the Indians of the North West in the scale of civilization."[5] The DIA monitored all missionary activity on reserves and in Indian schools and each year published information on these activities in its Annual Reports. At the same time, missionaries observed the activities of the department's employees and did not hesitate to articulate their concerns when they believed their interests in relation to other denominations were in jeopardy[6] or when they felt their moral influence and example were compromised by the department or one of its employees.[7] Occasionally, to the dismay and indignation of the DIA, church representatives went to the media and allowed their criticisms to enter the public's field of view.[8]

[. . .]

Despite local conflicts, it is clear that the department at Ottawa went to some length to maintain friendly relations with all denominations and to protect its public image of religious equality. The glowing report of Frederick Abbott, Secretary to the US Board of Indian Commissioners, attests to the success of the department's public relations efforts when the author wrote that a "splendid spirit of cooperation exists between the various religious denominations in Canada and the government."[9] The churches too, went some way to maintaining good relations with Ottawa so that, for example, when Anglican missionary A.E. O'Meara, a vocal advocate for Indigenous rights, was critical of the DIA's inability to fulfill its written promises and objectives and publicly labelled "one of its officers a liar . . . he was called to order very strongly by the Primate" of the Anglican Church.[10]

In addition to the DIA, the police too, particularly the NWMP [North West Mounted Police], were interested in the activities of various churches, especially if they believed that public peace was in jeopardy. When, for example, the Siksika voiced their dissatisfaction regarding compulsory attendance at the school on their reserve, Anglican missionary J.W. Tims recommended "a force of 200 or more men located on the border of the Reserve as a check to their present behaviour."[11] It is unlikely that such a large proportion of the force would ever be committed to such an assignment, but soon it was not necessary. A week later NWMP Commissioner Herchmer was able to report that the "departure of Rev. Tims has removed all cause of complaint and Indians are now perfectly quiet."[12] The same year, when NWMP Superintendent S.B. Steele found that children at the school at St. Paul's Mission on the Kainai reserve were being locked in at night, he warned the priest/principal that if lives were lost in the event of a fire, he would be tried for manslaughter.[13]

There was sectarian discord, differences in opinion regarding tactics within various denominations, and disputes between individual missionaries and police, and missionaries and DIA employees. There were few in either region, though, who presented any serious challenge to what was believed to be the natural correctness of individual land tenure and property ownership, to the belief that Indigenous people were not yet advanced enough to be permitted to reap any benefits liberalism had to offer, or that adherence to Christianity was a necessary prerequisite not only for civilization but for human development. Further, missionaries were employed by government officials to pacify Indigenous residents. For example, in preparation for the arrival of NWMP policemen and American troops into their territories to mark off the boundary between the United States and Canada, missionary John McDougall was sent to the Blackfoot to advise them of "the good will of the Queen" and to ask them "to regard the Force with a friendly eye."[14] On a larger scale, adherence to Christianity seems to have gone some way toward the DIA

objective of fostering quietude. As Chief at Cayuse Creek, a Lil'wat community, reported to missionary and DIA employee McDougall in 1910:

> We never leased land. We never gave away our right to game and salmon. They, the white men, took it from us. We did not get mad. The white people did all this. We did not get mad. No—Christ said "do not get mad."[15]

POLICE SURVEILLANCE

Though there were other police and investigative bodies involved with law enforcement in western Canada, these duties fell mainly to the NWMP east of the Rockies, and to the British Columbia Provincial Police [BCPP] to the west. Like the representatives of the various churches, the BCPP and the NWMP observed the movements and activities of First Nations peoples within their jurisdictions.

The BCPP formed in 1858, 16 years before the NWMP, and was the first territorial police force in Canada. While the immediate impetus for the creation of the force was the need to control the tens of thousands of gold seekers that arrived in the Fraser River watershed in 1858, it had a myriad of law enforcement duties during its existence.[16] That the British Columbia police were primarily responsible for ensuring the orderly development of liberal capitalism is evident from the particular attention it paid to working-class people, especially union organizers and the unemployed.[17] Undoubtedly, the increased surveillance of these individuals is a direct result of the demands of settlers, businessmen, and their political representatives for increased policing.

The provincial government felt that since "Indians" were a federal responsibility the cost of their surveillance should be borne by the government at Ottawa. Nevertheless, the BCPP continued to keep a watch on Indigenous people.[18] Indeed, the 1901 diary of a constable stationed in the southern Okanagan includes such regular entries as: "watched actions of party of half breeds," "large gathering of Indians on reserve," and "patrolled reserve all day."[19] Similarly, 10 years later, the constable in the district visited at least some reserves once a week.[20] The BCPP was also active in locating and returning truant students to boarding schools for Indigenous children including the Kamloops Indian Residential School.[21]

Job actions by Indigenous people, in concert with white workers, also brought them more directly under the supervisory gaze of lawmakers and police in the early twentieth century. The Fraser River fishery strikes of 1900 and 1901 are cases in point. As was reported to the Attorney General "over forty white and [I]ndian patrol boats, manned by ten men each now on the river intimidating destroying property and preventing fishing."[22] Here, as in the province's coal mines, Asian workers were co-opted into acting as strike breakers. This strategy, coupled with the declaration of martial law and the employment of special constables, militia men, and the BCPP to protect the Japanese fishers and so the interests of the cannery owners, ultimately defeated the action taken by striking Indigenous and white fishers.

It was not only overt resistance, however, that caused Indigenous people to be singled out as the primary reason for requesting additional policing. As one settler argued:

[m]y contention in this matter is, that the Govt.—in localities like this where the halfbreed element and Siwash element so largely prevail—should consider itself bound to see that the whites who keep up the country with their enterprise and taxes are allowed to live in comparative comfort and freedom from annoyance.[23]

For a short time, there was also a provincial police force in Alberta. When the RNWMP, apparently unwilling to enforce provincial prohibition regulations, cancelled its contract with the province in 1916, Alberta established its own provincial police which operated until the RCMP [Royal Canadian Mounted Police] reassumed policing responsibilities in 1932. While there was some surveillance of the First Nations of southern Alberta by the Alberta Provincial Police [APP], the continued responsibility of the Mounties for matters concerning Indigenous people insured that these activities were even less substantial than those of the provincial police in British Columbia.[24]

[. . .]

John A. Macdonald began preparing the ground for the formation of a mounted police force as the situation in the prairie west began to deteriorate in 1869, partly as a result of the lack of consultation with First Nations and Métis inhabitants regarding the transfer of Rupert's Land from the Hudson's Bay Company to Canada. The force began to take shape with an order-in-council in April 1870 in which provision was made for a mounted force which, like the Royal Irish Constabulary, would be under the central control of Ottawa and not territorial or regional governments.[25] While the resistance centred at Red River was over in 1870, the desire to establish Canadian authority over the west remained. In September of 1873, nine commissioned officers were appointed to a "Mounted Police Force for the North-West Territories" and by 3 November a further 150 men were recruited to the force.[26] In 1874, 300 Mounties marched west and arrived in the area that became southern Alberta to establish Fort Macleod in 1874 and Fort Calgary in 1875. The conspicuous expansion of Anglo-Canadian liberal values in this region and the formal surveillance network in preparation for the western settlement was initiated in advance of any treaty or agreement with resident First Nations.

The NWMP were an essential part of Macdonald's national policies.[27] In turn, the success of the national policies took precedence over not only treaty promises but also the basic human rights of Indigenous people.[28] The primary role of the Mounted police was to facilitate the peaceful occupation of the west by Anglo-Canadians and to allay their fears of Indigenous people once they arrived. Without farmer-settlers both the railway and the NWMP themselves would be redundant.[29]

Even more than the BCPP, the NWMP and its successors were required to fulfill a host of enforcement responsibilities at different times: from the Leprosy Act to the Explosives Act and from the Bank Act to the Canada Temperance Act. The Mounted police also, of course, enforced the Indian Act and other pieces of legislation both on and off the reserves. Further, despite the extent of the panoptic machinery that the DIA had in place, the NWMP and its successors provided them with a myriad of services.[30] They were a major force in laying the ground work for the acceptance of Treaty 7 and were a presence, along with their cannon, at the negotiations for the treaty.[31] In the years that followed they also provided an escort for the annuity money guaranteed in 1877.[32] The Mounted police could be called in at short notice at the request of the department to enhance its capacity in the case of a perceived threat. As occurred at the signing of the treaty, the Mounted police, by patrolling or merely by being visibly present, provided a show of force that could be very persuasive in "encouraging" Indigenous people to meet their will and that of the DIA.

[. . .]

The relationship between the police and the DIA, both institutionally and at the local individual level, was not always smooth, but both agencies had the same long-term objectives. Both were primarily interested in paving the way for non-Indigenous settlement and advancing Anglo-Canadian cultural and economic interests. Neither believed it necessary, or even feasible, to extend the rights and freedoms apparently guaranteed by liberalism to Indigenous people.

THE PASS SYSTEM

The restriction on the right of Indigenous people to travel freely provides perhaps the clearest illustration of the operation of exclusionary liberalism in western Canada. This restriction is best seen as a matrix of laws, regulations, and policy meant to "elevate" Indigenous people while simultaneously securing the interests of non-Indigenous newcomers. Like colonialism itself, this restrictive complex was creative and adaptable and so could adjust as political, economic, or social conditions changed. The most notorious element of this network was the "pass system," a DIA policy that had no legal basis, but nonetheless required reserve residents to secure a pass from their Indian agent before leaving their reserve for any reason.

The restriction of Indigenous movement seems to have originated with a NWMP concern regarding the potential consequences of cross-border movement by Canadian Indigenous people to hunt buffalo and steal horses. In the late 1870s, the NWMP was concerned primarily with proving they were able to exercise authority over Canadian territory and especially over Indigenous people. The worry was that Canada might provide a staging area for military action against the US army, which could then result in a US military incursion into Canadian territory in retribution. Brian Hubner confirms that the NWMP built forts Walsh and Macleod to this end.[33] By 1882, correspondence between the US and Canada led to the passage of an Order in Council in April by which Canada would propose to the US "that individual permits be granted by the authorities of both nations to their respective Indians who may wish to cross the border."[34]

In 1882 as well, NWMP Commissioner Irvine specifically recommended that Indian agents be vigilant in preventing large groups from leaving their reserves.[35] In November 1883, Deputy Superintendent General of Indian Affairs [DSGIA] Vankoughnet wrote to Macdonald to express his concern about Indigenous women camped near towns in the North-West and suggested that the problem could be rectified "in a very simple manner by the Mounted Police . . . requiring that the owner of any tepee produce a permit from the local Indian agent for his or her having the tepee at that point."[36] Macdonald agreed that the presence of women, especially near settler towns and villages, needed to be restricted. In his annual report for that year Macdonald offered the opinion that the location of the Tsuu T'ina so close to Calgary "operates detrimentally, to their improvement" and causes "demoralization of their women." In view of formulating a strategy "for checking this evil" Macdonald ordered the establishment of a dialogue between the Indian Commissioner for the North-West Territories and the Commissioner of the NWMP "with a view to the adoption of some plan to prevent the indiscriminate camping of Indians in the vicinity of towns and white settlements in the North-West Territories. . . . "[37]

The correspondence of the early 1880s indicates that there was desire and action at all levels of both the DIA and NWMP hierarchies to restrict Indigenous movement prior to 1885, but that a universally applied pass system as such did not yet have official approval. In 1885, though, "the [North West] Rebellion brought the pass system to life with a jolt."[38]

In May 1885, Major-General Frederick Middleton asked Dewdney, "[w]ould it not be advisable to issue proclamation warning breeds and Indians to return to their Reserves and that all those found away will be treated as rebels. I suppose such a proclamation would be disseminated without difficulty." Dewdney responded immediately that he had "issued a notice advising Indians to stay on Reserves and warning them of risks they run in being found off them but have no power to issue proclamation as you suggest."[39] The notice warned "all good and loyal Indians should remain quietly on their Reserves where they will be perfectly safe and receive the protection of the soldiers and that any

Indian being off his Reserve without special permission in writing from some authorized person, is liable to be arrested on suspicion of being a rebel, and punished as such."[40]

By June, with the resistance mostly subdued, Dewdney wrote of the futility of attempting to restrict Indians to reserves "when, if they do leave them, there is no law by which they can be punished and our orders enforced."[41] This does not necessarily mean that he was opposed to restricting Indigenous movement, only that, in his opinion, without supporting legislation, the pass system was inoperable. The Indian Commissioner then turned to his assistant, Hayter Reed, and requested that he put into writing some suggestions regarding "the future management of the Indians in the North West Territories."[42]

Following the instructions of his superior, and as Dewdney confirmed "only after careful consultation between myself and my assistant," Reed made 15 proposals. Of special interest here is Reed's seventh recommendation that "no rebel Indian should be allowed off the Reserves without a pass signed by an ID [Indian Department] official."[43] Significantly, Reed's suggestions were amplified as they moved up the DIA hierarchy. Indian Commissioner Dewdney, supported Reed's recommendation and suggested that "another year" legislation might be enacted in support.[44]

Apparently encouraged by Dewdney's support, Reed reported from Battleford in August, "I am adopting the system of keeping the Indians on their respective Reserves + not allowing any leave them without passes—I know this is hardly supportable by any legal enactment but one must do many things which can only be supported by common sense and by what may be for the general good—I get the Police to send out daily and send any Indians without passes back to their Reserves." Reed complained though "unless one is at their heels Police duties here are done in a half hearted manner."[45]

In June of 1886 Dewdney was sent "a form of pass proposed to be given to Indians when allowed to absent themselves from their Reserves" and in September he was sent the 50 books of passes that he had apparently requested. The following month Reed sent out the books of passes to Indian agents and the pass system was officially launched.[46] Throughout the remainder of the 1880s the DIA and NWMP generally co-operated to apply the policy in the Treaty 7 area as they did in the prairie west to the east despite the fact that no Treaty 7 First Nation participated in the events of 1885.

[. . .]

In 1890, the DIA acquiesced to NWMP requests to make the pass system more restrictive. Vankoughnet assured NWMP Comptroller White that agents would be told to issue passes only to those who convinced the agent that the reason for requesting leave was "a legitimate one".[47] He pledged further that Kainai Agent Pocklington would be instructed to withhold passes from anyone who was previously found using alcohol when away from the reserve.[48] The NWMP were particularly concerned about the Kainai, who Superintendent Deane admitted the police were unsuccessful in restricting to their reserve. According to Deane "[t]he Bloods think that they are the cream of creation, and it is time for them to begin to imbibe some modification of the idea."[49]

The pass system was part of a coercive and flexible matrix meant to restrict Indigenous movement in the interests of white settlers and it must be seen in that light. It took time for the pass system to find its place within this network and within the larger complex of exclusionary liberalism. Even though Canada never had the capacity to forcibly restrict all off-reserve movement, the will of both the police and the DIA to do what they could in this regard is evident, even if some in the upper echelons of the former were sometimes uncomfortable. There were cases of Indigenous people forcibly returned

to their reserve, but even when passes were used solely as instruments of surveillance or as demonstrations of state control, they remained bereft of any legal justification. Both the DIA and the mounted police wanted to be seen as responding to settler fears, first of the military threat, and later the annoyance, posed by Indigenous people.

RESTRICTION OF MOVEMENT IN BRITISH COLUMBIA

In British Columbia, there was no operational pass system nor was there the same degree of restriction of movement generally as there was in the prairie west. Secwepemc elders confirm that the period under discussion here is before "Indian Affairs had really taken hold of the Indians" in this area.[50] Since the "demands of war [World War I] coupled with our remoteness delayed the full effect of the system until a decade after the war," the Secwepemc were "just beginning to come under the domination of the Indian agent" at the end of this period.[51] For example, at various times the agent at Kamloops and Okanagan had to send advance notice of his coming to ensure that residents would be present on their reserve when he arrived. Sometimes he even met community leaders in hotels in town.[52] As British Columbia's Indian Superintendent Arthur Wesley Vowell reminded DSGIA Frank Pedley in 1903, "[i]n connection with the Indians in British Columbia it is well to recollect that they consider themselves as a self-supporting people, mixing freely wherever they please, and may expect to find profitable employment, amongst the whites, as independent so long as they obey the laws governing the Dominion and the Province."[53] As noted, there were only a few treaties in British Columbia and none in the southern interior. As a result there were no annuity payments, programs of farm instruction, or regular provision of foodstuffs and, coupled with the absence of the mounted police and far fewer DIA employees, there was less opportunity for coercion.

This does not mean that disciplinary surveillance was not applied in aid of the expansion of liberalism in British Columbia. Rather the point is only that the official structures to facilitate it were not as well developed nor as well staffed as they were in southern Alberta, at least in the period under discussion here and especially away from southern Vancouver Island and the Lower Mainland. As was the case in the prairie region, though, even those few First Nations who entered into the Douglas Treaties in the 1850s found that guarantees for freedom of movement in pursuit of economic activity were gradually eroded.[54]

As in the Treaty 7 region as well, special attention was paid in the interior of British Columbia to the movements and activities of Indigenous women.

Most attention appears to have been directed at keeping Indigenous women away from settler population centres of Victoria and the Lower Mainland. To this end, Indian Superintendent A.W. Vowell wrote to coastal steamship companies the following spring and requested that they "refuse passage to all Indian women unless they have permits from their Agents to take passage on the Steamer or other boats, to certain points of destination." While the initial responses from these companies seemed to indicate that they were willing to comply, as long as the other firms did as well, Superintendent Vowell reported that "so long as an Indian woman is able and willing to pay her fare upon any of these boats passage will not be denied her."[55] Like many east of the Rockies, Agent Pidcock remained in favour of a generalized restriction akin to the pass system but Superintendent Vowell argued that such a system would be "practically inoperative and the cause of much disquietude to all the Indians in the Province" since "many bands of Indians are beyond the reach of the Agents, who are the only representatives of the law known in some of these out of the way places, as far as the exercise of any immediate supervision over their actions is concerned."[56] This position was accepted by SGIA Thomas Mayne Daly who recognized that the distance between Indigenous people and their agents in British Columbia would make it impractical to obtain a pass before leaving their reserve to obtain work.[57]

Pidcock changed tactics and had a petition apparently signed by 31 Kwakwaka'wakw men stating "we are not able to stop the shameful traffic with Indian women without the assistance of the law" and requested that steamers only be allowed to transport women with the approval of the agent or designate. To this, the department responded that its employees would always help, "when requested by the husband or brother or any one having proper authority, to stop a woman from going away."[58] It is impossible to know for sure the circumstances that led to the creation of this document or the actual feelings of the community regarding the sentiments expressed in it. It seems unlikely though that any community would willingly turn over the right of its members to move freely to an outside authority and the incident involving the forcible restraint by the BCPP supports this interpretation. Women's freedom of movement was still an issue in 1909 when J.E. Rendle, a missionary on the coast, requested that the DIA "order the Indians to all live in their village." While the DIA passed on their own concerns to British Columbia, the province's attorney general reported that things were "not in such a bad state as the Indian Department would lead us to believe."[59]

MOUNTED POLICE

In both these regions of western Canada, racialized constructions of liberalism, which served to fundamentally exclude Indigenous people from land ownership, were backed up by the force of direct military intervention when necessary. For, as Reverend George

McDougall confirmed before the arrival of the NWMP in western Canada, "experience has taught us that Proclamations without a civil force to enforce them are not worth the paper they are written on."[60] But such interventions were extremely rare in the history of Canada. The main disciplinary mechanism and the principal reformatory apparatus was unquestionably, in fact could only be, surveillance.

While everyone in liberal Canada was under observation at some level, no single group experienced the intensity or continuity of surveillance that Indigenous people did. In addition to those groups and individuals mentioned above, who clearly made the observation of First Nations people a priority, only those defined as "Indians" had an entire government department dedicated to observing their actions and behaviour, and relieving them of their land and resources, while at the same time was charged with minimizing "the risk of a rebellion or of great dissatisfaction."[61]

NOTES

1. Appendix C of "Report of the Government of British Columbia on the Subject of Indian Reserves" in British Columbia, *Papers Connected to the Indian Land Question, 1850–1875, 1877* (1875 and 1877). Rpt. 1987, 14.

2. Hayter Reed, Circular, 9 February 1891, Library and Archives Canada (LAC), RG 10, vol. 1137.

3. Harry W. Gibbon Stocken to Baring-Gould, 21 February 1899. See also, H.G.W. Stocken's *Among the Blackfoot and Sarcee* (Calgary: Glenbow Institute, 1976), v, vii, xii.

4. For an example of the conflict in relation to a proposed hospital on the Nakoda reserve see correspondence in LAC, RG 10, vol. 3993, file 186,790.

5. "Indian Proselytism," *Calgary Herald*, 15 April 1891. "Why Not More Co-operation among the Churches," *Calgary Herald*, 8 June 1895.

6. Alex, Archbishop of St. Boniface, O.M.I. to Governor General in Council, 28 July 1889, LAC, MG29 E106, vol. 16, file "Church-Dept. Relations, 1887–1895."

7. Hayter Reed to Lucas, Indian Agent, Bears Hills, 18 December 1888 M699/4; Dewdney to Rev. Canon Newton, Edmonton, 31 May 1890, M699/4 and Lucas to Alonzo Wright, MP Ottawa County, 21 January 1891, M699/5, Glenbow, Lucas Family Fonds.

8. "Correspondence Regarding Communications Made to Newspapers by Ministers of the Gospel Criticizing Indian Affairs Government Officials in the Northwest Territories," LAC, RG 10, vol. 3753, file 30,613.

9. From the Report of Frederick Abbott, Secretary to the U.S. Board of Indian Commissioners, in regard to the relations between the church and government in Canada, Frederick H. Abbott, *The Administration of Indian Affairs in Canada* (Washington, DC: n.p., 1915), 25.

10. S.H. Blake to DSGIA Frank Pedley, 19 October 1908, LAC, RG 10, vol. 4024, file 289,032-2.

11. Tims to Indian Commissioner, 27 June 1895, LAC, RG 18, vol. 110, file 517-95.

12. Herchmer to Comptroller, telegram, 3 July 1895, LAC, RG 18, vol. 110, File 517-95. On Tims' unpopularity see J.R. Miller, *Shingwauk's Vision: A History of Native Residential Schools.* (Toronto: University of Toronto Press, 1996), 129–30.

13. Comptroller Frederick White to Commissioner L.W. Herchmer, 16 October 1895, LAC, RG 18, vol. 112, file 665-95.

14. Alexander Morris to John McDougall, 20 June 1874, LAC, MG 29 C23.

15. "Minutes of meeting held with Indians of Bonaparte, Pavilion and Fountain reserves on the 11th, 12th, 13th, and 14th August, 1910," LAC, RG 10, vol. 3750, file 29858-11.

16. British Columbia Archives (BCA), GR-0099, box 4, file K-18 and Hatch "The British Columbia Police," 1–18.

17. BCA, GR-0056, box 12, file 12.

18. Lynne Stonier-Newman, *Policing a Pioneer Province: The B.C. Provincial Police 1858–1950* (Madeira Park, BC: Harbour Publishing, 1991), 38.

19. Entries for 30 April, 8 June and 9 June 1901, BCA, GR-1728, vol. 2.

20. See, for example, entries for 5, 11, and 24 May 1911; 3, 10, 28, and 30 September and 3, 6, 10, and 17 November 1911, BCA, GR-1728, vol. 3.

21. Daily Journal, 1914, entries for 25, 26, and 27 1914 and Daily Journal, 1915, entry for 11 November, 1915. LAC, RG 10, vol. 1325.

22. H. Bell Irving, W. Farrel to D.M. Eberts MPP, telegram, 8 July 1901, BCA, GR-0429, box 7, file 3, item 2314/01. See also F.S. Hussey to D.M. Eberts, AG, telegram, 8 July 1901, item 2317/01.

23. H.D. Phen Armthrop to Hussey, 25 October, 1904, BCA, GR-0063, box 2, file 5.

24. Zhiqiu Lin and Augustine Brannigan, "The Implications of a Provincial Police Force in Alberta and Saskatchewan," in *Laws and Societies in the Canadian Prairie West, 1670–1940*, Louis A. Knafla and Jonathan Swainger, eds (Vancouver: UBC Press, 2005), 1; and Howard Palmer with Tamara Palmer, *Alberta: A New History* (Edmonton: Hurtig Publishers, 1990), 176.

25. S.W. Horrall, "Sir John A. Macdonald and the Mounted Police Force for the Northwest Territories," *Canadian Historical Review*, LIII, 2 (June 1972): 183.

26. Horrall, "Sir John A. Macdonald," 195–6.

27. R.C. Macleod, *The North-West Mounted Police and Law Enforcement, 1873–1905* (Toronto: University of Toronto Press, 1976), 3.

28. John Jennings, "The North West Mounted Police and Indian Policy After the 1885 Rebellion," in *1885 and After: Native Society in Transition*, F. Laurie Barron and James B. Waldram, eds (Regina, SK: Canadian Plains Research Center, University of Regina, 1986), 315; Sarah Carter, *Lost Harvests: Prairie Indian Reserve Farmers and Government Policy* (Montreal and Kingston: McGill-Queen's University Press, 1990), 155.

29. Gerald Friesen, *The Canadian Prairies: A History* (Toronto and London: University of Toronto Press, 1993), 181; and Sarah Carter, *Lost Harvests: Prairie Indian Reserve Farmers and Government Policy* (Montreal and Kingston: McGill-Queen's University Press, 1990), 52.

30. Scott to Stewart, 28 October 1927, LAC, RG 10, vol. 6822, file 494-1-2 pt. 1.

31. R.C. Macleod, *The North-West Mounted Police and Law Enforcement, 1873–1905* (Toronto: University of Toronto Press, 1976), 28; and Treaty 7 Elders and Tribal Council with

Walter Hildebrandt, Dorothy First Rider, and Sarah Carter, *The True Spirit and Original Intent of Treaty 7* (Montreal and Kingston: McGill-Queen's University Press, 1996), 80, 117, 136–7, and 378–9.

32. NWMP, "Annual Report for 1883," paper no. 12 in Canada, Sessional Papers, 1884, 15.

33. Frederick White in "North-West Mounted Police," Appendix D of Report of the Secretary of State in Canada, *Sessional Papers*, 1877, 21; Jennings, "The North West Mounted Police," 228; and Brian Hubner, "Horse Stealing and the Borderline: The NWMP and the Control of Indian Movement, 1874–1900," *Prairie Forum* 20, 2 (Fall 1995): 286–8.

34. Copy of Order in Council, 24 April 1882, Canada, DIA, *Annual Report, 1882*, xliv–xlv. John A. Macdonald's annual report as SGIA for that year indicates his early support for the idea of passes to restrict Indigenous movement, DIA, *Annual Report, 1882*, xi.

35. Commissioner A.G. Irvine in "North-West Mounted Police Force," Part III of *Annual Report of the Department of the Interior, 1882* in Canada, Sessional Papers, 1883, 11–12.

36. Vankoughnet memorandum to Macdonald, 15 November 1883, LAC, RG 18, vol. 1009, file 628.

37. DIA, Annual Report, 1883, lii. Macdonald's report is dated 1 January 1884.

38. Jennings, "The North West Mounted Police," 290–1.

39. Middleton to Dewdney, 6 May 1885 and Dewdney to Middleton, 7 May 1885, LAC, Dewdney Papers, MG 27 I C4, vol. 4, pages 1658–1660. See also B. Bennett, *Study of Passes for Indians to Leave Their Reserves* (n.p.: Treaties and Historical Research Centre, 1974), 1–2; and Carter, *Lost Harvests*, 150.

40. Dewdney, "Notice," 6 May 1885, LAC, RG 10, vol. 3584, file 1130.

41. Dewdney to J.M. Rae, Agent at Battleford, 23 June 1885, LAC, Dewdney Papers, MG 27 I C4, vol. 5, pages 1948–9. See also Bennett, "Passes for Indians," 3; and Carter, *Lost Harvests*, 150.

42. Dewdney to Macdonald, 1 August 1885, LAC, RG 10, vol. 3710, file 19550-3.

43. Dewdney to Macdonald, 1 August 1885 and Reed "Memorandum for the Hon[ble] the Indian Commissioner relative to the future management of Indians," 20 July 1885, LAC, RG 10, vol. 3710, file 19550-3.

44. Reed's Memorandum of 20 July 1885, LAC, RG 10, vol. 3710, file 19550-3; Carter, *Lost Harvests*, 146; and F. Laurie Barron, "The Indian Pass System in the Canadian West, 1882–1935," *Prairie Forum* 13, 1 (Spring 1988): 27–8.

45. Reed to Dewdney, 16 August 1885, LAC, Dewdney Papers, MG 27 I C4, vol. 5, pages 2076–87. Quote at 2078–9.

46. Unsigned letter to Dewdney, 4 June 1886, and unsigned Memorandum to McNeil, 1 September 1886, vol. 3710, file 19550-3. The date written on the first letter is 1866 but this must be an error. Bennett, "Passes for Indians," 3–4.

47. Vankoughnet to White, 21 October 1890, LAC, RG 18, vol. 44, file 784-90.

48. Vankoughnet to White, 17 October 1890, LAC, RG 18, vol. 44, file 782-90.

49. NWMP, *Annual Report, 1889*, 42.

50. Harvey Jules, interview with author Joyce Dunn at Chase, British Columbia, 1983. Copy of tape recording in author's possession.

51. George Manuel and Michael Posluns, *The Fourth World: An Indian Reality* (New York: Macmillan Publishing Co., 1970), 54, 1.

52. Kamloops Agent Daily Journal, 1898, entries for 30 March and 17 May 1898; Daily Journal for 1912, entries for 8 March, 29 June, and 1 July 1912 and Daily Journal, 1913, entries

for 20 May 17, 18, and 23 June, LAC, RG 10, vol. 1325.

53. Vowell to Pedley, 30 June 1903, LAC, RG 10, vol. 3944 file 121698-54.

54. For an example of restrictions on fishing imposed on the Lekwungen (Songhees) near Victoria, see John Lutz, *Makúk: A New History of Aboriginal-White Relations* (Vancouver: UBC Press, 2008), 257–62.

55. A.W. Vowell, I Supt to Capt J.D. Warren, Victoria, 3 March 1890; Warren to Vowell, 21 March 1890; Jon Irving to Vowell, 11 March 1890 and Vowell to Vankoughnet, DSGIA, 25 March 1890, LAC, RG 10, vol. 3816, file 57,045-1.

56. Pidcock to Vowell, n.d, (marked received 4 March 1891) LAC, RG 10, vol. 3816, file 57,045-1.

57. T. Mayne Daly to Senator W.J. Macdonald, 10 May 1895, LAC, RG 10, vol. 3816, file 57,045-1.

58. Vowell to DSGIA, 11 May 1895, and DSGIA to Vowell, 20 May 1895, LAC, RG 10, vol. 3816, file 57,045-1.

59. J.E. Rendle, Methodist missionary, Quatiaski Cove, BC, to Vowell, 29 October 1909, BCA, GR-0063, box 5, file 3.

60. George McDougall to D.A. Smith, 8 January 1874, LAC, RG 10, vol. 3609, file 3278.

61. Blake to Oliver, 6 February 1907, LAC, RG 10 vol. 4023, file 289,032-1.

---

4 From Sarah A. Carter, "Creating 'Semi-Widows' and 'Supernumerary Wives': Prohibiting Polygamy in Prairie Canada's Aboriginal Communities to 1900," in M. Rutherdale and K. Pickles, eds, *Contact Zones: Aboriginal and Settler Women in Canada's Colonial Past* (Vancouver: UBC Press, 2005), 131–59. Reprinted with permission of the Publisher © University of British Columbia Press 2005. All rights reserved by the Publisher.

Historically and culturally specific meanings of masculinity and femininity, and grave concern about alternate meanings of these, profoundly shaped the policies that Canada's Department of Indian Affairs (DIA) devised to "civilize" Aboriginal people living on reserves in western Canada in the post-1870 era. Legal, political, and missionary authorities shared the view that a particular marriage model—of lifelong monogamy in the tradition of the Christian religion and English common law—symbolized the proper differences between the sexes and set the foundation for the way both sexes were to behave. Sustained efforts were made to introduce and perpetuate this marriage model, and this endeavour is clearly illustrated in the 1890s resolve of the DIA to abolish polygamy.[1] Yet there were limitations and challenges to the authorities' ability to impose and enforce one marriage model. Aboriginal marriage law proved tenacious, because of the determination of

Aboriginal people, but also because of the limited capacity of the state to control the domestic domain. While constrained and never fully accomplished, however, these interventions caused considerable turmoil and rupture in Aboriginal communities.

Prohibiting polygamy among the Aboriginal people of western Canada was not an isolated, or unique development, and this study points to the concerns Canadian colonizers shared with the broader colonizing world about the "intimacies of empire."[2] In other colonial settings, polygamy was similarly condemned, but the nature, timing, purpose, and outcomes of programs of intervention varied widely. In western Canada, as in other colonial contexts, ideologies of gender and sexuality were a foundation of the colonial regime, but this was an unstable foundation.

Plains Aboriginal marriages were varied and complex, and they were not well understood by newcomers to western Canada.[3] The ceremonies and protocol involved differed from the Christian and English common-law model. In Plains societies, marriage was more of a process than a particular defining moment. Among the Blackfoot, marriages were family affairs—both sets of relatives had to give their consent. The relationship involved reciprocal obligations among the sets of relatives. The marriage was validated, and the reciprocal obligations of both parties established, through an exchange of gifts that could be initiated by either set of relatives. It became a matter of pride for the family receiving the first gifts to return gifts of greater value. Obligations were ongoing; they did not end with a defining wedding moment.

There were a variety of ideal types of conjugal union, not just one as in Euro-Canadian society. Lifelong, monogamous unions were common, but there were other kinds of marriages, seen not as a departure from a norm, but as a desirable family unit. Many of the leading men in Plains societies had more than one spouse. The term "polygamy" does not have a parallel in the Cree or Blackfoot languages, suggesting that it was not seen as a separate, distinct departure from a norm but as one of several possible forms of marriage. Often sisters were married to the same man. A man might also marry his deceased brother's widow, adopting the children and preserving the relationship with the grandparents and extended family. Only hardworking men of wealth could maintain these large households, so parents sought these marriages for their daughters.

Cree and Blackfoot sources indicate that subsequent wives were brought into a family generally after consultation with, and with the approval of, the first wife. These domestic arrangements provided economic assistance, companionship, and enhanced status for the senior wife. In 1891 Chief Red Crow of the Kainai (Blood) of southern Alberta described marriage practices to Indian agent R.N. Wilson, saying that the first wives seldom objected to the presence of other wives and that it was very often they who proposed that sisters or other relatives become second or third wives.[4]

Cree Chief Fine Day provided a detailed description of marriage practices in his 1934 sessions with anthropologist David Mandelbaum.[5] Fine Day's father had two wives, his mother being the second wife, and he said that the two got along well. Fine Day stressed that permission was required from the first wife, and that the acquisition of a second wife was a joint decision in recognition of the needs of the first wife. According to Fine Day, if a wife required assistance running her household, the husband would say, "How would you like to have a helper?" If she said yes, they then both would pick out some likely girl. He would ask her again, "Would you be kind to her?" She would say, "Yes, that's why I want her." Then he would go and get the other woman. But the first wife was always the boss.[6] Fine Day stressed the authority of the wives to determine the size and nature of the family unit:

It was not a man's abilities as a hunter that determined the number of wives he had, but upon the arrangements he made with his wife. Both a man and his wife paid for the second wife. Young girls would not want to be married to a man that was of no account. They wanted to marry a Worthy Man because they know that there would be no quarrelling—he would stop it.

If a man wanted to take a third wife, his first would usually agree but his second would often say no. That usually would settle it.[7]

If the permission of the wives had not been obtained there were consequences. Fine Day noted that if a man married a third wife without the permission of his first two, they would never be friendly toward her. According to Red Crow, if a husband brought home a second wife to the disgust of the first, she would "keep up a continual row until the newcomer was sent away."[8]

Kainai historian Beverly Hungry Wolf wrote that women did a tremendous amount of work, and it was thought to be desirable for a young woman to marry a prominent man with several wives as this eased the burden of work.[9] Work was divided. A 73-year-old Blackfoot woman, Middle Woman No Coat, who was interviewed in 1939, recalled the division of labour in her father's household with five wives. The first two wives "are older and do all the tanning. Younger wives do the cooking. In winter, all take turns getting wood; someone always present to take care of the fire."[10] Other advantages for the co-wives were that women in polygamous marriages tended to have fewer children, and the mothers of the sister co-wives were often part of the household.[11]

Among the Blackfoot the first and generally the oldest wife was known as the "sits-beside-him" wife, and this was a position of honour. She was the female head of the household and she had an important role in ceremonies such as those involving sacred bundles. She accompanied her husband to feasts and ceremonies, and she directed the other wives in their work. The other wives did not have as high a standing in the community as the "sits-beside-him" wife. These marriages were not always successful, but such incidents seem to have been the exception in an environment in which co-operation and sharing was vital, and in a society where women did almost all of their work communally. [. . .] According to Beverly Hungry Wolf, there were occasions when a younger wife in a large household and with a much older husband suffered from loneliness and a desire to be loved. She noted that some older husbands sanctioned outside relationships as long as they were discreet and brought no public disgrace.[12]

Church, government, political, and legal authorities severely censured what they understood as polygamy in Aboriginal societies. It was seen as deviant and morally depraved. Polygamy became a towering example of the shortcomings of Aboriginal societies, which were understood to subordinate women, in contrast to the ideal of monogamous marriage, cherished by Europeans as an institution that elevated women. Polygamy was viewed as a system that exploited and degraded women, depriving them of respect and influence. It was thought that jealousy and friction among the wives was inevitable. The husbands were seen as idle, debauched, and tyrannical. The sexual desires of the husband were seen as a main motivation for polygamy. Missionaries were among the most outspoken critics. They were deeply concerned about the propriety of a host of customs involving sexuality, marriage, and divorce. Aboriginal marriage, even when monogamous, was misunderstood and condemned as a heartless business transaction without love, courtship, or ceremony—a commodity simply changed hands.[13] But polygamy topped the list of forces that allegedly degraded women. As Methodist missionary John Semmens wrote in his 1884 memoirs, multiple wives were "general slaves, subject to the behests of the most thoughtless and relentless of taskmasters."[14]

These views were common throughout the imperial world in the late nineteenth century. In a book entitled *Women of the Orient*, Rev. R.C. Houghton described his thoughts on polygamy: "Deceit, bickerings, strife, jealousies, intrigues, murder and licentiousness have followed in its train; true love has, in its presence, given place to sensual passion, and woman has become the slave, rather than the companion of man. The word home, as symbolical of confidence, sympathy, rest, happiness and true affection, is not found in the vocabulary of polygamous lands. Polygamy is subversive of God's order; and, beginning by poisoning the very sources of domestic and social prosperity, its blighting influences are felt and seen in every department of national life."[15]

While missionaries and other reformers were ostensibly concerned with what they depicted as the despotism and degradation that Aboriginal women had to contend with from the men who were their "ruthless taskmasters," there was at the same time a contradictory and muted recognition that these women had some freedoms and privileges not enjoyed by non-Aboriginal women. Sexual freedom before marriage was tolerated. Divorce was relatively easy. People separated and divorced for reasons of incompatibility, physical abuse, laziness, or lack of support. Among the Blackfoot a marriage was dissolved when a wife left, returning to her parents or an older brother, taking her property, which included the tipi, with her. Children normally stayed with the mother following a divorce.[16] [. . .] Esther Goldfrank concluded that Blackfoot women had considerable power and influence, emphasizing also their central role in sacred ceremonies. Women "enjoyed a comparatively strong position . . . a woman could lead a war party; she could own property, receive and exercise medicine power, and give names. She was a necessary part of every ceremonial transfer; she was the custodian of the bundles that her husband bought. The pubic initiation of the Horn Society still dramatized the man's dependence. It is the wife who receives the power from the seller. Her husband can only gain possession from her."[17]

In contrast to widely held assumptions about their servitude and misfortunes, Aboriginal wives enjoyed more options and autonomy than Canadian women of the nineteenth century married under English common law. Legal historian Constance Backhouse has described this form of marriage as "very rigid, overbearing [and] patriarchal."[18] Husbands were expected to wield all the power, and wives were denied independence or autonomy. Under the "doctrine of marital unity," the very existence of the wife was legally absorbed by her husband. Her property became his property. Divorce was almost unknown; marriages were regarded as virtually indissoluble. Divorce was also expensive, and it carried a social stigma, attached strongly to the divorced woman regardless of the cause of marital breakdown. If a divorce did occur, the woman risked the loss of custody of children.

It was the missionaries in western Canada who made the first efforts to discourage polygamy. Their methods, however, and the enticements at their disposal (refusal to baptize, excommunication) were not particularly compelling. Missionaries were also uncertain about how best to proceed, and there was concern especially for the "discarded" wives and their children. These perplexing issues were discussed at the highest church levels. Anglican missionaries of the Church Missionary Society (CMS) were instructed not to baptize any man who had more than one wife, but the wives, perceived as victims, could be baptized. Although the policy was confirmed at the Lambeth Conference of 1888, it was not without considerable discussion of perplexing conundrums that might arise. [. . .]

Missionaries in western Canada were not in agreement about how to proceed when dissolving polygamous marriages. Which wife should be retained? How should the "semi-widows" or "abandoned" wives and children be provided for? Methodist missionary E.R. Young regretted the fate of the abandoned ones, but claimed in his memoirs that he felt obliged to enforce the rule that the first wife must take precedence over a later one, even if the first was childless and the later wife had a larger family.[19] John Semmens, however, felt that while the rule favoured the claim of the senior wife, there were "many instances . . . in which the right is waived voluntarily in favour of the younger women."[20] He felt the husband should care for the younger children, permitting the abandoned wives to earn a living. The Hudson's Bay Company, he noted, felt charitable toward these "semi-widows," allowing them job opportunities where others were refused. The children of a first wife, Semmens wrote, would be grown up and able to support their mother. In his memoirs of missionary life, Anglican John Hines wrote that he "followed no definite rule in deciding which wife should be retained, but that those with the greatest number of small children had the strongest claim."[21] Hines found that it was generally the eldest wife who left the marriage, moving to the homes of grown-up daughters.

While missionaries sought to eradicate polygamy from the beginning of their work on western Canadian Indian reserves after the 1870s era of treaties, federal government administrators were, until the 1890s, hesitant, even reluctant, to pursue any concerted efforts. The Indian agents, farm instructors, inspectors, school officials, teachers, and bureaucrats in Regina and Ottawa worked within the legal framework of the Indian Act and pursued a cluster of policies that together were to have the effect of imposing gender roles and identities drawn from the experiences of the colonizers. Men were to be yeoman farmers, and for a time the residential

and industrial school system trained them for other trades such as shoemaking or blacksmithing. Women were to be farm homemakers, undertaking their tasks of butter-making, sewing, cleaning, and cooking individually in permanent (not mobile) homes. (Women were also to be mothers, but their capacity in this regard was viewed by authorities as suspect, necessitating the residential school system.) These homes were to house nuclear families, and there would be decent partitions allowing privacy.

As part of this program, administrators wanted to impose what they regarded as legal, permanent, and monogamous marriages. The Indian Act was of some assistance in imposing this model of marriage. Under this legislation a widow could inherit her husband's property only if she could prove she was of good moral character and had lived with her husband until he was deceased.[22] A DIA official, most likely the Indian agent, would decide whether the widow was "moral" and so qualified. Also helping to impose the patriarchal and monogamous model of marriage was a clause of the act which stipulated that annuities (annual payments promised under treaties) and any interest money (which might arise from the sale of reserve land) could be refused any Indian "who may be proved, to the satisfaction of the Superintendent-General, to have been guilty of deserting his or her family and the said Superintendent-General may apply the same towards the support of any family, woman or child so deserted." The superintendent-general could also "stop the payment of the annuity and interest money of any woman having no children, who deserts her husband and lives immorally with another man."[23] These laws, which reflected a range of stereotypes about Aboriginal women, particularly their potential for "immorality," were aimed at keeping women within monogamous, lifelong marriages.

Based on legal advice from the Department of Justice, however, DIA authorities found that it was not possible to simply impose their marriage model. Indian agents expressed grave concern about what they perceived as a tenuous, invalid, impermanent form of marriage, as divorce was permitted. Yet they could not abolish or prohibit Aboriginal marriage. Not to recognize these as marriages, to proclaim them all invalid, would mean that married persons would feel free to consider their relationships null and void. The children would be illegitimate. There was also no one to perform civil or Christian marriages in many regions of the west. The superintendent inspector for Manitoba, Ebenezer McColl, complained in 1893 that couples were "living illegally together, according to the unorthodox custom of their pagan ancestors," but he was forced to admit that people did not have the money to obtain licences, and that the visiting missionary seldom remained long enough to enable the banns to be published the requisite number of times to legalize a marriage. "Hence," wrote McColl, "they have either to postpone indefinitely the regular consummation of their nuptials or live unlawfully together without having any authorized wedding ceremony performed."[24]

The resistance of Aboriginal people, who showed a preference for their own marriage laws, also hampered any program of intervention. According to the Fort Macleod *Gazette*, the first marriage of an Aboriginal couple in southern Alberta to be solemnized through obtaining a marriage certificate took place in 1895.[25] Two years later on the Blackfoot reserve, the first marriage of a Siksika couple at that mission was performed according to the rites of the Catholic Church, over 50 years after the first Catholic missionaries arrived on the prairies, and after twenty years of reserve life.[26] The DIA could do little to impose a new regime, although officials were instructed to work to end "tribal customs and pagan views," and to facilitate an understanding of the "true nature and obligations of the marriage tie."[27]

An 1888 Department of Justice opinion on Indian marriage and divorce established the policy that the DIA would pursue well into the twentieth century. "[Marriages of] Pagan Indians which have been contracted in accordance with tribal customs should be treated by your Department as *prima facie* valid and the issue of such marriage as legitimate," wrote a law clerk in 1888. "If, however, an Indian so married deserts the woman who is recognized or is entitled to recognition as his wife, and during her life time lives with and has children by another woman, the Minister does not think that such cohabitation should in any case be recognized as marriage, unless there has been an actual divorce from the first wife. The resulting issue should therefore be treated as illegitimate and as having no right to share in the annuities of the band."[28]

By about 1900 a complicated situation had emerged in which Aboriginal marriage law was recognized as valid if both parties were of that ancestry, and if the marriage conformed to the ideal of a monogamous, lifelong bond. Aboriginal divorce law was not regarded as valid. This policy, and the way in which it was interpreted by many reserve administrators, caused upheaval and instability in a society that had easily permitted remarriage in the event of marriage breakdown. Those who were divorced or deserted by their spouses were without their former option of forming a new family. "Legal" divorce was a virtual impossibility for reserve residents, and it was rare at this time for all Canadians.[29] Indian agents had tremendous power to decide which couples were legally married, which were living together "immorally," in their view, and which children were legitimate. For the purposes of annuity payments, the agents decided what constituted a valid family unit. Agents gave and denied permission for couples to marry, and they also refused permission for people to remarry in the event of divorce according to Aboriginal law. At times agents, the North West Mounted Police, and school principals took concerted action to break up what they saw as illegal marriages.[30]

DIA officials took few steps to abolish polygamous marriages until the early 1890s, and even then no action was taken against those who had entered into treaty in these circumstances. Annuity paylists indicate that leading men had two, three, or four adult women in the household. It was hoped that the practice would die naturally under the influence of missionaries and under the new conditions of reserve life. Officials did take steps to discourage any new polygamous marriages. An 1882 departmental circular established a policy that was intended to achieve this goal. Indian superintendent J.F. Graham wrote: "There is no valid reason for perpetuating polygamy by encouraging its continuance in admitting any further accessions to the number already existing, and I [illegible] to instruct you not to recognize any additional transgressions by allowing more husbands to draw annuities for more than their legal wives."[31] There is no indication that Indian Affairs officials were aware that until 1890 no statute existed that explicitly asserted that polygamy was illegal in Canada; a comprehensive antipolygamy bill was only introduced in 1890 in response to the arrival of Mormons in Alberta.

Why did the DIA decide that more active intervention was necessary by the early 1890s? In other colonial settings, programs of intervention were motivated by economic factors and the desire for Indigenous labour. In Natal and southern Rhodesia, for example, colonial authorities argued that married men would not be compelled to work while they were permitted to live "idly" at home with their wives doing all the work for them. Thus polygamy was understood to deprive the settler colony of African male labour, undermining the economic progress of the region. Men would have to seek wage labour if they could no longer accumulate many wives.[32] In the US west, punishing polygamists was a means of undermining the authority of many of the leading Native American men. The Court of Indian Offenses, established in 1883, took

aim at polygamy. Judges were to be selected from among the leading men of the reservations, but a polygamist could not serve as a judge. Polygamists were to be fined or to serve time with hard labour. As historian John D. Pulsipher has written, the Court of Indian Offenses was designed to strike at the heart of the power of Native American male leaders: "As with Mormons, polygamists in Native groups were usually the leading men of their tribes. By barring polygamists from judicial service—monogamy being the only qualification for serving on the bench—and actively prosecuting anyone who tried to take multiple wives, the Bureau could hope to subvert the existing tribal power structures and replace them with structures which were properly subsumed under federal authority."[33]

In western Canada there was little demand for the labour of Aboriginal males, so this factor can be ruled out. By the late nineteenth century in Canada, however, there was a widespread fear that the nuclear family and the home, the central institutions of the social order, were disintegrating in the wake of industrialization, rural depopulation, and urbanization. Reformers and leaders in Canada took steps to reinforce the institution of marriage. As historian James G. Snell has written, "in particular, Canadian leaders pressed for a stronger role by the state in defending marriage and in punishing any deviations from the moral code and social order associated with marriage."[34] The forces of industrialization, rural depopulation, and urbanization were somewhat remote from western Canada in the 1890s, when policymakers remained desperate to attract agriculturalists. But in this new region of the Dominion, the imperative to reinforce the institution of life-long monogamous marriage took on added dimensions and urgency. The nuclear family, centring on a husband and wife, was to be the basic building block of the west. This goal was embedded in the Dominion Lands Act and the homestead system that established the economic and social foundation of the prairie west. Yet there were challenges to this marriage and family model, not only from Aboriginal residents, but also from recent immigrants. In the late 1880s, missionaries had publicly voiced concern about the morality of some of the white men of the west who had a sequence of Aboriginal wives and were not supporting their children.[35] Some prominent men had cast aside women married according to Aboriginal law and had remarried newly arrived white women. Immigrants had marriage customs and domestic units that departed from the cherished single model. These multiple definitions posed a threat, endangering convictions about the naturalness or common sense of the European family formation. The arrival of the Mormons in southern Alberta in the late 1880s, however, combined with the Blackfoot's open resistance to and defiance of interference in their domestic arrangements, altered the situation. Charges of polygamy also in some cases permitted DIA authorities to depose, or threaten to depose, chiefs who challenged government authority.

The presence of the Mormons in Canada caused fear and anxiety. They also had supporters, as they were viewed as excellent dry land farmers, but support fell away after their request to continue in their polygamous marriages.[36] There was concern that Canadian men might be tempted to join up, and these fears seemed to be realized in 1889 when Anthony Maitland Stenhouse, a member of the British Columbia legislative assembly, tendered his resignation, renounced his own faith, and joined the Mormons in southern Alberta. He vocally and vigorously defended polygamy in the press (although he himself remained unmarried).[37] It was Stenhouse who read the Canadian statutes and discovered a loophole: marrying two wives at the same time did not violate existing laws.[38] Other concerns were that the Mormons would proselytize, dragging young non-Mormon girls into lives of degradation. But polygamy was seen as a deeper threat to

the very fabric of the young nation. As one Ontario Liberal parliamentarian declared in the House of Commons during the 1890 debate on "An Act respecting Offences relating to the Law of Marriage," polygamy was "a serious moral and national ulcer."[39]

Amendments to Canadian law, passed in 1890, imposed a five-year prison sentence and a fine of $500 on any person guilty of entering into any form of polygamy, any kind of conjugal union with more than one person at the same time, or what the "persons commonly called Mormons" knew as "spiritual or plural marriage". Any kind of ceremony, rite, or form practised by any society, sect, or denomination, religious or secular, or mere mutual consent could qualify—a binding form of marriage recognized by law did not have to have taken place.[40]

[. . .]

Given the public attention to the issue of polygamy, the widespread anxiety about the disintegration of the nuclear family, the proximity of the Mormons to a reserve community where polygamy was practised, and the new legislation that specifically prohibited polygamy, the time had come for the DIA to act. Also motivating action was evidence that new polygamous marriages were being contracted. A final factor to be considered is that in the early 1890s in western Canada, the land on fertile Indian reserves was being subdivided at great expense into 40-acre lots that were to be the small-scale farms and homes of nuclear families.[41] This plan was inspired in part by the US Dawes Severalty Act, as well as by Canada's Dominion Lands Act, but it was not precisely the same as either. It was similar, however, in that the ideal of a self-sufficient, independent family in which the male was the breadwinner and the farm wife his helpmate served as a rationale for the scheme. Large extended families of several wives, grandmothers, and many children could simply not survive on these miniature farms. In the United States, the implementation of the Dawes Act became an effective method of undermining polygamous households.

Yet measures aimed at eradicating polygamy remained reluctant and hesitant: In 1892 Indian Commissioner Hayter Reed asked his Ottawa superior for an opinion from the Department of Justice on questions that could guide a possible criminal prosecution "to suppress polygamy among our Indians," as cases still continued to occur "and the question arises whether some more stringent measures than heretofore resorted to should not now be adopted."[42] Not receiving a reply, Reed wrote in a similar vein the next year, saying that "their pernicious practices" were "far from showing sign of the gradual eradication which was expected," and asking for an opinion on questions including: "Is an Indian liable to criminal prosecution, if, in accordance with the customs of his Band, he lives with more than one wife?"[43]

In a December 1893 circular letter, each of the Indian agents in western Canada was asked to report on the state of polygamy in their agencies by ascertaining the numbers, and recording the names, of husbands and wives and recording the number of years of marriage. Agents were also to fully explain the law on the subject. In preparing the lists, Assistant Commissioner Amedée Forget emphasized "the necessity for the utmost carefulness, in order that injustice may not be inadvertently done to anyone named therein."[44] What Forget may have meant was that there was great potential for misunderstanding in drawing up these lists; not all of the households with more than one adult woman were necessarily polygamous. [. . .]

The initial lists of polygamous families were submitted to Ottawa in September 1894, but any action was delayed as bureaucrats there asked that further information be supplied as to the "ages of the Indians shown to have added to the number of their wives since entering into Treaty."[45] [. . .]

The people of southern Alberta's Treaty 7, however, stood out from the others in the persistence of polygamy. There were 76 polygamous families on the Blood Reserve, and 49 on the Blackfoot Reserve.[46] The list of polygamous marriages entered into since the treaty were 23 Blood, 41 Blackfoot, and 49 Peigan.[47]

Resolve to take legal action was strengthened when new cases of polygamous marriages continued in the Blood agency, despite the fact that in the summer of 1894 the people had been notified that no plural marriages would be permitted for the future.[48] Indian agent James Wilson reported that marriages were defiantly continuing.[49] Two young men had taken second wives and "upon [Wilson's] ordering them to obey instructions of the Department they refused." Wilson had warned them they were liable to be sent to prison, and he was refusing the families rations until they obeyed. He wanted to send them up before a judge and felt that "a little coercion" was necessary now to "put a stop to what is probably one of the greatest hindrances to their advancement." Threats of legal action and withholding rations worked in two cases, but a man named Plaited Hair refused to give up his second wife. Wilson sought permission to place the second wife in a residential school, and Forget agreed with this course of action.[50] Forget stated that threats of prosecution had been made for years, that regard for the "prestige of the law" would be lessened if they did not proceed, and that their wards might be emboldened by what would seem to them to be evidence of weakness if no action was taken.[51]

In all the correspondence concerning the eradication of polygamy, DIA officials expressed almost no concern about the fate of the "semi-widows" who would be the result of a successful policy or prosecution. There is no indication of the kind of discussion of the conundrums that bedevilled the missionaries, such as which wife would be regarded as legitimate and which would have to go, and were they able to remarry. The records also contain almost no indication of the thoughts or reactions of the wives. Concern that women were treated within their own society as chattels, to be moved about at will, seems hollow when officials were prepared to remove them from their homes and place them in residential schools without any apparent consultation or permission. A central rationale for eradicating polygamy was that women were to be saved from lives of slavery, yet if the initiatives were successful, the "semi-widows" or "supernumerary wives" and children were to be abandoned.

[. . .]

DIA administrators became ever more determined to take stringent measures as new cases of polygamy arose. It was also reported that girls were being promised in marriage as a means of preventing them from being sent to residential schools.[52] Before proceeding with the uncertain criminal prosecution, consideration was given to the tactic of placing girls in residential schools under the compulsory education clauses of the Indian Act. In 1895 Forget was wondering whether this might be more successful, causing "less friction than by proceeding to prosecute for bigamy under the Criminal Code." The linking of the residential school program with the campaign to abolish polygamy further inflamed protests on reserve communities of southern Alberta.

[. . .]

By the late 1890s, DIA officials were worried about the determination of the Blackfoot to resist interference in their domestic relations. Chief Red Crow of the Kainai continued to live with his four wives despite the fact that in 1896 he was baptized into the Roman Catholic Church and was married in a Catholic ceremony to his youngest wife, Singing Before. [. . .]

As evidence of new cases of polygamy accumulated in 1898, Indian Commissioner Forget wrote the new Deputy Superintendent General of Indian Affairs, James Smart, requesting "a definite and unqualified authorization to take measures of repression. Department's sanction of proceedings in such cases having hitherto been so qualified as to practically nullify same."[53] J.D. McLean, acting secretary, replied that the department was willing to leave the matter in his hands. Newcombe's 1895 opinion was quoted, and Forget was told that if he felt it was in the best interests of the Indians, and of public morality, he could take the necessary proceedings.[54] Forget was determined to take action, as he was convinced that "unless severe measures are taken it will be many years before the evil is eradicated."[55] In 1898 Indian agent James Wilson reported that notwithstanding all his efforts on the Blood reserve, six or seven young men had taken second wives, and he felt others would follow this example.[56]

In the Treaty 4 district, Cree Chief Star Blanket was reported in the fall of 1898 to have taken another wife.[57] The File Hills Indian agent informed the chief that more was expected of him as he had only recently been reinstated as chief. According to the agent, Star Blanket said that "he would rather give up the Chiefship [sic] than give the woman up."[58] After several months, Star Blanket complied with DIA policy to some extent by giving up his first wife, who appealed to the department for assistance as she was in a state of destitution.[59] Star Blanket was regarded as "difficult" to handle as he was opposed to policies on schools. It was recommended that he be deposed.

Forget decided to focus on the Blood Reserve after first giving the parties reasonable notice that they would be prosecuted unless they abandoned polygamy. He hoped that with firmness and the "hearty co-operation" of the police, the law would be enforced. In August 1898 Forget instructed agent Wilson to collect and submit information regarding all the new cases of polygamy to the Crown prosecutor, C.F. Conybeare of Lethbridge.[60] [. . .]

The Kainai were determined to resist. By November 1898 [the Crown prosecutor] Wilson could report no changes, despite numerous meetings on the subject. He tried another tactic by refusing to pay the wives their annuities.[61] Wilson explained to Forget that the Indian Act "gave power to refuse payment to women who deserted their families and lived immorally with another man, and that as these women knew what they were doing they were equally guilty with the men." Wilson told Red Crow that the paylist books would be kept open for ten days, and that during that time the chief was to hold a meeting with the women to persuade them to give up their marriages. A meeting was held, but it was reported that Red Crow's position was that the new rules about marriage should apply only to the graduates of the schools.[62] Wilson declared that the young people were bound to obey and that Red Crow should insist they obey. The chief refused to do this. Once again the young men were given one month to withdraw from the position they had taken. Wilson reported that the tactic of holding back annuities worked with a number of the wives, but three refused to comply or to give up their marriages. Wilson sought permission to continue to withhold annuities. In his view, these women were "living immorally" as they had "undoubtedly" left their families to reside with another married man. Two of the women were widows with children when they remarried. Forget permitted Wilson to withhold the annuities of the women who "still persist to live immorally."[63]

By December 1898 Wilson was determined that legal proceedings should be taken to "enforce the law as those young men still refuse to obey."[64] In consultation with Conybeare, he decided to proceed against Bear's Shin Bone, a scout for the North West Mounted Police and the man who had most recently entered into a polygamous marriage. Bear's Shin Bone was brought before Judge C. Rouleau at Fort Macleod on 10 March 1899 on a charge of practising polygamy with two women, an offence under Section 278 of the Criminal Code.[65] His wives were Free Cutter Woman and Killed Herself, and there is no indication that any evidence was

taken from them during the trial. To do so would have raised the question of whether they were competent to, or could be compelled to, testify against their husband. If, as in *Regina v. Nan-e-quis-a-ka*, the second wife was found not to be a valid wife, the case for the prosecution for polygamy would be weakened. Conybeare had to prove that there was a form of contract between the parties, which they all regarded was binding upon them. M. McKenzie for the defence argued that this section of the statute was never intended to apply to Indians (as discussed earlier, it was originally designed to address Mormon polygamy).[66] The court held that the law "applied to Indians as well as whites," and that the marriage customs of the Bloods came within the provisions of the statute and were a form of contract, recognized as valid by the case of *Regina v. Nan-e-quis-a-ka*. Both marriages had to be recognized as valid in order to invalidate the second marriage. This anomaly was recognized in the local newspaper's coverage of the case, in which it was noted that "Bare-Shin-Bone, the Blood Indian charged with polygamy, was convicted and allowed to go on suspended sentence, being instructed to annul his latest marriage (?) and cleave to his first spouse and none other."[67] If he did not, he would be brought up at any time for sentencing.[68]

The DIA regarded this as a test case, with the goal being not to punish, but to make the prisoner and the others obey the law. The DIA agreed to pay for the defence barrister, even though the Kainai had raised a sum of money for that purpose. Wilson also sought and received permission to pay arrears for the 1898 annuities withheld from the women who refused to give up their marriages. Wilson further sought permission to have the children listed as legitimate, allowing them to draw rations and annuities. These measures would, in Wilson's view, "help to allay the feeling of soreness which one or two of them feel at having to give up their second wives."[69] Permission was granted, and newly appointed Indian commissioner David Laird was advised from Ottawa that the offspring of these marriages would be considered legitimate and not only rationed, but also placed on the paylist.[70] DIA accountant Duncan Campbell Scott endorsed these measures, writing in a memorandum that "the right of the women themselves to payment of annuity is not impugned by the relation referred to, and if we were to consider the offspring of such unions illegitimate it would hardly be possible to advance just grounds for our decision, as a great number of adult Indians and children throughout Manitoba and the North West are the fruit of such marriages. The effect of leniency in these cases will assist in furthering an easy transition to civilized ways of matrimony."[71]

The 1890s flurry of activity aimed at prohibiting polygamy, which culminated in the Bear's Shin Bone case, did not entirely result in the desired goal. There was much "unfinished business". The 1901 census for the Blood Reserve indicated over 30 polygamous families.[72] Not all of these would have been marriages contracted before or at the time of Treaty 7, as some involved younger men and women. Indian agents continued to report polygamous marriages, although concerns about divorce and cases of bigamy became the more frequent complaints.[73] The 1890s prohibition campaign was one chapter in a lengthy saga of efforts, using diverse tactics, rewards, and punishments, which were aimed at imposing monogamous morality and "proper" gender roles. The concerted resistance and defiance demonstrated by the Kainai did not continue after Bear's Shin Bone, but Aboriginal people continued to challenge and contest interference in the domestic domain. Although unfinished and not always successful, however, these interventions continued well into the twentieth century.

NOTES

1. The term "polygamy" embraces both "polygyny" (one husband taking multiple wives) and "polyandry" (one wife taking multiple husbands). Plains Aboriginal societies practised polygyny (as did the Mormons), but non-Aboriginal people at the time and since have referred to this as polygamy. In Blackfoot and Cree there are no words for polygamy, polygyny, or polyandry.

2. Ann Laura Stoler, "Tense and Tender Ties: The Politics of North American History and (Post) Colonial Studies," *The Journal of American History* 88, 3 (December 2001): 829–65.

3. Jane Fishburne Collier, *Marriage and Inequality in Classless Societies* (Stanford, CA: Stanford University Press, 1988).

4. R.N. Wilson Papers, vol. 1, edited and annotated by Philip Godsell, p. 118, Glenbow Archives.

5. David G. Mandelbaum field notes, Fine Day # 1B, 6 August 1934, pp. 4–5, Canadian Plains Research Center.

6. Ibid., 4.

7. Ibid., 5.

8. Glenbow Archives, Wilson Papers, 118.

9. Beverly Hungry Wolf, *The Ways of My Grandmothers* (New York: Quill, 1982), 201.

10. Sue Sommers Dietrich typescript of 1939 interviews on the Blackfoot Reservation, Montana, p. 4, Marquette University Archives. Thanks to Alice Kehoe for this reference.

11. John H. Moore, "The Developmental Cycle of Cheyenne Polygyny," *American Indian Quarterly* (Summer 1991): 311–28, at 311.

12. Hungry Wolf, *Ways of My Grandmothers*, 27.

13. Sarah Carter, *Capturing Women: The Manipulation of Cultural Imagery in Canada's Prairie West* (Montreal and Kingston: McGill-Queen's University Press, 1997), 163–6.

14. John Semmens, *The Field and the Work: Sketches of Missionary Work in the Far North* (Toronto: Methodist Mission Rooms, 1884), 163.

15. Rev. Ross C. Houghton, *Women of the Orient: An Account of the Religious, Intellectual and Social Condition of Women* (Cincinnati: Hitchcock and Walden, 1877), 190–1.

16. L.M. Hanks Jr. and Jane Richardson, *Observations of Northern Blackfoot Kinship*, Monographs of the American Ethnological Society, no. 9, A. Irving Hallowell, ed. (Seattle: University of Washington Press, 1944), 23.

17. Esther Goldfrank, *Changing Configurations in the Social Organization of a Blackfoot Tribe during the Reserve Period*, Monographs of the American Ethnological Society, no. 8, A. Irving Hallowell, ed. (Seattle: University of Washington Press, 1944), 47.

18. Constance Backhouse, *Petticoats and Prejudice: Women and Law in Nineteenth-Century Canada* (Toronto: Women's Press, for the Osgoode Society, 1991), 176.

19. John Webster Grant, *Moon of Wintertime: Missionaries and the Indians of Canada* (Toronto: University of Toronto Press, 1984), 235.

20. Semmens, *The Field and the Work*, 166.

21. John Hines, *The Red Indians of the Plains: Thirty Years' Missionary Experience in the Saskatchewan* (Toronto: McClelland, Goodchild and Stewart Ltd., 1916), 158–9.

22. Sharon H. Venne, ed., *Indian Acts and Amendments, 1868–1975: An Indexed Collection* (Saskatoon: University of Saskatchewan Native Law Centre), 94.

23. Ibid., 139–40, Sections 72 and 73.

24. Canada, "Ebenezer McColl's report on the Manitoba Superintendency, 18 October 1893," in "Department of Indian Affairs report for 1893," *Sessional Papers*, no. 14, vol. 27, 45.

25. *Macleod Gazette*, 25 January 1895.

26. M.B. Venini Byrne, *From the Buffalo to the Cross: A History of the Roman Catholic Diocese of Calgary* (Calgary: D.W. Friesen and Sons, 1973), 50.

27. Canada, "Annual Report of the Superintendent-General of Indian Affairs," in "Department of Indian Affairs Report for 1898," *Sessional Papers*, no. 14, vol. 33, xxv.

28. "Questions on Indian Marriage," pp. 3–4, Records of the Department of Justice, Record Group (RG) 13, vol. 2406, file 1299–1914, Library and Archives Canada (LAC).

29. James G. Snell, *In the Shadow of the Law: Divorce in Canada, 1900–1939* (Toronto: University of Toronto Press, 1991).

30. See Records of the Department of Indian Affairs, RG 10, vol. 3559, file 74, pt. 4, LAC.

31. Circular letter of J.F. Graham, 24 July 1882, Records of the Department of Indian Affairs, RG 10, vol. 3602, file 1760, LAC.

32. Diana Jeater, *Marriage, Perversion and Power: The Construction of Moral Discourse in Southern Rhodesia, 1894–1930* (Oxford: Clarendon Press, 1993), 78.

33. John D. Pulsipher, "The Americanization of Monogamy: Mormons, Native Americans and the Nineteenth-Century Perception that Polygamy Was a Threat to Democracy" (PhD dissertation, University of Minnesota, 1999), 162.

34. James G. Snell, "'The White Life for Two': The Defence of Marriage and Sexual Morality in Canada, 1890–1914," in *Canadian Family History: Selected Readings*, Bettina Bradbury, ed. (Toronto: Copp Clark Pitman Ltd., 1992), 381–400, at 381.

35. Sarah Carter, "Categories and Terrains of Exclusion: Constructing the 'Indian Woman' in the Early Settlement Era in Western Canada," *Great Plains Quarterly* 13 (Summer 1993): 147–61, at 150.

36. Ibid.

37. Robert J. McCue, "Anthony Maitland Stenhouse, Bachelor Polygamist," in *American History and Life* 23, 1 (1990): 108–25.

38. Dan Erickson, "Alberta Polygamists? The Canadian Climate and Response to the Introduction of Mormonism's Peculiar Institution," *Pacific Northwest Quarterly* 86, 4 (Fall 1995): 160.

39. Quoted in Brian Champion, "Mormon Polygamy: Parliamentary Comments, 1889–90," *Alberta History* 35, 1 (Spring 1987): 10–17, at 13.

40. Ibid., 16.

41. Sarah Carter, *Lost Harvests: Prairie Indian Reserve Farmers and Government Policy* (Montreal and Kingston: McGill-Queen's University Press, 1990), 193–236.

42. Hayter Reed to Deputy Superintendent General of Indian Affairs (DSGIA), 8 September 1892, Records of DIA, RG 10, vol. 3881, file 94-189, LAC.

43. Reed to DSGIA, 25 September 1893, ibid.

44. Circular letter, Assistant Commissioner Amédée Forget to Indian Agents, 19 December 1893, ibid.

45. M. McGirr to A. Forget, 26 September 1894, ibid.

46. These figures are from the copies of the 1893 agents' reports prepared by A. Forget. The statements for the Peigan are incomplete and unclear (ibid.).

47. These figures are from the "Statement showing ages of Indians who have entered into polygamous relations since taking treaty," ibid.

48. J. Wilson to A. Forget, 21 January 1895, ibid.

49. Ibid.

50. Wilson to Forget, 20 February 1895, ibid.

51. Forget memo, n.d., ibid.

52. Magnus Begg to Forget, 23 March 1895, Records of DIA, RG 10, vol. 3881, file 934, 189, LAC.

53. Forget to J. Smart, 15 April 1898, Records of DIA, RG 10, vol. 3881, file 934, 189, LAC.

54. J.D. Mclean to Forget, 22 April 1898, Records of DIA, RG 10, vol. 3559, file 74, pt. 3, LAC.

55. Forget to McLean, 8 August 1898, Records of DIA, RG 10, vol. 3881, file 934, 189, LAC.

56. Wilson to McLean, 23 July 1898, ibid.

57. Forget to the Secretary, DIA, 13 September 1890, Records of DIA, RG 10, vol. 3559, file 74, pt. 6, LAC.

58. Ibid.

59. Forget to Indian agent, File Hills agency, 20 January 1899, ibid.

60. Forget to Wilson, 18 August 1898, Records of DIA, RG 10, vol. 3559, file 74, pt. 3, LAC.

61. Wilson to Forget, 4 November 1898, ibid., file 74, pt. 19.

62. Ibid.

63. Forget to Wilson, 10 December 1898, ibid.

64. Wilson to Forget, 6 December 1898, ibid.

65. Brian Slattery, *Canadian Native Law Cases*, vol. 2, 1870–1890 (Saskatoon: University of Saskatchewan Native Law Centre, 1981), 513. See also Backhouse, *Petticoats and Prejudice*, 26.

66. Wilson to Forget, 13 March 1899, Records of DIA, RG 10, vol. 3559, file 74, pt. 19, LAC.

67. *Macleod Gazette*, 11 March 1899.

68. Wilson to Forget, 13 March 1899, Records of DIA, RG 10, vol. 3559, file 74, pt. 19, LAC.

69. Ibid.

70. S. Stewart, Secretary, to Indian Commissioner David Laird, 1 April 1899, ibid.

71. Duncan Campbell Scott, memorandum, 29 March 1899, ibid.

72. 1901 Census Data, Canada Census Records, Glenbow Archives.

73. Records of the Department of Indian Affairs, RG 10, vol. 3559, file 74, part 3-30, LAC.

Chapter 3

Resisting the New Order

READINGS

Primary Documents

Historical Interpretations

INTRODUCTION

Canada's rush to take hold of its new possessions during the generation or so after Confederation brought a determined response from the Métis and, to a less spectacular extent, from settlers and Indigenous residents in the northwest. In 1869–1870 at Red River, and again in 1885 in the Saskatchewan River country, the Métis questioned the authority of the Canadian government. Both instances culminated in sending an armed force to quell the resistance; in 1885, the troops saw action. The enigmatic and charismatic Louis Riel played a significant role in the events, setting up provisional governments on both occasions. In 1870, a deal was worked out to create the province of Manitoba, which preserved at least some of the rights the Métis valued. Land was allocated to them, and significant numbers went north and west to appropriate it. The Métis who moved west ended up living in a territory that was under the federal government's authority. By 1885, they had formed communities in these new spaces, and eventually their interest in consolidating what they had meshed with Canadian settlers' desire for stronger representation in Ottawa and with Cree convictions that the treaties signed in the 1870s were inadequate. The primary sources reproduced here come from this second resistance period (1884–1885). Although unsigned, the "St Laurent Petition" was written by Louis Riel. It referred to the economic challenges faced by Indigenous people in the region, summarized the grievances of the Métis and colonial settlers alike, and demanded the creation of a new province as a way to address all the issues raised in the petition. The other primary source is a narrative of two white women captured by some men from the band of Mistahimaskwa (Big Bear). The capture occurred on the fringes of the resistance in 1885, when Aboriginal agitation to renegotiate the treaties of the 1870s found expression but was not coordinated with Métis efforts. The women referred to some of the military engagements between the NWMP/Canadian forces and the Métis, but these events took second place to their own predicament. Even though the battles raged nearby, the captives were mostly concerned with escape and rescue, and less willing to explain the nature of the alliance between their captors and the Métis. In the first of our historical interpretations, J.R. Miller investigates the reasons that led the Métis and some Indigenous people to take up arms in 1885. He highlights the distinctiveness of the Métis and Indigenous grievances in the region and argues that Riel played an essential role in the outbreak of violence. Our final reading from Ted McCoy highlights the ways in which resistance was punished. The courtroom dramas that played out in the summer and fall of 1885 show how ideas long present in the British legal tradition—for example, mercy—could be significantly reinterpreted in the light of racial and cultural differences, as well as the goals of the still-young Dominion.

QUESTIONS FOR CONSIDERATION

1. Why did the St Laurent petitioners believe that the creation of a new province in Saskatchewan would address their grievances?
2. What seem to be the greatest fears of the women held captive by Big Bear's band?
3. Why and how did Indigenous people participate in the rebellion?
4. What role did Louis Riel play in the advent of the North-West Rebellion?
5. What does the punishments given to the Indigenous men participating in the 1885 resistance tell us about the way "mainstream" Canada viewed the west and the Indigenous people living there?

SUGGESTIONS FOR FURTHER READING

Albert Braz, *The False Traitor: Louis Riel in Canadian Culture* (Toronto: University of Toronto Press, 2003).

J.M. Bumsted, *Louis Riel v. Canada: The Making of a Rebel* (Winnipeg: Great Plains Publications, 2001).

Sarah Carter, *Capturing Women: The Manipulation of Cultural Imagery in Canada's Prairie West* (Montreal and Kingston: McGill-Queen's University Press, 1997).

Thomas Flanagan, *Louis "David" Riel: Prophet of the New World* (Toronto: University of Toronto Press, 1996).

Frits Pannekoek, *A Snug Little Flock: The Social Origins of the Riel Resistance of 1869–70* (Winnipeg: Watson and Dwyer, 1991).

Jennifer Reid, *Louis Riel and the Creation of Modern Canada: Mythic Discourse and the Postcolonial State* (Albuquerque: University of New Mexico Press, 2008).

A.I. Silver, "Ontario's Alleged Fanaticism in the Riel Affair," *Canadian Historical Review* 69, 1 (1998): 21–50.

George F.G. Stanley, *The Birth of Western Canada: A History of the Riel Rebellions* (London and New York: Longmans, Green and Co., 1936).

Blair Stonechild and Bill Waiser, *Loyal Till Death: Indians and the North-West Rebellion* (Calgary: Fifth House, 1997).

Primary Documents

1   From "St Laurent Petition, December 16, 1884," reproduced in *The Collected Writings of Louis Riel*, Vol. 3: 5 June 1884 to 16 November 1885, Thomas Flanagan, ed. (Edmonton: University of Alberta Press, 1985), p. 45.

To His Excellency the Governor General, of canada [sic], in Council.

We, the undersigned, your humble petitioners, would respectfully submit to Your Excellency-in-Council, the following as our grievances:

1. that the Indians are so reduced that the settlers in many localities are compelled to furnish them with food, partly to prevent them from dying at their door, partly to preserve the peace of the Territory;

2. that the Half-breeds of the Territory have not received 240 acres of land, each, as did the Manitoba Half-breeds;

3. that the Half-breeds who are in possession of tracts of land have not received patents therefor;

4. that the old settlers of the N.W.T. have not received the same treatment as the old settlers of Manitoba;

5. that the claims of settlers on odd numbers, prior to survey, and on reserves, prior to the proclamation of such reserves, are not recognized;

6. that settlers on cancelled claims are limited to eighty acres Homestead and eighty acres of pre-emption;

7. that settlers are charged more than one dollar per acre for their pre-emptions;

8. that settlers are charged dues on timber, rails and firewood required for home use;

9. that custom duties are levied on the necessaries of life;

10. that settlers are not allowed to perform the required amount of breaking and cropping on their pre-emption, in lieu of their Homestead, when, as frequently happens in the vicinity of wooded streams, it is convenient to have farm buildings and grain fields on separate quarter sections;

11. that purchasers of claims from bona fide settlers who have not completed the required time of actual residence, do not get credit for the term of actual residence, by settlers;

12. that contracts for public works and supplies are not let in such a manner as to confer upon the North west producers as large a benefit as they might derive therefrom, consistent with efficiency;

13. that public buildings are often erected on sites little conducive to the economical transaction of public business;

14. that no effective measures have yet been taken to put the people of the North west in

direct communication with the European Markets, via Hudson's Bay;

15. that settlers are exposed to coercion at elections, owing to the fact that votes are not taken by ballot;

16. that while your petitioners wish to give the eastern government every credit for the excellent liquor regulations which obtain in the N.W.T. yet they must express their anxiety, lest those beneficial restrictions should be loosed, more specially as the country is sparsely settled and the Indians numerous and dissatisfied;

17. that they may humbly state their case, without intending to intermeddle with the affairs of Manitoba and other parts of the N.W.T. your petitioners respectfully submit:

(a) that in /70, when, on invitation of the Dominion, the Delegates of the N.W. arrived in Ottawa, claiming the control of its resources as one of the conditions of the entry of the Territory into Confederation, they were arrested;

(b) that after releasing those Delegates, at the interposition of the Imperial authorities, after explicitly acknowledging and receiving them, "as the Delegates of the North west" the Dominion treated with them amid preparations for war; and dispatched to the Northwest an expedition of federal troops while the negotiations were pending;

(c) that a Commissioner of the Then Governor General and of His government having averted the conflict which he saw would be the consequence of these hostilities, by giving his word of honor as commissioner that however threatening the outlook of the situation might appear, Canada would act in good faith, the response to that peace preserving act was repudiation;

(d) that an understanding having thus [been] arrived at with the Delegates, subject to the consent of the North west, the order in council by which the Queen annexed the Northwest Territory and Rupert's Land to the Dominion of Canada bears date 23d June/70, at which time that consent had not been obtained;

(e) that having thus dispensed with one of the most important conditions of the "Union" the imperial government seems to have followed, ever since, a policy calculated in the opinion of your humble petitioners, to make the Northwest a mere appendage to Canada;

(f) that although the existence of the above-mentioned word of honor and extraordinary treaty has been established, four years after, by special inquest of the House of Commons of Canada, supported, another year later, by the government and recorded in the most conclusive official documents, there are nevertheless, to day, in that part of the N.W. called Manitoba extant proofs of their continual violation;

(g) that although, by the last clause of the "Manitoba Act" Rupert's land and the North West Territories were to have been under temporary government until the 1st of January 71 and untill [sic] the end of the session then next succeeding, those

(h) Territories are, nevertheless, to day, under a government which has remained temporary for fifteen years and which, by the nature of its constitution is destined to remain temporary for an indefinite period;

(i) that the N.W.T. although having a population of 60,000, are not yet granted responsible government, as was Manitoba, when she had less than 12,000 of a population;

(j) that the N.W.T. and its Premier Province are not yet represented in the cabinet, as are the Eastern Provinces;

(k) that the North west is not allowed the administration, of its resources as are the eastern Provinces and British columbia [sic].

In submitting this as a fundamental grievance, your petitioners would disclaim any intention of defrauding the Federal government of the monies which they may have contributed to the improvement of the N.W.

In conclusion, your petitioners would respectfully state that they are treated neither according to their privileges as British subjects nor according to the rights of people and that consequently as long as they are retained in those circumstances, they can be neither prosperous nor happy;

You humble petitioners are of the opinion that the shortest and the most effectual methods of remedying these grievances would be to grant the N.W.T. responsible government with control of its own resources and just representation in the Federal Parliament and Cabinet.

Wherefor [sic] your petitioners humbly pray that your excellency in Council would be pleased to cause the introduction, at the coming session of Parliament, of a measure providing for the complete organization of the District of Saskatchewan as a province, and that they be allowed as in 70, to send Delegates to Ottawa with their Bill of rights; whereby an understanding may be arrived at as to their entry into confederation, with the constitution of a free province, And your humble Petitioners will not cease to pray.

---

2 From Theresa Delaney and Theresa Gowanlock, *Two Months in the Camp of Big Bear* (Regina: Canadian Plains Research Center, 1999), 14–22, 30–1, 33–5, 68–9, 71–5. Originally Published by the University of Regina Press (1999).

[from Theresa Gowanlock's account]

THE MASSACRE

Now come the dreadful scenes of blood and cruel death. The happy life is changed to one of suffering and sorrow. The few months of happiness I enjoyed with the one I loved above all others was abruptly closed—taken from me for ever—it was cruel, it was dreadful. When I look back to it all, I often wonder, is it all a dream, and has it really taken place. Yes, the dream is too true; it is a terrible reality, and as such will never leave my heart, or be effaced from off my mind.

The first news we heard of the Duck Lake affair was on the 30th of March. Mr. Quinn, the Indian Agent, at Frog Lake, wrote a letter to us and sent it down to our house about twelve o'clock at night with John Pritchard, telling my husband and I to go up to Mr. Delaney's on Tuesday morning, and with his wife go on to Fort Pitt, and if they saw any excitement they would follow. We did not expect anything to occur. When we got up to Mr. Delaney's we found the police had left for Fort Pitt. Big Bear's Indians were in the house talking to Mr. Quinn about the trouble at Duck Lake, and saying that Poundmaker the chief at Battleford wanted Big Bear to join him but he would not, as he intended remaining where he was and live peaceably. They considered Big Bear to be a better man than he was given credit for.

On the 1st of April they were in, making April fools of the white people and shaking hands, and they thought I was frightened and told me not to be afraid, because they would not hurt us. My husband left me at Mr. Delaney's and went back to his work at the mill, returning in the evening with Mr. Gilchrist. We all sat talking for some time along with Mr. Dill, who had a store at Frog Lake, and Mr. Cameron, clerk for the Hudson's Bay Company. We all felt perfectly safe where we were, saying that as we were so far away from the trouble at Duck Lake, the Government would likely come to some terms with them and the affair be settled at once. The young Chief and another Indian by the name of Isador said if anything was wrong among Big Bear's band they would come and tell us; and that night Big Bear's braves heard about it and watched them all night to keep them from telling us. We all went to bed not feeling in any way alarmed. About five o' clock in the morning a rap came to the door and Mr. Delaney went down stairs and opened it, and John Pritchard and one of Big Bear's sons by the name of Ibesies were there.

Pritchard said "There [sic] trouble."

Mr. Delaney said "Where?"

Pritchard *"Here!* Our horses are all gone, the Indians deceived us, and said that some half-breeds from Edmonton had come in the night and had taken them to Duck Lake, but Big Bear's band has taken them and hid them, I am afraid it is all up."

My husband and I got up, and Mrs. Delaney came down stairs with a frightened look. In a few minutes Big Bear's Indians were all in the house, and had taken all the arms from the men saying they were going to protect us from the half-breeds, and then we felt we were being deceived. They took all the men over to Mr. Quinn's, and my husband and I were sitting on the lounge, and an Indian came in and took him by the arm saying he wanted him to go too; and he said to Mrs. Delaney and I "do not to be afraid, while I go with this Indian." We stopped in the house, and while they were gone some of the Indians came in and went through the cupboard to find something to eat. They opened the trap door to go down cellar, but it was very dark, and they were afraid to venture down. Then the men came back and Mrs. Delaney got breakfast. We all sat down, but I could not eat, and an Indian asked Mr. Gowanlock to tell me not to be afraid, they would not hurt us, and I should eat plenty. After breakfast they took us out of the house and escorted us over to the church; my husband taking my arm, Mr. and Mrs. Delaney were walking beside us. When we got to the church the priests were holding mass; it was Holy Thursday, and as we entered the door, Wandering Spirit sat on his knees with his gun; he was painted, and had on such a wicked look. The priests did not finish the service on account of the menacing manner of the Indians; they were both around and inside the church. We were all very much frightened by their behaviour. They then told us to go out of the church, and took us back to Mr. Delaney's, all the Indians going in too.

We stopped there for awhile and an Indian came and told us to come out again, and my husband came to me and said "you had better put your shawl around you, for its [sic] very cold, perhaps we will not be gone long." We all went out with the Indians. They were going through all the stores. Everything was given to them, and they got everything they could wish for and took us up the hill towards their camp. We had only gone but a short distance from the house when we heard the reports of guns, but thought they were firing in the air to frighten us; but they had shot Quinn, Dill and Gilchrist, whom I did not see fall. Mr. and Mrs. Delaney were a short distance ahead of my husband, I having my husband's arm. Mr. Williscraft, an old grey-headed man about seventy-five years of age came running by us, and an Indian shot at him and knocked his hat off, and he turned around and said, *"Oh! don't shoot! don't shoot!"* But they fired again, and he ran screaming and fell in some bushes. On seeing this, I began crying, and my husband tried to comfort me, saying, "my *dear* wife be *brave* to the end," and immediately an Indian behind us fired, and my husband fell beside me his arm pulling from mine. I tried to assist him from falling. He put out his arms for me and fell, and I fell down beside him and buried my face on his, while his life was ebbing away so quickly, and was prepared for the next shot myself, thinking I was going with him too. But death just then was not ordained for me. I had yet to live. An Indian came and took me away from my dying husband [sic] side, and I refused to leave. Oh! to think of leaving my *dear* husband lying there for those cruel Indians to dance around. I begged of the Indian to let me stay with him, but he took my arm and pulled me away. Just before this, I saw Mr. Delaney and a priest fall, and Mrs. Delaney was taken away in the same manner that I was. I still looking back to where my poor husband was lying dead; the Indian motioned to where he was going to take me, and on we went. I thought my heart would break; I would rather have died with my husband and been at rest.

WITH THE INDIANS

Hardly knowing how I went or what I did, I trudged along in a half conscious condition. Led a captive into the camp of Big Bear by one of his vile band. Taken through brush and briar, a large pond came to view, we did not pass it by, he made me go through the water on that cold 2nd of April nearly to my waist. I got so very weak that I could not walk and the Indian pulled me along, in this way he managed to get me to his tepee. On seeing Mrs. Delaney taken away so far from me, I asked the Indian to take me to her; and he said *"No, No,"* and opening the tent shoved me in. A friendly squaw put down a rabbit robe for me to sit on; I was shivering with the cold; this squaw took my shoes and stockings off and partly dried them for me. Their tepees consisted of long poles covered with smoke-stained canvas with two openings, one at the top for a smoke hole and the other at the bottom for a door through which I had to crawl in order to enter. In the centre they have their fire; this squaw took a long stick and took out a large piece of beef from the kettle and offered it to me, which I refused, as I could not eat anything after what I had gone through.

Just then Big Bear's braves came into the tent; there were nearly thirty of them, covered with war paint, some having on my husband's clothes, and all giving vent to those terrible yells, and holding most murderous looking instruments. They were long wooden clubs. At one end were set three sharp shining knife blades. They all looked at me as I eyed those weapons (and they well matched the expression of their cruel mouths and develish [sic] eyes) thinking my troubles would soon be over I calmly awaited the result. But they sat down around me with a bottle full of something that looked like water, passing it from one Indian to the other, so I put on a brave look as if I was not afraid of them. After this they all went out and the most bloodcurdling yells that ever pierced my ears was their war-whoop, mingled with dancing and yelling and cutting most foolish antics.

[. . .]

After I had been there for four hours, Louis Goulet and Andre Nault came in, and Goulet said to me "Mrs. Gowanlock if you will give yourself over to the half-breeds, they will not hurt you; Peter Blondin has gone down to where the mill is, and when he comes back he will give his horse for you." I asked them to interpret it to the Indians in order to let me go to Pritchard's tent for awhile, and the Indians said that she could go with this squaw. I went and was overjoyed to see Mrs. Delaney there also. After getting in there I was unconscious for a long time, and upon coming to my senses, I found Mrs. Pritchard bathing my face with cold water. When Blondin came back he gave his horse and thirty dollars for Mrs. Delaney and me. He put up a tent and asked me to go with him, but I refused; and he became angry and did everything he could to injure me. That man treated me most shamefully; if it had not been for Pritchard I do not know what would have become of me. Pritchard was kinder than any of the others.

After I had been a prisoner three days, Blondin came and asked me if could ride horse back, and I said "yes," and he said if I would go with him, he would go and take two of the best horses that Big Bear had and desert that night. I told him I would *never* leave Pritchard's tent until we all left, saying "I would go and drown myself in the river before I would go with him".[. . .]

PROTECTED BY HALF-BREEDS

On the 3rd of April Big Bear came into our tent and sitting down beside us told us he was very sorry for what had happened, and cried over it, saying he knew he had so many bad men but had no control over them. He came very often to our tent telling us to "eat and sleep plenty, they would not treat us like the white man. The white man when he make prisoner of Indian, he starve him and cut his hair off." He told us he would protect us if the police came. The same day Big Bear's braves paid our tent another visit, they came in and around us with their guns, knives and tomahawks, looking at us so wickedly.

Pritchard said, "For God sake let these poor women live, they can do no harm to you; let them go home to their friends."

The leaders held a brief consultation.

An Indian stood up and pointing to the heavens said, "We promise by God that we will not hurt these white women; we will let them live."

They then left the tent.

Every time I saw one of Big Bear's Indians coming in, I expected it was to kill us, or take us away from the tent, which would have been *far worse* than death to *me*.

But they did not keep their word.

On the third night (Saturday, the 4th April,) after our captivity, two Indians came in while all the men and Mrs. Delaney were asleep, I heard them, and thought it was Pritchard fixing the harness, he usually sat up to protect us. A match was lighted and I saw two of the most hedious [sic] looking Indians looking over and saying where is the *Monias* squaw, meaning the white women. I got so frightened I could not move, but Mrs. Delaney put out her foot and awakened Mrs. Pritchard, and she wakened her husband, and he started up and asked what they wanted, and they said they wanted to take the white women to their tent, and I told Pritchard they could kill me before I would go, and I prayed to God to help me. Pritchard and Adolphus Nolin gave their blankets and dishes and Mrs. Pritchard took the best blanket off her bed to give to them and they went off, and in the morning the Wood Crees came in and asked if those Indians took much from us, and Pritchard told them "No"; the Indians wanted to make them give them back. After that Pritchard and other half-breeds protected us from night to night for we were not safe a single minute.

During the two days which had passed, the bodies of the men that were murdered had not been buried. They were lying on the road exposed to the view of everyone. The half-breeds carried them off the road to the side, but the Indians coming along dragged them out again. It was dreadful to see the bodies of our *poor dear* husbands dragged back and forth by those demoniac savages.

On Saturday the day before Easter, we induced some half-breeds to take our husbands' bodies and bury them. They placed them, with those of the priests, under the church. The Indians would not allow the other bodies to be moved. And dreadful to relate those inhuman wretches set fire to the church, and with yelling and dancing witnessed it burn to the ground. The bodies, I afterwards heard, were charred beyond recognition.

Upon seeing what was done the tears ran profusely down our cheeks and I thought my very heart would break. All the comfort we received from that unfeeling band was, "that's right, cry plenty, we have killed your husbands and we will soon have you." [. . .]

THEY TAKE FORT PITT

[. . .]

On Sunday the 12th of April they returned from the Fort flush with victory. They had captured that place, killed policeman Cowan, taken the whites prisoners, and allowed the police to escape down the river, all without loosing [sic] an Indian or half-breed. The prisoners were brought in while we were at dinner. Mr. and Mrs. Quinney came to our tent. Mrs. Quinney said she was cold and wet. She sat down and put her arms around me and cried. I gave her a cup of hot tea and something to eat. Shortly after the McLeans and Manns came in. It was a great relief to see white people again.

It was not long before they moved camp about two miles from Frog Lake. Mrs. Delaney and I, walking with Mrs. Pritchard and family, through mud and water: my shoes were very thin, and my feet very wet and sore from walking. The Indians were riding beside us with our horses and buckboards, laughing and jeering at us with umbrellas over their heads and buffalo overcoats on. We would laugh and make them believe we were enjoying it, and my heart ready to break with grief all the time. When we camped, it was in a circle. A space in the centre being kept for dancing.

I asked Blondin if he had any of our stockings or underclothing in his sacks. He told me no, and shortly afterwards took out a pair of my husband's long stockings and put them on before me, he would change them three and four times a week. He had nearly all my poor husband's clothes. Two men came in one time while Blondin was asleep and took one of my husband's coats out of his sack and went out; Blondin upon missing it got very angry and swore before me, saying that some person had come in and taken one of his coats, and all the time I knew whose coat it was they were quarrelling over. I wished then I could close my eyes and go home to God. [. . .]

ANOTHER BATTLE

Was it the distant roar of heaven's artillery that caught my ear. I listened and heard it again. The Indians heard it and were frightened.

A half-breed in a stage whisper cried, "a cannon! a cannon!"

An Indian answered, "a cannon is no good to fight."

I looked at them and it showed them to be a startled and fear-stricken company, notwithstanding that they held the cannon with such disdain as to say "cannon no good to fight." That night was full of excitement for the Indians; they felt that the enemy was drawing near, too close in fact to be safe. The prisoners were excited with the thought, that perhaps there was liberty behind that cannon for them, and taking it all round, there was little sleep within the tepees.

The next morning I awoke early with hopefulness rising within my breast at the thought of again obtaining my liberty. The first

sound I heard was the firing of cannon near at hand; it sounded beautiful; it was sweet music to my ears. Anticipating the prospect of seeing friends once more, I listened and breathed in the echo after every bomb.

The fighting commenced at seven o'clock by Gen. Strange's troops forcing the Indians to make a stand. It was continued until ten with indifferent success. The troops surely could not have known the demoralized condition of the Indians, else they would have compelled them to surrender. The fighting was very near, for the bullets were whizzing around all the time. We thought surely that liberty was not far away. The Indians were continually riding back and fro inspiring their followers in the rear with hope, and we poor prisoners with despair. At last they came back and said that they had killed twenty policemen and not an Indian hurt. But there were two Indians killed, one of whom was the Worm, he who killed my poor husband, and several wounded. We were kept running and walking about all that morning with their squaws, keeping out of the way of their enemies, and our friends. We were taken through mud and water until my feet got so very sore that I could hardly walk at all.

The Indians ordered us to dig pits for our protection. Pritchard and Blondin dug a large one about five feet deep for us, and they piled flour sacks around it as a further protection; but they dug it too deep and there was two or three inches of water at the bottom. They then threw down some brush and we got into it, twenty persons in all, with one blanket for Mrs. Delaney and me. McLean's family had another pit, and his daughters cut down trees to place around it. Mr. Mann and family dug a hole in the side of the hill and crawled into it. If I had my way I would have kept out of the pit altogether and watched my chance to escape.

We fully expected the troops to follow but they did not; and early in the morning we were up and off again. Some of the Indians went back to see how about the troops, and came back with the report that the "police" (they call all soldiers police) had vanished, they were afraid. When I heard it, I fairly sank, and the slight spark of hope I had, had almost gone out. Just to think that succor was so near, yet alas! so far. But for Mrs. Delaney I would have given way and allowed myself to perish. [. . .]

HOPE ALMOST DEFERRED

Almost a week afterwards, on a Saturday night, the fighting Indians gathered around a tepee near ours and began that never ending dancing and singing. It was a most unusual thing for them to dance so close to our tent. They had never done so before. It betokened no good on their part and looked extremely suspicious. It seemed to me that they were there to fulfil the threat they made some time previous, that they would put an end to us soon. The hour was late and that made it all the more certain that our doom had come. I became very nervous and frightened at what was going on. When all at once there was a scattering, and running, and yelling at the top of their voices, looking for squaws and children, and tearing down tents, while we two sat in ours in the depths of despair, waiting for further developments. I clung to Mrs. Delaney like my own mother, not knowing what to do. The cause of the stampede we were told was that they had heard the report of a gun. That report was fortunate for us, as it was the intention of the Indians to wrench us from our half-breed protectors and kill us.

[. . .]

OUT OF BIG BEAR'S CAMP

Monday morning, May 31st, was ushered in dark and gloomy, foggy and raining, but it proved to be the happiest day we had spent since the 31st of March. As the night was passing, I felt its oppressiveness, I shuddered with the thought of what another day might bring forth; but deliverance it seems was not far away; it was even now at hand. When the light of day had swallowed up the blackness of darkness, the first words that greeted my ears was Pritchard saying "I am going to watch my chance and get out of the camp of Big Bear." Oh! what we suffered, Oh! what we endured, during those two long months, as captives among a horde of semi-barbarians. And to think that we would elude them, just when I was giving up in despair. It is said that the darkest hour is that which preceedes [sic] dawn; weeping may endure for a night, but joy cometh in the morning. So with me, in my utter prostration, in the act of giving way, God heard my prayer, and opened a way of deliverance, and we made the best of the opportunity.

*"No foe, no dangerous path we lead,
Brook no delay, but onward speed."*

Some of the Indians it seems had come across General Strange's scouts the night before, and in consequence, all kinds of rumors were afloat among the band. They were all very much frightened, for it looked as if they were about to be surrounded. So a move, and a quick one, was made by them, at an early hour, leaving the half-breeds to follow on. This was now the golden opportunity, and Pritchard grasped it, and with him, five other half-breed families fled in an opposite direction, thereby severing our connection with the band nominally led by Big Bear.

We cut through the woods, making a road, dividing the thick brush, driving across creeks and over logs. On we sped. At one time hanging on by a corner of the bedding in order to keep from falling off the waggon. Another time I fell off the waggon while fording a stream; my back got so sore that I could not walk much. On we went roaming through the forest, not knowing where we were going, until the night of June 3rd the cry was made by Mrs. Pritchard with unfeigned disgust, "that the police were coming." Mrs. Delaney was making bannock for the next morning's meal, while I with cotton and crochet needle was making trimming for the dresses of Mrs. Pritchard's nine half-breed babies.

I threw the trimming work to the other end of the tent, and Mrs. Delaney called upon Mrs. Pritchard to finish making the bannocks herself, and we both rushed out just as the scouts galloped in.

RESCUED

Rescued! at last, and from a life worse than death. I was so overjoyed that I sat down and cried. The rescuing party were members of General Strange's scouts, led by two friends of my late husband, William McKay and Peter Balentyne of Battleford. We were so glad to see them. They had provisions with them, and they asked us if we wanted anything to eat. We told them we had bannock and bacon, but partook of their canned beef and hard tack. It was clean and good; and was the first meal we enjoyed for two months.

I could not realize that I was safe until I reached Fort Pitt. The soldiers came out to welcome us back to life. The stories they heard about us were so terrible, that they could scarcely believe we were the same.

The steamer was in waiting to take us to Battleford. Rev. Mr. Gordon took my arm and led me on board. The same gentleman gave us hats, we had no covering for our heads for the entire two months we were captives. We were very scant for clothing. Mrs. Delaney had a ragged print dress, while I managed to save one an Indian boy brought me while in camp. Upon reaching Battleford we were taken to the residence of Mr. Laurie.

Coming down on the steamer, on nearing a little island, we saw a number of squaws fishing and waving white flags. All along wherever we passed the Indians, they were carrying white flags as a token that they had washed off their war paint and desired rest.

[from Theresa Delaney's account]
Up to this point, I might say, the Indians showed us no ill-will, but continually harped upon the same chord, that they desired to defend and to save us from the half-breeds. So far they got everything they asked for, and even to the last of the cattle, my husband refused nothing. We felt no dread of death at their hands, yet we knew that they were excited and we could not say what they might do if provoked. We now believed that the story of the half-breeds was to deceive us and throw us off our guard—and yet we did not suspect that they meditated the foul deeds that darkened the morning of the second of April, and that have left it a day unfortunately, but too memorable, in the annals of Frog Lake history.

When I now look back over the events, I feel that we all took a proper course, yet the most unfortunate one for those that are gone. We could have no idea of the murderous intentions on the part of the Indians. Some people living in our civilized country may remark, that it was strange we did not notice the peculiar conduct of the Indians. But those people know nothing either of the Indian character or habits. So far from their manner seeming strange, or extraordinary, I might say, that I have seen them dozens of times act more foolishly, ask more silly questions and want more rediculous [sic] things—even appear more excited. Only for the war-paint and what Big Bear had told us, we would have had our fears completely lulled by the seemingly open and friendly manner. I have heard it remarked that it is a wonder we did not leave before the second of April and go to Fort Pitt; I repeat, nothing at all appeared to us a sign of alarm, and even if we dreaded the tragic scenes, my husband would not have gone. His post was at home; he had no fear that the Indians would hurt him; he had always treated them well and they often acknowledged it; he was an employee of the Government and had a trust in hand; he would never have run away and left the Government horses, cattle, stores, provisions, goods, &c., to be divided and scattered amongst the bands, he even said so before the council day. Had he ran [sic] away and saved his life, by the act, I am certain he would be then blamed as a coward and one not trustworthy nor faithful to his position. I could not well pass over this part of our sad story without answering some of those comments made by people, who, neither through experience nor any other means could form an idea of the situation. It is easy for me to now sit down and write out, if I choose, what ought to have been done; it is just as easy for people safe in their own homes, far from the scene, to talk, comment and tell how they would have acted and what they would have done. But these people know no more about the situation or the Indians, than I know about the Hindoos, their mode of life, or their habits.

[. . .]

Imagine yourself seated in a quiet room at night, and every time you look at the door, which is slightly ajar, you catch the eye of a man fixed upon you, and try then to form an idea of my feelings. I heard that the human eye had power to subdue the most savage beast that roams the woods; if so, there must be a great power in the organ of vision; but I know of no object so awe-inspiring to look upon, as the naked eye concentrated upon your features. Had we but the same conception of that "all seeing eye," which we are told, continually watches us, we would doubtlessly be wise and good; for if it inspired us with a proportionate fear, we would possess what Solomon tells us i[s] the first step to wisdom—"The fear of the Lord is the beginning of wisdom."

But I never could describe all the miseries I suffered during those few weeks. I was two months in captivity; and eight days afterwards we heard of Major-General Strange's arrival, I managed to escape. The morning of our escape seemed to have been especially marked out by providence for us. It was the first and only time the Indians were not upon the close watch. Up to that day, we used to march from sunrise to sunset, and all night long the Indians would dance. I cannot conceive how human beings could march all day, as they did, and then dance the wild, frantic dances that they kept up all night. Coming on grey dawn they would tier [sic] out and take some

repose. Every morning they would tear down our tent to see if we were in it. But whether attracted by the arrival of the soldiers—by the news of General Strange's engagement—or whether they considered we did not meditate flight, I cannot say—but most certainly they neglected their guard that day.

Some of them came in as usual, but we were making tea, and they went off. As soon as the coast was clear we left our tea, and all, and we departed. Maybe they did not know which way we went, or perhaps they were too much engaged with their own immediate danger to make chase, but be that as it may, we escaped. It was our last night under the lynx-eyed watchers. We went about two miles in the woods, and there hid. So far I had no covering for my head, and but scant raiment for my body. The season was very cold in April and May, and many a time I felt numb, chill, and sick, but there was no remedy for it; only "grin and go through." In the last part of my captivity, I suffered from exposure to the sun. The squaws took all my hats, and I could not get anything to cover my head, except a blanket, and I would not dare to put one on, as I knew not the moment we might fall in with the scouts, and they might take me for a squaw. My shawl had become ribbons from tearing through the bush, and towards the end I was not able to get two rags of it to remain together. There is no possibility of giving an idea of our sufferings. The physical pains, exposures, dangers, colds, heats, sleepless nights, long marches, scant food, poor raiment, &c., would be bad enough,—but we must not loose [sic] sight of the mental anguish, that memory, only two [sic] faithful, would inflict upon us, and the terror that alternate hope and despair would compel us to undergo. I cannot say which was the worst. But when united, our sad lives seemed to have passed beneath the darkest cloud that could possibly hang over them.

[. . .]

After our escape, we travelled all day long in the same bush, so that should the Indians discover us, we would seem to be still with them. We had nothing to eat but bread and water. We dare not make fire as we might be detected by the savages and then be subjected to a stricter *surveillance*, and maybe punished for our wanderings. Thus speaking of fire makes me think of the signals that the bands had, the beacons that flared from the heights at stated times and for certain purposes. Even before the outbreak, I remember of Indians coming to my husband and telling him that they were going on a hunt, and if such and such a thing took place, they would at a certain time and in a certain direction, make a fire. We often watched for the fires and at the stated time we would perceive the thin column of smoke ascend into the sky. For twenty and thirty miles around these fires can be seen. They are made in a very peculiar manner. The Indian digs a hole about a foot square and in that start the flame. He piles branches or fagots up on a cone fashion, like a bee-hive, and leaving a small hole in the top for the smoke to issue forth, he makes a draught space below on the four sides. If the wind is not strong, that tiny column of blue smoke will ascend to a height often of fifty or sixty feet. During the war times they make use of these fires as signals from band to band, and each fire has a conventional meaning. Like the *phares* that flashed the alarm from hill-top to hill-top or the tocsin that sang from belfry to belfry in the Basse Bretagne, in the days of the rising of the Vendee, so those beacons would communicate as swiftly the tidings that one band or tribe had to convey to another. Again, speaking of the danger of fire-making, I will give an example of what those Indians did with men of their own tribe.

A few of their men desired to go to Fort Pitt with their families, while the others objected. The couple of families escaped and reached the opposite side of a large lake. The Indians did not know which direction the fugitives had taken until noon the following day, when they saw their fire for dinner, across the lake. They started, half by one side and half by the other side of the lake, and came up so as to surround

the fugitives. They took their horses, blankets, provisions, and camps, and set fire to the prairie on all sides so as to prevent the unhappy families from going or returning. When they thus treated their own people, what could white people expect on their hands?

[. . .]

It was upon Friday morning that we got into Fort Pitt, and we remained their [sic] until Sunday. On Friday night the military band came down two miles to play for us. It was quite an agreeable change from the "tom-tom" of the Indians. Next day we went to see the soldiers drill. If I am not mistaken there were over 500 men there. Sunday, we left per boat, for Battleford, and got in that night. We had a pleasant trip on the steamer "The Marquis". While at Fort Pitt we had cabins on board the very elegant vessel "North West". We remained three weeks at Battleford, expecting to be daily called upon as witnesses in some cases. We travelled overland from Battleford to Swift Current, and thence by rail to Regina. At Moose Jaw, half way between Swift Current and Regina, we were greatly frightened. Such a number of people were collected to see and greet us, that we imagined it was Riel and his followers who had come to take us prisoners. Our fears were however, soon quelled. We remained four days at Regina; thence we came to Winnipeg. There we remained from Monday evening until Tuesday evening. Mostly all the people in the city came to see us, and I cannot commence to enumerate the valuable presents we received from the open-hearted citizens. We stoped [sic] with a Mrs. Bennett; her treatment to us, was like the care of a fond mother for her lost children.

We left on Thursday evening for Port Arthur, and thence we came by boat, to Owen Sound. A person not in trouble could not help but enjoy the glorious trip on the bosom of that immense inland sea. But, although we were overjoyed to be once more in safety, and drawing nearer our homes, yet memory was not sleeping, and we had too much to think off [sic] to permit our enjoying the trip as it could be enjoyed. From Owen Sound we proceeded to Parkdale by train. Parkdale is a lovely spot just outside of Toronto. I spent the afternoon there, and at nine o'clock that night left for home. I said good-bye to Mrs. Gowanlock; after all our sorrows, troubles, dangers, miseries, which we partook in union, we found it necessary to separate. And although we scarcely were half a year acquainted, it seemed as if we had been playmates in childhood, and companions throughout our whole lives. But, as we could not, for the present, continue our hand-in-hand journey, we separated merely physically speaking—for "time

has not ages, nor space has not distance," to sever the recollections of our mutual trials.

I arrived home at 6 o'clock on Monday morning. What were my feelings as I stepped down from the hack, at that door, where three years before I stepped up into a carriage, accompanied by my husband! How different the scene of the bride leaving three years ago, and the widow returning today! Still, on the first occasion there were tears of regret at parting, and smiles of anticipated pleasure and happiness—on the second occasion there are tears of memory, and yet smiles of relief on my escape, and happiness in my safe return.

3   Photographs

Library and Archives Canada/C-001873

Figure 3.1 Mistahimaskwa (Big Bear)

Figure 3.2 Big Bear and Poundmaker in detention

Figure 3.3 Gabriel Dumont

Library and Archives Canada/C-003450

Figure 3.4 Louis Riel, a prisoner in the camp of Major F.D. Middleton, c. 16 May 1885, Batoche

Library and Archives Canada/ C-1879

Figure 3.5 Louis Riel's trial

Historical Interpretations

8 From J.R. Miller, "The North-West Rebellion," in *Skyscrapers Hide the Heavens: A History of Indian-White Relations in Canada,* 3rd edn (Toronto: University of Toronto Press, 2000), 225–53. Reprinted with permission of the publisher.

The rebellion that broke out in the spring of 1885 has been the subject of a great deal of misunderstanding and myth-making. Among the many distorted views of that event, none is more ingrained than the notion that the rebellion was the consequence of the meeting of two distinct ways of life.[1] According to this view, both the Red River Resistance of 1869 and the trouble in the Saskatchewan country in 1885 are best understood as the lamentable consequences of the clash of a sophisticated society with more primitive peoples. Both represented futile attempts by technologically backward peoples to resist the march of more advanced societies. In Saskatchewan in 1885 the Métis and the Indians used force to defend a fading way of life against the expansion of commerce and agricultural settlement. Led by Louis Riel, the Métis precipitated a rebellion in which some of the Indian nations joined, both groups being motivated by a desire to repel the advance of agriculture. [. . .] Such interpretations, while seductive in their simplicity, fail to appreciate the complexity of the events and the variety of the actors' motives in the North-West Rebellion.

A proper understanding of these events requires careful consideration of at least three distinct elements: the Indians, the Métis communities of the Saskatchewan, and Louis Riel. The behaviour of each was quite distinguishable from that of the others, particularly in the preliminary stages of the armed struggle. And, in the case of the Indians, there were important differences among the various nations; the use of force; for example, was confined to the more northerly bands. It is impossible to understand why some Cree killed people, while others remained quiet, without analyzing the situation in which the western Indians found themselves between the signing of Treaty 7 in 1877 and the outbreak of violence in 1885. And it is impossible to appreciate why a peaceful Métis struggle for redress of grievances culminated in rebellion without careful examination of both the people who had grievances and the individual whose leadership they sought. Such an analysis will demonstrate that there was no Indian rebellion in the North-West in 1885; there were only sporadic and isolated reprisals by small groups from some bands. It will also illustrate that Louis Riel was the spark that caused the mixture of Métis and government to explode.

If any people in the North-West Territories had reason to rebel in the 1880s, it was the Indians.[2] They saw the basis of their economy shattered in the 1870s, and then watched in the 1880s as the new relationship with the Dominion of Canada which they had negotiated in the 1870s failed to provide them with the relief and assistance on which they had counted. Moreover, they watched as Ottawa deliberately and systematically violated its treaty promises in order to coerce the Indians into adopting the government's plans for settlement rather than following their own. Finally, they endured great hardship as Ottawa implemented policies of retrenchment that bore savagely on them. The underlying cause of the Indians' problems was the disappearance of the bison. It had come under greater pressure after the 1820s, as the Métis increasingly shifted into the provisioning trade for the

Hudson's Bay Company and attempted to satisfy the expanding market for buffalo robes. Other factors that accounted for the depletion of the herds included the arrival of modern weapons, such as the repeating rifle, and the completion of the transcontinental railway in the United States which brought to the plains the "sports" hunter whose only interest was the acquisition of a trophy. Buffalo hides were also in demand in eastern factories for use in the belts that drove machinery.

One final factor was American policy toward the Indians south of the 49th parallel. In the 1860s and 1870s the United States was still engaged in military campaigns against various Indian nations. Among the most spectacular of these was the ill-fated foray of General G.A. Custer and the Seventh Cavalry which resulted in their annihilation at the hands of Sitting Bull, Crazy Horse, and their warriors on the Little Big Horn River in 1877. The aftermath was the flight of Sitting Bull and hundreds of his followers across the "medicine line"—as the international boundary was called by Indians who recognized its importance in demarcating a land of refuge from a territory in which they could be hunted. Sitting Bull's presence in what is today southwestern Saskatchewan added to the strain on the food resources of the region and encouraged the American military to undertake operations designed to compel him to stay in Canada or starve him into submission in the United States.[3] At times in the late 1870s American forces burned the prairies in an effort to prevent the southern bison herd from trekking into Canada, where it might help to sustain the fugitive Sioux.

The result of this combination of factors was the near-extinction of the bison by the 1880s. Of the herds that had impeded travellers on the prairies and parkland for days at a time in the 1840s, mere hundreds were known to exist by the end of the 1870s. In 1879 a Hudson's Bay Company man wrote in shock of "the total disappearance of buffalo from British territory this season." By 1884 only 300 bison hides were sold at St Paul, and by 1888 an American game report said that "only six animals were then known to be in existence!"[4] The horror of starvation, never totally absent from Indian societies, now became all too familiar in the lodges of both Plains and Woodlands bands. [. . .]

The devastating hardships that the Plains peoples faced as a result of the disappearance of the bison were compounded by the government's response. As the Indians, especially the Cree, moved southward into the Cypress Hills in search of game and a base from which to pursue the buffalo herds, the Canadian authorities became increasingly alarmed. When the Cree, led by Piapot, Little Pine, and Big Bear in particular, began to press for contiguous reserves in the region of the hills, Ottawa's man on the spot became determined to prevent such a concentration. The fact that all three of these Cree leaders had refused to adhere to Treaty 6 when it was signed in 1876, and that Big Bear in particular had expressly rejected submission to Canadian law, made their actions a source of concern to uneasy officials.[5] The disappearance of the buffalo and the consequent hardships provided Edgar Dewdney, lieutenant governor of the North-West Territories, with his opportunity.

Dewdney, who was also commissioner of Indian affairs for the territories after 1879, could use the Indians' plight to defeat their diplomatic campaign for the creation of an Indian territory and to disperse them into other parts of the territories where they might be more easily controlled.[6] In deliberate violation of treaty provisions that covered at least Piapot and Little Pine, Indian Affairs officials refused them the reserves they requested in the south. At the same time, the government used denial of food aid to the starving bands as a weapon to drive them out of the Cypress Hills. In 1882 they were informed that they would get no more rations in the Cypress Hills, and in 1883 Fort Walsh, the Mounted Police post, was closed. The bands were forced to make their way north to lands in the Saskatchewan country. One by one the recalcitrants accepted reserves; even Big Bear entered treaty in 1882, and in 1884 seemed ready to accept a reserve well away from Little Pine and Poundmaker in the Battleford district to secure assistance for his starving people.[7] Piapot was moved, amidst much hardship to his people, to the Qu'Appelle Valley. But these apparent retreats by Piapot and Mistahimaskwa were merely a strategic withdrawal, not a surrender.

Over the next few years the Cree chieftains tried to unite the Plains Indians so as to force a revision of the treaties. The first step by the treaty chiefs was to complain to the Crown that the treaties were not being honoured, apparently in the belief that Queen Victoria or her Canadian government would remedy the shortcoming once informed of it. At Fort Carlton in 1881, Chief Mistawasis, one of the powerful proponents of entering treaty in 1876, informed Lord Lorne, the governor general and, not insignificantly, son-in-law of the Great White Queen in London, of the hardship the Cree had suffered: "Many a time I was very sad when I saw my poor people starving, and I could do nothing for them." His colleague Chief Ahtakakoop added, "I remember right at the treaty it was said that if any famine or trouble came the Government would see to us and help."[8] As it became ever clearer that treaty skeptics such as Mistahimaskwa had understood the Queen's Canadian government better than some others, Plains leaders shifted to a diplomatic campaign to unite the First Nations and pressure Ottawa for improvements. Piapot in the south and Big Bear and Little Pine in the Saskatchewan district attempted to persuade various bands of Indians—even such traditional enemies as the Blackfoot and Cree—to combine in a united front in their dealings with the federal government. Gradually, through personal appeals and the use of thirst dances, which were designed to unite different groups through communal ritual

observances, headway was made on this diplomatic offensive. In the summer of 1884 an Indian Council was held at Duck Lake by leaders of 12 bands to protest the snail-like pace with which the government was honouring its treaty promises on agricultural assistance. This was evidence of the success that Big Bear and others were achieving in their drive to secure reserves in the same areas as well as other revisions of the treaties. These consummate diplomats were confident that next spring, 1885, would see the triumph of their strategy when the Blackfoot joined them in a council on Little Pine's reserve.

The reason for the reliance of senior chiefs such as Piapot and Mistahimaskwa on diplomacy instead of more warlike preparations was simple: they were bound by their treaty promises. This was true in at least two senses. First, during the 1870s, most of them had faced the question of what posture to adopt toward the oncoming numbers and power of Canadian society. Would it be resistance or co-operation? When they took treaty they opted for co-operation; they chose to share their lands and resources rather than to resist the Canadians. Second, their taking of treaty occurred within a framework of spiritual practices—most notably the pipe ceremony that preceded most treaty talks—that signified that their discussions and agreements were overseen by the Great Spirit. To break commitments made in such a solemn manner for anything but the most dire of reasons was dishonourable and offensive to everything in which the First Nations believed. Consequently, when it became unmistakable that Canada was not living up to its treaty commitments, they reacted with protest and pressure. Such, at any rate, was the strategic choice of senior leaders such as Big Bear and Piapot.[9] The problem was that their younger followers were becoming impatient with the slow pace at which the diplomatic campaign proceeded. So far as the elder leaders' chosen path of peaceful diplomacy was concerned, progress could not come too soon.

During the winter of 1884–1885, the worst on record, younger Indians were becoming very restive.

Indian Affairs officials such as Edgar Dewdney had not been sitting idly by while the Cree attempted to do again by diplomacy what they had tried but failed to accomplish in the Cypress Hills in the late 1870s. Dewdney used a policy of "no work; no rations" to try to force the Indians into adopting agriculture speedily and to assert the government's control. At the same time, his officials and the Mounted Police did whatever they could to interfere with the movements of the Indian diplomats. Where possible, they prevented chiefs from travelling to councils or disrupted council meetings. They also instructed their agents and farm instructors to use rations to force a speedy transition to agriculture. In the south, some chiefs were taken by the new railway to visit Regina and Winnipeg so that they would become acquainted with the numbers and power of the white population.

This tendency toward coercion was made all the more painful for the Indians by Ottawa's decision after 1883 to implement a policy of retrenchment that would necessitate a reduction in assistance to Indians. A combination of renewed recession and mounting demands on the government treasury for the completion of Canadian Pacific Railway created a strain on the federal budget that led to cuts in many government departments, including Indian Affairs. Officials on the spot warned the department that such measures were false economy, but Macdonald's deputy minister was convinced by a quick tour of the region he made in 1883 that such reductions were possible. And the prime minister was too busy with other matters and too little informed about western affairs to overrule his senior bureaucrat. Such parsimony was as unwise as it was inhumane, given the situation that prevailed among the Indians of the western interior in 1883 and 1884.

[. . .] Indian Affairs Commissioner Dewdney had one final weapon that he proposed to use in the mid-1880s to cow and control the Indians of the plains and the Pacific. Convinced that the policy of harassing Indian diplomats and applying pressure by restricting the flow of rations was only partially successful, Dewdney urged Macdonald to adopt a policy of "sheer compulsion" in dealing with the leaders of those Indian bands who refused to behave as the department desired.[10] His efforts to prevent Indian leaders from meeting in 1884 had been thwarted by the small numbers of officials and police, and the absence of legislation enabling them to control Indians' movement. More police would be recruited by 1885, and the Indian Act would be amended to outlaw the potlatch of the Pacific Indians and to authorize officials to arrest Indians who were on reserves other than their own without department permission. Dewdney was confident that, when these amendments came into effect in 1885, he would be equal to the challenge posed by the likes of Big Bear, Piapot, and Little Pine.

While Big Bear had been manoeuvring and Dewdney had been countering, increasing dissatisfaction had arisen within some of the Cree bands, discontent that threatened to supplant the traditional leadership and rise up against government authority. Experienced leaders like Big Bear and Piapot understood the need for a united front and the futility of armed action, but some of their younger followers did not. Or, if they did, they inclined to the view that it would be better to meet extinction fighting than starving. These less-experienced men found it hard to bear with stoicism the suffering caused by want and the indignities resulting from the actions of overbearing bureaucrats. By 1883 their anger was approaching the boiling point, and in the summer of 1884 there were confrontations on reserves, such as that of Yellow Calf in the Qu'Appelle area, between hungry Indians and outnumbered policemen. In such disputes it was all that cooler, more mature heads could do to prevent the slaughter of the constable or agent. Another near-conflagration occurred in the "Craig incident" of 1884, when police and Indian Affairs officials foolishly barged into a thirst dance in the Battleford area in search of suspects. Big Bear complained at the 1884 council in Duck Lake that he was losing control of his band to more militant young men, such as Little Poplar, who advocated an all-out war as an alternative to diplomacy.

All the same, the older chiefs remained committed to a peaceful strategy, as they explained during a revealing meeting that some of them had with an Indian Affairs official at Fort Carlton in August 1884. After listing a number of specific grievances related to treaty commitments, they added that "requests for redress of these grievances have been again & again made without effect. They are glad that the young men have not resorted to violent measures to gain it . . . [I]t is almost too hard for them to bear the treatment received at the hands of the Government after its 'sweet promises,' made in order to get their country from them. They now fear that they are going to be cheated." They told the official that they would "wait until next summer to see if this council has the desired effect, failing which they will take measures to get what they desire. (The proposed 'measures' could not be elicited, but a suggestion of the idea of war was repudiated.)"[11] The Cree chiefs could not have been clearer about their peaceful intentions.

Though it did not have to be that way, it was in fact the grievances of the Métis, in combination with the influence of Louis Riel, that brought armed rebellion to the Saskatchewan country in 1885. The mixed-blood population of the region were largely Manitoba Métis who had migrated westward in search of a new home in which they could pursue their customary life of hunting, fishing, casual employment, and some agriculture. In the 1870s, while white settlers were establishing the nearby town of Prince Albert, some 1500

Métis founded villages such as St Laurent and Batoche in the South Saskatchewan Valley.

Both the Métis and the Euro-Canadians of the Saskatchewan had grievances with the federal government in the 1880s. The white farmers objected to the slowness of the land registry system, the failure of the transcontinental railway to make its expected way through their region, and the hardships resulting from several bad seasons. They responded by participating in the 1884 formation of the Manitoba and North West Farmers' Union, and joining with the Métis in a campaign to pressure the federal government to deal with their problems. The Métis not only shared in the whites' disgruntlement with government and economic adversity but had additional concerns of their own. As usual, land was at the heart of most of their grievances. The Saskatchewan Métis, as in Manitoba earlier, feared that the arrival of a land registration system from Ottawa might jeopardize their customary title to river-lot farms. They could not get assurances from an ominously silent federal government that their title would be respected. Some of them also believed that they had a claim for compensation for loss of Aboriginal title in the territories. They argued that the dominion had by treaty dealt with the Indians' title to the lands, but not theirs. Before extensive development occurred, Canada should recognize in Saskatchewan, as it had in Manitoba, that the Métis shared in Aboriginal title, and should compensate them for their loss of this interest in the land. Finally, some of the Saskatchewan Métis argued that they or their children had unresolved claims against the Dominion for land grants as a result of the promises made to future generations of Métis in the Manitoba Act of 1870.

The problems the Métis experienced in advancing their case in the early 1880s were similar to those that white farmers encountered: Ottawa never seemed to deal with their complaints. In part the problem was that federal politicians were preoccupied with other, to them more important, matters. There was also the fact that the ministers responsible for western matters, David Macpherson and later Sir John A. Macdonald, knew little about western problems. In Macdonald's case the problem was still further compounded by his age. "Old Tomorrow" was getting on. He was 63 when he returned to power in the general election of 1878; he was running out of energy; and he had little sympathy for the Métis. Macdonald mistakenly believed that much of the talk of land compensation from the Métis was nonsense that had been inspired by white land speculators who were stirring up the people of Batoche or St Laurent. So far as a repetition of the Manitoba Act's promise of land to mixed bloods by virtue of their partial Indian ancestry was concerned, he was having no part of such schemes. The promise of the Manitoba Act had been a disaster to fulfill, not least because the slowness, dishonesty, and incompetence of federal officials delayed the distribution of land so long that many Métis gave up and sold their land scrip for a pittance to speculators. Macdonald was, if possible, even more unsympathetic than he was uninterested in the complaints from the Saskatchewan country.

The response of both Métis and whites to their failure to get the federal government to deal with their grievances was a decision to ask Louis Riel to return to Canada to lead their movement. Both parties were clear that what they wanted was Riel's experience and skill in dealing peacefully with an unresponsive government. To obtain his help with their movement for redress of grievances, they sent a party south to Montana at the beginning of June 1884 to ask him to come to their assistance. Had they thought about his response to their request for any length of time, they might have been troubled about what they were doing. "God wants you to understand that you have taken the right way," said Riel when he met the delegates, "for there are four

of you, and you have arrived on the fourth of June."[12]

What Louis Riel's cryptic response to the invitation imperfectly disguised was the fact that the Riel who accepted the invitation in June 1884 was a very different man from the Riel who had led the resistance 15 years earlier. Riel had felt himself ill-used by the Canadian government in 1870. Forced to flee, denied the amnesty he had been promised, elected to Parliament but unable to take his seat for fear for his life, he was finally banished from the country for five years in 1875. The distressing events of the 1870s had unhinged him mentally. Riel was now convinced that he had a divine mission. Like the poet-king of Israel, David, whose name he adopted, he had been chosen by God. His mission was to prepare the world for the second coming of Christ and the end of life on earth by transferring the papacy from Italy to the New World, replacing the bishop of Rome with the Ultramontane bishop of Montreal, and ultimately locating the Holy See at St Vital, his home parish in Manitoba. The North-West was to become a new homeland in which the oppressed peoples of Europe could join the Métis and Indians to live in peace during a millennium that would precede the final end of the world.[13]

Like most prophets, Riel found himself without honour in his own land once he began to act on the revelation of his divine mission. He spent two periods of incarceration in asylums for the mentally ill in Quebec in the 1870s, and, when he was released, he was told that his cure would last only if he avoided involvement in matters that excited him. He moved to the United States, married, became an American citizen, participated in American politics, and settled down to the life of a mission school teacher in the west. However, he had not forgotten his mission; he continued to look for a sign that it was time for its fulfillment. When, on 4 June 1884, four delegates from the Métis of Saskatchewan invited him to return with them, he knew it was the signal he sought.

In the initial months after his return with his wife and children to Canada, Riel played the role he had been asked to rather than the role he knew God ultimately intended for him. He served as an adviser and organizer of legal protests, attending meetings and helping with the preparation of yet more petitions to Ottawa. He was even at Duck Lake at the time of the Indian council in 1884, but, although he met with Mistahimaskwa, there is no record that he sought to incite either the Indians or his own followers to acts of rebellion. It was only gradually during the winter of 1884–1885 that his purpose became known to the Oblate priests with whom he was in frequent contact. One of them claimed that Riel said he had personal claims—no doubt based on the terms of the Manitoba Act—that the federal government should redress. The priest informed Ottawa, but the prime minister declined to play the game of bribery, if that was the game Riel intended.[14] But the clerics were convinced that Riel was heretical if not completely deranged, as they became aware of his peculiar religious ideas. They would be the first in the community to turn against him; they would be followed during that winter by the white settlers who set their face against the conversion of the movement from peaceful protest to armed struggle.

It was clearly Riel—not the community at large, not even the Métis as a group—who pushed events in the direction of rebellion in the early weeks of 1885. For many months he had simply advanced the existing agitation; a petition of December 1884 did not include his own exalted claim for a land grant to the Métis by virtue of their sharing in the Aboriginal title to the country. By March, Riel was poised to attempt a recreation of the strategy that had worked so well in 1869. His pretext was the lack of response from Ottawa. In fact, in January the federal government decided to appoint a commission to inquire into the grievances of the Métis, and, while they made that decision known to Riel through an intermediary, they did not follow up their actions until two months later when the members of the commission were appointed. By that time Riel had raised the stakes, proclaiming a provisional government, of which he would be the prophet and Gabriel Dumont the adjutant-general. The insurgents demanded the surrender of Fort Carlton and its police detachment.

If Riel thought he was re-enacting the events at Red River in 1869, he miscalculated. The two situations were starkly different. In 1869 he had enjoyed clerical support and the backing of a reasonably united community. In 1885 the priests turned against him and the white settlers' support evaporated. It might have been possible in Rupert's Land in 1869, especially after McDougall's abortive proclamation of Canadian authority, to argue that there was a vacuum of legal authority that justified a provisional government. In 1885 there was little doubt that Canada was the effective government in the North-West Territories. Red River had been distant and vulnerable, partly because Ottawa feared that the Americans had designs on the region and partly because of the season in which the resistance occurred. Batoche in 1885 was geographically more remote, but in actuality more accessible, thanks to the nearly complete Canadian Pacific Railway. If the Dominion chose in 1885 to crush Riel rather than negotiate, his rising was doomed. That, of course, was precisely what Canada decided to do.

It was largely a matter of coincidence—certainly not a matter of design—that a series of Indian actions occurred about the same time that Riel and the Métis confronted the police.[15] In the camp of Big Bear, effective power had shifted to the young men in the warrior society by March 1885. This transition, by no means unusual in the fluid and subtle political systems of Plains Indian communities, meant that the authority of the elderly diplomat, Big Bear, was greatly lessened, while the ability of men such as his son Imasees and the war chiefs Little Poplar and Wandering Spirit to carry the band on their more war-like policy was increased. Irritation had been building up against some of the white men at Frog Lake, where Big Bear's band was established, and, when news arrived of a Métis victory over the police at Duck Lake, some of the young warriors attacked the Hudson's Bay Company storekeeper and the Indian agent. Big Bear attempted to restrain them when he became aware of what was going on, but before he could make peace prevail, nine whites lay dead.

The incident, essentially a bloody act of vengeance against unpopular officials, became unjustifiably known as the Frog Lake Massacre. That it was nothing of the sort was illustrated by the fact that not all the Euro-Canadians were killed; one Bay man and two white women were spared, thanks in part to Big Bear. Moreover, though these people were prisoners in Big Bear's camp for weeks, they were not harmed at all. If the death of nine people and the humane treatment of three others constitute a massacre, then, and only then, was Frog Lake a massacre.

But the impression that prevailed at the time was that the Indians were rising in response to the Métis initiative. The rout of police at Duck Lake had been followed by the "massacre" at Frog Lake. Panic set in, nowhere more obviously than in the Battleford district, where white settlers fled for refuge to the fort. A few days before trouble broke out, the industrial school principal noted during his visit to nearby reserves that the "Indians appear to be well disposed toward white men."[16] Yet when groups from Poundmaker's band who were travelling to the post in search of badly needed food looted some abandoned homesteads near the fort, these relatively innocent events became, in the minds of the settlers and the government, a "siege" of the fort by Poundmaker and the Cree. Again, it was nothing of the sort, as Poundmaker's retreat to his own reserve clearly illustrated. Nonetheless, the Canadian government was convinced, and set about convincing others, that the entire North-West was threatened by a combined Métis-Indian rising.

Canada's military response was devastating and indiscriminate. In all, some eight thousand troops, militia, and police were dispatched into the region along three routes: from Qu'Appelle north against the mixed-blood community in the valley of the South Saskatchewan; from Swift Current north to "relieve" Battleford; and from Calgary north to Edmonton. The only fighting of any consequence occurred at Fish Creek, Batoche, and Cut Knife Hill. At Fish Creek, Dumont persuaded Riel to let him attack the military column from hiding, but then nullified the advantage of surprise by prematurely revealing his position. The final stand came at Batoche, where the Métis dug rifle pits and established fortifications from which they rained a withering fire on their attackers. Unfortunately for the Métis, the defenders quickly exhausted their ammunition and were reduced to using makeshift projectiles. The attacking Canadian forces, both troops and militia, greatly outnumbered the few hundred armed Métis. Moreover, they were equipped with ample arms and ammunition, not even counting the Gatling gun that the American military had thoughtfully provided for field testing or the steamer that the commander attempted to use as a diversionary naval force. Finally, the ill-disciplined militiamen, tired of three days of feinting and long-range firing, and fed up with their general's cautious probes of Batoche, ignored their orders and overran the rifle pits.

Louis Riel, who had behaved throughout the encounters at Duck Lake and Batoche as though he was conducting a religious service rather than leading a revolt, now surrendered. The truth was that, at least in his own mind, his was a religious cause. He could not fail because he was carrying out God's mission. If the deity had arranged for a defeat, it could only be because Riel was to make his case at a trial after the surrender. Dumont, practical fighter that he was, hurriedly left for the United States.

The other military actions of the North-West campaign involved Poundmaker and Big Bear. When Colonel Otter's column "relieved" Battleford, its leader decided to set off in search of Poundmaker, whom all held responsible for the "siege" that had never happened. Otter caught up to Poundmaker's people at Cut Knife Hill and attacked. He and his men soon found themselves in trouble as the Cree fired from protected positions at the soldiers who were silhouetted on a hillside. The troops were astounded when they were able to retreat in an orderly fashion without suffering further losses. What they did not know was that Poundmaker had persuaded his men not to pursue and inflict any more damage on Otter's battered soldiers.

Big Bear and his followers spent much of May evading yet another Canadian force led by T.B. Strange in the bush country north of Frog Lake. The aftermath of the "massacre" had been the gradual restoration of the old leader's authority, and he used his control to follow his traditionally pacific paths. He allowed a frightened contingent of police to vacate Fort Pitt safely, and then he tried to take his people away from all trouble, including advancing troops. Strange caught up to Big Bear once, to his sorrow, near Frenchman's Butte, in the Fort Pitt area. Strange had to withdraw to Fort Pitt. Eventually, after Big

Bear had led the soldiers a merry chase in the northern bush, his forces began to melt away. Big Bear returned to the Fort Carlton area and surrendered early in July. With Riel and Poundmaker already in custody, Big Bear's surrender marked the end of the rebellion.

At least as significant as who participated in the rising was who did not. Piapot in the Qu'Appelle area did not take up arms, perhaps because the government quickly stationed troops on his reserve to discourage his men from violence. [. . .]

Nor did the Blackfoot Confederacy in the southwest take up arms. Part of the explanation lies in how weakened the southern tribes were by hardship, hunger, and disease by 1885. Here, again, the pacific influence of older chiefs such as Crowfoot and the sense of commitment to treaty obligations were part of the explanation. But so, too, was the southern Indians' familiarity with whites and their power. The Blackfoot, four of whose chiefs had earlier travelled by train to Regina and Winnipeg at Dewdney's invitation, appreciated the general significance of the large numbers of Euro-Canadians and the military potential of the railroad.[17] The non-participation of the southern Indians, arguably the people who had suffered most since the making of the treaties and the disappearance of the bison, was further evidence that the events of 1885, whatever Edgar Dewdney said they were, were not an Indian rising. [. . .]

NOTES

1. The earliest, and still the best, treatment of the rebellion as the clash of two ways of life is G.F.G. Stanley, *The Birth of Western Canada: A History of the Riel Rebellions*, 2nd edn (1936; Toronto: University of Toronto Press, 1960). University of Toronto Press issued a new edition, with an introduction by Thomas Flanagan, in 1992.

2. Essential in understanding the limited role of First Nations in the rebellion is Blair Stonechild and Bill Waiser, *Loyal till Death:*

Indians and the North-West Rebellion (Calgary: Fifth House, 1997). I am grateful to Professors Stonechild and Waiser, who have generously shared their insights with me.

3. G. Pennanen, "Sitting Bull: Indian without a Country," *Canadian Historical Review* 51, 2 (1970): 123–41.

4. Stanley, *Birth of Western Canada,* 220, 221; G. Friesen, *The Canadian Prairies: A History* (Toronto: University of Toronto Press, 1984), 250.

5. J.L. Tobias, "Canada's Subjugation of the Plains Cree, 1879–1885," in J.R Miller, ed., *Sweet Promises: A Reader on Indian-White Relations in Canada* (Toronto: University of Toronto Press, 1991), 216–17.

6. This account is based on Tobias, ibid., 216ff.

7. J.R. Miller, *Mistahimusqua (Big Bear)* (Toronto: ECW Press, 1996), 90–6.

8. National Archives of Canada [NAC], RG 10, Records of the Department of Indian Affairs, vol. 3768, file 33642, Notes of Governor General Lorne's meeting at Fort Carlton, 1881.

9. Spiritual considerations might also have contributed to the law-abiding behaviour of plains First Nations between treaty and 1885. Rod Macleod reports that the NWMP did not fire a single shot in anger at an Indian or Métis before 1885. R.C. Macleod, *The North West Mounted Police, 1873–1919* (Ottawa: Canadian Historical Association, 1978), 8. Macleod and another researcher have also found that settlers were five times as likely as Indians to be tried on a criminal charge in the territories between 1878 and 1885. R.C. Macleod and Heather Rollason [Driscoll], "'Restrain the Lawless Savages': Native Defendants in the Criminal Courts of the North-West Territories, 1878–1885," *Journal of Historical Sociology* 10, 2 (1997): 157–83.

10. Quoted in Tobias, "Subjugation," 221–2.

11. NAC, RG 10, vol. 3697, file 15423, J. Ansdell Macrae to department, 25 August 1884.

12. Quoted in Friesen, *Canadian Prairies,* 227.

13. The best account of Riel's millenarian thought is T. Flanagan, *Louis "David" Riel: Prophet of the New World* (Toronto: University of Toronto Press, 1979).

14. T. Flanagan, *Riel and the Rebellion: 1885 Reconsidered* (Saskatoon: Western Producer Prairie Books, 1983), chap. 5. How accurate the priest's report was is impossible to determine.

15. The following account relies heavily on Stonechild and Waiser, *Loyal till Death.*

16. Saskatchewan Archives Board, Saskatoon office, A718, Thomas Clarke Papers, file 1.1, diary entries of 23–24 March 1885.

17. H.A. Dempsey, "The Fearsome Fire Wagons," in Dempsey, ed., *The CPR West: The Iron Road and the Making of a Nation* (Vancouver: Douglas & McIntyre, 1984), 65.

9   From Ted McCoy, "Legal Ideology in the Aftermath of Rebellion: The Convicted First Nations Participants, 1885," *Histoire sociale/Social History,* 42, 83 (May 2009): 175–201. Reprinted with permission of the publisher.

In early October 1885, Winnipeg's train depot played host to an unusual arrival. Hundreds of curious onlookers crowded the platform and surged forward as the train pulled in. Excitement peaked as a large group of First Nations men disembarked in shackles. Among them were the famous Cree chiefs Big Bear, Poundmaker, and One Arrow. Many of the men still wore traditional dress, including blankets drawn closely around their bodies. A newspaper reporter suggested that their appearance did not disappoint the thrill-seeking crowd: "a more lawless looking set can hardly be imagined."[1] The men were taken to a local provincial jail before being transported by wagon to Manitoba Penitentiary the next day.

These men were Cree, Assiniboine, Dakota, and Blood individuals who had been tried and convicted for their participation in the 1885 North-West Rebellion. The legal aftermath of the rebellion played out in three primary settings: in the courtroom, on the gallows at Fort Battleford, and inside the walls of Manitoba Penitentiary (also known as Stony Mountain). The events in each of these settings demonstrate a response to First Nations defendants that was informed by British legal ideology and transformed by the unique colonial setting of the Canadian North-West, and they reveal sites of struggle between First Nations people and the Canadian state that enhance our understanding of the early legal history of western

Canada. At these sites of trial and punishment, First Nations defendants and their kin negotiated the legal ideologies of majesty, justice, and mercy in a setting in which these elements of the Canadian law were far from established or understood. Judicial and religious rhetoric and ritual invoked the majesty and mercy of the law, while capital punishment and penitentiary sentences revealed these ideologies in practice.

[. . .] Events demonstrate that legal ideology must be understood in specific historical, colonial, and geographic contexts. It will come as no surprise to Canadian historians that justice in Regina and Battleford required unique adaptations of the British legal customs and traditions on which Canadian law was based. However, interrogating the legal proceedings and punishment that followed the North-West Rebellion reveals a unique social context in which the law unfolded. [. . .]

In many ways, discussion of the rebellion's aftermath reveals an emergent hegemony in western Canada. Though the post-rebellion period is but one small part of this wider history, we must also uncover the instances in which this early domination was challenged and resisted by First Nations people. To do so, we must see more than pure terror, look beyond the majesty, justice, and mercy of the Canadian courts, and understand the social relations between the Canadian state and the First Nations as something more complex than an ever-expanding "subjugation." As E.P. Thompson suggests, hegemony does not impose an "all embracing domination upon the ruled," eclipsing the possibility of resistance or correction.[2] The experience of the convicted First Nations participants in 1885 is one example of how this hegemony played out on the stage of the criminal law. Uncovering examples of this experience, even in the darkest days of the post–Rebellion North-West, suggests the possibility of resistance in all areas of the relationship between First Nations people and colonial authorities.

If we are to understand why law and punishment operated as they did in the aftermath of the rebellion, it is useful to look back to the Bloody Code of eighteenth-century England. Though separated by a century from the establishment of Canadian law in the North-West, the legal ritual and ideology underlying Canadian law can be found in this history. Douglas Hay proposes that majesty, justice, and mercy were at the centre of the law's power in eighteenth-century England. Enforced by the Bloody Code, which featured the death penalty as its moral centre, the division of property by terror was effective and resonated with the population because it was complemented by ideologies of majesty, justice, and mercy. These ideologies were expressed in rituals that enriched and mystified the law and gave it emotional and psychic grounding. These rituals helped define contemporary social and class relations to help ensure a broader political conformity in England.[3] It would be obvious to state that the same ideological constructs resonated differently as they were translated into the colonial setting of British North America, but the historical facts demonstrate that British legal authorities attempted such a translation repeatedly in the nineteenth century. [. . .]

Theorists in the eighteenth century argued that the law must be structured in certain ways to establish its legitimacy. It should be "known and determinate, instead of capricious and obscure."[4] This permanence and impartiality supported the fiction that social class played no role in the operation of the law. This gave the law an important ideological weapon even when it did not operate uniformly. In nineteenth-century Canada, particularly in colonial settings, the concept of justice was adapted to the purpose of introducing the Queen's law to First Nations people in an even-handed and non-biased way. The very idea of justice thus became an important colonial tool. However, historians of colonial contexts argue that the law takes on different forms to maintain the legitimacy of its underlying ideology.

[. . .] Tracking the contradictory and unusual applications of the law in this way has allowed historians to examine justice as a legal ideology. Closely related and central to the experience of First Nations people meeting British law was the ideology of mercy.

In eighteenth-century England, mercy gave legal authorities the power of discretion to take into consideration, for instance, poverty or other extenuating circumstances. Rather than diminishing the terror and authority invested in capital punishment, legal discretion gave authorities an extra measure of power over the letter of the law by "creating the mental structure of paternalism" toward the condemned. Incidences of mercy helped to validate capital punishment to the poor by demonstrating the supposed sensibility of the law to mitigating circumstances.[5]
[. . .]

Most accounts of the First Nations' participation in the North-West Rebellion focus on the role played by Big Bear's Plains Cree, who had been wintering northeast of Edmonton at Frog Lake. Although Métis leader Louis Riel was in contact with Cree leaders throughout late 1884, the events involving Big Bear's band were among the first instances of serious conflict involving a First Nations group. Big Bear returned to Frog Lake in early April 1885 to find a horrifying scene.[6] While he had been away on a solitary hunting trip, his war chief Wandering Spirit and other young men, including Miserable Man and Imasees (Big Bear's son), planned to take hostages from the tiny settlement of Frog Lake and obtain desperately needed food and supplies. The plan was quickly derailed when Indian Agent Thomas Quinn refused to agree to the Cree demands. A standoff ensued between Quinn and Wandering Spirit, which escalated into a bloody *mêlée*. Big Bear pleaded for peace, but the situation spiralled toward a violent resolution. [. . .] Nine white men were killed by Cree warriors who then took the survivors prisoner and burned Frog Lake to the ground. This debacle occurred days after the Métis victory against the North West Mounted Police (NWMP) at Duck Lake and sparked fears across the country of a First Nations uprising inspired by Louis Riel. The government responded to news of the Frog Lake uprising with extreme military force. Three militia columns were deployed across the North-West to stamp out the rebellion.

As fear gripped the region, residents of the Fort Pitt and Battleford districts wired for help from inside barricaded forts and waited for the militia to arrive. The hysteria throughout the North-West also drew Cree chiefs Poundmaker and One Arrow into armed conflict. After terrifying the residents of Battleford (barricaded inside Fort Battleford) with the mere presence of his band, Poundmaker found his camp attacked three weeks later by an overzealous militia column under the command of Colonel W.D. Otter.[7] From this point, Poundmaker's band became more deeply embroiled in the events of the uprising, finding themselves in the middle of a massive confrontation between the Métis and the Canadian militia. While the primary militia column under General Middleton fought Riel's Métis forces at Batoche, the remaining columns pursued Cree chiefs Big Bear and Poundmaker. After a summer of being pursued by the militia, the majority of the exhausted Cree surrendered or were captured. In the summer and fall of 1885 the rebellion participants encountered the Canadian legal system in a series of criminal trials.

The government prepared cases against the captured and surrendered First Nations men throughout the summer of 1885 and charged 81 people with various crimes, ranging from arson and murder to treason-felony. The initial trials took place in Regina before the senior court in the North-West Territories, presided over by Stipendiary Magistrate Hugh Richardson. At the centre of the government prosecution were Cree chiefs Poundmaker, Big Bear, and One Arrow, all charged with treason-felony for their roles in the uprising. [. . .] Following the treason-felony trials, the venue moved to Battleford, where Stipendiary Magistrate Charles Rouleau presided over murder trials for those men accused of the Frog Lake murders as well as other isolated murder trials. During the trials, the judges invoked majesty through the spectacle of legal ritual and the use of rhetoric by which, as Hay notes about English law, "the powers of light and darkness [were] summoned into the court."[8] When First Nations defendants came before the court at Regina, this metaphor stood for the invocation of colonial authority.

Judge Rouleau excelled at lecturing in these tones, admonishing Itka and Man Without Blood at their murder trial: "you were foolish enough to rebel against the government, foolish because the government could send soldiers here until they were numerous as mosquitoes."[9] At the trial of Bad Arrow and Miserable Man, Rouleau expanded on these themes in an elaborate speech explaining the need for peace between whites and the First Nations. He asked the prisoners, "what object had you in killing the whites? If the whites withdrew from the country you would starve in a year, but the white man could live without the Indians."[10] Rouleau repeatedly invoked emotional language that gave his courtroom speeches the element of a religious sermon preached in the secular realm. Although the entire community of Battleford felt the events of the rebellion personally, Rouleau's emotionalism was likely heightened when he received a telegram in April from Indian Commissioner Edgar Dewdney laconically informing him, "your house burnt by Indians yesterday."[11] When Rouleau summoned colonial paternalism at the sentencing of Wandering Spirit, it was clear that he was addressing the multitude of First Nations groups in the North-West as well as whites who badly needed reassurance about the stability of government authority throughout the region. Rouleau lectured:

You were murdering while others were burning houses and committing other crimes. You could not expect any good results to follow your acts. . . . Instead of listening to wise men, you preferred to listen to the advice of bad men who were as poor as yourselves, and who could not help you if they wanted to, and who only got you in trouble. The Government do not want to destroy the Indians, but they wish to help them to live like white men but as far as murderers in cold blood are concerned, the Government has no pity for them. If a white man murders an Indian he must hang, and so must an Indian if he kills a while man.[12]

Here the eighteenth-century concept of justice, originally intended to inure the ruling class from suggestions of favouritism, was adapted to explain to a First Nations population that culture or race bore no influence on the operation of law. After the rebellion, this left First Nations people at a distinct disadvantage because many of the defendants, including Poundmaker and Big Bear, defended themselves in court based on their particular circumstances or cultural misunderstandings.[13]

This raises a question about how such legal rhetoric was received by the First Nations defendants. Is it possible to gauge the effectiveness of such ideological categories through the limited sources detailing the reaction of those men who came before the court? We can make some assumptions and believe, as E.P. Thompson suggested, that people are not so stupid as to be mystified by the first man to don a wig.[14] It is not clear that First Nations defendants were awed by these paternalist messages or the larger majesty of the law. In all likelihood, the messages contained in Rouleau's courtroom rhetoric were not novel to most of the Cree defendants. [. . .]

Some of the convicted men were despondent when sentenced. When Little Runner was sentenced to four years for horse-stealing, he replied, "I am glad to hear that. I have been longing to know what was to be done with me."[15] Though his execution was later commuted, Louison Mongrain responded to his death sentence, "I am not guilty of the charge, and hope God will receive me, as the charges against me are not true; I prepare myself to be resigned to my fate. After I am sentenced I would like to write to my mother and wife; I have no children, for which I am thankful. I pity the old man who was sentenced today."[16] Other defendants were belligerent or offhanded. Big Bear addressed the court for nearly an hour at his sentencing, ending with a plea for the welfare of his people.[17] Clearly aware that he was responding to a legal official vested with the full power of the Canadian state, Big Bear used the opportunity to deliver the last serious speech of his political career. Poundmaker responded to his accusers with a poignant majesty of his own. "I am a man," he said. "Do as you like. I am in your power. You did not catch me."[18] As he was sentenced to three years in the penitentiary, his offhandedness boiled over, and while being dragged from the court he shouted, "I would rather be hung than put in that place."[19] These responses, particularly Big Bear's, exemplified their defiance, despite their position of subjugation to the Canadian courts. Others would speak as forcefully or eloquently as their political leaders, but the limited number of recorded responses demonstrates that the defendants understood with some subtlety the court's majesty and were not merely overwhelmed by it, placing their experience beyond the realm of "awe."

Several other elements contributed to the haphazard nature of the trials and compromised the sense of majesty and justice surrounding them. At Regina, most of the men had no legal representation before the court and could not understand the proceedings in English. One Arrow famously responded to the translation of his treason-felony charge by asking, "Are you drunk?"[20] Catholic priest Louis Cochin was disgusted by the impossible position of the defendants. After One Arrow's trial he complained, "The poor old man didn't understand a word of it."[21] Cochin was further distressed at reports that the prosecutors and the judge were determining the sentences between themselves beforehand and then applying them to each defendant at trial. Missionaries on the scene counselled the men to plead guilty to all charges, effectively forfeiting any claim to a fair trial. "Does the government know of this?" Louis Cochin demanded in a letter to the Archbishop. "Or if it does know of it, how can it put up with such things?"[22] As the trials concluded, the government made plans to execute eight First Nations men at Fort Battleford.

In the aftermath of the North-West Rebellion, the death penalty was intended not only to punish, but to re-assert government authority throughout the region. It is not clear that the one-time event of mass execution at Battleford terrorized First Nations people as Canadian legal and government authorities had intended. Evidence from the courtrooms and the scene of execution indicates that the hangings, carried out as public spectacle, were met with a mix of ambivalence, sadness, and outrage by First Nations defendants and their kin.[23] Peter Linebaugh notes that public hanging in Britain represented a rare meeting of many levels of government united with church and legal authorities for a common purpose.[24] The Battleford hanging signified an important moment of this convergence in western Canada. Although it was the first execution under Canadian authority in the North-West, the common elements shared with hangings in other British and American jurisdictions indicate that the Canadian authorities were familiar with the script of the execution pageantry. In the weeks leading up to the execution, the original plan to hang the men two at a time was altered so that all eight men would die at once.

The hanging was carefully planned as a public spectacle at Fort Battleford to demonstrate visibly the government's power over

First Nations people. Prime Minister John A. Macdonald, also Minister of Indian Affairs, informed Dewdney, "the executions . . . ought to convince the Red Man that the White Man governs."[25] Assistant Indian Commissioner Hayter Reed agreed with the prime minister and suggested to Dewdney that First Nations people must witness the hanging as confirmation of their "sound thrashing". The hanging would "cause them to meditate for many a day and besides have ocular demonstration of the fact."[26] Curiously, government officials drew the line at what constituted *too much* intimidation. Indian Commissioner Edgar Dewdney stipulated that the execution could not occur on Cree reserves near the site of the crimes for fear that superstition would overtake the people and cause them to abandon their settlements.[27] The government's plan to intimidate and demoralize the Cree was not simply a response to the rebellion but part of a longer pattern of Cree "subjugation" stretching back to the signing of the numbered treaties. In the year before the rebellion, Cree efforts at organization and political solidarity had alarmed Indian Affairs officials so much that they quietly planned the arrest and immobilization of dissident Cree leaders like Big Bear and Poundmaker in the fall of 1884.[28] If it is generally accepted that in 1883 and 1884 the government executed a campaign of intimidation and subordination of the Plains Cree, the execution appears as a final and decisive blow to Cree political efforts.

[. . .]

As newspapers across Canada justified the impending execution scheduled for 24 November, at Fort Battleford the dialogue between the clergy and the prisoners centred on more personal and religious matters.

In the days before the hanging, Catholic priests A.H. Bigonesse and Louis Cochin attempted to convert the condemned men to Christianity. Their ministry is chronicled in *The Reminiscences of Louis Cochin,* published more than 40 years after the events.[29] Though clearly embellished, the narratives of the priests portray a conversion experience that demonstrates the role of religion in the pageantry of death frequently seen before the execution of First Nations people under British law. In their accounts, the priests strove to infuse the experience of the Cree and Assiniboine men with religious meaning. Christianity was depicted as the force bridging civilization and savagery in the face of the awesome power of capital punishment. [. . .] Religious writers in the post-Rebellion North-West employed religious solemnity as a powerful narrative tool to demonstrate the centrality of capital punishment in the developing relationship between the state and First Nations people. In Cochin's narrative, Wandering Spirit filled the role of the terrible savage against which Christianity's redemptive power was pitted. The War Chief was well suited to the part, as the press and government recognized him as the murderous leader of the Frog Lake Massacre. At his sentencing, Judge Charles Rouleau called Wandering Spirit "the greatest killer ever to walk on two legs in America."[30] A popular account of the final days of the prisoners, written by eye-witness William Cameron, repeated many of the savage portrayals of Wandering Spirit. Cameron's account frequently described the War Chief as "cruel" and "evil" in an attempt to sensationalize his role in the events of 1885. According to Bigonesse, Wandering Spirit refused to acknowledge the priests until the day before execution when he experienced a spiritual awakening.[31] Wandering Spirit finally accepted Christianity, thus shedding the savagery that had characterized his path to condemnation.

However, other evidence suggests that Wandering Spirit was deeply remorseful over the events at Frog Lake, and his interest in Christianity may have sprung from the grief that overtook him during the summer of 1885. Elizabeth McLean, taken prisoner by Big Bear's Cree at Fort Pitt, described Wandering Spirit as a deeply dejected and depressed individual who morosely asked them, "what would your God do to a man who had done what I did?"[32] McLean described the sight of a solitary and sad Wandering Spirit walking slowly into the camp of the Wood Cree prior to his capture, his hair turned from deep black to almost totally white.[33] He attempted to kill himself shortly after his capture and spent his final days dejectedly protesting his minor role in the uprising, telling Cameron, "I fought against it. Imasees nor the others would not let me go . . . it seemed it was to be—I was singled out to do it."[34] Unsurprisingly, this regret is never noted by the priests' narratives. Instead, their account emphasizes the power of conversion to effect change by highlighting the contrition of the Cree and Assiniboine prisoners.

In fact, although some of the men made conciliatory remarks from the gallows before their deaths, Little Bear and Itka both shouted menacing last words. They urged the people gathered in the square at Fort Battleford to remember how the whites had treated them and to make no peace. Further, they urged the spectators to show their contempt for the punishment they were about to witness. This scene certainly did not fit the script of conversion and contrition offered in the priests' version of the execution.

As the eight men ascended the scaffolding to be hanged, one of them allegedly said to Cochin, "Father, we do not know any Christian hymns, but we are anxious, however, to die singing. I pray you, allow us to sing in our own fashion." Cochin stated that he allowed them to do this "with good heart."[35] Cochin thus constructed another important element of the execution pageantry in his narrative—the confession. What other writers identified only as Cree and Assiniboine death chants and songs, Cochin transformed into improvised Christian prayers. When the trap dropped, Cochin saw it not as sending the men to their death, but sending them "together into eternity, where we have the sweet confidence they rejoiced in the favour of the infinite mercy of God."[36] The punitive elements of the execution that characterized government rhetoric fell away in these descriptions as the priests suggested a majesty rooted in Christian solemnity.

However, there are strong indications that this majesty and the terror it accompanied were not as immediately apparent to either the condemned men or the First Nations people who witnessed the hanging. While the government may have wanted the Cree to witness the execution, it is likely the Cree people from surrounding reserves would have been at the event for their own personal reasons. The singing of traditional death songs from the gallows is another strong indication of the specific First Nations understanding of these events. At the hanging of 38 Dakota men following the Minnesota Uprising in December 1862, the *St. Paul Pioneer* noted that upon the scaffold the hooded and bound men grasped for each other's hands and sang out their own names and the names of their friends as if to say "I'm here ! I'm *here!*"[37] At Battleford many of the condemned men sang to assembled family members and friends present at the execution.[38] One newspaper claimed the predominating sound was the "wails of the wives of the condemned braves."[39] These reports complicated the notion of the terror created by the Battleford hanging by demonstrating that First Nations people attended the execution for their own personal reasons. The spectators may well have been terrorized by the traumatic scene, but their role in the event was more than a passive one. A similar perspective should be employed for the actions of the condemned men. In a position of ultimate subordination and helplessness, they remained more than either characters in a spiritual passion play or signifiers of government power and authority.

Historians have examined the process of mercy following the rebellion less frequently than they have commented on the terror of the executions, but it formed an important feature of the legal landscape in the case of capital convictions. Three of the eleven men sentenced to death by Judge Rouleau did not hang in 1885. The practical application of state terror was sometimes mediated in subtle ways. In the aftermath of the rebellion, a sensitivity to Cree culture determined the process of mercy for the defendants Dressy Man and Charlebois. The two men were in Big Bear's camp following the uprising, during which time a woman named She-wins turned into a Windigo.[40] When the woman warned the camp that she was "bent on eating human flesh before the sun went down," Dressy Man, Charlebois, and a man named Bright Eyes agreed to murder She-wins, and the act was witnessed by 40 or 50 of Big Bear's men as well as Hudson's Bay Company factor William McLean. At the murder trials, Judge Rouleau attempted to instruct the jury on the differences between the charges of murder and manslaughter in an effort to accommodate some consideration of the Cree spiritual beliefs that had motivated the crime. He cautioned jury members that they could only convict for murder if they decided the crimes surrounding the Cree spiritual beliefs had been committed with malice. The jury deliberated for 20 minutes and brought back murder verdicts for Dressy Man and Charlebois and manslaughter for Bright Eyes. Dressy Man and Charlebois were sentenced to death and Bright Eyes to 20 years at Manitoba Penitentiary.[41] Two weeks before the Battleford hanging, the Governor General commuted the death sentences for the Windigo killers to life imprisonment in Manitoba Penitentiary.[42]

This sensitivity to First Nations cultural considerations suggests a number of questions surrounding the operation of mercy. When Judge Rouleau instructed the Frog Lake Massacre suspects that they would be treated without bias, he invoked a concept of justice based on equality before the law for First Nations people. To create a perception of impartiality to racial differences, it was essential that the court be seen to treat First Nations offenders with the same severity as whites. This was one example of how justice was regarded as "the great equalizer."[43] For both ideological and practical reasons, Canadian law was concerned with not only the appearance of impartiality, but also the transmission of British values throughout the North-West. The magisterial rhetoric from the bench was premised on this notion, and it precluded sensitive consideration of the meaning of murder based on racial factors.

However, there are also numerous historical examples in which considerations of cultural differences played an important role in the exercise of mercy in capital trials of First Nations people.[44] This occurred not at the trial stage but at the executive level. As Tina Loo argues, cultural considerations were not given formal weight in reaching verdicts, but were used in recommendations of mercy and addressed in post-trial reports written by magistrates.[45] Although he had lectured on the impartiality and justice of the law, in the case of Dressy Man and Charlebois, Rouleau was able to see the need for both impartial justice and mercy based on mitigating cultural circumstances. The judge's and politicians' cultural sensitivity in the rebellion aftermath resembled what Loo dubbed "savage mercy," confirming racial differences between whites and the First Nations by granting judges and the executive the power to decide which cultural elements to consider, a process heavily dependent upon stereotypes.[46] Further, the murder of a Cree woman by Cree offenders was easier to pardon than the murder of settlers or government officials because it did not threaten the emerging Canadian order in the North-West. The Windigo murder remained in the realm of the "savage," and this helps to explain the unique instances of government mercy. Making similar conclusions on the pardon of the Windigo killers, Carolyn Strange argues, "capital punishment could be an instrument of racist terror, yet selective mercy toward First Nations capital offenders was no less racially informed or politically hued."[47] When mercy appeared in this way, it could only help to reinforce the "mental structure of paternalism" toward First Nations people, ironically aided by attention to their specific cultural circumstances. Although the Windigo killers were spared by the prerogative of mercy, their commutation sent them to Stony Mountain Penitentiary and placed the men into the grip of a different form of legal punishment.

[. . .]

In the late 1870s and 1880s, an increasing number of First Nations men in the North-West were sentenced to federal penitentiaries. [. . .] By the time the rebellion prisoners arrived in late 1885, the prison administration at Manitoba Penitentiary had experience with First Nations inmates and offered a program of instruction not dissimilar to government industrial schools for younger First Nations boys. In the late 1870s, Warden Samuel Bedson adopted the view that the penitentiary could be used as an instrument of "civilization" and instituted a special education program for First Nations prisoners. Some of the programs reveal how the "civilizing" nature of the penitentiary, more than any other post-rebellion punishment, attempted to integrate First Nations people into the hegemonic landscape of white settlement in the North-West. If First Nations people crudely understood the subtleties of majesty, justice, and mercy in other forms of legal ritual and terror, the officials at Manitoba Penitentiary possessed the means to make these messages more direct.

[. . .]

In spite of the intentions of penitentiary authorities, the structural deficiencies and sanitary conditions at Stony Mountain undercut positive efforts at education and reform. Manitoba Penitentiary was a ramshackle building barely completed by the Department of Public Works before the first federal inmates moved to the site in 1877. The Inspector of Penitentiaries visited Manitoba two years after it opened and reported, "anything more unsuited to the purpose of a penitentiary it were difficult to conceive."[48] The worst shortcomings found by the inspector involved matters of cleanliness and hygiene. [. . .]

The 44 First Nations prisoners who arrived at Manitoba Penitentiary in October 1885 along with 36 Métis prisoners caused an immediate problem of overcrowding.[49] Respiratory disease infected the rebellion prisoners soon after their arrival. Overcrowding forced the men to share tiny cells or to sleep in hallways, which made segregation of the sick impossible. In any case, the penitentiary had no formal hospital facilities, and sick prisoners were confined to "hospital" within their cells mixed with the general population. The rebellion prisoners succumbed to disease in far greater numbers than the white prisoners for a number of possible reasons. The men likely entered the penitentiary in depleted health after a year of hardship, starvation, and military confrontation.[50] A pattern of vulnerability among First Nations prisoners was noted in prison records throughout the 1880s. The prison recorded the first death of a First Nations inmate in 1882, when a 19-year-old man named Ka-Ka-wink died of debility caused by scrofula.[51] Within the next two years, three more First Nations men, all under the age of 30, died in the Manitoba Penitentiary. [. . .]

Despite intimate knowledge of the dreadful sanitary condition within penitentiaries, officials relied on stock Victorian ideologies regarding the degenerated health of the First Nations to explain higher than normal incidences of disease and mortality.[52] Transmittable (and preventable) respiratory disease re-imagined as racial defect became the standard response to First Nations' sickness within the penitentiary and formed the basis of a powerful stereotype about the way they reacted to imprisonment. [. . .]

Mercy played a role again as the government began to consider pardons for the rebellion prisoners in 1886, largely as a result of their failing health. Anger surrounding the rebellion had subsided considerably by 1886, and the majority of prisoners ceased to be perceived as threatening or politically relevant. In these cases, political pragmatism carried the day over cultural considerations, particularly as officials realized throughout 1886 that many of the prisoners were terminally ill. The first 11 rebellion prisoners, including Chief Poundmaker, were released in March of 1886.[53] Catholic priest Albert Lacombe broke the news to the pardoned prisoners at Stony Mountain and recalled later, "they were so happy, like little children."[54] For the most part, the fear of political scandal over prisoners' deaths motivated these pardons. The press noted that the released men were very weak and sickly, and some were even unable to walk. Among the men released that spring was Chief One Arrow, who made it only as far as St Boniface before dying four days later.[55]

The inclusion of Poundmaker in the first group of pardoned prisoners also reveals the influence of political considerations. [. . .] The fear of a future insurgency among the Blackfoot caused government officials to treat Poundmaker with unusual deference. Dewdney wrote to the prime minister just after Poundmaker's trial expressing the anxiety that something more might come of the personal relationship: "I hope no understanding will be come to between the Crees & Blackfeet through Poundmaker—that is what I have been afraid of, but I think the light sentence will prevent that [. . .]."[56] The politics surrounding Poundmaker foretold the treatment he would receive from prison and government officials throughout his incarceration.[57] Indeed, some newspapers interpreted Poundmaker's treatment on his release in March 1886 as adulation. Once again, Poundmaker's relationship with Crowfoot served him well. Dewdney received a telegram from the prime minister in late February 1886 informing him that Poundmaker was to be released "at Crowfoot's intercession."[58] The penitentiary organized a banquet to celebrate the first release of the rebellion prisoners, and Warden Bedson presented Poundmaker with

a gold watch. The unusual fêting of the pardoned prisoners made the event seem more like a graduation ceremony than a release from a federal penitentiary. Poundmaker was granted a meeting with Indian Commissioner Edgar Dewdney the day of his release, and, after leaving the prison, the men slept at the mansion of Archbishop Taché before beginning the trip back to the Treaty 6 area.[59] [. . .] However, Poundmaker did not escape the disease endemic to Stony Mountain. He died at the age of 45, three months after his pardon. [. . .]

In striking contrast, First Nations politics in the North-West worked against Big Bear during his time at Stony Mountain. Big Bear languished at Manitoba Penitentiary throughout 1886 with several other Cree prisoners. Although about two dozen additional rebellion prisoners were quietly released from prison in the summer of 1886, Big Bear was not among them. In early 1887, Cree chiefs including Mistawasis, Ahtakakoop, James Twatt, and John Smith petitioned the government for Big Bear's release. The petition paid tribute to the government and gave assurances that the chiefs considered that the prison sentences would have "the happy effect of deterring other evil disposed persons from attempting to disturb the peace of the country in the future."[60] [. . .] Playing a deft political card, the chiefs emphasized the "loyal" status bestowed upon them by Hayter Reed following the rebellion.[61] Significantly, the language of the petition also marginalized Big Bear's standing among Cree leaders in the North-West by emphasizing their disapproval of his crimes.

However, Dewdney and Reed showed little interest in a pardon for Big Bear. Following the rebellion his band was scattered, and several of his followers sought sanctuary from the law in Montana.[62] Writing to the Superintendent of Indian Affairs, Reed initially rejected the petition based on the fear that the former members of Big Bear's band would leave their present settlements to join him. Evidently, the government still feared the political viability of Big Bear and opted to keep him imprisoned.[63] Reed also considered that Big Bear would need to be released eventually and suggested to the Superintendent, "[If] the Authorities decide to release him, I beg to suggest that the release should be made prominently to appear as having been obtained through the exertions of the loyal chiefs, since that tends to give them more influence with Big Bear."[64] Vankoughnet agreed that the release of Big Bear in 1887 would be premature and that a pardon should be deferred. Authorities were left with little choice only a month later when Big Bear's failing health caused the penitentiary surgeon to urge his release as soon as possible.[65] Big Bear was released in February 1887 and died less than a year later on the Little Pine reserve.

Big Bear's release put a symbolic bookend on the entire legal aftermath of the North-West Rebellion. The thunderous rhetoric of law and order, punishment and revenge that characterized the legal response to the rebellion ended in this way, with the slow degeneration of an elderly former chief waiting for government mercy. What transpired in between is a demonstration of the mutability of these ideological categories. Although government and legal authorities grounded their actions and responses in the ideological tenets of English law, the process revealed something quite different: a paternalist regime willing to resort to striking brutality in its response to opposition. [. . .] Although the North-West Rebellion violence ended in the early spring of 1885, the government did

not hesitate to open a new front against First Nations people in the legal realm. In this way the government used punishment to decapitate politically the most oppositional First Nations bands in the North-West.

Canada's legal response to the convicted First Nations participants suggests that, beneath an overarching colonial agenda, the law operated in complex and contradictory ways. The rebellion court cases, capital punishment, and penitentiary sentences reveal a process of colonization in which the majesty, justice, and mercy of the law unfolded, although seldom in the manner legal authorities intended. Elements of punishment, including executions and incarceration, demonstrate the different ways law and punishment were used to subordinate First Nations people. However, this subordination did not occur as directly as some writers have suggested. Domination was far from absolute in the shattering days after the North-West Rebellion. Productive and colonial relations were badly shaken by the uprising. In the aftermath, we see these relations reconstituted not only by brute state force but through the mediating effect of the ideological tenets of law. This legal response and the complex ways in which it unfolded tell us much about the emerging colonial relationship that figured forcefully in precipitating the rebellion and even more about an emergent Canadian hegemony afterward. The experience of the convicted First Nations participants of the North-West Rebellion is found in the midst of this history. Revealing their participation in these sites of struggle provides an essential contribution to our understanding of how Canadian hegemony in the North-West was challenged.

NOTES

1. Prince Albert *Times,* 9 October 1885.
2. E.P. Thompson, "Eighteenth-Century English Society: Class Struggle without Class?" *Journal of Social History* (May 1978): 133–65, quoted in Bryan Palmer, *The Making of E.P. Thompson: Marxism, Humanism,* and History (Toronto: New Hogtown Press, 1981), 95.
3. Douglas Hay, "Property, Authority, and the Criminal Law," in Douglas Hay, Peter Linebaugh, John G. Rule et al., *Albion's Fatal Tree* (New York: Pantheon Books, 1975), 49.

4. Ibid., 33.

5. Peter Moogk, "The Liturgy of Humiliation, Pain, and Death: The Execution of Criminals in New France," *Canadian Historical Review* 88, 1 (March 2007): 42.

6. Big Bear was a chief of the Battle River Cree. This group hunted in the Fort Pitt area of present-day Saskatchewan. Declining to sign Treaty 6 in 1876, Big Bear instead waged a political campaign against government for the next six years to obtain better terms for the settlement of First Nations people into the colonial relationship. Believing the Cree should speak in a single voice, Big Bear attracted other discontented Cree throughout the 1870s and 1880s. Although he signed Treaty 6 in 1882, he continued to refuse settlement on a reserve until late 1884, when his followers, numbering nearly 500, were reluctantly settled alongside the Wood Cree at Frog Lake, northeast of Edmonton, in present-day Alberta (Hugh Dempsey, *Big Bear: The End of Freedom* [Vancouver: Greystone Books, 1984], chap. 5 and 6).

7. Blair Stonechild and Bill Waiser, *Loyal till Death: Indians and the North-West Rebellion* (Calgary: Fifth House Ltd., 1997), chap. 7, "Making History," 126–45.

8. Hay, "Property, Authority, and the Criminal Law," 27.

9. *Saskatchewan Herald,* 5 October 1885.

10. *Saskatchewan Herald,* 12 October 1885.

11. Library and Archives Canada [hereafter LAC], MG 27, IC4 Volume 7, E. Dewdney to C. Rouleau, 24 April 1885.

12. *Saskatchewan Herald,* 28 September 1885.

13. See Sandra Estlin Bingaman, "The Trials of Poundmaker and Big Bear, 1885," *Saskatchewan History* 28, 3 (1975): 81–94; Waiser and Stonechild, *Loyal till Death,* chap. 10, "Snaring Rabbits," 214–37.

14. E.P. Thompson, *Whigs and Hunters: The Origins of the Black Act* (New York: Pantheon Books, 1975), 262.

15. *Saskatchewan Herald,* 28 September 1885.

16. Ibid.

17. William B. Cameron, *Blood Red the Sun* (Calgary: Kenway Publishing Company, 1926), 199.

18. *Saskatchewan Herald,* 7 September 1885.

19. Quoted in Bingaman, "The Trials of Poundmaker and Big Bear," 86.

20. Quoted in Stonechild and Waiser, *Loyal till Death,* 200.

21. Saskatchewan Archives Board [hereafter SAB], Taché Papers, R–E3641, L. Cochin to A. Taché, 14 August 1885, Regina. Some accounts of One Arrow's courtroom experience expand on his difficulty with English. According to Waiser and Stonechild, when the charge for treason was translated to the chief, he understood he was accused of "knocking off the Queen's bonnet and stabbing her in the behind with a sword" (*Loyal till Death,* 200).

22. SAB, Taché Papers, R–E3641, L. Cochin to A. Taché, 14 August 1885.

23. The idea of the terrible spectacle of the death penalty has been best studied by Peter Linebaugh and Michel Foucault, among many others. Peter Linebaugh, *The London Hanged: Crime and Civil Society in the Eighteenth Century* (Cambridge: Cambridge University Press, 1992), and "The Tyburn Riot Against the Surgeons" in Hay et al., eds, *Albion's Fatal Tree,* 65–119; Michel Foucault, *Discipline and Punish: The Birth of Prison,* Alan Sheridan, trans. (New York: Vintage Books, 1995).

24. Linebaugh, *The London Hanged,* xx–xxi.

25. Glenbow Archives [hereafter GA], Dewdney Papers, box 2, f.38, 587-88, J.A. Macdonald to E. Dewdney, 20 November 1885.

26. GA, Dewdney Papers, box 2, f.57, H. Reed to E. Dewdney, 6 September 1885.

27. SAB, Macdonald-Dewdney Correspondence. R–70, E. Dewdney to J.A. Macdonald, 3 September 1885.

28. This argument is found in John L. Tobias, "Canada's Subjugation of the Plains Cree, 1879–1885," *Canadian Historical Review* 64, 4 (1983): 519–48, and echoed in Stonechild and Waiser, *Loyal till Death.*

29. Louis Cochin and A. Bigonesse, *The Reminiscences of Louis Cochin, O.M.I.: A veteran missionary of the Cree Indians and a prisoner in Poundmaker's camp in 1885* (Battleford: North-West Historical Society, 1927).

30. *Saskatchewan Herald,* 26 October 1885.

31. There are at least two other accounts recording the spiritual conversion of Wandering Spirit. According to prison records, he was baptized by Catholic priest G. Cloutier of Stony Mountain Penitentiary while serving a sentence for horse-stealing in 1884 (*Sessional Papers,* 1885,

No. 15, S.L. Warden Samuel Bedson, *Annual Report of the Wardens,* "Report of the Roman Catholic Chaplain [translation]," 80). Cameron's book also notes that Wandering Spirit was baptized in captivity after the Rebellion three weeks prior to his execution.

32. Elizabeth M. McLean, "The Siege of Fort Pitt," *The Beaver,* December 1946, 22–41.

33. Stonechild and Waiser, *Loyal 'till Death,* 211.

34. Cameron, *Blood Red the Sun,* 207.

35. Cochin and Bigonesse, *The Reminiscences of Louis Cochin,* 42.

36. Ibid., 40.

37. *St. Paul Pioneer,* 28 December 1862.

38. Cameron, *Blood Red the Sun,* 80.

39. *New York Times,* 28 November 1885.

40. Among a variety of First Nations groups, including Cree and Ojibwa, the Windigo is thought to be an anthropomorphic monster that feeds on human flesh. The Windigo is traditionally destroyed by a spiritually powerful individual. In the late nineteenth and early twentieth century, Canadian courts heard a number of cases involving the murder of Windigos. See Sidney Harring, *White Man's Law: Native People in Nineteenth Century Jurisprudence* (Toronto: University of Toronto Press, 1998), chap. 8.

41. Stonechild and Waiser, *Loyal till Death,* 261–3.

42. LAC, RG 13, Series B–1, Volume 1423, File 206A, "Charlesbois, Charles (alias: Ducharme) (also: Dressy Man)."

43. Hay, "Property, Authority, and the Criminal Law," 32–40.

44. These two interpretations are explored in articles by Tina Loo. See "The Road from Bute Inlet: Crime and Colonial Identity in British Columbia" in Jim Phillips, Tina Loo, and Susan Lewthwaite, eds, *Essays in the History of Canadian Law: Volume V, Crime and Criminal Justice* (Toronto: University of Toronto Press, 1994), and "Savage Mercy: Native Culture and the Modification of Capital Punishment in Nineteenth-Century British Columbia," in Carolyn Strange, ed., *Qualities of Mercy: Justice, Punishment, and Discretion* (Vancouver: University of British Columbia Press, 1996), 104–29.

45. Loo, "Savage Mercy," 108.

46. Ibid., 110.

47. Carolyn Strange, "The Lottery of Death: Capital Punishment in Canada, 1867–1976," *Manitoba Law Journal* 23, 3 (1996): 593–619.

48. "Third Annual Report of the Inspector of Penitentiaries of the Dominion of Canada for the Year 1878," *Sessional Papers,* 1879, No. 27, p. 15.

49. The approximate inmate population of Manitoba Penitentiary before the arrival of the Rebellion prisoners was 100.

50. Additionally, most of the Plains Cree were unable to obtain much-needed buffalo resources throughout the 1880s and particularly in the era after their settlement on reserves. Several accounts note that the winter of 1884–1885 had been particularly difficult for the Cree, as they tried to obtain what wild game they could in the midst of widespread cutbacks in government rations throughout the North-West.

51. "Return of Deaths in Manitoba Penitentiary Hospital," *Sessional Papers,* 1883, No. 29, p. 133.

52. Anne McClintock explores the discourse of degeneration in an imperial context. She argues that social crisis in Britain in the 1879s and 1880s caused a eugenic discourse of degeneration predicated upon the fear of disease and contagion. Ruling elites classified threatening social groups (working-class and racialized people) in biological terms that pathologized their perceived shortcomings and potential to threaten the riches, health, and power of the "imperial race". Anne McClintock, *Imperial Leather: Race, Gender, and Sexuality in the Colonial Contest* (New York: Routledge, 1995), 46–51.

53. *Saskatchewan Herald,* 8 March 1886.

54. Katherine Hughes, *Father Lacombe: The Black-Robe Voyageur* (New York: Moffat Yard and Company, 1911), 308–9.

55. *Saskatchewan Herald,* 30 August 1886.

56. SAB, R70, Macdonald-Dewdney Correspondence, E. Dewdney to J.A. Macdonald, 23 August 1885.

57. Chief Crowfoot had adopted Poundmaker for a time in his youth to replace a son lost in battle. This was a customary reciprocity between warring tribes. After the last hostilities between the Cree and Blackfoot ended, the adoptive relationship between the two chiefs forged a strong political alliance. Although the Blackfoot did not participate in the Rebellion, the government understood that feelings within Blackfoot communities were strongly in favour of the Cree participants.

58. SAB, R70, Macdonald-Dewdney Correspondence. J.A. Macdonald to E. Dewdney, 24 February 1886.

59. *Saskatchewan Herald,* 8 March 1886.

60. LAC, RG 10, Vol. 3774, File 36846, "Petition of Cree Chiefs Requesting Big Bear's Release," January 15, 1887.

61. Following the Rebellion, Hayter Reed compiled a list of "band behaviour" in which he detailed the activities of each First Nations group and branded them as either "loyal" or "disloyal". The designations had wide-ranging implications and determined levels of assistance, government monitoring, and permission to possess firearms.

62. A large number of Big Bear's followers, including his son Imasees, fled the North-West for Montana following the Rebellion. Imasees stood trial in the 1890s for his role in the Frog Lake Massacre, but was not convicted. Despite American military attempts to dislodge them from Montana, the Cree under Imasees never returned permanently to Canada. Michel Hogue, "Disputing the Medicine Line," *Montana* 52, 4 (2002): 2–17.

63. LAC, RG 10, Vol. 3774, File 36846, H. Reed to Superintendent of Indian Affairs, 29 January 1887.

64. Ibid.

65. Quoted in Dempsey, *Big Bear,* 195.

Chapter 4

Canadians at Work

READINGS

Primary Documents

INTRODUCTION

Although we could describe today's capitalist economy more elaborately, much of it involves people selling either goods or services (like physical or mental labour) in the marketplace. Regulations and trade agreements have tamed the marketplace somewhat, but the basic pattern of people working for compensation has been only reinforced over time. In the nineteenth century, when a much larger proportion of the Canadian population was involved in activities like farming and fishing, our social safety net was still a distant dream, and the wage worker's best protection against unfair labour practices was to join a union. Many employers resisted attempts to unionize, and did not view keeping employees healthy and well-paid as a necessary cost of doing business. With unions that managed to bargain on behalf of their members and governmental measures to set minimum labour standards, working conditions generally improved, but these advances did not materialize for all workers at the same time or to the same degree. Working life also intersected with workers' leisure and community pursuits. Just as their jobs determined how workers spent their wage-earning time, the money they had available and the social pressures of their class and neighbourhood determined how they lived while away from the shop floor. It was, therefore, difficult to escape the constraints of the wage economy, even in the saloon or in church. Our primary sources address working conditions in two fundamentally different ways: from the perspective of what the worker might expect on the job (hours, breaks, etc.) and from the perspective of what was to be done for the worker. In the first instance, Jean Thomson Scott's report on labouring women in Ontario, we see in some detail what was expected of workers in the last decade of the nineteenth century. The existing regulations are perhaps more notable because Scott observes ways in which the regulations were not followed. In our other example, Stephen Leacock's gaze fell on western society's problems in the wake of the First World War, and his solution was ambitious: doing away with inequality of opportunity. Central to his scheme for reform was the re-making of the workplace through minimum wages and a shortened workday. Lately, however, labour historians have focused less often on working conditions and more on working-class culture. In the historical interpretations featured here, Paul Laverdure and Melissa Turkstra examine work, leisure, and religion. In Laverdure's piece, the Roman Catholic Church becomes increasingly concerned with Sunday work. Though Quebec had long shunned the sabbatarianism that was commonly held by many Protestant leaders, industrialization and immigration led many Catholic clerics to favour stricter Sunday observance. For her part, Turkstra examines how Ontario workers related to religion, particularly the act of worship. At times, workers thought that churches were not doing enough to encourage employers to behave in a Christian fashion, yet those same workers had grown up in a Christian society and drew inspiration from the gospel message, especially when the gospel called for the fair and equitable treatment of one's fellow man.

QUESTIONS FOR CONSIDERATION

1.   What were some of the factors motivating workers or employers to bend the labour regulations that Scott describes?
2.   Do Leacock's plans for social reform seem practical?
3.   Has the way we determine or define social class changed much since the period covered by these sources?
4.   What factors led to calls for stricter Sunday observance in Quebec?
5.   Why was religion so important to the labour movement when labour's main goal was to change the material lives of workers?

SUGGESTIONS FOR FURTHER READING

Bettina Bradbury, *Working Families: Age, Gender, and Daily Survival in Industrializing Montreal* (Toronto: University of Toronto Press, 2007).

Christina Burr, *Spreading the Light: Work and Labour Reform in Late-Nineteenth-Century Toronto* (Toronto: Toronto University Press, 1999).

Terry Copp, *The Anatomy of Poverty: The Condition of the Working Class in Montreal, 1897–1929* (Toronto: McClelland and Stewart, 1974).

Ruth A. Frager and Carmela K. Patrias, *Discounted Labour: Women Workers in Canada, 1870–1939* (Toronto: University of Toronto Press, 2005).

Judy Fudge and Eric Tucker, *Labour before the Law: The Regulation of Workers' Collective Action in Canada, 1900–1948* (Toronto: University of Toronto Press, 2004).

Craig Heron, *The Canadian Labour Movement: A Short History* (Toronto: Lorimer, 1996).

——— and Steve Penfold, *Workers' Festival: A History of Labour Day in Canada* (Toronto: University of Toronto Press, 2005).

Gregory S. Kealey, *Workers and Canadian History* (Montreal and Kingston: McGill-Queen's University Press, 1995).

——— and Bryan D. Palmer, *Dreaming of What Might Be: The Knights of Labour in Ontario, 1880–1900* (Cambridge: Cambridge University Press, 2005).

Suzanne Morton, *Ideal Surroundings: Domestic Life in a Working-Class Suburb in the 1920s* (Toronto: University of Toronto Press, 1995).

Joan Sangster, *Transforming Labour: Women and Work in Post-War Canada* (Toronto: University of Toronto Press, 2010).

Mariana Valverde, *The Age of Light, Soap, and Water: Moral Reform in English Canada, 1885–1925* (Toronto: McClelland & Stewart, 1991).

Primary Documents

1 From Jean Thomson Scott, *The Conditions of Female Labour in Ontario* (Toronto: Warwick & Sons, 1892), 9–31.

Victor Hugo has fitly called the present age the "Women's Century"; for although the annals of history have always contained the names of great women yet the position of women as a factor in the economic conditions of social life seems peculiar to recent times.

In this paper some attempt will be made to discuss the conditions under which women are working in the Province of Ontario; referring, perhaps, more particularly to the city of Toronto, which has afforded the most convenient field for observation.

When Harriet Martineau visited America in 1840, she relates that she found only seven employments open to women; namely, teaching, needlework, keeping boarders, working in cotton mills, type-setting, work in book-binderies and household service. Although women still retain their positions in these employments, they have vastly extended the number of their vocations. According to the latest census returns in the United States, women have now secured a footing in 4,467 different branches of various industries. While Ontario can not boast of such large numbers, the various callings entered by women in this Province are rapidly increasing in number. In some cases the establishment of new industries, especially within the last fifteen years, has led to their further employment. In others they have entered fields hitherto, for the most part, occupied by men. New employments are continually opening up with advancing civilization, which require but slight experience and seem adapted for women.

There are various reasons why women are ready for the numerous occupations which are continually offering themselves. In a large number of instances, circumstances make it a matter of necessity for them to earn their living. Often a desire to live up to a certain standard of comfort will lead girls, for a short time at least, to go into employments in which, while living at home, they can partially support themselves, or at least supply themselves with pin-money. Again, the social conditions of life in Canada are such that women find it necessary to prepare themselves for emergencies: they often begin to learn some occupation so as to be prepared for future risks, and then their circumstances and the occupation becomes a permanent one.

For these and other reasons we find a large and increasing number of women employed as wage-earners; and Ontario, following the example of older countries, has found it necessary to subject their labour to various restrictions in order to protect the interests of society.

SECTION I.—LEGISLATION IN ONTARIO

(1.) The employment of women and girls in *manufacturing* establishments in Ontario is regulated by the *Ontario Factory Act* of 1884 and the *Amendment Act* of 1889.

In passing such Acts Ontario was but following the example of older countries. Factory legislation in Great Britain has been in existence for more than half a century, and has been codified by the *Factory and Workshops Act* of 1878, with subsequent amendments. The example of Great Britain has been followed by other countries; in Europe by Austro-Hungary, in 1859; by France, in 1874; by Switzerland, in 1877; and by Germany, in 1878. In America factory legislation has been of very recent growth, but, although recent, it has been rapid. Massachusetts was the pioneer state in this respect, having passed a *Factory Act* providing for inspection in 1882. Ohio followed in 1884; so that Ontario compares favourably, in point of time, with the various states of the Union.

The principal sections of the *Ontario Factory Acts* which are pertinent to this enquiry may be summarized as follows:—

1. Under the word "Factory" only *manufacturing* establishments are included.

2. In order to come under inspection, there must be at least *six* persons employed in a factory.

3. No boy under *twelve* and no girl under *fourteen* shall be employed in any factory.

4. No child (defined as a person under the age of fourteen) or female shall be employed more than *ten* hours in one day, or more than *sixty* hours in one week; unless a different apportionment of the hours of labour per day has been made for the sole purpose of giving a shorter day's work on Saturday.

5. If the inspector so directs, meals shall not be eaten in the work-rooms, but in suitable rooms to be provided for the purpose.

6. Boys under twelve and girls under fourteen may be employed during the months of July, August, September and October in any year in such gathering-in and other preparation of fruits and vegetables for canning or desiccating purposes as may be required to be done prior to the operation of cooking, or other process of that nature requisite in connection with the canning of fruits or vegetables.

7. Employers shall allow each child, young girl and woman not less than one hour at noon of each day for meals, but such hour shall not be reckoned in the ten hours to which labour is restricted.

8. Children and women are not allowed to clean machinery while in motion.

9. Where the exigencies of certain trades require that women should be employed for a longer period than above stated, an inspector may give permission for such exemption, under the following limitations:—(a) No woman, young girl or child shall be employed before six o'clock in the morning, nor after the hour of nine in the evening (i.e., while employed during the day). (b) The hours of labour shall not exceed twelve hours and a half in any one day, nor more than seventy-two and a half in one week. (c) Such

exemption shall not comprise more than six weeks in any one year. (d) During the continuance of such exemption, there shall, in addition to the hour for the noon-day meal, be allowed to every woman, young girl or child so employed to an hour later than seven o'clock, not less than forty-five minutes for another meal between five and eight o'clock in the afternoon. (e) Women only may be employed to a later hour than nine, where the work relates to the canning or desiccating of fruits or vegetables, for twenty days during the summer months.

10. Provision is made for separate conveniences for women, and for the proper ventilation of the work-rooms.

11. A register of the children, young girls and women employed in any factory shall be kept by the employer for the reference of the inspector.

12. Notices of the hours between which children, young girls and women are to be employed shall be hung up in a conspicuous place in the factory.

After the passing of this Act it was found necessary to provide means for seeing that it was carried out, and in 1887 three inspectors were appointed in Ontario under the Act.

As has been intimated, the *Factory Act* in Ontario deals exclusively with those employed in manufacturing establishments, and not with those in mercantile or mechanical employments.

[. . .]

SECTION II.—EFFECTS OF LEGISLATION AND INSPECTION

1. Limitations of Inspection

The provisions of the "Factories Act" do not apply (a) to any factory employing not more than *five* persons; (b) where children, young girls or women are employed at home in a private dwelling, wherein the only persons employed are members of the family dwelling there. Originally the limit was placed at twenty; but as soon as the inspectors entered on their work it was found that the smaller places of business were more in need of inspection than the larger; and on their recommendation the Act as amended placed the limit at *five*.

Thus there are numerous small places of business employing four and five women, particularly small dressmaking and millinery establishments, which are excluded from the benefits of the Act. But it cannot be doubted that some system of inspection is needed for *all* places where women and children are employed. There is no reason why some places should be inspected and others not. That only one or two women are employed in any capacity is no reason why they should be subject to whatever conditions their employers see fit to impose. It would be advisable to do away with the number-limit altogether.

2. Child Labour

Section 6 prohibits the employment of boys under twelve and girls under fourteen in any factory coming under the Act; and in the case of boys under fourteen the employer is obliged to keep a certificate signed by the parent or guardian of the birth-place and age of each child, or else the written opinion of a registered physician that such child is not under age. But boys and girls under age are allowed to work during the summer months in such gathering in and other preparation of fruits and vegetables for canning or desiccating purposes as may be required to be done prior to the operation of cooking or other processes of that nature. Such employment is, of course, only temporary, owing to the perishable nature of the material; and, as the employment is light, children are as well able to do it as older persons, but whether it is really as profitable to employ them is a matter for the employers to decide. In some cases, such as the operation of shelling peas, machinery has taken the place of manual labour, thus lessening the employment of children.

That some legislation was necessary to limit the employment of children in Ontario was seen long before the passing of the Act. In 1881 the Dominion Government appointed a Commission to make inquiry into the working of mills and factories in Canada and the labour employed therein. The Commission visited and reported upon 465 factories, in which over two thousand children under fourteen years of age were found, and nearly two hundred of these were under *ten* years of age. The Commissioners state that considerable difficulty was found in obtaining with accuracy the ages of the children; for there was no record required to be kept, and in many instances the children, having no education, were unable to tell their ages—this more particularly among the very young children of eight and nine years. It was found, too, that wherever children were employed they invariably worked as many hours as the adults, and if not compelled were at least requested to work overtime; so that the condition of the young workers in the latter part of the day, especially during the warm summer weather, was anything but desirable. In some cases they were obliged to be at work as early as 6.30 AM, necessitating their being up much earlier for their morning meal and walk to work, and this in winter as well as in summer. This was unquestionably too heavy a strain on growing children, and was condemned by all except those who were directly benefited. As late as 1886–7 the Royal Labour Commission reported that child labour under legal age was still largely employed, the *Factory Act* not having got into working order. That the enforcement of this Act has been the means of largely decreasing the amount of child labour may be seen from the Inspectors' Reports. Wherever boys and girls under age have been found the employer has been

notified; and when the practice has been continued they have been prosecuted. In the report for the Western District for 1888 there were found about two hundred and fifty boys between twelve and fourteen, while in the report for the ensuing year only one hundred and sixty-nine were recorded. One reason given for the decrease was that the canning factories were not as active in the latter year. In some cases the employers preferred not to employ the children because of the trouble attached to procuring certificates. The chief resistance indeed comes from the parents of the children who, either from necessity or greed, are so anxious to get employment for them that they will sometimes furnish false certificates.

Sometimes children under legal age were employed by persons who took contracts for work and who, although working in a factory, argued that because the number they employed was less than constituted a factory under the law they were exempt from its provisions, although the total number of persons employed in such factory would cause it to be classed under the Act.

In some cases where children under age were found it was pleaded as an excuse that they were only a month or two under the required age. Parents too, complained that their children would not go to school, and were better at work than running about in the streets.

Of the boys between twelve and fourteen quite a number work in saw-mills where dangerous machinery is used. The Inspector for the Eastern District has suggested that the legal age for boys employed in saw-mills be raised to fourteen. In Quebec the legal age for boys in saw-mills is sixteen. Seeing that the whole number of boys between twelve and fourteen employed in factories is comparatively small, it would be no great revolution to raise the age for boys employed in any kind of factory to fourteen, and also prohibit their employment in any kind of dangerous work before sixteen. It would simplify the labours of the Inspectors considerably in the matter of requiring certificates, and also diminish the responsibility of the employers, who, in many cases, are importuned by the parents or even by the children themselves to give employment. A saving clause might be added to allow a boy to work where it could be shown that such work was necessary either for his own support or for the support of his family.

The factories found employing girls under age at the first visit of the Inspectors were principally cotton, woollen and knitting mills, which are run generally the full sixty hours a week, and where the work is purely mechanical as well as extremely monotonous. For a girl of fourteen or thereabouts to work continuously for ten hours a day and six days a week cannot but prove injurious to her health. Where factories are running for ten hours a day no girls under sixteen ought to be employed, or if they are, only for a short period. In Quebec the employment of boys under sixteen and girls under eighteen is prohibited in any factory named for that purpose by the Lieutenant-Governor in Council as unhealthy or dangerous. The list at present contains the names of twenty-eight kinds of manufactures which are considered dangerous on account of the dust, obnoxious odours, or danger from fire. Among these are tobacco factories and saw-mills; and boys under fourteen and girls under fifteen are altogether prohibited from working in cigar factories.

Scarcity of labour cannot be pleaded as an excuse for the employment of children as long as able-bodied men are seeking employment; and, of course, the gradual restriction of child labour widens to some extent, if not in the same proportion, the field for adult labour.

While child labour is thus partially restricted in Ontario in factories, there is still not the slightest restriction set upon their employment in shops and offices. Numerous children find employment as cash and parcel boys and girls in retail stores. This evil, however, does not exist now to the same extent as formerly owing to the introduction of machinery for carrying cash and even parcels to the desks and wrapping counters. Boys in Toronto find employment in selling newspapers on the street; but although girls did engage in such employment at one time they are now, very properly, prohibited from doing so.

It is to be hoped that the restrictions under the *Factories Act* in regard to child labour will be applied to their employment in mercantile and mechanical establishments as soon as possible. If child labour is to be effectually restricted the compulsory school law and the *Factories Act* must work together. If the school law compels all children between eight and fourteen to be in attendance at some school it is plain that they cannot be employed in any work during school hours. But to carry out the *Education Act*, far more abundant and efficient inspection must be provided than at present, and school accommodation, even if of a temporary character, must be promptly furnished in growing suburbs.

3. Hours of Labour

Sub-section 3 of section 6, of the *Factory Act* enacts that no child, young girl or women shall be employed in a factory for more than *ten* hours a day or more than *sixty* hours in any one week; unless a different apportionment of the hours of labour per day has been made for the sole purpose of giving a shorter day's work on Saturday. Sub-section 4 requires that every employer shall allow each child, young girl and women not less than one hour at noon of each day for meals.

In addition to these regular hours for work, exemptions may be granted by the Inspectors, where the exigencies of certain trades demand it, for working overtime; but in such cases no child, young girl or women shall work longer than twelve and a half hours a day or seventy two and a half in any one week; and such exemption shall not comprise more than six weeks in any one year, nor shall the time fixed for meals be diminished. During the period of such exemption, every child, young girl or woman, employed in any factory to an hour later than seven in the evening shall be allowed not less than forty-five minutes for an evening meal between five and eight o'clock in the evening. While working overtime, women are not to be employed before six in the morning, nor later than nine in the evening, except in canning factories where they may work later than nine in the evening for not more than twenty days in a year.

In those places coming under the *Factories Act* where women are employed comparatively few work for the full sixty hours a week. In a list comprising eighty factories in Toronto, only ten worked for sixty hours a week; fourteen worked less than sixty but over fifty-five; thirty worked from fifty to fifty-five hours; and the remainder from forty-four to fifty. One cause of the reduction of hours in Toronto is the general adoption of the Saturday half-holiday. Outside Toronto it is not so general, and the hours of labour per week reach a higher average. It is to be hoped that fifty-five hours will be made the limit instead of sixty; and so cause the hours of labour to be nine hours a day, or else five and a half days a week.

The clause in the Act which allows a different apportionment of the hours per day in case of shorter hours on Saturday is an unfortunate one, because it would permit an average of eleven hours a day for five days in the week— far too long a period for women to work.

Those factories which work the full sixty hours are principally cotton, woollen and knitting mills, where expensive machinery is employed.

Before the *Factories Act* came into force many factories worked longer than ten hours

a day; so that the results of inspection have been thus far beneficial.

Another loop-hole in the law is the clause concerning the noon meal hour. It reads, "the employer shall allow not less than one hour at noon," which has been interpreted to mean that the employees may take less if they choose, and in some cases this has been done, either in order to stop work earlier in the evening or to lessen the hours of work on Saturday. It need hardly be said that shortening the meal hour is poor economy in the way of preserving one's health. In this matter the girls themselves are not the best judges; for the majority of them would even prefer to take only a half hour at noon if by so doing they could stop working in the evening. In some cases where girls made such a request the employers wisely advised against it; and in one case a compromise of three-quarters of an hour was effected. It would be better if the law were more absolute in the matter, especially where the full ten hours a day is insisted on.

Still another matter in which the law is indefinite is that of night labour for women and children. The law *does* state that where, under the exemption women work longer than ten hours a day they are not to be employed before six in the morning nor later than nine in the evening, but it does not prohibit night labour *per se*. As a matter of fact girls in Toronto have been employed for a few months from eleven o'clock in the evening till five or six in the morning in setting type at the Central Press Agency for the cable despatches to country newspapers. The Deputy Attorney-General was appealed to for the interpretation of the law, but it was decided that nothing in the Act prevented the night employment of women. Fortunately for the women themselves, in the case referred to they found the work too arduous, and have ceased working (since September 18th, 1891).

The *Factory Law* in Switzerland is more definite in this matter and states that "under no circumstances shall women work on Sunday or at night work." The law of Massachusetts is "no corporation or manufacturing establishment in this commonwealth shall employ any minor or women between the hours of ten o'clock at night and six in the morning." The *Quebec Factories Act* as amended states "that the day of ten hours work shall not commence before six in morning nor end after nine in the evening." According to the new English Act, the employment of women must now be brought within a specified period of twelve hours, taken between 6 AM and 10 PM, with an hour and a half off for meals, except on Saturday, when the period is eight hours with half an hour off. It is to be hoped that the law in Ontario will be so amended that night labour for women will be prohibited.

Complaint has frequently been made to the Inspectors that women in millinery and dressmaking establishments are employed over ten hours a day; but of course as long as the legal limit of sixty hours per week is not exceeded by any one employee, the Inspector cannot interfere. It seems usual during the busy season to ask part of the staff to remain after six o'clock, the usual hour for closing, one part taking turn with another. There is generally no allowance made for an evening meal in such cases, the girls preferring to work till they finish rather than go home and come back again; but to work from one till eight or nine in the evening without food is certainly not conducive to health. Legislation on the subject seems to be called for. According to the English *Factory Act* no women can be employed for more than four and a half hours without an interval of half an hour at least for a meal. The overtime occurs only during the busy season or on Saturdays. Employers argue that it is not always possible to foresee what work is coming in, and that in order to oblige their customers they have to promise the work at a certain time. Some establishments make it a rule never to work overtime; and when urgent work comes in, other work is put

aside for a time. It would be well if all would make this the rule. A little more forethought too, on the part of customers would lessen the evil. Ladies could often wait a day or two for a bonnet or gown; or, if not, could give their order earlier. Conversation with those in the business reveals the fact that it is not orders for dresses for weddings or funerals which cause overtime—but those for balls and parties, this of course in establishments doing a trade of that kind. The general desire again on the part of many to have a new gown or bonnet for Sunday makes Saturday the busiest day for dressmakers and milliners. In England no woman can be employed in such establishments after 4 PM on Saturdays. It is not customary to pay for such overtime in Toronto. The matter seems to be looked on as only occasional, but there is a danger of too much of it being done if some restriction is not placed on the length of time in any one day during which a woman may be employed.

All that has been said hitherto in regard to the hours of labour only applies to manufacturing establishments where girls and women are employed.

The *Factories Act* in Ontario does not include mercantile or mechanical employments in its provisions. The *Shops Regulation Act* however prohibits the employment of boys under fourteen and girls under sixteen for a longer period than twelve hours a day including meal hours, or than fourteen hours a day on Saturday also including meal hours. *Such an enactment makes no regulations whatever for girls over sixteen as far as the hours of work are concerned, and as the majority of girls employed in shops are over that age the Act is not very far-reaching.* As has been already stated there is no system of inspection under this Act. In some towns the shopdealers have combined under the early closing by-law and close their shops at seven in the evening; but this is not as general as could be wished.

2   From Stephen Leacock, *The Unsolved Riddle of Social Justice* (Toronto: S.B. Gundy, 1920), 124–52.

WHAT IS POSSIBLE AND WHAT IS NOT

Socialism . . . will not work, and neither will individualism, or at least the older individualism that we have hitherto made the basis of the social order. Here, therefore, stands humanity, in the middle of its narrow path in sheer perplexity, not knowing which way to turn. On either side is the brink of an abyss. On one hand is the yawning gulf of social catastrophe represented by socialism. On the other, the slower, but no less inevitable disaster that would attend the continuation in its present form of the system under which we have lived. Either way lies destruction; the one swift and immediate as a fall from a great height; the other gradual, but equally dreadful, as the slow strangulation in a morass. Somewhere between the two lies such narrow safety as may be found.

[. . .]

When we view the shortcomings of the present individualism, its waste of energy, its fretful overwork, its cruel inequality and the bitter lot that it brings to the uncounted millions of the submerged, we are inclined to cry out against it, and to listen with a ready ear to the easy promises of the idealist. But when we turn to the contrasted fallacies of socialism, its obvious impracticality and the dark gulf of social chaos that yawns behind it, we are driven back shuddering to cherish rather the ills we have than fly to others we know not of.

Yet out of the whole discussion of the matter some few things begin to merge into the clearness of certain day. It is clear enough on the one hand that we can expect no sudden and complete transformation of the world in which we live. Such a process is impossible. The industrial system is too complex, its roots are too deeply struck and its whole organism of too delicate a growth to permit us to tear it from the soil. Nor is humanity itself fitted for the kind of transformation which fills the dreams of the perfectionist. The principle of selfishness that has been the survival instinct of existence since life first crawled from the slime of a world in evolution, is as yet but little mitigated. In the long process of time some higher cosmic sense may take its place. It has not done so yet. If the kingdom of socialism were opened to-morrow, there are but few fitted to enter.

But on the other hand it is equally clear that the doctrine of "every man for himself," as it used to be applied, is done with forever. The time has gone by when a man shall starve asking in vain for work; when the listless outcast shall draw his rags shivering about him unheeded of his fellows; when children shall be born in hunger and bred in want and broken in toil with never a chance in life. If nothing else will end these things, fear will do it. The hardest capitalist that ever gripped his property with the iron clasp of legal right relaxes his grasp a little when he thinks of the possibilities of a social conflagration. In this respect five years of war have taught us more than a century of peace. It has set in a clear light new forms of social obligation. The war brought with it conscription—not as we used to see it, as the last horror of military tyranny, but as the crowning pride of democracy. An inconceivable revolution in the thought of the English speaking peoples has taken place in respect to it. The obligation of every man, according to his age and circumstance, to take up arms for his country and, if need be, to die for it, is henceforth the recognized basis of progressive democracy.

But conscription has its other side. The obligation to die must carry with it the right to live. If every citizen owes it to society that he must fight for it in case of need, then society owes to every citizen the opportunity of a livelihood. "Unemployment," in the case of the willing and able becomes henceforth a social crime. Every democratic Government must henceforth take as the starting point of its industrial policy, that there shall be no such thing as able bodied men and women "out of work," looking for occupation and unable to find it. Work must either be found or must be provided by the State itself.

Yet it is clear that a policy of state work and state pay for all who are otherwise unable to find occupation involves appalling difficulties. The opportunity will loom large for the prodigal waste of money, for the undertaking of public works of no real utility and for the subsidizing of an army of loafers. But the difficulties, great though they are, are not insuperable. The payment for state labor of this kind can be kept low enough to make it the last resort rather than the ultimate ambition of the worker. Nor need the work be useless. In new countries, especially such as Canada and the United States and Australia, the development of latent natural assets could absorb the labor of generations. There are still unredeemed empires in the west. Clearly enough a certain modicum of public honesty and integrity is essential for such a task; more, undoubtedly, than we have hitherto been able to enlist in the service of the commonwealth. But without it we perish. Social betterment must depend at every stage on the force of public spirit and public morality that inspires it. So much for the case of those who are able and willing to work. There remain still the uncounted thousands who by accident or illness, age or infirmity, are unable to maintain themselves. For these people, under the older dispensation, there was nothing but the poorhouse, the jail or starvation by the roadside. The narrow individualism of the nineteenth century refused to recognize the social duty of supporting somebody else's grandmother. Such charity began, and ended, at home. But even with the passing of the nineteenth century an awakened sense of the collective responsibility of society towards its weaker members began to impress itself upon public policy. Old age pension laws and national insurance against illness and accident were already being built into the legislative codes

of the democratic countries. The experience of the war has enormously increased this sense of social solidarity. It is clear now that our fortunes are not in our individual keeping. We stand or fall as a nation. And the nation which neglects the aged and infirm, or which leaves a family to be shipwrecked as the result of a single accident to a breadwinner, cannot survive as against a nation in which the welfare of each is regarded as contributory to the safety of all. Even the purest selfishness would dictate a policy of social insurance.

[. . .]

The attitude of the nineteenth century upon this point was little short of insane. The melancholy doctrine of Malthus had perverted the public mind. Because it was difficult for a poor man to bring up a family, the hasty conclusion was reached that a family ought not to be brought up. But the war has entirely inverted and corrected this point of view. The father and mother who were able to send six sturdy, native-born sons to the conflict were regarded as benefactors of the nation. But these six sturdy sons had been, some twenty years before, six "puling infants," viewed with gloomy disapproval by the Malthusian bachelor. If the strength of the nation lies in its men and women there is only one way to increase it. Before the war it was thought that a simpler and easier method of increase could be found in the wholesale import of Austrians, Bulgarians and Czecho-Slovaks. The newer nations boasted proudly of their immigration tables. The fallacy is apparent now. Those who really count in a nation and those who govern its destinies for good or ill are those who are born in it.

It is difficult to over-estimate the harm that has been done to public policy by this same Malthusian theory. It has opposed to every proposal of social reform an obstacle that seemed insuperable—the danger of a rapid overincrease of population that would pauperize the community. Population, it was said, tends always to press upon the heels of subsistence. If the poor are pampered, they will breed fast: the time will come when there will not be food for all and we shall perish in a common destruction. Seen in this light, infant mortality and the cruel wastage of disease were viewed with complacence. It was "Nature's" own process at work. The "unfit," so called, were being winnowed out that only the best might survive. The biological doctrine of evolution was misinterpreted and misapplied to social policy.

But in the organic world there is no such thing as the "fit" or the "unfit," in any higher or moral sense. The most hideous forms of life may "survive" and thrust aside the most beautiful. It is only by a confusion of thought that the processes of organic nature which render every foot of fertile ground the scene of unending conflict can be used to explain away the death of children of the slums. The whole theory of survival is only a statement of what is, not of what ought to be. The moment that we introduce the operation of human volition and activity, that, too, becomes one of the factors of "survival". The dog, the cat, and the cow live by man's will, where the wolf and the hyena have perished.

[. . .]

The fundamental error of the Malthusian theory of population and poverty is to confound the difficulties of human organization with the question of physical production. Our existing poverty is purely a problem in the direction and distribution of human effort. It has no connection as yet with the question of the total available means of subsistence. Some day, in a remote future, in which under an improved social system the numbers of mankind might increase to the full power of the natural capacity of multiplication, such a question might conceivably disturb the equanimity of mankind. But it need not now. [. . .]

I lay stress upon this problem of the increase of population because, to my thinking, it is in this connection that the main work and the best hope of social reform can be found. The children of the race should

be the very blossom of its fondest hopes. Under the present order and with the present gloomy preconceptions they have been the least of its collective cares. Yet here— and here more than anywhere—is the point towards which social effort and social legislation may be directed immediately and successfully. The moment that we get away from the idea that the child is a mere appendage of the parent, bound to share good fortune and ill, wealth and starvation, according to the parent's lot, the moment we regard the child as itself a member of society—clothed in social rights—a burden for the moment but an asset for the future—we turn over a new leaf in the book of human development, we pass a new milestone on the upward path of progress.

It should be recognized in the coming order of society, that every child of the nation has the right to be clothed and fed and trained irrespective of its parents' lot. Our feeble beginnings in the direction of housing, sanitation, child welfare and education, should be expanded at whatever cost into something truly national and all embracing. The ancient grudging selfishness that would not feed other people's children should be cast out. In the war time the wealthy bachelor and the spinster of advancing years took it for granted that other people's children should fight for them. The obligation must apply both ways.

[. . .]

Few of us in mind or body are what we might be; and millions of us, the vast majority of industrial mankind known as the working class, are distorted beyond repair from what they might have been. In older societies this was taken for granted: the poor and the humble and the lowly reproduced from generation to generation, as they grew to adult life, the starved brains and stunted outlook of their forbears—starved and stunted only by lack of opportunity. For nature knows of no such differences in original capacity between the children of the fortunate and the unfortunate. Yet on this inequality, made by circumstance, was based the whole system of caste, the stratification of the gentle and the simple on which society rested. In the past it may have been necessary. It is not so now. If, with all our vast apparatus of machinery and power, we cannot so arrange society that each child has an opportunity in life, it would be better to break the machinery in pieces and return to the woods from which we came.

Put into the plainest of prose, then, we are saying that the government of every country ought to supply work and pay for the unemployed, maintenance for the infirm and aged, and education and opportunity for the children. No modern state can hope to survive unless it meets the kind of social claims on the part of the unemployed, the destitute and the children that have been described above. And it cannot do this unless it continues to use the terrific engine of taxation already fashioned in the war. [. . .]

But all of this deals as yet only with the field of industry and conduct in which the state rules supreme. Governmental care of the unemployed, the infant and the infirm, sounds like a chapter in socialism. If the same regime were extended over the whole area of production, we should have socialism itself and a mere soap-bubble bursting into fragments. There is no need, however, to extend the regime of compulsion over the whole field. The vast mass of human industrial effort must still lie outside of the immediate control of the government. Every man will still earn his own living and that of his family as best he can, relying first and foremost upon his own efforts.

One naturally asks, then, To what extent can social reform penetrate into the ordinary operation of industry itself? Granted that it is impossible for the state to take over the whole industry of the nation, does that mean that the present inequalities must continue? The framework in which our industrial life is set cannot be readily broken asunder. But we can to a great extent ease the rigidity of its outlines. A legislative code that starts from

sounder principles than those which have obtained hitherto can do a great deal towards progressive betterment. Each decade can be an improvement upon the last. Hitherto we have been hampered at every turn by the supposed obstacle of immutable economic laws. The theory of "natural" wages and prices of a supposed economic order that could not be disturbed set up a sort of legislative paralysis. The first thing needed is to get away entirely from all such preconceptions, to recognize that the "natural" order of society, based on the "natural" liberty, does not correspond with real justice and real liberty at all, but works injustice at every turn. And at every turn intrusive social legislation must seek to prevent such injustice.

[. . .] Let us take, as a conspicuous example, the case of the minimum wage law. Here is a thing sternly condemned in the older thought as an economic impossibility. It was claimed, as we have seen, that under free contract a man was paid what he earned and no law could make it more. But the older theory was wrong. The minimum wage law ought to form, in one fashion or another, a part of the code of every community. It may be applied by specific legislation from a central power, or it may be applied by the discretionary authority of district boards, or it may be regulated—as it has been in some of the beginnings already made—within the compass of each industry or trade. But the principle involved is sound. The wage as paid becomes a part of the conditions of industry. Interest, profits and, later, the direction of consumption and then of production, conform themselves to it.

True it is, that in this as in all cases of social legislation, no application of the law can be made so sweeping and so immediate as to dislocate the machine and bring industry to a stop. It is probable that at any particular time and place the legislative minimum wage cannot be very much in advance of the ordinary or average wage of the people in employment. But its virtue lies in its progression. The modest increase of to-day leads to the fuller increase of to-morrow. Properly applied, the capitalist and the employer of labor need have nothing to fear from it. Its ultimate effect will not fall upon them, but will serve merely to alter the direction of human effort.

Precisely the same reasoning holds good of the shortening of the hours of labor both by legislative enactment and by collective organization. [. . .] Seven o'clock in the morning is too early for any rational human being to be herded into a factory at the call of a steam whistle. Ten hours a day of mechanical task is too long: nine hours is too long: eight hours is too long. I am not raising here the question as to how and to what extent the eight hours can be shortened, but only urging the primary need of recognizing that a working day of eight hours is too long for the full and proper development of human capacity and for the rational enjoyment of life. [. . .]

The shortening of the general hours of work, then, should be among the primary aims of social reform. There need be no fear that with shortened hours of labor the sum total of production would fall short of human needs. This, as has been shown from beginning to end of this essay, is out of the question. Human *desires* would eat up the result of ten times the work we now accomplish. Human *needs* would be satisfied with a fraction of it. But the real difficulty in the shortening of hours lies elsewhere. Here, as in the parallel case of the minimum wage, the danger is that the attempt to alter things too rapidly may dislocate the industrial machine. We ought to attempt such a shortening as will strain the machine to a breaking point, but never break it. This can be done, as with the minimum wage, partly by positive legislation and partly collective action. Not much can be done at once. But the process can be continuous. The short hours achieved with acclamation to-day will later be denounced as the long hours of to-morrow. The essential point to grasp, however, is that society at large has nothing to lose by the process.

The shortened hours become a part of the framework of production. It adapts itself to it. Hitherto we have been caught in the running of our own machine: it is time that we altered the gearing of it.

The two cases selected—the minimum wage and the legislative shortening of hours—have been chosen merely as illustrations and are not exhaustive of the things that can be done in the field of possible and practical reform. It is plain enough that in many other directions the same principles may be applied. The rectification of the ownership of land so as to eliminate the haphazard gains of the speculator and the unearned increment of wealth created by the efforts of others, is an obvious case in point. The "single taxer" sees in this a cure-all for the ills of society. But his vision is distorted. The private ownership of land is one of the greatest incentives to human effort that the world has ever known. It would be folly to abolish it, even if we could. But here as elsewhere we can seek to re-define and regulate the conditions of ownership so as to bring them more into keeping with a common sense view of social justice.

But the inordinate and fortuitous gains from land are really only one example from a general class. The war discovered the "profiteer". The law-makers of the world are busy now with smoking him out from his lair. But he was there all the time. Inordinate and fortuitous gain, resting on such things as monopoly, or trickery, or the mere hazards of abundance and scarcity, complying with the letter of the law but violating its spirit, are fit objects for appropriate taxation. The ways and means are difficult, but the social principle involved is clear.

We may thus form some sort of vision of the social future into which we are passing. The details are indistinct. But the outline at least in which it is framed is clear enough. The safety of the future lies in a progressive movement of social control alleviating the misery which it cannot obliterate and based upon the broad general principle of equality of opportunity. The chief immediate direction of social effort should be towards the attempt to give to every human being in childhood adequate food, clothing, education and an opportunity in life. This will prove to be the beginning of many things.

Historical Interpretations

3 From Paul La Verdure, "Sunday in Quebec, 1907–1937," *CCHA, Historical Studies*, 62 (1996): 47–61.

When representatives of the Toronto-based Lord's Day Alliance rushed on Ottawa in 1906 to have the Lord's Day Bill made into law, Roman Catholics and Anglicans opposed Presbyterian and Methodist attempts to make Canada righteous by force of law. Under Henri Bourassa's leadership, French Canadians arguing for the rights of conscience and provincial autonomy in the Lord's Day debate of 1906 opposed English Protestant desires for a uniform Canadian day of rest. An amendment, sponsored mainly by Quebec's Roman Catholic members of parliament, gave the administration of the 1906 Lord's Day Act to the Attorney-General of each province. This guaranteed that Quebec could ignore the Lord's Day Act. Furthermore, just before the federal act came into effect in 1907, Quebec passed a considerably watered-down provincial law that guaranteed individuals, Jews or Seventh-Day Adventists, for example, the right to work on Sunday if their consciences forced them to rest on some other day. Quebec in effect passed a weak provincial Sunday law to take precedence over the stricter federal law. Quebec legislated Sunday as the common rest day if no other day was chosen by the individual. Protestants through the Lord's Day Alliance could well try to enforce a sabbatarian version of a Christian Canada in other provinces, but not in Quebec. All of this began to change soon after the First World War.

A form of Catholic sabbatarianism had grown out of Quebec's answer to the challenges of industrialization and urbanization. An organized Catholic sabbatarianism was a later development in Canadian life than Protestant sabbatarianism because, unlike Protestant sabbatarians, Roman Catholics did not base their Sunday claims entirely on a literal biblical interpretation. Very much like Protestant sabbatarianism, however, after initial successes, it rapidly withered in the political arena.

In 1910, a Jesuit, Léonidas Hudon, reformed the League of the Sacred Heart, a prayer society, and linked it to other Catholic societies to become a lobby group and a force in Quebec.[1] Hudon's successor as chaplain to the League of the Sacred Heart was another Jesuit, Joseph-Papin Archambault. [. . .] On taking over the League of the Sacred Heart, Archambault concentrated on more education for the Catholic laity in the practical application of Roman Catholic teachings in the Canadian context.[2] Using Belgian and Dutch Jesuit examples, Archambault promoted intense closed monastic retreats during the First World War. In these retreats, where his knowledge and small intimate talks offset his speaking voice, prayer, fasting, and readings from the Bible alternated with the study of European Catholic Action principles, authors, and techniques.[3]

After the First World War, highly sen-
sitized retreatants crept out from their
self-imposed monastic silence to propose
an articulate Catholic critique of Quebec
society. Archambault emerged as the pre-
eminent theorist of Catholic Action and
went on to organize the "Semaines sociales"
(Social Weeks) beginning in 1920. These
almost annual conferences brought several
members of the Catholic elite—clergy, bishops, religious, and lay people—together to
renew the intense educational experiences of
the retreat and to spread these teachings to a
wider audience.[4] Archambault himself spoke
little but chose many of the speakers and the
topics. The 1920 conference studied Pope Leo
XIII's *Rerum novarum* of 1891 and touched on
issues which would occupy Quebec labour
unions for the next 40 years.[5] For example,
the 1920 speakers called for the 6-day and
the 48-hour work week.

Two of the 1922 Social Week talks about
capital and labour dealt with Sunday. The first
talk presented the biblical and church texts,
from Genesis to Leo XIII, that established
Sunday as a day of physical and social rest for
divine worship. The second talk, by the Vicar
General of Chicoutimi, Eugène Lapointe,
claimed that Sunday work in Quebec's factories and the pulp and paper industries
destroyed workers' health, home, and spiritual
lives.[6] Immediately, the Social Week executive
approached the episcopate of Quebec for their
leadership on the Sunday problem.[7]

On 18 April 1922, the bishops of Quebec published a pastoral letter on Sunday's
importance. The letter had three sections.
The first section set out the theory of Catholic
Sunday observance. The theory emphasized
attendance at religious services—as opposed
to the strict sabbath rest observance of the
Jews and the Protestants—and argued this
position from the Bible, Thomas Aquinas, the
Plenary Council of Quebec and, naturally,
Leo XIII's *Rerum Novarum*.

The second section spoke to employers in
general and argued that Sunday desecration

was a willful social sickness tempting God's
punishment. On a practical note, the letter
also stated that Sunday rest could be useful in keeping workers content while it also
allowed time for worship and religious services. The bishops warned employers that if
workers were not given the chance to rest and
to go to religious services, God's punishment
would come from revolutionary, dechristian-
ized workers breaking down the social order.
Although communism was not mentioned,
the recent Russian Revolution and the Winnipeg General Strike were not far from everyone's thinking. The bishops recommended
to employers a strict observance of rest from
midnight Saturday to midnight Sunday. In
an oblique reference to the Jews, the bishops
called upon the civil power to ensure that
non-Christians did not require work from
Christians.

The third section declared that all those
who missed Sunday Mass, especially those
who missed Mass for excursions, theatre
shows, and professional sports, were in mor-
tal sin. Excursions, innocent entertainments,
and sports in themselves were not sinful;
they were permissible on Sundays but only
after all obligations to God had been fulfilled.
The bishops concluded that Sunday observance brought honour to the parish, strength
to the family, and blessings on the nation.[8]
The comments about the permissibility of
innocent amusements and the appeal to the
Roman Catholic Church's authority marked
the only Catholic differences with the Protestant Lord's Day alliance view of Sunday.

The bishops had also given the signal that the time for study was over. An ad
hoc committee in the city of Quebec then
successfully prosecuted Sunday theatres.[9]
To coordinate the ad hoc prosecutions, on
16 April 1923, Archambault brought 50 people together in the basement of the Gesù, the
Jesuit-run parish church in downtown Montreal. Representatives of the main Montreal
Catholic societies, many of them former
retreatants, attended. [. . .][10] A constitution

for the new Ligue du Dimanche, drafted by Archambault, was approved and so the Ligue du Dimanche was born.

The Ligue accepted individuals and organizations as members. Members signed a pledge not to work on Sundays, not to employ anyone on Sundays, not to go to theatres on Sundays, to fight Sunday work by any means, and to follow directives from the Ligue du Dimanche.[11] Only practising Catholics were allowed to join and the League restricted itself to Quebec where the majority of Canada's Catholics lived. The Ligue's goal was to have the Sunday laws enforced and Sunday observed according to Church law and teachings. To do this, the League continued to study Sunday work, educate lay people through conferences, tracts, newspaper articles, congresses, and local committees, and lobby the government through petitions. Its central organization was divided into three major urban and ecclesiastical committees: Montreal, Trois-Rivières, and Quebec City. Montreal, the largest city of French Canada, was the seat of the central committee. Montreal provided the secretary, most of the executive officers, and the chaplain: Joseph-Papin Archambault.

The first targets of the Ligue du Dimanche's Catholic Action crusade were the pulp and paper mills. Quebec's Cardinal Louis-Nazaire Bégin wrote a pastoral letter on May Day 1923, a traditional labour holiday and the feast of St Joseph the worker, advising all workers to quit their jobs when forced to work on Sundays. Montreal's Archbishop Georges Gauthier directed his clergy to instruct the faithful in their Sunday duties.[12] Monseigneur Eugène Lapointe of Chicoutimi urged immediate political action against the Price Paper Company.[13] Surviving documents show that the Quebec committee alone amassed over 6700 members and gathered resolutions against Sunday work from 211 municipalities. The pressure from so many Catholic organizations culminated in a visit by a delegation from the Ligue du Dimanche to Quebec's Liberal Premier Louis-Alexandre Taschereau.[14] In alarm, the pulp, flour, and glass mills appealed to Taschereau to recognize that their particular industries required Sunday work. They gained a slight reprieve while the government studied the situation.[15] Throughout 1924, the pressure on Taschereau mounted higher. *Le Soleil, Le Droit, Le Devoir, Le Colon, La Patrie, La Presse, Le Canada, Le Bien Public, L'Action Catholique, L'Étoile Du Nord*, and *Le Nouvelliste* published articles, editorials, and letters in June and July of 1924 all in favour of Sunday laws.[16] Also in 1924, Archambault published a pamphlet *Contre le travail du dimanche* in the Catholic Action series, *L'Oeuvre des Tracts*. The League, he declared, was founded to prevent people from becoming industrial slaves. Why did the transportation industry insist on working Sundays? Why did factories run until 4 or 6 AM on Sunday and start again at 4 or 6 PM? Money, he answered in disgust! In one of the 1925 Social Week conferences, a speaker complained that the provincial law did not allow the full severity of the Mosaic law to fall upon Sunday transgressors: death.[17] Public opinion became so insistent that Premier Taschereau wrote to the pulp and paper companies that the provincial law, ignored in the past, would be enforced against them in future.

Each company promised to stop work on Sundays, but each had its own way of interpreting the law. The Saint-Maurice Pulp and Paper Company cleaned machines for six hours after shutting down at midnight Saturday and then spent another six hours before Sunday midnight in preparation for the week. The International Paper Company spent the morning in repairs and began work again at 4 PM. The St Lawrence Paper Company began repair work at 8 AM. The Wayagamack shut down from 8 AM to 3 PM. Sunday. The same half-hearted attempts to comply with the letter of the law could be seen at Laurentide, Price Brothers, Eddy, Booth, International, and Canada Cement.[18] A 1926 provincial

commission of inquiry into Sunday observance in the pulp and paper industry exerted
additional pressure on the companies, but
unsuccessfully.[19] The mills were too powerful in isolated regions of Quebec where
their rule was law. The Ligue du Dimanche
published a small book, *Le Repos Dominical,* in 1927. Archambault, of course, wrote
the introduction; the conclusion insisted on
government intervention. Finally, in 1927
Taschereau started prosecutions against factories that refused to close.[20] It had been
almost five years since the Semaine Sociale
and the pastoral letter of 1922. Fortunately
for the companies, the fines were so small
that the prosecutions were ignored.

Cases against theatres, instigated by
English-speaking Quebeckers, had periodically dragged through the reluctant courts.[21]
Between four and five o'clock on Sunday afternoon, the 9th of January 1927, a fire broke
out in Montreal's Laurier Palace Theatre.
Seventy-eight children between the ages of 5
and 16 years of age suffocated or were tram-
pled to death. More were injured. The shock
forced a provincial commission of inquiry. All
Catholic organizations, unions, and the press
joined the Ligue du Dimanche in asking for
Sunday theatre closings.[22] From the moment
the ashes cooled until the commission's final
report, the Montreal diocesan newspaper,
La Semaine Religieuse, called for the closing of
all theatres on Sundays and for the exclusion
of children from the theatres at all times. The
fire, said militant Catholics, was a punishment from God for the theatres' Sunday desecration.[23] The Retail Merchants Association
and the international labour organizations
protested, the former for profitable motives,
the latter to provide entertainment to people
who did not want to go to Mass.

The Laurier Palace Theatre Commission
examined the reasons why films were so popular that people would ignore their priests'
anathemas. It concluded that immorality, free
love, adultery, divorce, thefts, murders, sui-
cides, and, more importantly, the depiction of

people flouting legal and religious authority
attracted paying customers. Although the federal 1906 law forbad Sunday theatrical shows
entirely, the Lord's Day Alliance request that
the stricter federal law be enforced was not
discussed. Perhaps the government realized
that it could not stop people from watching films. Still, the Roman Catholic Church
insisted that the portrayal of unpunished
immorality promoted disrespect for authority. Since both church and state were able to
agree that children's respect for authority was
important, on August 30, after the 1927 provincial elections were safely won, the judge
recommended that children be denied entry
into theatres. Although the Laurier Palace
Theatre had been overcrowded, badly ven-
tilated, and had had too few exits, building
safety standards were never discussed in the
report. The Taschereau government introduced a law forbidding entry into theatres
to children under the age of 16. This legislation implied that Sunday shows were legal for
everyone over 15, in spite of the 1906 federal
Lord's Day Act which outlawed all Sunday
shows.

This new legislation angered the bishops so much that their sabbatarianism took
an extreme direction. All of the bishops and
archbishops of Quebec signed another pastoral letter which denounced all Sunday activities, even those raising money for charity.
"If need be," the bishops wrote, "use the civil
law, and if it is again successfully avoided, we
are sure our legislators will dutifully amend,
refine, strengthen, and give the law effective
penalties."[24] Clearly, if Taschereau's Liberals
were slow to close the theatres, the bishops
were prepared to support another set of legislators who would.[25] Taschereau began a new
series of prosecutions. Only one prosecution
forced a theatre to close in 1929.[26]

In the late 1920s, the sabbatarians turned
to another target. A Ligue du Dimanche
investigation showed that many small Jewish businesses were open both Saturdays and
Sundays. The Quebec Sunday law allowed

Jews to do business on Sunday if for conscience's sake they did not do business on Saturday and did not disturb anyone in their own Sunday rest. Jews were allowed to work on Saturday or on Sunday but not on both.[27] As conspiracy theories and the publication of anti-Semitic books and newspapers flourished, Ligue members saw Jews behind every evil. The Ligue du Dimanche thought it saw Jews owning the pulp and paper mills and forcing good French-Canadian Christians to work on the holy day of Sunday. Looking closely at the theatres, the Ligue saw Jewish owners or film makers tempting the morals of Canadian Catholic youth.[28] Finally, looking closely at the little shops of St-Laurent Boulevard and Sherbrooke Street in Montreal, spy squads of Catholic Action members could see the Jews working both Saturdays and Sundays. This put stores owned by French Canadians, supposedly working only six days in the week, at a competitive disadvantage. Montreal's courts began to condemn Jew after Jew for petty Sunday offences.[29]

In 1929, Archambault instituted "le mois du dimanche" (Sunday month) and dedicated the entire month of April to Sunday observance. Every Catholic liturgical celebration on every day in April was taken up with the Sunday question. Schools were asked to set assignments and exams with Sunday as their topic. Songs were composed, poems and stories were written, prayers were said. Every pope's pronouncement was brought out; every bishop's pastoral was studied again; every saint who had ever said anything about Sunday was brought forward for veneration. Over 60 monthly magazines and over 50 weekly and daily newspapers participated. The Sunday month was in the middle of the provincial election. Both political parties promised to do their utmost to enforce the provincial and the federal Sunday laws. The month's campaign was a resounding success.[30] Once re-elected, the Taschereau government named two Sunday law inspectors, both men recommended by the Ligue du

Dimanche, to travel the province. Ironically, both men worked Sundays. In memory of this outpouring of public opinion, the Ligue du Dimanche promoted a "Semaine du dimanche" (Sunday week) every year from 1930 to 1960, similar to the Alliance's Lord's Day Week in the rest of Canada.

As the Depression descended on Quebec, an avalanche of complaints about the Jews poured into the Ligue's offices. The president of the Fédération Nationale Saint-Jean-Baptiste, Marie Gérin-Lajoie, known for her women's suffrage position, wrote to the Ligue du Dimanche pledging her personal support and her organization to the Ligue in its fight against the Jews.[31] Newspapers as diverse as the right-wing *L'Action Catholique,* the liberal *Le Progrès du Saguenay,* and Adrien Arcand's fascist *Le Miroir* published articles against the Jewish exemption clause.[32]

The flash point occurred when Allan Bray, president of the City of Montreal's executive committee, stated that since the Jews celebrated New Year's on Saturday, 21 September 1930, and closed their stores on that day, they could open their stores on the following Sunday.[33] The campaign against the Jews took on new dimensions. The Ligue du Dimanche again entered the political arena to pressure the City of Montreal to reverse its decision. Mr Bray reassured the Ligue du Dimanche that Montreal had been busy with over 148 Sunday cases in the preceding six months, most of them involving Jews. The Ligue complained that the number of cases against the Jews was too low; Catholic Action squads had discovered 134 more cases in one day in only one area of Montreal.[34] The Confédération des Travailleurs Catholiques du Canada, the Knights of Columbus, the Fédération des Ouvriers du Canada, and other organizations called for the repeal of the provincial law so that Quebec would fall under the stricter federal law.[35] Maurice Duplessis, the Conservative from Trois-Rivières, pledged his support to the Ligue du Dimanche and was duly enrolled as an honorary member.[36] When the

Catholic youth group, Jeune Canada, com-plained loudly and irrationally that the fed-eral Lord's Day Act was used only to persecute French Canadians while English-speaking Jews were left alone, the provincial govern-ment prepared a confidential study about recent prosecutions.

The secret study found that only three per cent of all cases in all of Quebec involved French Canadians. The vast majority involved Jews. The rest were Italians, Greeks, and English-speaking Canadians. The government commissioned the report in order to prove that it was not party to an anti-French federal cam-paign; it proved instead that the provincial and municipal governments of Quebec condoned an anti-Jewish campaign.[37] The records of the Montreal courts from 1930 to 1932 were a roll call of the Jews of Montreal. Jews were allowed to open stores on Sunday; but if they sold on both Saturday and Sunday, they were prose-cuted. If they employed non-Jews or if they sold to non-Jews on Sundays, they were pros-ecuted. If they did anything besides selling on Sundays to Jews, they were prosecuted—making criminals of almost all of the Jewish storekeepers of Montreal.[38] Although there was evidence that many French-Canadian shops also kept open, very few of these were prosecuted. Jewish storekeepers said nothing, paid the fines, and often closed their doors, working five days a week instead of their com-petitors' six.[39] The French Catholic organiza-tions still demanded the repeal of the Jewish exemption clause. The Lord's Day Alliance, writing from Toronto on behalf of Quebec's English Protestants, happily wished the Ligue du Dimanche success in suppressing the Jew-ish exemption clause.[40]

Archambault asked the secretary of the Ligue du Dimanche to write to the premier of Quebec formally asking that the Jewish exemption clause be stricken from Quebec's Sunday law. The idea of Jews working on Sunday was "against the spirit of our legisla-tion based on Christian principles and con-trary to good order."[41] A threat of unforeseen

consequences, of civil disorder, and of riots underlay the demand. Adrien Arcand openly stated that his fascist followers were prepared to beat up Jews that opened on Sundays.[42] Taschereau bargained for time by replying that the provincial government could not repeal a statutory clause recognized by the federal government.[43] When the Ligue turned to the federal authorities, the federal lawyers strongly and unhesitatingly argued that Que-bec had the right to repeal the clause without asking federal permission.[44] Obviously, the federal government did not wish to bring the touchy religious issue into the federal arena.

In May 1935, Maurice Duplessis and his colleague, Jean-Paul Sauvé, again brought the question of the Jewish exemption clause into the Quebec legislature. Taschereau out-flanked the demand by staging a success-ful majority vote to submit the question to Quebec's Court of Appeal. This move bought Taschereau the chance to hold another elec-tion during which he could promise to repeal the clause if the courts decided that he could. He obviously preferred not to abolish pro-vincial and civil rights so hard won by Henri Bourassa and Quebec's Liberals many years before while Taschereau had been a younger and more idealistic parliamentarian. The Ligue du Dimanche's lawyer, Antonio Per-rault, a professor of civil law at the University of Montreal, claimed that the Attorney-General of Quebec (in this case, Premier Taschereau) had absolute control over the provincial law and administrative authority over the federal law. It was Taschereau's right to repeal the Jewish exemption clause in the provincial law. The provincial court agreed.[45] Although the case was heard in October, the ruling was postponed until December 3, con-veniently after the November 25 elections. Taschereau returned to power with a slim six-seat majority.

During that campaign, the Union Natio-nale party headed by Maurice Duplessis had insisted on the immediate repeal of the Jewish exemption clause. This helped to win

the clergy's endorsement of the Union Nationale. Taschereau bowed to the politically
inevitable. By declaring that he really had
no objections to repealing the exemption,
he hung on to some of his followers ready
to defect to the growing Union Nationale.[46]
The Jewish exemption clause was repealed on
10 June 1936.[47] The disintegration of the
Quebec Liberal Party, the stress of a declining
majority in the legislature, and perhaps the
abandonment of principles for which he had
previously fought led Taschereau to resign
the next day.

Against the factories, against the movies, and against the Jews, Quebec's Ligue du
Dimanche had successfully applied encyc-
lical, pastoral, and sermon to form a united
Catholic Action movement. Joseph-Papin
Archambault educated a Catholic laity,
organized it, affiliated it with Catholic organizations across Quebec, inspired it and,
leading from behind, urged it to create a
Catholic Quebec. The Ligue du Dimanche
used Duplessis against an aging, weakening
Liberal government to legislate the morals of
a Quebec nation in which Catholicism and
the Ten Commandments would form the
constitution of the nation. Instead, Duplessis
successfully used the Ligue as one of his tools
in gaining power.

The similarities of Quebec's experiences
to early battles by the Lord's Day Alliance are
striking. Catholic Action groups were rather
like English Canada's social gospellers in
using government power for religious ends.[48]
Ironically, too, the democratic creation of a
Catholic Christian day of rest, like Canada's
Lord's Day, also meant the coercion of dissident Christians and Jews. Those who refused
to comply with the law were prosecuted and
fined or jailed. The Ligue du Dimanche was
a youthful, Quebec version of the Lord's
Day Alliance, willing to do battle with all
and sundry for Christian civilization. In the
interests of uniformity within Quebec, the
provincial Sunday law of Quebec had been
shorn of the Jewish exemption clause which

had distinguished Quebec from the rest of
Canada. In the first half of the twentieth century, Quebec's Catholic Action paralleled the
Canadian Protestant social gospel battles to
create a uniform, righteous and Sabbatarian
nation.[49] Maurice Duplessis gained power
with the help of the Sunday law issue. Yet,
under Duplessis, although Sunday morning
activities were prosecuted so that religious
services were the only activities permitted,
no prosecutions were allowed against afternoon activities. The theatres slowly reopened
and the pulp and paper companies went on
their unimpeded way and in 1937 there
were over 120 cases against the mills. Price
Brothers Paper Company ignored the law
in 1937 and, in 1938, was fined 50 dollars
under the Lord's Day Act.[50] Recognizing
that the penalties needed to be increased,
the Ligue turned to the federal parliament.
A private member's bill was amended almost
out of existence.[51] Neither the federal nor
the Duplessis government wanted to hamper companies bringing in needed capital
and jobs during the 1930s. The Sunday law
inspectors' salaries went unpaid. Duplessis
became unavailable for Ligue interviews. His
assistant instructed the inspectors to ignore
the major companies and concentrate on
closing small businesses, such as pool halls,
in the towns, during Mass times.[52] The Ligue
du Dimanche had to content itself with prosecuting weak minorities, such as the Jews.

Prophetically, Chicoutimi's Monseigneur
Eugene Lapointe castigated the Ligue for
allowing itself to be deflected from its original mission against the inhuman pulp and
paper mills employing thousands of Roman
Catholics. [. . .] He said: "We are deluding
ourselves when we say that we have won anything in this 20-year struggle against Sunday
work. We have won nothing, or so little that
it might as well be nothing. The present situation, this Depression, caused less Sunday
work. That's all!"[53]

As the 1930s slipped by, and the failure of the Sunday campaign became more

apparent, fewer members attended Ligue du Dimanche meetings. People resigned to join other crusades, such as the one against communism.[54] Of the original members, only Archambault was left and he was often busy with other meetings, retreats, and "Semaines Sociales". Few fought "atheistic communism" and "anarcho-jewish socialism" with the same fervour as did Archambault and his retreatants. Overall, Quebec's national Sunday became much less important than the struggle against "Jewish-inspired" communism being waged in Franco's Spain. . .

All that remained to defend Quebec's hothouse sabbatarianism was a skeleton organization that met weekly, then monthly, then seasonally. The Duplessis government had been elected with the help of Sunday votes, yet the people of Quebec continued to work on Sundays, go to hockey games, sometimes to the theatre, and occasionally stopped at the shop after Sunday Mass. The Ligue du Dimanche had gone into the political arena and, to defeat the Liberal government, had transferred its hopes, its moral authority, and its power to the Duplessisgovernment. Now they were left with nothing as the Duplessis government and the people of Quebec ignored the Ligue du Dimanche in favour of other, more pressing secular problems. By 1937, Quebec went to work or play on Sunday, much as it had done in 1907 after the passage of the Lord's Day Act. Organized Roman Catholic sabbatarianism was a short-lived movement in Quebec.

NOTES

1. Joseph-Papin Archambault, SJ, "Les trois phases de l'École Sociale Populaire," *Les vingt-cinq ans de l'École Sociale Populaire. 1911–1936. Une oeuvre de doctrine et de salut*, École Sociale Populaire, vol. 269–70 (juin–juillet 1936), pp. 42–50; also Archives of the French-Canadian Province of the Society of Jesus, Record Group 3, Joseph-Papin Archambault, SJ, Papers, boxes 34–46 (abbreviated hereafter as JPA, box number-file number, item number) JPA, 38-5,1-32, in which Archambault's sermon plans about Sunday observance were published in the *Bulletin de la Ligue du Sacré Coeur* (1914), p. 180, and in other religious newspapers.

2. Archambault, *La Question Sociale et nos Devoirs catholiques*. II. École Sociale Populaire: vol. 66 (Montreal 1917), p. 37. I am indebted to the Rev. Fr. Joseph Cossette, SJ, former archivist of the French Canadian Province of the Society of Jesus, for this description of Archambault.

3. Archambault, *L'Organisation ouvrière catholique en Hollande*, École Sociale Populaire: vol. 1 (Montreal 1911): 29p.; JPA, 39-1, 38, "L'Observation du Dimanche" in *Le Bulletin des Directeurs* (August–September 1912); Archambault, *La Villa St. Martin. Retraites Fermées pour les Hommes* (Abord-à-Plouffe, 1922), 24p.; *Figures Catholiques. Préface du Juge Thomas Tremblay* (Montreal 1950), 192p.

4. An ideological analysis is available in Richard Jones, *L'Idéologie de L'ACTION CATHOLIQUE (1917–1939)* (Quebec 1974).

5. *Rerum Novarum* 1920; Unions 1921; Capital and Labour 1922; The Family 1923; Property 1924; Justice 1925; Authority 1927; The Economic Problem 1928; The City 1929; The State 1931; The Christian Social Order 1932; The Land Problem 1933; Social Education 1935; Professional Organization 1936; Cooperation 1937; For a Christian Society 1938; The Christian in the Family 1940; Catholic Action and Social Action 1941; Democracy 1942; Temperance 1943; Colonization Congress 1943; Social Restoration 1944; Liberty and liberties 1945; Youth 1946; Rural Life 1947; Peace 1948; Work and Leisure 1949; The Home 1950.

6. École Sociale Populaire, *Semaines Sociales du Canada. IIIe Session . . . Ottawa 1922 Capital et Travail. Compte rendu des Cours et Conférences.* (Montreal: Bibliothèque de l'Action française, 1923); "Le Repos du Dimanche. Principes—Avantages," by the Rev. Fr. Trudeau, O.P.,

pp. 112–31; "Le Travail du dimanche dans notre industrie" by Mgr Eugène Lapointe, pp. 132–49.

7. Archambault, *Contre le travail du dimanche. La Ligue du Dimanche* (Montreal: 1924), pp. 8–9.

8. JPA, 34-5,5, "Lettre Pastorale de Son Eminence Le Cardinal Louis-Nazaire Bégin, Archevêque de Québec, et de Nos Seigneurs les Archevêques et Evêques de la province Ecclésiastique de Québec sur La transgression du devoir dominical," (18 April 1922): 12p.

9. Lord's Day Alliance of Canada Papers, Manuscript Collection 129 of the Thomas Fisher Rare Book Library, University of Toronto (hereafter LDA) box 155, *Quebec Chronicle*, 4 October 1922, "Lord's Day Act To Be Enforced. Legal Action To Be Taken Against Theatre Proprietors For Opening On Sundays." Sir F.-X. Lemieux, Chief Justice of the Superior Court, Hon. Nemèse Garneau, Rev. Fr. Philippe Casgrain, etc., were members of the powerful committee.

10. JPA, 34-5,7, "La Ligue du Dimanche, Fondation." The Central committee was the Rev. Fr. Edmour Hébert, Adélard Dugré, SJ, Alfred Bernier of the A.C.V., and the lawyer and V.P. of the S.S.J.B., Jean-Chrysostome Martineau. Others recruited the following day were Judge Edouard Fabre-Surveyer, the President General of the Saint Vincent de Paul Conferences of Montreal, M. Julien, the lawyer Arthur Laramée, the businessman Paul Joubert, Wilfrid Déziel, Edgar Genest, the secretary of the Syndicats catholiques, Gérard Tremblay, the notary Beaudoin, J.-W. Cadieux, and the editor of *Le Devoir*, Omer Héroux.

11. JPA, 34-5,6 "Statuts et Règlements de La Ligue du Dimanche."

12. JPA, 45-4,1, 26 [October?] 1923 to Judge Dorion, President of the Ligue; LDA 153, Montreal Gazette, I May 1923, "Lord's Day Observance. Cardinal Begin Sends Pastoral Letter to Workers"; *Lord's Day Advocate* (Newspaper published by the Lord's Day Alliance of Canada. New Series Vol. I:1-XXII:12 [1903–1926]) (hereafter ADV) XIX:7 (July 1923) "Quebec"; LDA 153, *Montreal Gazette*, 28 May 1923, "Labor On Sunday Matter of Inquiry"; Mandements. *Lettres Pastorales et Circulaires des Evêques de Montréal* vol. 17 (21 November 1922): p. 103.

13. JPA, 34-5,23, Lapointe to Adélard Dugré, SJ, 7 October 1923.

14. JPA, 34-5,27, Ernest Moreau to Martineau, secretary of the Ligue du Dimanche, 22 November 1923. Also JPA, 34-5,28-30 and National Archives of Quebec (hereafter NAQ), E17-410, files 4288, 4289, 4290, and 4306; E17 Indexes show that from 1919 to 1931, the pulp and paper mills caused the most complaints.

15. JPA, 45-2 and 45-3,2, Lapointe to the Ligue du Dimanche, 13 October 1924.

16. E.g. LDA 157, *Le Nouvelliste* of Trois-Rivières, 7 April 1924, "Peut-on Arreter Le Travail Du Dimanche?"; 13 May 1924 "Pas De Solution. Les Compagnies Et Le Travail Du Dimanche. Elles ne voient pas comment l'état de choses actuel pourrait être modifié" quoting James Murray of International Paper Co.; National Archives of Canada, RG 13 A2, vol. 369, file 152, "Lord's Day Act. Sundry questions. Consolidated fyle": City Clerk, Montreal to the Secretary of State, 8 November 1923; Secretary-Archivist, Knights of Columbus, Shawinigan Falls to the Minister of Justice, 1 December 1923; Vol. 282, file 1827, Municipal Council of Shawinigan Falls to the Minister of Justice, Sir Lomer Gouin, 22 October 1923. For an excellent summary of newspaper opinions on both sides of the Quebec Sunday debate, see Antonin Dupont, *Les relations entre l'Église et l'État sous Louis-Alexandre Taschereau 1920–1936* (Montreal: 1973), pp. 145–74.

17. "With what force, even today, would the priest's voice penetrate the soul if, at the foot of the pulpit stood a vengeful judge able to emprison the heartless masters who build their hateful fortunes on the souls' ruin!" Simon Lapointe, "La Justice et la sanctification du dimanche," École Sociale Populaire, *Semaines Sociales du Canada. . . . Trois-Rivières 1925. La Justice* (Montreal: 1925), p. 314 [my translation].

18. JPA, 34-5,63, Taschereau to Pulp and Paper Makers, September 1926; JPA, 34-5,76, "Le Travail du dimanche. Dans l'industrie de la Pulpe et du Papier"; 41-12,20, Fr. Joseph Bonhomme, OMI, to Archambault, I1 October 1926.

19. NAQ, E17-509, file 1532, "Report of Inquiry," 4 March 1926.

20. ADV XXII:2 (February 1926) "The Tide Turns"; e.g. NAQ, E17-1479, file 6202, Report re Harricanna Mines, 8 September 1928.

21. NAQ, E17-1469, file 1C26-1414A, Index for 1918, and files 363, 365, 366, etc.; ADV XV:6 (July 1919) "It was a Famous Victory."

22. École Sociale Populaire, *Dimanche vs Cinéma (les articles publiés dans la Semaine Religieuse du 20 janvier au 14 juillet 1927)* (Montreal: 1927); also NAQ, E26-35, 223-1, 12 May 1927.

23. JPA, 34-5,81, "Le Travail Du Dimanche," broadsheet originally published in *Le Bien Public*, 25 January 1927.

24. JPA, 34-5,88, "Lettre Pastorale de Nos Seigneurs les Archevêques et Evêques de la Province civile de Québec, sur la Sanctification du Dimanche" (21 November 1927), p. 65 [my translation].

25. "Le dimanche et le cinéma," *La Semaine Religieuse de Montréal* vol. 88:23 (6 June 1929), praised the provincial government which, under Duplessis' pressure, forbad Sunday theatres.

26. *Marin v. United Amusement Corpn.* 1929.

27. "Les Juifs sont la prudence même: quelques-uns ne vendent, le dimanche, qu'à leurs core-ligionnaires": Archambault, *Contre le travail du dimanche* (1924), p. 5.

28. *La Semaine Religieuse de Montréal* vol. 86:35 (1 September 1927): "After the conclusions from the cinema investigation," the editor wrote, "Let us admit that the Jews and the Greeks opening their shops on Sunday have been lucky!" [my translation]. NAQ, E171478, "Index 1927"; E17-1479, "Index 1928."

29. *Rex v. Levinson* 1924; NAQ, E17-481, item 236, *Eugene Bond v. Recorder of Montreal* 1925; other cases against Jews: see E17-1477, "Index 1926."

30. JPA, 39-2,2, Archambault, *Le mois du dimanche* (Montreal: L'Oeuvre des Tracts no. 117, 1929), 16p.; also Antonin Dupont, p. 163; politicking: 35-1,9, Guy Bolduc, Secretary Treasurer of the Village and Parish of Ste-Anne-de-Beaupré to J.-C. Martineau, Secretary of the Ligue du Dimanche, 4 May 1929; 35-1,16, L.-P. Lévesque, C.Ss.R., Rector of Ste-Anne-de-Beaupré, to M. Rodolphe Godin, Secretary-General of the Association Catholique de la Jeunesse Canadienne-française—Montréal, 15 May 1929.

31. JPA, 35-2,45, 9 March 1932.

32. JPA, 43-1,1-108 and 43-7,54, *Montreal Herald*, 2 December 1930; a systematic summary of newspaper articles in Dupont, pp. 145–74.

33. "Le travail du dimanche. Autour d'une fausse manoeuvre," *La Semaine religieuse de Montréal* vol. 89:40 (2 October 1930).

34. JPA, 44-4,1, 4, 9, and 36, correspondence between de la Rochelle and Bray, beginning 7 October 1930.

35. JPA, 43-1,58, *L'Action catholique*, 13 December 1934, "L'abrogation de la loi qui permet aux Juifs . . . "; pp. 44-4,100-41.

36. JPA, 35-2,9, Duplessis to the Secretary of the Ligue, 26 January 1932; 35-2,136, "Rapport des Activités Generales du Comité Regional Trifluvien de la Ligue du Dimanche pour l'année 1932," 14 January 1933.

37. NAQ, E17-793, file 475, memorandum, 20 December 1933.

38. NAQ, E17-2150, "Infractions à la loi du 38 dimanche"; and E17-1485, file 1301.

39. David Rome, *The Jewish Congress Archival Record of 1936. With a report on Sabbath Rest (in lieu of a Preface)* (Montreal: 1978), p. 1, and Rome, *Jewish Archival Record of 1935. With Preface by Victor Sefton* (Montreal: 1976), p. ix; JPA, 43-1,100, *Montreal Gazette*, 19 December 1938, "Observance of Sunday Is Urged Upon Jews." The Ligue so often promoted and participated in anti-Semitic campaigns that Betcherman went so far as to label it fascist, but with little other evidence: *The Swastika and the Maple Leaf* (Toronto: 1975), p. 39.

40. JPA, 35-2,193, Huestis to de la Rochelle, 23 May 1933.

41. JPA, 44-4,68, Archambault to de la Rochelle, 3 March 1933.

42. For Arcand, see Rome, *The Jewish Congress Archival Record of 1936*; pp. 5A, 12A, 13A, 22A; and for Laurendeau: p. 17A.

43. National Archives of Canada, RG 13 A2, vol. 400, file 406, 12 March 1934, the Attorney-General of Quebec to the Minister of Justice, 12 March 1934; "Note concernant la demande d'abrogation de l'article de la Loi du dimanche (S.R.Q., 1925, c.199)," 20 June 1934.

44. National Archives of Canada, RG 13 A2, vol. 44 400, file 406, "Memo . . . for Mr. Edwards," 12 July 1934.

45. For the arguments, NAQ, E17-989, file 3836, "Mémoire soumis par Maitre Antonio Perrault" and "Mémoire soumis par Mtre. L.E. Beaulieu, soutenant la negative." Perrault had practised his Sunday arguments in Archambault's 1927 book, *Le Repos Dominical.*

46. JPA, 43-1,64, *L'Action Catholique,* 3 May 1935, "Débat sur l'observance du dimanche dans la province. M. Jean-Paul Sauvé présente une motion pour faire disparaître l'article légal . . . "; JPA, 43-1,72, *Le Devoir,* 4 December 1935, "L'arrêt de la Cour d'appel au sujet du privilege juif . . . "; JPA, 43-1,73, *Le Devoir,* 5 December 1935, "La question du travail des Juifs, le dimanche. M. Taschereau n'aurait aucune objection à voter le rappel de l'article 7"; 44-4,166, de la Rochelle to Taschereau, 23 May 1935; *Statutes of the Province of Quebec,* 1 Ed. VIII, ch.4, "An Act to repeal Section 7 of the Sunday Observance Act"; Dupont, preface; Rome, 1936, pp. 25A, 26A.

47. The Jewish exemption clause is discussed at length in Paul Laverdure, "Sunday Secularism? The Lord's Day Debate of 1906," *Canadian Society of Church History. Papers* 1986, pp. 85–107.

48. Everett C. Hughes, "Action Catholique and Nationalism: A Memorandum on the Church and Society in French Canada, 1942," in Stewart Crysdale and Les Wheatcroft, eds, *Religion in Canadian Society,* (Toronto: 1976), pp. 173–90.

49. Richard Allen, *The Social Passion. Religion and Social Reform in Canada 1914–28* (Toronto: 1971), p. xxiii, noted certain similarities between the two movements.

50. For indexes, NAQ, E17-1487, "Index 1936" and E17-1489, "Index 1937"; Price Bros.: E17-1286, file 3515, 8 Avril 1938.

51. Debates of the House of Commons (1937) pp. 1758, 2405, 2599, (1938) pp. 104, 835, 837, 2639, 4351–2, (1939) pp. 137, 1301–6, 1643; press clippings in JPA, 41-13.

52. JPA, 35-4,77, Arthur LaRue to de la Rochelle, 29 October 1936; NAQ, E17-1241, file 515, Assistant Procurer General reply to the Report of the Inspector for Trois-Rivières, 6 September 1938.

53. JPA, 35-3,89, Lapointe to de la Rochelle, 10 October 1934 [my translation].

54. JPA, 38-4,66, Jules Dorion, "Le Dimanche et sa semaine," *L'Action Catholique,* 5 May 1937.

4   From Melissa Turkstra, "Constructing a Labour Gospel: Labour and Religion in Early Twentieth-Century Ontario," *Labour/Le Travail* 57 (Spring 2006): 93–130. Reprinted by permission of the publisher.

On 14 December 1900, just under 50 working men gathered in the lecture hall of James Street Baptist Church in Hamilton, Ontario, to meet with its pastor, Rev. J.L. Gilmour. Rev. Gilmour's primary objective in organizing this meeting was to solicit the opinion of workers in order to gain a better understanding of why more working men did not attend church. What is most striking about this meeting is how animated and frank these men were in their responses to the minister. Most of the men conceded that the church did have a message for workers; one worker even admitted that, in his opinion, Christianity was the only answer for the current social and labour problems while another quoted from the Bible to demonstrate that it had many relevant messages for workers. At the same time, the general consensus was that the churches were not successfully reaching the masses. Part of the problem, the men claimed, was the presence of "unchristian" manufacturers in the high offices of the church. Long hours and hard work were also cited as key factors keeping men from attending church. The men offered several suggestions of how the churches could amend this situation. First, ministers had to concentrate less on the spiritual welfare of the people and more on their temporal welfare. This meant, for example, that church leaders needed to join in the fight for the shorter workday and denounce the present competitive system. Ministers also had to return to the simple practical doctrine preached by Christ. Despite these criticisms, it was clear that working men were not completely alienated from the church. One worker questioned why working men were being singled out because, in his opinion, they were just as likely to regularly attend church as professionals and businessmen. Another worker stated that the working class had a responsibility to attend church even if it did have faults. Samuel Landers, future editor of the Hamilton *Labor News*, acknowledged that there were a few churches that attracted working men and attributed this to two factors: the attentiveness of these churches to workers' needs, and the concerted effort made by the pastors of these churches to visit their congregants. Probably the most remarkable statement at the conference was the response to Rev. Gilmour's concluding question; he asked, "How do men, who never attend church, know what is going on inside of them?" He was informed that the men discuss the sermons in the workshop.[1]

The views that were expressed at the working men's conference in Hamilton in 1900 were not exceptional. Both moderate and radical labour leaders voiced similar ideas in various labour publications in early twentieth-century Ontario. Like the working men at the Hamilton conference, these labour leaders were not shy about revealing where the churches had failed when it came to the working class. In the labour press, editors did not hesitate to portray the established churches as symbols of capitalist wealth and clergymen as puppets controlled by their wealthy constituents. They were also quick to point out that their strong critique of the churches did not imply a rejection of Christianity by carefully distinguishing between a true Christianity and a hypocritical "Churchianity".[2] While they underlined this distinction, this did not mean there was no interaction between labour leaders and the churches. Some labour leaders praised

and co-operated with those clergymen who were willing to denounce the injustices of the industrial capitalist system and champion labour issues.

[. . .]

The purpose of this paper is not only to provide examples of the presence of religion in the formally organized labour movement in early twentieth-century Canada, but to consider why religion continued to influence the thought and actions of labour leaders during this period. It will first explore labour leaders' disillusionment with the established churches and look at what changes they required the churches to make if they hoped to establish stronger ties with labour. It will then examine the non-sectarian, activist Christianity articulated by many labour leaders and consider how these beliefs helped them frame the issues they were concerned about. It will conclude with a close look at the alliances that developed between church and labour bodies at the national level and between labour-friendly clergy and a small group of labour leaders in industrial centres in southern Ontario. It will carefully look at who in the labour movement was most committed to building these cross-class alliances, determine what they hoped to achieve from this co-operation, and examine the irreparable cracks in the foundation of these alliances as a result of the opposing positions of the churches and labour on a number of important issues. While this labour gospel helped moderate and radical labour leaders in interpreting and constructing the issues they were concerned about, any rapprochement between organized labour and the churches during this period was modest.

To better understand the relationship between organized labour and religion, I have examined a number of labour newspapers including the *Industrial Banner*,[3] *Tribune*,[4] the Hamilton *Labor News*,[5] and the *Labor Leader*,[6] as well as *Cotton's Weekly*,[7] the official organ of the Social Democratic Party of Canada [SDP].[8] The Annual Report of the Proceedings of the Trades and Labor Congress of Canada has been particularly helpful in understanding the alliances that developed between the churches and labour leaders at the national level. With the exception of the socialist *Cotton's Weekly* and the more conservative labour weekly, the *Labor Leader*, which were national publications, the other papers were regional and local Ontario labour newspapers. In the pages of these newspapers, readers were informed about the social and economic injustices of the industrial capitalist system like child and female labour, unemployment, Chinese immigration, and poverty. They could learn about workers who were striking for better wages and shorter hours, the labour reforms organized labour was fighting for, the appeal of trade unionism, and party platforms. For the editors of these papers, including the radical, anti-capitalist W.A. Cotton, these publications were an important vehicle to promote working-class solidarity and teach workers that through trade unionism and the ballot workers could achieve their goals.[9] Although these labour publications are a useful window through which to examine the relationship between labour and religion, it is important to note that in looking at these papers I am, for the most part, analyzing the voices of the organized, articulate, and earnest intellectual leadership of the labour movement, not the rank-and-file. I am also focusing on a particular group of leaders within the labour movement. In many cases, the leaders I refer to were from southern Ontario. They were class-conscious craftworkers who had a particular idea of how the labour movement would evolve. They were moderate labour reformists who sought to secure a respected place for labour within industrial capitalist society through collective bargaining and labour representation in legislative bodies. These labourists, along with some socialists in the SDP, believed that social transformation would take place gradually through reforms, not revolution. With respect to religion, these men repeatedly insisted that it was not their role to intervene in the religious lives of workers because religion was a private matter and churches private institutions.[10] Despite the avowed policy of the labour press to avoid this subject, it was not difficult to find references to religion in the pages of their newspapers. It is also important to point out that the references to religion very rarely differentiated between denominations or even between the Protestant and Catholic churches. They discussed the Christian "church" broadly speaking. It is clear, however, that labour leaders were really concerned with the Protestants, particularly the Methodists, Presbyterians, and Congregationalists, to whom they turned for alliances.[11]

LABOUR, CHRISTIANITY, AND THE CHURCHES

Like the Knights of Labor and other labour movements before them, labour leaders in the early twentieth century characterized the established churches as symbols of capitalist wealth and, therefore, part of the exploitive industrial capitalist system they were working so arduously to change.[12] What they found particularly appalling were the wealthy capitalists who had monopolized the churches and used their power to control ministers. As one worker in a letter to the editor of the *Tribune* resentfully explained, "There is no getting away from the fact that the Church at present is for the class, not the mass."[13] Joseph Marks, editor of the *Industrial Banner*, voiced a similar complaint at a 1906 Labor Forward meeting, arguing that the working class was absent from the church because it catered to wealthy congregants.[14] In a letter to the editor of the *Industrial Banner* in 1913, an observer characterized the religion in the churches as a charity religion that was becoming increasingly dependent on the contributions of wealthy congregants who, as a natural consequence, guided the policy of the churches and silenced its ministers. The writer complained, "The church practically teaches that God made this world not for the children of men, but for a special few, so that these favourites could live by the sweat of their neighbour's face."[15]

[. . .]

Also contributing to labour's disillusionment with the churches was the apathy of clergymen with regard to labour issues. One trade unionist expressed his disappointment to the editor of the *Tribune*, writing, "of the twelve years that I have been a trade unionist, I have never seen a clergyman come and ask to be allowed to have a five minute conversation with them on any of their meeting nights, yet they wonder why the large majority do not attend the church."[16] [. . .]

If the churches wanted to mend relations with labour, they would have to do more than just show an interest in labour issues; labour believed it was the duty of the churches and its ministers to join labour in its fight for more just conditions for workers. The *Industrial Banner* questioned why the preachers of Toronto were not supporting the strike of female operatives at the Adams Shoe Company in 1912 who, without notice, received a serious reduction in wages. It noted the hypocrisy in this silence: "What can be said of the kind of civilization that can stand for it in a city where hundreds of church spires point upward to the skies, and where peace upon earth and good will towards men is openly proclaimed from its myriad pulpits on every Sabbath morn."[17] In addition to supporting strikes, labour expected churches to endorse labour legislation. An article entitled "The Church's Opportunity" invited churches in Ontario to take an interest in the workmen's compensation for injuries act because it was essentially a moral and religious question. Such legislation was necessary, it argued, because hundreds of workers were sacrificed every year as a result of industrial accidents and the widows and children of these workers deserved protection from destitution. [. . .]

Although labour was clearly frustrated with the inaction of churches, it believed that the churches were not only capable of but had a vital role to play in eliminating the injustice pervading society. Articles explicitly set out what changes the churches had to make if they were sincerely interested in amending their relationship with labour. Instead of remaining neutral in matters that concerned capital and labour, it was the duty of the churches to be involved in and publicize important moral and religious issues that affected the welfare of the people. The issues the churches were expected to address were quite progressive and included increases in wages and a decrease in hours of work, the abolition of child labour in factories, and equal pay for men and women for equal work or service.[18] This assistance also meant action. Churches had to take an aggressive stance against exploitive capitalists and make social and economic issues a priority. An article published in *Cotton's Weekly* in 1913 summoned the churches "to prepare the rich man for Heaven by condemning a system that allows some men to get rich while other men are starving," insisting that "the church has got to go into economic conditions or go out of existence." It proceeded to call on ministers "to go into the workshop as Christ did and condemn the owners of the slave pens."[19] [. . .]

The labour press, in the early twentieth century, described to their readers what it believed was wrong with the present state of the churches. The fundamental obstacle impeding the churches' relations with workers was the inability of the churches to detach themselves from the exploitive industrial capitalist system. The labour press portrayed the churches as synonymous with this system; the control of the churches and its ministers by wealthy capitalists was simply an extension of capitalists' abusive power. This did not mean that the churches were dismissed completely; it just meant that they were on trial. The message labour editors wanted to convey to their readers regarding the established churches was that they were a useful but not a necessary tool in workers' efforts to secure a more equitable economic and social system.

CHRISTIANITY IN LABOUR'S MESSAGE

Whether the established churches did or did not join with organized labour in its fight to establish a more just society had little bearing on its view of religion. The labour press made a conscious effort to distinguish between rejecting the "churchianity" it identified with the churches and the true Christianity that gave meaning to the daily struggles of workers.[20] The *Labor News*, for example, explained that workers were vacant from the pews not because they were infidels and materialists but because they saw the church "as a tool of the employing class."[21] And irregular church attendance, according to the *Labor Leader*, did not automatically qualify a person as a non-Christian.[22] [. . .]

Not only did labour leaders reject the notion that it was anti-religious, they articulated a radical social gospel that applied their interpretation of Christian teaching to workers' struggles and insisted that social and economic regeneration precede individual regeneration.[23] This labour gospel was both a direct assault on the unrestrained individualism of laissez-faire capitalism and the individualist gospel that focused on the relationship between God and man.[24] For workers, particularly skilled workers whose craft traditions and autonomy were being threatened during this period by dramatic industrial changes like the concentration of capital, new scientific management practices, technological innovations, and new manufacturing industries that relied on huge pools of unskilled and semi-skilled immigrant labour, this labour gospel helped to frame the issues they were concerned about.[25] [. . .]

The majority of religious references in the labour press were centred, not on the divinity of Jesus, but on the temporal significance of his life.[26] Labour newspapers emphasized Jesus' working-class origins. Articles in labour newspapers pointed out the parallels between the life of Jesus and the lives of workers, noting that he was born into poverty and that his trade until the age of 30 was that of a hard-working carpenter.[27] An article printed in the Christmas issue of the *Labor Leader*, entitled "Jesus in Overalls," asked readers to remember that the clothes they stripped from his body before he was nailed to the cross were the clothes of a working man: "What! Jesus in overalls? Sure! He wore them. His overalls smelled of human sweat, and the soil of untarrying toil was upon them."[28] Jesus was an ideal representative of the working class. It was because of his authentic experience as a worker that Jesus was able to honestly understand workers' struggles, needs, and goals.[29]

In addition to establishing his working-class origins, the labour press depicted Jesus as a heroic social reformer and the first great successful labour leader and invoked his ethical teachings and bold actions to fuel opposition to modern-day social and economic problems.[30] Exploitive employment practices, for example, were inimical to Jesus' teaching. An article entitled "The People Want to Know" questioned what the Christian life meant in the twentieth century and asked "if the Saviour of mankind, Who blessed little children, would approve of their exploitation by Christian employers who confine them in unsanitary factories" or "if a Christian employer who pays his female help one half the wages paid to men for the same work is honest or actuated by the spirit of his Master."[31] Labour leaders also looked to Christianity to frame their critique of the use of immigrant labour and workplace safety. Demonstrating the deep ethnic division in the labour movement during this period, labour leaders characterized the efforts made by the Canadian Manufacturers' Association to overstock the labour market by giving bonuses to immigration agencies and transportation companies as "neither Christian, civilized, nor decent."[32]

Labour leaders also drew on Jesus' ethical teachings to target the unequal distribution of wealth. These teachings were often used to garner support for the single tax, the panacea for land monopolization.[33] The *Industrial Banner*, for example, printed several speeches by W.A. Douglas, a vociferous proponent of the single tax, who often drew on the example of Jesus to reinforce his attacks on land speculation. In 1913, Douglas used the pulpit of King St Methodist Church in Toronto to speak out against those land owners who had amassed their wealth from land monopoly. He queried, "What would Christ's answer be to the question, 'What is the greatest obstacle to the progress of the kingdom of God?' If he were to come, do you think he would be the guest at the homes of the very rich?" Jesus, Douglas continued, would probably ask, "Where is that brotherhood I came to this world to found?" and respond with the statement, "I cannot see it as I go among the people. In every city that I visit, the mansions at one end are like the palaces of princes, while the homes of the hard working people who produce the abundance of the wealth are of the poorest character."[34]

Labour leaders also drew on Jesus' teachings and other biblical lessons and characters to illustrate the effectiveness of labour unions and to underline that workers themselves were the agents that would effect a more just and equitable society. An article entitled "Trade Unionism Stands for the Open Door" tried to impress upon wage earners the need to join trade unions by noting the similarities between unionism and the early church. Both were wide open to new members; trade union organizers were the missionaries preaching the benefits of affiliation; both provided better improved conditions through brotherly co-operation and mutual assistance; both

uplifted moral standards; and both faced the malevolence of and persecution by bitter opponents.[35] While labour leaders did not hesitate to identify with the early churches, they argued that the present churches, while providing important theories like the Golden Rule and the law of love, lacked legitimacy because they were not solving social and economic problems. Trade unionism, on the other hand, was a legitimate institution because it was acting out the teachings of the Bible. For example, by emancipating children from exploitive labour practices, trade unionism was obeying the command, "Inasmuch as ye have done it unto one of the least of these my brethren, ye have done it unto me"; "Suffer little children, and forbid them not to come unto me; for of such is the kingdom of Heaven."[36]

Socialists also drew on an activist Christianity to frame their calls for an alternative society. *Cotton's Weekly*, on several occasions, identified socialism with Christianity, stating that "socialism is simply applied Christianity. The golden rule applied to everyday life"[37] or that socialism "has for its foundations the very elements of Christianity."[38] It also noted that "the ethics of socialism are identical with the ethics of Christianity"[39] and "socialism is Christianity put into practice."[40] [. . .]

Religious discourse was present in the labour press in early twentieth-century Canada because moderate and radical labour leaders understood that one way they could effectively reach workers with their message was through religion. The activist Christianity that labour leaders drew on to interpret and construct labour issues helped make workers aware of the injustices of the industrial capitalist system and cultivate in them a desire to change this system. [. . .] In the early twentieth century, labour leaders articulated an activist Christianity that helped them frame the social and economic problems that were of concern to them. This labour gospel was distinctive to the working class and became part of these leaders' attempts to change the industrial capitalist society.

THE CHURCHES AS LABOUR'S ALLIES

In 1911 the *Industrial Banner* acknowledged the friendship between organized labour and the churches when it responded to a letter published in the *Globe* by Moses Baritz, organizer for the Socialist Party of Canada. Baritz had challenged the statement of Methodist Superintendent S.D. Chown that socialism was founded upon the teachings of Christ. Not only was socialism opposed to all religions, according to Baritz, but all religions would be abolished with the establishment of a socialist regime. While the *Industrial Banner* assured its readers that Baritz was entitled to his private opinion, it chastised him for antagonizing the church, a force that was friendly to the labour movement.[41] This defensive response by the *Industrial Banner* is not surprising given that its editor was among the few labour leaders who saw building alliances with progressive clergymen in the Protestant churches as a practical and effective way to secure middle-class support for labour reforms.[42] While the presence of this cross-class alliance must be appreciated, it is important to point out that the labour leaders I refer to below were, for the most part, from southern Ontario, their efforts to build an alliance was most evident in the years leading up to World War I, and their alliance with the churches was tenuous as a result of deep divisions between labour and the churches on a number of issues.

Before World War I, the Trades and Labor Congress of Canada [TLCC] and labour leaders in southern Ontario allied with various church bodies and clergymen because they saw this collaboration as an opportunity to assist the advancement of labour. One of the first examples of co-operation between organized labour and the churches was between the TLCC and the Lord's Day Alliance [LDA], an organization formed by the Protestant churches in 1889 which sought legislation to secure the day of rest. Seeing that both groups had similar aims, labour wanted workers to have one free day from work and the Alliance wanted one free day to worship, organized labour not only lent a supportive voice but several prominent labour advocates were members of the alliance which was successful in securing the passage of the Lord's Day Act in 1906.[43] Co-operation between these two groups continued after this legislation was passed.

Although labour exchanged fraternal delegates with the LDA and expressed enthusiasm for its support of labour initiatives, labour leaders made it clear that their support of one day free from work was based on economic not religious grounds.[44] Commenting on legislation to secure the day of rest, the *Industrial Banner* in 1906 stated that this legislation was "absolutely necessary for the welfare of the working masses." This legislation should be supported, it continued, not on religious grounds but because workers have a right to have one day of rest to spend as they desire.[45] [. . .] The *Industrial Banner* was trying to be neutral on the question of religion as labour unions were made up of Protestants, Catholics, a large number of non-Christians like Jews who regarded Saturday as their sacred day, adherents of other religions, as well as free thinkers.[46]

Co-operation between labour leaders and the church continued in the church-led Moral and Social Reform Council of Canada [MSRCC].[47] Like the LDA, several prominent labour leaders were members of the MSRCC.[48] Clergymen representing the MSRCC were also welcomed at the annual meetings of the TLCC. Labour leaders also attended the meetings of various local church bodies and used church platforms to publicize and educate people on labour issues. [. . .]

In addition to co-operating with labour-friendly church bodies and clergymen, the labour press praised enlightened ministers who aggressively spoke out against the social injustices in society. [. . .] Before World War I, labour leaders in the southern Ontario labour movement built an alliance with progressive clergymen at the national and local levels; in the years directly following the war, these leaders were becoming more convinced that the churches, with their call for industrial democracy, were sincere in their sympathy for workers and their struggles. The resolutions of the Methodist Church in 1918 which called for a co-operative system of service to replace the present competitive system of profits elicited the most optimistic response from these leaders. An article in the 18 October 1918 issue of the *Labor News* entitled "Methodists Out for the Common People" and the headline of a 17 January 1919 issue of the *Industrial Banner*, "Far Reaching Pronouncement Outlines a Basis for Economic Reconstruction: A Great Church Insists That Business Shall Be Run No Longer For Corporation Profits,"[49] demonstrated that organized labour was encouraged by the radical recommendations of the Methodist Church.[50] Labour leaders believed this call for social reconstruction would not only result in future co-operation with the churches but would inevitably lead to great political, economic, and industrial changes.[51] That some of these leaders viewed the churches' statements with optimism was also evident in a statement in the *Labor News*: "If the Methodist ministers follow up the platform laid down by the Conference some of us fellows might have to start going to church again."[52]

The alliance that was being built between progressive clergymen in the Protestant churches did not include all members of the labour movement, however; there were deep divisions between labour and the churches on a number of important issues. There were differences between organized labour and the churches on the Sabbatarian issue starting in the late nineteenth century. Although the TLCC initially endorsed the prohibition of Sunday streetcars in Toronto in 1891, it was the conservative wing of the TLCC that joined forces with the LDA; workers in Toronto were strongly opposed to this prohibition. When

the question of streetcars arose again in subsequent years, the TLCC listened to their followers and did not support the Sabbatarian cause.[53] After the Lord's Day Act was passed in 1906, and especially after World War I, the differences between the two sides became apparent. Organized labour firmly believed that Sunday was a day for workers to do what they wanted, like attend sports.[54] Organized labour, in fact, became one of the major critics of the Alliance because of the Alliance's insistence on enforcing legislation and restricting recreation on Sundays.[55]

An even greater obstacle undermining this alliance was the powerful opposition of radical members of the TLCC in the west. As early as 1911 these members demonstrated that they were a serious force to be reckoned with, when they almost ended the Congress' affiliation with the MSRCC. At the annual meeting in Calgary in 1911, delegate McVety of the Vancouver Trades and Labor Congress and delegate Stubbs proposed an amendment to end affiliation with the Council. The amendment was narrowly defeated by a vote of 50 to 52.[56] Just four years later, at the annual meeting in Vancouver, the Congress again voted to withdraw from the Council. Despite the strong opposition from James Simpson, the recommendation was adopted by a vote of 72 to 66.[57] Although the formal separation between the TLCC and MSRCC was a definite setback for those labour leaders who saw the practical advantages of an alliance with the churches, the most potent force preventing any long-term co-operation between these two groups was prohibition.

Prohibition was the most hotly contested form of moral critique of working-class life. While prohibition was one of the great moral crusades of the Protestant churches, for organized labour, it was an issue where there was a distinct difference of opinion. A number of labour leaders applauded the sober morality of Protestant religion, speaking out against drinking in saloons and some even supporting prohibition, particularly those who were members of the MSRCC.[58] Other labour leaders, however, resented the temperance societies that ignored the economic and social causes of drinking. Those who worked in the alcohol business were especially opposed to prohibitive measures like the reduction of licences because they feared losing their jobs. Many leaders also saw prohibition as class-biased legislation that targeted the social lives of working men. The only option for working men, they argued, was to drink in hotel saloons because they could not afford to drink at home or in private clubs. By World War I, organized labour vocally opposed prohibition and by 1919 was rallying around the demand for beer.[59] Organized labour's fight to drink moderately and responsibly collided with the demand by the Protestant churches for a dry regime and was another example of the divisions between churches and the labour movement.

If Sabbatarianism, prohibition, and east-west divisions in the Canadian labour movement led to increasing tension between the churches and the labour movement by World War I, the deterioration of the relationship between organized labour and the churches in the immediate post-war period can be attributed to the inability of the churches to act on their proclamations and a resurgent labour movement that relied less on middle-class support for labour's cause. [. . .]

The widening rift between organized labour and the churches came at a time when labour was more confident, united, and class-conscious than ever before. Starting in 1916, and for the next four years, union membership rose rapidly and workers joined together in an unprecedented number of strikes.[60] The Winnipeg Strike and the general strikes taking place across Canada in May, June, and July of 1919 were a testament to the wave of nationwide resistance. This was also a period of increased radicalism in the labour movement, especially in the west, where at the Calgary Labour Conference in the early spring of 1918, the One Big Union

was formed.[61] This resistance was accompanied by a renewed interest in independent political action. There was a significant increase in the number of independent labour parties at both the municipal and provincial level. In Ontario, the Independent Labour Party joined the United Farmers of Ontario to form a coalition government in 1919.[62]

The 1921 Toronto printers' strike was the final blow that ended the alliance between the churches and labour. [. . .] At the centre of this conflict were the Methodist Book Room and its intransigent superintendent, S.W. Fallis, who refused to give in to the printers' demand for a 44-hour week. [. . .] That this strike caused irreparable damage to the alliance between labour and the churches was clear. The *Labor News* argued that the actions of the Methodist Book Room contradicted the 1918 Methodist General Conference resolutions. The *Industrial Banner* stated, "The position of the Methodist Book Room in the strike of the printing trades is nothing less than tragic. It is a position from which the Church will not recover during its lifetime, and which can only be partly effaced when Church union is brought about and a new name is given to the united churches."[63] The noticeable decline in the number of references to the churches in the labour press also attests to the negative impact the strike had on the relationship between organized labour and the churches.[64]

[. . .]

CONCLUSION

In early twentieth-century Canada, labour leaders were not reticent in their denunciations of the churches, which they saw as symbols of capitalist wealth. Nor were they afraid to excoriate clergymen who were indifferent or openly hostile to labour's cause. This deep resentment did not mean, however, that they abandoned religion. The labour movement during this period may not have been imbued with religiosity like the Knights of Labor in the late nineteenth century, but religion was present. Both moderate reformist and radical labour leaders believed in an activist Christianity and interpreted and constructed social and economic problems in light of these beliefs. This labour gospel helped make workers better understand these problems, build opposition to the present industrial capitalist system, and attract workers to their respective movements.

In addition to drawing on an activist Christianity to frame the issues they were concerned about, this paper has looked at the alliances that developed between labour leaders in southern Ontario and the churches. The examination of these alliances suggests a richer relationship between the churches and labour than the work of other historians would suggest. While future research must look at alliances in other regions of Canada, it is evident that labour leaders in southern Ontario co-operated with church bodies at national and local levels, sang high praises for those socially conscious churches and clergymen who championed the cause of labour, and readily admitted the benefits of the alliances with the churches.[65] Yet, support for a cross-class alliance was not shared by all members of the labour movement. This can be attributed to the deep divisions between the churches and labour on issues like Sabbatarianism and prohibition, but also to regional differences and the national and regional dynamics and diversity of the Canadian labour movement.

The purpose of examining labour leaders' criticism of established churches, their promotion of an activist Christianity, and the alliances they formed with various church bodies and clergymen has not been to measure the extent of religious belief of organized labour. Some labour leaders were churchgoers, but certainly not all were. Some rejected organized religion but espoused an activist Christianity. Some were non-believers, but supported Christian principles. What is evident from this examination of labour publications is that, while labour leaders may have had a diverse range of religious beliefs or even non-belief, Christianity was present in the labour movement.

NOTES

1. *Hamilton Spectator*, 13 December 1900; *Hamilton Evening Times*, 13 December 1900.
2. "Churchianity" was a term used to describe the church's obsession with creed, ritual, and wealth. See *Cotton's Weekly*, 28 January 1909.
3. Kevin Brushett, "Labour's Forward Movement: Joseph Marks, the *Industrial Banner* and the Ontario Working-Class, 1890–1930," (MA thesis, Queen's University, 1994), 21, 66, 146; Ron Verzuh, *Radical Rag: The Pioneer Labour Press in Canada* (Ottawa 1988), 97–8; *McKim's Canadian Newspaper Directory* 1920, 87.
4. The *Tribune* was the mouthpiece of the Toronto District Labor Council.
5. James Naylor, *The New Democracy: Challenging the Social Order in Industrial Ontario, 1914–1925* (Toronto 1991), 67–8.
6. *The Labor Leader*, 18 December 1925; 17 December 1926.
7. Edward Penton, "The Ideas of William Cotton: A Marxist View of Canadian Society, 1908–1914," (MA thesis, University of Ottawa, 1978), 14.
8. Janice Newton, *The Feminist Challenge to the Canadian Left, 1900–1918* (Montreal and Kingston 1995), 32.
9. Brushett, "Labour's Forward Movement"; Penton, "The Ideas of William Cotton"; and *Dictionary of Hamilton Biography*, vol. 2, 1992, "Samuel Landers," by Craig Heron.
10. *Industrial Banner*, November 1911; *Labor News*, 10 March 1916; *Labor Leader*, 26 September 1924; *Cotton's Weekly*, 21 January 1909.
11. Jacques Rouillard, *Histoire de la CNS,1921–1981* (Montreal 1981).
12. Gregory S. Kealey and Bryan D. Palmer, *Dreaming of What Might Be: The Knights of Labor of Ontario, 1880–1900* (Toronto 1987), 311; Lynne Marks, "The Knights of Labor and the

Salvation Army: Religion and Working Class Culture in Ontario, 1882–1890," *Labour/Le Travail*, 28 (Fall 1991), 108; Lynne Marks, *Revivals and Roller Rinks: Religion, Leisure, and Identity in Late-Nineteenth-Century Small Town Ontario* (Toronto 1996), 63.

13. *Tribune*, 4 November 1905.

14. *Industrial Banner*, March 1906.

15. *Industrial Banner*, 6 June 1913.

16. *Tribune*, 4 November 1905.

17. *Industrial Banner*, 29 November 1912.

18. *Industrial Banner*, August 1904, October 1904, October 1907.

19. *Cotton's Weekly*, 12 June 1913.

20. Ian McKay, *For a Working-Class Culture in Canada: A Selection of Colin McKay's Writings on Sociology and Political Economy, 1897–1939* (St John's 1996), 6.

21. *Labor News*, 25 October 1918.

22. *Labor Leader*, 13 February 1920.

23. McKay, *For a Working-Class Culture in Canada*, 56, 67; Peter Campbell, *Canadian Marxists and a Search for a Third War* (Montreal and Kingston 1999), 128.

24. Gene Homel, "James Simpson and the Origins of Canadian Social Democracy," (PhD thesis, University of Toronto, 1978), 66; McKay, *For a Working-Class Culture in Canada*, 6–7.

25. Naylor, *The New Democracy*, 4–5, 16–17; Brushett, "Labour's Forward Movement," 54.

26. Kealey and Palmer, *Dreaming of What Might Be*, 312.

27. *Cotton's Weekly*, 24 December 1908; *Labor Leader*, 25 May 1928.

28. *Labor Leader*, 26 December 1924.

29. *Industrial Banner*, 19 March 1912, 29 August 1913.

30. *Industrial Banner*, November 1908. Several historians have similarly noted that labour leaders and socialists invoked Christ's example in their fight against societal injustices. See Norman Knowles, "Christ in the Crowsnest: Religion and the Anglo-Protestant Working Class in the Crowsnest Pass, 1898–1918," in Michael Behiels and Marcel Martel, eds, *Nation, Ideas, Identities* (Don Mills 2000), 67; McKay, *For a Working-Class Culture in Canada*, 6–7; W.W. Knox, "Religion and the Scottish Labour Movement c.1900–1939," *Journal of Contemporary History* 23 (1988): 615.

31. *Industrial Banner*, May 1906.

32. *Industrial Banner*, February 1906.

33. The "single tax," which taxed unearned land values, was an important issue for organized labour well into the twentieth century. See Allen Mills, "Single Tax, Socialism and the Independent Labour Party of Manitoba: The Political Ideas of F.J. Dixon and S.J. Farmer," *Labour/Le Travailleur* 5 (Spring 1980): 33–56.

34. *Industrial Banner*, 2 May 1913.

35. *Industrial Banner*, January 1906, October 1911.

36. *Industrial Banner*, October 1911.

37. *Cotton's Weekly*, 25 February 1909.

38. *Cotton's Weekly*, 4 March 1909.

39. *Cotton's Weekly*, 11 March 1909.

40. *Cotton's Weekly*, 13 February 1913. See also Homel, "James Simpson and the Origins of Canadian Social Democracy," 278.

41. *Industrial Banner*, January 1911.

42. Craig Heron, "Labourism and the Canadian Working Class," *Labour/Le Travail* 13 (Spring 1984): 64; Homel, "James Simpson and the Origins of Canadian Social Democracy," 390.

43. Sharon Meen, "The Battle for the Sabbath: The Sabbatarian Lobby in Canada, 1890–1912," (PhD thesis, University of British Columbia, 1979), 318; *Industrial Banner*, January 1906, November 1911.

44. Christopher Armstrong and H.V. Nelles, *The Revenge of the Methodist Bicycle Company* (Toronto 1977), 62; Meen, "The Battle for the Sabbath," 42, 119; Homel, "James Simpson and the Origins of Canadian Social Democracy," 280.

45. *Industrial Banner*, January 1906.

46. *Industrial Banner*, January 1906, August 1908.

47. The MSRCC was later named the Social Service Council of Canada in 1913. Nancy Christie and Michael Gauvreau, *A Full-Orbed Christianity: The Protestant Churches and Social Welfare in Canada, 1900–1940* (Montreal and Kingston 1996), 198, 208–9.

48. NA, Canadian Council of Churches, Moral and Social Reform Council of Canada Minutes; NA, Canadian Council of Churches, Minutes of the Annual Meeting of the Social Service Council.

49. *Industrial Banner*, 17 January 1919.

50. *Labor News*, 18 October 1918.

51. *Industrial Banner*, 14 March 1919.

52. *Labor News*, 25 October 1918.

53. Armstrong and Nelles, *The Revenge of the Methodist Bicycle Company*, 61–3, 102, 177; Meen, "The Battle for the Sabbath," 120–1.

54. See Barbara Schrodt, "Sabbatarianism and Sport in Canadian Society," *Journal of Sport History*, 24 (Spring 1977): 22–33; Homel, "James Simpson and the Origins of Canadian Social Democracy," 282.

55. Meen, "The Battle for the Sabbath," 272.

56. *Report of the Proceedings of the Annual Trades and Labor Congress of Canada* 1911, 96.

57. *Report of Proceedings of the Annual Meeting of Trades and Labor Congress of Canada* 1915, 106–7.

58. Homel, "James Simpson and the Origins of Democracy," 283–4.

59. See Craig Heron, *Booze: A Distilled History* (Toronto 2003), 219–31; Homel, "James Simpson and the Origins of Canadian Democracy," 283–93.

60. Douglas Cruikshank and Gregory Kealey, "Canadian Strike Statistics, 1891–1950," *Labour/Le Travail*, 20 (1987): 85–145; Heron, "National Contours: Solidarity and Fragmentation," in Craig Heron, ed., *The Workers' Revolt in Canada 1917–1925* (Toronto 1998), 269–70.

61. Tom Mitchell and James Naylor, "The Prairies: In the Eye of the Storm," in Craig Heron, ed., *The Workers' Revolt in Canada 1917–1925* (Toronto 1998), 177.

62. James Naylor, "Striking at the Ballot Box," in Heron, ed., *The Workers' Revolt*, 155–63.

63. *Industrial Banner*, 8 July 1921.

64. Christie and Gauvreau, *A Full-Orbed Christianity*, 211–12.

65. Lynne Marks, "Exploring Religious Diversity in Patterns of Religious Participation," *Historical Methods*, 33 (Fall 2000): 247–54.

Chapter 5

The First World War

READINGS

Primary Documents

1   From "The Duty of Canada at the Present Hour: An Address Meant to Be Delivered at Ottawa in November and December 1914, but Twice Suppressed in the Name of 'Loyalty and Patriotism,'" Henri Bourassa

2   From "Canada Will Answer the Call: Sir Robert Borden's Inspiring War-Message to the Canadian People: Speech Delivered at Toronto, Dec. 5th, 1914," Robert Laird Borden

Historical Interpretations

3   From "'He Was Determined to Go': Underage Soldiers in the Canadian Expeditionary Force," Tim Cook

4   From "Uncovering the Enemy Within: British Columbians and the German Menace," Peter Moogk

INTRODUCTION

Commitment to an undertaking such as war is both collective and personal, so it should not be surprising that the First World War had national and regional political repercussions but also deeply affected the families that sent troops overseas and tried to manage at home without their sons, husbands, and fathers. Committing to war did not always bring with it harmony or good-will, despite the fact that fighting a war would be easiest if longstanding grievances, animosities, and anxieties could be set aside. One of the most important things that students of history can do when looking at war and wartime life is to recognize that First World War participants suffered during and after the war from the shock of living at the centre of battle for months on end; the deployment of troops, tactics of battle, and coping with casualties were only part of the experience. New approaches to understanding the war continue to yield stories and historical data that testify to a transformation of the entire society along with the more frequently cited transformation of Canada's foreign and domestic relations. On the homefront during the First World War, the struggle to keep Canadians enlisting and producing highlighted ongoing divisions. One of these, the gulf between French- and English-speaking Canada, became wider over the issue of conscription, and is illustrated by our primary sources. Henri Bourassa was to deliver the speech presented here late in 1914, a time of relative optimism about the war. Bourassa questions Canada's participation in the war, urging his audience to think critically about leaping headlong into the conflict, and admonishing the Canadian government for putting out a special call to French speakers. Prime Minister Borden's speech, although not presented as a direct response to Bourassa, shows he was convinced of the righteousness of war against Germany and its allies, and did not wish to acknowledge that there was much difference of opinion about the war, either within Canada or the Empire. The historical interpretations here deal with two widely separated aspects of wartime life. Tim Cook brings the question of underage soldiers into focus, examining the reasons young men may have joined—some of which were hardly patriotic—and showing how Canada's need for soldiers could trump concern for the innocence of youth. In Peter Moogk's article, we see how the First World War affected Canadians of German and Austrian-Hungarian origins. Wartime hysteria led the German population of British Columbia, which had been in the process of integrating itself into the wider Protestant community, to be reclassified as dangerous outsiders. Many German-born men were interned in labour camps and a cloud of suspicion fell on all persons known or assumed to be of German heritage.

QUESTIONS FOR CONSIDERATION

1.   What were Bourassa's main objections to the way the First World War was "sold" to Canadians in various parts of the country?
2.   Borden pointed to Germany's nineteenth-century history to justify Canada's participation in the war? Why?
3.   What seems to be the main social or cultural factors that motivated Canada to increase its participation in the war?
4.   What were some of the forces pushing adolescents to enlist?
5.   How did the war exacerbate or re-order ethnic tensions in British Columbia?

SUGGESTIONS FOR FURTHER READING

Nic Clark, *Unwanted Warriors: The Rejected Volunteers of the Canadian Expeditionary Force* (Vancouver: UBC Press, 2016).

Tim Cook, *Canadians Fighting the Great War, 1914–1918* (Toronto: Viking Canada, 2007).

Sarah Glassford and Amy J. Shaw, *A Sisterhood of Suffering and Service: Women and Girls of Canada and Newfoundland during the First World War* (Vancouver: UBC Press, 2013).

Geoffrey Hayes, Andrew Iarocci, and Mike Bechthold, eds, *Vimy Ridge: A Canadian Reassessment* (Waterloo: Wilfrid Laurier University Press, 2007).

Andrew Iarocci and Jeffrey Keshen, *A Nation in Conflict: Canada and the Two World Wars* (Toronto: University of Toronto Press, 2015).

Bohdan S. Kordan, *No Free Man: Canada, the Great War, and the Enemy Alien Experience* (Montreal and Kingston: McGill-Queen's University Press, 2016).

Susan Mann, *Margaret Macdonald: Imperial Daughter* (Montreal and Kingston: McGill-Queen's University Press, 2005).

Brock Millman, *Polarity, Patriotism, and Dissent in Great War Canada, 1914–1919* (Toronto: University of Toronto Press, 2016).

Desmond Morton, *Fight or Pay: Soldiers' Families in the Great War* (Vancouver: UBC Press, 2004).

———, *When Your Number's Up: The Canadian Soldier in the First World War* (Toronto: Random House, 1993).

Robert Rutherdale, *Hometown Horizons: Local Responses to Canada's Great War* (Vancouver: UBC Press, 2004).

Brian Douglas Tennyson, *Canada's Great War, 1914–1918: How Canada Helped Save the British Empire and Became a North American Nation* (Lanham: Rowman & Littlefield, 2014).

Jonathan F. Vance, *Death So Noble: Memory, Meaning, and the First World War* (Vancouver: UBC Press, 1997).

Timothy C. Winegard, *For King and Kanata: Canadian Indians and the First World War* (Winnipeg: University of Manitoba Press, 2012).

Primary Documents

1 From Henri Bourassa, "The Duty of Canada at the Present Hour: An Address Meant to Be Delivered at Ottawa in November and December 1914, but Twice Suppressed in the Name of 'Loyalty and Patriotism,'" Montreal, January 1915.

Canada, an Anglo-French community, bound to Great Britain and France by a thousand ties, ethnical, social, intellectual and economic, has a vital interest in the preservation of France and Britain, in the maintenance of their prestige, power and action in the world. It is therefore the national duty of Canada to contribute in the measure of her resources and by such means of action as she may command, to the success and above all to the *endurance* of the combined efforts of France and Great Britain. But if we want our contribution to be effective, if we mean to keep up the effort, we must face with clearsighted resoluteness the grim realities of the situation; we must calculate the exact measure of our means of action, and secure first the internal safety of Canada, before we attempt to settle the affairs of the world.

Whether Canada has or has not a strict obligation to help, directly or indirectly, the cause of France and England, one fact is indisputable: the effects of this tremendous conflict will be deeply felt in Canada as in the rest of the world. It will be particularly disastrous in Canada on account of certain local and accidental causes: intense immigration in late years, exclusive dependence upon British capital, extravagant speculation, excessive borrowings by public bodies and individuals, etc., etc. Canadians are just on the point of realising how poor Canada is, financially speaking. They are just beginning to perceive that they have been living extravagantly on borrowed money, which they are called upon to pay back at the very moment they are unable to do it. The crushing weight of the burden will be increased in proportion to our direct contribution to the war: the larger that contribution the greater the strain upon our meagre financial resources, not to speak of the stoppage of our industries and the weakening of our military forces, which may be needed to preserve internal peace.

If a general collapse is to be avoided, these aspects of the situation call for the immediate attention and co-operation of all men of good will. And they must be viewed primarily from the point of Canada's interests.

CANADA FIRST

To some, the Empire is all and every thing; others think of France only; another category, logical but narrow in their Canadian exclusiveness, see nothing beyond the borders of Canada: they seem to ignore our most conspicuous world's responsibilities.

These various feelings indicate a singular absence of a truly national patriotism. They show a marked contrast with that strong and practical sentiment which binds in one solid mass the people of other countries, the moment the vital interests of the nation are at stake. Since the outbreak of the war, the country has been flooded with "patriotic" speeches and writings; but those words have been followed with very few deeds for the good of Canada.

This marks all the difference between the thoughtful action of sovereign peoples, masters of their destinies, conscious of their responsibilities, and the thoughtlessness of a child-nation, deprived of international status, unable to measure the consequences of its actions and even to foresee the repercussions of the movements of other nations, including that from which it depends.

Everyone speaks of the duties of Canada to Great Britain or France. Who has thought of the duties of Canada to herself?

It may be objected that it is too late to consider the question: the parliament and people of Canada have decided upon it, emphatically and unanimously; the active participation of Canada in the European war is settled; to pursue that participation with full strength and celerity is all that remains to be done.

The answer to that objection is that it is never too late for nations or individuals to think of the consequences of their actions.

We are yet at the beginning of the war. If, as generally asserted and as decreed by parliament with apparent unanimity, Canada is bound to share actively in this war, it is assuredly the duty of the Canadian government to make our participation as efficient as possible, and to minimize the grave effects of that participation upon the economic and social life of the country.

It is also the duty of all citizens to help the government with such advice and information as may guide its movements. In all national crises, the government is not to be considered as a mere group of politicians of doubtful or diverse ability, temporarily invested with authority. The men in office represent the power of the nation. They ought to be enlightened, informed and advised. They must even be supported till they are guilty of betrayal. National accord demands the adjournment of party quarrels and acrimonious discussions; it does not however impose silence in face of danger, nor complicity in any crime or error; nor does it call for any sacrifice of principle.

ECONOMIC ASPECTS OF THE WAR

When a country means to make war, or to share in war, the first duty of its rulers is to take the necessary steps to keep up the economic life of the country. "Battles are won with pounds sterling as much as with bullets," as was very truly said by the genial Chancellor of the Exchequer. That they are won with wheat sheaves still, more than with gold, he might well have added,—had he not meant, of course, that with her enormous wealth and reserve of gold, Great Britain is well able to purchase corn and other foodstuffs.

There is something ludicrous and painful at the same time in contrasting the ineffectiveness of war preparation in Canada with the practical and effective methods followed in the countries of Europe.

In France and England,—not to speak of Germany where it was carried to the point of perfection—, no single regiment was put on foot, no man-of-war despatched for action, before the most elaborate and effective measures had been adopted and put into execution in order to maintain the credit of the country and its financial institutions, to provide for the storing of foodstuffs, to prevent the cornering of food and the rise of prices, to keep up the trade and industries of the country, and even to profit by the exclusion of German trade from foreign markets.

In this peaceful, mercantile and rural community, apart from a few measures of finance, nothing has been done except a tremendous display of wordy patriotism, with a view to enlisting as many men as possible, fit or unfit for warfare.

The determination of the Canadian Government, as enunciated in Winnipeg by the Solicitor General, is to bankrupt Canada to save the Empire. Considering that practically all the creditors of Canada are London bankers, and that the British government is most anxious to maintain the credit of the United Kingdom, the execution of that patriotic program would hardly contribute to the strength, glory and prestige of the Empire.

[. . .]

To keep up the credit and the prosperity of Canada, first, for the sake of Canada, and, secondly, for the benefit of Great Britain and her allies, ought to be the main object of every level headed and truly patriotic Canadian.

It is but a few weeks since one of the most authoritative London journals, the *Westminster Gazette*, was obliged to remind us that we could render better service to the Motherland and the Empire by growing wheat than by raising soldiers.

In the first weeks of the war, one of the most thoughtful and practical statesmen of the Empire, Lord Milner, warned Great Britain, the British Empire, and the world at large, of the dire menace of famine, which is sure to follow in the footsteps of war.

[. . .]

"GET BACK TO THE LAND!"

"Get back to the Land!" Such is the timely and pressing advice given by many patriotic politicians and publicists, though in no greater hurry to go and till the soil than they are of shouldering their muskets for war, in spite of their tremendous efforts to induce other people to enlist.

The advice is excellent; but if it is to be followed by any large number of unemployed city dwellers, it requires something more than verbal commendations. In so far as it applies to the great rural provinces west of Lake Superior, where the production of wheat could be increased on the largest scale, the situation has been aptly illustrated in a cartoon published in the *Grain Growers' Guide*. One unfortunate city man, attracted by the cry: *"Get back to the Land!"* starts in search of a farm lot. He climbs to the top of a telegraph post along the track of the Canadian Pacific Railway. As far as his sight can reach, he is unable to find one single foot of free land. On each lot is planted a post with a sign: *"Canadian Pacific Railway Lands,"*—*"Hudson's Bay Company Lands," "Canadian Northern Railway Lands"*—and the whole series of grabbing firms and so-called Colonisation Societies, created during the last quarter of a century by our politicians, much to their own profit. At the foot of the telegraph post, a patriotic cur yaps and yelps to its heart's content: *"Get back to the Land!"*

[. . .]

UNEMPLOYMENT AND FOOD PRODUCTION

If the government and parliament are sincere in their wish to help Great Britain, France and Belgium, if they really want to bring our people *back to the land*, to diminish unemployment and misery, and stimulate the production of food, they have a clear duty to perform: let them put the State, temporarily at least, and without disbursement, in possession of a portion of the immense waste lands cornered by the CPR, the CNR, the Hudson's Bay Company and the multitude of real estate companies, most of which include among their directors, shareholders and profit grabbers, a large portion of our *patriotic* statesmen, politicians and publicists. That being done, efficient and strong measures should be adopted to enlist and organise the "civil army". This was the first care of the Patriotic Committee in France; it was immediately followed with practical action and fruitful results. The unemployed of our large cities should be enrolled and put in active service on the land. That army should be equipped with building material and farm implements *made in Canada*, with horses and cattle, seed, etc. Naturally, it cannot be hoped that this work could be accomplished without a certain waste of money and boodle,—though less, I think, than in the raising of an army; for, in military organisation, the exigencies of "loyalty" and "patriotism" forbid any inquiry into, or the slightest comment upon, the profitable operations performed under shelter of devotion to the Empire.

Such or similar measures of practical patriotism should have been taken the very first day war was declared, whether Canada participated in it or not. They have been rendered more imperative on account of the enormous expenditure connected with our participation, and the consequent increase of the economic disturbance of the country. Were they adopted immediately, in spite of the deplorable loss of so many weeks of precious time, numerous and fruitful results would accrue.

THE RESULTS

First, the production of food being largely increased, both the consumers of Canada and those of the allied nations would be partially protected against the frightful inflation of prices which is bound to take place within a few months.

Last year, the government and parliament thought it necessary to create a Commission of enquiry in order to ascertain the cause of the then growing cost of living. Is nothing to be done when the people of this country are face to face with the certainty of a much higher cost synchronizing with general stagnation in business, unemployment of labour and financial stringency?

The second good result of these measures would be the decongesting of large centres. The burden upon municipal exchequers and private charity would be materially alleviated. Thousands of unproductive consumers, threatened with hunger and misery, an easy prey to the temptations of debauchery and disorder, would be turned into active and contented producers. Let there be no delusion: if nothing is done in that sense, there will be riots in more than one Canadian city, before one year or even six months are over.

A third result would be to stimulate several industries, now at a standstill.

The construction of cottages, barns and stables would require building material of various sorts: timber, lumber, bricks, cement, corrugated or galvanised iron-sheeting, etc., etc. Most of those articles would come from our soil and forests, and pass through the various manipulating processes of our factories. Before they were used by the rural producer, their extraction and fabrication would have given bread to the woodman, the brickmaker and the factory labourer; our carrying trade would be enhanced by their transportation.

Those farm implements, shovels, picks, axes, etc., would be the output of our factories.

In August last, the Massey-Harris firm, excluded from its vast European markets, temporarily threw out of employment 5,000 Canadian employees and labourers. If the Federal government, with the help and co-operation of the governments of Alberta, Saskatchewan and Manitoba, undertook to stock five, ten or fifteen thousand new farms the farm implement factories could keep running during the whole winter and save from misery thousands of Canadian men, women and children.

And what about the permanent and ultimate result? By the placement, in the midst of the virgin prairie, of ten or fifteen thousand new homesteads, the State expenditure would be eventually paid back a hundredfold. This would be true national colonisation, far more useful than the wholesale import of foreign immigrants, carried on at a very high cost for the last fifteen years. A similar effort could be attempted on a smaller scale, in their respective spheres of action, by the governments of Ontario, Quebec, New Brunswick and British Columbia, where vast stretches of land could be opened to settlement.

[. . .]

"KEEP THE FACTORIES RUNNING"

In order to face the grave situation confronting the country, another series of practical measures should have been devised and could yet be adopted with a view to keeping up industrial production and fostering the export of manufactured goods. Naturally, to be fruitful, such measures require the active co-operation of public powers and leaders in finance, industry and trade. In this respect, as in the matter of agricultural production, there has been much talk but very little

action. Just as the employed were advised to get back to the land without anything being done to give them land and help them in putting those lands in a state of production, likewise, our talking economists have limited their activities to empty words: *"Capitalists, keep your factories running"—"Consumers, curtail your expenses, and buy nothing but home-made goods."* Very good mottoes, no doubt; but the pious and patriotic warning to be frugal and buy nothing but home-made goods, is singularly weakened by the knowledge that the Canadian volunteers were supplied, at the expense of Canada, with razors made in Germany and purchased at a cost considerably higher than the retail price before the war!

As to the demand that factories be kept running, it must not be forgotten that factories cannot be operated with patriotic expostulations: manufacturers need money as well as raw materials; they need also a consuming market for their goods, and means of transportation to reach those markets.

[. . .]

THE NUMBER OF MEN

As to the number of men, it is more than doubtful if the Canadian government acted wisely in pledging themselves to send to the front one, and perhaps two or three hundred thousand men. Such an effort surpasses, in proportion, what is being done by Great Britain herself. In his parliamentary statement of the 17th of September, Lord Kitchener declared that the total number of British forces then at the front was "rather more than six divisions of infantry and two divisions of cavalry." That was equivalent to about eighty-five thousand men; let us say one hundred thousand.

If Canada sends 100,000 men, out of a population of 8,000,000, the United Kingdom, with its 46,500,000 people should keep at least 600,000 men at the front. This is precisely double the figure which Lord

Kitchener, on the 25th of August, indicated as the total to be reached the month of February or March.

What are the available military resources of the United Kingdom?

Before the war broke out, the Regular Army stationed in the British Isles counted in round numbers 300,000 men; the Territorial, a trifle less. In his last speech in the House, on the 16th of November, Mr Asquith declared that 700,000 new recruits had joined the Regulars, and 300,000, the Territorials. This would place the total land forces of the United Kingdom at nearly 1,600,000 men, out of which less than 15 per cent are fighting at present on the battlefields of Europe.

[. . .]

THE DUTY OF "FRENCH CANADA"

With regard to the decision of parliament to bring Canada into this war, I have little to say at present, except this, that the question should never have been placed on the ground of races.

To make a direct and special appeal to the French Canadians, because French and English are fighting side by side in Europe, is to pave the way to most dangerous possibilities. If the French Canadians are led to believe that they have a special duty to perform, because of the casual co-operation of their two "motherlands,"—as England and France are now called in the Province of Quebec— where will they be the day England is again the enemy of France, as she has been during seven centuries, as she was yet in the days of Fashoda?

If this unfortunate appeal to racial feelings is persisted in, let it be done at least with something akin to truth and justice.

All sorts of nasty comments have been passed upon the small proportion of French Canadians enlisted at Val Cartier. If this

and all future Canadian contingents are to be classified by races and nationalities, a distinction should be established, not only between French- and English-speaking volunteers, but also between Canadian-born and British-born. If all British-born soldiers were counted out from the first contingent, it would be found that French-speaking Canadians enlisted in larger proportion than English-speaking Canadians. Out of less than 6,000 Canadian-born recruits, over 2,400 were French. If English Canada is to be credited with all the English-speaking soldiers gone from Canada, then French Canada has the right to count to her credit all the Frenchmen and Belgians, residents of Canada, who have joined their colours or enlisted in their native lands. They are Canadians, just as much as the newcomers from the British Isles. It may be objected that, under the military laws of France, all Frenchmen living in Canada were *obliged* to go and serve. But apart from the fact that those laws could not reach them here, the objection has no value in the mouth of those Imperialists who claim that all Canadians have a strict duty to participate in this war.

Whatever the duty of Canada in this grave contingency, that duty commands the whole of the Canadian people, irrespective of race, creed or language.

CONSTITUTIONAL ASPECT

Another point of great importance has been raised, in connection with Canada's participation in the war. It has been stated, in Parliament and out of it, that Canada, as part of the British Empire, is in duty bound to participate actively in every conflict in which Great Britain may be drawn.

That doctrine is contrary to all traditions, to the basic principals [sic] upon which rests our constitution, to the long standing agreement between the motherland and her self-governing colonies.

Canada, as a mere irresponsible dependency of Great Britain, has no moral or constitutional *obligation*, nor any *immediate interest* in the present war.

Great Britain has entered the conflict of her own free will, in consequence of her entanglements in the international situation. She has framed her policy and decided her action with a sole view to her own interests, without consulting her colonies or considering in any respect their peculiar situation and local interests.

The territory of Canada is not exposed to the attacks of any of the belligerent nations. An independent Canada would be today in absolute safety. The dangers to which her trade may be exposed result from the fact that she is a British possession, subject to the consequences of British policy and the risks of a military intervention decided by the Imperial government upon their exclusive authority and responsibility. It is therefore the duty of Britain to defend Canada and not the duty of Canada to defend Britain. Such was the doctrine laid down in 1854, in 1862, in 1871, by Sir John A. Macdonald, Sir George Cartier, Sir Alexander Campbell. It still holds good, in law and in fact.

Besides, in protecting the territory and trade of her colonies, Great Britain makes sure of her own subsistence.

---

2 Robert Laird Borden, "Canada Will Answer the Call: Sir Robert Borden's Inspiring War-Message to the Canadian People: Speech Delivered at Toronto, Dec. 5th, 1914," Ottawa: Federal Press Agency, [1914].

Mr Chairman and Gentlemen,—

Today there is but one thought in our hearts, and it is fitting that I should speak to you of the appalling struggle which has been forced upon our Empire. I say forced upon us, because I am convinced that no nation ever desired peace more sincerely than the nations which compose the British Empire; that no statesmen ever wrought more to avoid war than the statesmen of Great Britain in the weeks which immediately preceded the conflict.

There is not time, nor is it necessary that I should dwell upon the occurrence which determined the issue. The great events which brought about the establishment and consolidation of the German Empire under Prussian domination are well known to you. Bismarck foreshadowed in a famous phrase the policy of the future. "The great questions are to be settled," he said in 1862, "not by speeches and majority resolutions, but by blood and iron." Then came, in quick succession, the war against Denmark in 1864, the downfall of Austria in 1866, and the overthrow of France in 1870. The policy of blood and iron seemed to consummate the realization of that which has been the dream of Germany for centuries. Germany became an Empire; the King of Prussia became its Emperor. The military spirit of Prussia dominated German thought and German ideals. The intoxication of victory aided by a propaganda preached to every child and every young man by the foremost thinkers of Germany imposed on its people an ideal and ambition which included the dominance of Europe, and, indeed, of the world.

INSIDIOUS TEACHING OF THE WAR ADVOCATES

The world has only recently come to realize the astonishing teaching to which the German people have listened for the last half century. Among many others, Treitschke, a great professor of history, whose influence upon the young men of Germany cannot be over-estimated, and Bernhardi, his disciple, have preached the religion of valour and might. War has been glorified as a solemn duty for the cause of national development. They proclaimed that the State is not only justified, but bound to put aside all obligations and to disregard all treaties insofar as they may conflict with its highest interest.

"War," said Bernhardi, "is in itself a good thing. It is a biological necessity of the first importance. . . . War is the greatest factor in the furtherance of culture and power; efforts to secure peace are extraordinarily detrimental as soon as they influence politics. . . . Efforts directed toward the abolition of war are not only foolish, but absolutely immoral, and must be stigmatized as unworthy of the human race. . . . Courts of arbitration are a pernicious delusion. The whole idea represents a presumptuous encroachment on natural laws of development which can only lead to the most disastrous consequences for humanity generally. . . . The maintenance of peace never can be or may be the goal of a policy. . . . Efforts for peace would, if they attained their goal, lead to degeneration. . . . Huge armaments are in themselves desirable. They are the most necessary precondition of our national health."

GERMANY HAS LONG BEEN A WORLD-MENACE

The profound influence of this teaching upon the German people may be realized from their unquestioning support of the enormous increase in their military and naval forces. Beyond question Germany is the greatest military power in the world. Without any such need as makes a great fleet imperatively necessary to ensure the safety and even the existence of the British Empire, she has built up in ships, personnel, dockyards, and all other essentials a powerful navy designed to challenge conclusions with that of Great Britain. What ambitions would not be open to Germany, what tribute could she not exact, if

dominating Europe with her army she could wage a successful naval campaign against Britain.

Within the past ten years the peace of Europe has been threatened by Germany on no less than three occasions. In 1905 France, at her dictation, was obliged to dismiss her Foreign Minister. In 1909 Germany shook her mailed fist and compelled Russia to bow to her will. In 1911, as the history of the Agadir incident recalls, she again attempted to coerce and humiliate France, and the situation was saved only by the interposition of Great Britain. Germany receded on that occasion from her first pretensions, but only to abide her time, which came in 1914.

CANADA'S OFFER MADE BEFORE WAR WAS DECLARED

The military autocracy of Germany have taught their people for more than twenty years that the British Empire stood chiefly in the path of German expansion, and that war was inevitable. No one could predict the exact occasion which would be seized but no one could doubt the intention of the Prussian militarists. There was the lesson of Denmark and Austria and France. In the end the storm broke suddenly and the country was confronted with responsibilities greater than those which it had ever faced. The situation demanded action; it demanded immediate and unhesitating action beyond the authorization of the law as it then stood; it was impossible for the Government to wait, and by Order-in-Council we promulgated necessary measures in advance of the meeting of Parliament. The people of Canada loyally acquiesced in these measures, and our course has been ratified by the necessary legislative sanction. On the first of August I sent to the British Government a secret telegram announcing Canada's desire to send an expeditionary force if war should ensue. The offer was not accepted until the 6th of August, but in the meantime steps in anticipation were taken and the raising and equipment of troops for such a force was authorized. On the 7th of August the suggested composition of the force was received from the British authorities, and was immediately sanctioned by Order-in-Council.

Recruiting in the meantime had already commenced, and on the 6th of August the preparation of the Valcartier Camp was begun. I visited that camp four weeks from the day on which work commenced, and I am proud that we possess in Canada the ability to achieve within so limited a period all that was accomplished within that month. [. . .]

TREMENDOUS WORK OF ORGANIZATION

I venture the assertion that the organization and arrangements of Valcartier Camp have not been excelled in any part of our Empire since the commencement of this war. It is unnecessary to describe in detail all the equipment, arms, accoutrements and other necessaries furnished. To equip the force sent forward and to make some provision for future contingents 290,000 pairs of boots and shoes have been provided; 100,000 forage caps, 90,000 great coats, 240,000 jackets and sweaters of various types, 235,000 pairs of trousers, 70,000 rifles, 70,000 bayonets, 80,000 oil bottles, 70,000 water bottles, 95,000 sets of valise equipment, and so on in like proportion over a list of sixty-six different articles. With the first expeditionary force we sent to Great Britain 21 thirteen-pounder quick-firing guns, 96 eighteen-pounder quick-firing guns, 10 breach-loading sixty-pounder guns, a large number of machine guns, motor lorries, transport wagons and vast quantities of ammunition. The force was ready for embarkation within six weeks from the outbreak of war, and could have been then despatched if arrangements for escort had been immediately possible. You, perhaps, do not realize how great an undertaking it was for a non-military country to assemble, organize, train, equip and despatch so large a force within that brief period. It is, I believe, the largest military force that ever crossed the Atlantic at one time. In the great Armada, which threatened the shores of Great Britain three centuries ago, there were less than 20,000 soldiers. The force which we have sent across the Atlantic is nearly 50 per cent greater than the total number of British troops under Wellington's command at Waterloo.

MUST BE HIGHLY TRAINED AND SEASONED

It would be not only useless, but unjust and cruel as well, to send untrained men to the front against highly trained and seasoned troops. They must also be hardened by exercise in the duties of a soldier's life until their physical condition will enable them to endure the hardships of active service. Thus our troops are receiving in Great Britain the same tests of training and of exercise which are prescribed for the volunteer army of the Mother Country. That they will acquit themselves worthily no one can doubt who saw them at Valcartier. In physique, in spirit, in courage, and in all qualities that are necessary for the soldier they will be found second to none.

If the training of a soldier is important, the training, the skill, and the experience of the men who command them are even more essential and imperative. The officers of the Canadian militia have all the necessary qualities that could be desired. They have given ungrudgingly of their time and their energy to fit themselves as far as possible for the duties of active service. But for them even more than for the men the training and experience at Valcartier and on Salisbury Plain are not only invaluable, but absolutely essential before they lead their men into action. In this grim struggle our forces will face the most highly organized military machine in the world.

SECOND CONTINGENT BEING PREPARED NOW

I have spoken of what Canada has done. The call of duty has not fallen upon unheeding ears in this country. East and west, every province and practically every community has responded with an ardour and spirit which emphasizes the strength of the ties that bind together the Dominions of this Empire. When the first contingent sailed from Canada we immediately announced that another would follow. During the delay which ensued before the War Office, in pressure of multitudinous affairs, could suggest its composition, it was announced that in addition to 8,000 men engaged in garrison and outpost duty, we would enlist and train 30,000 men; and that from these a second contingent would be despatched as soon as the necessary arms and equipment could be provided and as soon as the War Office would be prepared to receive them. The number under training has recently been increased to 50,000 men and it is arranged that as soon as each contingent goes forward a corresponding number of men will be enlisted to take its place. This will proceed regularly and continuously until peace is achieved, or until we are satisfied that no more men are needed. Our forces under arms in Canada and abroad will soon exceed 100,000 men. That number has frequently been mentioned in the press. In this war which we are waging against the most powerful military organization the world ever knew, I prefer to name no figure. If the preservation of our Empire demands twice or thrice that number, we shall ask for them, and I know that Canada will answer the call. But remember that men cannot be sent forward more rapidly than the British authorities are prepared to receive them and to undertake their final training. Moreover, we have not in Canada, as in countries organized on a military basis, great stores of equipment, arms, accoutrements, ammunition and guns. These must be provided, and they are being provided with all possible expedition. Both here and in Great Britain these requisites are lacking upon the tremendous scale which is now necessary. Without thorough training, without arms, equipment and all the essentials of warlike preparation, men sent into this awful maelstrom of war are but an incubus and danger rather than an aid.

ONLY ONE ISSUE, BUT NOT A SPEEDY ONE

There can be but one issue to this war, but do not expect that it will be a speedy issue. I have reason to know that the results hitherto attained have been all that were anticipated by the Allies; but so far as can be foreseen there is a long struggle before us.

The justice of the Allies' cause is generally understood and recognized among our kinsmen in the great neighbouring nation, and we are proud of their sympathy. [. . .] The people of this Dominion are eager and determined to take their part in a struggle which involves the destiny of their Empire, and, indeed, its very existence. They are quite prepared and willing to assume all responsibilities which that action involves and they have reasonable confidence in Canada's ability to defend her territory.

[. . .]

UNITY OF THE EMPIRE IS WELL DEMONSTRATED

And this war has demonstrated the essential unity of the Empire. When the book is closed and the story has been told, we shall at least owe that to the Kaiser. It was to fall asunder as soon as he girded on his shining armour. But instead it has become tense with unity and instinct with life and action. Our decadent race was to flee in terror before his victorious troops, but the plains of Belgium and France tell no story of decadence. The history of British arms contains no annals more glorious. It is our hope and our confidence that Canada's record will not be less worthy.

In the bitterness of this struggle let us not forget that the world owes much to German thought, endeavour, and achievement in science, literature, the arts and every other sphere of useful human activity. I do not doubt that the German people, misled as to the supposed designs of Great Britain, impressed for the time being by the Prussian military spirit, and not truly comprehending the real causes of the conflict, are behind their Government in this war. Nevertheless, it is in truth a war waged against the military oligarchy which controls the Government of Germany. The defeat of that military autocracy means much for the world, but it means even more for Germany herself. Freed from its dominance and inspired by truer ideals, the German people will attain a higher national greatness then before.

CANADA BELIEVES THAT BRITAIN'S CAUSE IS JUST

Canada is united in the strong conviction that our cause is just and in an unflinching determination to make it triumphant. This appalling conflict was not of Britain's seeking. Having entered upon it, there is but one duty, to stand firmly united in an inflexible resolve to force it to a victorious and honourable conclusion. Reverses may come, but they must only inspire us with a deeper courage and greater determination. Our fortitude and our endurance must equal all demands that the future shall make upon us. All that our fathers fought for and achieved; all that we have inherited and accomplished, our institutions and liberties, our destiny as a nation, the existence of our Empire, all are at stake in this contest. The resolution, the determination, the self-reliance which never failed Canada in the stress and trials of the past will assuredly not fail her now.

Historical Interpretations

3 From Tim Cook, "'He Was Determined to Go': Underage Soldiers in the Canadian Expeditionary Force," *Social History* 41, 81 (2008): 41–74. Reprinted with permission of the publisher.

Thousands of adolescents fought with the Canadian Expeditionary Force (CEF) during the Great War. Historians have overlooked their service because it has been difficult to distinguish them from their older comrades, since most of these young soldiers lied about their age in order to enlist. A sense of adventure, peer pressure, and fierce patriotism impelled young and old to serve. Most underage soldiers who enlisted were 16 or 17 (and later 18 when age requirements were raised to 19), but at least one cheeky lad enlisted at only 10 years old, and a 12-year-old made it to the trenches.[1]

As many as 20 000 underage soldiers served overseas.[2] Canadians under the age of 19 constituted an important segment of the population during the Great War, one of the most traumatic experiences in Canadian history, but their history remains largely unknown.[3] Studying the reaction of these soldiers to the war effort and their interaction with parents, society, and the military forces reveals that young Canadians were approvingly incorporated into and became a significant part of Canada's war effort.

ENLISTMENT

The British and Canadian military had a long history of accepting into the ranks a small number of boy soldiers and sailors in apprenticeship roles, often as buglers, drummers, and young sailors. These boy soldiers and sailors, some as young as 10 or 12, were taken on strength with the regiment or ship, where they were part of the regimental family, eating, serving, and sleeping in the same barracks. Within the family officers tended to take a paternal attitude to these boys, and educational activities were offered or foisted on them to improve their lot in life.[4] Strict discipline and corresponding punishment for flouting regulations were also a part of their service in the rigid hierarchy of military service.[5] They were also in harm's way, with boy sailors fulfilling a variety of roles on a ship and drummer boys leading men into battle.

In Canada, the King's Regulations and Orders for the Canadian militia specified that boys of "good character" between the ages of 13 and 18 could be enlisted as bandsmen, drummers, or buglers.[6] However, since the Canadian permanent force was a mere 3000 before the war, there were very few boy soldiers, although the various and scattered militia units across the country had no compunction about turning to juveniles to fill their always thin ranks. Still, the vast majority of the thousands of adolescents who would enlist in the Great War were not pre-war boy soldiers, but chose to serve for a variety of reasons.

To understand the role of serving adolescents in the Great War, one must acknowledge the constructed nature of childhood.[7] For much of the nineteenth century, little thought or worry was given to the emotional life of young people or the necessity of a childhood filled with play and exploration. Childhood was hard and dangerous in working-class families. All children, no matter their class or ethnicity, were sadly acquainted with death in and out of the workplace. Few families escaped the tragedy of losing children or siblings to disease or accident. Education remained a privilege for most, with youngsters often pulled from schools to support the family. Yet these pre-war working boys and adolescents were also toughened by their hardship, and it was not uncommon for them to mobilize in the workplace, demanding greater rights.[8] Despite their age, they were tough customers who eagerly embraced all aspects of their emerging masculinity, smoking, drinking, and fighting in a rough-and-tumble environment.

At the time, there was no accepted classification for what age designated a child or adolescent, although the state—both at the federal and provincial levels—attempted to define young Canadians through the creation of various forms of legislation. Since 1871, legislation had required that students stay in school until the age of 12, but by the decade before the war this had been raised to 14 or 16, depending on province, as well as on city and rural jurisdictions.[9] However, many young people left school before the legislation allowed and were employed in full-time jobs. There was legislation to control youth from flooding the market, both for their health and to defend against a dilution of the workforce, but this, too, was applied differently across the country, no doubt affected by provincial economies.[10] While labour laws varied, delinquent children and adolescents were defined and normalized in the 1908 Juvenile Delinquents Act, in the attempt to punish transgressive behaviour by youthful deviants. Under the act, delinquents were classified as between the ages of 7 and 16 (18 in some provinces), but children under 12 were treated more leniently under the law.[11] Thus, in the eyes of probation officers and the courts, adolescents fell somewhere between the ages of 12 and 18. While state actors attempted to define childhood, adolescence, and adulthood, the constructed nature of these classifications was also shaped by region, class, and ethnicity. Most young

Canadians were involved in adult activities long before the age of 18. Any attempt to define youth invariably led legislators into contested terrain, although 21 was the required age of adult citizenship.[12]

Since the late nineteenth century, women's groups, educational reformers, and a constellation of reform-minded Canadians had aimed to improve the lot of children's and adolescents' health and spiritual well-being, no matter their age.[13] These groups engendered vast improvements in society and helped to shape the nature of childhood by demanding that the state and society recognize the difference between adolescence and adulthood. While many adolescents were rescued from the gutters, some would soon march straight into the trenches.

Canada went to war in August 1914, carried forward by a swell of patriotic excitement. For some boys in menial jobs or back-breaking work, the transition from a brutal, dangerous industrial profession to the military was viewed as a safe move, especially since few expected the war to extend past Christmas. Trading coal dust for healthy marching did not raise the objections of many in society. Soldiers, both young and old, spoke approvingly of having three solid, if monotonous, meals. The $1.10 a day for privates, plus the chance to serve a seemingly noble cause, were also incentives that drew lads from across the country.

Like all Canadians, adolescents had a myriad of reasons to enlist. "When the war broke out . . . The country went mad!" recalled Bert Remington, who immediately enlisted at age 18, but with a physical appearance, in his words, of "five foot nothing and 85 pounds."[14] Adolescents were just as susceptible to the hyper-patriotism of the period, yet, unlike older men, most did not have good jobs or a family to temper the heady thoughts of serving King and country. Added to these factors was the inherent belief by most young people that they were nearly indestructible.[15] Others had pre-war militia training that

made them more inclined to serve and fight, and before the war some 40 000 school boys had enrolled in the cadets, an institution accused by critics of militarizing childhood and adolescence.[16]

Even those youth who did not march in khaki or carry the .22 cadet Ross rifle had, for the most part, been raised at home and in school on stories of victorious campaigns that had won Britain her empire. While class mitigated some of the messages, insofar as boys and adolescents of working-class families would likely be engaged in paid work rather than education, much of the popular culture of literature, music, and toys for male children was infused with ideals of manliness. Military service in the imperial ranks caught the imagination of most boys at one time or another. Parades, marches, and flag-waving were all normal activities at school or in the community. When war came, many adolescents were eager to carve out their own heroic future.[17]

Despite the sense of naïve adventure and pre-war masculine culture, one cannot discount genuine patriotism and a belief in the widely disseminated liberal ideals underpinning the British war effort. [. . .]

Multiple layers of masculinity thus drove adolescents to enlist. They ached for honour, sacrifice, and an opportunity to prove their manhood. Young boys instantly became men in their own eyes and those of others by signing their names to the legally binding attestation form. A 16-year-old student was treated the same as the 25-year-old baker or the 29-year-old clerk. In moving from short pants to military trousers and puttees, an adolescent moved from being a boy to a man.

This embracing of adulthood began with enlistment. Across the country, hopeful men of all ages made their way to the armouries. While militia orders stipulated that recruits were to be between the ages of 18 and 45, overage and underage Canadians provided fabricated birth dates for official documentation to serve.[18] There was a loophole, however, as adolescents under the age of 18 could enlist if they had a parent's signed letter of consent.

Many parents waived their right to veto their son's choice. Activist and author Nellie McClung was filled with fear and anger when she watched the "first troops going away. I wondered how their mothers let them go." But then her son, Jack, who was also there to see the soldiers off, turned to her with expectant eyes, asking, "Mother, when will I be eighteen?"[19] It was a blow and a realization that the war would affect everyone, but especially the mothers left behind, forced to wait, worry, and watch their eager sons enlist for war. Jack would eventually serve overseas, with McClung's blessing; he survived, although in his mother's eyes he lost his youth on the battlefields of the Western Front.

Jack was lucky; thousands did not return. Percy McClare, who enlisted in April 1915, six weeks after his seventeenth birthday, wrote a pleading letter to his mother asking that she sign the consent form. He had been impressed by a recruiting sergeant who informed McClare "that the men at the [front] are happy as can be . . . Said they had a Jolly time. All I need is your concent [sic]."[20] His mother eventually agreed to his service, as did many parents, who were no doubt pressured by patriotic messages in speeches and posters. As one recruitment poster aimed at the "Women of Canada" demanded: "When the War is over and someone asks your husband or your son what he did in the great War, is he to hang his head because you would not let him go?"[21] Many parents did not need such shaming techniques, as they firmly believed in the war, but it is also clear that some parents allowed their underdeveloped and too-young sons to enlist because they assumed their boys could not possibly be accepted into the ranks of men.[22] Most were soon shocked to find their sons in uniform. McClare served and, as the sergeant noted, was indeed happy in the ranks; but he was killed a month after arriving on the Western Front. Many parents

and adolescent soldiers spent what was left of their lives regretting their choices. Young Private Donald Gordon marched with the 8th Battalion and had lied about his age when he enlisted against his parents' wishes. On April 15, 1915, a sniper's bullet took his life. Among his personal possessions was a Bible with the inscription: "Goodbye, Mother, Forgive me."[23]

While adolescents showed up at recruiting stations clutching letters of consent, often they were turned down because of their size or unsuitability for soldiering. The age requirement of at least 18 seems to have been used as a guide rather than a rule, however, and no one in the heady patriotic environment of 1914 and 1915 inquired too deeply about the influx of adolescents into the ranks. Perhaps the arbitrary assignment of an age—18 and later 19—seemed at odds with the situation of most adolescents who were out of school and working in the capacity of young adults. Whatever the case, thousands of youths disregarded the rule, which was almost impossible to enforce since few recruits had birth certificates, and no one was required to produce one as proof of age. One should also not discount the prevalence of Canadians who did not know their own birthdate. Nonetheless, bluster and brass often allowed many youngsters to elude serious scrutiny during the already inconsistent enlistment process, although parents had the right to pull their underage sons from the forces until the summer of 1915, when this privilege was quietly dropped after a court ruled that the militia had made a pact with a soldier, no matter his age.[24]

Queuing before the recruiting sergeant could be a nerve-wracking exercise. Forty-nine-year-olds with newly dyed hair and 16-year-olds standing erect and sweating under a borrowed jacket and bowler hat watched anxiously as recruiting sergeants jotted down their names and birthdates. Depending on the circumstances of the unit, and especially if it needed more men to hit its quota to go overseas, recruiting sergeants often turned a blind eye to an obviously too-young lad or the deeply lined face of an older man.

Some boys did not know the age requirements and so gave honest responses to the question of their birth date, revealing that they were 16 or 17, or occasionally even younger. One official CEF report noted that underage soldiers who were later questioned about how they got overseas gave consistent responses: these new recruits, when they had given their proper age, were told to "run around the block, think over [their] age, and come back again."[25] Most did, offering a birthdate that fell within the required age range. Yet most adolescents knew that they had to be 18 or 19 to enlist. A study at the end of the war noted that, when the underage soldiers came forward with their real ages, as indicated on their birth certificates, a comparison with the initial attestation paper revealed that ages had most often been inflated to 19.[26] Another study of these soldiers indicated that the number of recruits who gave their age as 19 was out of proportion to any other age group represented in the British Expeditionary Force, likely because it consisted of several age groups, including those who were 16, 17, and 18.[27]

Not all had their wishes come true. Thomas Raddall, who would later become an eminent Nova Scotia novelist and historian, remembered wearing his first pair of trousers at age 15. Having shed his children's clothes, he walked confidently into a recruiting station. "Several boys from Chebucto School had [already] done so and gone overseas," he recounted in his memoirs. "One of our neighbour's sons had enlisted at sixteen and was killed in France at seventeen. But I was recognized by the recruiting sergeant who knew my father [who would be killed overseas], and he told me bluntly to go back to school."[28] However, even if a soldier was turned down, since there was no cross-referencing of rejected men, a determined youth could and

did move from regiment to regiment in search of one that needed to fill its quota. Rejection for an obstinate youth only meant a trip down the street or re-enlisting on another day, with a different sergeant and under a new name, and it was not uncommon to find soldiers who tried to enlist two or three times before they were accepted. [. . .]

The act of enlistment was a two-step process, and being accepted by officers and sergeants did not guarantee service. Recruits still needed to pass a medical examination. The quality of the inspecting medical officers varied at the armouries and depots across the country. Throughout the war, several hundred thousand potential recruits were turned down by medical officers—and this number might have been as high as 40 per cent of all who attempted to enlist.[29] Anything from poor eyesight to flat feet to bad teeth could keep a man out of the service. Age was a factor, but it stopped fewer men than it should have. It was not an easy task to distinguish adolescents from men. A husky farm boy or a lad who had been working at hard labour for years might be in far better shape than a pasty 20-year-old bank clerk. A gangly boy might not stand out, especially in mid-1915 when height requirements were dropped to 5 feet to allow the malnourished and malformed to enlist. [. . .]

The medical screening process remained notoriously unreliable throughout the war. A cursory visual inspection of the naked body was a humiliating event: sunken chests were poked, genitals examined, flat feet kneaded, eyesight tested through distance charts.[30] Thomas Rowlett, an underage signaller, enlisted in Nova Scotia with two pals. Both naked friends were asked the same question by the medical officer: "Are you 19 years old?" Both replied in the affirmative. To the taller one the medical officer nodded; the other he rejected with a dismissive glance.[31] While medical officers were experienced in sizing up a man or boy with a glance and a bit of prodding, this haphazard approach led to regular complaints in England that the weak, too-youthful, and aged were being accepted into the ranks. One diligent medical officer in England was nearly apoplectic about the nature of the recruits by the end of 1915. He lamented that he had examined a tunneller, C.J. Bailey, who had deformed feet, with most of the toes amputated; a J.J. McDonald of the 4th Company, Canadian Engineers, who was missing both of his thumbs; and the 79-year-old W.J. Clements, who had "advanced arterosclerosis" and was barely able to stand erect.[32]

The problem of keeping unfits and undesirables (as the army in England called them) out of the service eventually rose to epidemic proportions, and by the end of 1916 there was a failed attempt to punish medical officers in Canada by having them pay the $120 cost of returning unfit men across the Atlantic. This was never implemented, as it was seen by military officials in Canada as detrimental to the already strained recruiting effort.[33] More successful was an order from the Overseas Ministry that a second examination be carried out on troops before they stepped off the boats in England.[34] However, this generally did not include the underage soldiers, who were often considered good troops; they would wait in England, training for battle, until the day they came of age. [. . .]

Searching letters from desperate parents evoking their rights under the law continued to pluck underage soldiers from their units, however, until the summer of 1915. Roy Macfie, who served with his two brothers, wrote home shortly after arriving in England: "There are two of the Cook boys from Loring here, and their mother sent to the General and told him that they were underage, and were not to go to the front so I think they will be sent home, they won't like it."[35] Sapper J.E. Lowe was likely even younger than the Cook brothers, having enlisted at 15 (although, of course, lying on his attestation paper, which gives his age as 18) as a bugler in a pioneer battalion. After six weeks in England, the tough

little Lowe, who stood 5 feet, 3 inches but had been a pre-war miner, was sent home.[36]

While an undisclosed number of young Canadians were pulled from the ranks, either because of parents' letters or by officers who now realized that the firing line was not the place for an adolescent, hundreds and then thousands of underage soldiers pleaded and cajoled their way into overseas service. Some openly threatened that, if sent home, they would only sign up again under an assumed name. Many officers relented and allowed the adolescents to continue serving, but others would have none of it, and those underage were put on ships and sent home.

Youth has never liked to be told how to act, and this was especially true for those returned to a country gripped with hyper-patriotism as exhibited through war posters, recruiting sergeants, politicians, and patriotic groups that assaulted every young man with the same message: do your bit. One student at the University of Saskatchewan wrote to his mother that he had been pressured to enlist because the other students "make you feel like two cents if you don't."[37] Eminent Canadians roared that "to live by shirking one's duty is infinitely worse . . . than to die."[38] Many men, both young and old, would have echoed Armine Norris's statement, "I enlisted because I hadn't the nerve to stay at home."[39] Norris was no coward and would be awarded the Military Cross for bravery in battle before being killed during the last months of the war.

The returned patriotic youth did not last long under this pressure. Opportunities were available to fight the "Hun" from the classroom floor through the writing of vitriolic essays, by throwing their increasing weight behind raising funds through the various patriotic movements, and, toward the end of the war, by working as "Soldiers of the Soil" to help farmers bring in the crops, but they could not avoid the increasingly aggressive questions and disapproving stares that lumped them together with other perceived slackers. Many re-enlisted, often under assumed names and against their parents' wishes. Enlisting under a false name meant that a soldier was effectively cut off from his loved ones. There would be no letters home, no news of the family, no death benefits should the worst occur. Those at home might never know what had happened to their sons should they fall in battle.

OVERSEAS

The Canadian Division arrived in France in February 1915 and was joined over the next year and a half by three more divisions to form the Canadian Corps, some 100 000 men strong. From the start, the Canadians soon encountered the harsh subterranean world of the Western Front. Million-man armies constructed vast trench systems in aerially eviscerated farmers' fields. The infantry had to endure rats, lice, and frozen feet in the winter and the same insect and rodent tormentors, as well as flies and thirst, in the summer. All year round there was the constant wastage of the trenches, where men were killed by shell and bullet, sickness, and poison gas.

In the firing line, an underage soldier was expected to be a soldier just like his elder mates. Certainly there was no distinction for the other death-dealing weapons that indiscriminately took lives in fearful numbers. Among the ranks, however, underage soldiers sometimes were treated differently by older men who often took younger ones under their wing. Canon Scott recounted the actions of one officer, who told Scott about his encounter with a young lad in his company:

[We] had to hold on, in a trench, hour after hour, under terrific bombardment. [The officer] was sitting in his dugout, expecting every moment to be blown up, when a young lad came in and asked if he might stay with him. The boy was only eighteen years of age, and his nerve was

utterly gone. He came into the dugout, and, like a child clinging to his mother, clasped the officer with his arms. The latter could not be angry with the lad. There was nothing to do at that point but to hold on and wait, so, as he said to me, "I looked at the boy and thought of his mother, and just leaned down and gave him a kiss. Not long afterward a shell struck the dugout and the boy was killed, and when we returned I had to leave his body there."[40]

[. . .]

In the mud and misery of the front-line trenches, officers often ensured that underage soldiers were excluded from the most dangerous duties like trench-raiding, but there were few safe places at the front. Infantryman William Now remembered that his commanding officer had removed an underage soldier from the front-line trenches to carry water in the rear. One night Private Now trudged toward the forward trenches and passed the young lad's "two horses lying dead on the cobbles and the cart all smashed up . . . the boy was not to be seen. He had evidently been picked up. I hoped that he had only been wounded and would survive but it was almost too much to expect. I could not see how he could have escaped, except by a miracle. Some Mother's Boy."[41] While some adolescents were put in "bomb-proof" jobs in the rear, more often underage soldiers were treated the same as their older companions. [. . .]

While some underage soldiers were awarded gallantry medals, including 17-year-old Tommy Ricketts of the Royal Newfoundland Regiment, a Victoria Cross recipient, more often the young soldiers simply did their duty. Herbert McBride recounted that, of the four other soldiers on his machine-gun crew, all were underage. "Some had enlisted at sixteen and not one of them was of voting age."[42]

None was a medal winner; nor did any ever crack in battle. All four would be killed by the end of the war. For those who survived, observed Private J.E. Cromwell, a 16-year-old in the No. 2 Construction Battalion, "You grew up in a hurry."[43] R.B. Henley of the 42nd Battalion enlisted at 13 years old, was caught and sent home, then re-enlisted. Finally making it to France, he reported, "I was scared and stayed scared all the time. But a scared soldier lives longer."[44] He survived, although he was wounded twice in battle.

Young soldiers continued to serve and endure with the help of their mates. The comradeship of the trenches was a key component in constructing and supporting the will to keep fighting through the most dire of circumstances. Not to let down one's companions drove many soldiers to hold on past their limits. It was no different for young soldiers, and perhaps even more important, since there was a desire among most adolescents to live up to the ideals of the masculine soldier. A.E. Fallen, a 17-year-old infantrymen serving with the 52nd Battalion, remembered his first time in the line, standing in mud and slush and wondering to himself, "I hope to God I can stand this. . . . I would have hated like hell to have cracked up as a kid."[45] He found the strength to endure, serving through some of the toughest battles of the war.

Issues of masculinity remained important for the young soldiers. There were norms and regulations to follow in emulating the masculine ideals. Young soldiers did not like to stand out as anything other than a companion in the ranks. Some obviously overcompensated. Nineteen-year-old Private John Lynch recounted that he and other young soldiers "wanted to impress the world with their toughness. We cursed louder, drank harder and behaved in a very boisterous manner, putting on a front for the veterans of the outfit, many of whom were older than our fathers."[46] While service conferred adulthood on young men, sometimes they felt the need to prove it. But the army saw no distinction and paid young lads as much as older men. As well, the young soldiers

received the same rights and privileges in the trenches. The daily issue of rum, in itself a tool for reinforcing discipline, hierarchy, and masculinity, was not denied to underage soldiers. Signaller William Ogilvie, who had enlisted at the age of 17 from Lakefield, Ontario, testified, "We juniors learned the ropes from our older and more experienced comrades and though we younger ones were far from serious drinkers, we were now caught up by the challenge."[47] The act of drinking was often understood to be one of the distinguishing marks between men and boys. Army-issued rum was powerful, syrupy, over-strength spirit that burned, as one soldier remarked, as if "he'd swallowed a red-hot poker."[48] After the first few sputtering attempts, an infantryman learned to hold his rum, and these young soldiers soon measured up to the group's expectations.

While rum was not withheld, neither was enfranchisement. "We had scores of fellows who had not yet reached voting age. We knew at least two who celebrated their sixteenth birthdays in France," remarked Fred Noyes, a stretcher-bearer. "Many gave 'official' ages which wouldn't have stood the test if the authorities had cared to investigate. . . . A remarkable feature of the election was the voting of our teen-old youngsters."[49] As well, young soldiers were sometimes elevated in rank above their older peers. Although it appears uncommon, there were cases like Corporal J.G. Baker of the 15th Battalion, who, at the age of 17, would have been in charge of a dozen men, all likely older.[50] John Hensley enlisted at the age of 16 in Halifax, serving through two years of warfare before he was killed at Passchendaele at the age of 18. During that time, he had risen to the rank of captain, responsible at times for 200 men in his company.

Of course, not all young soldiers survived the emotional and mental rigours of the trenches. Lieutenant William Gray recounted watching one adolescent come unstrung during a heavy drumfire bombardment: "He laughed rather hysterically and babbled incoherently. Suddenly he jumped up, climbed into the open, his sole thought to get away but there, a scant hundred yards, we saw him fall."[51] While anecdotal evidence suggests that young soldiers often had a better chance of withstanding the psychological pressures of war, many soldiers eventually broke under the prolonged stress. One report on British courts martial revealed the shocking statistic that 32 minors had been executed during the war, and that 10 of them had used shell shock as a defence for why they had deserted from the front.[52] None of the 25 Canadians executed was underage, but for all soldiers, from the young in the prime of their lives to the ancient 39ers (the nickname for older men who had lied about their age), enduring the strain of war depended on the man, the circumstances, and the ability to draw on those internal and external resources.[53]

With the constant lack of sleep, the never-ending agony of scratching at lice, and the threat of dismemberment by shell fire, many soldiers eventually began to pray for their release from the front lines. Unlike older soldiers, however, underage ones had an escape route, since by 1916 trench rumours had swirled through the ranks passing on valuable information that underage soldiers could reveal their age and be pulled from the line. Corporal Harry Hillyer wrote to his sister about her son, only a few months before Hillyer was shot in the head and killed in battle:

How old is Eddie? You know if he is under 18 you can claim him out by writing to the OC of the Regiment. I think you would be wise in doing so if his age warrants it as the fighting is liable to increase in fierceness from now on, in fact, we have noticed the difference already. This has happened in 3 cases quite recently in our own regiment. One of the boys claimed out is one of our best scouts but he is to go

just the same although he was very loathe to leave us. Of course, it is immaterial to me, but if he was my brother I would not let him go through what is in store for us here.[54]

Adolescents who had enlisted and embraced the army life, who had even lied to get into it, were torn in a silent battle between doing their duty and supporting their comrades, and the release that they would have received by revealing their real age.

[. . .]

CONCLUSION

The Commonwealth War Graves Commission, tasked with caring for the graves of over a million British and Commonwealth service personnel, has a total of 1412 identified Great War Canadian adolescents under the age of 19 in its care. Of these, 1027 were 18 years old, 296 were 17, 75 were 16, and 14 of the dead were aged 15.[55] Most were killed on the Western Front. Since only about 61 per cent of the total CWGC entries show the age of death, however, it would be logical to assume that about 2270 underage soldiers died during the war. Of course, the number was likely higher, since soldiers who enlisted at 16 or 17 but were killed at 19 would not be classified as underage soldiers in this exercise. They warrant some acknowledgement, even if their number is unquantifiable. Since there were roughly 60 000 Canadian deaths for those in service, one in 26 was an underage soldier. Extrapolating again, of the 424 000 Canadians who served overseas, one in 26 would yield a number of almost 16 300 underage servicemen. Yet many of these underage soldiers never made it to France, and it is therefore likely that they would not have suffered the same casualty rate as those who lie buried in the CWGC cemeteries. Thus the figure of total underage enlistees under 19 was even higher, likely over 20 000. While these figures are necessarily soft, considering that underage soldiers often enlisted using a false age, it is clear that the country had relied heavily on its adolescents during the Great War.

These underage soldiers grew proficient at hiding themselves in their units to escape detection during the war. However, in the post-war years, the adolescents were left increasingly in the forefront of the ever-dwindling ranks of surviving veterans as their more elderly comrades succumbed to age. By the beginning of the twenty-first century, as the last veterans marched into history, it appeared that these now ancient heroes representing the great mass of veterans were all boys when they fought in the Great War. That, of course, is untrue: the average age of the Canadian Great War soldier was 26.3.[56] But the notion of wasted youth, of a lost generation, remains a powerful trope surrounding the Great War.[57] The war "murdered the nation's youth and turned youth into murderers," recounted one bitter veteran in his post-war memoirs.[58] The loss of more than 60 000 Canadians, and perhaps especially those who were underage soldiers, forever marked a generation.

Most veterans survived, however. Crashing back to Canada in wave after wave in 1919, they found jobs scarce in the post-war years as a country mired in debt was little able to fulfill its promise of creating a "land fit for heroes." Furthermore, an 18-year-old who had seen two years in the trenches, prematurely aged and perhaps embittered, did not easily return to being a stock boy or even to live under his parents' roof and rules. There were also the wounded, among whom there would have been some 6500 underage adolescents.[59] Some would never be the same. William Mansley had enlisted at 14 in the second year of the war. At 4 feet, 11 inches and 95 pounds, he could not deny his youth, but still he served in the trenches with the Royal

Canadian Regiment, even if it was only for the last three months of the war and to escape a jail term for stealing a bike. While in the trenches he suffered no physical wounds, but remained psychologically scarred and unable to hold down a job after the war, even though other veterans often tried to intervene on his behalf. In 1930 he wrote to Sir Arthur Currie, his former corps commander, "[O]wing to my age and sacrificing all in life, all I have now is my discharge and medals."[60]

At least some of the underage soldiers who served in the trenches never recovered from their ordeals. These adolescents sacrificed their youth; others, their middle and old age as well. Meacham Denyes had enlisted underage and served with the 102nd Battalion in the summer of 1918 until his death on the battlefield. A post-war commemorative text reflecting on his service observed, "[N]ow that we are at peace again it seems inconceivable that young students barely on the threshold of manhood should take part in such indescribable carnage."[61] Indeed, while these young Canadians faced the firestorm of combat, they were fully supported by a constellation of groups at home, which, despite post-war regret, had actively facilitated the service of these young soldiers. The patriotic discourse during the war encouraged and pressured young men to enlist and urged their parents not to hold them back. The increasingly unlimited war effort was supported by politicians, leaders of society, and even the clergy. The recruiting sergeants and medical officers who turned a blind eye to a nervous boy with no facial hair and an undeveloped body were clearly accountable, but they too had been pressured by their society to take all who could carry a rifle. Of course, the lads themselves must be held responsible for their own actions, as they presented themselves time and time again to enlist, refusing to be infantilized. We cannot, however, read history backwards through the lens of the twenty-first century, which includes Canada's well-respected recent record of attempting to ban child soldiers around the world and to provide support to those brutalized by war. While Canada has its own past of child soldiers, this history must be understood within the context of the time.

NOTES

1. Desmond Morton, *When Your Number's Up* (Toronto: Random House, 1993), 279.
2. See the conclusion for an analysis of available data.
3. For a recent important work that offers some insight into the role of children, see Desmond Morton, *Fight or Pay* (Vancouver: UBC Press, 2004).
4. A.C.T. White, *The Story of Army Education, 1943–1963* (London: George G. Harrap, 1963), chap. 2–3.
5. A.W. Cockerill, *Sons of the Brave* (London: Leo Cooper, in association with Seceker & Warburg, 1984), 41–4.
6. King's Regulations and Orders (1910), para. 243, 246.
7. Cynthia Comacchio, *The Dominion of Youth* (Waterloo: Wilfrid Laurier University Press, 2006), and *Nations Are Built of Babies* (Montreal and Kingston: McGill-Queen's University Press, 1993).
8. For an example of boy miners, see Robert McIntosh, *Boys in the Pits: Child Labour in Coal Mines* (Montreal and Kingston: McGill-Queen's University Press, 2000), chap. 7–8.
9. Marta Danylewycz and Alison Prentice, "Teachers' Work: Changing Patterns and Perceptions in the Emerging School Systems of Nineteenth- and Twentieth-Century Central Canada," *Labour/Le Travail* 17 (1986): 140; R.D. Gidney, *From Hope to Harris: The Reshaping of Ontario's Schools* (Toronto: University of Toronto Press, 1999), 13.
10. Robert McIntosh, "Boys in the Nova Scotian Coal Mines, 1873–1923," in Nancy Janovicek and Joy Parr, eds, *Histories of Canada's Children and Youth* (Toronto: Oxford University Press, 2003), 77.
11. Joan Sangster, *Girl Trouble: Female Delinquency in English Canada* (Toronto: University of Toronto Press, 2002), 15–16.
12. See Robert Mcintosh, "Constructing the Child: New Approaches to the History of Childhood in Canada," *Acadiensis* 28, 2 (1999), for an overview of the literature.
13. See Ramsay Cook, *The Regenerators: Social Criticism in Late Victorian English Canada* (Toronto: University of Toronto Press, 1985); Sharon Anne Cook, *Through Sunshine and Shadow: The Woman's Christian Temperance Union, Evangelism, and Reform in Ontario, 1874–1930* (Montreal and Kingston: McGill-Queen's University Press, 1995).
14. Daphne Read, ed., *The Great War and Canadian Society: An Oral History* (Toronto: New Hogtown Press, 1978), 90–1.
15. David Silbey, *The British Working Class and Enthusiasm for War, 1914–1916* (London and New York: Frank Cass, 2005), 81.
16. Desmond Morton, "The Cadet Movement in the Moment of Canadian Militarism, 1909–1914," *Journal of Canadian Studies* 13, 2 (1978): 56–69.
17. Mark Moss, *Manliness and Militarism: Educating Young Boys in Ontario for War* (Toronto: Oxford University Press, 2001); Michael Paris, *The Great War and Juvenile Literature in Britain* (Westport, CN: Praeger, 2004).
18. See Directorate of History and Heritage, 74/672, Edwin Pye papers, folder 4, Militia Order No. 372, 17 August 1914.
19. Nellie McClung, *The Next of Kin: Those Who Wait and Wonder* (Toronto: Thomas Allen, 1917), 33, 48.
20. Dale McClare, *The Letters of a Young Canadian Soldier during World War I* (Kentville, NS: Brook House Press, 2000), 1.
21. Toronto, Archives of Ontario, C232–2–0–4–263, "To the Women of Canada" [poster]. See also Jeff Keshen, *Propaganda and Censorship during Canada's Great War* (Edmonton: University of Alberta Press, 1996), 42.
22. Peter Simkins, *Kitchener's Army: The Raising of the New Armies, 1914–16* (Manchester: Manchester University Press, 1988), 182–3.

23. Bruce Tascona, *Little Black Devils* (Winnipeg: Frye Publications for Royal Winnipeg Rifles, 1983), 77.

24. Colonel A.F. Duguid, *Official History of the Canadian Forces in the Great War, 1914–1919, General Series, Volume I* (Ottawa: J.O. Patenaude, Printer to the King, 1938), 430–1; Library and Archives Canada (LAC), RG 9, III, vol. 2893, 160–33, clipping, *Montreal Gazette*, 18 October 1916.

25. LAC, RG 9, III, vol. 37, 8–2–10, 2 pts., Officer in charge of Medical Board Department, Folkestone, to Director of Recruiting, 22 August 1916.

26. LAC, RG 9, III, vol. 1765, file U–I–13, pt. 16, Captain G.A. Dann to OC, YSB, 13 September 1918.

27. Richard Van Emden, *Boy Soldiers of the Great War* (London: Headline, 2005), 33.

28. Thomas H. Raddall, *In My Time: A Memoir* (Toronto: McClelland & Stewart, 1976), 42–3.

29. See Ian Hugh MacLean Miller, *Our Glory and Our Grief: Torontonians and the Great War* (Toronto: University of Toronto Press, 2002), 76–80.

30. Ilana R. Bet-El, *Conscripts: Lost Legions of the Great War* (Stroud, UK: Sutton Publishers, 1999), 33–35.

31. Thomas P. Rowlett, "Memoirs of a Signaller, 1914–1918" (Canadian War Museum Library, unpublished memoir, n.d.), 12–13.

32. LAC, RG 9, III, 8–2–10, 2 pts., Officer in charge of Medical Board Department, Director of Recruiting to Carson, 12 July 1916.

33. Sir Andrew Macphail, *Medical Services: History of the Canadian Forces* (Ottawa: F.A. Acland, 1925), 157–8.

34. LAC, RG 9, III, vol. 30, 8–1–60, Director of Recruiting and Organization to Carson, 5 June 1916.

35. John Macfie, *Letters Home* (Meaford, ON: Oliver Graphics, 1990), 12.

36. See LAC, RG 150, Accession 1992–93/166, box 5768–11, John Lowe; L.C. Giles, *Liphook, Bramshott, and the Canadians* (Preservation Society, 1986), postscript.

37. John Thompson, *Harvest of War: The Prairie West, 1914–1918* (Toronto: McClelland & Stewart, 1978), 42.

38. Quote by Robert Falconer, president of the University of Toronto, cited in Keshen, *Propaganda and Censorship*, p. 23.

39. Armine Norris, *Mainly for Mother* (Toronto: Ryerson Press, n.d. [1919]), 133.

40. Frederick G. Scott, *The Great War as I Saw It* (Ottawa: CEF Books, reprint 2000), 94–5.

41. William Now, *The Forgotten War* (self-published, 1982), 30.

42. Herbert McBride, *A Rifleman Went to War* (Plantersville, SC: Thomas Samworth, 1935), 7.

43. Calvin Ruck, *The Black Battalion, 1916–1920: Canada's Best Kept Military Secret* (Halifax: Nimbus Publications, 1987), 45–6.

44. Cockerill, *Sons of the Brave*, 139.

45. LAC, RG 41, Records of the Canadian Broadcasting Corporation, research transcripts for radio program *Flanders Fields*, vol. 15, 52nd Battalion, A.E. Fallen, 3/1–2.

46. John W. Lynch, *Princess Patricia's Canadian Light Infantry, 1917–1919* (Hicksville, NY: Exposition Press, 1976), 59.

47. William Ogilvie, *Umty-Iddy-Umty: The Story of a Canadian Signaller in the First World War* (Erin, ON: Boston Mills Press, 1982), 40.

48. LAC, RG 41, vol. 8, 7th Battalion, J.I. Chambers, 1/7.

49. F.W. Noyes, *Stretcher Bearers at the Double* (Toronto: Hunter Rose Company, 1937), 175, 183.

50. Desmond Morton and Glenn Wright, *Winning the Second Battle: Canadian Veterans and the Return to Civilian Life, 1915–1930* (Toronto: University of Toronto Press, 1987), 74.

51. William Gray, *A Sunny Subaltern: Billy's Letters from Flanders* (Toronto: McClelland, Goodchild & Stewart, 1916), 164.

52. Gerald Oram, *Military Executions during World War I* (London: Palgrave, 2003), 62.

53. On Canadian executions, see Andrew B. Godefroy, *For Freedom and Honour?* (Nepean, ON: CEF Books, 1998); Teresa Iacobelli, "Arbitrary Justice? A Comparative Analysis of Canadian Death Sentences Passed and Death Sentences Commuted during the First World War" (MA thesis, Wilfrid Laurier University, 2004).

54. Norma Hillyer Shephard, ed., *Dear Harry: The Firsthand Account of a World War I Infantryman* (Burlington, ON: Brigham Press, 2003), 204.

55. I am indebted to Richard Holt for compiling and helping to interpret the information from the Commonwealth War Graves Commission.

56. Morton, *When Your Number's Up*, 278.

57. Jay Winter, *Sites of Memory, Sites of Mourning* (Cambridge, UK: Cambridge University Press, 1995); Jonathan Vance, *Death So Noble* (Vancouver: UBC Press, 1997).

58. Pierre Van Paassen, *Days of Our Years* (New York: Hillman Curl Inc., 1939), 81.

59. The ratio of death to wounded was about one in four during the Great War, and surprisingly consistent among most armies.

60. LAC, MG 30 E100, Sir Arthur Currie Papers, vol. 23, file 92, Mansley to Currie, January 23, 1930 and February 17, 1930; RG 150, 1992–93/166, 5904–14, W.T. Mansley.

61. Walter S. Herrington and Rev. A.J. Wilson, *The War Work of the County of Lennox and Addington* (Napanee, ON: The Beaver Press, 1922), 211.

4   From Peter Moogk, "Uncovering the Enemy Within: British Columbians and the German Menace," *BC Studies* 82 (Summer 2014): 45–72. Reprinted with permission of the publisher.

The stress of war brings out the best and the worst in human beings. This effect was evident in British Columbia after the British Empire (including Canada) went to war with the European Central Powers on 4 August 1914. War assists nation building by promoting solidarity, egalitarianism, and altruism within the dominant cultural group.[1] This was certainly true for British Canadians. Two-thirds of British Columbians were British by origin and, before the establishment of Canadian citizenship in 1947, all Canadians were simply British subjects. The declaration of war inspired a show of loyalty, generosity, and a zeal to serve. There was an immediate outburst of British pride and demonstrations of Canadian patriotism. Parades and military band concerts encouraged the flow of recruits to local militia regiments and to the naval reserve as units were brought up to wartime strength before being sent overseas. Many people who, because of age, family obligations, or disability, could not enlist formed paramilitary groups for the defence of Canada. The Canadian division of the Legion of Frontiersmen and the North Vancouver Rifle Association augmented self-constituted Home Guard associations.[2] Money was collected through patriotic funds to support the dependents of soldiers who had gone overseas and through the Red Cross Society to provide comforts and nursing care for servicemen. These charities were later supplemented by the Canadian Field Comforts Commission. When it was apparent that Britain's enemies were better equipped with automatic firearms, the Machine Gun Fund was established in 1915 to arm Canadian troops with Maxim machine guns.[3]

At first, the population's mood was optimistic and confident. Local newspapers boasted of the British Empire's might. [. . .] The war was expected to be a swift, glorious march to victory with few casualties.

In 1914 the immediate, external threat to British Columbia came from Admiral Maximilian von Spee's German East Asia Squadron, originally based at the Chinese concession port of Tsingtao. These German warships were active in the Pacific Ocean. It was feared that an enemy cruiser might attack shipping and shell coastal installations, such as the Esquimalt naval base. In the first weeks of war the BC press speculated about the probable movements of German cruisers in the Pacific Ocean. In response, the coastal gun batteries at Victoria-Esquimalt were readied for action, and improvised gun batteries were set up at Vancouver and at Seymour Narrows. Two submarines, purchased by the provincial government, were added to Canada's training cruiser *Rainbow* and the two sloops-of-war already guarding the coast. The late August arrival of British, Australian, and Japanese warships on the Pacific coast provided a reassuring presence. The departure of the German naval squadron from the Pacific and its destruction off the Falkland Islands in December 1914 removed that external threat.

Fear of an internal threat remained, and this fear revealed the dark side of human nature. The 22 August 1914 War Measures Act gave Canada's federal cabinet the power to issue regulatory orders-in-council "with the force of law" without parliamentary approval. This act allowed the central government to censor all communications, to seize property, and to arrest and detain without bail anyone who is an "alien enemy, or upon suspicion that he is an alien enemy."[4] In British Columbia the provincial government set up a secret service and the British Columbia Provincial Police (BCPP) swore in special constables to secure vital facilities.[5] Armed guards were placed at strategic facilities to prevent sabotage. [. . .]

Those immigrants from Germany and the Austro-Hungarian Empire who had settled in the province, but had not become naturalized British subjects, were now enemy aliens. The 1911 census identified 17 687 people of German or Austro-Hungarian ancestry in British Columbia—4.5 per cent of the province's population.[6] The province's 11 880 German - Canadians were a long-established group—only 25.7 per cent had been born in continental Europe. Most were British subjects by birth or naturalization, which shielded them from legal discrimination at the war's beginning. They were concentrated in the cities and included professionals, retailers, hotel keepers, and skilled craftspeople. The immigrants from the Austro-Hungarian Empire were mostly recent arrivals, overwhelmingly single men who were still foreign nationals. They had found employment as itinerant railway workers, miners, and loggers. Compared with the German-Canadians, they had less formal education and fewer industrial skills.

To deal with these foreigners the Government of Canada issued a proclamation on 15 August 1914. This proclamation, like the later War Measures Act, authorized the arrest of anyone, especially enemy subjects, who attempted to leave Canada to join their homeland's armed forces. [. . .] The proclamation gave assurance that "all persons in Canada of German or Austro-Hungarian nationality, so long as they quietly pursue their ordinary avocations[, would] be allowed to continue to enjoy the protection of the law and be accorded the respect and consideration due to peaceful and law-abiding citizens." Those caught fleeing from Canada or "attempting to engage in espionage and acts of a hostile nature" in support of the enemy were to be arrested and detained. The property of fugitives could be confiscated. Notices in English were placed in BC newspapers directing citizens of the enemy powers to register with the local police. Police officers were authorized to demand that any enemy national sign a written undertaking to report regularly to the authorities and to refrain from any hostile or disloyal act. Those who refused to sign this document were liable to imprisonment under military guards.[7] Registered enemy aliens were to report to the local police or government agents once a month. There was a rush in applications for naturalization in order to escape the obligation to register and report, but the government authorities were reluctant to grant these requests.

[. . .]

It was naïve to assume that these foreigners would read about the rules in English-language newspapers and obey them. Publications in an enemy language were now forbidden. "Austrian" and German workers at the Rogers Pass Tunnel failed to register or to sign the neutrality declaration because they could not read English.[8] Enemy nationals of military age were supervised by the Canadian army's Department of Enemy Reservists in Victoria, run by Major (later Lieutenant-Colonel) William Ridgway-Wilson. Under a federal order-in-council of 3 September 1914, enemy residents were also expected to surrender any firearms, ammunition, and explosives in their possession. All these provisions seem reasonable and justifiable, but their application was increasingly harsh, punitive, and unselective.

What encouraged a hard interpretation of the rules was the changed perception of Germans and Germany. At the century's beginning the German Empire had been regarded as an upstart power—it was barely 40 years old—testing British patience by its colonial ventures, the rapid expansion of its navy, and aiding the South African Boers in their resistance to the absorption of the Transvaal and Orange Free State into the Empire. On the other hand, the British royal family had kinship ties to Germany and was descended from Hanover's kings. The much-lamented Prince Albert was German, and King George V's consort, Mary of Teck, belonged to an aristocratic German family. The king's family name was indisputably German: von Saxe-Coburg Gotha. Kaiser Wilhelm II of Germany was a grandson of Queen Victoria of Great Britain. Germans were foreigners but not as foreign as other Europeans. [. . .]

Germans were admired for their scientific, industrial, and medical achievements and for their contributions to orchestral music. They were among the preferred nationalities recruited in continental Europe by Canadian immigration agents because of their cultural kinship with the British. They were expected to assimilate easily into Christian "Anglo-Saxon civilization." According to the racial theories of the time, Germans were close cousins of "the Anglo-Saxon Race." [. . .] Drawing on his experience in Manitoba, the Reverend James S. Woodsworth wrote: "Even those who detest 'foreigners' make an exception of Germans, whom they classify as 'white people like ourselves.' The German is a hardworking, successful farmer . . . [T]hey are among our best immigrants. In one sense they are 'easily assimilated,' . . . [N]otwithstanding some faults, we welcome the German."[9] Immigration by German speakers to what became Canada began in the 1750s, and British Columbia's first German-speaking settlers came by way of California in the late 1850s. They provided services for the mining population as "grocers, shopkeepers and brewers." They furnished transportation to the goldfields and even gave the mining town of Barkerville its popular dancing girls.[10]

[. . .]

German origins were not a bar to social acceptance before 1914. Dr John Sebastian Helmcken of Victoria, born in England of German parents, was a member of the province's social elite. David Oppenheimer, a German Jew, was elected mayor of Vancouver in 1888 and served as president of the city's Board of Trade. Henry F.W. Behnsen, a cigar manufacturer from Hanover, represented Victoria City in the provincial legislature for three terms despite his ancestry and past service in the German army. In Vancouver, Gustav Konstantin "Alvo" von Alvensleben was a popular host who had made a fortune in real estate, established a German social club, and was a co-founder of the city's stock exchange. Members of the Loewen and Grauer families succeeded in a variety of fields. "For all these people," writes B. Ramsay, "the process of integration was rapid and easy. Within a generation they were not only part of the community, but leaders of it."[11] The September 1912 visit to British Columbia of the governor general, the Duke of Connaught, and his German wife[12] was an opportunity for German-born Canadians to display their dual loyalty to the British Crown and to their fatherland. There seemed to be no conflict in these allegiances in 1912.

How did the industrious German become the bestial "Hun"? Across Canada, wrote John Herd Thompson, "the home-front propaganda war imprinted a new negative stereotype of the German to replace the positive pre-war image."[13] Calling Germans "Huns" likened them to the feared nomadic and warlike peoples from Central Asia who had ravaged Europe in the fourth and fifth centuries. Ironically, the Germanic tribes were among their victims. [. . .] "Hun" was a new addition to the vocabulary of prejudice, and it had the sanction of wartime patriotism. [. . .]

"Kaiser Bill" became the embodiment of aggressive German militarism, or "Prussianism." In August 1914, Vancouverites burned the Kaiser in effigy.[14] Prime Minister Robert Borden's early assurance that "we have absolutely no quarrel with the German people" was soon forgotten.[15] The belief grew that all Germans were collectively guilty. The assumption that the Germans had started the war was established as early as 1914. The role of Serb nationalists in sparking a conflict with Austria-Hungary, Germany's ally, was ignored. The allies of Serbia were Russia and France, and, in order to strike a quick blow against the French before the Russians could mobilize their vast resources, the German army attacked France through neutral Belgium. The open terrain of Belgium and northern France provided the easiest invasion route. German violation of Belgian neutrality, guaranteed in 1839 by the European powers—including Britain—was indisputable. Reports of the German soldiers' conduct in Belgium were far more shocking. Canadians read stories of how the invaders had looted homes, set fire to towns, and shot civilians whenever they encountered armed resistance. [. . .]

The belief that the Germans had departed from all norms of civilized behaviour was reinforced by events in early 1915. In January, German Zeppelin airships started to bomb British coastal towns, killing civilians. Air raids against cities, far from the battlefront, were a terrifying innovation. The war's ferocity touched Canadians too. In February, the First Canadian Contingent arrived in France, and, in April, these soldiers were deployed in the Ypres Salient. Between attacks, constant shelling and sniping took their toll. Nearly six thousand Canadian soldiers were killed, wounded, or captured in April 1915. On 7 and 8 May, British Columbia's principal newspapers published two Canadian casualty lists showing that over four hundred men were wounded and that around three dozen were killed or missing.[16] Local men who had died were highlighted in the press. The terrible cost of war was now evident. The departure of the Second Canadian Contingent was hastened by the need to make up the losses. When the German army launched two attacks against the Ypres Salient in April, using poisonous chlorine gas—an unprecedented and horrifying weapon—belief in Prussian barbarism was reinforced. [. . .]

This confirmed the damning picture of Germans established by the sinking of the British liner *Lusitania* and the consequent death of twelve hundred passengers, including women and children, on 7 May 1915. The ship was hit by a torpedo fired, without warning, from a German submarine. That torpedo and a secondary explosion caused the vessel to sink within 20 minutes. The language used in the press to report this event was bound to excite emotions: Germany was the "mad dog of Europe" led by "Wilhelm the accursed." The sinking was "savage and barbaric" piracy, another "Teuton outrage" over which these "savages" gloated. The *Victoria Daily Times* outdid other newspapers in its use of inflammatory language. Its 8 May headline read "1,364 WERE MURDERED BY THE GERMANS." Other articles on the same front page bore the titles "Powers of Hell are Arrayed with Huns" and "Germany Knows No Law of God or Man." [. . .]

Thus, the First World War was transformed from being a conflict of rival empires into "The Great War for Civilisation," which is what was inscribed upon the victory medal issued to Canada's military veterans. Elevating the struggle to a confrontation between Christian civilization and ruthless German "kultur" gave lustre to Canada's participation and helped justify the sacrifices being made. This was not just a war: it was now a holy crusade against "a nation of murderers." The transformation of a benign view of German-speakers into a hostile caricature was a radical change in perspective. The corollary of war's beneficial effect in promoting solidarity among members of the "in-group" is the rejection of those seen as belonging to the "out group."[17] German-Canadians were reclassified as dangerous outsiders.

"A Nation of Murderers" was the heading given to the first of a series of anti-German editorials by John P. McConnell of the *Sun* after the *Lusitania* sinking. He wrote: "We cannot see . . . that ANY GERMAN in Canada deserves the slightest recognition as a human being unless he forswears his native land . . . [T]he word 'German' stinks in our nostrils and . . . any man who retains the slightest connection with the German nation is beyond the pale." McConnell disavowed the destruction of German-owned property and proposed, instead, that all German- and Austrian-owned businesses be boycotted. Because the Vancouver police would not give him the names of enemy nationals who had to report to the authorities, he invited readers to provide that information: "The people of Vancouver have the right to know who are Germans and who are not and [the *Sun*] will publish any bona fide letters on this subject." He warned that German proprietors hid behind businesses with English names, such as the "Kew Gardens" owned by the Schumanns and "the Dominion Bakery" run by Messrs Schmid and Kruck. The latter, he alleged, showed their disloyalty by refusing to put war tax stamps on their cheques.[18] Schmid and Kruck engaged a law firm to demand a retraction of the story as they were naturalized British subjects who had lived in British Columbia for over a decade and because only one cheque had lacked a war tax stamp.[19]

[. . .]

One might ask why Anglo-Canadian outrage focused on the Germans rather than on Austrians, Germany's allies among the Central Powers. Canadian troops were fighting Germans in Flanders and France, not Austro-Hungarian troops. Immigrants from the Austro-Hungarian Empire were not as numerous as were German-Canadians. Moreover, the dual monarchy of Austria and Hungary was more difficult to comprehend because of the diverse and intermixed nationalities it ruled. Canadians, frankly, were ignorant of that Empire's complexity. Just as all immigrants from India were called "Hindoos"—Sikhs included—the term "Austrian" encompassed Czechs, Slovaks, Hungarians, Croats, Slovenes, as well as those Ukrainians and Poles who lived under the dual monarchy. [. . .]

In addition to ignorance of Europe's complexity, English speakers in early twentieth-century Canada had a pseudo-Darwinian view of nations. Nations were seen as biological species whose members had inherited physical *and* social characteristics. Influential writers, such as the historian Francis Parkman, spoke of the character traits of "the Anglo-Saxon Race" and "the French Celts."[20] Each group was deemed to have innate behavioural tendencies. The ascendancy of Great Britain and the United States through warfare and territorial expansion in the 1890s had demonstrated the superiority of Anglo-Saxons over other peoples. Canadians of the early twentieth century did not make a clear distinction between heredity and acquired social traits. They also believed in national, religious, and racial stereotypes. Jokes of the time played upon the assumed character and manners of a race or ethnic group—for example, the romantic and excitable Frenchman or the penny-pinching Scot.

Ethnic and physical stereotyping explains why some of the reports received by the BCPP denounced people for disloyalty because they had "the appearance of a German" or behaved or sounded like Germans, as the informants imagined them to be.[21] Speaking in a foreign language or in English with a strong foreign accent were grounds for suspicion.[22] Scandinavians were accused of being Germans.[23] Jews, who often had Germanic surnames, could be denounced for being enemy aliens or pro-German. The garbled spelling of German surnames in the police correspondence reveals an ignorance of the German language. [. . .]

Pre-existing strains within BC society shaped popular reactions to wartime conditions. This is evident in the BCPP records of the period. Labour radicalism unnerved "the respectable element" and suspicion fell easily upon people associated with the Industrial Workers of the World (which promoted working-class solidarity among skilled and unskilled labourers of all origins) or radical political groups. Some migrant workers from eastern Europe were recruited by social democrats and communists. There was also anxiety that the large-scale immigration of East European Slavs might dilute the British character of western Canada's population. Some of the "Austrians" suspected of engaging in seditious activity had Slavic surnames.[24] The organizer of a "Yugo Slav Society" had advised Slavs from the Austro-Hungarian Empire to describe themselves as Serbs to avoid having to report as enemy aliens (Serbia was an ally of Great Britain).[25]

[. . .]

Regular contributions to the Canadian Patriotic Fund, the Red Cross Society, or to the Victoria Patriotic Aid Society became a test of loyalty.[26] In June 1918, Margaret Gordon of Naramata refused to pay her water rates for irrigation because, she said, the water company's agent, Hans Salting, was an insolent German who "refuse[d] to pay one cent towards any of our various patriotic and Red Cross societies" and yet "he [was] cunning enough not to *say* anything sufficiently disloyal to intern him." Salting was found to be a Dane and a socialist "who [did] not believe in war." Since a lack of enthusiasm for the war was a hallmark of disloyalty, pacifists were despised.[27]

The newspapers fed paranoia about the internal menace by publishing reports of the arrest of alleged enemy spies and saboteurs in France and Britain. Enemy agents, spies, and saboteurs were assumed to be everywhere.

[. . .] The provincial police were forced to investigate alarming reports of flashing lights at night, mysterious vessels offshore, hidden firearms, supposed caches of explosives, suspected radio installations, disloyal talk, and the presence of enemy nationals close to telegraph lines, railway bridges, and train tunnels.

What were innocuous activities in peacetime could be seen as sinister deeds in wartime, at least to the distrustful mind. For example, when the German-Canadian Graff brothers, farming near Vesuvius on Salt Spring Island, were said to be setting up radio aerials and sending smoke signals to unseen vessels, it was revealed that they were really erecting a wire fence and burning the old wooden rails that it replaced.[28] [. . .]

Detecting the enemy within also gave homefront patriots a feeling that they were playing an active and useful role in the conflict. This show of patriotic zeal may have raised their social status as well as their self-esteem. Being unable to retaliate against those who were killing Canadian and British Empire troops, civilians in Canada directed their anger and hostility at those linked by ancestry to the enemy. After one more false denunciation of someone for being a German agent or for being pro-German, Captain G.E. Robertson of the Marine Department wrote: "I hardly think it fair that hearsay should be the means of possibly doing a man harm."[29] [. . .]

Many Germans and Austrians had a nostalgic affection for their birthplace and, in Canada, some must have sympathized with the Central Powers during the war. Social clubs, choral societies, church congregations, and two newspapers had kept the German language alive in British Columbia. Because the open expression of pro-German sentiment was dangerous in wartime Canada it is impossible to document this natural sympathy for one's homeland. Reserve officers of the German Imperial Army were most likely to return to their country of birth. Those who remained in Canada were reluctant to enlist in the Canadian army to fight against their homeland, and they resisted conscription in 1917. [. . .]

The war allowed people to give a patriotic veneer to private disputes with those who had come from enemy countries. [. . .] The chief constable at Prince Rupert was in favour of arresting all German residents "before any damage [was] done," and the Haida of Skidegate, an Indian agent reported, had volunteered to "go to Lawn Hill and kill the Germans." [. . .]

A case of a vendetta with a patriotic colour arose in early 1917. [. . .] A. Dohlie, a German, had been running a general store at Parksville, and his low prices attracted customers. This offended L. Compton Reade, who wrote to the provincial premier in February 1917 to complain about the "4 alien Germans" who were allowed to move freely about the municipality. In fact, two were naturalized British subjects and a third was an American citizen. Compton Reade described Dohlie as "an unnaturalised pure German" and thought it was scandalous that soldiers' dependents who were receiving financial assistance from the Canadian Patriotic Fund spent their money at Dohlie's store. By contrast, one of the two partners in a rival "British Store here" was in the army "at the front" and his associate was liable to be called to serve in the armed forces. His departure, according to Compton Reade, "would leave the field practically open to a German to wax fat in the Community." The investigating chief constable interviewed Compton Reade and other residents, who "describe[d] him [i.e., Reade] as somewhat of a 'crank' on this subject" and concurred with an earlier decision of a policeman and an army officer that Dohlie need only report to the local justice of the peace regularly *even though he was a naturalized citizen.* The policeman did not endorse Compton Reade's wish to see Dohlie interned.[30]

[. . .]

Dismissing employees who had come from enemy countries had a precedent. In the mother country, immediately after the declaration of war, the Vancouver *Daily Province* reported that "British families [were] discharging German servants, governesses and chauffeurs."[31] It made sense to remove enemy nationals from defence-related jobs, and, at the Esquimalt Dockyard, an Austrian worker identified as "Poney Bryan" had been discharged in September 1914.[32] In the next year "a German named Schmidt, and a dangerous character," working as "one of the shore gang on [the warship] HMS *Kent*," was arrested and sent to the Saanich Prison Farm. Upon investigation, it was discovered that this "dangerous character" was British-born, had served in Britain's territorial army, and had earned the Queen's South African medal "with five clasps" in the Boer War. He aroused suspicion by discarding his German surname (there was only a newspaper notice about his name change) and then adopting the name "Stanley Macdonald."[33]

Less justifiable were the dismissals from purely civilian occupations. [. . .] The war exacerbated an older ethnic conflict among workers in the copper mines at Phoenix. According to Greenwood's constable: "There are two factions in Phoenix, the Austrians and Slavs or 'Bohunks' as they are commonly called, and the Welshmen and their sympathizers, this has been smouldering for some time and almost culminated in a riot on Dec. 27th 1912." After newspapers reported that the "Austrians" had raised their flag at Phoenix, the investigating officer found that this report was untrue and, in reality, that "six or eight Austrians . . . after being paid off [i.e., dismissed], bought a keg of beer and were sitting around in the evening, drinking, dancing and playing the goat generally." The copper mines laid off single men from Austria-Hungary first. "A large number . . . have already left Phoenix and, in a short time, will be scattered over the country looking for work. A number have been trying to cross the line into the United States, but have been turned back by the American Immigration authorities."[34]

By January 1916, Superintendent Colin Campbell of the BCPP had come to the conclusion that, even if there were no official objection to the employment of "Aliens of Enemy Nationality as long as they behave themselves," it would be "good policy" not to employ them at all "for fear of causing trouble in the [workers'] camp." A day later, he wrote to Greenwood's chief constable and, in addition to the list of enemy aliens already received, asked the chief constable to let him know if there were "any British Subjects in the district who could do the work that these Alien Enemies [were] doing."[35] Under a federal order-in-council of 28 June 1915, unemployed enemy aliens were to be interned, so these men lost both their jobs and their freedom of movement.[36] Dismissing men from their jobs or confining them deprived families of their principal breadwinner, adding to welfare cases. The BCPP superintendent then wondered if the federal government was going to support the indigent dependents of interned men.

Fear of discrimination and, possibly, dismissal from work led a few families to change their surnames. An editorial in the *Sun* had advised German-born residents: "If [you] are Canadians at heart . . . in some instances [you should] go to the length of changing [your] names, for everything German is today revolting to decent people."[37] Like Stanley Macdonald, formerly Schmidt, the Koenigs became Kingsleys and the Reinharts became Ryans. The German origins of some long-established Canadian families were already obscured by the Anglicization of their names: Baumann became Bowman, Neumann was altered to Newman, Schuhmacher evolved into Shoemaker, and Krause was transformed into Crouse. The reason for abandoning a German surname was made clear in the case of A. "Bloomhagen" or "Bloemhagen," a waiter at the Glacier Hotel

near Golden. In December 1915, when the local chief constable investigated the waiter's apparent disappearance, it was discovered that Bloomhagen had changed his name and was now employed in shovelling snow off the hotel's roof: "Bloomhagen was advised last spring by Mrs Young, Manageress of the Glacier Hotel, to change his name to Brown, as his name sounded too much German, and Brown would look better on the hotel payroll, and that he was likely to be discharged if the Suprintendent [sic] of CPR Hotels knew he was a German."[38]

Rather than deflecting hostility, name changes aroused greater distrust, and they were investigated by the police. A German-American tourist from Minnesota, Rowena Busch, registered at the Victoria YWCA as "Regana Rush." That led to a search of her possessions and her bedroom.[39] She was placed under surveillance until her return to the United States. Changing the name of the Victoria's Kaiserhof Hotel to the "Blanchard [sic] Hotel" did not protect it from anti-German rioters in May 1915. [. . .]

The official distinction between enemy nationals and naturalized British subjects of German or Austrian origin faded. In April 1915, Major William Ridgway-Wilson, who was in command of the Department of Enemy Reservists, recommended the arrest and removal of Reinhold "Hipkes" or "Hipkoe" until his reliability and naturalization could be verified. He was a resident of Chilliwack River who had received a German-language newspaper from the United States and, reportedly, "became very jubilant" after reading about "the [German naval] bombardment of Scarborough," England. [. . .] J.B. Watson, Port Renfrew's postmaster, was of the same mind. In April 1916, he informed the BCPP superintendent, Colin Campbell, that there were an Austrian and one German (and, possibly, others) working for the Iowa Lumber Company. "They both claim to be naturalized," Watson wrote, "but as it is said a dead Indian is always a good Indian, I should think an interned Enemy alien, will likely prove good too."[40]

[. . .]

By 1917, any association with Germany was a liability. Berlin, Ontario, was renamed "Kitchener";[41] the town of Prussia, Saskatchewan, became "Leader"; and Carlstadt, Alberta, was transformed into "Alderson" to honour the first commander of the Canadian Corps in Europe. Dozens of other Canadian places were purged of their Teutonic names. The British royal family changed its surname in July 1917 from "Saxe-Coburg Gotha" to "Windsor." [. . .]

In 1918, the belief that the First World War was a moral struggle between Christian civilization and Teutonic evil started by the Germans and led by a kaiser bent on world domination was deeply entrenched in Canada. The United States was officially neutral before it joined the Allied cause in April 1917. An American citizen, Walter C. Barnes, was hired in 1917 as an "Instructor in History" by the University of British Columbia to replace a faculty member who had enlisted in the army and was on a leave of absence. Barnes's BA from the University of Colorado was supplemented by an Oxford University baccalaureate obtained as a Rhodes Scholar, making him a respectable recruit for the history department.

During the spring of 1918, Barnes tried to get his Canadian students to take a more detached view of the war. At a university that had been mobilized to support Canada's war effort, this enterprise was bound to cause trouble. According to one of his students, Chester Field, who wrote home to his cousin at Brisco in the Columbia River Valley:

Our University History Professor who is a liberal minded American, not a German American, says that the Germans are not to blame for this war, indeed it was partly forced on them. The German newspapers charge the British with similar atrocities with which they are charged. As for the

violation of Belgian neutrality, all the European nations have done the like things before, even England to a certain part of Africa. Moreover Germany knew that the struggle was one for her existence. If she did not take a short cut thru [sic] Belgium there would be no longer a German Empire.

Field concluded that "the only reason why Britain wont [sic] accept the German peace terms is because they [sic] want to totally crush Germany, and get all her boundless wealth. Her motives are not as unselfish as the newspapers are forced to say they are." This novel view of the war undermined Field's support for military conscription: "It is a mighty hard thing for a young fellow with all his life to look forward to [and to] die for nothing except the jealousy between nations. Of course you have the chance of coming home disabled and dependent upon friends for food to eat, and then you are called a hero."[42]

This letter came to the attention of Field's uncle at Brisco, who passed it on to the chief constable at Golden, who commented: "[It] looks as though German propaganda [is] being taught in the University of British Columbia." The evidence was delivered to the deputy attorney general of the province, who demanded an explanation from the university.[43] The university's Board of Governors responded that it had "made careful inquiry into . . . the charges against Mr Barnes . . . in respect to his teaching concerning the cause and conduct of the war" and had interviewed three students from the classes he taught, as well as hearing from Chester Field. An investigating committee reached "the unanimous conclusion that the charges against Mr Barnes were not proven" and the Board of Governors accepted its report "unanimously."[44] Given the intensely partisan climate in wartime Canada, this defence of academic freedom seems courageous. On the other hand, Barnes was a temporary appointee and his employment at the university was abruptly terminated on 31 May 1918, well *before* the war had ended.

The post-war odium of being connected with Germany was evident in the sharp drop in the number of Canadians who were prepared to acknowledge their German origins. In 1911, there were 393 320 residents of German origin. By 1921, only 294 636 Canadians were prepared to identify themselves as being of German ancestry.[45] The number of people claiming to be Swiss-, Belgian-, Danish-, Austrian-, and Dutch-Canadians doubled in a decade during which immigration was hindered by war. [. . .]

The First World War was a traumatic experience for Canadians of German origin and for those who spoke German at home. They had been a welcome addition to the dominant British-Canadian population before 1914. The attitude of Anglo-Canadians toward German - Canadians had been cordial. In the war's course people of German ancestry became "outsiders"—the enemy's kin and the spawn of a murderous and brutal race. It was a dramatic loss of status. This transformation was the other side of a war that brought out so many admirable impulses in the dominant cultural group.

[. . .]

NOTES

1. Michal Bauer, Alessandra Cassar, Julie Chytilova, and Joseph Henrich, "War's Enduring Effects on the Development of Egalitarian Motivations and Group Biases," *Psychological Science* 25, 1 (April 2014): 47–57.

2. On the Home Guard associations, see James Wood, *Militia Myths: Ideas of the Canadian Citizen Soldier, 1896–1921* (Vancouver: UBC Press, 2010), 222.

3. Castell Hopkins, *Canadian Annual Review of Public Affairs,* 1915 (Toronto: Annual Review Publishing, 1916), 207–12.

4. "An Act to confer certain powers upon the Governor in Council and to amend the Immigration Act," 5 George V, chap. 2 (assented to 22 August 1915), *Statutes of Canada* (Ottawa: King's Printer, 1914).

5. Superintendent Colin S. Campbell to John L. Sullivan of the Secret Service, 28 April 1916, British Columbia Archives (hereafter BCA), GR 61, vol. 64, p. 669.

6. Canada, *Fifth Census of Canada, 1911,* 6 vols (Ottawa: C.H. Parmelee printer, 1912–1913), 1: 368, 2: 370, 440–41. There were also 479 people of Turkish or Bulgarian origin who, despite their link with Canada's enemies, were ignored by the police.

7. Proclamation of 15 August 1914, BCA, GR 57, vol. 11, file 111.

8. Lieutenant-Colonel H.S. Tobin to Colin S. Campbell, Superintendent of the Provincial Police, 30 October 1914, BCA, GR 57, vol. 9, file 38.

9. J.S. Woodsworth, *Strangers within Our Gates* (Toronto: University of Toronto Press, 1972), 84.

10. B. Ramsay, "The Germans," in John Norris, ed., *Strangers Entertained: A History of the Ethnic Groups of British Columbia* (Vancouver: Evergreen Press, 1971), 98–9.

11. Ibid., 100.

12. Canada's governor general in 1911–1916, the Duke of Connaught, was married to Princess Louise Marguerite of Prussia.

13. John Herd Thompson, *Ethnic Minorities during Two World Wars* (Ottawa: Canadian Historical Association, 1991), 6.

14. "City Stirred by News of Battle . . . Kaiser Burned in Effigy." *Daily Province,* 6 August 1914.

15. Canada, Sessional Papers, Special War Session, p. 14, quoted in Tracy Raynolds, "A Case Study in Attitudes towards Enemy Aliens in British Columbia, 1914–1919,"(MA thesis, UBC, 1973), 35.

16. "Casualties among Canadian Soldiers," *Victoria Daily Times,* 7 May 1915; "Canadian Casualty List," *Daily Province,* 8 May 1915.

17. Bauer et al., "War's Enduring Effects," 3.

18. *Vancouver Sun*, 10 May 1915. The writer states: "the German nation has branded itself as a nation of murderers."

19. "An Explanation," *Vancouver Sun*, 12 May 1915.

20. Francis Parkman, *The Old Régime in Canada* (Boston: Little Brown and Co., 1898 [1874]).

21. T.P. Brazil, Justice of the Peace at Port Renfrew, telegram to C.S. Campbell, 7 October 1914, BCA, GR 57, vol. 8, file 7. The man who had "the appearance of a German" was a Mr Braim, a BC Electric Railway motorman who had come to British Columbia from Ontario. Eric Albrecht, a German subject who tried to go to Seattle, was described as "very erect and steps quickly . . . has the appearance of an army man, but says he is not."

22. Report of Sergeant O'Leary, 15 April 1916, BCA, GR 57, vol. 8, file 3. The report pertains to a man called Jones who was buying chemicals and who "[spoke] with a foreign accent" and "look[ed] very much like Captain Bloomquist [a Swede?]." Among the damning charges made against a man in a Port Alberni hotel in March 1916 was the fact that he exchanged "a few words in a foreign language" and said, in English, something like "anyone would be a fool to say anything in this country."

23. Letters of J.B. Watson, postmaster at Port Renfrew, to C.S. Campbell, 13 March and 18 April1916, BCA, GR 57, vol. 8, file 7.

24. See Chief Constable G. Welsby, Fernie, to C.S. Campbell, 31 October 1916, BCA, GR 57, file 11. This letter is about John Konjelava, who was suspected of aiding an escape from the internment camp at Morrissey. A Mr Luckovitch was discussed in Constable Keir, Duncan, report to C.S. Campbell, 27 July 1915, BCA, GR 57, vol. 9, file 35.

25. Inspector T.G. Wynn, Vancouver, to C.S. Campbell, 19 February 1917, BCA, GR 57, vol. 9, file 35.

26. BCA, GR 61, vol. 62, p. 808; BCA, GR, 61, vol. 64, p. 883.

27. Chief Constable J.A. Fraser, Vernon, to C.S. Campbell, 14 November 1916, BCA, GR 57, vol. 11, file 113.

28. C.S. Campbell to F. Fryer, provincial constable, Ganges, 8 December 1914, BCA, GR 57, vol. 9, file 45; report of Constable Fryer, 19

March 1915, BCA, GR 57, vol. 9, file 45. Looking for a reported radio transmitter in the home of Felix Fruehauf of Pender Harbour, the police found that his wife had a practice key for learning telegraphy. See Thomas Smith, Chief Constable at Vancouver, to C.S. Campbell, 14 May 1915, BCA, GR 57, vol.9, file 34.

29. G.E.A. Robertson to Commander F. James, RN, 31 August 1915, BCA, GR 57, vol. 10, file 82.

30. L. Compton Reade to the premier, 6 February 1917, BCA, GR 57, vol. 11, file 118; Chief Constable W.R. Dunwoody to C.S. Campbell, 17 February 1917, BCA, GR 57, vol. 11, file 118.

31. *Daily Province,* 6 August 1914.

32. Commander Walter Hose, Esquimalt, to Attorney General Bowser, 25 September 1914, BCA, GR 57, vol. 8, file 15.

33. Constable Hugh Allan to C.S. Campbell, 5 June 1915, BCA, GR 57, vol. 10, file 65; Commander F. James to C.S. Campbell, 6 June 1915, BCA, GR 57, vol. 10, file 65.

34. John Simpson, Chief Constable at Greenwood, report to C.S. Campbell, 14 August 1914, BCA, GR 57, vol. 13, file 1265-A.

35. C.S. Campbell to Superintendent and Justice of the Peace T.B. Brazil, Port Renfrew, 13 January 1916, BCA, BC series, GR 61 (Provincial Police Papers, Letter Books), vol. 62, pp. 745 and 790; C.S. Campbell to Chief Constable John Simpson, Greenwood, 14 January 1916, BCA, GR 61, vol. 64, p. 267.

36. Raynolds, "Case Study," 58–60, describes the crisis for the welfare services created by all these dismissals. Premier William Bowser of British Columbia advocated the automatic internment of all enemy nationals, whether employed or unemployed.

37. *Vancouver Sun*, 12 May 1915.

38. Chief Constable R.J. Sutherland, Golden, to C.S. Campbell, 15 December 1915, BCA, GR 57, vol. 9, file 38. Superintendent Campbell's letter of 9 December 1915, about Bloomhagen's apparent disappearance, is in the same file.

39. Letters of 26 and 27 October 1915, BCA, GR 57, vol. 10, file 83 deal with the Rowena Busch case, as does BCA, GR 61, vol. 61, pp. 168–170 and 182.

40. J.B. Watson, Port Renfrew, to C.S. Campbell, 18 April 1916, BCA, GR 57, vol. 8, file 7.

41. Field Marshal Earl Kitchener of Khartoum was the British secretary of war at the beginning of the First World War.

42. Chester Thomas Field, Vancouver, to Ralph Segart, Brisco, 4 April 1918, BCA, GR 57, vol. 13, file 1265-D.

43. Chief Constable R.J. Sutherland, Golden, to Superintendent William G. McMynn, Victoria, 30 April 1918, BCA, GR 57, vol. 13, file 1265-D; and Provincial Secretary, memo to Deputy Attorney General, 9 May 1918, BCA, GR 57, vol. 13, file 1265-D. Information about Walter Barnes comes from *1917 Yearbook* (Vancouver: University of British Columbia, 1917), 24.

44. Board of Governors, University of British Columbia, to the Hon. J.D. MacLean, Minister of Education and Provincial Secretary, 31 May 1918, BCA, GR 57, vol. 13, file 1265-D.

45. Canada, *Sixth Census of Canada, 1921*. Vol. 1 (Ottawa: F.A. Acland, 1924), 354. The same trend was noted in K.M. McLaughlin, *The Germans in Canada* (Ottawa: Canadian Historical Association, 1985), 12–13.

Chapter 6

Environmental History and the Canadian North

READINGS

Primary Documents

1 From *Report of the Royal Commission Appointed by Order-in-Council of Date May 20, 1919 to Investigate the Possibilities of the Reindeer and Musk-Ox Industries in the Arctic and Sub-Arctic Regions of Canada,* John Gunion Rutherford, James Stanley McLean, and James Bernard Harkin

2 From "The Flu Epidemic," edited by Margaret M. Thom and Ethel Blondin-Townsend

Historical Interpretations

3 From "A Broken Frontier: Ecological Imperialism in the Canadian North," Liza Piper and John Sandlos

4 From "The Cold War on Canadian Soil: Militarizing a Northern Environment," P. Whitney Lackenbauer and Matthew Farish

INTRODUCTION

While European imperialism has impacted the Canadian North through the fur trade and exploration since the late seventeenth century, it played out differently than in the southern regions of Canada. The barren land and inhospitable climate of the Arctic and sub-Arctic regions hindered the development of agriculture and limited the expansion of settler society there. The harshness of the physical environment, however, did not prevent Euro-Canadians from exploring, exploiting, and planning for the development of those regions. This chapter focuses on the relationship between humans and nature in the Canadian North. It shows that this relationship has always been complex. While the physical environment restricted what Canadians could do in the Arctic and sub-Arctic regions, they still transformed these regions' geography, vegetation, and wildlife. By introducing micro-organisms such as viruses and bacteria, seeds, and animals to the regions, as well as by building infrastructure such as highways, airfields, and radar stations, Canadians fundamentally altered the physical geography and the different ecosystems. They also deeply affected the Indigenous people living there. Our first primary document is an excerpt from the report of a royal commission of inquiry appointed in 1919 to investigate the possibilities of developing the reindeer and musk-ox industries in the Canadian North. It focuses on the possibility of importing reindeer herds to Canada. It shows that though the importation of some species were accidental (such as viruses and some seeds), others were desired and planned. The second primary document discusses the influenza epidemic that spread along the Mackenzie River in the spring and summer of 1928 from the point of view of a five-year-old boy. The flu virus arrived with a Hudson's Bay Company ship and spread quickly thanks to spring gatherings that brought together Indigenous and white people. Since Indigenous people had never been exposed to this specific strain of influenza before, they lacked proper immunity to the pathogen. In total, at least 10 per cent of the region's Dene population died from the epidemic. Although unintentional, the epidemic is an example of the impact of Euro-Canadian imperialism in the Canadian North. Our first historical interpretation puts these primary documents in their historical context. In their article, Liza Piper and John Sandlos explain how Euro-Canadian imperialism transformed the northern environment and affected the lives of Indigenous people over the last two centuries. Finally, P. Whitney Lackenbauer and Matthew Farish discuss the militarization of the Canadian North in the context of the Cold War. They show how the region was strategically important to the military, and how the military promoted the modernization of the region.

QUESTIONS FOR CONSIDERATION

1. Why did the Royal Commission assume that it was possible to bring reindeer herds to the Arctic and sub-Arctic regions?
2. What would be the advantages of importing reindeer herds to the Canadian North?
3. According to Piper and Sandlos, why were Indigenous people in the northern regions so susceptible to infectious diseases in the nineteenth and twentieth centuries?
4. Why did the Canadian military participate in the modernization of the North? How?
5. How important is it to take into consideration the relationship between humans and our environment when we try to understand the past?

SUGGESTIONS FOR FURTHER READING

Tina Loo, *States of Nature: Conserving Canada's Wildlife in the Twentieth Century* (Vancouver: UBC Press, 2007).

Laurel Sefton MacDowell, *An Environmental History of Canada* (Vancouver: UBC Press, 2012).

Liza Piper, *The Industrial Transformation of Subarctic Canada* (Vancouver: UBC Press, 2010).

John Sandlos, *Hunters at the Margin: Native People and Wildlife Conservation in the Northwest Territories* (Vancouver: UBC Press, 2008).

John Thistle, *Resettling the Range: Animals, Ecologies, and Human Communities in British Columbia* (Vancouver: UBC Press, 2015).

Graeme Wynn, *Canada and Arctic North America: An Environmental History* (Santa Barbara, CA: ABC-CLIO, 2006).

1 From John Gunion Rutherford, James Stanley McLean, and James Bernard Harkin, *Report of the Royal Commission Appointed by Order-in-Council of Date May 20, 1919 to Investigate the Possibilities of the Reindeer and Musk-Ox Industries in the Arctic and Sub-Arctic Regions of Canada* (Ottawa: F.A. Acland Printer to the King's Most Excellent Majesty, 1922), 18–24, 27–8, 33–4.

REINDEER

Possible Maintenance in Canadian Arctic and sub-Arctic—

There is no reasonable doubt as to the possibility of reindeer being able to live and thrive in most parts of northern Canada.

The experience of the United States authorities in Alaska, that of the Grenfell herds in Newfoundland and Labrador, the presence of the wild caribou in large numbers in many different parts of the north and the ample evidence which has been obtained as to the nature of the different areas and the vegetation and other natural conditions found therein, all indicate that while there may be difficulties in the way, these are neither fundamental nor insuperable.

That the wild caribou, which is a member of the same species, with very few points of difference, and these insignificant, can exist in large numbers in the Arctic and sub-Arctic regions of Canada, furnishes practically indisputable evidence as to the suitability of these regions for the maintenance of reindeer herds.

Necessity of Restraint—

In this connection, however, it must not be forgotten that if the reindeer is to retain his quality of domestication, which is, after all, the only argument in his favour as against the caribou, he must of necessity be kept under a measure of restraint.

The caribou, ranging at will from season to season and from place to place, has a distinct advantage not only in the matter of grazing areas, but in being able to avoid insect pests and other conditions which may from time to time interfere with his well-being.

Grazing Problems—Parasitical Infestation—

As evidence that the United States Government is beginning to appreciate this phase of the question, it is noteworthy that Dr. E.W. Nelson, Chief of the United States Bureau of Biological Survey, in giving evidence before the House Committee on Appropriations at Washington in December last, stated that the reindeer herds in Alaska had undergone serious depreciation from various causes, the Bureau of Education, under whose control these herds had been until last year, having made no investigation of the diseases and parasites of the animals, nor any study of the grazing problems connected with the industry.

It had been found that reindeer grazing in the same area for ten years had become very seriously infested with parasites of five or six different kinds, whereas, reindeer herds grazing by themselves over a distant and freer range, were practically free from such parasites.

Grazing Unit—

The United States authorities are now studying the range and endeavouring to determine a grazing unit, that is to ascertain how much land, under the forage conditions of that country, one reindeer needs to maintain it for a year.

Reindeer Moss—

From a statement regarding "Reindeer in Norway," prepared by Mr. N. Width for the information of the Bureau of Education of the United States Department of the Interior, the following is quoted:

> "The reindeer moss (*Cladonia rangiferinas*) is greyish-white when dried, but with a greenish shade when moist; it takes its nourishment chiefly from the air, avidly absorbing the humidity, which makes it swell and become elastic; in a dry condition, however, it is very brittle. It contains flour and gelatin stuff which makes it nourishing to the reindeer and cattle.

> "It grows very slowly. When eaten by the reindeer, which eat only the tops and fine parts of the plants, the moss requires about twenty years to regain its full size. If taken up with the roots, it will hardly grow again."

There would seem to be a considerable divergence of opinion as to how long this reindeer moss or lichen takes to reproduce itself after being closely grazed. Mr. James White, F.R.G.S., Assistant to the Chairman of the Commission of Conservation, states that in Norway the period of recovery is from five to seven years.

The question would seem, however, to be largely one of locality, as the nature of the soil, the amount of precipitation and the extent to which the lichen is eaten down are all factors of importance, while the fact that when in grass producing districts, the reindeer is largely independent of the lichens, is one of great importance in arriving at any decision as to what constitutes a grazing unit.

Large Herds—Difficulties Arising from Necessity for Restraint—

There are now over 200,000 reindeer in Alaska, all of which, in addition to the tens of thousands which have been killed for meat, have come during the last twenty-eight years from the original importation of 1,280 animals, purchased in the years 1892 to 1902 inclusive. This is a remarkable showing, but it is worthy of note that as the animals increase in number and the herds in size, unforeseen difficulties are encountered and that most of these result from the restraint which it is necessary to impose on the domesticated reindeer as compared with the caribou in its natural state of freedom.

The caribou, in his relation to the reindeer industry is dealt with fully elsewhere in this report, but at this juncture it should be noted that he unquestionably constitutes the greatest obstacle in the way of establishing herds of domesticated reindeer in Northern Canada, and especially in that portion of the mainland which lies between Hudson bay on the east and the Alaskan boundary on the west.

Much evidence was secured as to the numbers and habits of the wild caribou which inhabit this region, and while this evidence is not as full and complete as it might be, it is quite clear that these animals exist in such numbers and are so widely distributed, that there will be constant danger of their attracting and absorbing any herds of domestic reindeer which may be established in this area.

Establishment of Experimental Herds—

While the difficulties are not to be ignored or minimized, your commissioners are of opinion that there is no doubt as to the advisability of establishing a number of experimental herds in the most suitable locations which can be selected, for the following reasons:

(1) The creation and development of such herds will provide reliable and economical food and clothing supplies for the natives, both Esquimaux and Indians.

As will be seen from the evidence submitted, there have been most distressing instances of actual starvation among these people, due to failure of their usual food supplies. In this connection it would appear to be necessary to provide further safeguards against the possible extermination of the caribou and other wild life, such as had already taken place in certain localities.

(2) To provide future food supplies for white men who may go in to develop or exploit, as the case may be, the mineral and other natural resources of the north.

It may be here pointed out that the food supply furnished by the reindeer herds in Alaska has proved to be a very valuable factor in the development of that country.

(3) To lay the foundation for a possible future commercial meat industry. From the evidence, as also from certain memoranda submitted with this report, it will be seen that such industries have already been established in Norway and in Alaska.

Your commissioners understand that the Hudson's Bay Reindeer Company is now inaugurating a commercial herd on the concession on Baffin island, granted a year ago to Mr. Vilhjalmar Stefansson. In view, however, of the enormous areas available, there is no reason why many similar enterprises should not be established in Northern Canada.

Further, should this scheme prove abortive or for any reason fail to succeed, much valuable time would be sacrificed, whereas the development by the Government itself, of several small experimental herds, in different carefully selected localities, would largely remove the elements of doubt and uncertainty, and so tend to encourage private enterprise and investment.

As a matter of fact, there is no limit to the possible extension of the industry, if gone about properly and on sound lines. There are, however, certain lessons to be learned from the experience of other countries.

Even in Norway, the home of the reindeer, there is, if we may judge from the evidence of Mr. Storker Storkerson, room for considerable improvement, at least in the matter of winter feeding.

In Alaska, as has already been pointed out, over-confidence and neglect of the first principles of animal husbandry, have produced a crop of parasitic and other troubles, which it will be our duty to avoid.

Dr. Grenfell's experience in Newfoundland with its discouraging sequel at Lobster bay, as also the ill-starred attempt to locate a herd of reindeer at Fort Smith, all point to the necessity for the employment of caution, care and foresight, as well as sound practical knowledge in any action which may be taken. [. . .]

Selection of Localities—

The evidence indicates that great care must be exercised in selecting locations for any herds which it may be decided to establish.

Vegetation—

In the first place, the district must be one in which the vegetation is of such a nature, and in such quantity, as to provide ample sustenance for the herd. The evidence of those witnesses best qualified to express an opinion, is to the effect that the reindeer and his relative the caribou, readily eat both grass and lichen, having apparently no special predilection for either, but utilizing whichever is most prevalent in the locality in which they may happen to be.

Herding—

The nature of the country must be such as will permit of effective herd control. The evidence indicates that in some districts man, either on foot or on horseback, would find it quite impossible, especially during the summer season, to travel over the surface in any given direction at such a speed as to permit of effective herding.

Flies—

While the evidence on this point is somewhat conflicting, it has been fairly well established that during the summer season, when the flies are bad, both reindeer and caribou endeavour to reach the seashore or betake themselves to higher and more open lands, where they have the advantage of such breezes as may offer.

Natural Shelter—

It is claimed by some witnesses that there is no tendency on the part of either the reindeer or the caribou to seek shelter in extreme weather. Be this as it may, the fact remains that the woodland caribou are much larger than those of the so-called barren land variety, their carcasses dressing out at from two hundred to two hundred and seventy pounds, while the carcasses of the barren land caribou do not weigh over one hundred and fifty pounds.

Of the barren land caribou, those herds which spend at least a portion of the year in the wooded country, are much larger and stronger than those found in the northern islands, the extreme example being the Peary caribou, found in Northern Grant island and Axel Heiberg island, which is a small light animal, very slim and with fragile bones, though there is no lack of lime in that area.

It is, therefore, reasonable to suppose that the existence of winter shelter would be an advantage.

Danger from Wild Caribou—

This is unquestionably the most important point to be considered in selecting the locations for reindeer herds, especially on the mainland.

Many witnesses readily admitted the danger of the absorption of a small herd of reindeer by a large herd of wild caribou, but the danger is by no means confined to the large caribou herds, as a small band of wild caribou would be quite as likely to lead off any reindeer not under close and constant observation and control.

Fencing—

In most parts of the north country, fencing would be a matter of great difficulty on account of frost conditions, while in any case it would add enormously to the cost of operation.

The difficulties in connection with the effective herding of reindeer have already been referred to. It is therefore plain that the selection of a location for a reindeer herd on the mainland will necessitate a very careful study of the area under consideration, so as to utilize to the best possible advantage, as means of control, any suitable valleys or other special topographical features which may be available.

[. . .]

Reindeer Meat—

As stated further on in this report, much valuable evidence was secured by your commissioners as to the undoubted nutritive value and palatability of caribou meat. From evidence, both direct and indirect, it was clearly shown that there is practically no difference between the meat of the reindeer and that of the caribou.

Information secured by Mr. Stefansson was to the effect that in Norway and Sweden there was developed during the war period an excellent market for reindeer meat, and that as the people became accustomed to its use the price increased with the growing demand, until it slightly exceeded those of both beef and mutton.

That it also finds a market in North America is shown by the following excerpt from a most comprehensive memorandum furnished by Dr. James White, F.R.C.S., from which more extensive quotations would have been made but for the fact that before it reached the Commission, much of the information which it contains had already been secured and compiled:

> "During 1919, about 1,000 reindeer carcasses, averaging 150 pounds each, were shipped from Nome to Seattle, making an aggregate of 150,000 pounds, or 75 tons. This meat sold for about 28 cents, f.o.b. Seattle, making the total value of the trade about $42,000.
> "The carcasses are shipped with the hides on, the hides being valued at about $5 each.
> "These shipments were made by the Lomen Company which owns about 16,000 reindeer.
> "The average value of reindeer in Alaska is about $25 per head."

Reindeer Skin—

The skin of the reindeer which, when properly dressed, is very soft and pliable, is the principal clothing material in use among the Lapps of Northern Europe and their kinsmen in Siberia. It is almost solely used for clothing purposes by those natives of Alaska who have reindeer, as also largely by the white inhabitants of that territory. The Esquimaux of Northern Canada use instead the skin of the caribou which is, of course, practically identical. In Ungava, owing to the disappearance of the caribou, the natives have been forced to wear cotton clothing, and as a consequence, endure great physical suffering and are very liable to disease.

Milk—

Although the yield from the domestic reindeer is small, the milk is richer than that of the cow, and among the Lapps reindeer milk and its various products form an important part of the diet.

[. . .]

ESQUIMAUX AS HERDERS

Much conflicting evidence was given as to the likelihood of the Esquimaux or the Indians developing into efficient herders. Most of the witnesses who have had an opportunity of studying the Esquimaux at close range, appeared to think that if properly trained by Lapp experts, they would develop into excellent herders.

This view is of course strongly supported by the experience of those in charge of the reindeer enterprise in Alaska, where the Esquimaux have clearly demonstrated their adaptability in this regard.

Mr. D. Jenness, Ethnologist, who spent one year in Alaska and two on Coronation gulf with the Canadian Arctic Expedition, was not sure that it would be at all an easy task to convert the native Esquimaux into efficient herders. While intelligent and trustworthy, they have been for generations hunters and fishermen, and as long as game, fish and seal are plentiful they will not, in his opinion, turn away from that life for the more humdrum life of herding. If, however, game became scarce, they would, he thought, develop into herders as they had done in Alaska.

Professor D.B. MacMillan also stated frankly that he could not imagine two or three Esquimaux guarding a herd of musk-ox or caribou, as such an occupation was entirely at variance with their usual mode of life. As he knew them in the far north, their summers were spent in hunting and laying up provisions for the winter, while the winter itself was a season of pastime, spent in visiting and other forms of Arctic enjoyment.

It was generally agreed, however, that the Esquimaux was more likely than the Indian to become a herder, but several of the most experienced missionaries thought that the latter could also be trained, though it would take some time and effort to make him reliable and efficient.

Your commissioners desire to emphasize the importance of securing the services of skilled Lapp herders to take charge of any reindeer herds which may be established, and to act as instructors to either white men or natives who may later be entrusted with the care of reindeer. [. . .]

---

2 From "The Flu Epidemic," in Margaret M. Thom and Ethel Blondin-Townsend, eds, *NahechoKeh, Our Elders* (Fort Providence, NWT: Slavey Research Project 1987), 59–61.

The Flu Epidemic of 1928 as seen through the eyes of a child of five years; by Jimmy Sabourin.

"My father said to me, once the snow melts we will break camp and go to town on the scow. As the weather grew warmer I used to climb aboard and I was amazed. I just couldn't imagine travelling on it at all! My father's mother, my granny made me a little paddle and said it was for me so I could help my father.

"When it was time to go and we loaded all our pelts and possessions onto the boat and set off. We drifted downstream and didn't even have to paddle. My father spotted a bear on the shore and he shot it. He and his older brother, Charles Sabourin took the canoe and paddled off to get it. When they returned granny noticed the bear had no ears. They looked as though they had been cut off with a knife. Everyone was very shocked and granny said it was a bad omen. We wanted to throw the carcass away but granny said we must wait and throw it away on dry land. When we came to shore for the night, the men cut the bear's stomach open and threw the carcass away into the bush.

"It was spring time then so the days were long. My father had seen a moose and went off to hunt it. I went along to carry the knife. When we tracked the moose down I went to look at its ear first. One of them was ripped down the middle. Again we thought it was a bad omen. It took all night to cut up the moose and haul the meat to camp. I helped too.

"When we got to town, we opened up our house. We even had a stove with an oven in it. My family were great trappers and had good luck. The men went to the trading post in town that had just opened up. When they came back they had bought a gramaphone. We were astounded and stood around the table listening to it all day.

"Now the treaty payments were about to begin and the fields were covered with teepees. There were so many people! The sickness came so suddenly. What could we do? We couldn't even run away. Gabriel Denetre's father was drumming to ask the sickness to go back to where it came from. By the next morning hardly anyone could stand.

"I saw the brothers driving a cart pulled by two cows. There were boxes on it but I didn't know why. When Jean Marie Sabourin came in I asked him and he said they were for the dead. I was really scared then.

"My parents were too sick to even move. They couldn't even sip water and of course there was no medicine. Granny asked me to get her some manure to boil. She said it was powerful medicine. I looked where my father had tied the dogs the previous year and found some.

"I was trying to light the fire for her when the trader's children Maurice, Louie and Alphonse and their sister Margaret came to help me. Granny tried to crawl out but she was too weak. We helped her put the manure in a lard pail, pour in water and set it on the fire. The children went back to their father and returned with some dried milk. They had things like that because their father was a white man. They mixed it with water and gave it to granny. She also drank the manure broth.

"The priest, the grey nuns and the brothers brought around watery oats and dried bread. They said it was for whoever was hungry.

"I started to get sick that night. My ears began to buzz and my head hurt. The next morning I was hungry but I didn't know where any food was. Jean Marie found something for me, dry meat, fish and a trout. He spoke to my parents. My father said he couldn't eat as he had a pain in his side. Jean Marie said he wanted to go back down river but he couldn't. He was needed to dig graves. There was no one to help him. He was covered with mud.

"My father said, what is happening? Then Jean Marie said, your brother died yesterday. When my father heard that he started screaming and crying. He and his brother had been the only two sons in that family.

"How is my sister Liza? He went on, she is sick.

"I noticed granny was not moving. I told my father and he took off her blanket. She

was no longer breathing. Even though he was so sick, my father laid her out himself.

"When the priest came by, my father told him what happened. The priest said, there have been so many people dying. The brothers will make a coffin for her and come and get her. Then he prayed over granny with his rosary and blessed her with water. He said, when you die, your body returns to dust but your breath and soul belongs to Jesus.

"I was so sad and there were tears in my eyes. Who could I call granny now?

"My father said that we would not burn her blankets but leave them the way they were. I wasn't scared, not after what the priest said. That night I went and laid my head on her blankets and fell asleep. The next morning I was better. I believed that my granny had helped me get well and that made me happy.

"Maurice and the other boys came by then and told me they had found something in the bushes and that I should go with them to see. It was a tent that had belonged to an old man who had died. Inside was a piece of white cloth on a pole with caribou antlers and a drum. There were also birch bark baskets and pans that you use for washing your face. The boys took the drum but I thought it might be dangerous. Maurice said he had heard the old man play his drum and he knew how to do it.

"We went down to the river bank and Maurice drummed for us and we danced. I asked him if he drummed medicine songs but he didn't know. They were just songs that he could remember.

"When we went to the fields there was not one teepee left. The police had advised people to leave because of the epidemic . . . Many things had been abandoned in the rush to get away; knives and beautifully made baskets.

"I sometimes think how I may well have been one of those put into a box and yet I survived . . . and here I am still walking around today."

Historical Interpretations

3   From Liza Piper and John Sandlos, "A Broken Frontier: Ecological Imperialism in the Canadian North," *Environmental History* 12, 4 (October 2007): 759–95. By permission of Oxford University Press.

In his narrative account of the expedition sent in the summer of 1899 to secure a treaty with the Cree and Chipewyan people who inhabited lands that would become part of northern Alberta, the Secretary of the "Half-Breed" Commission, Charles Mair, suggested that the lower reaches of the Athabasca River offered ideal conditions for agricultural settlement within Canada's northern territories. "The future of the Athabasca," Mair wrote, "is more assured than that of Manitoba seemed to be to the doubters of 30 years ago. In a word, there is fruitful land there, and a bracing climate fit for industrial man, and therefore its settlement is certain." Most importantly, there was, according to Mair, "ample room" for new immigrants who were willing to work the land; the time had come to extend the reaches of Canada's agricultural frontier into the fur trapping and trading frontiers of the high northern latitudes.[1] Mair's vision of a taiga forest and tundra landscape transformed into a productive and fertile plain was repeated time and time again in government survey reports and popular narratives over the next two decades. For the promoters and dreamers of northern expansion, the time had come to extend the farming and settlement frontier to the northward reaches of the country.[2]

In retrospect, the general enthusiasm for the agricultural potential of Alberta's northern forests appears to be largely misplaced. Extreme winter temperatures, the risk of summer frost, the long distances from major markets, the variable quality of the soils, and a relatively brief growing season ensured that there was little land suitable for large-scale agriculture in the Canadian prairie provinces above the 56th parallel. As one moves farther north and east to the vast Arctic tundra region, extreme temperatures, continuous permafrost, and nutrient deficiencies in the soils suggest that agricultural production of any kind is a futile undertaking. [. . .]

At first glance, then, the Canadian North seems a poor candidate for a study of the ecological dimensions associated with European imperialism. Certainly the wholesale ecological changes that Alfred Crosby has identified with the introduction of European plants, animals, and disease micro-organisms in New World environments did not occur on the same broad scale in Canada's North as in the temperate latitudes of North America.[3] Throughout the large expanse of the Canadian Arctic tundra and sub-Arctic forests there are few introduced species of plants: native flora such as jack pine (*Pinus banksiana*) and Labrador tea (*Ledum groenlandicum*) dominate even the most southerly extensions of the boreal forest region. In addition, large populations of native wildlife such as caribou, moose, and muskoxen are still the most prominent faunal assemblages in the tundra and boreal environments. In terms of human populations, the Aboriginal people continue to form a demographic majority over much of northern Canada (in 2001, for example, First Nations and Inuit people comprised 85.2 per cent of the population in Nunavut and 50.5 per cent in the Northwest Territories, the two largest northern political jurisdictions in Canada).[4] Thus, in many respects, the Canadian North can be characterized as a region where ecological imperialism has failed. [. . .]

In spite of these underlying environmental conditions, foreign biological invaders arrived in sub-Arctic and Arctic Canada in much the same ways that they arrived in temperate North America. Disease micro-organisms travelled in the bodies of Europeans and seeds arrived mixed with the straw used by the Hudson's Bay Company for packing. The intentional introduction of food plants such as barley and animals such as oxen meant that European portmanteau biota travelled widely across the North and were assisted by Europeans in adapting to northern New World environments. [. . .]

Throughout the Canadian North, recognizable processes of ecological imperialism precipitated significant social and environmental change on a local or regional scale without necessarily producing a Neo-Europe. Sporadic attempts to introduce European plants and exotic animals to the tundra and sub-Arctic forest regions often carried profound ecological consequences in local environments. In addition, the accidental introduction of countless disease organisms beginning in the eighteenth century drastically altered Aboriginal communities and their relationships to the natural environment with social and economic repercussions spread throughout the Canadian North. The purpose of this essay is to assess the tentative success of ecological imperialism in the region. Our investigation of major categories of alien species introductions in northern Canada—diseases and animals—suggests that ecological imperialism was an important historical process that produced variable and often localized ecological changes in a region located outside of the temperate Neo-Europes. Here the simultaneous progression of colonization and environmental change occurred not as an all-encompassing invasion along a single line of advance, but as series of sporadic and limited changes on the uneven border of a broken frontier.

DISEASE

In 1942, work crews on the Alaska Highway brought measles into the Teslin Lake district,

infecting 129 people within a population of 135. This outbreak was followed in 1943 by dysentery, jaundice, German measles, and finally meningococcic meningitis, which caused the largest number of fatalities. There were also sporadic cases of mumps, tonsillitis, and ear infections.[5] Ten years later, in the eastern Arctic, measles devastated Inuit communities along Ungava Bay and on southern Baffin Island. Doctors with the National Department of Health and Welfare traced the source of infection to children living at the Goose Bay air base in Labrador. Inuit returning to Fort Chimo (Kuujjuaq) and Frobisher Bay (Iqaluit) from the base brought the measles with them, leading to two separate outbreaks during which 99 per cent of those exposed to the virus fell ill and 75 people died. In 1954, doctors Peart and Nagler described the mortality rates of 7 per cent in the Ungava district and 2 per cent on Baffin Island as "unprecedented in modern times."[6] In *Ecological Imperialism*, Alfred Crosby uses these outbreaks to introduce the larger discussion of the effects of disease in the New World and as evidence of his main thesis, that "when isolation ceases, decimation begins."[7] The notion that the North was isolated previous to the middle of the twentieth century obscures a much longer interaction of northerners with foreigners, international politics and markets, and most importantly "invading" alien pathogens. The Alaska Highway and Ungava epidemics were two among several major twentieth-century epidemics that represent the culmination, not the onset, of the process of ecological imperialism in the Canadian North.

The effects of introduced infectious epidemic diseases upon Indigenous populations are well documented in the historical literature and do not bear repeating in detail here. The estimated impact of these diseases suggests that they killed between 90 and 95 per cent of the Indigenous American population. The Indigenous peoples of northern Canada were not spared from the devastating effects of exogenous diseases upon individuals and communities.[8] As elsewhere, pre-contact health history is uncertain but Indigenous northerners certainly suffered from lower respiratory tract diseases and illness from tapeworms and other parasites prior to the arrival of Europeans. [. . .] Martin Frobisher's explorations in the eastern Arctic in 1576 and Vitus Bering's explorations and contact with the Aleuts from the west in 1741 created the earliest connections to European disease pools. These contacts sufficed for the transmission of infectious epidemic diseases although little evidence of the first epidemics survives. [. . .]

Beginning in the late eighteenth century a pattern of epidemic intensity and diffusion emerges within the documentary record that positions the North squarely within the model of ecological imperialism. In 1782 Samuel Hearne appended a note to his published journal describing a smallpox epidemic in northern Canada. Hearne claimed, "the Northern Indians, by annually visiting their Southern friends, the Athapuscow Indians, have contracted the small-pox, which has carried off nine-tenths of them, and particularly those people who composed the trade at Churchill Factory."[9] Many nineteenth-century northern epidemics, as well as the eighteenth-century epidemic Hearne described, were the distant end of major North American outbreaks. Measles and whooping cough epidemics reached the Petit Nord—the area between the Great Lakes, Lake Winnipeg, and the Hudson Bay lowlands—in 1819 and continued northwest, causing significant fatalities south of Great Slave Lake by 1822. Concurrent epidemics of influenza, measles, and dysentery hit the Petit Nord in 1846. In that year, traders reported influenza and measles along the western shore of Hudson Bay, while measles diffused north to Fort Chipewyan and west to the Cordillera region.[10]

These epidemics spread north along corridors of disease transmission that corresponded with the movements of whalers and fur traders. [. . .]

The extent to which these outbreaks led to depopulation in the North has been vigorously debated.[11] In combination with the impact upon northern demography, epidemics profoundly disrupted Indigenous societies. Accounts of starvation, hunger, and poor hunts appear alongside accounts of disease. Epidemics with high adult mortality destabilized social groupings, resulting in the loss of expertise and authority, while small northern populations made it difficult to replace these losses. Shepard Krech has argued that epidemic disease in combination with inter-ethnic hostilities and faunal depletion made the western sub-Arctic more like than unlike other regions of the New World that had faced the ecological onslaught of Europeans.[12]

Yet one crucial element distinguished the role of epidemic disease in northern history. Ecological imperialism in temperate environments involved both the disruption (through death, social disorganization, and depopulation) and replacement of Indigenous populations with agricultural settlers. In the Canadian North, not only did European fur traders depend upon Native men and women for their role as trappers, middlemen, and provisioners in the fur trade, but there were also far fewer people interested in settling frozen soils of the Canadian North than the St Lawrence Valley or the prairie lands to the south. Thousands of people did go north in pursuit of mineral riches. During the Klondike Gold Rush, the population of Dawson City in the Yukon ballooned to 40 000 in 1898. Similar surges of newcomers arrived for mineral rushes further east in the Mackenzie District during the 1920s and 1930s. The resource economy attracted more transient labour than actual settlers, however. By 1902 Dawson's population was down to 5 000 and across the North the influxes of newcomers associated with mining developments appear as little more than isolated peaks in a longer steadier demographic history.

In the absence of a nineteenth-century demographic takeover by Euro-Canadians, northern populations remained small and isolated, and the epidemic transition of the North was delayed. [. . .] Geography, isolation, and small populations were the principal factors which led to variable disease diffusion, rather than northerly latitudes per se. Certain diseases, most notably scarlet fever, may not have arrived in the North until the second half of the nineteenth century.[13] More commonly, epidemics arose in the North when only mild outbreaks if any manifested themselves further south. This is best evidenced by the frequency of epidemics during the late nineteenth century and into the twentieth century.[14] The epidemic diseases most devastating to Indigenous populations were crowd diseases (infections that required large populations in order to survive, in endemic form, in human communities). Small populations in the North limited the number of susceptibles and crowd diseases would spread as epidemics and then fade out. As diseases travelled north periodically from urban centres, adults and children within particular communities may not have been previously exposed, leading to increased morbidity and mortality.[15]

Major epidemics occurred in the Canadian North through much of the twentieth century. In addition to the Alaska Highway and Ungava epidemics described earlier, which were among the last major northern outbreaks, epidemic influenza, measles, dysentery, typhoid, diphtheria, and even smallpox each killed many Natives and to a lesser extent newcomers in the North. Influenza was particularly fatal in the twentieth century.[16] The Spanish influenza pandemic had a surprisingly limited impact in the northern interior, although it destroyed coastal communities such as Brevig Mission in Alaska and Okak in Labrador. The southern Yukon and Alaska Panhandle were among the regions hardest hit, with Native communities disproportionately affected.[17] Quarantine measures implemented by Royal North-West Mounted Police officers, post managers, and

missionaries helped keep the Spanish influenza out of the Mackenzie Valley.[18] The successes of 1918–1919 were not repeated ten years later when this district faced an influenza epidemic of its own. At least one in ten people living along the Mackenzie River died in 1928; Fort Providence lost 20 per cent of its population and many families and some camps were completely destroyed.[19] The influenza arrived on board the Hudson's Bay Company supply ship the S.S. *Distributor* which provided speed and range, but the fuller dispersion of the virus came as a result of spring gatherings including Treaty payments that brought Native peoples, white trappers, and traders together. Then again in 1949, an influenza outbreak among the 84 Inuit inhabitants of Cambridge Bay on Victoria Island led to 17 deaths with an additional 37 people admitted to hospital.[20]

High mortality among Natives distinguished northern epidemics from their southern counterparts in the twentieth century. In part this reflected the demography of northern settlements where often the only non-Natives were a handful of police officers, missionaries, and traders. Furthermore, non-Natives generally had better access to medical care, fewer dependants, and could leave the community during an epidemic. The greater susceptibility of Natives to infectious diseases struck contemporary observers and later chroniclers, suggesting to each that these were what Crosby describes as virgin-soil epidemics.[21] The presence of twentieth-century virgin-soil epidemics in the North would support the argument that, outside of the temperate zone, harsher environments kept foreign invaders at bay until more recently when their final isolation ceased. Relative to more southerly urban populations there is no doubt that northerners had less exposure to these diseases. [. . .] There is considerable evidence, however, that by the twentieth century many northern Native populations had suffered multiple exposures to introduced diseases. These exposures produced acquired immunity in the late nineteenth century to infections such as measles and whooping cough. In outbreaks of infectious disease other than influenza, which mutates frequently enough to thwart acquired immunological defenses, observers often noted both survivors and fatalities who had been previously exposed.[22] The use of the term "virgin soil" is at best partly accurate in describing populations and individuals who had experience with the pathogens that devastated northern communities in the twentieth century.

Referring to twentieth-century outbreaks as virgin-soil epidemics also obscures the other causes of infectious disease epidemics in the Canadian North. [. . .] In the twentieth century, the synergistic impact of concurrent disease outbreaks were typically a pre-requisite to major incidences of widespread sickness and devastating mortality rates among northern Aboriginal populations. The simultaneous spread of measles and influenza, for instance, exacerbated the mortality and morbidity rates associated with Alaska's Great Sickness in 1900 and the Ungava epidemic of 1952.[23] More commonly, it was the debilitating effects of endemic tuberculosis that compounded the impact of infectious diseases among Native northerners. Tuberculosis and its close cousin syphilis had arrived in the North by the end of the eighteenth century. By the 1860s tuberculosis was identified as the foremost killer of native northerners from the Petit Nord to Frobisher Bay (Iqaluit) on Baffin Island.[. . .] Malnutrition was a major factor in disease mortality, particularly so in northern environments where the cold climate and labour necessary for food production required high energy diets, and where shortages of hares, fish, big game, or other dietary staples were common.[24] At times a vicious circle emerged, where disease intensified malnutrition as food producers fell ill and the resultant hunger caused additional sickness when people consumed meat from rotting animal carcasses or other spoiled foods.[. . .] In the early

twentieth century, moreover, white trappers and resource workers competed with Native northerners for increasingly scarce fish and game resources.[25] Exposure and sub-zero temperatures also had more direct effects in contributing to mortality during epidemics. Climate, nutrition, and the compounding effects of other diseases each contributed more to high Native mortality in the twentieth century than a lack of acquired immunity due to prolonged isolation. Finally, the poor quality of medical and nursing care contributed to high mortality rates. The Canadian government insisted upon taking greater responsibility for northern health care in the early twentieth century but failed to discharge its obligations with either adequate treatments or sufficient personnel.[26]

Major changes at mid-century diminished the frequency and severity of epidemic diseases. New medical treatments, in particular the use of antibiotics to treat tuberculosis and vaccination against measles, mumps, and diphtheria, became available beginning in the 1940s. The Dene population began to increase dramatically in the 1950s and the non-Native population focused at Whitehorse and Yellowknife grew as mining and other resource activities expanded. By 1971, Whitehorse had a population of more than 11 000 and Yellowknife almost 6 000.[27] The relative isolation of northern communities retreated in the post–World War II period as increasing numbers of transient seasonal workers kept one foot in urban disease centres and another in northern towns. Government provided additional medical resources to service the growing non-Native population. Transportation links such as the Mackenzie and Dempster highways (completed in 1948 and 1979 respectively) and new aviation routes increased the speed, frequency, and range of movements between northern communities and southern population centres. By the end of the twentieth century, the population of northern Canada had become well integrated with urban disease pools.

The persistence of post-contact epidemics well into the 1950s ensured that disease micro-organisms had the opportunity to interact with new agents of economic and cultural imperialism that emerged during the same period. For many Native communities, the twentieth-century epidemics are historical markers for the transition from "traditional" to "modern" worlds. The 1928 influenza, for example, killed many Dene elders and accounted for the absence of their medicine power in the modern world.[28] [. . .] The Great Sickness of 1900, the Alaska Highway epidemics, and the 1952 Ungava Bay measles outbreak each corresponded with major resource developments in their respective regional environments, in effect facilitating the partial removal of Aboriginal occupants and their attendant material cultures from the path of an emerging industrial economy in northern Canada.

Ecological imperialism had different effects in the Canadian North that were out of synch with the rhythms of post-contact relations in the temperate Neo-Europes. Yet there is no doubt as to the transformative power of the spread of Euro-Canadian diseases when coupled with social and economic colonization in the sub-Arctic and Arctic. Native northerners had experience with introduced diseases dating to the first contacts of the sixteenth century and introduced diseases had similar devastating effects upon northern populations as they did further south. The extent of depopulation remains an open question. What is certain is that agrarian settlement did not follow in the wake of early epidemics. Resource economies—first oriented around furs and later fish, minerals, and oil—extended northward up to the end of the nineteenth century largely relying upon, rather than displacing, Native peoples. Small populations and relatively isolated communities characterized settlement in the Canadian North through the twentieth century. Infectious disease epidemics also persisted into the twentieth century, in part due to the

immunological effects of the continued isolation of northerners, but more importantly as a result of malnutrition, the synergistic effects of concurrent infections and tuberculosis in particular, the physical stresses of life in a cold and extreme climate, and the social, economic, and medical dimensions of Canadian colonization. Disease preceded and accompanied all phases of Euro-Canadian imperialism in the North, collaborating most effectively in the 1928–1929 epidemic when influenza catalyzed the transformation of traditional fur trading societies into more sedentary communities with greater ties to southern cultural norms and commercial institutions.

ANIMALS

The prospect of raising domesticated livestock in the extremely cold and isolated regions of Canada's northern forests might appear, at first glance, to be a questionable undertaking. From the 1890s to the 1940s, however, a combination of land hunger, railway development, and dry conditions in the southern prairies encouraged would-be settlers to colonize an agricultural fringe that stretched along the southern edge of the boreal forest from Quebec to the interior valleys of northern British Columbia.[29] Although these farmers were primarily grain growers, taking up dairy farming and meat production only reluctantly when wheat prices plummeted, some locations nevertheless provided the combination of suitable grazing lands and ready access to local markets or rail lines that was a prerequisite to the successful introduction of cattle ranches to the northern boreal region.[30] Cattle were raised on a small scale, for instance, in the clay belt regions of northeastern Ontario and Quebec after World War I, where abundant lumber and mining camps provided local markets form eat and dairy products.[31] Cattle also were raised for commercial purposes on several Native reserves in Manitoba's Interlake region beginning in the 1890s.[32] The most productive grazing area in the southern boreal fringe, however, was undoubtedly the prairie and forest parkland of northeastern Alberta's Peace River country. Raising livestock was not easy here: Deep snow and harsh climatic conditions rendered winter grazing difficult for even the hardiest breeds of cattle, and large amounts of imported or locally produced hay were required to carry the animals through to the spring. Nonetheless, the Peace River region was the most active area of agricultural settlement in Canada from the 1930s to the mid-1960s, and many of these farmers imported European livestock in significant numbers after 1941, when government subsidies supported the conversion of wheat fields to pasture.[33] By 1976 the livestock population in the Peace River Country had reached 480 000 head of cattle, 75 000 pigs, and 24 000 sheep. In four decades the Peace River country had become the most successful among the discrete islands of livestock production that emerged in the southern fringe of the boreal forest.[34]

Despite the isolated successes in the southern boreal forest, raising livestock in the taiga forest and Arctic tundra north of the 60th parallel proved to be a more intractable undertaking. Small numbers of cattle were introduced, for example, as a supplemental source of meat and dairy products in communities along the Mackenzie River route after the advent of steam navigation in 1887, but the limited availability of suitable grazing areas or hay lands and the long distance from markets and processing facilities prevented any major expansion of commercial animal husbandry north of the 60th parallel.[35] Sporadic attempts to develop cattle operations in the Northwest Territories beginning in the 1970s also failed due to factors ranging from the poor health of one herd owner to the constant harassment of livestock by summer flies. [. . .]

In the early twentieth century, senior bureaucrats within the Dominion Departments of the Interior and Agriculture began to consider ways of overcoming the inherent limitations associated with ranching European livestock in the Far North. They gave serious consideration to the idea of domesticating northern wildlife on a large scale as the basis for settled agriculture in the region. Animals such as caribou and especially muskoxen, it was thought, could better withstand the harsh climate and survive on the sedges and lichens that dominate the Arctic prairie. The federal government also established breeding programs designed to cross cattle with bison or yak to create a new range animal that could easily tolerate cold climates.[36]

These programs yielded few practical results, but the enthusiasm for stocking northern environments with exploitable game populations was such that from 1925 to 1928 wildlife officials with the National Parks Branch and the Northwest Territories and Yukon Branch collaborated on a program to introduce close to 7000 plains bison from southern Alberta to the northern wood bison range in Wood Buffalo National Park. In the short term, the program was meant to alleviate overcrowding on the grazing range at the fenced-in Buffalo National Park near Wainwright, Alberta, but the commercial potential of bison ranching was never far from the minds of those who promoted the project. Maxwell Graham, chief of the Animal Division in the federal government and the most fervent promoter of the bison transfer among senior wildlife officials, argued for the creation of the original wood bison preserve because "a reserve stock of pureblood bison of the highest potency should be kept in reserve, so that the ultimate fixed type of new range animal may continue to pass on to successive generations the potent qualities of the true bison, hardiness, thriftiness, a valuable robe, and first-class beef qualities."[37] The addition of the plains bison to Wood Buffalo National Park would, according to Graham, allow for "re-stocking vast areas suitable for the propagation of bison at comparatively little cost."[38] Within three decades, Graham's dream of productive bison pastures in the northern forests of Alberta and the Northwest Territories had largely been realized. By 1950 there were 12 000 bison within Wood Buffalo National Park and the federal government began to cull between 200 and 800 animals each year until cost overruns and frequent flooding in the two park abattoirs prompted a cessation of the program in 1967. In part the slaughters were meant to control the spread of the tuberculosis bacilli that had arrived with the Wainwright bison, but the annual culls quickly developed into a commercial program that actively sought to develop markets for bison meat in southern Canadian hotels and packing houses. Although the commercial slaughter program remained a small-scale operation and certainly did not live up to earlier dreams of using native animals as an agricultural base for settlement in the Canadian North, by the 1950s the bison population of Wood Buffalo National Park was clearly managed as if it was part of a large game ranch. This agricultural approach to wildlife management implied not only the intensive supervision and control of the bison herds, but also the effective colonization of local human relationships to wildlife as Aboriginal hunters were forbidden to kill a traditional source of food that had been appropriated for the purposes of state-sponsored commercial production.[39]

Game ranching was not the only economic activity that federal officials proposed as a pathway leading toward northern agricultural development. Nothing, in fact, captured the imagination of bureaucrats and private promoters in the early twentieth century more than the idea of importing domesticated reindeer from northern Europe as the vanguard of a settled and prosperous agricultural civilization in northern Canada. In large measure, the enthusiasm for reindeer introductions among senior politicians and bureaucrats within the Departments of the Interior and Indian Affairs was a response to the success of American attempts to transform Inuit hunters along the western coast of Alaska into reindeer herders. [. . .] Vilhjalmur Stefansson offered additional inspiration for the reindeer introductions in Canada. Through late 1918 and early 1919, the famous northern explorer lobbied intensively in Ottawa to persuade senior Canadian politicians and bureaucrats that a combined program of reindeer importation and muskoxen domestication not only would save the Native hunter from privation, but also provide a cheap food supply to fuel the growth of industry in the Canadian North.[40]

It was much easier, however, to dream of an expanding commercial empire based on reindeer ranching than to actually create one. Despite several state-led initiatives and the implementation of a Dominion policy in July 1918 granting free grazing leases to those willing to undertake the risky enterprise of Arctic ranching, all attempts to establish a viable reindeer population in the region before the end of the 1920s failed dramatically. [. . .] A Royal Commission established in 1919 to examine the economic potential of reindeer and muskoxen industries in northern Canada responded three years later to these early failures by recommending that reindeer be introduced to northern grazing ranges only after careful botanical investigations of proposed sites.[41]

By the mid-1920s the Department of the Interior had identified the Mackenzie Delta as one possible location for an experimental herd. The site was attractive not only because of the abundant forage for reindeer but also because the wild caribou herds had been decimated in this region to supply whaling ships with meat in the late nineteenth century. Senior officials in the Department of the Interior thus presumed that the introduction of even a small reindeer herd could provide badly needed food and clothing and also introduce a new modern industry to help advance Inuit hunters in the region beyond their "primitive" state.[42] In 1929 the

Dominion government purchased 3000 rein-deer from the US-based Lomen Reindeer Company, which in turn hired a Sami herder, Andy Bahr, to deliver the animals overland to the Mackenzie Delta from Kotzebue Sound in western Alaska. Bahr spent an astonishing six years driving the surviving 2382 reindeer across the northwestern Arctic mainland, delivering them to their grazing preserve on the west side of the Mackenzie River only in February of 1935.[43]

The introduction of reindeer to the Mackenzie Delta seemed at first to be an un-qualified success. The herd increased to 4585 animals by 1938, and one major goal of the program was fulfilled when 900 reindeer were separated from the main body of ani-mals to become the first Inuit-owned herd. Five additional Native-owned herds were es-tablished over the next two decades and the reindeer population totalled 9000 animals by 1943.[44] An information pamphlet published by the Department of the Interior in 1938 celebrated the adoption of herding among the Inuit, noting that "the change from hunter to husbandman is necessarily a gradual process but progress has been made and the admin-istration looks for further advances in this line."[45] This assessment proved to be overly optimistic, however, as all the Native herds but one had declined in numbers and each was sold back to the main government herd by 1956. By 1958 the total herd had declined to approximately 6000 animals and in 1960 the government sold the herd to private inter-ests.[46] The Canadian Wildlife Service briefly assumed control over the herds after they had declined to just over 2700 animals in 1968, but the herd was sold again in 1974 and has remained a small operation in private hands ever since.[47] The Canadian government's goal of transforming the northern Aborigi-nal economy from hunting and trapping to herding clearly lay in tatters by the end of the 1950s.

Why did the reindeer herds fail to ex-pand in population and geographic range?

Certainly there is ample evidence to suggest that social and ecological conditions in the Arctic precluded the possibility of European reindeer acting as a significant agent of coloni-zation and economic change throughout the region. Not only were there significant losses of reindeer to wolf predation, but the most prominent threat to the reindeer operation was the tendency of the animals to run off with their genetically identical cousins that populated the resurgent wild caribou herds of the Mackenzie Delta.[48] In order to mini-mize these losses, the Sami herders employed at the reindeer station adopted the close herd-ing techniques that were common in their homeland. Under this rigorous regime of su-pervision, herders kept the reindeer tightly packed together by moving constantly in a circle around them. While this technique was effective when applied to the family-owned herds of 300 animals that were the norm in Scandinavia, the monotonous labour re-quired to supervise several thousand animals made it difficult to attract local Inuit to the reindeer project, many of whom preferred the independent lifestyle associated with hunting and trapping.[49] The close herding system also carried with it undesirable ecological conse-quences: The concentration of grazing activ-ity near the base camp of the herders did in some instances lead to overgrazing on slowly regenerating fields of lichen that form the reindeer's main winter food.[50] In 1964 a pri-vate owner introduced an open herding sys-tem involving minimal supervision to allow for more efficient grazing patterns and labour practices. An aerial survey in 1967 revealed that the new management regime was hardly a success: The reindeer population had de-clined from approximately 8000 to just over 2000 animals, most likely the result of an increase in predation and straying from the main herds. The Mackenzie Delta reindeer herders thus faced an irresolvable dilemma. If they left the herd largely to its own de-vices, its population would be regulated by predators and chance encounters with wild caribou that might "carry off" significant portions of the reindeer population, but if they practised close herding they were more likely to strip optimal winter grazing ranges of vegetation and alienate the local Inuit, who were supposed to be the main beneficiaries of the project. The reindeer were, somewhat paradoxically, both too wild and too dependent on human labour to serve as an effective broad-scale colonizer of a remote New World environment.[51]

Nonetheless, the local social, economic, and cultural impact of reindeer introductions in the Canadian North should not be underestimated. Since their arrival in 1929, the reindeer have provided important employment opportunities and a source of relatively inexpensive meat for the Inuvialuit of the Mackenzie Delta. In 1953, for example, the reindeer industry employed 21 Inuvialuit and 10 years later roughly 90 Inuvialuit declared herding as their main source of livelihood. The amount of meat produced was also significant. Although reliable figures are difficult to obtain, between 1935 and 1974 approximately one million kilograms of meat and thousands of hides were distributed for sale to mission hospitals, residential schools, and to individuals through informal sales and the extensive distribution network of the Hudson's Bay Company.[52] The reindeer also have served as an important medium of cultural exchange between the Inuvialuit and the Sami herders. The present owner of the herd, Lloyd Binder, is the grandson of Mikkel Pulk, one of the original Sami herders, and the son of Otto Binder, one of the first Inuvialuit reindeer herders. As Binder's background suggests, the presence of reindeer has created a hybrid culture among many Inuvialuit, one where hunting and trapping is still valued but also one where the alien rhythms associated with herding, calving, roundup, and slaughter have come to play an important role in the seasonal round of economic activity. As of the year 2000, Binder's reindeer herd numbered 6500 animals and there

are plans to expand the herd to nearly twice that number. The reindeer evidently continue to shape the social, economic, and ecological relationships among Indigenous people, local wildlife, and the grazing ranges of the Mackenzie Delta, constituting the most northerly and the most distinctive of the small pockets of European animal husbandry that dot the broad expanse of northern Canada.[53]

[. . .]

CONCLUSION

Over the past three decades, environmental historians have tended to equate colonial environmental change with the radical transformation of New World environments. Although many of the canonical texts within the field have refined Crosby's theory to place more emphasis on economic and cultural factors as important agents of environmental change in colonial environments, few have questioned the assumption that the process of ecological imperialism in North America produced environmental change only in the temperate zones with no discernible effect in other regions.[54] And yet prominent pillars of ecological imperialism [. . .] were clearly present in the non-temperate Canadian North; each produced environmental changes that aided the process of colonization in the region. Many of the impacts of invasive species in the Canadian North were similar to those in the temperate latitudes: European livestock provided a subsistence base for settlers in the boreal fringe, semi-domesticated European animals were introduced as a means to provide Aboriginal people with a more settled and civilized occupation, and diseases undermined the traditional cultures of the region's Aboriginal people. Although few of these northern portmanteau biota produced broad-scale environmental changes (and almost none other than disease produced any effect at all in the tundra region north of the tree line), their introduction to the region did allow for the creation of a disaggregated network of Neo-European settlement and ecological transformation throughout the Canadian North. The evidence from Canada's North further emphasizes how Crosby's broad biogeographical strokes drawn principally according to climate (temperate vs tropical, Arctic, alpine, desert settings) are only broadly accurate. Just as there were significant local successes in the North, there were also likely significant local failures in temperate environments, a better understanding of which has largely fallen by the wayside as scholars have embraced Crosby's approach. In order to better understand the process of ecological imperialism in both temperate and non-temperate settings, it is thus crucial to analyze the various combinations of factors that acted to precipitate localized and broad-scale ecological changes across different regional environments.

[. . .]

NOTES

1. Charles Mair, *Through the Mackenzie Basin: A Narrative of the Athabasca and Peace River Treaty Expedition of 1899* (Toronto: Briggs, 1908), 148.

2. John Schultz, "Report of the Select Committee of the Senate Appointed to Inquire into the Resources of the Great Mackenzie Basin." Appendix I, *Journals of the Senate of Canada*, 1888; J.W. Tyrrell, "Report on the Country North and East of Great Slave Lake," 1901. RG 85, vol. 1087, file 401–22, pt. 1, Library and Archives Canada [hereafter LAC]; Ernest J. Chambers, ed., *Canada's Fertile Northland: A Glimpse of the Enormous Resources of Part of the Unexplored Regions of the Dominion* (Ottawa: Government Printing Bureau, 1907).

3. See Alfred W. Crosby, *The Columbian Exchange: Biological and Cultural Consequences of 1492* (Westport, CT: Greenwood Publishing Co., 1972); "Virgin Soil Epidemics as a Factor in the Depopulation of the Americas," *The William and Mary Quarterly* 33 (April 1976): 289–99; and *Ecological Imperialism: The Biological Expansion of Europe, 900–1900* (Cambridge: Cambridge University Press, 1986).

4. Statistics Canada, *2001 Census of Canada: Analysis Series. Aboriginal Peoples of Canada: A Demographic Profile* (Ottawa: Industry Canada, 2003).

5. John F. Marchand, "Tribal Epidemics in the Yukon," *Journal of the American Medical Association* 123 (1943): 1019–20; Julie Cruikshank, "The Gravel Magnet: Some Social Impacts of the Alaska Highway on Yukon Indians," in K. Coates, ed., *The Alaska Highway: Papers of the 40th Anniversary Symposium* (Vancouver: UBC Press, 1985), 172–87.

6. A.F.W. Peart and F.P. Nagler, "Measles in the Canadian Arctic, 1952," *Canadian Journal of Public Health* 44 (April 1954): 146–56, quotation on 154.

7. Crosby, *Ecological Imperialism*, 196–7.

8. Henry F. Dobyns, *Their Number Become Thinned: Native American Population Dynamics in Eastern North America* (Knoxville: University of Tennessee Press, 1983); William H. McNeill, *Plagues and Peoples* (Garden City: Anchor Press, 1976); Paul Hackett, *A Very Remarkable Sickness: Epidemics in the Petit Nord, 1670–1846* (Winnipeg: University of Manitoba Press, 2002); Robert T. Boyd, *The Coming of the Spirit of Pestilence: Introduced Infectious Diseases and Population Decline among Northwest Coast Indians, 1774–1874* (Vancouver: UBC Press, 1999); Theodore Binnema, *Common and Contested Ground: A Human and Environmental History of the Northwestern Plains* (Norman: University of Oklahoma Press, 2001); R. Cole Harris, "Voices of Disaster: Smallpox Around the Straight of Georgia in 1782," *Ethnohistory* 41 (1994): 591–626; Jody Decker, "'We Should Never Be Again the Same People': The Diffusion and Cumulative Impact of Acute Infectious Diseases Affecting the Natives of the Northern Plains of the Western Interior of Canada, 1774–1839," (PhD diss., York University, 1989).

9. Samuel Hearne, *A journey from Prince of Wale's fort, in Hudson's Bay, to the Northern Ocean* (London: A. Strahan and T. Cadell; sold by T. Cadell Jun. and W. Davies, 1795), 178.

10. John Franklin, *Narrative of a Journey to the Shores of the Polar Sea, in the Years 1819, 20, 21, and 22* (London: John Murray, 1823), 137, 158; Shepard Krech III, "The Influence of Disease and the Fur Trade on Arctic Drainage Lowlands Dene, 1800–1850," *Journal of Anthropological Research* 39 (Summer 1983): 127–8; Hackett, *A Very Remarkable Sickness*, 199, chap. 7; Renée Fossett, *In Order to Live Untroubled: Inuit of the Central Arctic, 1550–1940* (Winnipeg: University of Manitoba Press, 2001), 159; Boyd, *Coming of the Spirit of Pestilence*, 145–60.

11. See June Helm, "Female Infanticide, European Diseases, and Population Levels among the Mackenzie Dene," *American Ethnologist* 7 (1980): 259–85; and Krech, "Disease and the Fur Trade," and "Disease, Starvation, and Northern Athapaskan Social Organization," *American Ethnologist* 5 (1978).

12. For a discussion of the relationship of ecological disruption to disease, see Krech, "Disease, Starvation, and Northern Athapaskan Social Organization," 711, 718–24; Krech, "Disease and the Fur Trade," 132, 135–8; and June Helm, "Bilaterality in the Socio-Territorial Organization of the Arctic Drainage Dene," *Ethnology* 4 (1965): 351–85.

13. Krech, "Disease, Starvation, and Northern Athapaskan Social Organization," 714; Hackett, *A Very Remarkable Sickness*, 187–9, 240.

14. Epidemics manifested in the North in each decade after 1850 until the end of the century. Many of these remain unidentified, others included scarlet fever (1862–1864, 1865, 1897), diphtheria (1880s), dysentery (1851, 1899), smallpox (1850, 1862), typhoid (1855, 1898), typhus (1892), and influenza (1889, 1893, 1896).

15. See Hackett, *A Very Remarkable Sickness*, Introduction; and Boyd, *Coming of the Spirit of Pestilence*, chap. 1, for definitions of terms; Linda A. Newson, "A Historical Ecological Perspective on Epidemic Disease," in William Balée, ed., *Advances in Historical Ecology* (New York: Columbia University Press, 1998), 48–9; McNeill, *Plagues and Peoples*, chap. 5.

16. As in the nineteenth century, problems with the identification of disease outbreaks continued in the twentieth century. Outbreaks of known diseases aside from those described in detail in the text include influenza (1935, 1943, 1944, 1946, 1948, 1950, 1956); measles (1900, 1902, 1916, 1935, 1948); whooping cough (1918, 1919, 1925–1926); dysentery (1900); diphtheria (1907, 1923–1924); typhoid (1902–1903, 1918, 1920). Smallpox was rare but certainly appeared in the west in 1900, arriving on board the steamers at Nome and spreading to Dawson in the Yukon. See Smallpox in the Yukon 1900–1912, RG 29, vol. 2, file 937013 Parts 1 & 2, LAC.

17. "Influenza Among Eskimo in the Arctic," May–June 1919 correspondence, RG 18, vol. 567, file G6, LAC; Mission Diary, January 29, 1919, St. Peter Hay River, Great Slave Lake, Anglican Diocese of the Mackenzie 70.387, MR 4/1c, (hereafter SPHR), PAA.

18. See Julie Cruikshank, *Life Lived Like a Story* (Lincoln: University of Nebraska Press, 1990), 130, n.62; Lyle Dick, *Muskox Land: Ellesmere Island in the Age of Contact* (Calgary: University of Calgary Press, 2001), 401–2; and M.K. Lux, "Disease and Growth of Dawson City: The Seamy Underside of a Legend," *The Northern Review* 3 (1989): 96–117.

19. For descriptions of the 1928 Mackenzie epidemic, see Influenza Epidemic at Good Hope, Norman, and Simpson, 1928, RG 85, vol. 789, file 6099, LAC; 12–22 July 1928, SNM, PAA; excerpts from Chick Ferguson, *Mink, Mary and Me*, Account of Father Antoine Binamé, OMI, at Fort Good Hope, Charles Parker, "Report for the year 1928, submitted to the Department of Indian Affairs," as printed in René Fumoleau, *As Long as this Land Shall Last: A History of Treaty 8 and Treaty 11, 1870–1939* (Toronto: McClelland and Stewart, 1975), 362, 460–74.

20. C.E. van Rooyen, L. McClelland, and E.K. Campbell, "Influenza in Canada during 1949, Including an Account of a Severe Epidemic at Cambridge Bay, Victoria Island, N.W.T., Interim Report to the Defence Research Board Being Part of Influenza Research Done Under Grant D.R.B. 82," RG 29, vol. 1192, file 311-J2, Part 1, LAC.

21. J.F. Moran wrote from Fort Norman in the midst of the 1928 epidemic: "The Indians have no resistance whatever." Extract from Mr. J.F. Moran's letter dated at Fort Norman 7th July 1928, File 5979; RG 85 C-1-a, vol. 789 file 6099, LAC.

22. For further discussion of the significance of new influenza viruses, see Hackett, *A Very Remarkable Sickness*, 179–80.

23. See Robert J. Wolfe, "Alaska's Great Sickness, 1900: An Epidemic of Measles and Influenza in a Virgin Soil Population," *Proceedings of the American Philosophical Society* 126 (April 1982): 91–121; Fortuine, *Chills and Fever: Health and Disease in the Early History of Alaska* (Fairbanks: University of Alaska Press, 1989), 215–26. For discussions of disease synergy in the Ungava epidemic, see Peart and Nagler, "Measles in the Canadian Arctic, 1952," 155.

24. See November and December entries, "Journal" [John Thomson], for an early nineteenth-century instance when a shortage of hares (likely cyclical) corresponded to a period of sickness, in Lloyd Keith, ed., *North of Athabasca: Slave Lake and Mackenzie River Documents of the North West Company 1800–1821* (Montreal and Kingston: McGill-Queen's Press, 2001), 143–5.

25. Helge Ingstad was one such trapper and described his and his neighbour's experiences with influenza in the summer of 1928 in Eugene Gay Tifft, trans., *Land of Feast and Famine* (New York: A.A. Knopf, 1933), 149–55.

26. Commissioner NWT, August 1, 1928, RG 85, vol. 789 file 6099, LAC; Angela Sidney's description of the 1942–1943 Alaska Highway epidemics emphasizes the lack of appropriate medical care, Cruikshank, *Life Lived Like a Story*, 134.

27. Helm, "Female Infanticide," 270; Bureau of Statistics, Yukon Statistical Profile (Whitehorse: Executive Council Office, n.d.), Table 2.4 "Yukon Population Figures, by Census Years, Yukon and Communities, (1901–1981)."

28. George Blondin, *Yamoria the Lawmaker: Stories of the Dene* (Edmonton: NeWest Press, 1997); George Blondin, *When the World Was New: Stories of the Sahtu Dene* (Yellowknife: Outcrop 1990); Margaret M. Thom, Ethel Blondin-Townsend, and Tessa Mackintosh

Wah-Shee, *Nahecho-Keh-Our Elders* (Slavey Research Project, 1997).

29. Burke G. Vanderhill, "The Passing of the Pioneer Fringe in Western Canada," *Geographical Review* 72 (April 1982): 200–17; Henry M. Leppard, "The Settlement of the Peace River Country," *Geographical Review* 25 (January 1935): 62–78.

30. See Zaslow, *The Northward Expansion of Canada, 1914–1967* (Toronto: McClelland & Stewart, 1988), 43–5; Donald Wetherell and Irene R.A. Kmet, *Alberta's North: A History, 1890–1950* (Edmonton: University of Alberta Press, 2000), 166–7.

31. See Zaslow, *The Northward Expansion of Canada*, 43–4.

32. Frank Tough, *As Their Natural Resources Fail: Native Peoples and the Economic History of Northern Manitoba, 1870–1930* (Vancouver: UBC Press, 1996), 170–1.

33. For an overview of cattle ranching in the Peace River district, see Wetherell and Kmet, *Alberta's North*, 166–67.

34. The livestock numbers were derived from Northern Alberta Development Council, "Agriculture in Northern Alberta," Discussion Paper (September 1978): 24–8.

35. For a summary of attempts to raise cattle in northern Canada, see William Dickson, "Northern Agriculture," in Carl A. Dawson, ed., *The New North-West* (Toronto: University of Toronto Press, 1947), 168–9.

36. For an overview of these experiments, see C. Gordon Hewitt, *The Conservation of the Wild Life of Canada* (New York: Charles Scribner's Sons, 1921), 136–42.

37. Maxwell Graham, *Canada's Wild Buffalo: Observation in the Wood Buffalo Park* (Ottawa: Department of the Interior, 1923), 12.

38. Maxwell Graham, "Finding Range for Canada's Buffalo," *The Canadian Field-Naturalist*, 38 (Dec. 1924), 189.

39. For an overview of the bison slaughters and the Wainwright transfer program, see Tina Loo, *States of Nature: Conserving Canada's Wildlife in the Twentieth Century* (Vancouver: UBC Press, 2006); Patricia A. McCormack, "The Political Economy of Bison Management in Wood Buffalo National Park," *Arctic* 454 (December 1992): 367–80; John Sandlos, "Where the Scientists Roam: Ecology, Management and Bison in

Northern Canada," *Journal of Canadian Studies* 37 (Summer 2002): 93–129; John Sandlos, *Hunters at the Margin: Native People and Wildlife Conservation in the Northwest Territories* (Vancouver: UBC Press, 2007).

40. For a summary of his ideas, see Vilhjalmur Stefansson, "Possible New Domestic Animals for Cold Countries." This memo was originally sent to Sir Richard McBride on 9 February 1917. A copy that Hewitt forwarded to Harkin on 28 November 1918 was found in RG 85, vol. 1203, file 401-3, pt. 1, LAC.

41. John Gunion Rutherford, James Stanley McLean, and James Bernard Harkin, *Report of the Royal Commission to Investigate the Possibilities of the Reindeer and Musk-ox Industries in the Arctic and Sub-Arctic Regions of Canada* (Ottawa: King's Printer, 1922).

42. See O.S. Finnie, director, Northwest Territories and Yukon Branch to W.W. Cory, July 21, 1926, RG 85, vol. 765, file 5095, pt. 1, LAC. For a published overview of the Department of the Interior's agenda with respect to the Mackenzie Delta reindeer project, see Alf Erling Porsild, "The Reindeer Industry and the Canadian Eskimo," *The Geographical Journal* 88 (July 1936): 1–17.

43. Notice of the arrival is contained in a telegram from Porsild to J. Lorne Turner, chair of the Dominion Lands Board, February 24, 1935, RG 85, vol. 765, file 5095, pt. 1, LAC.

44. See the report, "Native Herd 1: Anderson River Area," no date, RG 10, vol. 4062, file 398746-3, LAC. For the herd numbers, see "Information for the Reindeer Committee," no date, RG 10, vol. 4062, file 398746-3, LAC.

45. Department of Mines and Resources, "Canada's Reindeer Experiment," (1938), RG 10, vol. 4062, file 398746-3, LAC.

46. The herd was sold to John Teal, an agricultural researcher from Vermont, and Alfred Oeming, the owner of a game farm in Alberta. For a summary, see Erhard Treude, "Forty Years of Reindeer Herding in the Mackenzie Delta, NWT," *Polarforschung* 45 (1979): 121–38.

47. See William Nasogluak and Douglas Billingsley, "Reindeer Industry in the Western Arctic: Problems and Potential," in *Proceedings: First International Symposium on Renewable Resources and the Economy of the North*, Banff, Alberta: May 1981, 86–95.

48. See Charles Krebs, "Population Dynamics of the Mackenzie Delta Reindeer Herd, 1938–1958," *Arctic* 14 (1961): 91–100. See also Treude, "Forty Years of Reindeer Herding," 127. For an overview of the interactions between caribou and reindeer, see David R. Klein, "Conflicts Between Domestic Reindeer and their Wild Counterparts: A Review of Eurasian and North American Experience," *Arctic* 33 (December 1980): 739–56.

49. References to the difficulty of attracting the Inuit to the reindeer herding project were found in several documents, including a correspondence from R.A. Gibson, deputy commissioner of the Northwest Territories, to J.A. Parsons, general foreman, Reindeer, Station, January 19, 1944, RG 85, vol. 939, file 12513, LAC. See, also, a report of the Branch Reindeer Committee, January 19, 1944, RG 85, vol. 939, file 12513, LAC. Finally, see "Extract from Annual Report by Mr. W.E. Hogan, Reindeer Station, 31 March 1945," RG 85, vol. 939, file 12513, LAC.

50. See Erhard Treude, "The Development of Reindeer Husbandry in Canada," *The Polar Record* 14 (1968): 17. For a scientific analysis, see Julian T. Inglis, "The Impact of Reindeer Grazing on Selected Areas of Winter Range in Successive Years, Mackenzie Delta Area, N.W.T., Canada," in Jack Luick, ed., *Proceedings of the First International Reindeer and Caribou Symposium, 9–11 August 1972, University of Alaska, Fairbanks, Alaska*, Biological Papers of the University of Alaska Special Report No. 1 (Fairbanks: University of Alaska, 1975).

51. See Treude, "Forty Years of Reindeer Herding," 130.

52. See Treude, "Forty Years of Reindeer Herding," 132–3.

53. For oral testimony on some of the local benefits and cultural changes associated with the reindeer herding project, see Gerald T. Conaty and Lloyd Binder, *The Reindeer Herders of the Mackenzie Delta* (Toronto: Key Porter, 2003). The reindeer population estimate for 2000 was located in Government of the Northwest Territories, Environmental Impact Review Board, *Public Review of Kuññek Resource Development Corporation's "Revitalization of the Western Arctic Reindeer Herd" Proposal*, Inuvik, 27 November 2000, 11.

54. See, for example, William Cronon, *Changes in the Land: Indians, Colonists and the Ecology of New England* (New York: Hill and Wang, 1983); Carolyn Merchant, *Ecological Revolutions: Nature, Gender and Science in New* *England* (Chapel Hill: University of North Carolina Press, 1989); and Virginia DeJohn Anderson, *Creatures of Empire: How Domestic Animals Transformed Early America* (New York: Oxford University Press, 2004).

4   From P. Whitney Lackenbauer and Matthew Farish, "The Cold War on Canadian Soil: Militarizing a Northern Environment," *Environmental History* 12, 4 (Oct 2007): 920–50. By permission of Oxford University Press.

On 15 February 1946, the "Moving Force" of Exercise Musk-Ox left Fort Churchill, Manitoba, and over almost three months traced a 5000-kilometre-long northern arc via Victoria Island and Norman Wells in the Northwest Territories to Edmonton, Alberta. Fort Churchill, later home to Canada's Defence Research Northern Laboratory, was by the end of the Second World War a site of significant research on military bodies, units, and technologies under adverse environmental conditions.[1] Musk-Ox was an extraordinary extension of these research interests. It was less a routine test of endurance than a public spectacle held within a territory of new strategic interest, a demonstration of the Canadian military's ability to travel across, and thus command, a challenging landscape. Staged at the outset of the Cold War, Musk-Ox offered no significant human enemies for its participants, or for the audiences digesting reportage of the event. Rather, the chief opponent was nature itself.[2]

The Cold War's first decade featured numerous northern exercises similar to Musk-Ox, part of a broader militarization of the North American Arctic capped by the Distant Early Warning (DEW) Line radar project. [. . .] The result of such interest, as signalled by the early example of Musk-Ox, was the systematic consolidation of nature as a military entity, but also an extension of the scope and terms of militarization to reflect the cautious longevity of the Cold War.

[. . .]

The global history of the American armed forces indicates increased attention during and after the Second World War to the world's hostile environments, terrain types which might, it was believed, be scenes of conflict under the umbrella of planetary struggles with fascism and then communism. This essay addresses one such environment: the Canadian North. Frequently combined with Alaska and Greenland to form a vaguely defined region, the Canadian North was a site of keen military concern throughout the Cold War. [. . .]

As a bastion between an apparently aggressive Soviet Union and the North American industrial heartland, northern Canada was a key component of Cold War strategic maps. During the 1950s, in particular, recognition of these cartographic conditions led to intense military and associated activity in the Arctic, a region that had, until the Second World War, been largely ignored by defence officials. The first decade of the Cold War witnessed a variety of attempts, some relatively minor, others extraordinarily ambitious, to overcome what was perceived to be an antagonistic environment. Military exercises, conducted in scores of Canadian locations from the Yukon to Labrador, were not only tests of individual and unit readiness for northern warfare against an invading force, but state-driven campaigns to document and respond to natural challenges. Meanwhile, the construction of radar lines and associated settlements undermined the perception of Canadian wilderness as inhospitable.

During this early wave of interest, "neither the United States nor Canada looked on the North as a place to be protected because of some intrinsic value," Kenneth Eyre observes. "Rather it was seen as a direction, as an exposed flank."[3] Until the late 1960s few proponents of northern militarization were concerned with what this process entailed beyond the outlines of perceived Cold War pressures. This limited vision was challenged, for a number of reasons, and from a number of perspectives, as the Cold War entered its third and fourth decades. But the seemingly unremarkable and yet singular perception of the North as a natural space readily subject to military forms of geographical vision did not diminish.

[. . .]

The environmental history of the Cold War Canadian North is best understood through the lens of military modernization, a particular version of a familiar narrative: that of a state (or, in this case, often two) working to make a landscape legible so as to enroll it more effectively into such classic political responsibilities, according to James C. Scott, as "taxation, conscription, and prevention of rebellion."[4] These did not drive the militarization of the Cold War North; geopolitics did. But put into practice, militarism in the North was similar to the non-military projects Scott documents in his compelling study *Seeing Like a State* (Yale, 1998), projects backed by the authority of reason and the latest technologies, designed at a distance and implemented without sufficient attention to local conditions. As the Cold War proceeded, this dynamic changed. Nevertheless, the fact that environmental assessment and remediation directly related to military activity initiated in the early Cold War period is still ongoing suggests that this activity was not only significant, but also that the power of the military's instrumental, oppositional approach to northern nature has not entirely diminished.

EARLY FORAYS

If the First World War heralded the dawn of the air age, air power still posed no serious threat to North American security. With this awareness, the Canadian government focused on domestic unity. The fledgling Royal Canadian Air Force spent much of its time mapping and charting in the North, but did not build permanent infrastructure in the region and never ventured into the high Arctic. The Royal Canadian Corps of Signals opened the first stations of the Northwest Territories and Yukon Radio System in 1923, installations that soon dotted the landscape and revealed how the military could be used as a tool to support national development programs in the North. Apart from this wireless communication infrastructure, the military's presence was insubstantial, and even if the region's environmental challenges were well known, it was not considered holistically in the language of strategy.[5]

The Second World War was a watershed in the militarization of the Canadian North. At the behest of American military planners interested in securing reliable access to Alaska, Canadian officials agreed to support the construction of northern airfields. The Northwest Airway, built from 1939–1941 to link Edmonton to Fairbanks, established airfields and radio sites at one hundred mile intervals. The subsequent Northwest Staging Route produced a larger series of airfields in the Yukon and provincial norths, as did highway and oil projects. In the eastern Arctic, the Crimson Route consisted of airbases built to ferry aircraft and supplies to Europe. These were constructed in Goose Bay, Fort Chimo, and Frobisher Bay in 1941, and at The Pas, Churchill, and Southampton Island the following year. Even when these facilities were not used as planned, they opened up new transportation routes to—and through—the North.[6] [. . .]

Disruptions were more profound in the western sub-Arctic, home to the Northwest

Defence Projects. The US Army Corps of Engineers and civilian contractors carried out most of the construction, with a view to short-term military goals. "This was a peaceful army of occupation," Coates and Morrison observed. "The main weapons were the shovel, not the rifle, and the bulldozer, not the tank. But such a force—more than 40 000 soldiers and construction workers—could not help but recast the sparsely populated and undeveloped Northwest."[7] The Alaska Highway soon linked an isolated American possession to the southern road network through the Yukon, northern British Columbia, and Alberta, while the Canol Pipeline extended from the oil fields at Norman Wells to a refinery in Whitehorse. These military mega-projects radically transformed the human and physical geography of the North. Bulldozers tore permafrost off the ground, disrupting ecosystems and creating impassable quagmires. Forest fires, logging, over-hunting, and over-fishing depleted resources in the region. Arriving workers brought diseases, from measles to VD, which devastated indigenous populations. Scientific and geographic surveys, telephone systems linking Edmonton to Fairbanks and Norman Wells, shortwave communication systems, small generating plants, and wage employment all furthered connections to distant centres of calculation.[8] But as with Cold War endeavours further north, engineering marvels did not master a distinct natural environment: unanticipated conditions and minimal understanding of the local terrain meant that the infrastructure was not up to proper standards. "Pioneer" roads had treacherous grades and disintegrated during spring thaws.[9]

[. . .]

A HOSTILE NATURE

The military presence in the North did not cease with declarations of Allied victory in 1945. In part this was because of the Cold War's sudden emergence, but the justifications for northern militarization, and related scientific inquiry, were dependent not only on particular geopolitical circumstances. Although the subjects of sovereignty and, more vaguely, continental defence were discussed in wartime Ottawa and Washington, the North was additionally becoming part of a more generic geography, a view which treated the region as both important and unknown. Institutions such as the American Air Force's Arctic, Desert, and Tropic Information Center (ADTIC), briefly discontinued at the end of the war, sprang into action once again to continue research on problems of survival and combat in non-temperate climates.

The Canadian North was a crucial component of this inquiry; it was proximate, strategically significant, but also mysterious. As the Director of the Arctic Institute of North America, Lincoln Washburn, argued in 1948, "in general the fundamental aims of Arctic exploration are purely scientific—to learn more about the North, to solve the many problems that confront us there and which must be solved before we are in a position to describe the North accurately and completely. From this point of view the North differs from no other region; where it does differ is in the fact that we know so little about it compared with most other parts of the world."[10]

Washburn did not mention that post-war scientific expeditions in the North were being funded overwhelmingly by military sources. It therefore made sense that journalistic articles about the Arctic during the early Cold War were filled with terms such as "assault" and "invasion".[11] But the "polar regions," a US Air Force researcher wrote in the preface to a 1953 ADTIC study of survival experiences in the north, "are not to be entered casually or in an unprepared state. The environment presents unique problems not met elsewhere in the world. Constant study and experimentation are needed to adapt machines, materiel, and men to its demands." The examples documented in the text did not result from contact with a human enemy; the "adversary in these episodes was the environment."[12]

Military activity in the Cold War North was thus not just a physical engagement with soil, muskeg, permafrost, water, and ice; it was critical to the formation of a new imaginative geography of the Arctic. Clear evidence of the transition is found in the numerous military exercises of the 1940s and 1950s, varying in duration, scale, and premise, which traced a series of scars across the region. The natural nordicity of these operations was apparent in their names: Musk-Ox, Lemming, Eskimo, Polar Bear, Sun Dog, and Sweetbriar. Although their cumulative imprint was still nowhere near as significant as that of concurrent radar construction, their sheer volume is testament to the direct interest of the Canadian and American armed forces in winter warfare. Indeed, the importance of these forays into the North is collective.

For Major Patrick Baird, a participant or observer on several winter warfare exercises in the 1940s, such repeated tests of equipment and endurance demonstrated that with appropriate technology and provisions military "operations in the barren grounds which represent one-third of Canada's area can be as unhindered as operations on the Libyan desert."[13] This was the premise which lay behind agencies such as ADTIC: to show that while the Arctic required specific study, it was, ultimately, only part of a set of hostile Cold War environments which spanned the globe, environments where the American armed forces might find themselves stationed. While Baird's adventures might have been motivated by the desires of Canadian officials to secure military experience on their own terrain, national defence was constantly overshadowed in the first decade of the Cold War by significant American pressure to share results and space. The United States had Alaska, of course, which effectively became a Cold War laboratory. But military exercises such as 1950's Sweetbriar, which crossed the Alaska-Yukon border and was deliberately designed as a binational event, demonstrated that political borders were far less important than a common natural environment.[14] This shared landscape would automatically unite Canada and the United States in the event of northern warfare, and thus in the planning for this potential combat.

While military exercises were planned and executed, more ambitious plans for Arctic defence were also developed. Although it would take a decade to be implemented, the vision of a radar line stretching across the northern edge of the continent was discussed as early as 1946, when US Army Air Force planners proposed a string of northern radar sites that could track waves of incoming Soviet planes.[15] When finally constructed in the late 1950s, this system, dubbed the Distant Early Warning Line, was an extraordinary intervention that likely did more to alter the lives of northern inhabitants than any other Cold War initiative.

The DEW Line was made possible by a comprehensive exercise in military geography: exhaustive terrain, climatic, and coastal surveys undertaken with the aid of the Canadian Joint Intelligence Bureau and arms of both national militaries. This was, in effect, a vast catalogue of environmental data designed to aid "all those who may be involved in the work of planning and installing the Distant Early Warning Line."[16] But like the sponsors and designers of ambitious high modernist projects considered by James C. Scott, the Line's creators were forced to grapple with the nuances of the northern environment.[17]

Articles in engineering journals tracing the progress of "Project 572"—as the DEW Line construction effort was initially known—are prefaced with the language of adventure, "the heights to which determination can aspire, in the face of frustrating odds . . . despite an uncooperative Nature." But these reports also testify to the limitations of "data" on northern landscapes, despite significant attempts at collection and consultation, in the early stages of the project. These gaps, it was believed, could be filled by field reconnaissance. Even then, when construction began, "no member of the 572 Project had set foot on any of the proposed locations, except the experimental sites in Alaska and a few native settlements in Canada."[18] "Hazardous aircraft flights over trackless wastes," landings on "unprepared and unmarked snowfields," encounters with "the Eskimo and his primitive life" in an "unmapped country," and surveying successes in "sub-zero temperatures" were all common components of the "fantastic" tale of the DEW Line, an "unparalleled" "full-scale attack on the Arctic" narrated within and beyond scientific communities.[19] Such colourful descriptions certainly tested the dispassionate terms of high modernism. More importantly, while these engineering stories began with drama and concluded with success, it was difficult to maintain a consistent tone: "many mistakes were made in the early stages of planning. Early issues of drawings incomplete or containing architectural-engineer conflicts resulted in erroneous material and tool procurement and shortages. Unavailability of information on site topography, layout and soils led to inadequate heavy equipment being furnished. . . . The errors resulting from the inability to complete plans caused delays in some components of the schedules which were costly and serious in relation to completion."[20]

Overcoming an arduous environment also became a typical narrative for media stories on the DEW Line, stories that similarly highlighted the successful application of modern solutions to treacherous terrain. [. . .]

Journalists who visited DEW sites under construction faced censorship, but their directives suggested that "difficulties due to terrain, weather, distance, [and] wild animals may be mentioned together with human interest stories on construction personnel." News writers were provided with stock anecdotes of nasty weather conditions, polar bear encounters, and the benefits of "Eskimo" clothing, which limited perspiration but kept workers warm—when it could be found in sufficiently large sizes.[21] Similarly, readers of their newspapers and magazines learned that the actual radar installations comfortably housed southern workers who enjoyed all the amenities of modern living while serving on the remote front lines of Cold War surveillance and detection.[22]

To prepare for a potential Soviet invasion, it was not enough to detect aircraft. Northern landscapes, low in population and sufficiently far from Soviet eyes, were seen as particularly suitable for Air Force training.[23] The development of jets, rockets, and missiles, as well as high-level bombing and fighter interceptor training, required a new Canadian air weapons centre, and in April 1951 Defence Minister Brooke Claxton informed Parliament that a bombing and gunnery range centred on Primrose Lake would encompass 4490 square miles.[24] This expanse of "unoccupied" Crown lands straddled the Alberta–Saskatchewan border along the 55th parallel, and the dense boreal forest and muskeg suitably resembled a potential battlespace over Europe and Siberia. Negotiations over the range focused on human geographies and little else. It would affect resource exploitation, commercial fishing, and trap lines, but would not encroach on any settlements. Hunters, fishermen, and trappers were compensated for their interests in the land, and some Aboriginal communities received additional money to offset partially the disruption of their traditional subsistence economies.[25]

For the first time, the Canadian Wildlife Service (CWS) expressed a direct interest in the "preservation of national wildlife values in connection with projects for defence training schemes." Dr Harrison Lewis was concerned that the bombing range plans had not been referred to the CWS so that "national interests in wildlife may receive consideration before action is taken." He pointed to the

US military's consultations with the US Fish and Wildlife Service prior to recent atomic tests and explosions in the Nevada desert as a model practice. Given provincial jurisdiction over natural resources, the issue was more complicated in Canada, but the federal Minister of Resources and Development reminded his Defence counterpart that military development and control of "large tracts of land for use as bombing ranges, training areas, or other defence purposes . . . may have important effects on the widely distributed wildlife resources of Canada." The CWS duly appointed a wildlife officer "of extensive military experience and appropriate military rank" to deal with National Defence on these matters. As negotiations for the air weapons range neared completion, Saskatchewan officials raised the possibility that an epidemic could break out amongst wild animals, should overcrowding occur when trapping and harvesting ceased on the property. "A large population, particularly natives, in this region of the north, depend almost entirely on trapping for their livelihood," one document noted, "and we are naturally anxious to avoid damage to the industry." The Department of Defence was unwilling to change its development plans to accommodate trapping because this would interfere with its training program. "The airport is nearing completion, buildings, including hangars, are under construction and public utilities are under way," the deputy minister reported. If the range were unavailable, the base would be of little use. Environmental concerns were quantified as financial compensation to trappers and the provinces for opportunity costs in resource development.[26]

Beginning in 1952, Alberta's Cold Lake air station became a major Cold War facility for pilot training and weapons testing. Two runways, each over a mile in length, "stretched across the muskeg, while massive hangars and buildings, showpieces of modern technology, rose [over what had once been] the haunts of coyotes. A large and modern community had thrust out the wild forests of jackpine and spruce." The station housed more than five thousand people, and featured many of the amenities of modern life: a hospital, tennis courts, a school, even a shopping centre.[27] Bombing practice, noisy overflights, and air-to-ground training on the 106 target complexes eventually established on the range produced intermittent "startle effects" in wildlife, and practice bombs, rockets, strafe, explosive ordnance, flares, marker marines, chaff, aerial targets, and tow wire resulted in terrain damage and vegetation impacts. "Academic range training" at Jimmy Lake posed the greatest disturbances: more than two hundred low-altitude sorties were flown over this location during a busy month, each typically involving six bombing passes, four rocket passes, four strafing passes, and two "dry passes." In addition to aircraft noise, firing rockets and cannons produced sonic shock waves that exceeded decibel levels associated with "startle effects." At the same time, the military's occupation served to limit outside resource exploitation and development. In subsequent decades, when oil and gas infrastructure and agricultural expansion engulfed neighbouring lands, the weapons range remained a heavily controlled yet protected boreal mixed wood habitat for species like moose, caribou, bison, and river otter. Indeed, the abundance of woodland caribou on the range suggested that they successfully habituated to training exercises.[28] The example of Cold Lake suggests that the study of military–environment relations requires a contextual interpretation that does not begin with assumptions of automatic degradation.

It does little good to confer present-day expectations on 50-year-old policies and their designers, as though they should have systematically contemplated the environment in current scientific and cultural terms. Equally, however, it is a mistake to conclude that rudimentary ecological principles—often unintentional byproducts of the nuclear arms race—were absent from political and military circles during the early Cold War.[29] The Canadian Department of National Defence (DND) relinquished its control over a high explosive weapons testing area near Watson Lake, Yukon, in 1954, and while it did not find any unexploded ordnance during its surface clean-up, it acknowledged the missiles or bomb fragments could still be present. The military ensured that the Department of Resources and Development did not anticipate major impacts on wildlife prior to establishing a danger area for surface-to-air guided missile testing in Hudson Bay, or a practice gunnery and bombing range at Grey Goose Island in James Bay. Given that the latter was a major migration route for Canada geese and snow geese, and "an important part of the food supply of the Indians who reside near the southern end of James Bay," the National Parks Branch requested that the air force curtail its activities during the summer and autumn migration periods.[30]

At the 1958 meeting of the Royal Society of Canada, Robert Legget (Director of the Division of Building Research at the National Research Council) proudly explained that the technological developments of the previous decade had changed the face of the North, and that engineers had "direct[ed] the great sources of power in Nature for the use and convenience of man."[31] This was the language of environmental modernization, which enrolled an increasingly *definite* region in national and continental maps even as its geopolitical limitations were becoming clear. Within the global purview of the Cold War, the colonial curiosity of military science in the North was shifting to other landscapes. New technologies, particularly intercontinental ballistic missiles, also redirected attention away from the region in the late 1950s. Canadian military activities in the region declined sharply. The DEW Line continued its vigil along the coast, but half of the radar stations were decommissioned in 1964 and DND transferred the infrastructure (and liability) to the Department of Indian and Northern

Affairs. Prime Minister John Diefenbaker's election rhetoric about a new northern national policy proved fleeting, and his tenure (1957–1963) was plagued by indecision and inaction. The Canadian Forces vacated Churchill, the Department of Transport took over many northern airfields, and the Northwest Highway System was transferred to civilian control. Apart from the annual maritime resupply of the DEW Line, this "new Mediterranean"—as the geographer Trevor Lloyd dubbed the Arctic Ocean in an era of jets and nuclear submarines—was a relatively quiet military space.[32]

Nevertheless, military actors remained prominent in new settlements established around bases and radar stations, with a host of cultural and environmental implications. Off-road vehicles damaged vegetation and organic matter, resulting in the melting of permafrost, in turn affecting hydrological systems. So too did the discharge of sewage onto the tundra, never mind the presence of new physical barriers (such as roads, airstrips, and landfills) on the landscape. Disruption of the local social order, whereby Aboriginal hunters did not procure food in a seasonal cycle as they had previously, and denser clusters of people around military sites meant more competition for resources. The DEW Line personnel were not allowed to hunt: their rifles were sealed unless polar bears, attracted to the site's garbage or food caches, needed to be shot for safety. There is no doubt, however, that the transient workers also violated hunting and fishing regulations, depleting local animal and fish stocks, not to mention visitors who "appear[ed] to believe game laws only apply to residents." Federal officials expressed serious concern with rumours that commercial pilots supplying the DEW Line buzzed caribou herds for amusement, given the "alarming" decline in caribou numbers. "It is difficult to say exactly what damage is done to a caribou herd that is harried by an aircraft," the deputy minister of Northern Affairs and Natural Resources noted, "but most wildlife experts are convinced that there are a number of undesirable results."[33] The full magnitude of these impacts cannot be determined, but anecdotes suggest that these activities—coupled with the concentration of Aboriginal groups around military installations—had devastating local impacts and disrupted the traditional Native subsistence economy.

[. . .]

CONCLUSION

Historians of modernization theory have demonstrated how its claims to objectivity were compromised by its Cold War origins and applications. The immediacy of geopolitical conflict meant that grandiose theories of democratization and economic liberalization often ran counter to seemingly necessary military incursions and tempting authoritarian stability.[34] The case of the Cold War Canadian North is similar insofar as militarization was frequently disguised behind loftier goals, whether of scientific enlightenment, economic and social development, or national pride. The most significant military project in the North, the Distant Early Warning Line, was a modern marvel designed to render a complex landscape legible, and in the process comfortable for southern visitors and workers. This meant overcoming and disguising the effects of northern nature on bodies and minds, with little consideration for the ways in which the Line was radically altering the human and physical geographies of the North, confirming once more an unfortunate correlation between toxins and race in North American environmental history.[35]

In writing this history, engineering endeavours such as the DEW Line, just one of a long list of military projects in the Cold War North, must be considered next to the more general issue of nature as a subject of military scrutiny. The contributions of the American and Canadian armed forces to the history of the Cold War North comprise more than a list of individual activities and subsequent effects. A map of "footprints"—some lingering, others fading—fails to illuminate two wider considerations. First, these footprints represent a fraction of the global military activity conducted in the name of the Cold War. Second, the identification of military sites or routes across the Canadian North points only to the material manifestations of a particularly powerful form of imaginative geography which treats an environment as both an opponent and a resource to be used, possibly to advantage, with the correct knowledge and training.

[. . .]

And yet the militarization of northern nature has been flexible enough to accommodate varying discourses of defence, protection, and security. Tracing the genealogy of the Cold War has been aided by the recognition that the famed military-industrial complex established in the middle of the twentieth century has not vanished. In addition to a lingering, terrifying global presence in soils, water, air, and species, it returned with a vengeance as Americans prepared for an indefinite war on terror. Cold War military activities in the Canadian North ultimately constitute part of a global "treadmill of destruction" tying militarism to environmental and political injustice.[36] [. . .]

As yet another wave of sovereignty and security concerns washes over the Canadian public, prompted by a global climate change crisis that some commentators anticipate will make commercial transnavigation of the Northwest Passage feasible within the next two decades, it will be crucial to consider how northern military activity will be justified—in the familiar language of national defence, or in the more complex terms of human and environmental security.[37] Beefing up defence spending and resisting compliance with international environmental agreements suggest that the Cold War is, paradoxically, being both perpetuated and forgotten. But as we have done in this essay with reference to the Cold War period, it will also be crucial to continue to consider the persistent militarization of northern landscapes in more philosophical terms—to ask how this militarization bears on the idea of nature more generally, especially when the Canadian North is still represented as geographically distinct.

NOTES

1. See *Defence Research Northern Laboratory, 1947–1965* (Ottawa: Defence Research Board, Department of National Defence, 1966).
2. On Musk-Ox, see Hugh A. Halliday, "Exercise 'Musk Ox': Asserting Sovereignty 'North of 60'," *Canadian Military History* 7 (1998): 37–44; and Kevin M. Thrasher, "Exercise Musk Ox: Lost Opportunities" (MA thesis, Department of History, Carleton University, 1998).
3. Kenneth C. Eyre, "Forty Years of Military Activity in the Canadian North, 1947–87," *Arctic* 40 (1987): 292–9; quote on 294.
4. James C. Scott, *Seeing Like a State: How Certain Schemes to Improve the Human Condition Have Failed* (New Haven: Yale University Press, 1998), 2.
5. Kenneth C. Eyre, "Custos Borealis: The Military in the Canadian North" (PhD thesis, Department of War Studies, Kings College, University of London, 1981), 45–79.
6. On these projects, see Stanley W. Dziuban, *Military Relations between the United States and Canada, 1939–1945* (Washington, DC: Office of the Chief of Military History, Department of the Army, 1959); C.P. Stacey, *Arms, Men and Governments* (Ottawa: Queen's Printer, 1970), 379–88; and Shelagh Grant, *Sovereignty or Security? Government Policy in the Canadian North, 1936–1950* (Vancouver: UBC Press, 1988).
7. Kenneth S. Coates and William R. Morrison, *The Alaska Highway in World War II: The U.S. Occupation in Canada's Northwest* (Norman: University of Oklahoma, 1992), 85.
8. The phrase is Bruno Latour's; for a spatial consideration, see Michael Heffernan "Mars and Minerva: Centres of Geographical Calculation in an Age of Total War," *Erkunde* 54 (2000): 320–33.
9. Coates and Morrison, *The Alaska Highway in World War II*, 67, 86–100, 158.
10. A.L. Washburn, "Geography and Arctic Lands," in G. Taylor, ed., *Geography in the Twentieth Century: A Study of Growth, Fields, Techniques, Aims and Trends*, 3rd edn (New York: The Philosophical Society, 1957), 267–87; quote on 267.
11. For an example, see Leslie Roberts, "The Great Assault on the Arctic," *Harper's* (August 1955), 37–42.
12. R.A. Howard, *Down in the North: An Analysis of Survival Experiences in Arctic Areas* (Maxwell AFB, AL: Arctic, Desert, Tropic Information Center, 1953), iii, 1.
13. Quoted in Hugh A. Halliday, "Recapturing the North: Exercises 'Eskimo', 'Polar Bear' and 'Lemming', 1945," *Canadian Military History* 6 (1997): 29–38; quote on 38.
14. On Sweetbriar, see "Joint Canadian-United States Exercise Sweetbriar, 1950," *Polar Record* 6 (1951): 258; Omond M. Solandt, "Exercise Sweetbriar," Speech to the Empire Club of Canada, March 30, 1950 (http://www.empireclubfoundation.com/details.asp?SpeechID=2633&FT=yes).
15. See T. Ray, *A History of the DEW Line* (Maxwell AFB, AL: Air Force Historical Research Agency, Air Defense Command Historical Study 31, n.d.).
16. *Distant Early Warning Line Military Geography Support Programme* (Ottawa, Joint Intelligence Bureau, January 1955), DHH File 79/82.
17. Scott, *Seeing Like a State*, 7.
18. James D. Brannian, Frank J. Donohue, and Attilio Baltera, "W.E. Engineering for the DEW Line—I. Siting Design and Construction," *Western Electric Engineer* 1 (1957): 2–11; quote on 3.
19. J.D. Brannian, "Siting the DEW Line Radar Stations," *Engineering and Contract Record* 70 (1957): 53–5, 171–8, 195–202, 207–11; quotes on 53.
20. M.S. Cheever, "Construction on the DEW Line," *Engineering and Contract Record* 70 (1957): 53–7, 193–19; quote on 53.

21. Joint Press Tour, DEW Line, 26 March–3 April 1956, DHH 181.009 (D6587).

22. See, for example, "Temperature, Vapors Kept under Control in DEW Line Buildings," *The Globe and Mail*, 24 April 1956; Rick Ranson, *Working North: DEW Line to Drill Shop* (Edmonton: NeWest Press, 2003), 7–18.

23. See Joseph T. Jockel, *No Boundaries Upstairs: Canada, the United States, and the Origins of North American Air Defence, 1945–1958* (Vancouver: UBC Press, 1987), and Andrew Richter, *Avoiding Armageddon: Canadian Military Strategy and Nuclear Weapons, 1950–1963* (Vancouver: UBC Press, 2002), 37–47.

24. House of Commons *Debates*, 19 April 1951, 2173–4. For background, see RG 10, v.6341, f.736-1 pt.1, Library Archives of Canada [LAC]; "Canadian Forces Base, Cold Lake, Alberta," (c1960s), DHH 112.3H1.009 (D279); Dan Black, "Combat at Cold Lake," *Legion Magazine* September/October 2002 (http://www.legionmagazine.com/features/militarymatters/02-09.asp).

25. See Indian Claims Commission, *Indian Claims Commission Proceedings vol. 1* (1994), 3–157; and P.W. Lackenbauer, *Battle Grounds: The Canadian Military and Aboriginal Lands* (Vancouver: UBC Press, 2007).

26. LAC, RG 22, vol. 836, file 84-11-11, part 1.

27. "Canadian Forces Base, Cold Lake, Alberta," DHH; T. Thompson, "Tales of the Bay and Chilly Pond," *Airforce* 25 (Summer 2001): 34–5.

28. See D.A. Westworth & Associates Ltd., *National Defence Environmental Assessment Cold Lake Air Weapons Range vol. 1: Natural Resource Inventory* (Edmonton, December 1994); Bel MK Engineering, *Department of National Defence Environmental Assessment of NATO Flying Training in Canada–4 Wing Cold Lake, Final Report* (Calgary, April 1997), 44–7.

29. See, among other sources, Laura A. Bruno, "The Bequest of the Nuclear Battlefield: Science, Nature, and the Atom during the First Decade of the Cold War," *Historical Studies in the Physical Sciences* 33 (2003): 237–60.

30. Assistant Chief, National Parks Branch, to G.W. Rowley, Secy, Advisory Committee on Northern Research, 10 February 1956, and 10 April 1957, LAC, RG 22, vol. 836, file 84-11-11, part 1.

31. Robert F. Legget, "An Engineering Assessment," in Frank Underhill, ed., *The Canadian Northwest: Its Potentialities* (Toronto: University of Toronto Press, 1959), 9.

32. Trevor Lloyd, "Canada's Northland," *Queen's Quarterly* 66 (Winter 1960): 529–37.

33. J.D. Ferguson, "A Study of the Effects of the Distant Early Warning Line upon the Eskimo of the Western Arctic of Canada," Northern Research Coordination Centre research project (April 1957), 48; Extract from Mr D.W. Bissett's Report for August and September, 1961, LAC, RG 85, vol. 1360, file 207-6 pt 2; Distant Early Warning Co-Ordinating Committee, Progress Report No. 6, LAC, RG 12, vol. 2407, file 14-13-9-1 pt 4; R.G. Robertson to Vincent W. Farley, Western Electric Company, 4 April 1956, LAC, RG 25, box 5928, file 50210-C-40 pt. 7; Ken Reimer, *The Environmental Impact of the DEW Line on the Canadian Arctic: Summary* (Victoria: Royal Roads Military College, Environmental Sciences Group), 29–30; William R. Morrison, *True North: The Yukon and Northwest Territories* (Toronto: Oxford University Press, 1998), 137. On illicit hunting, see, for example, Lynden T. (Bucky) Harris, "A Failed Polar Bear Hunt," and Larry Wilson, "DEW Line War Stories vol. 1," both at www.lswilson.ca/warstories.htm.

34. See, for instance, Nils Gilman, *Mandarins of the Future: Modernization Theory in Cold War America* (Baltimore: Johns Hopkins University Press, 2003).

35. Carolyn Merchant, "Shades of Darkness: Race and Environmental History," *Environmental History* 8 (2003): 380–94.

36. Gregory Hooks and Chad L. Smith, "The Treadmill of Destruction: National Sacrifice Areas and Native Americans," *American Sociological Review* 69 (2004): 558–75.

37. See, for example, Rob Huebert, "Climate Change and Canadian Sovereignty in the Northwest Passage," *Isuma* (Winter 2001): 86–94. For a dissenting opinion, see Franklyn Griffiths, "The Shipping News: Canada's Arctic Sovereignty Not on Thinning Ice," *International Journal* 58 (Spring 2003): 257–82. On climate change and the Arctic, see Arctic Climate Impact Assessment (ACIA), *Impacts of a Warming Arctic* (Cambridge: Cambridge University Press, 2004).

Chapter 7

Anti-Asian Hostility

READINGS

Primary Documents

Historical Interpretations

INTRODUCTION

Although Canada is often called a nation of immigrants (a description that ignores First Nations' prior claims), for a long time these immigrants came from a rather limited slice of the world. Augmenting the colonial migrations dominated by France and Great Britain, most people who migrated to the Dominion before the turn of the twentieth century left European nations, predominantly the British Isles and Western Europe. This pattern began to shift noticeably in the 1890s, as it became more likely for Southern and Eastern Europeans to make the trip. The Asian workers arriving in the first couple of decades after Confederation were another notable exception to the general pattern, but their numbers remained small in comparison to the visible majority of whites around them. In terms of outward appearance and cultural practices like religion, there was not much difference between most new arrivals and the families who had been in Canada for several generations. However, this demographic dominance by the "white race" did not lessen discrimination. Racism flourished in a variety of ways, from individual acts of suspicion and disrespect to formally enacted laws and policies designed to drive out or limit the prospects of racial minorities. We have chosen sources here that highlight reactions to the presence of South and East Asians, mainly because most early-twentieth-century white Canadians viewed Asian immigration as a threat to national prosperity, but also because historians have been able to tap a rich vein of evidence detailing anti-Asian measures. Emily Murphy was a magistrate in Edmonton, and was perhaps best known for her role in promoting women's rights. She also concerned herself with the problem of drug trafficking in Canada and, despite taking some care to present her remarks as detached and scientific, had some strong opinions regarding various racial and ethnic groups and their involvement in the trade. The 1923 Chinese Immigration Act set out the conditions under which Chinese migrants would be allowed to enter Canada, and these conditions excluded all but a handful of privileged groups with prior ties to Canada. The 1923 law eliminated the notorious "head tax" of 1885 entirely, possibly in the hope that the number of Chinese eligible to pay such a tax would soon become insignificant. We return to the theme of drugs with Catherine Carstairs' s article on the conflation of race and vice in the public imagination. Penalties for drug use increased during the 1920s, and were seemingly tailored to the sort of drug use prevalent in the Chinese community. Isabel Wallace's article examines the case of the *Komagata Maru*, a Japanese vessel whose Indian passengers were denied entry into Canada in 1914. Wallace notes that specious arguments regarding public health protection were invoked by government officials to strengthen the case for excluding fellow British subjects from enter-ing the Dominion. It is important for students of history to recognize that in many ways, drug legislation, immigration regulations, and public health initiatives were merely new stages on which the old script of racism was played out.

QUESTIONS FOR CONSIDERATION

1. How does Emily Murphy represent the Chinese-Canadian community as a divided one?
2. What sort of immigrant could make it into Canada under the 1923 Act?
3. Given the effort made to discriminate between Euro-Canadians and others, what did white Canada fear?
4. How does Carstairs define a "moral panic," and how does a moral panic gain momentum?
5. What measures were taken by Canadian authorities to exclude immigrants from British India?

SUGGESTIONS FOR FURTHER READING

Kay J. Anderson, *Vancouver's Chinatown: Racial Discourse in Canada, 1875–1980* (Montreal and Kingston: McGill-Queen's University Press, 1995).

Constance Backhouse, *Colour-Coded: A Legal History of Racism in Canada, 1900–1950* (Toronto: University of Toronto Press, 1999).

David Goutor, *Guarding the Gates: The Canadian Labour Movement and Immigration, 1872–1934* (Vancouver: UBC Press, 2007).

Ali Kazimi, *Undesirables: White Canada and the Komagata Maru* (Vancouver: Douglas & McIntyre, 2011).

Hugh Johnston, *The Voyage of the* Komagata Maru: *The Sikh Challenge to Canada's Colour Bar,* revised edition (Vancouver: UBC Press, 2014).

Lisa Rose Mar, *Brokering Belonging: Chinese in Canada's Exclusion Era, 1885–1945* (Oxford: Oxford University Press, 2010).

John Price, *Orienting Canada: Race, Empire, and the Transpacific* (Vancouver: UBC Press, 2011).

Patricia E. Roy, *Oriental Question: Consolidating a White Man's Province, 1914–42* (Vancouver: UBC Press, 2003).

Timothy J. Stanley, *Contesting White Supremacy: School Segregation, Anti-Racism, and the Making of Chinese Canadians* (Vancouver: UBC Press, 2011).

Peter Ward, *White Canada Forever: Popular Attitudes and Public Policy toward Orientals in British Columbia* (Montreal and Kingston: McGill-Queen's University Press, 2002).

Primary Documents

1   From Emily Murphy, *The Black Candle* (Toronto: Thomas Allen, 1922), 178–99.

INTERNATIONAL RINGS

Secret path marks secret foe.
—Sir Walter Scott

The Christianized Chinese in Canada and the States are also anxious to clear up crime or misbehaviour among their compatriots, and so are proceeding to make these conform to the provisions of the white man's laws.

Fussy folk, and self-opinionated ones, can be found who claim there is no such thing as a Christianized Chinaman, and that his profession is one of entire hypocrisy, just as though Jehovah's arm were shortened and His ear heavy when the suppliants' color was just a shade deeper than their own.

Knowing many men from the Flowery Kingdom who exhibit all the traits of Christian gentlemen, we are prepared to take them as such until the contrary is proven. What Sa'di, the Persian, said of the morals of the dervishes is here applicable: "In his outward behaviour I see nothing to blame, and with the secrets of his heart I claim no acquaintance."

We believe that the letter here following was written by a Chinaman who desires to be a good citizen, and who has the same desires for his compatriots. At any rate, he speaks to the point and is no trembler. This was received by us a few months ago, and is interesting as showing the ideals and expressions of a naturalized Oriental:—

> Magistrate Murphy,
>   The Police Court,
>   Edmonton, Alberta.
>
> DEAR MAGISTRATE:—
>
> I have information that the China Town of this City, has lots of gambling houses and opium smokers. Things around here are so quiet just now, and hard times coming soon. I do not like the people around here getting starving, because I found out lots of poor labourers lost all their money for play the Chinese gamble which is called "fine tin"* and waste up their good money for smoking opiums and so let their families, such as their father, mother, sisters, and young brothers starving at China.

*fan-tan.

And I am also afraid that the peoples around here spoil their own condition, and spoil all business in this city too, because the peoples lost their money, but they must betting lazy, then they must go stealing any things for their lives around this town, and getting all kinds of troubles here.

I am now wish you to stop all the China gambles houses at once, and would like to show you all the gambling houses address to arrest them.

If you spent a month time for the gambling houses, I believe the all gambling houses be stop so all the gamblers have to work for their own foods and every body have take care their families. Then I say "Amen".

I think you would be glad to do this for me. If you want any help let me know soon.

Yours sincerely,

. . ..

(Chinaman)

It came about this year in Vancouver that the Chinese merchants and leading members of the colony, with the support of the Chinese consulate, joined in the citizens' campaign to clean up Chinatown both morally and physically.

Realizing that their actions might lead to reprisals and to financial loss—that "the ungodly might bend their bow"—they still decided to wage war on those elements which had brought disrepute and opprobrium upon all Chinamen in the Province of British Columbia.

The advantages of such co-operation with the citizens has been set forth in an article in a Western daily paper by a reporter with a well-oiled mind. "The members of the Colony" he says, "have the inside information. They know where the drugs are coming from; who is getting them into Vancouver; the underground methods by which they are being brought in; who has the financial interest in the drug ring; the methods of distribution in this and other cities; all the ramifications of the drug traffic are known to them. And they will tell all they know to the proper authorities. It is to be open warfare and they will do all in their power to combat the drug-ring."

It is claimed that in some of the anti-narcotic campaigns, men who have financial interest in the Ring are among the most active workers, whether these are joining for sinister purposes, or merely to divert suspicion from themselves, it would be difficult to say. Probably their purpose includes both, but, be this as it may, it was a clever move to secure the co-operation of the reputable members of the Oriental Colony as allies in this campaign.

In Vancouver and Victoria during the present year, mass meetings have been held and committees appointed to take active steps in the organization of every public service body in Canada for a fight against the activities of the Ring. The local organizations then proceeded to get in touch with all kindred branches in other cities in the Dominion, emphasizing the need of their taking a definite stand on the question.

Some of the organizations back of the movement in the cities are the Board of Trade, Ratepayers' Association, Women's Institutes, Women's Press Club, War Heroes' Association, Victorian Order of Nurses, Kiwanis, Rotary, Kwannon and Gyro Clubs, Parent-teachers' Association, Woman's New Era, and the One Hundred Per Cent Clubs, the Women's Church Temperance Union, the Imperial Order of the Daughters of the Empire, Trades and Labor Council, University Women's Club, King's Daughters, The Maccabees, Child Welfare Association, Orangemen, American Women's Club, the Great War Veterans, the Local Council of Women, the "Y" Associations, the Medical Association, as well as the municipal and provincial authorities, and a hundred churches.

In Seattle, believing that organization is the key to success, they are also combining their forces in a drive on addictive drugs. In

Seattle, they too, have a branch of the White Cross Association. This Association has done more than any other agency to combat the drug evil, and at a lesser expense. In seven months last year, one paid agent caused 275 arrests, some of the persons convicted received heavy fines and others terms of imprisonment of from one to four years. It is claimed by White Cross workers that police departments cannot appropriate the sums required for the detection of pedlars in that most of the police officials are known to the drug runners, and hence large sums must be spent to secure arrests.

The White Cross are agitating that the Harrison Anti-Narcotic law be so amended as to permit of sentences of from seven to twelve years. The organization declares that short terms and fines are no deterrent in that the Ring has abundant money with which to pay the fines while the pedlar has no fear of from thirty to sixty days imprisonment. Besides, he is well rewarded for his temporary incarceration in jail.

In January of this year, a Narcotic Drug Control League was formed in New York, this League comprising the most notable organizations and workers in the State. The secretary is Joseph P. Chamberlain, Columbia University, New York City.

The objects of their anti-drug League as set forth on the invitation sent out are as follows:—"To marshal representative forces against the world menace of drug addiction. The Narcotic Drug Control League represents the first organized movement against this evil which has reached alarming proportions and is producing a growing horde of incompetents and criminals involving even the youth of our country."

"Habit forming drugs are destroying and enslaving a steadily increasing number of our people. The toll of victims among the youth of the country is the striking development of recent years. The people do not know the facts. Our program is definite and constructive. Its success demands the aid of the churches,

the judiciary, the medical profession, and public-spirited citizens representative of every class in the community. Patriotic people must unite to remove this scourge from our land and from the world."

This claim that the people do not know of the terrifying growth of the narcotic evil, was referred to recently by Dr. J.A. Drouin of the State of Vermont who said, "Most of us have been lulled to sleep by the usual so-called hospital reports, and other 'official' reports, regarding the fast disappearing drug addicts in the United States, especially after the enactment of the *Harrison Narcotic Act*."

In Canada, our federal officers declare that the people would be astounded if they comprehended the extent of the illicit traffic and the foothold it has gained.

That this method of organized public effort is a good one cannot be disputed. A Presbyterian clergyman, in Canada, speaking of this matter said the Drug Ring is successful in its operation because its brains are pooled and concentrated. Occidental ingenuity and Oriental craftiness are dangerously combined. Unless all the different public bodies become organized into a single fighting force, and the best brains of our camp centralized and concentrated as the directing mind, the fight will be futile. To carry on successfully the crusade, monetary backing is necessary also. It will take money to fight money.

In a previous chapter it was stated that white men of every clime and color were engaged in this traffic, and it was rumored that Japanese and German interests were chiefly responsible. As the Germans have not been trafficking in any goods with the people of this continent, for several years past, it would seem that the charge must be impossible of proof. Indeed, in communicating with the Chiefs-of-Police in the United States concerning the ravages of drug-intoxication, it was markworthy that those bearing German names were especially prompt and thorough in reply to my enquiries, and in making suggestions as to the applications of practical remedies.

It is true that the finest grade of cocaine in the world is manufactured in Germany and is known as "Mercks". Buyers claim—with what verity we cannot say—that this is now exported into Spain and shipped to this continent as "No. I Spanish". It is alleged on excellent authority that a kilo of cocaine (about two-and-a-fifth pounds) can, at the present time, be purchased in the Province of Alberta, Canada, for $18.00 or at about seventy-five cents an ounce. This seems incredible, in view of the prices paid by the addicts, but the Ring are not telling their secrets, nor registering their profits, so that we have no means of exactly verifying these figures.

On the other hand, we know that there are more narcotic drugs in Europe at the present time than in pre-war days, and that the market for these is in England, the United States and Canada, among the Anglo-Saxon races.

In Germany itself, the use of narcotic drugs is "verboten," so that almost their entire traffic must be with other countries. Indeed, the same remark is practically applicable to all the European countries, a fact which is dealt with more fully elsewhere in this volume.

It is also true that while no Japanese ever becomes an addict, yet it is claimed he is the most active and dangerous of all the persons forming the Ring in that he keeps well under cover and is seldom apprehended.

We know, however, that several large seizures of contraband drugs have been made on Japanese steamers on the western coast of America. In March of this year, narcotics worth, at the wholesale price of $20,000, and a considerable quantity of Japanese whiskey were seized at Portland, on the Japanese steamer *Miegyi Maru*. The Japanese seamen hurled overboard a large number of sacks which were believed to have contained bottles.

The United States have made, this year, a formal protest to the Japanese Government against the smuggling of opium, morphine, heroin and other narcotics into America. Replying to this complaint, the Tokio foreign office has informed the American Government that efforts will be made to prevent illegal traffic in drugs and has requested Japanese ship owners to co-operate in the suppression of the same.

Returning to the matter of the alleged participation of German persons in this traffic, one of the authorities claiming this is Dr. Erwin C. Ruth, head of the Narcotic division of the International Revenue Department of Boston. He alleges that the opium and cocaine traffic is financed largely by interests in Germany and Great Britain, and that certain Germans have powerful corporations operating in South America, which deal in coca leaves, from which is produced cocaine.

Concerning the operations of Drug Rings in Asia especially in relation to opium, Dr. Ruth states that the opium traffic in Asia has grown to immense proportions and has become one of the greatest industries in the world, being organized with Standard Oil efficiency. In Persia, Turkey and India, immense plantations are operated by powerful interests, while great banking institutions for financing the drug traffic are well established.

Among the pedlars who are the agents of the Ring, the traffic is chiefly in the hands of Americans, Canadians, Chinese, Negroes, Russians and Italians, although the Assyrians and Greeks are running closely in the race.

It is claimed also, but with what truth we cannot say, that there is a well-defined propaganda among the aliens of color to bring about the degeneration of the white race.

Maybe, it isn't so, after all, the popular dictum which has something to do with a flag and a bulldog.

Oh! yes! it is the one which declares, "What we have we'll hold." The trouble with most bulldogs is that their heads are only developed in the region of the jaw and that any yellow terrier can hamstring them from behind.

We have no very great sympathy with the baiting of the yellow races, or with the belief that these exist only to serve the Caucasian, or to be exploited by us. Such a belief was exemplified in a film once shown at a five-cent theatre in Chicago, and was reported by Jane Addams.

In the pictures, a poor woman is surrounded by her several children, all of whom are desperately hungry, and hold out pleading hands for food. The mother sends one of the boys on the streets to beg but he steals a revolver instead, kills a Chinaman, robs him of several hundred dollars, and rushes home with the money to his mother.

The last scene portrays the woman and children on their knees in prayer thanking God for His care and timely rescue of them.

The Chinese, as a rule are a friendly people and have a fine sense of humor that puts them on an easy footing with our folk, as compared with the Hindu and others we might mention.

Ah Duck, or whatever we choose to call him, is patient, polite, and persevering. Also he inhales deeply. He has other peculiarities such as paying his debts and refraining from profanity. "You sabe?"

The population of China amounts to 426,000,000 or one-third of the human race. Yes! it was a New York citizen who, looking up from an encyclopedia exclaimed with deadly earnestness, "In this household, we shall not have more than three children seeing this book says every fourth child born in the world is a Chinaman."

Still, it behooves the people in Canada and the United States, to consider the desirability of these visitors—for they *are* visitors—and to say whether or not we shall be "*at home*" to them for the future.

A visitor may be polite, patient, persevering, as above delineated, but if he carries poisoned lollypops in his pocket and feeds them to our children, it might seem wise to put him out.

It is hardly credible that the average Chinese pedlar has any definite idea in his mind of bringing about the downfall of the white race, his swaying motive being probably that of greed, but in the hands of his superiors, he may become a powerful instrument to this very end.

In discussing this subject, Major Crehan of British Columbia has pointed out that whatever their motive, the traffic always comes with the Oriental, and that one would, therefore be justified in assuming that it was their desire to injure the bright-browed races of the world.

Naturally, the aliens are silent on the subject, but an addict who died this year in British Columbia told how he was frequently jeered at as "a white man accounted for". This man belonged to a prominent family and, in 1917, was drawing a salary of six thousand dollars a year. He fell a victim to a drug "booster" till, ultimately, he became a ragged wreck living in the noisome alleys of Chinatown, "lost to use, and name and fame."

This man used to relate how the Chinese pedlars taunted him with their superiority at being able to sell the dope without using it, and by telling him how the yellow race would rule the world. They were too wise, they urged, to attempt to win in battle but would win by wits; would strike at the white race through "dope" and when the time was ripe would command the world.

"It may sound like a fantastic dream," writes the reporter, "but this was the story he told in one of the brief periods when he was free from the drug curse, and he told it in all sincerity."

Some of the Negroes coming into Canada—and they are no fiddle-faddle fellows either—have similar ideas, and one of their greatest writers has boasted how ultimately they will control the white men.

Many of these Negroes are law-abiding and altogether estimable, but contrariwise, many are obstinately wicked persons, earning their livelihood as free-ranging pedlars of poisonous drugs. Even when deported, they make their way back to Canada carrying on their operations in a different part of the country.

2 From *An Act Respecting Chinese Immigration* (Ottawa: F.A. Acland, 1923), 301–15.

13–14 GEORGE V.
CHAP. 38.
An Act respecting Chinese Immigration.
  [Assented to 30th June, 1923]

His Majesty, by and with the advice and consent of the Senate and House of Commons of Canada, enacts as follows:—
[. . .]

ENTRY AND LANDING

5. The entry to or landing in Canada of persons of Chinese origin or descent irrespective of allegiance or citizenship, is confined to the following classes, that is to say:—

(*a*) The members of the diplomatic corps, or other government representatives, their suites and their servants, and consuls and consular agents;

(*b*) The children born in Canada of parents of Chinese race or descent, who have left Canada for educational or other purposes, on substantiating their identity to the satisfaction of the controller at the port or place where they seek to enter on their return;

(*c*) (1) Merchants as defined by such regulations as the Minister may prescribe;

(2) students coming to Canada for the purpose of attendance, and while in actual attendance, at any Canadian university or college authorized by statute or charter to confer degrees; who shall substantiate their status to the satisfaction of the Controller at the port of entry subject to the approval of the Minister, whose decision shall be final and conclusive; provided that no Chinese person belonging to any of the two classes referred to in this paragraph shall be allowed to enter or land in Canada, who is not in possession of a valid passport issued in and by the Government of China and endorsed (*visé*) by a Canadian Immigration Officer at the place where he was granted such passport or at the port or place of departure.

6. No person of Chinese origin or descent shall enter or land in Canada except at a port of entry.

7. No person of Chinese origin or descent other than the classes mentioned in paragraphs (*a*) and (*b*) of section five and sections twenty-three and twenty-four of this Act shall be permitted to enter or land in Canada elsewhere than at the ports of Vancouver and Victoria.

PROHIBITED CLASSES

8. No person of Chinese origin or descent unless he is a Canadian citizen within the meaning of paragraph (f) of section two of *The Immigration Act* shall be permitted to enter or land in Canada, or having entered or landed in Canada shall be permitted to remain therein, who belongs to any of the following classes, hereinafter called "Prohibited classes":—

(*a*) Idiots, imbeciles, feeble-minded persons, epileptics, insane persons and persons who have been insane at any time previously;

(*b*) Persons afflicted with tuberculosis or leprosy in any form, or with any loathsome disease, or with a disease which is contagious or infectious, or which may be or become dangerous to the public health, whether such persons intend to settle in Canada or only to pass through Canada in transit to some other country;

(*c*) Persons who have been convicted of, or admit having committed, any crime involving moral turpitude;

(*d*) Prostitutes and women and girls coming to Canada for any immoral purpose and pimps or persons living on the avails of prostitution;

(*e*) Persons who procure or attempt to bring into Canada prostitutes or women or girls for the purpose of prostitution or other immoral purpose;

(*f*) Professional beggars or vagrants;

(*g*) Persons who in the opinion of the Controller or the officer in charge at any port of entry are likely to become a public charge;

(*h*) Persons of constitutional psychopathic inferiority;

(*i*) Persons with chronic alcoholism, or addicted to the use of drugs;

(*j*) Persons not included within any of the foregoing prohibited classes, who upon examination by a medical officer of the Department of Health are certified as being mentally or physically defective to such a degree as to affect their ability to earn a living;

(*k*) Persons who believe in or advocate the overthrow by force or violence of the Government of Canada or of constituted law and authority, or who disbelieve in or are opposed to organized government, or who advocate the assassination of public officials, or who advocate or teach the unlawful destruction of property;

(*l*) Persons who are members of or affiliated with any organization entertaining or teaching disbelief in or opposition to organized government, or advocating or teaching the duty, necessity, or propriety of the unlawful assaulting or killing of any officer or officers, either of specific individuals or of officers generally, of the Government of Canada or of any other organized government, because of his or their official character, or advocating or teaching the unlawful destruction of property;

(*m*) Persons who have been found guilty of high treason or treason for an offence in connection with the late war, or of conspiring against His Majesty, or of assisting His Majesty's enemies during the war, or of any similar offence against any of His Majesty's allies;

(*n*) Persons over fifteen years of age, physically capable of reading, who cannot read the English or the French language or some other language or dialect. For the purpose of ascertaining whether aliens can read, the immigration officer shall use slips of uniform size prepared by direction of the Minister, each containing not less than thirty and not more than forty words in ordinary use printed in plainly legible type in the language or dialect the person may designate as the one in which he desires the examination to be made, and he shall be required to read the words printed on the slip in such language or dialect. The provisions of this paragraph shall not apply to persons residing in Canada at the date of the passing of this Act nor to Canadian citizens;

(*o*) Persons who have been deported from Canada, or the United States, or any other country, for any cause whatsoever.

9. The Minister may authorize the admission to Canada of any person of Chinese origin or descent without being subject to the provisions of this Act, and such admission shall be authorized for a specified period only, but may be extended or cancelled by the Minister in writing.

POWER OF CONTROLLER

10. (1) The Controller shall have authority to determine whether an immigrant, passenger or other person seeking to enter or land in Canada or detained for any cause under this Act is of Chinese origin or descent and whether such immigrant, passenger or other person, if found to be of Chinese origin or descent, shall be allowed to enter, land or remain in Canada or shall be rejected and deported.
[. . .]

11. There shall be no appeal from the decision of the Controller, as to the rejection or deportation of any immigrant, passenger or other person found to be of Chinese origin or descent seeking to enter or land in Canada when such decision is based upon a certificate of the examining medical officer to the effect that such immigrant, passenger or other person of Chinese origin or descent is afflicted with any loathsome disease, or with a disease which may be or become dangerous to the public health, or that he comes within any of the following prohibited classes, namely, idiots, imbeciles, feeble-minded persons, epileptics and insane persons: Provided always that Canadian citizens and persons who have left Canada with the declared intention of returning thereto under the provisions of section twenty-three hereof and are seeking re-entry in accordance with the provisions of section twenty-four hereof, shall be permitted to land in Canada.

12. In all cases other than those provided for in the next preceding section an appeal may be taken to the Minister against the decision of the Controller if the appellant within forty-eight hours serves written notice of such appeal upon the Controller. Such notice of appeal shall act as a stay of all proceedings until a final decision is rendered by the Minister.

[. . .]

15. Every person of Chinese origin or descent, brought to Canada by a transportation company and rejected by the Controller, shall be sent back to the place whence he came by the said transportation company and the cost of his maintenance while being detained at an immigrant station, as well as the cost of his return, shall be paid by such transportation company.

[. . .]

17. (1) The Controller shall deliver to each Chinese immigrant who has been permitted to land in or enter Canada a certificate containing a description and photograph of such individual, the date of his arrival and the name of the port of his landing, and such certificate shall be *prima facie* evidence that the person presenting it has complied with the requirements of this Act; but such certificate may be contested by His Majesty or by any officer if there is any reason to doubt the validity or authenticity thereof; or of any statement therein contained; and such contestation shall be heard and determined in a summary manner by any judge of a superior court of any province of Canada where such certificate is produced.

(2) The Chief Controller and such controllers as are by him authorized so to do shall each keep a register of all persons to whom certificates of entry have been granted.

18. Within twelve months after the coming into force of this Act and subject to such regulations as may be made by the Governor General in Council for the purpose, every person of Chinese origin or descent in Canada, irrespective of allegiance or citizenship, shall register with such officer or officers and at such place or places as are designated by the Governor General in Council for that purpose, and obtain a certificate in the form prescribed: Provided that those persons who may, during the time fixed for registration, be absent from Canada with authority to return, may register upon their return.

19. No vessel carrying Chinese immigrants to any port in Canada shall carry more than one such immigrant for every two hundred and fifty tons of its tonnage.

20. (1) It shall be unlawful for the master of any vessel carrying persons of Chinese origin or descent, whether immigrants, passengers, stowaways, officers or crew, to any port in Canada to allow any person of Chinese origin or descent to leave such vessel until a permit so to do stating that the provisions of this Act have been complied with has been granted to the master of such vessel by the Controller. Should such master permit any such person to leave the vessel without such permit he shall upon demand pay to the Controller or officer in charge at the port of entry one thousand dollars for each such person so permitted to leave the vessel.

(2) No controller at any port shall grant a permit allowing any person of Chinese origin or descent to leave the vessel until the quarantine officer has granted a bill of health, and has certified, after due examination, that no leprosy or infectious, contagious, loathsome or dangerous disease exists on board such vessel; and no permit to land shall be granted to any person of Chinese origin or descent prohibited entry under section eight of this Act.

(3) No vessel shall be granted clearance papers pending the determination of the question of the liability to the payment of such fine, or while the fine remains unpaid; nor shall such fine be remitted or refunded unless in the opinion of the Minister a mistake has been made. Provided that clearance may be granted prior to the determination of such question upon the deposit of a sum sufficient to cover such fine.

21. (1) Every conductor or other person in charge of any railway train or car bringing persons of Chinese origin or descent into Canada shall, immediately on his arrival, deliver to the Controller or other officer at the port or place of arrival a report containing a complete and accurate list of all persons of Chinese origin or descent arriving by or being on board of the railway train or car of which he is in charge, and showing their names in full, the country and place of their birth, their occupation and last place of domicile; and he shall not allow any such persons of Chinese origin or descent to disembark from such train or car until after such report has been made.

[. . .]

22. Persons of Chinese origin or descent may pass through Canada in transit from one port or place out of Canada to another port or place out of Canada: Provided that such passage is made in accordance with and under such regulations as are made for the purpose by the Governor in Council.

23. (1) Every person of Chinese origin or descent, who wishes to leave Canada with the declared intention of returning thereto, and who establishes to the satisfaction of the Controller that he was legally landed in Canada, and is lawfully resident therein, shall give written notice of such intention to the controller at the port or place whence he proposes to sail or depart at least twenty-four hours before the intended date of his departure; in which notice shall be stated the foreign port or place which such person wishes to visit and the route he intends taking, both going and returning; and such notice shall be accompanied by a fee of two dollars.

(2) The form of such notice shall be in accordance with such regulations as are made from time to time for the purpose by the Governor General in Council.

(3) The Controller shall enter in a register to be kept for the purpose the name, residence, occupation and description of the person making the declaration, and such other information regarding him as is deemed necessary under such regulations as are made by the Governor General in Council for the purpose.

24. (1) The person so registered shall be entitled on his return, if within two years of such registration, and on proof of his identity to the satisfaction of the controller, to re-enter; but if he does not return to Canada within two years from the date of such registration, he shall be treated in the same manner as a person making application for admission as an immigrant.

(2) Every person of Chinese origin or descent who leaves Canada and does not register shall be subject on his return to the provisions of this Act as in the case of a first arrival.

(3) Every person of Chinese origin or descent, who registered out between April 1st, 1914, and March 31st, 1919, and who, under the provisions of an Order in Council of the 2nd April, 1919 (P.C. 697), was accorded the privilege of prolonging his return to Canada until one year after a proclamation had been published in the *Canada Gazette* declaring that a state of war no longer exists, shall be entitled to re-enter if he returns to Canada within one year from the date of the coming into force of this Act, and substantiates his identity to the satisfaction of the Controller.

Notwithstanding the provisions of the said Order in Council P.C. 697, every person of Chinese origin or descent who registered out between April 1st, 1914, and March 31st, 1919, and who does not return to Canada within one year from the date upon which this Act comes into force shall be subject on his return to the provisions of this Act as in the case of a first arrival.

25. (1) Any person of Chinese origin or descent who has been legally admitted to Canada and who is employed as a member of the crew of any vessel which operates between Canadian and United States ports, shall in order to retain his right of re-entry to Canada on his return with such vessel from such United States ports register with the controller and obtain a certificate of registration, which certificate shall be in the form prescribed and under such regulations as may be made by the Governor General in Council, and shall be produced at any time when demanded by an officer; such registration shall be for a period not to exceed two years and a fee of two dollars shall be charged by the controller for each registration card issued.

(2) Every person who fails to register in accordance with the provisions of this section shall be subject on his return to Canada to the provisions of this Act as in the case of a first arrival.

(3) Any transportation company, master, agent, or owner of any vessel who employs on such vessel a person of Chinese origin or descent without such person having complied with this section shall pay to any controller or officer demanding the same the sum of two hundred and fifty dollars for each such person. Pending the determination of the question of the liability to the payment of such fine, which question shall be decided by the Minister, no such vessel shall be granted clearance: Provided that clearance may be granted prior to the determination of such question upon deposit with the controller or officer in charge of a sum sufficient to cover such fine.

OFFENCES AND PENALTIES

26. Whenever any officer has reason to believe that any person of Chinese origin or descent has entered or remains in Canada contrary to the provisions of this Act or of the *Chinese Immigration Act*, chapter ninety-five of the Revised Statutes of Canada, 1906, or any amendment thereof, he may, without a warrant apprehend such person, and if such person is unable to prove to the satisfaction of the officer that he has been properly admitted into and is legally entitled to remain in Canada, the officer may detain such person in custody and bring him before the nearest controller for examination, and if the controller finds that he has entered or remains in Canada contrary to the provisions of this Act or of the *Chinese Immigration Act* or any amendment thereof, such person may be deported to the country of his birth or citizenship, subject to the same right of appeal as is provided in the case of a person applying for original entry to Canada. Where any person is examined under this section the burden of proof of such person's right to be or remain in Canada shall rest upon him. Where an order for deportation is made under this section and in the circumstances of the case the expenses of deportation cannot be charged to the transportation company, such expenses shall be paid by the person being deported if able to pay, and, if not, by His Majesty.

27. (1) Every person of Chinese origin or descent resident in Canada at the date of the coming into force of this Act, who was admitted under the provisions of any Act now or heretofore in force, and did not secure such admission by fraudulent misrepresentation, and does not belong to any of the prohibited classes of persons described in section 8 of this Act, shall be deemed to be entitled to continue to reside in Canada: Provided, however, that any such person who was, subsequent to the 25th day of July, 1917, admitted without payment of the head tax because of his being a merchant and who has ceased to belong to such class, shall pay into the Consolidated Revenue Fund of Canada the sum of five hundred dollars, and if he refuses or fails to make such payment he shall *ipso facto* forfeit his right to remain in Canada, and may be arrested by any officer without a warrant and brought before a Controller for examination, whereupon he shall be dealt with to all intents and purposes in the same manner and subject to the same provisions as in the case of a person apprehended under section 26 of this Act.

(2) Any person admitted under this Act who at any time after admission ceases to belong to any of the classes admissible under this Act shall, unless he is a Canadian citizen, *ipso facto* forfeit his right to remain in Canada and may be arrested by any officer without a warrant and brought before a Controller for examination, whereupon he shall be dealt with to all intents and purposes in the same manner and subject to the same provisions as in the case of a person apprehended under section 26 of this Act.

[. . .]

32. (1) Every person of Chinese origin or descent who—

(*a*) lands or attempts to land in Canada contrary to the provisions of this Act;

(*b*) wilfully makes use of or attempts to make use of any forged or fraudulent certificate, or of a certificate issued to any other person for any purpose connected with this Act is guilty of an offence, and liable to imprisonment for any term not exceeding twelve months and not less than six months, or to a fine not exceeding one thousand dollars and not less than three hundred dollars, or to both imprisonment and fine, and shall be deported.

(2) Every person who wilfully aids and abets any person of Chinese origin or descent in any evasion or attempt at evasion of any of the provisions of this Act is guilty of an offence and liable to imprisonment for a term not exceeding twelve months and not less than six months, or to a fine not exceeding one thousand dollars and not less than three hundred dollars, or to both imprisonment

and fine, and shall be deported unless of Canadian citizenship.

[. . .]

34. Any person of Chinese origin or descent who fails to register as required by section eighteen of this Act or any order or regulation made hereunder shall be liable to a fine not exceeding five hundred dollars or to imprisonment for a period not exceeding twelve months, or to both. In any prosecution under this section where the accused alleges that he is not a person of Chinese origin or descent, the onus of establishing that fact shall be upon the accused.

35. Every person who takes part in the organization of any sort of court or tribunal composed of Chinese persons for the hearing and determination of any offence committed by a Chinese person, or in carrying on any such organization, or who takes part in any of its proceedings, or who gives evidence before any such court or tribunal, or assists in carrying into effect any decision, decree, or order of any such court or tribunal, is guilty of an offence and liable to imprisonment for any term not exceeding twelve months, or to a fine not exceeding five hundred dollars, or to both; but nothing in this section shall be construed to prevent Chinese persons from submitting any differences or disputes to arbitration, if such submission is not contrary to the laws in force in the province in which such submission is made.

[. . .]

38. No court and no judge or officer thereof shall have jurisdiction to review, quash, reverse, restrain or otherwise interfere with any proceeding, decision or order of the Minister or of any controller relating to the status, condition, origin, descent, detention or deportation of any immigrant, passenger or other person upon any ground whatsoever, unless such person is a Canadian citizen, or has acquired Canadian domicile.

[. . .]

41. Notwithstanding any provision of this Act or any order or regulation made thereunder, any person of Chinese origin or descent who is at the date of the coming into force of this Act en route to Canada and presents himself for admission within three months from said date, shall if admissible under the provisions of the *Chinese Immigration Act* or any amendment thereof, be permitted to enter Canada upon payment of the head tax therein provided: Provided that if he belongs to any of the exempt classes he may be admitted exempt from the head tax.

Historical Interpretations

3 From Catherine Carstairs, "Deporting Ah Sin to Save the White Race: Moral Panic, Racialization, and the Extension of Canadian Drug Laws in the 1920s," *Canadian Bulletin of Medical History* 16, 1 (June 1999): 65–88. Reprinted with permission from University of Toronto Press (www.utpjournals.com).

In the early 1920s, newspapers, women's groups, social service organizations, labour unions, fraternal societies, and church congregations all joined in a campaign to eradicate what they described as the "drug evil." Blaming Chinese-Canadians for degradation of white youth through drugs, they demanded harsh new drug legislation, as well as Chinese exclusion. As a result of their campaign, maximum sentences for trafficking and possession increased from one year to seven in 1921. In 1922, Parliament passed legislation that allowed judges to order the deportation of any aliens convicted of possession or trafficking. That same year, the Honourable Members decided that people convicted of possession or trafficking offences should serve jail terms of at least six months. Police were given the right to search all locations except a "dwelling-house" without a warrant if they suspected drugs were present. In 1923, codeine and marijuana were added to the Schedule of Restricted Drugs without debate. The same legislation limited the right to appeal a conviction for possession or trafficking.[1] This legislative flurry marked a significant turning point in Canada's approach to drug use. By the mid-1920s, drug use had been thoroughly criminalized, both by the law and within the public mind.

[. . .]

The term "moral panic" has been used extensively by scholars to describe periods of public alarm about deviant behaviours, such as drug use. The term was first coined by Stanley Cohen in his 1972 book, *Folk Devils and Moral Panics*. Cohen described moral panics as follows:

> A condition, episode, person or group of persons emerges to become defined as a threat to societal values and interests; its nature is presented in a stylized and stereotypical fashion by the mass media: the moral barricades are manned by editors, bishops, politicians and other right-thinking people; socially accredited experts pronounce their diagnoses and solutions; ways of coping are evolved or (more often) resorted to; the condition then disappears, submerges or deteriorates and becomes more visible.[2]

[. . .]

Moral panics reproduce and in some cases reify or worsen the social inequalities that gave rise to them in the first place. The moral panic about drug use in the early 1920s stigmatized an already marginalized Chinese population and created legal precedents (including the right to search people and places without a warrant and limiting the right to an appeal) that potentially limited the human rights of all Canadians who interacted with the criminal justice system. For this reason, it is important to understand which social groups participated in the panic and for what reasons, whether their concern was proportionate to the actual harm involved, and why the issue of drug use gained currency at this particular point in time.

The other important term in this discussion is racialization. As Kay Anderson described in her book, *Vancouver's Chinatown*, racialization is the process by which attributes such as skin colour, language, and cultural practices are given social significance as markers of distinction.[3] The effectiveness of the drug panic depended on the creation of a racial drama of drug use that featured "innocent" white youth and shadowy Asian traffickers who turned them into morally depraved "dope fiends."[4] This drama was believable because it took shape in the middle of a concerted drive to exclude the Chinese from Canada, segregate their children in west-coast schools, and place restrictions on their business enterprises and land ownership.[5] Examining the racialization of drug panic helps explain why anti-drug crusaders called for strict penalties for possession and trafficking and at the same time wished to establish treatment facilities for the poor (white) drug addicts for whom they had so much sympathy. It also explains why parliamentarians, many of whom were trained lawyers, were willing to overlook traditional civil liberties in their desire to pass harsh legislation to counter what they regarded as a "Chinese" menace.

THE EARLY DEVELOPMENT OF CANADA'S DRUG LAWS

Canada's first drug law was the indirect result of anti-Asian riots on the west coast in 1907. The government sent Deputy Minister of Labour William Lyon Mackenzie King to investigate the riots and claims for compensation. One of the claims was by several opium manufacturers who up until that time had been operating openly and legally on the west coast. When he was in British Columbia, members of a Chinese anti-opium league called upon King and asked for the government's help in their efforts to discourage and prevent the manufacture and sale of opium. King subsequently tabled a report that warned that opium smoking was not just confined to the Chinese in British Columbia and that it was spreading to white women and girls. He quoted a newspaper clipping that told the story of a pretty young girl who had been found in a Chinese den. His report reviewed the progress of the anti-opium movement in China, the United States, England, and Japan, leaving the impression that Canada was far behind in this international moral reform movement.[6] Less than a few weeks later the Minister of Labour introduced legislation prohibiting the manufacture, sale and importation of opium for other than medicinal purposes. The legislation passed without debate.

Three years later the government prohibited the use of opium and other drugs. In 1911, the sale or possession of morphine, opium, or cocaine became an offence carrying a maximum penalty of one year's imprisonment and a $500 fine. There was no minimum penalty. Smoking opium was a separate offence and carried a maximum term of $50 and one month imprisonment. Again, there was no minimum penalty. There were several reasons behind the new legislation. First of all, the 1908 legislation had not stopped opium smoking in Canada and the police felt that more drastic measures were needed. Chief Rufus Chamberlain, the Chief

Constable of the Vancouver City Police, recommended that opium smoking and possession of opium should be offences under the law. Secondly, Mackenzie King, who introduced the legislation, had attended the 1909–1910 International Opium Commission in Shanghai. The Commission was an American initiative meant to help China eradicate the opium traffic. Canada's 1911 legislation was intended to bring its legislation in line with the Resolutions passed by the international meeting.[7] [. . .]

The 1908 and 1911 laws were the result of a number of different factors including a growing unease about psychotropic substance use in a prohibitionist era, changing medical practices which created fewer cases of iatrogenic addiction, and the international anti-opium movement. The fact that opium was perceived to be used by working-class Chinese, and cocaine by underclass Montrealers also contributed to the notion that these drugs, like the people who used them, needed to be controlled and regulated. However, there was a significant difference between this legislation and the legislation of the 1920s. Fines were the norm in the 1910s. After the drug panic of the 1920s, an increasing number of drug users were imprisoned.

THE CANADIAN DRUG PANIC

Canada was not alone in passing severe laws against drugs in the 1920s. Countries around the world were outlawing the use of opium and other drugs. Nonetheless, Canada's laws were among the most severe in the world, and for this reason, it is important to look at the specifics of the Canadian situation.[8] Drug crusaders claimed that the drug situation was especially troubling in Canada, but this does not seem to have been the case. In 1923–1924, based on a survey of doctors and police departments, the Division of Narcotic Control estimated that there were 9500 drug addicts in the country: 2250 in British Columbia, 3800 in Quebec, and 1800 in Ontario, with small numbers in every other province except Prince Edward Island.[9] This estimate cannot be regarded as definite and did not seem to include Chinese opium smokers, but it indicated that only one in every 1000 Canadians was an addict. Adding Chinese opium smokers, many of who seem to have smoked recreationally and were probably not addicted, would not have noticeably increased the per-capita rate of addiction.[10]

Drug scholars have generally dated the beginning of the drug panic to 1920, when the practised social reformer, Emily Murphy, published a series of five articles in *Maclean's* magazine. Murphy was a leading suffragist, a temperance activist, and a popular writer under the pen-name "Janey" Canuck. She was also a key player in eugenic debates, and a staunch supporter of the Sexual Sterilization Act in Alberta, which sterilized the mentally disabled.[11] In 1916 she was appointed police magistrate for Edmonton, and then for Alberta, becoming the first female magistrate in the British Empire. It was as a judge that she first became interested in drug use. She followed her 1920 articles with two additional articles in *Maclean's* in 1922 and her book *The Black Candle*. In 1923, she nominated herself for a Nobel Prize for her work in this area.[12] Although Murphy's articles marked the beginning of a sustained anti-drug campaign, she had little impact on the Vancouver drug panic, and her importance has been overstated both by herself and by subsequent drug historians. The Division of Narcotic Control had little respect for Murphy, and the Vancouver parliamentarians who played a leading role in drug legislation paid far more attention to the anti-drug crusade in their own city.[13] Nonetheless, Murphy's articles did mark a turning point and her book, which drew heavily on the Vancouver campaign and was dedicated to the Vancouver drug investigators, brought the Vancouver drug panic to a larger Canadian audience.[14]

Murphy's first article was entitled "The Grave Drug Menace". The first page delineated that this was a Chinese menace. It featured a threatening drawing of a hand with long fingernails holding a Chinese tablet, a picture of a wizened Asian man with smoke coming out of his ears, and a photo of an Asian man smoking a pipe. The text itself focused primarily on white female addicts and warned that "all folks of gentle and open hearts should know that among us there are girls and glorious lads who, without any obliquity in themselves, have become victims to the thrall of opiates."[15] Murphy explained that drug use posed a serious threat to the white race, as it accounted for most cases of miscegenation.[16] In subsequent articles, Murphy accused the Chinese of continuing their nefarious activities behind locked doors and hidden passages despite the Opium and Narcotic Drug Act.[17] Several times she referred to her imaginary Chinese characters as "Ah Sin,"[18] a quick shorthand for describing the moral failures of the Chinese, and had them engage in what was clearly meant to come across as "foreign" behaviour. In her fourth article she described one drug user's quest for religious help for a drug habit:

> In this place [a joss house in Vancouver] there was a serving altar on which stood huge vases of pewter and enamel and over which hung banners and peacock feathers. These banners, the Chinese explained, were extremely efficacious in the case of opium sickness, and so were carried to the sick room whenever required. On the serving altar, there is also a rubber stamp used to impress the paper taken away by men suffering from insomnia. "Debil, him keep China boy not sleep," explained the servitor.
> Yes! It is quite certain we do not understand these people from the Orient, nor what ideas are hid behind their dark inscrutable faces, but all of us, however owl-eyed, may see pathos in the picture

of the hapless drug victim—often a mere withered stalk of pain, stealing away in to the streets with his piece of sacred paper trying to make believe that, instead of the pipe, this will give sleep to his tortured eyes and still more tortured brain.[19]

Everything in this passage served to mark the "otherness" of the Chinese—the pidgin English, the religious practices, the "dark inscrutable faces," even the assumption that whites would be "owl-eyed" upon observing such activities. She used her pity as a tool by which to validate her racist description of Chinese religious practices. The fact that she expressed sympathy for the Chinese drug user (something she did not do in other places) and the inability of his religion to help him highlighted what she considered to be the inadequacy and peculiarity of Chinese methods for dealing with addiction.

In her 1922 book, Murphy took care to distance herself from what she considered to be prejudice or racism. "We have no sympathy with the baiting of the yellow races, or with the belief that these exist only to serve the Caucasian, or to be exploited by us," she wrote. "The Chinese as a rule are a friendly people," she condescendingly pronounced "and have a fine sense of humor that puts them on an easy footing with our folk, as compared with the Hindu and others we might mention. Ah Duck, or whatever we choose to call him, is patient, polite and persevering." Despite her favourable assessment of what she viewed as the Chinese character, she assumed that it was her right to name the Chinese, and to tell the "truth" of their character.

She followed this up with the statement that

> it behooves the people in Canada and the United States, to consider the desirability of these visitors—for they are visitors—and to say whether or not we shall be "at home" to them for the future. A visitor

may be polite, patient, persevering, as above delineated, but if he carried poisoned lollypops in his pocket and feeds them to our children, it might seem wise to put him out.[20]

By complimenting the Chinese and criticizing their exploitation, she gave greater credibility to her view that the Chinese were outsiders who threatened the well-being of Canadian children through drugs.

Murphy was one of Canada's best-known writers and her monthly feature in Canada's national news magazine garnered attention in newspapers across the country.[21] However, her campaign was dwarfed by a far more important anti-drug campaign in Vancouver. Vancouver was the primary location for anti-Chinese organizing, which was gathering steam in the years immediately following World War I. It also had the largest number of drug arrests and the biggest Chinese community in Canada. In 1917, an African-Canadian drug user had killed the Chief of Police, leading to a certain amount of hand wringing about the drug menace.[22] In the spring of 1920, coinciding with Murphy's campaign in *Maclean's*, the *Vancouver Sun* ran a brief campaign against the drug traffic, and in editorials, it called for the abolition of Chinatown. One declared that it is "absolutely necessary to prevent the degrading of white boys and girls who are being recruited into the ranks of drug addicts. If the only way to save our children is to abolish Chinatown, then Chinatown must and will go, and go quickly."[23] [. . .]

The catalyst for the first major anti-drug campaign occurred in March 1921, when returned soldier Joseph Kehoe pleaded guilty to eight charges of robbery with violence and was sentenced to five years in the Penitentiary and 24 lashes. According to the fast-growing *Vancouver Daily Sun*,[24] which covered the issue intensively, this unlikely "hero" was 28 years old and came from a "good family" in Nova Scotia. According to the paper, Kehoe

had been a medical student when he enlisted at the very start of the war. In April 1915 he was gassed and taken prisoner at Ypres. The Germans put him to work in a munitions factory, but he refused to take part in work that would be used to harm his fellow allied soldiers and eventually convinced his fellow prisoners to break his arm so that he could no longer work. He was brought before a military tribunal and sentenced to 15 years imprisonment in a military prison. At the end of 16 months his health was so poor that he was sent to England in an exchange of prisoners. He was discharged in 1919 and after his return to Canada he started using drugs.[25]

[. . .] A few weeks later a general meeting of the Comrades of the Great War passed a resolution opposing light sentences in the case of dope peddlers.[26] As it had the previous year, the coverage quickly took an anti-Chinese turn. In a front-page article on 12 April, entitled "Dope Peddler King Is Taken," the *Vancouver Sun* told its readers that prominent Chinese businessman Wong Way boasted that he was turning over more than half a million dollars' worth of drugs each year and that he drove one of the best limousines in the city. This fit in well with business complaints that Chinese merchants were competing unfairly with whites.[27]

A week later, Vancouverites held a mass meeting to demand "drastic federal action" to defeat the "dope traffickers."[28] The meeting was organized by the Returned Soldier's Council and included the Mayor, the Chief of Police, the City Prosecutor, Oakalla Prison Farm officials, and service club representatives. A week later, a second meeting called for minimum two-year sentences for first-time traffickers and five years and the lash for a second trafficking offence. Participants demanded that all aliens convicted of selling drugs be deported, and wanted the police to have the right to search for drugs without a warrant.[29] The enormous headline proclaimed "DEATH ON DOPE: CITIZENS PLAN BIG CAMPAIGN TO SMASH

UP THE DRUG RING." Beginning 3 May, the newspaper hired a former drug addict to carry on a special investigation into the traffic. J.B. Wilson described himself as a "successful young businessman" before he started using drugs. Now cured, he was anxious to "devote my talents and my energies to assisting in rescuing others who have fallen victims to the drug ring." Wilson argued that police were doing everything they could to stamp out the drug traffic, but that the "Chinese dope peddler is about the most cunning human being and the smartest of them all."[30] In a later article he commended the RCMP who "are bending their energies to rid our Canadian soil of the Oriental filth of the drug traffic."[31]

Several weeks after the first Vancouver meeting, the Minister of Health introduced legislation to amend the Opium and Narcotic Drug Act. H.H. Stevens, a Conservative MP from Vancouver South who had been an active participant in the Vancouver meetings, proposed two new amendments to the Act: 1) that a person found guilty of an offence be liable on indictment to imprisonment for seven years; and that 2) a person convicted of giving or distributing to a minor be liable to whipping as an additional penalty. This was the first time the House of Commons discussed drug use as a serious social menace. Stevens introduced his amendment with the announcement that drug traffickers were distributing drugs to high school children and even to children in the higher grades of elementary school.[32] [. . .]

[T]he Vancouver drug panic temporarily disappeared from the headlines, but there was still considerable backstage activity. In the spring of 1921, the Rotary, Gyros, and Kiwanis Clubs established an Investigating Committee into the Drug Traffic.[33] That summer the *Vancouver Sun* published Hilda Glynn Ward's novel *The Writing on the Wall*. The plot featured wealthy Vancouver citizens who became addicted to drugs and subsequently co-operated with the Chinese in their drive for the domination of Canada.[34] At the beginning

of 1922, the Investigating Committee had a great opportunity to expose their findings when the *Vancouver Daily World*, Vancouver's oldest newspaper,[35] launched a campaign that far exceeded the one launched by the *Sun* a year earlier. This newspaper highlighted the drug issue on its front page for months and increased its circulation by one third.[36] As a result, over 300 groups in Vancouver passed resolutions asking for mandatory sentences for drug possession and trafficking and the deportation of naturalized aliens who participated in the drug traffic.[37]

From the day the *World* campaign began, it was clear that they blamed Asians for the spread of the drug habit. The first day featured two front-page articles. The headline article proclaimed "Drug Soaked Addicts Pass on the Way to Jail." The article commenced with the case of Yung Yuen "an ivory faced Chinese." He was sentenced to a year in prison for procuring three packages of drugs for a "white victim." The next paragraph highlighted the case of Lim Gum, "an undersized bald-headed little Chinese" who was found with four tins of opium. The descriptions of the Chinese addicts were unflattering and attempted to draw attention to the physical ways in which the Chinese were perceived to be different from whites. At his trial, Yung was said to have written his name on a piece of paper and burned it with a match while mumbling "Chinese rigmarole to the effect that so might his soul burn after death if he failed to tell the truth." This depiction highlighted the "foreign" nature of the Chinese and their customs.[38]

[. . .]

The anti-Asian discourse in Canada during this time period consistently emphasized the intelligence of the Chinese and their craftiness as reasons for why they should not be permitted to immigrate to Canada. The idea that the Chinese were consummate drug smugglers, on account of their ingenuity and cleverness, would not come as any surprise to the citizens of

Vancouver. Most were already convinced that the business acumen of the Chinese posed a serious threat to white enterprise. The article below "Drug Soaked Addicts" announced that "All Boats from Asia Bring in Illicit Drugs," and was subtitled "Oriental Crews Largely Engaged in Traffic." Asian traffickers were described as "wily" and the newspaper proclaimed that innocent passengers were sleeping on top of drugs hidden under berths and stitched into mattresses. Obviously, Vancouverites needed to wake up to the danger. The following day, the article "Dying Lad Tells How Boys and Girls Are Made Drug Addicts" asserted that most of the drugs came from Chinatown. One dealer, the young addict confided, had a secret code whereby the purchaser would request drugs by number, lessening the chance of being caught over the phone.[39] Under such circumstances, it would not be easy to catch "cunning" Asian drug traffickers. The entire community needed to unite to defend itself.

On the third day of their campaign, the newspaper announced its solution to the drug problem. The headline blared "Deport the Drug Traffickers." The article asserted (wrongly) that 1778 Asians were convicted of drug offences in the Vancouver Police Court in 1921.[40] Since most received fines and only a few went to jail, they all became free again to "commit the same sin against society." The article concluded "Vancouver's first move in abolishing the drug traffic must be the absolute banishment by deportation of every Oriental who lends himself to the drug ring."[41] Over the months that followed, the *World* encouraged organizations throughout Vancouver to pass resolutions to that effect. Thousands of Vancouverites signed petitions requesting that aliens including naturalized aliens be deported if convicted of selling drugs. The measure was included in the 1922 amendments to the *Opium and Narcotic Drug Act* and in fact was even stricter than requested since deportation could be applied

to people convicted of possession as well as trafficking.

The third day contained the announcement that the Child Welfare Society was joining the fight against the "drug evil," despite the "fact" that other officials had received threats against their lives when they opposed the "drug ring" and that "actual attempts have been made on the lives of government officials engaged in the fight against the big influences at work behind the scenes."[42] [. . .] The frequently repeated idea that the Chinese might bring about the destruction of the white race through drug use appeared in a particularly blatant form in a front-page story about a wealthy addict who was "dragged down by drugs." This addict asserted that the Chinese drug sellers "taunted him with their superiority at being able to sell the dope without using it. Taunted him by telling him that the yellow race would rule the world. That they were too wise to attempt to win in battle but that they would win by wits. That they would introduce drugs into the homes of the Caucasians; would strike at the white race through 'dope,' and that when the time was ripe they would take command of the world."[43] On 29 January, less than two weeks after the start of the *World* campaign, 2000 Vancouverites attended a meeting held at the Empress Theatre, where they passed a unanimous resolution asking for the elimination of fines as a penalty and the substitution of prison sentences of not less than six months, and not more than 10 years, with lashes, and the deportation of aliens.[44] The *World* reported that women openly wiped tears from their eyes, as the self-styled drug investigator Charles E. Royal told the audience about young girls in their teens who sold themselves to Chinese, Japanese and "Hindoos" to get money for drugs. The newspaper continued,

They shuddered when he pointed out that many of them came from the best families in Vancouver and in the Dominion and when he told of a young boy of this city, himself an addict, who had, at the instigation of the Chinese traffickers, started his sister on the drug habit, and then had used her to pander to the passions of these self-same traffickers in order to get the money to buy drugs, women turned pale, while men clenched their hands and gripped their lips with their teeth to keep down the anger that fought for an outlet.[45]

The following day, the city council and the Mayor both endorsed the anti-drug campaign.[46]

[. . .]

In May 1922, New Westminster Unionist W.G. McQuarrie introduced a motion into the House of Commons asking for the government to take "immediate action with a view of securing the exclusion of Oriental immigration."[47] Vancouver South Liberal-Conservative Leon Ladner gave a long speech highlighting the discoveries of the Vancouver Investigating Committee. He concluded that the drug traffic was reason enough to stop all Chinese immigration.[48] While most members participating in this debate stressed economic issues, three other members also emphasized the dangers of the drug traffic.

The government introduced new drug legislation at the beginning of June. By this time, no parliamentarian asserted that the drug panic was overblown. Members from a variety of parties urged the Health Minister to take even more stringent steps against the drug traffic. In introducing the legislation, the Minister Henri Beland indicated that numerous requests had reached him from benevolent, charitable, and religious bodies as well as parliamentarians from both sides of the House, to abolish the option of a fine.[49] At the first reading, Progressive Archibald Carmichael, from Kindersley, Saskatchewan, asked for an amendment deporting all Asians found guilty of trafficking in drugs.[50] Vancouver MP Leon Ladner, who had spoken at

several of the Vancouver mass meetings, advised the government to pass an amendment allowing for the lash.[51] [. . .]

In the debate that followed, the anti-Asian racism of the Vancouver campaign had a clear impact. Leon Ladner told the story of a girl of 16 who had come before the investigation committee in Vancouver. The girl was a morphine or cocaine addict. Infected with venereal disease, she worked as a prostitute with Chinese men. Ladner concluded "this traffic is carried on in a cool and calculating way. The men who sell the drug do not themselves use it; they know its terrible effects, but they exercise all their resourcefulness and ingenuity to induce others to acquire the habit."[52] Fully persuaded, Dr Robert Manion, who had been opposed to the lash the previous year, admitted that "I believe that the hon. Gentlemen who represent British Columbia in this House are more familiar with this question than perhaps the rest of us, even those who are in the medical profession" and agreed to support the lash.[53] Although there were still a few such as United Farmer Oliver Gould who opposed the lash on humanitarian grounds, even he felt compelled to state that the traffic "is one of the greatest evils extent in this country."[54] In the discussion over deportation it was clear the "foreigners" to be deported were Chinese. Health Minister Henri Beland pointed out that "so far as a provision for deportation is concerned the committee will realize that it would not very well apply to Canadians. Only to Chinese who have not been naturalized could it apply."[55] He did not even consider the possibility that citizens of other countries might be deported by this legislation, although once the legislation was implemented, large numbers of Americans were also deported.

In 1923, not long after the passage of the 1923 Chinese Immigration Act, which initiated Chinese exclusion, the anti-drug consensus resulted in yet another set of revisions to the Opium and Narcotic Drug Act. By this time, the panic also had spread to Toronto and Montreal. That spring large meetings of prominent citizens were held at the Loew's Roof Garden Theatre in Toronto and at the Mount Royal Hotel in Montreal.[56] In the House of Commons debate that followed, the government passed legislation that restricted people's right to an appeal, increased the fine for smoking opium, and increased the maximum penalty for being found in an opium den and for the possession of opium equipment. This debate was short, but the anti-drug consensus was clear. Mr E.M. Macdonald stated that "we are all agreed that this nefarious traffic, which saps the mind and body of the people can only be dealt with in the strongest possible way."[57] Dr Manion, who opposed the measure to restrict appeals on constitutional grounds, made sure to indicate that his failure to support the amendment was not because he was "soft on drugs." "I presume," he clarified, "there is no member of this House, whatever may be his party affiliations who is not just as eager as my hon. friend to do away with the illicit use of any of these habit-forming drugs."[58]

Although the "panic" ended in 1923, the tropes that guided it had been firmly established and regularly reappeared in magazine and newspaper articles throughout the decade. In 1929, the debate over the consolidation of the Act, which added whipping at the discretion of the judge to all trafficking offences, showed how clearly the discourse of the innocent addict and the nefarious trafficker had permeated the public mind. Mr Edwards described a murderer as "white as the driven snow in comparison with the low, degraded human beast who for a few dollars' profit will gradually murder his fellow-man by selling to him habit forming drugs."[59] By contrast, the addict was described as a "poor creature."[60] Minister of Health James King declared that addicts were not being prosecuted under the Act.[61] However, in that year, more than half of the convictions under the Act were for smoking opium or for frequenting an opium den, two provisions which were

clearly aimed at drug users, not at drug traffickers.[62] What he meant when he said that they did not prosecute the addict was that they did not prosecute the imaginary white "victims" of drugs. However, they were prosecuting working-class drug users of all races.

Interestingly, in the 1929 debate, there was no mention of the race of traffickers. Did this mean that the racialization of drug use was on the decline? Perhaps, although the connection between drugs and Asians was still strong in the popular press.[63] In fact, the 1929 debate was short, and by this time parliamentarians may not have felt the need to stress the culpability of the Asian trafficker, since it was already well established in the public mind, and the Chinese Exclusion Act had all but ended Chinese immigration. However, the lack of attention to race in the 1929 debate also marked a transition point. By this time, the panic was over, but the public remained fully convinced that drug use was dangerous and drug traffickers immoral. Perhaps it was no longer necessary to exploit anti-Asian sentiment to pass strict laws against drugs.

The government never did act to provide treatment facilities, even for the innocent young addicts who incurred so much sympathy and who inspired such a strict legislative response to drugs. Throughout the decade, the Minister of Health and the Division of Narcotic Control asserted that treatment was a matter of provincial jurisdiction. They encouraged the provinces to pass legislation allowing for compulsory treatment of drug addicts in provincial mental institutions, but only Alberta and Nova Scotia passed such legislation and only Alberta put it into effect.[64] Ultimately, white drug users were rarely the promising young men and women of the middle classes who were featured in anti-drug campaigns. Many female drug users were prostitutes, and the men were often vagrants who had had previous encounters with the law.[65] These "dope fiends" received little notice in anti-drug campaigns and police officers and health officials who came into contact with them regarded them as difficult and noisy prisoners and patients. Although "innocent" white addicts served as an effective rhetorical tool for anti-drug crusaders who wanted stricter laws against drug use, neither the government or social service organizations were willing to spend money on the treatment and rehabilitation of the socially disadvantaged "dope fiend."

CONCLUSION

The link between drug use and the Chinese was a key factor in the demonization of drugs that took place in the early 1920s. It was no accident that the most important campaign against drug use in Canada took place at the same time as a concerted drive for Chinese exclusion. In this intolerant environment, an understanding of drug use emerged in which Chinese drug traffickers were vilified, Chinese drug users were ignored or regarded as a moral contagion, and white drug users were regarded as tragic victims. This imagery provided one more excuse for keeping the Chinese out of Canada, and resulted in the passage of severe drug legislation.

Racism does not "hurt us all," as an ad campaign declared in the mid-1990s. It hurts some much more than others. However, as Elizabeth Comack, Patricia Roy, and many others have noted, racism often divides the working class, and as such it can work to the disadvantage of people of all races. Although the middle and upper classes also used drugs, especially alcohol, to excess, by the 1920s, the drugs prohibited under the Opium and Narcotic Drug Act seem to have been used primarily by working-class people. The middle- and upper-class people who did use opiates and cocaine often were able to obtain supplies through doctors. They had little contact with the illicit market and rarely faced criminal sanctions for their drug use. This was not true for working-class users.

In the 1920s, as Clayton Mosher has pointed out, Chinese men convicted of drug offences often faced more lenient penalties than working-class white users of drugs. This was because they often were charged with opium smoking, or being found in an opium den, rather than possession. These charges were easier to prosecute, and served to raise revenue for the judicial system. However, Mosher's emphasis on sentencing downplays the extent to which drug laws were used to persecute the Chinese population. Between 1923 and 1932, 761 Chinese were deported as a result of the deportation provision passed in 1922, representing almost 2 per cent of the total Chinese population in Canada.[66] On average, people deported under the Act had been in Canada for almost 17 years.[67] Moreover, the police regularly raided opium dens. In 1922, 1117 Chinese were convicted under the Act, meaning that nearly 3 per cent of the total Chinese population was convicted under the Opium and Narcotic Drug Act that year alone.[68] In some cities, the arrest rates were even higher. These exceptionally high rates of arrest show the extent to which the Opium and Narcotic Drug Act was used as a tool against the Chinese population of Canada.

Nonetheless, drug laws did hurt all drug users, and even all Canadians. By the mid-1930s opium smoking had all but died out, and the mostly white drug users caught violating the law were sentenced to at least six months in prison for possession. Moreover, the Opium and Narcotic Drug Act contained provisions for corporal punishment, limited the right to an appeal, and allowed the police extensive power to search without a warrant. These provisions were dangerous precedents for the human rights of all Canadians, regardless of whether or not they used drugs.

The drug panic of the early 1920s had all the hallmarks of a "moral panic." Concern about drug use spread widely throughout society. There was a vastly increased level of hostility toward the Chinese men associated with the traffic, the concern was disproportionate to the apparent harm caused by drug use, and it erupted quite suddenly. Most importantly, this racialized drug panic had an important impact on Canadian civil rights and liberties.

NOTES

1. An Act to amend the Opium and Narcotic Drug Act, Statutes of Canada 1921, c.42; An Act to Amend the Opium and Narcotic Drug Act, Statutes of Canada 1922, c.36; and An Act to Prohibit the Improper Use of Opium and Other Drugs, Statutes of Canada 1923 c.22.

2. Stanley Cohen, *Folk Devils and Moral Panics: The Creation of the Mods and Rockers* (Oxford: Martin Robertson, 1980), 9.

3. Kay Anderson, *Vancouver's Chinatown* (Montreal and Kingston: McGill-Queen's University Press, 1991), 18.

4. Catherine Carstairs, "Innocent Addicts, Dope Fiends and Nefarious Traffickers: Illegal Drug Use in 1920s English Canada," *Journal of Canadian Studies* 33, 3 (Fall 1998): 145–62.

5. The literature on anti-Asian racism on the West Coast includes Peter Ward, *White Canada Forever* (Montreal and Kingston: McGill-Queen's University Press, 1978); Patricia Roy, *A White Man's Province* (Vancouver: University of British Columbia Press, 1989); and Gillian Creese, "Exclusion or Solidarity? Vancouver Workers Confront the 'Oriental Problem,'" *BC Studies* 80 (Winter 1988–89).

6. "A Report by W.L. Mackenzie King, Deputy Minister of Labour, on the Need for the Suppression of the Opium Traffic in Canada," *Sessional Papers of Canada 1908*, Paper No. 36b.

7. G.F. Murray, "Cocaine Use in the Era of Social Reform: The Natural History of a Social Problem in Canada, 1880–1911," *Canadian Journal of Law and Society*, 2 (1987): 29–43.

8. David Musto, *The American Disease: The Origins of Narcotic Control* (New Haven: Yale University Press, 1973); Andrew Blake, "Foreign Devils and Moral Panics: Britain, Asia and the Opium Trade," in Bill Shwartz, ed., *The Expansion of England: Race, Ethnicity and Cultural History* (London and New York: Routledge, 1996); T.O. Reins, "Reform, Nationalism and Internationalism: The Opium Suppression Movement in China," *Modern Asian Studies* 25, 1 (1991): 101–42.

9. *Annual Report of the Department of Health for the Year Ended March 31, 1924*, 36.

10. The population of Chinese in Canada in 1921 was 39 587. It is impossible to know how many of them smoked opium (Peter S. Li, *The Chinese in Canada* [Toronto: Oxford University Press, 1988]).

11. Byrne Hope Sanders, *Emily Murphy: Crusader* (Toronto: Macmillan, 1945), 186; and Christine Mander, *Emily Murphy: Rebel* (Toronto: Simon and Pierre, 1985), 117.

12. Michael Bliss, *The Discovery of Insulin* (Toronto: McClelland and Stewart, 1982), 225.

13. National Archives of Canada (NAC), RG 29, Vol. 602, File 325-1-3.

14. Murphy's dedication read: "To the members of the Rotary, Kiwanis and Gyros Clubs and to the white Cross Associations who are rendering valiant service in impeding the spread of drug addiction, this volume is respectfully dedicated."

15. Emily Murphy, "The Grave Drug Menace," *Maclean's*, 15 February 1920, 9.

16. Murphy, "The Grave Drug Menace," 11.

17. Madge Pon, "Like a Chinese Puzzle: Constructions of Chinese Masculinity in Jack Canuck," in Joy Parr and Mark Rosenthal, eds, *Gender and History in Canada* (Toronto: McClelland & Stewart, 1996), 88–100.

18. Murphy, "The Underground System," *Maclean's*, 15 March 1920, 55; and "Fighting the Drug Menace," *Maclean's*, 15 April 1920, 11.

19. Emily Murphy, "What Must Be Done," *Maclean's*, 15 June 1920, 14.

20. Emily Murphy, *The Black Candle* (Toronto: Thomas Allen, 1922), 187–8.

21. In its introduction to the second article, the editors of *Maclean's* wrote that newspapers across the country commented on the first article and commented that the editors of *Maclean's* had received a large number of letters as a result.

22. See "Chief MacLennan Is Shot Dead in Battle with Negro Desperado," *Vancouver Daily Sun*, 21 March 1917, 1.

23. "Chinatown—or Drug Traffic?" *Vancouver Daily Sun*, 22 March 1920, 6. See also "Chinatown and the Drug Traffic," *Vancouver Daily Sun*, 31 March 1920, 6.

24. The *Vancouver Daily Sun* was the fastest growing newspaper in Western Canada (*The Canadian Newspaper Directory* [A. McKim, 1922], 418).

25. "War Veteran to Be Given Lashes," *Vancouver Daily Sun*, 18 March 1921, 1.

26. "Dope Peddlar King Is Taken," *Vancouver Daily Sun*, 12 April 1921, 1.

27. Ward, *White Canada Forever*, 124–8; and Anderson, *Vancouver's Chinatown*, 110–13.

28. "War Opens on Drug Traffickers: Mass Meeting of Citizens Demand Federal Action," *Vancouver Daily Sun*, 21 April 1921, 1.

29. "Death of Dope," *Vancouver Daily Sun*, 28 April 1921, 1.

30. "Ex-Crook and Reformed Drug Fiend Aids City Police in Fight on Dope Ring," *Vancouver Daily Sun*, 3 May 1921, 1.

31. "Drug Exposure Causes Mass Meeting to Be Called to Fight Evil," *Vancouver Daily Sun*, 12 May 1921, 1.

32. House of Commons, *Debates*, 3 May 1921, 2897.

33. "Clubs to Report on "Dope" Probe," *Vancouver Daily Sun*, 28 January 1922, 3.

34. Hilda Glynn Ward, *The Writing on the Wall* (Toronto: University of Toronto Press, 1974; 1st edn, 1921).

35. The circulation of the *Vancouver Daily World* averaged 16 182 in 1921 (*The Canadian Newspaper Directory*, 463).

36. In an advertisement in the newspaper directory, the newspaper claimed that its circulation for February 1922 was 21 353, much higher than it had been for the year ended 30 September 1921.

37. "Call on Liberal Executive to Take Action on Drugs," *Vancouver Daily World*, 7 March 1922, 9.

38. "Drug Soaked Addicts Pass on Way to Jail," *Vancouver Daily World*, 16 January 1922, 1.

39. "Dying Lad Tells How Boys and Girls Are Made Drug Addicts," *Vancouver Daily World*, 17 January 1922, 1.

40. Statistics kept by the Dominion Bureau of Statistics were for the year ended 30 September. Statistics on race were not published until 1922. In the year ended 30 September 1922,

519 Chinese were convicted of drug offences in British Columbia. For the year ended 30 September 1921, 649 people of all races were convicted of drug offences in British Columbia, meaning that the newspapers' statistics were far off.

41. "Deport the Drug Traffickers," *Vancouver Daily World*, 18 January 1922, 1.

42. "Waterfront Open Gate for Drugs; Child Welfare Society Joins Fight," *Vancouver Daily World*, 18 January 1922, 1.

43. "Dragged Down by Drugs from Post Giving Big Pay," *Vancouver Daily World*, 21 January 1922, 28.

44. "Ten Years for Drug Sellers Demanded by 2000 Citizens," *Vancouver Daily World*, 30 January 1922, 1, 13.

45. "Ten Years for Drug Sellers Demanded by 2000 Citizens," 1.

46. "Mayor and Council Endorse World's Anti-Drug Campaign," *Vancouver Daily World*, 31 January 1922, 1; and "City to Join in the Drug Crusade," *Vancouver Daily Sun*, 31 January 1922, 2.

47. House of Commons, *Debates*, 8 May 1922, 1509.

48. House of Commons, *Debates*, 8 May 1922, 1529–31.

49. House of Commons, *Debates*, 15 June 1922, 3014.

50. House of Commons, *Debates*, 12 June 1922, 2824.

51. House of Commons, *Debates*, 12 June 1922, 2824.

52. House of Commons, *Debates*, 15 June 1922, 3015.

53. House of Commons, *Debates*, 15 June 1922, 3016.

54. House of Commons, *Debates*, 15 June 1922, 3017.

55. House of Commons, *Debates*, 12 June 1922, 2824.

56. Letter from F.W. Cowan to Elizabeth MacCallum, 9 April 1923, in NAC, RG 29, Vol. 605, File 325-4-7.

57. House of Commons, *Debates*, 23 April 1923, 2132.

58. House of Commons, *Debates*, 23 April 1923, 2117.

59. House of Commons, *Debates*, 12 February 1929, 62.

60. House of Commons, *Debates*, 12 February 1929, 65.

61. House of Commons, *Debates*, 29 May 1929, 2971.

62. Dominion Bureau of Statistics, *Annual Report of Criminal and Other Offences for Year Ended September 30, 1929*, 148–9.

63. Anne Anderson Perry, "The Dope Traffic in Canada," *The Western Home Monthly*, August 1929; and Thomas Warling, "Canada's Greatest Menace," *Canadian Home Journal*, August 1930.

64. NAC, RG 29, Vol. 326, File 324-1-2, Parts 1–3.

65. Clayton Mosher's thesis shows that 85.9 per cent of people convicted of drug offences in five Ontario cities between 1921 and 1928 were working class or had no occupation ("The Legal Response to Narcotic Drugs in Five Ontario Cities 1908–1961," [PhD dissertation, University of Toronto, 1992]).

66. *Annual Report of the Department of Pensions and National Health for 1932–33*, 70.

67. Answer to a question in the House of Commons, 27 February 1929 asking for the average length of time deported aliens had been in Canada (*Debates*, 508–9).

68. Dominion Bureau of Statistics, *Annual Report of Criminal and Other Offences for the Year Ended September 30, 1922*.

4   From Isabel Wallace, *"Komagata Maru* Revisited: 'Hindus,' Hookworm, and the Guise of Public Health Protection," *BC Studies* 178 (Summer 2013): 33–50. Reprinted with permission of the publisher.

Between May and July 1914, Canadian Department of Immigration officials prevented most of the ss *Komagata Maru's* 376 South Asian passengers from landing in Vancouver. Although this action was challenged in court, the British Columbia Court of Appeal upheld the decision and affirmed the validity of the newly reinstated orders-in-council P.C. 23, P.C. 24, and P.C. 897, the three acts of legislation maintaining South Asian exclusion.[1] The Canadian naval ship HMCS *Rainbow* escorted the *Komagata Maru* from Canada on 23 July. This article offers a new perspective on this much discussed incident by studying what Erika Lee terms "law at its bottom fringes," and it broadly addresses Tony Ballantyne's recent call for revisionist scholarship on the early South Asian immigrant experience. Drawing upon a previously unexplored government file on South Asian immigration, it shows for the first time how Canadian officials secretly initiated unprecedented health screening for South Asian arrivals in 1912 and, in anticipation of the arrival of the *Komagata Maru,* prepared a contingency plan to test for the curable disease of hookworm, a bacterial parasite that affects the small intestine and causes lethargy and anemia but that was not formally classified as a contagious or loathsome disease under the Immigration Act.

Approximately 5000 first-wave South Asian immigrants landed in British Columbia between 1904 and 1907, joining close to 35 000 Chinese and Japanese settlers in the province. Soon after, labour leaders, politicians, and other Asian exclusionists began to view the new arrivals, who were mostly Sikhs from the Punjab, as competitors for white labour. The exclusionists argued that immigrants from India were unsuited to Canada's climate and suffered from medical conditions and diseases that were specifically attributable to their race. These ideas were initially subsets of a larger argument that South Asians were unassimilable because they accepted a lower standard of living, had caste prejudices, spoke a foreign language, and were potential anti-imperial activists who would fight for Indian independence. Quickly, however, the climate and disease arguments took on lives of their own and became key components of the argument against further immigration from India. For example, in late 1906, Victoria's Trades and Labour Congress resolved that Indians posed "a constant danger" to public health because they carried "bubonic plague, smallpox, Asiatic Cholera and the worst forms of venereal diseases."[2]

In January 1908, shortly after a major anti-Asian riot in Vancouver, Prime Minister Wilfrid Laurier introduced an order-in-council (P.C. 920) barring immigrants who had not arrived in Canada by continuous journey from their land of birth or citizenship, along with a second order-in-council (P.C. 926) requiring that Asian arrivals possess at least two hundred dollars upon entry to Canada.[3] Since it was impossible for residents of India to travel to Canada without changing ship in Japan or Hong Kong, this provision cleverly excluded South Asians without naming them specifically and thus exacerbating anti-imperial political tensions in India. [. . .]

Newly arrived immigrants from Asia already faced closer medical scrutiny and a greater probability of detention than Europeans. Between 1881 and 1904, most vessels from Asia, and many from San Francisco, underwent primary inspection at William Head quarantine station on an isolated headland near Victoria before proceeding to their destination. However, 1905 legislation allowed vessels from US Pacific coast ports to skip this step, and, while the quarantine station would continue to operate on a reduced scale for another five decades, by 1910 improved mainland port inspection facilities also allowed most vessels from Asia to proceed directly to Vancouver and Victoria. The small number of Europeans travelling on these vessels in steerage, and passengers in first- and second-class, generally passed inspection on the day of their arrival, but medical inspectors detained Asians at least 24 hours for observation because, as one inspector at Vancouver explained in 1910,"the crowded condition of the Asiatic steerage" and "the susceptibility of Asiatics" to trachoma, a contagious eye infection, necessitated extra time in detention "before the medical inspection [could] be satisfactorily completed." This additional level of inspection included checking for trachoma

by flipping back the eyelid. In 1906, the superintendent of Vancouver's immigrant detention hospital reported to Ottawa that *"Genuine cases of Trachoma are not so frequent* [among South Asians] *as among the Chinese or Japs,"* yet inspectors at BC ports attempted to reject as many South Asians as possible for medical reasons, especially after the summer of 1907, when A.S. Munro, medical inspector at Vancouver, gave South Asian arrivals a "rigid physical examination" on Minister of the Interior Frank Oliver's orders.[4]

In British Columbia, as in the American Pacific coast states, all Asian groups encountered widespread levels of resistance and hostility. As Patricia E. Roy and others have shown, virulent and sustained anti-Asian activism throughout British Columbia had brought about a prohibitive Chinese head tax in 1885 (increased in 1900 and 1903), and immigration from Japan was governed by a 1907 "gentleman's agreement" under which Japan limited immigration to Canada by restricting the granting of passports to its citizens. [. . .]

In 1910, Department of Immigration officials began developing a dossier that is an invaluable source of documents pertaining to public health issues of South Asian immigration in Canada. Frank Oliver, Liberal minister of the interior under Laurier until 1911, originally opened it to monitor the American response to US Public Health Service physician M.W. Glover's September 1910 discovery that many South Asian arrivals at California's Angel Island Quarantine Station had hookworm.[5] As historians Joan Jensen and Nayan Shah have shown, American immigration officials subsequently used hookworm testing to facilitate what Jensen calls a policy of South Asian "executive restriction"—a stringent, often questionable interpretation of immigration legislation—before Congress finally legislated South Asian exclusion in 1917. However, as Oliver's file demonstrates, Glover's discovery also had an important impact in Canada, where government officials, like their American counterparts, eagerly seized upon and implemented Glover's findings at Pacific ports. For Oliver and for the Canadian medical inspectors at BC's ports, the American discovery of hookworm in South Asian immigrants confirmed a key tenet of early twentieth-century tropical medicine, which Alexandra Stern explains was "deeply connected to the production of colonial and racial difference."[6]

Shortly after Glover released his findings from Angel Island, Oliver ordered Canadian border agents to reject any prospective immigrants of South Asian origin with hookworm coming from the United States.[7] When P.H. Bryce, chief medical officer of the Department of Immigration, visited the Pacific coast a year later, G.L. Milne, the department's immigration inspector in Victoria, recommended a more formalized inspection policy to check for the disease. However, after leaving the coast, Bryce learned that hookworm could only be transmitted through direct exposure to infected fecal matter, something that was unlikely in North America and thus appeared to be questionable grounds for rejection. Yet, since South Asian legislative exclusion in Canada meant that Canadian inspectors had not yet had the opportunity to test South Asians for the disease, he was insistent that Canada should verify that any future South Asian arrivals did not have hookworm. He thus permitted Milne to order a microscope and other equipment for the "*careful* examination of the bowel contents in Hindus or other immigrants whom you may deem suspicious."[8]

There the matter rested until April 1912, when William Charles Hopkinson, the department's immigration agent responsible for political surveillance of the province's South Asian population, received information that three to four hundred South Asians were bound for BC ports on the SS *Orterio*. Since the vessel was travelling directly from India, the potential immigrants could not be legally prevented from landing. In a telegram

to Deputy Minister of the Interior W.W. Cory, Hopkinson suggested that medical examiners at Vancouver and Victoria "confidentially" test the *Orterio*'s South Asians for hookworm as this had proved "effective" in barring hundreds of South Asians at US ports. Cory approved and ordered "a special Medical inspection" to ensure that all were "carefully examined," though not without the following proviso: "It is important that this matter should be kept private."[9] Immigration superintendent W.D. Scott's instructions to Milne and Malcolm J. Reid, immigration inspector at Vancouver, made it clear that this order was to apply only to South Asians. His terse telegram read: "Request Medical Inspector examine Hindu passengers 'Orterio' specially for hookworm. This is *confidential*." A week later, it transpired that the *Orterio* carried no South Asians.[10] [. . .]

According to historian Nayan Shah, the use of "biopolitical techniques" like the hookworm test gave medical inspectors, for the first time, the ability to "extend the boundaries of the human body beyond its epidermal container to its wastes," to "coax 'truth' from the recalcitrant body and to interpret that truth." By such means they sought to ascertain physical fitness in order to predict an immigrant's future as "worker" and "citizen." Early twentieth-century bacteriological testing "collapsed the identification of a parasite organism within the body with the status of being a social parasite and dependent" as those infected would presumably require state aid. Historian Amy Fairchild agrees that, at Pacific coast ports in the pre-war period, bacteriology had "both social and medical implications" as government officials argued that an immigrant's infection would likely impair her/his potential labour productivity. Just as pathogens caused disease in healthy bodies, so diseased immigrants "infected the economic body."[11]

[. . .]

By 1913, British Columbia's South Asian population had dwindled from the approximately 3000 remaining at the time of the1911 census to fewer than 2500.[12] Yet, at summer's end, Scott expressed his concern that P.C. 920 and P.C. 926 were insufficient controls on Canada's South Asian community. In July, Hopkinson had informed the department that nine South Asians, five of whom were new to Canada, arrived on the SS *Sado Maru* with prepaid tickets purchased in Victoria in 1912. The five had "fully complied" with the Immigration Act by coming on tickets previously purchased in Canada, but they were detained "a day or so at the Immigration Hall with a view to a strict medical examination—more especially for 'Hookworm.'" Yet all were landed at Victoria at the end of July. At the same time, a mistake by a Canadian immigration commissioner at Ellis Island, who had allowed eight South Asians arriving at New York to proceed to New Brunswick, indicated that a general and nationwide order-in-council was necessary to keep South Asians out of Canada. Accordingly, Scott called for a new regulation "framed in such a way that it would apply without any question."[13]

The arrival of the Japanese steamer SS *Panama Maru* at Victoria in October triggered a brief immigration crisis.[14] Though immigration officials rejected 39 of the ship's 56 South Asian passengers for failing to meet the continuous journey provisions of P.C. 920, the BC Supreme Court found a technical inconsistency in the wording of the order-in-council and allowed all but five of the passengers rejected for standard medical reasons (likely trachoma) to land. The decision dominated the province's newspaper coverage for almost a month, and federal Member of Parliament for Vancouver H.H. Stevens and others wondered if the vessel was the harbinger of a larger plan to circumvent the Canadian Immigration Act. What never made the papers, however, was the fact that Milne and his assistant medical inspector, H.B. Rogers, had secretly initiated non-standard fecal testing on the detained passengers for hookworm—a test previously performed only on

the South Asians of the SS *Sado Maru*—and requested funds to hire a tropical disease expert.[15]

After examining a fecal sample taken from passenger Jewalla Singh, Dr W.P. Walker of Victoria reported that there were no mature hookworms present but that he had found "numerous segmented non-opercular ova" that were "most probably" of the hookworm parasite. Walker could not be sure of these results and noted that a mature worm specimen could only be passed from the body after the patient had taken an anthelmintic solution like thymol, which he recommended administering before taking another fecal sample.[16] In the end, Department of Immigration staff were unable to prove that Singh had hookworm. The BC Supreme Court ruling on the *Panama Maru* came only a few days after Dr Walker submitted his initial report. The immediate release of the vessel's passengers—paired with the fact that four of the five men ordered deported for other medical reasons escaped from detention before deportation—deprived the specialist of the opportunity to re-test the patient.

It is clear that Milne opposed the Supreme Court's decision. His letter to W.D. Scott later in December offers insight into his perspective as a gatekeeper of Dominion public health, and, more important, into departmental-level policy approaches to South Asian immigration during the immediate pre-war period.[17] Milne opined: "The more I consider the question of Asiatic immigration to this coast, the more am I convinced that the only really effective restriction would be obtained by thorough examination for hookworm disease." Yet, in order to test future South Asian arrivals, Victoria's detention quarters required facilities for ensuring that passengers could be monitored during defecation. During the *Panama Maru* crisis, Milne had been unable to obtain fecal samples from most of the detainees because "the Hindus were rather rebellious, and it was rather difficult for us to segregate them." Milne's staff had secured Singh's sample only because he had been detained separately from the others while he recovered from a cold. Anthony Caminetti, the US commissioner general of immigration, had informed Milne that US authorities along the Pacific coast were now checking every Asian immigrant for hookworm and were finding the parasite in about 90 per cent of cases. Milne noted that, if Canada adopted the same practice:

> *I have no doubt that we would find 90% of Asiatics, & particularly Hindus, infested with this disease* . . . You will, therefore, see that if we were to proceed on these lines, & were able to reject 90% of these people, the object of the Gov. would be attained. The rejection of immigrants under this cause would not be followed by so much criticism by the general public; in fact, on the other hand, it would appeal to them strongly as a measure for the protection of the public health.[18]

Replying to Milne, Scott agreed that, "in view of the importance of the subject," Milne should continue to test South Asians for hookworm. If the parasite were found in "any" Indian immigrant, then it would be "in order to hold up every individual Hindu until his case can be decided." Milne later sent Scott a circular on hookworm that Caminetti had recently dispatched to his immigration officials, addressing a newly released Rockefeller Sanitary Commission report, which estimated that 60 to 80 per cent of India's population had hookworm. Scott then distributed the flyers to his BC agents.[19]

By Nayan Shah's account, the discovery of the hookworm parasite in the stool of South Asians at Angel Island dramatically influenced inspection policies at that quarantine station. In the midst of a crisis over station management, the high rate of infection among a sample of South Asian arrivals enabled Public Health Service officials to use bacteriology as a means of "sidestepping other strategies of border control and exclusion." Official "confidence in hookworm's predictive value was dubious" as infection was possible in those displaying no outward symptoms of the disease. Yet inspectors at Angel Island "emphasized the unassailable expertise of the medical examiner's diagnosis" that an immigrant with hookworm endangered public health.[20] BC politicians eagerly adopted these views on South Asians and hookworm as non-debatable "truth."

In November 1913, Vancouver MP H.H. Stevens informed reporters that he planned to ask Cabinet to hire a bacteriologist to study the "many serious diseases" of Pacific coast Asians, whom he believed were "infested with several bacterial diseases," including hookworm, which had existed in Asia for hundreds of years. Like Milne, Stevens concluded that "the health side of the Asiatic problem is just as important as the industrial, racial and social." Yet Stevens seems to have been slow to act; after spending a month in central Canada, he told reporters that he was still planning to raise the inspection issue.[21]

Stevens's continued use of the disease argument demonstrates how it prevailed even in the face of contradictory evidence. In 1913, Alberta physician E.H. Lawson informed the editor of the *Victoria Colonist* that having served as ship's surgeon on CPR vessels during the height of Indian immigration to Canada before 1908, he had personally inspected many of the immigrants landing at British Columbia. As Lawson recalled:

> Although at first I was strongly prejudiced against them I lost this prejudice after thousands of them had passed through my hands and I had compared them with the white steerage passengers I had seen on the Atlantic. I refer in particular to the Sikhs and I am not exaggerating in the least when I say that they were 100 per cent cleaner in their habits and freer from disease than the European steerage passengers I had come into contact with.

The Sikhs impressed me as a clean, manly, honest race.

Lawson added that his recent medical work with white workers in mining camps, which were "rife" with immorality, had "increased [his] respect for the Sikhs." He concluded that he had "not yet seen one good reason why they should not be permitted to bring their families in as freely as the European immigrants."[22]

[. . .]

Early in 1914, when Chief Medical Officer P.H. Bryce planned to visit British Columbia to find first-hand evidence of "Hindu hookworm," Scott suggested this might be unnecessary as Caminetti's circular had apprised all BC agents of the South Asian–hookworm connection. Shortly thereafter, however, Scott changed his mind on hearing that several South Asians in Yokohama were purchasing through tickets for a charter vessel that would depart for Vancouver. From the timing of this report and the follow-up correspondence on the matter, it is virtually certain that the vessel in question was the SS *Komagata Maru*.[23]

Scott quickly instructed Milne to "pay special attention" while screening the incoming South Asian passengers of this vessel for hookworm. In a letter to his direct supervisor W.W. Cory, Scott stated that, in light of the "probability of a number of Hindus applying for admission to Canada at Vancouver," he recommended the use of a specialist to "detec[t] the parasite or ova of the Hook-worm in the case of Hindus or other immigrants from India." Scott also approved Milne's November request for "a properly equipped place" to detain immigrants for defecation. Cory granted Scott's suggestion to prepare the Vancouver office for the South Asians, and Scott authorized both Milne in Victoria and Inspector Malcolm J. Reid in Vancouver to hire tropical disease experts.[24]

Scott's instructions came in spite of the recent findings of Dr W. Bapty of BC's Provincial Board of Health, who reported that the province had received no complaints that resident South Asians had or were spreading hookworm. Bryce made a similar report after his BC mission in March, during which he had interviewed the medical teams of both Milne and A.S. Munro (the medical inspector of immigrants at Vancouver) and consulted with a physician attached to Vancouver's US Public Health Service branch. [. . .] Bryce asserted that, while hookworm infection was a serious health risk in India, where people often went barefoot and lived without proper sanitation: "It does not follow that we are to be satisfied that these are reasons why immigrants from these infected countries should be excluded from Canada unless it can be shown, that similar habits of life will be followed here and that therefore the dangers through contamination through the spread of the disease are similar." [. . .]

Soon thereafter, the Department of Immigration reversed its policy and abandoned its plans to test the coming *Komagata Maru* passengers for hookworm. Bryce's conclusion likely played no role in this decision as Scott still intended to seek ministerial approval for wide-scale testing a full week after the chief medical officer submitted his report. Three other factors appear to have quashed the plan. The first of these was its cost. Although Milne could collect stool from patients and do some microscopic work, he did not have the expertise to analyze the test results himself. Dr Walker in Victoria was the natural choice for the project, but when Reid asked Walker for a quote for testing in anticipation of the *Komagata Maru's* arrival Walker replied that "the proposed examination of Hindu or other immigrants from India" for hookworm would cost $2.50 per case for 50 passengers or more. At $2.50 for each of the vessel's 376 passengers, the cost would be almost $1000, close to what W.C. Hopkinson earned in an entire year.[25]

Walker may have inadvertently given the Department of Immigration a second reason to back off the hookworm strategy. In conversation with Reid, he admitted that passengers could cheat the hookworm test by taking an initial dose of thymol while still en route from Asia. Since, in his estimation, the timing of the dose would flush out worms and allow hookworm ova to cling to the intestine in a later test, an immigrant with a severe infection could disguise his or her condition.[26] There is insufficient evidence to prove the influence of this point on policy [. . .] but a third factor caused the department to abandon its plan to screen the *Komagata Maru's* passengers for hookworm. On 31 March, order-in-council 1914–897 passed, barring non-farming "artisans and labourers" from landing at BC ports; this was a renewed version of legislation the government had passed the previous December after hearing the rumour that a steamship line was considering opening a direct service between British Columbia and India. Two weeks after forwarding Bryce's and Reid's reports for ministerial approval, Scott advised Reid that "the provisions of P.C. 897 would appear to be sufficient to dispose of this matter for some time." Borden tellingly reissued this order-in-council the day after his government learned that the *Komagata Maru* had left Hong Kong for Canada. The Department of Immigration later followed this exact course, using P.C. 897, along with the newest incarnations of the continuous journey (P.C. 23) and two-hundred-dollar requirement provisions (P.C. 24), to exclude most of the vessel's passengers.[27]

When the vessel anchored off Vancouver on 23 May, Canada's parliamentarians, still in session in Ottawa, voiced their dismay at the arrival of the South Asians. The outcry extended across party lines as members from the ruling Conservatives and the Liberal opposition alike agreed that Canada should reject the passengers. Minister of the Interior W.J. Roche declared: "We are going to stand by the immigration law in its fullness." This despite Liberal Frank Oliver's criticism that the government had been slow to resolve the situation using the Immigration Act. Oliver also opined that excluding South Asians was necessary in order to protect Canada against a "population that shall hamper and deter" the nation's "ideals of civilization": "[It is] under those principles that, for my part, I desire to see this law administered."[28] This reaction typified Oliver's approach to immigration, which he had implemented as minister of the interior between 1905 and 1911. His 1906 Immigration Act had dramatically increased the health requirements of immigrants and expanded the definition of an "undesirable" immigrant. His precept that South Asians were wholly at odds with Canadian society reflected the prevailing viewpoint of both parties on Parliament Hill in 1914.

[. . .]

Returning to the standby of public health protection, Roche replied to Oliver that the *Komagata Maru's* passengers had been "undergoing a very critical medical examination" and that "a good many of these" were infected with trachoma and other eye diseases. Roche later informed the House that 90 of the men had been rejected for physical reasons—reasons that Hugh Johnston has identified, in most cases, as trachoma. There is no record of medical examinations or of the detention of *Komagata Maru* passengers in Vancouver as only the ship's physician and his family and 20 returning immigrants were allowed to disembark. Without such documentation it is difficult to ascertain the health of the passengers when they first arrived on BC's coast. Norman Buchignani, Doreen Indra, and Ram Srivastiva argue that the government's discovery of trachoma at Vancouver was "an old trick" designed to "make deportation certain" by "finding non-existent disease in prospective immigrants." However, the authors offer no evidence to support this claim.[29]

Although, in 1912, the Department of Immigration had prepared for hookworm testing on the South Asian passengers of the ss *Orterio,* and, in 1913, initiated testing on South Asians from the ss *Sado Maru* and the ss *Panama Maru,* immigration officials abandoned the hookworm inspection plan a month before the *Komagata Maru* reached Canada. In the end, and despite the fact that Munro's staff may have found that some of the men aboard the *Komagata Maru* had trachoma, disease was not a determining factor in the rejection of any of the passengers. This is shown in July 1914's BC Supreme Court ruling in the case of Munshi Singh, a representative of the *Komagata Maru's* passengers whose appeal case represented all on board. This ruling upheld the government's finding that the vessel's passengers were excludable not for health reasons but, rather, because they did not meet the provisions of P.C. 23, P.C. 24, and P.C. 897. The government's November 1914 report on the incident confirmed that the passengers had been deported for the sole reason that they failed to satisfy the stipulations of these orders-in-council.[30]

The 1914 resolution of the *Komagata Maru* crisis and the BC Supreme Court's affirmation of legislative exclusion removed the need for Dominion officials to continue hookworm testing. Although American officials continued testing most Asian arrivals for hookworm until 1919, the inconclusive 1913 test of Jowalla Singh was Canada's last test in a decade. Then Milne reintroduced fecal inspection for hookworm at Victoria in order to deport a group of Chinese actors; however, his ruling was reversed immediately by Bryce's successor J.D. Page. Testing was suspended and Milne was reprimanded for "committing an injustice" by using a positive hookworm test to bar otherwise healthy immigrants. Page concluded, just as Bryce had in 1913, that hookworm was not "a menace to public health"—a truth that Department of Immigration officers had ignored in their quest to bar South Asians between 1912 and 1914.[31]

[. . .]

NOTES

1. P.C. 1914-23 stipulated that immigrants arrive in Canada by "continuous journey" from their country of birth and/or nationality, and P.C. 1914-24 ordered that Asian immigrants, except those whose entry was governed by other legislation (Chinese and Japanese nationals), have two hundred dollars in their possession upon arrival. These January 1914 orders-in-council replaced P.C. 920 and P.C. 926 of 1910, which were updated versions of the original orders-in-council P.C. 920 and P.C. 926 of January 1908. P.C. 1913-897 of 31 March 1914 is discussed later.

2. Three hundred and eighty-seven South Asian immigrants arrived in the 1905–6 season, followed by 2124 in 1906–7, and 2623 in 1907–8. See Joseph Pope to Martin Burrell, "Draft Minute on Asiatic Immigration," 22 January 1912, Library and Archives Canada (hereafter LAC), RG 25, vol. 1118, file 66-1912; Secretary F. Grey, Victoria Trades and Labour Congress to W.D. Scott, 15 October 1906, LAC, RG (Record Group) 76, vol. 384, file 536999, pt. i.

3. Government of Canada, P.C. 920, 8 January 1908, which prohibited immigrants who did not arrive in Canada by continuous journey from the land of their birth or citizenship, and P.C. 926, 3 June 1908,which effectively added a two-hundred-dollar requirement to all Asians except Chinese and Japanese.

4. Linda M. Ambrose, "Quarantine in Question: The 1913 Investigation at William Head, BC," *Canadian Bulletin of Medical History* 22, 1 (2005): 143–5; J.H. MacGill to W.D. Scott, 30 September 1910, 1; Robert McKechnie, Superintendent Detention Hospital, to W.D. Scott, 9 December 1906, 2. Emphasis in original. The last two references are both in LAC, RG 76, vol. 306, file 281230 Vancouver, pt. 1. See also A.S. Munro to Frank Oliver, 14 September 1907, LAC, RG 76, vol. 384, file 536999, pt. 1.

5. The file "Prevalence of Hook Worm among Hindus Applying for Admission to US and among the Negroes (Blacks) of the US" is housed in LAC, RG 76, vol. 584, file 820636.

6. See Joan Jensen, *Passage from India: Asian American Immigrants in North America* (New Haven, CT: Yale University Press, 1988), 113; and Nayan Shah, *Contagious Divides: Epidemics and Race in San Francisco's Chinatown* (Berkeley: University of California Press, 2001), 190.

7. *Victoria Times,* 17 October 1910; Frank Oliver to W.D. Scott, 18 October 1910, LAC, RG 76, vol. 584, file 820636.

8. G.L. Milne to P.H. Bryce, 14 November 1911, and P.H. Bryce to G.L. Milne, 28 December 1911, 1-2, LAC, RG 76, vol. 584, file 820636. Emphasis in original.

9. W.C. Hopkinson to W.W. Cory, 15 April 1912; and W.W. Cory to W.D. Scott, 16 April 1912. The foregoing references are both in LAC, RG 76, vol. 384, file. 536999, pt. 5. See Jensen, *Passage from India,* and Hugh Johnston, *The Voyage of the* Komagata Maru (Oxford: Oxford University Press, 1979), for a detailed discussion of Hopkinson's key role in South Asian immigration inspection and community surveillance before his 1914 assassination.

10. W.D. Scott telegrams to G.L. Milne and Malcolm J. Reid, 17 April 1912, LAC, RG 76, vol. 384, file 536999, pt. 5. Emphasis in original; G.L. Milne to W.D. Scott, 20 April 1912, LAC, RG 76, vol. 584, file 820636; M.J. Reid to W.D. Scott, 18 April 1912; M.J. Reid to W.D. Scott, 27 April 1912. The last two references are both in LAC, RG 76, vol. 384, file 536999, pt. 5.

11. Nayan Shah, *Stranger Intimacy: Contesting Race, Sexuality and the Law in the North American West* (Berkeley: University of California Press, 2011), 200–2; Shah, *Contagious Divides,* 180 and 196; Amy Fairchild, *Science at the Borders: Immigrant Medical Inspection and the Shaping of the Modern Industrial Labor Force* (Baltimore: Johns Hopkins University Press, 2003), 39,1 81–2.

12. Census data in F.C. Blair to Sir J. Pope, 25 July 1922, LAC, RG 25, G1, vol. 1300, file 1011, FPi.

13. W.D. Scott Memorandum, 30 September 1913, 1–2; W.C. Hopkinson to W.W. Cory (confidential), 1 August 1913. Both of the foregoing are in LAC, RG 76, vol. 385, file 536999, pt. 6. See also *Ottawa Free Press,* 8 October 1913. The South Asians were admitted on 30 July 1913. See arrivals for that vessel on http://www.ancestry.ca.

14. Johnston, *Voyage,* 20-2L

15. Ibid., 17–21. See also G.L. Milne to W.D. Scott, 26 November 1913, LAC, RG 76, vol. 385, file 536999, pt. 8; *Vancouver Province,* 23 October 1913; *News-Advertiser,* 24 October 1913; W.C. Hopkinson, 25 October 1913; and G.L. Milne to W.D. Scott, 27 October 1913. The last two references are both in LAC, RG 76, vol. 385, file 536999, pt. 6. W.D. Scott to W.W. Cory, 28 October 1913, in RG 76, vol. 385, file 536999, pt. 6. Ministerial permission granted in W.D. Scott to G.L. Milne, 8 November1913, in RG 76, vol. 385, file 536999, pt. 6.

16. W.D. Scott to W.W. Cory, 28 October 1913, in ibid. Ministerial permission granted in W.D. Scott to G.L. Milne, 8 November 1913, in Ibid; W.P. Walker, Victoria, to G.L. Milne, 18 November 1913, LAC, RG 76, vol. 584, file 820636. "Jewalla" Singh was almost certainly the 35-year-old "Jowalla Singh" described in the department's passenger manifest. See "Jowalla Singh," passenger of the SS *Panama Maru,* which arrived 17 October 1913 (see Canadian Passenger Index, http://www.ancestry.ca); W.H. Schultz, "A Study of the Relative Efficiency and Danger of Thymol as Compared with Certain Other Remedies Proposed for Hookworm Disease," *Journal of the American Medical Association,* 57, 14 (1911): 1102–6. See also *New York Times,* 7 October 1911. In 1911, US government pharmacologist Dr W.H. Schultz was credited with being the first to widely publicize the effectiveness of thymol, a natural derivative of the herb thyme, in treating hookworm.

17. *Victoria Colonist,* 28 November 1913. See P.C. 2642, 8 December 1913.

18. G.L. Milne to W.D. Scott, 12 December 1913, 1–2, LAC, RG 76, vol. 584, file 820636. Emphasis in original.

19. W.D. Scott to G.L. Milne and M. Reid, 7 January 1914, LAC, RG 76 vol. 584, file 820636; "Circular No. 30, Distribution of Hookworm Inspection," 1 November 1913, 1, forwarded by Milne to Scott on 26 December 1913, LAC, RG 76 vol. 584, file 820636; Scott requested more circulars in W.D. Scott to John H. Clark, 19 December 1913, LAC, RG 76 vol. 584, file 820636.

20. Shah, *Stranger Intimacy,* 200–2; Shah, *Contagious Divides,* 180.

21. *Toronto Mail and Empire, Toronto News,* and *Montreal Gazette,* 11 November 1913; *Montreal Gazette,* 4 December 1913. By December, Stevens had unaccountably switched his focus to lung fluke.

22. E.H. Lawson, MD, Highland, Alberta, letter to *Victoria Daily Colonist,* 25 September 1913.

23. W.D. Scott to P.H. Bryce, 24 January 1914; P.H. Bryce to W.D. Scott, 26 January 1914; W.D. Scott, Memo to W.W. Cory, 2 February 1914; and W.D Scott, Memo to W.W. Cory,19 February 1914. All of the foregoing are in LAC, RG 76, vol. 584, file 820636. (Hopkinson and Cory's memos are described in W.D. Scott to W.W. Cory, 19 February 1914.) Hugh Johnston explains that, at this time, Gurdit Singh was soliciting passengers and securing the vessel. The vessel did pick up passengers at Yokohama. See Johnston, *Voyage,* 25, 26 and 33.

24. W.D. Scott, Memo to W.W. Cory, 10 February 1914, 1–2; W.D. Scott to G.L. Milne, 10 February I914. Both of the foregoing are in LAC, RG 76, vol. 385, file 536999, pt. 8. See also W.D. Scott to M. Reid, 2 March 1914; H.E. Young to W.J. Roche, 21 February 19L4. Both of the foregoing are in LAC, RG 76, vol. 584, file 820636. See also W.D. Scott to C.J. Davidson, Act. British Consulate General, Yokohama, 26 February 1914, LAC, RG 76, vol. 385, file 536999, pt. 8.

25. See (RUSH) M.J. Reid to W.D. Scott, 31 March 1914,172, LAC, RG 76, vol. 584, file 820636; See also W.D. Scott to W.W. Cory, 1 April 1914, LAC, RG 76, vol. 584, file 820636; After an original annual salary of $1200 in 1909, Hopkinson's salary became $18oo in March 1912. See W.W. Cory to W.D. Scott, 26 February 1912, LAC, RG 76, vol. 561, file 808722, pt. 1; Hugh Johnston, "The Surveillance of Indian Nationalists in America, 1908–1918," *BC Studies* 78 (1988): 16.

26. (RUSH) M.J. Reid to W.D. Scott, 31 March 1914, 1–2, LAC, RG 76, vol. 584, file 820636.

27. W.D. Scott to W.W. Cory, 1 April 1914; W.D. Scott to M.J. Reid, 14 April 1914. Both of the foregoing are in LAC, RG 76, vol. 584, file 820636. For the legislative history of P.C. 1914-897 (formerly P.C.1913-2642), see Bruce Ryder, "Racism and the Constitution: The Constitutional Fate of British Columbia Anti-Asian Immigration Legislation, 1884–1909," *Osgoode Hall Law Journal* 29, 3 (1991): 670; Sir Francis May, Governor of Hong Kong, Telegrams to Duke of Connaught, 31 March 1914 and 6 April1914, LAC, RG 25, G1, vol. 1138, file 1914-40C. See P.C. 3432 23 (September 1914).

28. House of Commons, 12th Parliament, 3rd Session, vol. 5, 26 May 1914, 4214; ibid., 27 May 1914, 4295. See also ibid., 30 May 1914, 4533; ibid., 1 June 19L4, 4562 and 4565.

29. House of Commons, 12th Parliament, 3rd Session, vol. 5, 1 June 1914, 4565 and 6 June 1914, 4954-55; Johnston, *Voyage,* 44. Seventy-seven of the 88 men rejected for physical reasons had trachoma. See House of Commons, 12th Parliament, 3rd Session, vol. 5, 8 June 1914, 5026; Johnston, *Voyage,* 36–37; *Vancouver News-Advertiser,* 22 May 1914; Shah, *Contagious Divides,* 61–63; Norman Buchignani, Doreen Indra, and Ram Srivastiva, *Continuous Journey: A Social History of South Asians in Canada* (Toronto: McClelland and Stewart, 1985), 44.

30. See Re Munshi Singh (6 July 1914), 20 B.C.R. 243 (BC Court of Appeal); and H.C. Clogstoun, *Canada: Commission to Investigate Hindu Claims Following Refusal of Immigration Officials to Allow Over 300 Hindus Aboard the* SS Komagata Maru *to Land at Vancouver* (Vancouver: Government of Canada, 1914).

31. See US Public Health Service Order, 7 March 1919, which removed hookworm from the list of "Loathsome and Contagious Diseases," in Washington, DC, National Archives and Records Administration, RG 85, vol. 54261, file 184; A. Joliffe, Memo to J.E. Featherstone, 5 April 1923; J.D. Page, Chief of Division of Quarantine, to G.L. Milne, 5 April 1923. The last two references are in LAC, RG 76, vol. 584, file 820636. Page was specifically referring to the case of Lai Hung Sang, whom Milne deported for hookworm without Page's consent.

Chapter 8

Dealing with Hunger and War

READINGS

Primary Documents

1   From "It's a Woman's War," Mattie Rotenberg

2   From *How to Eat Well Though Rationed*, Josephine Gibson

Historical Interpretations

3   From "'If You Had No Money, You Had No Trouble, Did You?': Montréal Working-Class Housewives during the Great Depression," Denyse Baillargeon

4   From "Under the President's Gaze: Sexuality and Morality at a Canadian University during the Second World War," Catherine Gidney

INTRODUCTION

For the better part of a generation, from 1929 to 1945, Canadians learned to live with privation and uncertainty. During the early 1930s, when the Great Depression was in full swing, unemployment soared and industrial growth ground to a halt in Ontario and Quebec. In the Atlantic region, the collapse of cod prices brought hardship, while on the prairies the Depression coincided with a severe drought. During the 1930s, most Canadians learned to make do with less and to live with an uncertain future. Marriages were put off and the birthrate declined. Many parents could not afford to send their children to school, and Canada's universities experienced a significant decline in enrolment. Unemployment largely disappeared during the Second World War, which lasted from 1939 to 1945, but rationing and uncertainty prevented most Canadians from enjoying wartime economic growth. Canada's involvement in the fighting in Europe and the north Atlantic was significant, but it tends to obscure the vital efforts on the homefront. During the Second World War, those who did not qualify for combat roles because they were women, too young, too old, or physically or mentally disabled; had crucial industrial or administrative skills; or were of a racial or ethnic origin considered suspect by the Canadian government nonetheless found themselves drawn into wartime rhythms of work or domestic life. This "total war" environment was plainly discernible in Canadian society, in its economic priorities, and in the cultural lives of Canadians. Plentiful jobs in war-related industries, housing shortages, unrelenting messages to work harder and more efficiently to further the war effort, and the abandonment of at least some leisure-time pursuits were all convincing evidence. Our primary sources involve two aspects of homefront life: the contributions and post-war prospects of women, and the struggle to feed a family under the strict regime of federal rationing. Broadcaster Mattie Rotenberg reminded her listeners that the world's women stood to lose as much as any nation if the war did not end in an Allied victory. She did not call for liberation from traditional gendered family roles, but asked women to do what they could to tackle the problems of "unemployment, housing, ignorance and want," which would continue when the war was over. In her cookbook, Josephine Gibson offered tips to Canadian homemakers on meal preparation in a rationed environment. Her recipes promised to "make a little go a long way," most notably through "meat stretching dishes." These tips would not have been unfamiliar to the working-class women whom Denyse Baillargeon examines in her piece. She insists that the survival strategies employed by women were essential to the household budget of the working class, and notes that underlying poverty prepared many Montreal women for the privations they faced during the Depression. Catherine Gidney's article studies the gender norms and work ethic imposed by government and institutions during the Second World War. Her work reveals the extent to which authorities took accusations of indolence and homosexuality seriously, especially when they were levelled at German nationals interned in Canada.

QUESTIONS FOR CONSIDERATION

1. How does Rotenberg depict home life under fascism?
2. How were wartime restrictions affecting the diet of Canadian families?
3. What role were women called to play in wartime Canada? How were women encouraged to fulfill this role?
4. What sort of survival strategies did Montreal working-class housewives pursue during the Depression?
5. What gender norms were imposed on Canadian men in the early to mid-twentieth century?

SUGGESTIONS FOR FURTHER READING

Denyse Baillargeon, *Making Do: Women, Family and Home in Montreal during the Great Depression* (Waterloo: Wilfrid University Press, 1999).

Timothy Balzer, *The Information Front: The Canadian Army and News Management during the Second World War* (Vancouver: UBC Press, 2010).

David Bercuson, *Maple Leaf against the Axis: Canada's Second World War* (Don Mills: Stoddart, 1995).

Ivana Caccia, *Managing the Canadian Mosaic in Wartime: Shaping Citizenship Policy, 1939–1945* (Montreal and Kingston: McGill-Queen's University Press, 2010).

Lara A. Campbell, *Respectable Citizens: Gender, Family, and Unemployment in Ontario's Great Depression* (Toronto: University of Toronto Press, 2009).

Serge Durflinger, *Fighting from Home: The Second World War in Verdun, Quebec* (Vancouver: UBC Press, 2006).

Magda Fahrni, *Household Politics: Montreal Families and Postwar Reconstruction* (Toronto: University of Toronto Press, 2005).

Carolyn Gossage, *Greatcoats and Glamour Boots: Canadian Women at War, 1939–1945* (Toronto: Dundurn Press, 1991).

Michiel Horn, *The Dirty Thirties: Canadians in the Great Depression* (Toronto: Copp Clark, 1972).

Paul Jackson, *One of the Boys: Homosexuality in the Military during World War II*, 2nd edn (Montreal and Kingston: McGill-Queen's University Press, 2010).

Jeffrey A. Keshen, *Saints, Sinners, and Soldiers: Canada's Second World War* (Vancouver: UBC Press, 2004).

Jody Perrun, *The Patriotic Consensus: Unity, Morale, and the Second World War in Winnipeg* (Winnipeg: University of Manitoba Press, 2014).

Katrina Srigley, *Breadwinning Daughters: Young Women in a Depression-Era City, 1929–1939* (Toronto: University of Toronto Press, 2009).

Primary Documents

1 Mattie Rotenberg, "It's a Woman's War," broadcast on *Trans-Canada Matinee*, CBC Radio, n.d. (1944). CBC Licensing.

Yes, it is a woman's war—in a special way. I don't mean so much that women and children are in the front line—that bombs and bullets are falling on them—though there is that, too. But this is a war to sweep Nazi tyranny from the world—to liberate the peoples who have been enslaved by it—and at the top of the list of those enslaved are women—all women. We hear a lot of what the Nazis have done to the Czechs, the Danes, the Dutch. We don't hear so much of what has happened to women under fascism, and yet, they were the first to suffer years ago in Italy, but most noticeably in Germany, because in the German Republic, women had gone far ahead in citizenship, in education, in the professions. There, the rights and privileges for which women had struggled for 50 years were swept aside

within a few months—for National Socialism is a movement of men, contemptuous of women; along with the doctrine of racial superiority goes that of women's inferiority. We've heard a great deal of Jews and Socialists being driven from their jobs, forbidden to practise their professions;—but the same thing happened to women, too—just because they were women—even to Nazi women who had worked for years to help Hitler. National Socialism doesn't believe in equality of opportunity in education for everybody. It preaches the law of inequality—it says that some people are by nature inferior, and must forever be hewers of wood and drawers of water for the German master-race. And among the inferior groups are women—all women. But there's even more to it than that. Nazi treatment of women is something more than reaction and suppression—more than throwing women doctors and teachers out of work. In Nazi Germany, women are being used, relentlessly moulded to the needs and ambitions of the State,—made into unthinking, obedient robots. So this is a woman's war. On its outcome depends the answer to the question, Are we women to move forward to a position of greater freedom, or lose what we have gained? We know what the fascist answer to that question is.

In fascist countries, any woman who wants a job, an education, a profession, is told that such things are not for her— contemptuously, she is sent back to "Kuche, Kinder, Kirche"—The kitchen, the children, the Church. These are the fields reserved for women—all other doors are closed. At first thought, this may not seem so bad—after all, for most of us women, these are our fields—but not the way the Nazis would have it.

Kuche—the kitchen—we do spend a lot of time in the kitchen, you and I, but we spend freely—we're glad to be able to provide sustenance and nourishment for our families. But we're glad to be able to give them bread that's spread with butter, and not with guns; food that is solid and nourishing, not "crabs," imitation,—the leftovers after the tanks and guns have been fed. You know how angry it would make you to have a stranger come into your kitchen and criticize what you're doing. Well, how would you like to have a lady feuhrer coming into your kitchen at any time she felt like it? Some petty official coming in, poking around to see what's in the pot, asking, where did you get that loaf of bread in the pantry, or what's this bone doing in the garbage can?—and you couldn't tell her to get out, either. That's what German women have to put up with. And that's not all. They interfere in everything. Not only tell you what to cook and

how to cook it; what to wear; but if you're not married, some official calls you on the carpet and wants to know why not. If you are married, you're ordered how many children to have, and when. The Nazis need an unending stream of boys to march, soldiers to die—and they're trying to make women provide them. We know this is a war for freedom—that's rather abstract, though. But when freedom means the privacy of your own house—the right to be boss in your own kitchen—well, that does bring it home to you that this is a woman's war.

And it's even more so when we think of the children—That's the second item in women's sphere, you know. Of course we want our children, but we want to bring them up our way, not to be cogs in an insatiable war machine. We don't want them brought up in the Nazi fashion, ignorant of everything but party doctrines, contemptuous of all other races and peoples, with narrow and darkened minds, fit only for blind obedience to the Feuhrer. We want our children to live by the light of learning; we want them to carry forward the heritage of our civilization; to make some of our dreams for a better world come true—to succeed where we have failed. A war to give our children this chance—that they may live as free men, not as dumb, driven cattle—that *is* a woman's war.

And lastly, in woman's sphere, is Kirche, the church—no wonder the Nazi leaves all that to women—He is busy resurrecting the old pagan gods, who will be more at home in the barbarian world he is trying to create. And religion would hamper him, too, in his career of lawless conquest. "Thou shalt have no other Gods before me"—against that, Hitler sets up the worship of the State. "Honour thy father and thy mother"—how can that be for Nazi children, taught to spy and inform, even on their parents? "Thou shalt not kill, thou shalt not steal, thou shalt not covet"—one after another the sacred tablets are smashed. Why, democracy itself, our way of life that is being challenged that's a religious idea. It's the recognition of the worth and dignity of every human life,—of the divine spark in every one of us. It is no accident, I think, that the British peoples are the ones now making the stand for the defence of democracy and religion. They have been brought up on the Bible—for centuries it has been read in their homes and churches—nurtured in its principles, theirs is the character that is now standing the test. This heritage has given them that significant spirit that made Dunkirk a modern miracle—it has given them the strength for inner self-discipline in these dark days—they don't need to be disciplined by a Duce or a Feuhrer—they can look after themselves.

And now, the very foundations of this life, this religion, are being attacked. It's been hard for people to believe such a thing—who would have thought it possible—that in the twentieth century, in our proud civilization, a powerful force would arise, deliberately bent upon dethroning the truth, abandoning justice, forsaking the rule of law—setting up brute force against the conscience of mankind? Yet, these are the issues. Shall *Mein Kampf* replace the Bible as the guide for human conduct? Shall the reign of truth give way to the reign of falsehood? We have all been taught—"Righteousness exalteth the nation"—must we forget that, to acknowledge instead that might is right? For a long time, men and women have prayed, "Thy will be done." Must they now bow to the dictator's "My will be done"? It is not only the privacy of our homes and the lives of our children that are at stake—not only the liberty to choose our religion, but the whole structure and principle of religion. Realizing that these are the issues, we women know that this is our war—and that knowledge raises in every heart the unshakable resolution to hold out till victory—we just can't think of humanity plunged back to the dark

ages, to start the slow, upward climb all over again.

Many people have been slow to realize that these really are the issues—they felt that Fascism and Nazism were just other political ways—of course, we preferred democracy, but perhaps they had something. You've heard people praise Mussolini,—he made the Italian trains run on time. But what good are trains *on time* if they take a people to destruction? And the Germans are efficient—yes—they're efficiently using modern science to take us quickly back to barbarism. This idea of German efficiency has spread far—their propaganda machine saw to that. Why, just this summer I was standing on the shores of a beautiful lake in Northern Ontario. Few people came there, because the road was bad. One day we were talking about how bad the road was, and a neighbour—she's no fifth columnist, she's as good a Canadian as any of us—she said to me, "I suppose if the Germans had this country, there'd be a good road here." Well, I felt a cold shiver go through me—because that remark showed how successful the Nazis had been in spreading the myth of themselves as supermen, of Hitler as a demigod, performing miracles with a magic wand. Have roads and buildings and a great war machine been built in his country? He had no magic wand—he used secret police and slavery, the torture chamber and the concentration camp. Nazi propaganda masks the horrible truth with fair words—they show their military pomp, but hide the slavery beneath. They want to sow doubt in our minds about democracy. To such doubts we must lock our minds, absolutely. That's what they want—to confuse us—they know that doubt and disunity are their opportunities. By appealing to ignorance and discontent, to racial and religious prejudice, they have gained entry for their ideas into every country of the world. Hitler himself says that his battles are fought with ideas, no less than with guns, and that he never attacks a nation until it has been demoralized from within. So that any hesitation, any doubt that our democratic way is better, any hospitality to racial or religious hatreds that divide our people—these open the door for the enemy.

Of course, that doesn't mean that our democracy is perfect—nobody knows that better than we women. We and our children are the ones who suffer from low wages and unemployment—we have seen people starving while food was being destroyed—living in slums while builders' hands are idle. We know we have many sicknesses to be cured—but that doesn't mean we should copy the methods of the totalitarian states. Whatever good thing they have taken—labour and unity and efficiency are good—they have corrupted, and you know the old saying, that the worst results come about through the corruption of what is good. They say they've solved unemployment but they've done it by making slaves of the people. They say they're more efficient than we are—but can their factories, where spies watch the workers and secret police watch the spies—can those factories be more efficient than ours? If every action is tangled in a web of government rules and restrictions—does that make for efficiency? With all its defects, democracy still offers the plain man and woman more security or hope than the slave states ever can. Hitler says he's introducing a new order into the world.—But there's nothing new about lawlessness, cruelty and slavery. What is new, is the new order we women want—justice, kindliness, brotherhood beyond the boundaries of race or creed—that's the new order we hope to see after the war— that's another reason why it's a woman's war.

And the time for us to start building that new order is now. Some people talk of waiting till after the war—to put our attention to it now, they say, would take away from our war effort. But they're wrong. Curing poverty and ignorance, righting injustice—that's part of our war effort. You can't put ideals into cold storage—they won't keep; unless they're put into action, made into reality, they shrivel and die. We've got to start right now to bridge the gap between our preaching and our practice; to tackle the questions of unemployment, housing, ignorance and want. Every step forward will heighten the wall of confidence and unity—will strengthen the whole nation as nothing else would.

So, in this woman's war, that's the woman's job. We want a better democracy, but we can't have it unless we make it ourselves—it won't do for a woman to say about a political question, "Oh, I don't know anything about that. You'll have to ask my husband." It's not easy to be a democratic citizen—there's so much to learn. You've got to study, to work, to think. But we'll have to learn to rule ourselves the way we want, or have others do it the way they want. And we've another job. In this struggle, we must muster all our resources,—and the greatest resources of a nation are its people. We have our mines and factories, our fields and forests, that's true. But what about our homes? Surely we must count the courage and cheerfulness, the tolerance and kindliness, found in every home across the land—surely we must count these among our resources—and of those resources, we women are the guardians. Oh, I know we must have the machines of war—but behind the armies and the navies stand the common people—it's their moral fibre that counts in the end. The Maginot line has proved that no material defence is worth much if the spirit behind it is feeble. And if we women can't go out and fight in the field—we can build up and guard the spirit at home. We can put on the armour of truth and of faith and in the knowledge that our homes, our children, our religion is at stake, we can resolve to stand fast, to build and endure until we can see the dawn of a clearer and brighter day. It's a woman's war! Yes! and we Canadian women are prepared to meet brute forces with the rightness of our cause, knowing that in the end it will be victorious.

2 From Josephine Gibson, *How to Eat Well Though Rationed* (Vital Publications, 1943), 2–12.

KEEPING YOUR FAMILY FIT IN WARTIME

The truest patriot is the healthy one. It's our civic duty to keep ourselves and our families fit and well in wartime, thus the home front can support the nation's war effort. Good food and plenty of it is the first step toward health. Only healthy people can work hard, do their jobs better and help us win the war sooner!

Men are daily rejected for service with the armed forces because of faulty nutrition and thousands of man-hours are lost on the production lines for lack of proper food. It's up to the women of Canada to change all this.

An official standard for eating has been adopted in the now-familiar slogan: "Know the Right Foods—Eat the Right Foods" Anyone regularly eating this basic group of foods (given below) will have everything needed for a good diet. One who doesn't won't secure an adequate diet. The essential foods are simple ones, many of them unrationed and all available in amounts necessary for health.

Remember:

I. Use a variety of foods daily.
II. The diet will be adequate in minerals and vitamins if liberal use is made of milk and cheese, eggs, vegetables, especially green leafy ones, fruits, especially citrus fruits and tomatoes, whole grain cereals, and Canada approved bread.
III. Protein needs (for building and repairing body tissue) require one daily serving each of meat or fish, or other meat substitute, and one of eggs or cheese. Milk may be used in quantities sufficient to supply the major portion of the protein required. Use milk especially to supplement dried beans and peas.
IV. When the basic needs have been taken care of, enough foods high in energy (fuel for the body) may be then selected to bring the diet up to the caloric value that makes a satisfying diet.

The simple plan given below offers an easy way for homemakers to select a daily family diet that will supply all nutritive essentials in adequate amounts, outlining first the foods needed each day. All tastes and pocketbooks, even with wartime food rationing, are covered.

"Know the Right Foods—Eat the Right Foods"

Milk:
Use as a beverage and also on cereals, in cocoa, in soups, cream sauces for vegetables, custards and puddings.

Eggs:
At least 3 or 4 weekly for adults.
1 daily for children.
(Use cooked, in custards, griddle cakes and waffles, cakes and puddings.)

Other Protein Foods:

1 serving daily from this group in addition to milk and egg allowance on Page 2.

beef	veal	kidneys
pork	fish or other seafood	sweetbreads
lamb	liver	cheese
mutton	heart	poultry

Fruits and Vegetables:

1 serving daily of citrus fruits or tomatoes, or
1 serving daily of other raw fruit or vegetable rich in vitamin C (see list of foods below).
1 serving daily of a green vegetable (leafy ones frequently).
1 or 2 servings daily of other fruits and vegetables, including potatoes. Use yellow vegetables often. Serve more fruits and vegetables when possible.

Fruits and vegetables are valuable for minerals, vitamins and bulk. Those starred in this list are the best sources of vitamin C.

*apples, depends on variety	grapes	*strawberries
apricots	*lemons	dried or stewed apricots
bananas	melons	dates
blackberries	*oranges	prunes
blueberries	peaches	figs
cantaloupe	pears	*black currants
cherries	pineapple	*tomatoes
*grapefruit	plums	potatoes
	*raspberries	

Green vegetables are excellent sources of vitamin A and iron. Use one every day.

beet greens	kale	lettuce
green string beans	spinach	parsley
broccoli	turnip greens	
dandelion greens	watercress	

All vegetables are important for minerals, vitamins and bulk. Use one or more every day.

asparagus	celery	turnips
lima beans	corn	squash
dried beans	cucumbers	sweet potatoes
beets	eggplant	tomatoes
brussels sprouts	parsnips	carrots
cauliflower	peas	

Breads and Cereals:

Whole grain or vitamin B Canada approved bread with every meal. A serving of cereals once a day. Use unrefined cereals and oatmeal often. Use dry cereals with added vitamin B.

Butter:

At least 2 tablespoons daily.

Sugars and Sweets:

As needed.

Use a variety—molasses, syrup, brown sugar, honey, jams and jellies.

Fats and Oils:

As needed.

Use in salad dressings, seasonings for vegetables, cakes and other desserts.

Desserts:

1 or 2 servings daily.

Use a variety—puddings, gelatin desserts, fresh fruits, pies and cakes (remember that cake made with good materials is an excellent food).

These foods are rich in iron, the mineral least likely to be found in sufficient amounts in the diet. Try to serve at least one of these every day.

eggs	kidney	lentils
whole grain cereals	navy beans	dried apricots
liver	lima beans	dried figs
heart	dried peas	dried dates

If yours is an average Canadian family of father, mother and two growing children under twelve years of age, your market order for the week should include all of the above essential foods. All are within the bounds of your ration allowances.

Suggested Weekly Market Order

(For parents and two children under twelve years)

1. FRUITS AND VEGETABLES

(Spend ⅕ or more of food money for this group of foods)

Potatoes and sweet potatoes	11 pounds
Dried peas and beans and peanut butter	1 ½ pounds
Oranges (or use grapefruit or tomatoes or tomato juice)	2 ½ to 3 dozen
Leafy, yellow and green vegetables	7 pounds
Dried fruit	1 ½ pounds
Other vegetables or fruit	8 pounds

2. MILK OR CHEESE (⅕ or less of food money)

Use pasteurized whole milk (or its equivalent)	18 quarts

3. MEATS, EGGS AND FISH (About ⅕ of food money)

Eggs .... 1 ½ dozen

Lean meat, fish and seafood ....6 pounds

4. BREAD AND CEREALS (⅕ or less of food money)

Bread, whole grain or enriched .... 5 ½-pound loaves

Assorted cereals .... 10 pounds

Oatmeal, wheat, rice, macaroni, cornmeal, flour, cakes, cookies
and crackers.

5. FATS, SUGARS AND ACCESSORIES (⅕ or less of food money)

Butter and other spreads ....1 ½ pounds

Lard, oils, salt pork, bacon...1 ½ pounds

Sugar..2 pounds

Molasses and syrup... ¾ pint

Coffee... ½ pound

Tea .... ⅛ pound

Cocoa.. ½ pound or less

Baking powder, salt, flavorings, etc. .... As needed

Cod-Liver Oil

(For each child under 12 years)

Study the above lists and charts for they will help you to plan well-balanced menus amid constantly changing conditions that necessitate quick alterations in marketing and eating habits. It is your responsibility, no matter how difficult the task, to see that your husband and children are well fed and happy when they come to the family table.

PLANNING RATIONED MENUS

In planning well-balanced family menus with food rationing and shortages, a working knowledge of nutrition is essential. On pages 2–3 we have listed the foods that should be included in every day's menus for every member of the family to assure good nutrition. If these foods are used in recommended amounts you can be certain that you are serving healthful meals.

The menus you plan and serve are as individual as the hats you choose. Almost never do two women purchase food or plan menus in exactly the same way. Family food preferences; the ages, occupations and activities of the members of your family; the locality in which you live; whether or not you have lunches to pack; and many other factors enter into your menu planning. For these reasons, it is impossible to plan menus that will be practical for every family.

The week's menus suggested here for a family of four are low in rationed foods and well balanced. They will serve as a general guide in menu planning but can be re-arranged and other foods substituted. In planning menus, consult chapters in this book on economical war-time meat dishes, main dishes without meat, sugar saving desserts, etc. These are recipes that will help you to eat well, though rationed.

A WEEK'S MENUS FOR A FAMILY OF FOUR

(At Moderate Cost)

SUNDAY

BREAKFAST
Orange Juice
Scrambled Eggs   French Toast
Coffee   Milk

DINNER
Stuffed Meat Loaf (Page 13)
Pan Browned Potatoes
Creamed (or Buttered) Green Peas
or Carrots and Peas
Mixed Fresh Fruit Salad
Apple Pie (Baked on Saturday)
Coffee

SUPPER
Waffles   Maple Syrup
Apple Sauce   Carrot Sticks
Old Fashioned Molasses Cookies (Page 40)
Hot Chocolate or Milk

MONDAY

BREAKFAST
Tomato Juice
Oatmeal   Milk
Toast   Fruit Preserves
Coffee   Milk

LUNCH
Scrambled Egg Sandwiches
or
Meat Loaf Sandwiches (meat from Sunday Dinner)
Baked Apples
Cocoa

DINNER
Beef Liver with Onions (Page 19)
Baked Potatoes
Green Beans Au Gratin
Mixed Vegetable Salad (Shredded carrots, celery
and onion)
Warm Gingerbread (milk or cream)

TUESDAY

BREAKFAST
Stewed Dried Prunes
Dry Cereal   Milk or Cream
Soft Cooked Eggs   Toast
Coffee   Milk

LUNCH
Cheese and Lettuce Sandwiches
Coleslaw
Gingerbread (from Monday Dinner)
Milk

DINNER
Lamb Stew (Page 17)
Buttered Peas
Celery and Apple Salad
Hot Muffins   Jam
Baked Indian Pudding (Page 41)

WEDNESDAY

BREAKFAST
Cooked Cereal   Milk or Cream
Toast   Marmalade
Coffee   Cocoa

LUNCH
Toasted Cheese Sandwiches
Lettuce with Russian Dressing
Fresh Pears
Milk or Tea

DINNER
Upside Down Meat Pie (Page 13)
Buttered Spinach
Creamed Carrots
Perfection Salad
Stewed Cherries
Honey Chocolate Chip Cookies (Page 39)

THURSDAY

BREAKFAST
Tomato Juice
Griddle Cake   Syrup
Coffee   Cocoa

LUNCH
Hard-Cooked Egg and Celery Salad
Bread and Butter Sandwiches
Carrot Strips
Chocolate Chip Cookies (Baked Wednesday)
Tea or Milk

DINNER
Stuffed Flank Steak (Page 18)
Mashed Potatoes
Cabbage Au Gratin
Gelatin Fruit Salad
(made with fresh fruits as orange, banana and
apple)
Chilled Baked Rice Pudding (Page 42)

FRIDAY

BREAKFAST
Halves of Grapefruit
Bacon   Poached Eggs
Toast or Coffee Cake (Made with prepared biscuit
mix)

continued

Grape Jelly
Coffe   Milk
LUNCH
Cream of Potato Soup
Toast with Grated Cheese
(Cheese melted in oven)
Lettuce   Russian Dressing
Chocolate Chip Cookies
(Baked Wednesday)
Tea or Milk
DINNER
Fish Fillets   Tartar Sauce
Scalloped Potatoes   Green Peas
Grape Jelly (Opened for Breakfast)
Chilled Tapioca Pudding
or
Lemon Meringue Pie

SATURDAY
BREAKFAST
Fresh Fruit (Apples, Pears, Etc.)
Dry Cereal   Milk or Cream
French Toast
Coffee   Milk
LUNCH
Macaroni with Cheese Sauce
Applesauce
Bread and Butter
Cookies
Milk
DINNER
Sausage
Creamed Potatoes   Buttered Onions
Tossed Green Vegetable Salad
Fresh Fruit Cobbler
Tea or Milk

THE WARTIME LUNCH BOX

Lunch box carriers are on the increase as Canada is on the march! They must be packed with the right foods—healthful, appetizing, and carefully planned for nutritional balance—for hit-or-miss lunches gamble with vital working power which the nation needs. The packer of lunches must learn all possible tricks to make these carried meals attractive and varied.

Suggestions for Packing a Lunch

1. Include in every lunch box the essentials of a varied meal: meat, fish, eggs, cheese or beans, some milk, some vegetables, fruits, bread or other cereal.
2. Wrap all sandwiches separately in waxed paper.
3. Use fillings that will not soak the bread, or wilt before eating.
4. Add something juicy to every lunch box—whether it be fruit, vegetable, salad or beverage. Sandwiches and cookies become awfully dry when eaten without plenty of liquid.
5. Tuck in a surprise like wrapped candy, stuffed prunes, a bag of potato chips or a relish that you know is well liked.
6. Be sure to include plenty of paper napkins in the box, and make them sizable ones. A salt shaker is a good addition.
7. Plan foods that will be easy for you to fix and varied and interesting to the one who eats them.
8. Leaves of lettuce wrapped in waxed paper to be added to sandwiches before eating will stay crisper than if put in sandwiches at time of making.
9. Cupcakes (baked in paper containers, if you like) instead of slices of cake, and turnovers instead of wedges of pie carry well in the packed lunch.

MEAT STRETCHING DISHES

There are two schools of thought on how to manage the meat ration. One might be called the "feast and fast" plan with a big steak or roast one day and no meat for several days afterward.

The second plan is to "make a little go a long way." With this plan you serve smaller amounts of meat but serve it almost every day.

For most families the second plan is much the better one. Base your menu on meat as usual but plan to extend that meat dish when necessary with vegetables, as in stews and meat pies; with cereals or bread dressings as in meat loaves and patties; or with sauces or gravies. Often half a pound of meat can be extended to serve four or five.

Really fine eating is provided by the stews, meat pies and casserole dishes that are a necessity now. Such homely dishes as boiled beef and cabbage, pot-roast and potato dumplings and hearty meat pies have made the reputation of more than one famous restaurant. So serve them with pride, even to guests. The secret of success is to make theme extremely well and serve them attractively.

Historical Interpretations

3 From Denyse Baillargeon, "'If You Had No Money, You Had No Trouble, Did You?': Montréal Working-Class Housewives during the Great Depression," *Women's History Review* 1, 2 (1992): 217–37. Reprinted by permission of the publisher Taylor & Francis Ltd, www.tandfonline.com.

[. . .] This article reports the results of an oral history study which was designed to [explore] the experience of a group of working-class Montreal housewives. Because women during this period bore the primary responsibility for feeding, clothing, and generally looking after the welfare of the family, a study of the domestic activities of working-class housewives during the 1930s provides an opportunity to introduce a new dimension. This study was designed to elicit information about the ways in which women engaged in a range of strategies in order to make up for the decline in their husbands' earning power and also to examine the way in which the Depression influenced motherhood, the working conditions of housewives, and the division of labour within the family.

The study is based on an analysis of interviews with 30 women, all of whom lived in Montreal. Montreal was selected as the locus of the study because it was the industrial centre of the province and because 60 per cent of unemployed Québécois lived there.[1] Because the Depression had its greatest impact on workers and especially on unskilled workers, I drew my sample from those women who had lived through the decade of 1929–1939 in a working-class district of Montreal. All my respondents were of French-Canadian origin, and were Roman Catholic. Since the study was designed to examine family life, all the women were married, and all had been married before 1934. The employment patterns of their husbands were variable: some of the husbands were employed during these years while others were unemployed.

[. . .]

AN INTRODUCTION TO THE RESPONDENTS IN THE SAMPLE

All the women interviewed were born between 1897 and 1916, 14 of them in rural areas. However, all lived in Montreal and Verdun (a working-class suburb of Montreal) at the beginning of the Depression. Most were daughters of workers or farmers, and most grew up in poor families with a relatively large number of children, where the low income and irregular employment patterns of the father rendered the work of the children critical to the family's survival:

We were not rich, not even well-off. We barely made ends meet. [. . .] In those days, wages were low. We managed, but I can't say that we were comfortable. In those days, people had no money. You started to work young. I think that my oldest sister began when she was twelve.[2]

For the majority of these women, school was but a brief interlude preceding their integration into the workforce. In fact, 21 of the women interviewed had left school on or before their fourteenth birthday. With the exception of three respondents who lived on the farm until their wedding and a fourth, raised by her well-to-do grandparents, all these women worked for a wage before they got married. A few were teachers or clerks in stores or offices, but most were employed as servants or workers. All these women were educated to become wives and mothers, but the interviews revealed that their early integration into the labour force did nothing to develop their skills as housewives. Indeed, being employed outside the home cut short the time during which they could have become familiar with the most complicated housework tasks, like cooking and sewing. Many respondents, but especially those who left school for the factory or the office, acknowledged that their skills in these areas were quite limited and that they felt ill-prepared to keep house once married. Actually, 16 of them did not know how to sew at that time, even though all their mothers were skilled enough to make most of the garments for their families. Seven would never acquire this skill, while the others would be forced to set about it after marriage, when a tight budget would give them no choice. [. . .]

Eighteen of the respondents were married before 1929, ten between 1930 and 1932, and the other two in 1933 and 1934, respectively. Two early weddings, celebrated after 1929, came as a result of unexpected pregnancies, and the bride of 1933 had to postpone her wedding day for three years because her fiancé was unemployed. Since the social network of Quebec youth during the early decades of the century was centred around the district or the village, a strong social and geographical endogamy governed the respondents' choice of marriage partners.[3] For instance, in 22 cases, the couples originated from the same or a neighbouring district or locality. Moreover, differences in income and living standard between the family of origin of the couples were slight: in 16 cases, the father and father-in-law of the respondents had a similar job or trade, while 17 of the couples were formed of wage-earners or the same category. Most of the couples married with slender means and settled with a minimum of belongings: the bride's trousseau, the wedding gifts and furniture for two or three rooms, generally second-hand or bought on credit. Lack of savings and low income made it necessary for 18 of them to co-habit with in-laws for some time, in most cases with the husband's side of the family.

A survey of the employment status of the husbands reveals that most were workers or low-echelon salaried employees, while three had a small business (one owned a barber shop, one a *restaurant-dépanneur*, and a third was the owner of two taxis). These last three men did not, however, enjoy a higher standard of living. Among the sample as a whole, only five of the men earned as much as $25 a week; some earned as little as $10 and more than half of them earned less than $20. Data from the Federal Department of Labour shows that in December 1929, a family of five in Quebec needed a minimum income of $20.18 a week to cover food, heating, lighting, and lodging.[4] This illustrates that even before the Depression set in most of these couples were living below the poverty level and suggests that even if the main provider of the family was employed, the family could not survive without intensified domestic production and a very tight rein on the budget. Even then, help was needed from in-laws and family; often, husband and wife had to take in additional work or resort to alternate strategies to bring in more cash.

Thirteen of the husbands had a "sideline" during the thirties. A mechanic repaired cars at home, an office clerk worked during the weekend on the maintenance of the sports club where he worked during the week. A third man organized small lotteries where the prize, advertised at his grocer's, was a checker board he had made, while another one sold hockey game score cards to his workmates, both in violation of the law prohibiting lotteries. A fifth man worked as a bookkeeper for a grocer in addition to his regular work as a municipal civil servant. The restaurant owner worked during the day as a salesmen in a shoe store while his wife worked in the restaurant. A man employed in a department store opened a little snack bar for his workmates, with the permission of the store owners. During the Second World War, he also made figurines for Christmas displays since the store could not order them from Italy. In addition to these regular side-lines, the husbands who became unemployed during the thirties engaged in other wage-earning activities such as excavation work or washing walls and ceilings for neighbours, removing snow in the well-to-do districts of the town, and selling homemade alcohol.

Most of the husbands of the respondents were unemployed, or under-employed during the 1930s. Of the three business owners, only one—the barber shop owner—kept his business: the other two had to sell out before going bankrupt. Cash flow difficulties brought them brutally back into the ranks of the unemployed, confirming that their ownership status did not set them apart from the other working people on whom they depended for their living. Among the salaried men, only four avoided unemployment, reduced time employment, or salary cuts. Four had to accept a shorter work week and three others suffered wage cuts of as much as 20 per cent. Seven were without steady jobs for more than three years, six for periods of one to two years, and the last, the luckiest one, was without work for a few months only. In all, 15 of these young couples lived on welfare for more or less prolonged periods.

There is, therefore, no doubt that most of the sample families saw their financial situation deteriorate during the 1930s. Further proof of this is that the welfare benefits represented only 50 per cent of what was necessary in 1933 to cover the basic needs of a family of five.[5] Obviously, the families of the unemployed could not subsist on welfare benefits and, to fill the gap, turned back to strategies they already knew or had to learn.

DOMESTIC WORK AND THE FAMILY ECONOMY DURING THE 1930S

For my respondents, maternity was in theory the prime object of marriage and sexuality, which is not surprising if one remembers the religious and medical dogmas of the time. As one of them said: "It was a woman's life to bear children" (R24). However, in actuality, bearing and raising children often became a very heavy burden, particularly when financial resources were severely limited. After two or three children, most women admitted they were hoping to postpone further additions to their families and despite the precepts of the Church, some of them did have recourse to methods of birth control: "After my third [child], I said: we should take a little break or we will never make it! We didn't have that much money in those days and with three children, there was a lot more to do" (R23).

On the whole, the 28 women in the sample who were able to bear children averaged five children each, which is two less than their mothers who averaged 7.2 babies. This average conceals, however, great differences between the women, five of whom had more than eight children, three had more than ten, and six had less than three. Most often, however, that is in 11 out of 28 cases, they had three to five children. The 15 women who controlled their fertility had an average of four children, while the others had six. The number of pregnancies is a little higher: 6.3 for all fertile women in the sample. Those who did not take contraceptive measures had 7.5 pregnancies, while for those who practised some form of family planning the figure was 5.4.

We can surmise that the respondents' decision to use contraception had some connection with the economic difficulties of the 1930s. In fact, the majority of couples who tried to control their fertility experienced cuts in wages or had to live on welfare for more or less prolonged periods. However, a complexity of motivations was involved. For instance, few women spoke only of economic reasons to justify their decision to limit the size of their family, but also referred to the amount of work a larger family would entail and to their wish to give proper care and education to each child. A typical response was as follows:

> I said to myself, God gave me children but I don't want to see them suffer later on. Larger families always meant hard times. [. . .] So I said, we could avoid that. My husband and I both decided that. Because my husband earned so much and I wanted to give them a good education. [. . .] I said, I prefer to have a small family and be able to give them what they need. I was thinking of their education. (R16)

On the other hand, several couples in the sample who also faced serious financial difficulties did not see fit to limit the number of their children, which indicates that a lower income is not always the main motivation for birth control. The families who practised contraception made a deliberate decision to do so, a decision that involved the co-operation of the husband: the contraceptive methods used—condoms in three cases,

or coitus interruptus in 8 cases out of 15—left the women no choice but to depend on their husbands. In the case of the Ogino–Knauss method, the goodwill of the husband was equally essential. For families who did not practise contraception, religious background combined with ignorance of birth control methods, a rural background, and a large number of children in both of the families of origin, appears to have produced a fatalistic acceptance of large numbers of children, in spite of the economic difficulties engendered by the Depression: "There was nothing and you heard of nothing to prevent pregnancies. Physically, it is tough being pregnant but you could not do otherwise. Sometimes you would think about it: if only there was something. Some had methods, or so they said, but I found out too late" (R3); "To prevent pregnancies was out of the question. It was the law of the Church. You had to have children" (R29).

For the women in the sample who did practise contraception, the Great Depression was in part responsible for a lessening of their work load as mothers. But it must be remembered that in the religious climate of the times, recourse to a contraceptive method created a profound moral crisis: most women had a deep sense of guilt in transgressing the Church's teaching and continued to confess their perceived "sin" to their priest, at the risk of not being shriven: "Going to confession was cruel. It was no picnic having to confess using birth control . . . I had no choice . . . The priests would lecture us" (R5). Some of them developed different strategies to be absolved without trouble, like whispering or going to confession at the end of the day, when the priests were tired and probably bored stiff. One of the women related:

> Once, during Holy Week, I went to confession with my husband. He said: I'll go before you, and when he came out, he nodded "no": he hadn't received absolution. Oh yes! They refused to give

us absolution! Once, we even saw three priests! Finally we found one . . . I don't know if he was tired, it was late, he was probably hungry and eager to get out of the confessional . . . Anyway, he was in such a rush that I don't even know if he heard our confession. Besides, we would whisper as low as possible . . . anyway. (R10)

On the other hand, those who did not use birth control often endured anxiety and discouragement throughout their pregnancies, feeling they could not fulfill their children's needs: "He worked until 1933 . . . After that there was no more construction, and there was a new born baby every year. That's tough. They had to be fed you know? When your man is out of work" (R12). Whatever the choice, it is obvious that for these women, maternity brought more anxieties than joys during the years of the Depression.

While several couples were willing to transgress the Church's rules in order to practise birth control, they generally refused to consider any new sharing of roles, even though their economic circumstances were considerably worsened. Having said this, it is necessary to point out that even before the Depression set in, family division of labour based on sex did not always scrupulously follow the pattern of a strict separation of the roles of male provider and female housewife. Indeed, when they got married, it was generally agreed that the wife should leave her job to take care of the house and of the expected children, while the husband should become the sole breadwinner. In practice, however, 18 women in the sample worked for pay during the 1930s. Five were employed outside the home, while the others carried on some type of paid activity in the home: for example sewing, laundering, taking in boarders, doing house cleaning, selling homemade pastries, or managing a small business. Therefore, most of those who contributed to the family income during the decade of the Depression

had begun to work even before their husband lost his job or suffered a cut in pay: only three respondents took paid employment because their husband was out of work.

On the other hand, nine husbands lost their jobs for periods of several months or several years and the question of their wives supplementing the family income never arose. The respondents offered many reasons for this, such as the number of dependent children in the family and the unlikelihood that the women would find work. However, opposition by the husband to the wife's employment appears constantly and often simultaneously in the testimonies, which reveal a great ambivalence on the part of the women interviewed. Women as well as men were reluctant to engage in a role reversal at variance with the socially accepted division of labour. One of them stated: "I wanted to go to work; he didn't want me to. Besides, the children were too young, and I could not leave them on their own. In those days, you didn't leave your babies" (R20). Thus, the presence of small children seemed to be a main deterrent, even if the unemployed father could have been available to look after them. Most of these women also said there was no work to be found, though they admitted not having tried to find any:

Back then, there was no more work for women than there was for men. Besides, I would have been at a complete loss going about looking for a job. My mother-in-law had never worked out of the home. As for myself, I guess I felt obliged to do the same thing. (R19)

In fact, in the nine couples where the wife had never contributed to the family income before the husband lost his job, the division of labour based on sex was such an inborn and rigid concept that it precluded any new outlook on seeking new sources of income.

A closer look at the five women who worked outside the home shows that only two of them became the main breadwinner. Moreover, they had a maximum of two children and someone other than the father took care of them, even though he was out of work. For their part, those women who took in paid work in the home before their husbands became unemployed continued and even intensified their work load whenever possible. But none of them even considered the possibility of exchanging paid work within the home for outside employment. According to their own statements, their husbands would not have allowed it. An informant declared: "During the crisis I sewed for others in order to make money for the household. I helped my husband a lot; he did the best he could and so did I." However, when asked if she considered working for wages she replied: "My husband would have never allowed me to. He would have said that a woman should not work outside . . . You could only be hired to work as a housekeeper"(R5).

Male inactivity due to unemployment did not bring about any increase in the men's sharing of housework. In the same way that women did not seek to replace their husbands as the main provider, the men did not take a greater part in the housework, except to do tasks that had already been incorporated into the family pattern (like shopping, looking after the children, or washing the floors). At any rate, according to their wives, they spent most of their time outside the home, looking for work. Moreover, it is clear that the women considered that the house was their domain and even if their husbands were unemployed, they did not ask for more help:

Oh no! Like I said, in those days men would never, ever have done housework. I would never have wanted him to either. I enjoyed doing my own thing. Women were all the same back then. I was an early bird and I always managed to get my work done in time, so there was no need for help. (R29)

Thus, if it can be said that the Depression did not modify the division of labour within the family along sex lines—that is no changes were made at all as to the roles and responsibilities that already prevailed in the family—this does not mean that they were strictly based on the breadwinner/housewife pattern. [. . .]

It is difficult to determine exactly what part of the total family income was provided by women. In most cases, the respondents could not remember very clearly what they earned because their work varied constantly as did the time devoted to it within any one week: "It was an extra; it didn't give me a steady income" (R22). Yet even these partial recollections allow us to estimate these contributions as between $3 to $10 a week—which in some cases was as much as 50 per cent of the breadwinner's wages. This money was all the more important because it could make the difference between living under or just a little above the poverty level. "It didn't pay much but it gave me a little income at the end of the week. When my husband didn't have enough, I would either help pay for the rent or buy clothes for the children" (R17).

According to a time honoured working-class tradition, in Quebec as elsewhere, women were generally the ones who managed the budget.[6] Despite what they were able to earn, the sums they were managing were generally very small because these supplements were in most cases added to very low incomes. Making ends meet was a real balancing act for the majority of the respondents. To achieve this goal, they established priorities which they respected most rigorously. Heading the list were those expenses which could not be tampered with, like rent and electricity, which they considered as debts that must be met. Next came food, fuel, and then whatever could be spent on clothing, transportation, insurance, or leisure, if they had any money left.

Checking and double-checking the prices, buying only the bare minimum, avoiding any waste and debts, were the *mots d'ordre* brought up constantly in the testimonies: "I never wasted anything" (R1); "Every cent was accounted for" (R2); "You know, we never bought anything we didn't need. We never wasted anything" (R26). This means that they were always doing very intensive housework, usually in the most inadequate conditions with inefficient appliances. The wood or coal stove was used for both cooking and heating. All meals were homemade, from soups to pastries, and many made preserves, pickles, and jams. Women who had learned to sew made most of their own clothes and those of their children, often re-making hand-me-downs. They also sewed all the household linen: sheets, tablecloths, tea towels, bed linens, bed covers, drapes, curtains, etc. Most of them owned a foot-pedal sewing machine, even if they only used it for repairing clothes, but most waited until after the second or third child before acquiring a washing machine. This means that, for varying lengths of time, most of the women did all their washing by hand with washboards, in tubs or bathtubs if they were lucky enough to have one in their lodgings.

What they could afford for rent might vary from $12 to $18 a month, which meant low quality lodgings: poor lighting, poor insulation, softwood floors that were hard to keep clean, etc. Lodgings were often infested with rats or cockroaches. While all these lodgings had municipal water and electric facilities, they were rarely connected to natural gas. Less than half of the respondents lived in lodgings with a bath and the vast majority could not afford to rent or buy a water heater. Inadequate income also meant that the lodgings were always too small and the parlour often had to serve as a bedroom. Some children even slept in the kitchen, or in the hallways on cots which were folded and made up daily.

This brief account shows that for these women, budgeting was practically an obsession, while housework represented harsh, physically demanding labour, which had to be done in unpleasant conditions, often without adequate facilities. In fact, their domestic work consisted of such a varied number of tasks and services that when the Depression came, it was hard to find anyway they could add anything to what they were already doing. Unlike women in the middle-income groups, who, for instance, could substitute their own labour for ready-made consumer products—like clothes or food—the majority of women in this sample had not yet become mass consumers. They could not return to methods of saving from which they had never departed. On the contrary, lack of income and inadequate welfare payments caused them to give up some of the work they used to do, such as making preserves, jams, or pickles, for in order to make these, they would have had to buy products in bulk which they could not afford: "We didn't have money to buy anything. How could we buy all it took to make ketchup and things like that? We were allowed only one sugar ration. In order to make jam you needed a lot more; so we didn't make any" (R19). However, there is no doubt that for these women, lower incomes and, above all, inadequate welfare benefits led to serious difficulties in providing food and clothing, and to a deterioration or at the least a lack of improvement in their working conditions.

Because they already bought only the bare necessities, the Depression days forced them to cut expenses in crucial areas, where alternatives had to be found. This is particularly true where food was concerned, since then the lack of money often meant looking for new sources of savings, which generally resulted in a lowering of both the quantity and quality of foodstuff. In order to get cheap meat, some did their shopping at the slaughterhouse rather than at the local butcher. A few dollars would get them several pounds of meat, but the nutritional value was not necessarily the best: "In those days, you could buy your meat [at the slaughterhouse]; soup bones were available and other such things as sausages, blood-pudding, nothing expensive as you can imagine, however 99¢ bought a whole lot" (R19). Others shopped at their regular butcher but late on Saturday evening. Few butchers had refrigeration in those days and often they preferred to cut prices rather than keep meats until Monday, which might have meant a total loss. Another way of cuttings costs in food was to buy damaged or no longer fresh fruits and vegetables, even if it took greater care and time to prepare them: "As you can imagine, it was a lot more work. Sometimes it was slightly spoiled. But as long as it was edible" (R5). Surprisingly, the respondents did not turn to baking their own bread. One said she tried three or four times, but it was a long and complicated task and lack of experience increased the risk of poor results and loss of costly ingredients. [. . .]

It is evident that it took considerable skill and imagination to prepare tasty and nutritious meals under those circumstances. Despite their care and inventiveness, many interviewees were often forced to eat only slices of bread—sometimes spread with mustard or sugar—or do without food at all for entire days in order to feed their children: "We can't say that we ate well. [. . .] We barely had enough to eat, and most of the time, we left what we had for the children" (R27). [. . .]

For the unemployed, buying clothes and sewing material were the first budget cuts they made. This meant that women and their husbands alike had to wear out their clothing completely in order to find money with which to dress their growing children. Two of the respondents, who had never sewed before, learned to do so because of the Depression:

That's when I learned to sew. At first, I bought clothes for my children but after, [when my husband lost his job] I couldn't afford to. I learned to sew by taking apart old clothes and remaking them. I didn't have a sewing machine, so in the evenings I would go to my mother's to sew while my husband looked after the children. (R12)

In most cases, however, women who did not know how to sew relied on parents or charity organizations such as the Salvation Army or Saint-Vincent-de-Paul.

Lower incomes forced half of the respondents to move, often more than once, to ever less expensive and less comfortable homes.[7] Thus the Depression generally lowered the standard of living of the whole family, but even more so that of the women for which home was at once both work and living space. For these women, moving also meant additional heavy work. The new home had to be found, possessions had to be packed and unpacked, and the new places had to be thoroughly cleaned. [. . .]

The Great Depression also deprived some of the interviewees of a number of home appliances. For instance, many could not get repairs done. Others saved on electric bills by reducing their use of electric appliances. Two of the respondents had their power cut off; this made their work all the more difficult, because they had to postpone tasks to the evening, as they could then illegally hook up the wires with less fear that the company inspector might drop in.[8] Finally, two went back to live on the farm because their husbands could not find any work. Without electricity or running water, they had to put their electric irons, toasters, and washing machines in storage and go back to making by hand a number of products that they were used to buying ready-made. [. . .]

Despite having to move more often, do laundry more frequently because they had fewer clothes, facing greater difficulties in feeding their families, and generally searching constantly for ways and means to satisfy the needs of all their family members, these women were not unanimous in their assessment as to how the Depression had affected their lives. Many felt that lack of money had not really entailed that much more work. Others conceded that they had to work more but hastened to add that they could cope with it very well: "Housework never bothered me"

(R6); "Yes, [it meant more work], but like I said, it was part of a routine. It didn't bother me. I managed to cook with what I had . . ." (R29). In fact, their testimonies attest once more to the courage and self-sacrifice of which women are capable as they raise their families and also their pride in overcoming whatever hardship they have to face. The evidence reveals that women have a very elastic conception of their working time and capacity, which renders the task of evaluating the impact of the Depression on their housework all the more difficult. More than a living memory of responsibilities, their statements reflect pride in having ensured their family's well-being in spite of adverse economic conditions.

It is obvious, however, that for most of these families, and especially for those who lived on welfare for many years, it would have been impossible to cope were it not for their parents' support. Of course family solidarity did not begin with the Great Depression; it was always present, particularly among low-income families.[9] Yet, the interviews indicate that there was a difference in kind during economic hard times. In normal times, for instance, shared child care and the exchange of clothing was natural enough, as well as the sharing of certain work tools, such as washing or sewing machines and the use of the telephone. The Great Depression increased the sharing of goods and services amongst family members, particularly gifts of food and fuel, as well as loans or gifts in money and the sharing of living space. Such help obviously went further than the traditional exchanges. Many of the respondents felt as humiliated by their need to seek such help as having to ask for government welfare assistance which was a last resort for most of them: "It was my mother who supported me. She would send us food and things, because we had nothing to eat and he didn't work" (R27); "That, I didn't like. It would have been okay if there had been only me but there was my husband and my son to consider" (R9).

The evidence from the respondents underlines the fact that the immediate family played an essential role in supporting those most stricken by the Great Depression. The rule was that government welfare only went to those who were absolutely destitute and who could not be helped by their families. In practice, however, families helped in many ways to fill the gap between the actual needs and what the welfare provided. Having exhausted their own resources and cut their expenses to the bone, couples then turned for help to their close families. The use of the traditional family network, which relied on the domestic work of the women of the previous generation, was therefore intensified during the Great Depression and it is clear that the contribution of these women to the well-being of families on the dole was as essential as that of the state. Thus all women within the extended family and not only the housewives whose husbands were unemployed bore the brunt of the Depression.

[. . .]

Most working-class families frowned on the use of credit, especially for consumer goods. In fact, the lack of social security measures to compensate for loss of income was such that these women and their partners were acutely aware of their financial limitations:

> We never had debts. I never bought anything on credit because I figured that if there was no money today, there wouldn't be any more tomorrow. If we had accumulated debts, I don't know how we could have paid for them. In our days we always wondered whether or not the salary would still be there tomorrow. There was nothing you know; you couldn't rely on anyone but yourself. That's why most of the time, we deprived ourselves of many things we wished for. (R17)

The poor labour market, particularly during the thirties, increased the fear of not being able to pay off their creditors. Avoiding credit was also considered as proof that the wife was a good manager and that a family could meet its essential needs.

During the Depression, a few of the respondents had bought clothing from travelling salesmen who offered credit, with interest payments, another few incurred debts at the grocer, to their landlord or with the doctor, but most preferred to turn to the Salvation Army or the Saint-Vincent-de-Paul for food, furniture, or clothing when the immediate family could not help. The amounts of the debts incurred were small indeed compared with today's standards; it rarely represented more than the wages of a week or two. In fact, it can be said that most of these households preferred to restrict their desires according to their means. For these women, the essential was to feed, clothe, and house the family.

Few of the interviewees complained about their precarious finances or the fact that the Depression further reduced their purchasing power. This can be attributed to a certain form of fatalism, but for the most part the women simply accepted that they were "living like everyone else." This is why, despite their many hardships, most of these women do not recall the 1930s as a particularly tragic period of their lives. The relative poverty of most of these households in the pre-Depression years meant that while family survival during the Depression itself involved cutting essential elements from the family budget, poverty had prepared them for deprivation: their previous experience had taught them to live frugally and to depend on the paid work, the domestic labour and the managing strategies of the wife in order to survive. Their pre-existing poverty meant that the conditions they endured during the Depression were not so drastically different from their previous standard of living. Moreover, most of the women had grown up in relatively poor households. Inured to poverty since childhood, they had learned to deal with it and knew ways and means to overcoming it.

[. . .]

NOTES

1. In 1931, 42.7 per cent of Quebec labour power was living in Montreal (Andrée Lévesque, *Virage à gauche interdit. Les communists, les socialistes et leurs ennemis au Québec, 1929–1939* [Montreal: Boréal Express, 1984], 15).

2. Excerpt from the interview with respondent number 29. Thereafter, each excerpt drawn from the interviews will be followed by an R and the number associated with the respondent (in this case: R29).

3. Horace Miner, *St.-Denis: un village Québécois* (Montreal: Hurtubise HMH, 1985); Lucia Ferretti, "Mariage et cadre de vie familiale dans une paroisse ouvrière montréalise: Saint-Brigide, 1900–14," *Revue d'histoire de l'Amérique française*, 39 (1985): 233–51.

4. *Annuaire Statistique (ASQ) 1930 and 1934* (Quebec, 1930, 1934), 400, 426; Canada, ministère du Travail, *La Gazette du Travail*, February 193, 249. Twenty dollars a week, which covers only the bare necessities, was thus a strict minimum for a family of five. It took $1500 a year, that is more than $28 a week, to attain a level of decency (Lévesque, *Virage à gauche*, 22).

5. For a family of five, the Montréal Unemployment Commission paid $8.50 for the rent to the landlord and gave $7.15 a week in winter and $6.55 in summer to cover all other expenses.

6. Meg Luxton, *More than a Labor of Love: Three Generations of Women's Work in the Home* (Toronto: Women's Press, 1980), 161–99; Veronica Strong-Boag, *The New Day Recalled: Lives of Girls and Women in English Canada, 1919–1939* (Toronto: Copp Clark Pitman, 1988), 133–44; Elizabeth Roberts, *A Woman's Place: An Oral History of Working-Class Women, 1850–1940* (Oxford: Basil Blackwell, 1984),

125–68; Pat Ayers & Jan Lambertz, "Marriage Relations, Money, and Domestic Violence in Working-Class Liverpool, 1919–39," in Jane Lewis, ed., *Labour and Love. Women's Experience of Home and Family, 1840–1940* (Oxford: Basil Blackwell), 195–219.

7. Marc Choko, *Les crises du logement à Montréal* (Montreal: Editions cooperatives Albert Saint-Martin, 1980), 109.

8. Rubert Rummily, *Histoire de Montréal* (Montreal: Fides, 1974), quoted in Claude Larivière, *Crise économique et contrôle social: le cas*

de Montréal, 1929–1937 (Montreal: Editions cooperatives Albert Saint-Martin, 1977), 175.

9. See Andrée Fortin, *Histoires de familles et de réseaux. La sociabilité au Québec d'hier à demain* (Montreal: Editions Saint-Martin, 1987); Marc-Adélard Tremblay, "La crise économique des années trente et la qualité de vie chez les montréalais d'ascendance française," in Académie des Sciences Morales et Politiques, *Travaux et Communications*, Vol. 3: *progress techniques et qualité de vie* (Montreal: Bellarmin, 1977), 149–65.

4 From Catherine Gidney, "Under the President's Gaze: Sexuality and Morality at a Canadian University during the Second World War," *The Canadian Historical Review* 82, 1 (March 2001): 36–54. Reprinted with permission from University of Toronto Press (www.utpjournals.com).

During the Second World War, Johann Schmidt, a young man recently released from an internment camp, entered one of Canada's many universities still holding denominational affiliation. Alone in a new culture and living amid strangers, Schmidt wrote to a companion in the camp. Following their mandate, immigration officials vetted the correspondence of the friends. Schmidt's letter contained the usual chitchat: inquiries as to how his friend was doing and when he would be released from the camp. The letter also reported on Schmidt's experiences in residence, in particular, the way in which college boys wasted their time, the immaturity of some students who had not been through what he had, and his delight at having an intelligent and friendly roommate. There were, however, two items in the letter which alarmed immigration officials. First, Schmidt's letter to his friend expressed a general appreciation for the male body. Second, having worked on a farm the summer before, as part of the war effort, Schmidt expressed his determination in the coming summer not to take a "steady job," but to work on successive farms as it suited him. Concerned about the moral fibre of the student, in terms of both his sexuality and his apparent laziness,

the director of the Immigration Branch, F.C. Blair, wrote to the president of the university, and a secretive investigation into the student's character ensued.

A number of historians have documented how Canadian universities have traditionally tried to regulate student behaviour and mores. In the nineteenth and early twentieth centuries, residences recreated the Christian home, university presidents and faculty expected Christian deportment, and chapel services and religious knowledge courses reinforced the role of religion on campus.[1] [. . .]

While the Schmidt case provides an illustration of the use of direct coercion to maintain "proper" deportment on campus, it must be understood within the broader project of creating Christian citizens. The middle decades of the century were a particularly anxious time for Canadians because of the disruption of traditional social and moral norms. Students had been pushing the boundaries of acceptable behaviour through the interwar period. The trend from single-sex socialization to co-ed activities, and from the surveillance of parlour courtship to a more anonymous culture of dating, led to the notion of sex for pleasurable consumption and marked the development of a new heterosexual culture. Fears about students' sexual purity merged with concerns during the Second World War about the increase of divorce rates, venereal disease, juvenile delinquency, and the growing number of women in the workforce, resulting in a general anxiety about the stability of the family and in calls for the moral regeneration of society.

Universities were one site where social and cultural values could be moulded. Although universities were each shaped by their own set of traditions—in this particular case the university was a small, urban, Protestant institution—by the twentieth century they also promoted certain common ideals. University administrators, for example, believed their institutions had a central role to play in the moral guardianship and training of Canada's future leaders. Although expectations of comportment were rarely laid out clearly, glimpses may be seen in residence rules or the reaction to an occasional lapse in good behaviour. Explicit references to students' sexual behaviour are even more limited. Indeed, presidents' reports, university correspondence, and even student newspapers generally avoided discussing sexual conduct.

One exception to this silence was the 1941 Hazen Conference on religion and life. In the face of growing concern over the moral fibre of Canada's youth, faculty, presidents, and deans of women from across English Canada convened to determine how to secure the proper development of Canadian students. Offering one of the rare glimpses into the views of university administrators on sexuality, the conference provides context for the Schmidt case and suggests that universities generally attempted to educate students and mould their conduct. Only in rarer cases, when educational methods failed, did coercion ensue.

In the context of increased societal fears over moral and sexual transgressions by Canadian youth, it is not surprising that, when the president was sent a copy of

Schmidt's letter, he immediately became distraught. Two issues were of particular concern: Schmidt's sexual references to other men and his attitude toward work. In his letter, Schmidt reminded his friend of a mutual acquaintance whose body he particularly admired. He went on to say that, while he still liked this acquaintance, he no longer thought of him as an ideal. Since he had been released from the internment camp, he related, he had met a new boy whose body he admired. Yet he also worried over his reaction, feeling that he liked this boy's body "too much". As Schmidt wrote to his friend: "I was a bit afraid that my experiences and impression in camp might have an influence on my sex life or rather attitude towards sex. However lately this trouble seems to disappear more and more, nevertheless I have to be a bit careful still in my thoughts and also my actions. Naturally nobody out here respects anything of that kind. It would be the last thing people think of. In the opposite, I am getting a reputation of being very interested in girls which by the way is quite true." Schmidt's letter suggests a young man attempting to understand and cope with his own sexuality. There is no explicit evidence of sexual relations, though certainly his writing is suggestive in its admiration for the male body. He was clearly worried about the effect of his camp experiences on his sexual conduct and believed that his feelings or experiences in the internment camp broke the moral or sexual codes of the university. Keeping his own activities in check would protect his reputation. So, too, would the fact that homosexuality was something few people knew about on campus. Ultimately, he believed, his reputation was secure through a genuine interest in girls.

Schmidt's letter raised further concerns because of his attitude towards summer work. Canadian students were being asked to work on farms as their part in the war effort, and the Immigration Branch felt that refugee students should be similarly employed. Attempting to remain in good standing with the branch, Schmidt had asked for permission to work on a farm. After spending a month with the university's Canadian Officers' Training Corps (COTC) contingent, he expected to perform farm work, as he had the previous year. However, in his letter to his friend he wrote: "This summer I shall probably be working on a farm again but it will be much nicer. I won't take a steady job but just work till I do not like it any more and then go on to another place. It will be different now that I have friends here."

[. . .]

The university and the broader Canadian community expected students, who were privileged not to be at the war front, to be serious and upright members of the community in both their social activities and their military training. As a result, student activities such as sports, social functions, and initiations at universities across Canada were limited by the faculty and the students themselves.[2] Those recreational activities that were allowed were expected to be frugal, simple, and quiet.[3] When the war broke out in 1939, dormant units of the COTC quickly re-formed.[4] Military training was initially voluntary, but by the fall of 1940 it entailed six hours a week of compulsory military training during the academic year and two weeks at the end of the year at a spring camp.[5] By mid-war, women were also compelled to participate in war work. Although some women volunteered for military corps, most took classes such as child care, first aid, or auto mechanics, and engaged in practical work such as knitting socks for the troops overseas.[6] Having fulfilled their military training, male students who remained in good academic standing could continue to the end of their undergraduate program without being called up.[7] Students attempting to evade military training were threatened either with having their grades withheld or, more seriously, with conscription.[8]

Nancy Kiefer discovered in research on the University of Toronto that leadership positions within university war work were based on personal character. Men accepted into the COTC were being trained as officers and expected, unlike those in the auxiliary corps, to possess moral and physical leadership abilities.[9] Similarly, women joining the Canadian Red Cross Corps required two character references and were expected to set an example for other female students.[10] Moreover, according to the national commandant, their uniform provided "an outward and visible sign of an inward and spiritual strength."[11] Such symbolism underlined the moral and religious expectations interwoven into the calls for students to do their duty through military training.

With students expected to take their academic activities and contributions to the war effort seriously, Blair felt offended by Schmidt's cavalier attitude to work. He had only one recommendation for Schmidt: if the president dismissed him, "we will return him to the refugee camp and keep him there until he can be sent back to where he came from." Blair's harshness toward Schmidt was not an isolated incident. Although the Immigration Branch fell under the jurisdiction of the Department of Mines and Resources, Blair, rather than the elderly minister Thomas Crerar, made and enforced much of the immigration policy when the Liberals came into power after 1935. He reflected the anti-immigration policies of the times, but historians have also argued that he rigidly enforced, and indeed strengthened, these policies against "undesirable" immigrants.[12] Department of Immigration bureaucrats had traditionally "carried out a clandestine and illegal immigration selection process, and deported immigrants according to their own informal and extralegal system of justice."[13] As part of this system, and as a result of his personal sense of responsibility for preserving the character of Canada, Blair personally scrutinized the documents and qualities of every potential immigrant. Schmidt, then, was only one individual who fell under Blair's scrutiny.[14]

At first the president's reaction was the same as Blair's: Schmidt had failed "to appreciate either the moral standards or the obligations which he should have assumed after release" and should be dismissed. The president ascribed Schmidt's moral lapses to his European background. Implying that Europeans had lower sexual standards than North Americans, the president claimed that Schmidt had "to be judged by European rather than by Canadian standards." Yet, even so, the president felt he could not afford such lapses in college residence, especially since he believed that a homosexual could, as he phrased it, "turn others". Despite the fact that several weeks later he had still not talked to Schmidt, the president continued to believe that he was a "real Problem." Apparently the president did not want to interview the student until officials from the Immigration Branch were ready to pick the boy up because, on the advice of the local RCMP, he believed that "such an interview would almost certainly result in his leaving college and taking to the open road." Moreover, while the president had "found no evidence that he has spread vicious practices," he still felt that "the evidence being what it is, he cannot return to college here."

The president directly linked sexual transgression with a lack of general moral soundness and also felt that Schmidt's moral lapses explained the young man's reluctance to take steady work during the summer. Ironically, the president understood that Blair would be acting not on the grounds of the student's "moral turpitude," but on the basis of his "hypocrisy." At the beginning of the correspondence between the president and Blair, then, Schmidt was to be returned to the camp because of his laziness rather than any sexual transgression.

Yet the president was also worried about the effect that returning Schmidt to camp would have on him. While he believed that "such persons" should not be allowed to immigrate to Canada, he was concerned that the "return of the boy to camp may only increase the temptation to and the opportunities for the vices of which he boasts." Moreover, he contended that the student's letter indicated that he had the potential to recover from his moral lapse. He was anxious not to send Schmidt off without a kind word, fearing that the experience might destroy "all hope of his return to normal living." Despite his optimism for Schmidt's future moral rectitude, the president also believed he had a duty to protect the moral fibre of his students. Good character was needed both for participation in the university community and for citizenship, and it was the president's unofficial duty to foster it. Faulty character could not be tolerated and, indeed, justified deportation.

Surveillance of youth was not new to wartime. Students in residence traditionally faced a variety of rules that they often enforced themselves. Women, in particular, endured strict curfews, restrictions that were linked to the belief in the need to preserve their moral character and sexual purity.[15] Men, while given more freedom, were prohibited from gambling or drinking and were constantly reminded of standards of dress and comportment.[16] Still, moral and sexual restraints were loosening during the interwar years. As Paul Axelrod discovered for the 1930s, students attended a multitude of dances, holding them off campus if they were prohibited at denominational institutions.[17] Students also began discussing sexual issues and holding lectures on birth control and preparation for marriage.[18] Administrators' acceptance of such topics was not always forthcoming. In the late 1920s, the Social Sciences Club at the University of British Columbia held a debate on birth control. Despite the fact that the club had engaged a local minister to give the proceedings a high moral tone, the Board of Governors gave the club a dressing down for having brought unfavourable publicity to the campus.[19]

The holding of dances as well as lectures on birth control attests to the fact that university students were beginning to take a more open approach toward heterosexual activity. Compared with their counterparts in the United States, however, Canadian students pushed gently at the boundaries of moral and sexual propriety. While American surveys of college students in the 1930s illustrate a high level of sexual experimentation, Axelrod has found in interviews with graduates that there was a greater degree of sexual restraint among Canadian students. He argues that this moderation was due at least in part to the continuing influence of denominational colleges.[20] Sexual and moral purity was expected of students at both denominational and non-denominational universities and was enforced in a number of ways, such as through residence rules and the censorship of club activities.

Expectations of a wholesome campus also extended to students' intellectual and political endeavours. For example, during the 1930s, when an editor of the University of Toronto *Varsity* described the campus as seething with atheism, the editor lost his job and the paper was suspended.[21] Such action on the part of the administration indicates, among other things, the continuing understanding of the university as a Christian institution. Administrators were not the only ones concerned about the tone of campus activities. Through much of the twentieth century the RCMP kept an eye on the Student Christian Movement and other left-wing campus groups believed to be involved in radical activities and to have Communist ties.[22]

If surveillance addressed breaches of proper moral conduct, the task of educators was also to provide students with the tools to attain sexual and moral maturity. As Canadians grew concerned about the moral regeneration of their society, educators took the opportunity to attempt to understand the needs of Canada's youth and create strategies to ensure youth's proper development. The First Canadian Hazen Conference, which, in 1941, brought together educators

who were not only involved in personal counselling but concerned about the place of religion in higher education, was one such attempt.[23] [. . .]

The conference report stated that, because students arrived at university in late adolescence, and not as fully formed adults, the purpose of liberal education should be to address the whole person—the social and physical side as well as the intellectual. Universities, it contended, needed to pay more attention to four aspects of students' development: emotional independence from their family, engagement in heterosexual relations, the discovery of a vocation, and acceptance of a philosophy of life.[24] Each element was important in and of itself, but all were necessary if the student was to become a well-adjusted adult.

This lengthy and detailed Hazen report makes explicit many of the assumptions in the correspondence between Blair and the president. The report began by placing much of the blame for students' emotional immaturity on their families. Most parents, it contended, had failed to wean their children fully before sending them to university. Children who had not been taught to be independent, who did not feel secure in the love of their parents, who had been overprotected, or who had either too much or not enough discipline became homesick and hysterical at university, or broadcast their insecurity and attempted to assert their independence by throwing "conventions to the winds" and trying "to be tough and 'wild.'"[25] The family, and then the schools, create self-directed, self-controlled, and self-reliant children. Only by stimulating a critical mind, the report argued, could students become full members of society.[26]

The Hazen report reiterated beliefs common among Protestants. The family formed the basis of Christian society, yet with young men and women away in the services or working in recently expanded war industries, with the increase of divorce and drinking, venereal disease, and juvenile delinquency, as well as the continuing poor housing and health conditions in Canada, the stability of the family lay in question.[27] This crisis in family life, many believed, foretold the ruin of Canadian society. Such concerns during the war anticipated investigations in the post-war period, such as those by the Canadian Youth Commission, in which educators and civil servants explicitly linked family life to active citizenship, national stability, and the preservation of democracy. As one late 1940s report stated, "If democracy is to be a reality in community and national affairs, it obviously must begin in the home."[28] The family was increasingly perceived as the cradle of democracy, where a child's independence could be carefully nurtured or just as easily squashed by an authoritarian or neglectful parent.[29]

As the Hazen report forewarned in the early war years, parents could not always be counted upon to provide children with the necessary tools to participate fully in the community. Nor were Canadian universities providing adequate services for students with emotional problems. The Student Health Services of American universities should be adopted in Canada.[30] Dealing with students' emotional problems, the report stated, was part of the role of a liberal education, and guidance was needed "for the student to achieve personal values in any adequate fashion." It was the responsibility of the university to aid the student's development "as a person."[31]

Ensuring proper sexual development was, in the Hazen report, part of this responsibility. Drawing on Freudian terminology, the conference report saw the sexual development of youth as progressing through various stages, culminating in maturity through heterosexual union. It stated that adjustment to the opposite sex was usually far from complete in boys and girls entering college and that, in fact, completion could only be reached in "a happy marriage." "If adolescents do not accept their characteristic sex role during the years of middle and late adolescence,"

the report went on, "they may never do so." The few students who arrived with no interest in the opposite sex were either exhibiting "delayed maturity" or had "deep-seated emotional problems" that could cripple their development. Yet those interested in the opposite sex also had problems to face. Dating, petting, masturbation, continence, selecting a mate, and adjusting to marriage were all issues that had to be faced. Few were equipped, the report continued, to handle "the psychological aspects of sex and marriage."[32] Clearly, the conference participants linked proper adjustment to family life, a connection that Schmidt's letter failed to embody.

[. . .]

While the report's section on heterosexual relations used psychological language to understand proper sexual conduct, comments about sexual adjustment cannot be taken out of the broader context of the conference report. Historians have tended to describe the early twentieth century, especially within the university, as an era marked by a shift from moral concerns to social scientific ones.[33] But the use of psychological language took place within broader moral assumptions, particularly Christian ones. The Hazen Conference is a good example of the slippage between a continuing ideal of moral guardianship and the expertise of a trained set of professionals (psychiatrists, psychologists, health services) whom the university would increasingly come to rely upon.

For the conference participants, sexuality was embedded in broader ideals about citizenship and Christianity. Students needed not only to reach sexual maturity but also to learn self-reliance, independence, discipline, and self-control.[34] Sexual development could be achieved through courses on sex and marriage, greater opportunities for healthy interaction between the sexes in, for example, student-run extracurricular activities, and a more progressive educational system that would encourage the critical thinking ideally begun within the home.[35] The end purpose of all this development in the university was an ethic of service. Students, educators argued, needed to become active participants in the community. Their technical or professional training was the tool that a liberal education could teach them to put to use in service to society. The concept of the socially minded citizen was, of course, a useful one that also had a long history within the Christian tradition.

The conference participants clearly perceived the personal physiological and psychological needs and desires of adolescents to be part of the broader need to find purpose in life or universal principles they could follow. This search for a "philosophy of life" was presented as an open one, without ties to a particular religion,[36] though it was clearly rooted in Christian ideals. If the end of university development was service, this was, the conference report stated, also the cornerstone of Christianity.[37] "One of the chief reasons why university education is not a liberating process for students is that it often negates the New Testament verse—'He that saveth his life shall lose it, and he that loseth his life shall save it.' No one can find full self-expression and full freedom except in so far as he freely gives himself in service for others. This is not preaching—it is merely good psychology."[38] For the Hazen Conference on religion and life, psychology and Christianity reinforced each other, at least on broad social values.

Such sentiments were generally expressed within Canadian universities. Increasingly during the twentieth century, administrators shared both purpose and rhetoric. As Patricia Jasen states, "by the interwar period, presidents and principals of most universities in English Canada had developed a common style of speech and policy-making which emphasized the service function of their institutions."[39] Such communities arose out of the predominance of two particular intellectual strands. During the first decades of the twentieth century, educators were influenced by social gospel ideals and philosophical idealism. The social gospel, with its imperative to create the Kingdom of God on earth, and the idealist emphasis on the interconnectedness of reality and life, gave credence to the notion that all should be active participants in the community. Indeed, before the First World War, this notion helped fuel the development of the social sciences out of which psychology emerged. As the Hazen Conference indicates, psychology had an influence on religious thought. Yes the notion of personality development also arose out of a more liberal theology. William McGuire King suggests that in the American context, the concept of "personality" was central to the social gospel. "The fundamental claim of the social gospel," he contends, was the belief " . . . that religious self-realization manifests itself as a religious enthusiasm for humanity."[40]

Linking psychological language, philosophical idealism, and the ethic of service, Robert Falconer, the president of the University of Toronto in the 1930s, stated, "the University is at once a source of individual culture and of public service. It deepens and enriches personality, and through the enriched personality of its members it can be a servant of the whole nation."[41] This emphasis on the importance of social citizenship and service to the nation was heightened during the Second World War. Falconer's successor, H.J. Cody, reassured students in 1941 that their studies were part of their "preparation to serve the state in this time of grave national crisis" and that it was through the production of "trained and educated men and women" that the university served the country.[42] These prominent educators were drawing on liberal theology as well as on the language of the new social sciences in emphasizing their vision of the role of the student and the university in society.

For many administrators, then, the need to defend the nation was not simply a secular service. The roots of democracy, many argued, were Christian.[43] Students needed to enter the work world realizing that they had "duties to God and man as citizens of a democratic community."[44] Students in college were expected to search for both intellectual and spiritual values to ground their life in the eternal, for it was only as individuals recognized and incorporated the divine spirit into their lives that society could reach a higher level.[45] Indeed, their duty would continue in the post-war years. "The task of you and your generation," one commentator told graduating students in 1945, "is to re-establish a civilization based upon the supremacy of intellectual, moral and spiritual values. This is the task for which men of our nation, men of this college, and men of your year have given their lives. By the sacrifice of their lives they have increased your responsibility."[46]

The connection between Christianity, democracy, and service was also forcefully articulated within the Protestant press. Where educators focused on the role of students in Canadian society, commentators in the popular Christian press linked education to broader world issues. For them, improper education resulted in the "barbarism and brutality"[47] not only of Nazi Germany but also of Communist Russia, a theme that would become particularly prominent in the post-war period. Democracy could only be renewed through a strong spiritual life,[48] and many considered "the highest standards of democracy" to be "the standards of Christian living."[49] Only through a proper education melding faith and duty would students recognize their responsibility to use their abilities to ensure peace and liberty.[50] Thus private faith and public endeavour intertwined on the university campus. University students were envisioned as the natural leaders of the nation, and, as such, they were being prepared in the university not only for service to their country but for a Christian service. To become active participants in Canadian society, educators believed, university students should ideally be educated in "the home, the church, the school, [and] the university."[51]

The home and church would provide the roots for healthy growth, and the university would allow the spirit to blossom so that students could enter the workforce, create a family of their own, and contribute to the prosperity of the country.

Yet not all students fit within this version of productive citizenship. A month after writing the letter to his friend, Johann Schmidt found himself charged with, as he stated, "the intention of violating rules by the Director of Immigration and also with an immoral behaviour, to be more explicit, with homosexuality." In an attempt to defend himself, Schmidt acknowledged that his letter showed him "in a very bad light," but maintained he was not guilty of the charges. He presented three main arguments in his defence. First, he contended it had not occurred to him that his statements about liking men could be understood in an ambiguous manner, as anything other than friendship. Second, he stated he had written the letter late at night, had been depressed, and had been reading an author who described "similar feelings" and explained them as "'unconsciously sexual and as a development of the adolescent stage of boyhood." Thus, contradicting his first defence, Schmidt in some sense admitted to fearing he was sexually attracted to men. But he also contended that he had never been engaged sexually with a man; "that anybody could suspect me of such immorality," he said, "makes me blush." Finally, Schmidt argued that if inquiries into his moral conduct were made, he would be found to be an upright individual. He challenged his investigators to make inquiries of the men in the internment camp, his professors at the university, his roommate, and the women in the female residence. As he stated, "Girls appeal very much to me. . . . I only went steady with a girl in my first term and in my second term I took many girls out but did not go steady." Before the Second World War, casual dating was the norm and indicated popularity.[52] Schmidt, then, used the notion of a vigorous heterosexuality as proof of his good moral conduct.

Schmidt also explained what he had meant in reference to changing jobs. He considered himself a conscientious worker and argued that the farmers he had worked for had wanted him back. But he had not liked his work the summer before (he did not explain why) and was looking forward to changing farms as the fruit seasons changed, to regular hours, and to the chance, if the RCMP agreed, of a trip to James Bay with his roommate. Schmidt realized what was expected of him as a potential citizen and as a student during the war. Students at Canadian universities had been told clearly that they should be serious and upright members of the community. Those who did not perform well at mid-terms were hauled off to military authorities or, if not eligible for service, to their parents. But Schmidt argued that he was fulfilling all that was expected of him and more—eagerly entering the COTC, working on a farm, and even becoming a blood donor. "I never intended to disregard any regulations," he stated. "In the opposite it was always my ambition to show my gratitude to this country."

After reading Schmidt's letter of defence, the president began to see the case in a new light, and, on making inquiries, he found that Schmidt's moral conduct was sound. He came to feel that most of the misunderstandings were due to the fact that English was Schmidt's second language. The president thus wrote to Blair stating, "if he is innocent, I certainly cannot be a party to driving him to despair and bitterness. He is too able a lad to be treated harshly." The student's fate was also determined by the president's own beliefs about homosexuality. As he observed:

I may say further that what little experience I have had with the kind of pervert that we at first suspected him to be leads me to doubt his guilt. It would be almost practically impossible for a pervert, who can be as often a medical case as a purely moral problem, to live in a men's residence for a year without giving rise to some suspicions at least. My inquiries among responsible students have revealed no such suspicions, and I am coming to feel that this is strong presumptive evidence that we were misled by his unfortunate language. As I have said earlier, I am not yet prepared to make a final judgement, but I am definitely hesitant about taking any drastic action.

While Schmidt's language had initially condemned him, lack of proof of any physical activity with another man vindicated him. The president's belief that homosexuals could not hide their sexual desires proved to be Schmidt's ultimate defence.

Despite the increasing influence of psychology, the president mixed medical and moral language in attempting to come to terms with sexual issues. As historian George Chauncey has revealed, "pervert" was a technical term used by such regulatory agents as the police and doctors as well as by moral reformers.[53] "Pervert" or "perversion" was first used in the late nineteenth century by psychologists.[54] The term pervert was used to define the conventionally masculine man transgressing proper sexual boundaries, who was condemned as psychologically and morally deficient.[55] Historians and sociologists of sexuality, while understanding psychologists' categorizations as judgmental or moral condemnations, rarely link these condemnations to the broader Protestant culture of British, American, or Canadian society. If the Hazen Conference rooted sexual transgressions in psychological terms, the president's description of Schmidt's sexuality as "moral turpitude" and "vicious practices," and the fear these qualities could be spread to others, suggest that the medical understanding of the homosexual as a particular personality type had still not become the dominant discourse. Gary Kinsman suggests that, in the 1950s, "psychiatric definitions of sex deviation and homosexuality became firmly established,"[56] but certainly in the early 1940s the language of social science and of morality continued to overlap.

Moral and medical discourses existed side by side for the president and for the authors of the Hazen Conference report, indicating that the medical language just being developed in this period could not be divorced from the Christian moral canvas on which it was inscribed. While psychologists saw homosexuality as a medical problem, many leaders within the Canadian universities and mainline churches of mid-century viewed it also as a moral one. This article reveals that, in wartime, university educators saw themselves as training the private individual for public service. As the head of a denominational university, the president understood himself to be playing an important public role. His college's involvement in such events as the Hazen Conference suggests that the university community perceived itself as engaged with other concerned Christians in the process of shaping future citizens.

If, in Gary Kinsman's phrase, sexuality and morality as "socially produced and regulated,"[57] it is evident that the university was one of the prime sites for such activity. The university helped construct, reinforce, and regulate the ideal of heterosexuality, seeing family as the outcome of proper relations between men and women. Its purpose was to recreate a particular type of citizen: industrious, Christian, heterosexual, capable of leadership—none of these elements could be missing from the whole, well-adjusted person. [. . .] The president, faculty, and even the students envisioned and worked to produce a particular type of student. But when such methods did not work, the coercive arm of the university was never far afield, as the secretive investigation of Johann Schmidt illustrates.

NOTES

1. See, for example, Michael Gauvreau, *The Evangelical Century: College and Creed in English Canada from the Great Revival to the Great Depression* (Montreal and Kingston: McGill-Queen's University Press, 1991); A.B. McKillop, *Matters of Mind: The University in Ontario, 1791–1951* (Toronto: University of Toronto Press, 1994); Marguerite Van Die, *An Evangelical Mind: Nathanael Burwash and the Methodist Tradition in Canada, 1839–1919* (Montreal and Kingston: McGill-Queen's University Press, 1989).

2. "President Stresses Need for Balanced Outlook," *Varsity*, 25 Sept. 1941, 7; "Klinck Urges Students Curtail Frosh Rites," *Ubyssey*, 24 Sept. 1940, 1.

3. Frederick G. Gibson, *"To Serve and Yet Be Free": Queen's University, 1917–1961* (Montreal: McGill-Queen's University Press, 1983), 181.

4. Nancy Kiefer and Ruth Roach Pierson, "The War Effort and Women Students at the University of Toronto, 1939–45," in Paul Axelrod and John G. Reid, eds, *Youth, University and Canadian Society: Essays in the Social History of Higher Education* (Montreal and Kingston: McGill-Queen's University Press, 1989), 162.

5. Gibson, *"To Serve and Yet Be Free,"* 185.

6. "Delta Gamma," Dalhousie *Alumni News*, April 1943, 18; Report of Dean of Women in the Annual Report of the President of the University of British Columbia, 1941–2, 40; Kiefer and Pierson, "The War Effort and Women Students," 162, 164, 175–6. For Ontario universities more generally, see McKillop, *Matters of Mind*, 523–6.

7. Kiefer and Pierson, "The War Effort and Women Students," 162.

8. University of British Columbia Archives, Klinck Papers, box 1, file 2, Address to Freshmen Students during Newcomers' Organizational Period, 18 Sept. 1942.

9. Kiefer and Pierson, "The War Effort and Women Students," 162.

10. Ibid., 168, 171–2.

11. Adelaide M. Plumptre, *Varsity*, 15 Oct. 1941, 2, quoted in Kiefer and Pierson, "The War Effort and Women Students," 170.

12. Irving Abella and Harold Troper, *None Is Too Many: Canada and the Jews of Europe, 1933–1948* (Toronto: Lester and Orpen Dennys 1983), 7–9.

13. Barbara Roberts, *Whence They Came: Deportation from Canada 1900–1935* (Ottawa: University of Ottawa Press, 1988), 3.

14. Abella and Troper, *None Is Too Many*, 7–9.

15. United Church of Canada/Victoria University Archives (UCA/VUA), Records of the President's Office, 89.130v, box 71–9, Residence Regulations 1945–6; University of King's College Students' Handbook, 1940.

16. UCA/VUA, Burwash Hall and Men's Residence Committee, 87.195v, box 1–5, Burwash Hall, 1935; ibid., box 1–1, Victoria University Men's Residences, 1946–7; University of King's College Archives, Calendars 1930–1, 1939–40. Such moral requirements remained in effect well into the twentieth century. See Dalhousie University Archives, MS-1-3, A226, Dalhousie President's Office, Buildings—Men's residence (Howe Hall), Dalhousie Men's Residence Handbook, c. 1959.

17. Paul Axelrod, *Making a Middle Class: Student Life in English Canada during the Thirties* (Montreal and Kingston: McGill-Queen's University Press, 1990), 113.

18. Ibid., 116.

19. Samuel Leonard Simpson, "The Social Sciences Club—A Study in Sex and Censorship," in Philip A. Krigg et al., *The Way We Were: Anecdote—Antic—Absurdity at the UBC* (Vancouver: UBC Alumni Association 1987), 36.

20. Axelrod, Making a Middle Class, 115.

21. Ibid., 137.

22. Catherine Gidney, "Poisoning the Student Mind? The Student Christian Movement at the University of Toronto, 1920–1965," *Journal of the Canadian Historical Association*, new series, 8 (1997): 150; S.R. Hewitt, "Spying 101: The RCMP's Secret Activities at the University of Saskatchewan, 1920–1971," *Saskatchewan History* (Fall 1995): 24.

23. UCA/VUA, SCM, box 84-53, file First Hazen Conference 1941, "The Influence of the University in Canada on the Life of the Student,"

24. UCA/VUA, SCM, box 84-53, file First Hazen Conference 1941, "The Influence of the University in Canada on the Life of the Student," 9–14.

25. Ibid., 9.

26. Ibid.

27. Editorial, "The Spirit Is Essential," *United Church Observer*, 15 Feb. 1943, 4; Editorial, "Christian Family Week," ibid., 1 May 1944, 4; Mrs Hugh MacMillan, "Reconstructing Family Life," ibid., 15.

28. Canadian Youth Commission, *Youth Speaks Out on Citizenship* (Toronto: Ryerson Press, 1948), 53.

29. Ibid., 104–5.

30. UCA/VUA, SCM, box 84-53, file First Hazen Conference 1941, "The Influence of the University in Canada on the Life of the Student," 10.

31. Ibid., 8.

32. UCA/VUA, SCM, box 84-53, file First Hazen Conference 1941, "The Influence of the University in Canada on the Life of the Student," 10.

33. See McKillop, *Matters of Mind*; Marlene Shore, *The Science of Social Redemption: McGill, the Chicago School, and the Origins of Social Research in Canada* (Toronto: University of Toronto Press, 1987); Doug Owram, *The Government Generation: Canadian Intellectuals and the State, 1900–1945* (Toronto: University of Toronto Press, 1986).

34. UCA/VUA, SCM, box 84-53, file, First Hazen Conference 1941, "The Influence of the University in Canada on the Life of the Student,'" 9.

35. Ibid., 10–13.

36. Ibid., 14.

37. Ibid., 9.

38. Ibid., 12.

39. Patricia Jasen, "The English Canadian Liberal Arts Curriculum: An Intellectual History, 1880–1950" (PhD dissertation, University of Manitoba, 1987), 203.

40. William McGuire King, "An Enthusiasm for Humanity: The Social Emphasis in Religion and Its Accommodation in Protestant Theology," in Michael J. Lacey, ed., *Religion and Twentieth-Century American Intellectual Life* (Cambridge: Woodrow Wilson International Center for Scholars and Cambridge University Press, 1989), 53.

41. Robert Falconer, "The Place of the University in National Life," *University of Toronto Quarterly* 4, 3 (1934–5). See also Gibson, *"To Serve and Yet Be Free": Queen's University, 1917–1961*, 202.

42. "President Stressed Need for Balanced Outlook," *Varsity*, 25 Sept 1941, 1.

43. Falconer, "The Place of the University in National Life."

44. Annual Report of the President of the University of Toronto, 1941–2, 17.

45. UCA/VUA, Records of the President's Office, 89.130v, box 37-14, Baccalaureate Service by Walter T. Brown, Principal Victoria College, 19 April 1942.

46. Ibid., Baccalaureate Service 1945, no author.

47. Principal J.G. Brown, Union College, "The Church's Present Educational Policy," *United Church Observer*, 15 Aug. 1942, 16.

48. Editorial, "Education," ibid., 1 Nov. 1942, 4; George E. Levy, "Democracy and Religion," ibid., 15 July 1942, 15; Editorial, "Education for Life," ibid., 1 Nov. 1944, 4. For the postwar period, see Canadian Youth Commission, *Youth Speaks Out on Citizenship*.

49. Ruth Brownbridge, "Building Today for a Christian World," *United Church Observer*, 1 Jan. 1945, 10.

50. David B. Roe, *King's College Record*, Encaenia 1946, 22.

51. "The President Looks at the University," University of British Columbia *Graduate Chronicle*, Jan. 1945. For a similar comment in the Christian press, see "Christian Family Week," *United Church Observer*, 15 April 1942, 5.

52. Beth L. Bailey, *From the Front Porch to Back Seat: Courtship in Twentieth-Century America* (Baltimore and London: Johns Hopkins University Press, 1988), 26.

53. George Chauncey, *Gay New York: Gender, Urban Culture, and the Making of the Gay Male World, 1890–1940* (New York: Basic Books 1994), 14, 145–6.

54. Jonathan Ned Katz, *The Invention of Heterosexuality* (New York: Dutton Books, 1995), 20–2.

55. Chauncey, *Gay New York*, 122–3.

56. Gary Kinsman, *The Regulation of Desire: Sexuality in Canada* (Montreal and New York: Black Rose Books, 1987), 115.

57. Ibid., 15.

Chapter 9

The Rise of the Welfare State

READINGS

Primary Documents

1   From *Report on Social Security for Canada*, Leonard Marsh

2   From *The Dawn of Ampler Life*, Charlotte Whitton

Historical Interpretations

3   From *Social Policy and Practice in Canada: A History*, Alvin Finkel

4   From "Africville and the Dynamics of State Power in Postwar Canada," Tina Loo

INTRODUCTION

In the period following the First World War, Canada, among a number of other nations, took some initial steps toward policies that we now consider to be the core of the welfare state. These included enacting veterans' and survivors' benefits and proposing unemployment relief for all Canadians. This trend accelerated during (and especially after) the Second World War. Part of the explanation for this acceleration was that Canadians (and others) had seen how effective the national government had been during wartime, and urged governments to tackle peacetime problems using the same sort of planning and vigorous action. This basic shift involved the argument that complex modern societies are more stable and prosperous when their working-age citizens do not have to fear starvation in the event of injury, illness, or unemployment, and when the aged do not have to fear poverty in their declining years. This shift had extended, by the 1960s, to a system of universal health care regardless of one's ability to pay. At least to some, the obvious provider of this social safety net was the state. But other people were not in favour of such drastic changes to the existing order. They feared that making life too easy for the average citizen would cause some to stop contributing to society, living on what the state provided rather than seeking work. This difference of opinion is evident in our primary sources. Leonard Marsh wrote his *Report on Social Security for Canada* as a kind of blueprint for the post-war era, and he clearly patterned his plan on the system set out for the United Kingdom by Sir William Beveridge. The basic idea of Marsh's plan was to guarantee a minimum level of income for citizens and their dependants, thus keeping the economy stable through consumer spending. Without such measures, he argued, economic times would become even tougher as people who were laid off could not buy goods and services, leading to even more layoffs. Charlotte Whitton disagreed with this idea, preferring to let local or provincial authorities take care of local welfare needs, and to let the market, rather than a board of experts, determine a decent living wage. In our first historical interpretation, Alvin Finkel tells the story of how Canada acquired a health care system that figured out a way of bringing doctors more patients. Canada's geography played a role in this story, pushing Canadians in remote areas to demand care that a market system would be unlikely to provide. Even if the expansion of the state after the Second World War had an overall positive impact on the lives of Canadians, not all of its interventions were entirely successful. In her article, Tina Loo discusses one of the more controversial state interventions of the 1960s: the destruction of Africville, Nova Scotia. The promoters of this municipal scheme hoped to improve the lives of an almost entirely black community, located at the north end of Halifax, by razing this destitute neighbourhood and relocating its inhabitants elsewhere in the city. Despite good intentions, this scheme destroyed a community without improving the lives of all Africvillers. This article highlights the nature and limitation of the Canadian welfare state as developed after 1945.

QUESTIONS FOR CONSIDERATION

1. Was Marsh advocating handouts to everyone?
2. Why did Whitton oppose the way that Marsh wanted to implement social security for Canadians?
3. Do Canada's size and sparse population make the welfare state a rather obvious choice?
4. What were some of the objections that doctors and other health professionals had to the idea of medicare?
5. What explains the failure of the Africville relocation?

SUGGESTIONS FOR FURTHER READING

Raymond Blake, *From Rights to Needs: A History of Family Allowances in Canada, 1929–92* (Vancouver: UBC Press, 2008).

Lara A. Campbell, *Respectable Citizens: Gender, Family, and Unemployment in Ontario's Great Depression* (Toronto: University of Toronto Press, 2009).

Nancy Christie, *Engendering the State: Family, Work, and Welfare in Canada* (Toronto: University of Toronto Press, 2000).

Alvin Finkel, *Social Policy and Practice in Canada: A History* (Waterloo: Wilfrid University Press, 2005).

Antonia Maioni, *Parting at the Crossroads: The Emergence of Health Insurance in the United States and Canada* (Princeton: Princeton University Press, 1998).

Dominique Marshall, *The Social Origins of the Welfare State: Quebec Families, Compulsory Education, and Family Allowances 1940–1955* (Waterloo: Wilfrid Laurier University Press, 2006).

Jennifer Nelson, *Razing Africville: A Geography of Racism* (Toronto: University of Toronto Press, 2009).

Jennifer Anne Stephen, *Pick One Intelligent Girl: Employability, Domesticity and the Gendering of Canada's Welfare State, 1939–1947* (Toronto: University of Toronto Press, 2007).

Shirley Tillotson, *Contributing Citizens: Modern Charitable Fundraising and the Making of the Welfare State, 1920–66* (Vancouver: UBC Press, 2008).

Primary Documents

1   From Leonard Marsh, *Report on Social Security for Canada*, 1943 (Ottawa: King's Printer, 1943), 6–19.

1. CANADIAN PERSPECTIVE

The war, or rather the unprecedented production effort that the war has called forth in Canada, has changed the face of the Dominion so far as social needs and social security problems are concerned. It is not only that mass unemployment has been eliminated, with such unemployment as still remains limited to special problems of transferring between jobs, production hold-ups in industrial plants, and other types of interruption of working time which do not leave workers completely without prospect of further employment. In spite of the heavy demands of the Treasury for revenue to finance the war, consumer incomes have increased in several sections of the population. Earnings in many families have been brought above their previous levels through better-paid or more regular work on the part of the main breadwinner, the employment of additional members of the family, or even in some cases through the allowances now payable from state funds for the members of that family who are serving the country in uniform. There are still broken families—in some respects more than ever

before—and not only because of the absence of fathers or sons overseas, but because members of the families have found work away from their hometowns, and again because many housewives are now full-time or part-time workers on one of the home fronts of the war effort. There are still problems of distress, for war bereavements have been added, and on a growing scale, to those of normal times. But full employment, whatever may be its special wartime pressures, has removed chief characteristic of the Canadian welfare picture as it was in the thirties. It has erased from the lives, if not the memories, of many thousands of families, the hopelessness and tragedy of seeing no means of making a livelihood in sight, and no means of maintenance other than doles from municipal or provincial governments, unskilled and dispiriting relief work, or assistance from the voluntary charitable agencies in the cities of Canada where these existed.

It is certain that the background of social and economic insecurity has not been entirely forgotten by many who are employed or contributing to family earnings now; and it is equally certain it must not be forgotten in projecting our minds forward to the post-war period, in planning in advance what measures should be taken to deal with the re-employment problems of that period, and on a wider plane seeking to give reality to the aspirations and hopes which the peoples of the world are more and more clearly voicing: that organized provision will be made in the post-war world for the risks and contingencies of family like that are beyond the capacity of most to them to finance adequately from their own resources.

These risks and contingencies are not solely those of unemployment. But it is understandable, against the background of the depression thirties, why unemployment should dominate most other considerations. If earning power stops all else is threatened. For the moment it is not necessary to pause to distinguish the differences in the risks of unemployment, sickness, accident, more normal but none the less serious events from the point of view of the working budget such as the increase in the number of children; and other factors. There are certain basic lessons to be learned from the experience of the thirties in which all the hazards of life—at least as they appear to the low and middle income groups—seemed to be swallowed up in the great vortex of unemployment.

The first is that provision for unemployment, both economically and socially, is the first and greatest need in a security program designed for the modern industrial economy. A second is that in the absence of organized provision for particular categories or types of need and contingency, unemployment relief—itself the extension of provision intended only for destitution of multiple forms—draws into itself all other kinds of need: sickness, disability, widowhood, desertion, loss of residence requirements and so forth. Provision for simple destitution without any particular analysis as to cause may be barely justifiable when the scale of such assistance is small, as it was in the small parish

or village of long ago when only a few persons in each community found themselves at any particular time without any means of subsistence and beyond the support of any relatives. It is completely indefensible, and of a nature to defeat efficient and constructive administration, once it attains national dimensions.

Canada has experienced all the problems of undifferentiated relief provision, and the consequence of having little or no measures designed for specific causes of distress and need. These deficiencies, in point of fact, are not solely in what is usually known as social security legislation. Some of them are due to the inability of municipal governments, whether in terms of finance or of administrative facilities, to handle many of the problems which constitutionally may still be interpreted as their responsibility. The basic framework of government itself has still not been adapted in any radical fashion—except recently for the vast effort of the war—from that which at the time of Confederation seemed proper for a country of the New World that did not know the modern problems of unemployment or public health or lack of economic opportunity, and was still in very large measure a constellation of small communities.

It would be a mistake to assume that a social security program is entirely a matter of specific pieces of legislation, each covering a field marked off for itself alone. Social insurance involves an administrative organization, which is important for Canada not solely because it is a federal community but because of its problems of sheer distance. The proper methods for decentralization and regional administration demand the most careful consideration. None the less this much is clear. The only rational way to cope with the large and complicated problem of the insecurities of working and family life is by recognizing and legislating for particular categories or areas of risk or need. One of the contributions made by the social insurances, almost without the change being observed, is the advent of classified maintenance or treatment, or what in some countries has been called categorical provision. As will be indicated later, there is still need for development or rationalization of some of these categories. But this much may be said in advance. The establishment of organized provision for even one defensible area of need, as, for example, through the institution of unemployment insurance of health insurance, makes immensely easier the handling and the sorting out of the other types of need which still remain.

The Method of Social Insurance

An explanation of these areas of social contingencies will be made in a succeeding Section. First, will be well to state simply what social insurance means, and why the approach through social insurance methods is appropriate. There are three basic reasons:

(a) In modern economic life there are certain hazards and contingencies, which have to be met, some of them completely unpredictable, some of them uncertain as to time but in other ways reasonably to be anticipated. They may be met in hit-and-miss fashion by individual families or may be met by forms of collective provision. Some of the risks may never strike any individuals or families; but we know from experience that, *collectively speaking*, these problems or needs are always present at some place in the community or among the population.

(b) For a large proportion of the population, incomes are not sufficient to take care of these contingencies through their own resources. It is no answer to this point to say that this would not be true if wage rates and earnings were higher than at present. As one of the Rowell-Sirois reports has summed up the matter, "It is impossible to establish a wage which will allow every worker and his family to meet the heavy disabilities of serious illness, prolonged unemployment, accident and premature death. These are budget-shattering contingencies that strike most unevenly." The inadequacy of even moderate incomes to provide for such things as major illnesses has now been measured by more than one authoritative investigation.

(c) The third principle, which really links together the first two, is that of the collective pooling of risks. Social insurance is the application on a much larger scale of the principle of pooling which has long been the basis of insurance in the more restricted sense (commercial insurance against fire, etc.). A great number of people may be liable to a certain risk, but only a few of them at any one time. At the time the hazard strikes, they may draw on the resources gathered through the contributions of many, including their own.

The understanding of social insurance, however, is still confused because too much emphasis is placed on the second word and too little on the first word of the phrase. Social insurance brings in the resources of the state, i.e., the resources of the community as a whole, or in a particular case that part of the resources which may be garnered together through taxes or contributions. It does not mean, more particularly for phenomena subject to such variability as unemployment, that there must be a precise actuarial adjustment of premiums to risk in each individual case. The contributors who do not draw on the fund help to aid the unlucky ones who suffer unemployment or some social casualty. Some social insurance provision may have to be frankly viewed as no more than the gathering together of a fund for a contingency whose total dimensions are uncertain, but whose appearance in some form or magnitude is certain. In any circumstances it is better than having no collective reserves at all, or leaving the burdens to be met by individuals in whatever way they can. Of course, the more refinement that can be made, in the light of experience, between revenues required and current disbursements, the more systematic and economical for its particular task the social insurance fund becomes. The most important and serviceable of these devices is the provision, now written into all modern legislation, for careful annual review of the finances of the scheme, and their relation to current contribution and benefit rates. [. . .]

As experience with social insurance has grown, there has been increasing recognition of the advantages of this pooling of individual risks by collective means along with state control and participation. [. . .]

It may be questioned why, if these extensions of the pooling idea are valid, social insurance should not be financed solely by taxation, rather than the contributory method. The answer depends a good deal on practical considerations. If a widely comprehensive and unified scheme is not possible immediately, contributions serve to demarcate the section of the population for which it is intended to cater. Secondly, they have certain distinct administrative advantages, through applications, records and other ways, relating the individual directly to the service rendered or benefit received, and serving to facilitate the enforcement of conditions attached to benefit. But whatever the method of assessing the contributions, since it is in the interest of the insured person to maintain them regularly, his relation to the administration is more likely to be a responsible one. Generally speaking, the wider the area over which it is sought to make benefits available, the more important this becomes. And the proprietary interest which citizens as contributors come to feel in the satisfactory working of the scheme is not without psychological as well as administrative virtues.

None of these considerations should obscure the possibility of combining both contributory and tax-revenue methods. In effect,

it is this combination which the Beveridge recommendations propose to develop extensively, and the combination has been effectively in operation in the comprehensive New Zealand system for several years. It is important to note, indeed, that state contributions or outright grants (e.g., in the form of marriage or maternity grants) administered in conjunction with an insurance system are much more likely to be payable without introducing the flavour of charity or the equal disability of irresponsible gratuity.

This is really the logical outcome of planning a better distribution of existing or anticipated income, both in point of time and as between the whole population or certain classes of it. Much of it is not necessarily additional expenditure, but the replacing of inefficient expenditures by more efficient methods. This is best recognized today in the case of health insurance. Large expenditures are already made both by governments and by citizens for medical care, much of it ill-advised, much of it in the later stages of an illness or disease when it is least able to be effective. Taxes in modern communities are similarly a major method of redistributing incomes, and of securing through individual contributions certain objects of collective expenditure. Social insurance administration, of course, brings to the disbursement of payments and services certain appropriate conditions. But the ability to put these conditions into effect on a fair and uniform basis is one of its major advantages. The genius of social insurance is that it enlists the direct support of the classes most likely to benefit, and enlists equally the participation and controlling influence of the state, at the same time as it avoids the evil of pauperization, and the undemocratic influence of excessive state philanthropy.

Relation to the Post-War World

The purpose of this report is to look forward, not backward. It would not serve this purpose if it were not geared closely to consideration of the vast economic and social changes which are going on now, and which must continue only with the difference of changes in purpose and direction, once the war is over. There have been certain compelling arguments for the community types of social provision ever since the growth of large industrial communities. But there are additional reasons, and some reasons which change the force of the old ones, for planning the overhaul and extension of our social legislation at this time.

The first is that social security has become accepted as one of the things for which the peoples of the world are fighting. It is one of the concrete expressions of "a better world" which is particularly real to those who knew unemployment, destitution, inadequate medical care and the like in the depression periods before the war. To others the idea of better social security measures may be less of a reaction from previous hard experience; but it is an intelligible recognition that it is one way of realizing nationally a higher standard of living, and of securing more freedom and opportunity through the use of such income as is available once social insurance has taken care of the minimum.

Whatever assessment may be placed on the first and rather broad interest in social security, a second one is completely realistic and timely. The end of the war means demobilization of much of the civilian as well as the uniformed population and, no matter how short may be the period of transition, there are risks and difficulties attached to the process of re-employment against which all appropriate facilities must be mobilized. It should not be forgotten, in this connection, that the re-employment problems of the post-war period include the reassembling of many thousands of families.

A third and equally realistic consideration is that the transition period will show in more marked contrast than any other, differences in respect of social provision for Canadian citizens when they are in the army or in some other branch of the services, and when in ordinary civilian life. The provisions which the state extends to its armed forces and their dependants in time of war,

and to ex-service men's families after war, go far along all the avenues of what is usually comprised in "social security"—provision for children's maintenance, widowhood, medical care, disability, unemployment, retraining, and other contingencies.

The standards and allowances and the attention given to many varieties of need will, rightly or wrongly, be measured against standards of livelihood and welfare in the civilian world. Some of these differences may be entirely justifiable. But nothing short of an objective appraisal of existing legislation, the requirements of transition, and the adjustment of such civilian deficiencies as may have been rendered more prominent by improved attention to groups affected by the pressure of war, will meet the situation.

The final point in gauging the need and validity of a social security program in post-war Canada is only indirectly a welfare matter at all, but it is a strategic factor in economic policy generally whose importance cannot be overemphasized. One of the necessities for economic stability is the maintenance of the flow of purchasing power at the time when munitions and other factories are closing down and war activity in many other spheres is being liquidated. Sound social insurance, which is a form of investment in physical health, morale, educational opportunities for children, and family stability, is a desirable and a comparatively easy vehicle of expenditure. It is not only an eminently appropriate peacetime alternative for expenditures now being devoted to destruction: it is also a form of using some of the deferred backlog of consumer expenditure to which reference is so often made only in terms of radios, frigidaires and other tangible consumers' goods. In this perspective, a wide and properly integrated scheme of social insurance and welfare provision of $100,000,000 or $500,000,000 is not to be regarded with the alarm which, with inadequate understanding, it might otherwise occasion.

[. . .]

Subjects Not Within the Scope of the Report

This report addresses itself particularly to those forms of individual and family need which arise when earnings are impaired or interrupted by unemployment, illness or accident; to the economic problems which are directly incurred by failing capacity through age, or loss of support through disability or death; and to the family contingencies requiring exceptional expenditure, particularly those connected with birth, death and marriage. There are, of course, a number of fields of social welfare provision which might be considered in any exhaustive survey of social facilities. Nutrition has become so important a matter in itself that it is now a separate chapter in any social welfare book. The proper provision of housing, and the elimination of

bad housing, is so universally recognized as a fundamental attack on many social ills that it also is a separate topic in itself. There are certain inventories—of hospitals, sanatoria, etc. or of institutions for orphans, crippled children, etc.—which raise questions of the adequacy of our capital equipment no matter what legislative provision there may be for care. The advent of health insurance will raise some of these questions more prominently. Education is of course a fundamental not only in social welfare but for many other aspects of civilian life. Better provision for passing the young worker from school to employment, and codes governing juvenile labour, would not be fully rounded out without attention to the treatment of juvenile delinquency. These and other problems will not be forgotten by anyone who has in mind for the future the fullest utilization of our human resources.

2 From Charlotte Whitton, *The Dawn of Ampler Life* (Toronto: Macmillan, 1943), 1–7, 9–10, 14–19.

A MEMO FOR CANADA

1. Some Definitions and Premises

Before discussing measures of social security, it might be well to attempt to define the term itself. In recent years, in the United States, and now in the Beveridge Report, the words have been given a special interpretation. "Social Security" is used by Beveridge to denote "the securing of an income to take the place of earnings when they are interrupted by unemployment, sickness or accident, etc. Primarily, Social Security means security of income up to a minimum."[1]

Surely, if Social Security is to be offered to men and women as an ideal to fire them to sacrifice and achievement it must be more than that. The world that fights this battle through will not be satisfied with anything so negative as stability or security, within or at some

position to which human progress has already advanced. Its people will want a concept of dynamic action lifting life forward in a great surge of freedom and unity of purpose. To the definition of such hopes might the term Social Security more properly be applied—something offering the vision of humanity secure and happy, enjoying that peace of mind which only a sense of safety can bring. The structure of a fuller life, in a freer, better world cannot be built upon the one pier of freedom from want: it must rest upon the cornerstones of all four freedoms—with spiritual stability in freedom of worship, intellectual strength in freedom of speech, political growth in freedom from fear, and economic security in freedom from want.

What has been so generally described as Social Security is therefore really not that at all but just "Income Security," in which narrower meaning the Beveridge Report really discusses it throughout.

Income Security calls for economic planning on the one hand and welfare planning on the other. Economic Planning should be directed to the gearing of the State's productive mechanism to assure to all, able to work, continuous gainful occupation, with such fair return for the use of the labour, skill or means of each, as to assure livelihood for the worker and the worker's dependants at a reasonable level of decency and security. Welfare Planning should seek to assure, within the State, the maintenance of such health, educational and welfare facilities as will bring the opportunity of their good use within the range of all people, but, about and behind these services, there must also be other resources, whereby in loss or impairment of income, the worker and his dependants are protected against preventable or unnecessary suffering or distress.

Some General Premises

Certain premises can probably be taken for granted in Canadian discussions of income security today. There will be general agreement that the purpose and organization of production, within the State, must be directed, to greater degree than in the past, to the maintenance of livelihood for all the people at a level consistent not only with survival but with decency and human dignity.

There will also be no question that this should be sought primarily by the maintenance, not so much of "full employment" (which unconsciously assumes a national economy, predominantly industrial and using human power on a wage basis) but of "gainful occupation" for all the population at the highest possible level, with continuity of work and remuneration, in wages, prices for goods or in other return sufficient to assure reasonable self-support.

There will be further concurrence that, no matter how well meshed or stringently controlled the organization of work opportunity, production and distribution may be,

exigencies will arise to throw the system out of gear and threaten the continuance of gainful occupation on a self-supporting basis, both over large groups and for the individual worker. The force of public conviction undoubtedly recognizes and accepts the obligation of collective responsibility to keep such exigencies to the minimum and to assure community provision for them when they do arise. [. . .]

There will be debate but not serious disagreement in Canada as to these requisites to national well-being:

1. The development of resources and production, geared to assurance of the highest possible level of continuous gainful occupation on a self-supporting basis for all workers, whether on wages or self-employed.
2. A basic system of Social Utilities, affording educational, health, and welfare services for all the people, under varying auspices and available on varying bases.
3. A correlated system of Social Assistance, paying allowances, grants, or relief against impairment of income, from non-predictable or individual contingencies, on a basis of means and need in each case, and, for circumstances and citizens, not coverable by insurance benefits or pensions.
4. A system of Income Insurance, paying benefits and pensions to afford protection against impairment of income from predictable and insurable exigencies and applicable to insurable elements in the population.

Where real question immediately arises, is in the fundamental objective to which this planning is to be directed, the extension of protection of these varying types of provision over the respective elements of the population, and the administrative, constitutional and financial processes involved therein.

2. The Canadian Scene

The Dominion of Canada is the achievement of a small people with a great faith in their own strength. Initiative and enterprise meant opportunity, and opportunity, with integrity and thrift, meant security. The years between the two wars dealt, ruthlessly and cruelly, with the Canadian's superb and simple confidence in his own destiny but they did not destroy the essential vigour and buoyancy of this country. For there is vitality in the land itself, in the vibrant silence of the forests, in the quiet sense of growth in the prairie soil, the pounding power in the rushing streams. Energy, ambition and the instinct of thrift still are bred in the people, as a whole, born of their background and renewed in the necessity of preparation, always, for the sharp, harsh changes of the seasons with constant adaptation to their needs. No plan for security, with freedom and opportunity, can be well imposed upon such a people: it must be a growth from the nature and background of the land itself, a fulfillment in which each different element in our life shall have contributed its strength.

It is well that in this process Canada should draw upon the experience of other peoples, older in story and schooled in the technique of protecting life against the buffeting of its exigencies. And, among all States, it is natural that this country should look particularly to the two with whom comparison is most valid—the United Kingdom, from whom many of the basic principles of our social legislation have derived side by side with the procedures of the Quebec Civil Code; and the United States of America, the tempo of whose life beats so insistently upon our own. But this should not mean the importation of the systems of other lands, and a straining to fit them to our needs. Rather, we should seek the evolution of a Canadian wrap, with the wool thereon as distinctively the product of our own experience as our own home-spun designs. This calls for knowledge and love of our land, inventive imagination and courage, if the fabric of our social planning is to afford protection against the thrusts of circumstance.

Canada must be seen for what she is, not in terms of the crowded, matured life of Europe's twenty odd States and five hundred and twenty millions of people on an area less extensive than our own; nor yet in those of the compact unified life of the United Kingdom, with almost four times our population, working 90 per cent in industry, business or commerce, on a base no larger than the average of a dozen of the larger counties of Ontario or Quebec, and affording an intimacy and efficacy of organization just unattainable in any land of our extent. Nor can the United States of America be our precept, for her great territory, continentally less than our own, is occupied by twelve times our population. Moreover, her balanced economy rests on the temperateness of the South whereas ours must meet the physical challenge of that two-fifths of our domain lying within the Yukon and the Northwest Territories and containing less population than a large USA or British town.

[. . .]

Across three thousand miles, from sea to sea, her population stretches in two narrow bands, contiguous to the main transportation systems, clotted at ports and junction points into heavy urban, even metropolitan, centres; dwelling, in the older farmlands, in pleasant friendly clusters; in others and in forest and hinterland as scattered, lone and isolated as the people of the Norwegian fiords or the Russian steppes. With her great water-power close to mineral and forest wealth, she supports the strange anomaly of heavy industrial development in the midst of wild, barely accessible and isolated lands, often incapable of providing the supplementary products essential to their indigenous industries. Two great cities now hold 20 per cent of all our population, while nearly a half dwells in villages of less than 500 persons or in the open country, or in these hinterlands; a third lives in the towns and smaller cities.

[. . .]

The relative life of the provinces varies widely. Ontario and Quebec are similar in their widely diversified and balanced activities. British Columbia also enjoys a fairly equitable economy. In the Maritime Provinces, nearly a quarter of the people are engaged in agriculture; and in the Prairie provinces, 45 per cent, Alberta and Saskatchewan having more than half, Manitoba 35 per cent of the population, agrarian.

Old and mature in their economic life, the five Eastern provinces, decades ago, developed characteristic services for the education and social protection of their people, all strongly integrated in their traditional local government on a municipal basis. Quebec incorporated the partnership of private, religious, charitable direction with a measure of public liability in finance and supervision. New Brunswick and Nova Scotia built on the public liability for the needy of the English poor laws. Ontario and Prince Edward Island modified the English practice but retained its principles and all four continued to rely upon a large measure of private citizen effort, both in administration and finance.

The Pacific Slope and the Northwest had remained for years under the direct administration of the Hudson's Bay Company. As all these great territories gradually opened to settlement, their extent, and the proportion of continental European population therein, tended to develop government along the highly centralized lines of Company administration, with the provincial authority, naturally, and to large measure necessarily, assuming many a responsibility and function which, in the older provinces, remained within municipal jurisdiction. Municipal government—and especially that extremely successful territorial intermediary between purely local and provincial government, the county—has tended to become the secondary agent in the West for many obligations and

duties for which it remains primarily responsible in the East, except in Prince Edward Island where, with a small population and territory, the provincial and municipal government are peculiarly supplementary.

In such an evolution of settlement and government, the Provinces remained the primary unit in Confederation in all matters of civil rights and, so, of education, health, welfare, and the area of social assistance and protection then dimly etched but now constantly enlarging. The same enactment as constituted the sovereignty of the Dominion government, in its spheres, confirmed the sovereignty of each respective province within the area of its jurisdiction. The diversified powers and responsibilities, therefore, of three levels of government in Canada are but the reflection of the diversified character of the land, its people and their occupations.

[. . .]

The basic criticism of the proposals offered by Dr Marsh for Canada, is that they attempt to direct this Dominion along the blueprints of the Beveridge plan and introduce certain suggestions emerging from a different social background when all the elements of the Canadian situation demand the evolution of realistic measures, grounded deep in the character of this country and its people.

4. The Canadian Objective

What then should be the purpose, form, and execution of such part of the planning for income security as may lie within the framework of the Canadian state? Simply stated the objective to which the Beveridge Report and Dr Marsh's suggestions for Canada are directed is the establishment and assurance of what is described as a national social minimum, or in specific terms an actual income budget in currency values which shall be assured to every individual in the state, by supplement or substitution for earned income to the degree that the latter fails. This social minimum is to be calculated on a budgetary basis, though Sir William Beveridge leaves the gravely difficult question of rent differentials in widely varying parts of the United Kingdom unsettled, and Dr Marsh appears to rest the very complicated question of differences between costs in different types of Canadian communities on a possible variation of 15 per cent between urban and rural budgets.[2] The social minimum in the closely similar Beveridge and Marsh proposals contemplates a minimum standard living budget in terms of the single adult worker, and the adult worker with one adult dependant, these budgets varying in their relation to social aid, as to whether the cause of the income impairment is of a presumably temporary or permanent nature, the latter scales (e.g., for aged) being lower than the former (e.g., in unemployment or temporary sickness). Variation in family needs is to be met by another device, straight cash grants or allowances by the State, in the Beveridge proposals, on behalf of all children of school age, save the first (which is included, however, if the parent is in receipt of social aid), and in the Marsh suggestions for all children under 16 or 17 years of age.

Whatever the merits of the case in an industrially mature population with a declining natural increase, there seems grave doubt as to whether in a young, vigorous, rich Canada, the most dynamic ideal that can be set before her people, is the attempted mathematical calculation of a social minimum in terms of weekly income in dollars and cents, and then the organization of the national life and production to assure that. In a land of such diversity of life and occupation, the practical possibility of such a device, equitable to all parts of the country and all elements in the population seems seriously open to question, even if theoretically desirable.

There is agreement among Canadians that no one within their citizenship should be suffered to exist at less than a decent level of life, and a real anxiety and purpose to realize such economic security for all our people. But it is suggested that in this conviction Canadians are not thinking of so many dollars and cents per head being required in currency within each home: they think rather of a simple, decent, sound wholesome family life, varying with the part of the country and the occupation in which the family finds itself. They think of the shelter, food, and clothing to be acquired within their individual effort, by sale of their labour, their skill or the goods they produce; they think, too, of all the things that mean well-being and opportunity, to them,—the "chance to make good" by development of land or fishing, or some personal enterprise, or by good training, education and employment. Health services, schools, the district or neighbourhood church—all these things are bound up together in the average Canadian's concept of what he means by a decent social minimum or standard of living; it is all something more far-reaching, vital and complex than the hope of a calculated amount of income in currency terms. Further, he wants the opportunity to provide these things by his own efforts, directly in return for what he has to sell, in so far as these individual needs are concerned and, directly, also through the creation of community services, in the provision and control of which he participates—good roads, good community facilities, good schools, hospitals, housing, etc. It is a harder way, than the calculation of a definite income, and supplementation from public funds where earnings are "sub minimum" but it is the dynamic way, not a defeatist counsel of acceptance of things as they are, and as such, it is submitted, one more consistent with the youth and vigour of this country.

[. . .]

The next line of social policy should be the organization of gainful occupation on such a basis as to offer to the conscientious and efficient worker, valid hope of an income from his effort, sufficient to maintain, in reasonable decency, the family obligations which he might normally be expected to require. This premise rejects the contention that "fundamentally insistence on relating a wage rate to family needs is illogical."[3] It is admittedly illogical to accept the premise that the remuneration of a worker should be automatically increased, without regard to his relative value in the occupation in which he is engaged, just because his dependants increase, by birth of more children or otherwise, but to deny that the basic rate, on which the value of human power should be remunerated (in wages or fees for skills or in prices for natural products) should be grounded in decent minimum living standards, is to reject the fundamental basis on which wage standards, and the effort to control price spreads, have developed on the North American continent since the opening of this century.

Whatever the practice in other lands, in the United States and Canada the theory of wages and prices has been predicated on the earnings of an adult worker being adequate to support, in reasonable decency, his wife and a "typical family" of two to three children of varying age. If an industry cannot be adjusted to that rate of remuneration for the human element in its relevant costs, granted the labour is efficient, the industry is deemed to require investigation to ascertain the cause of its inability to do so. Similarly, if the production of primary goods cannot yield reasonable subsistence and the hope of progress for an adult, of comparable responsibilities, it is recognized that inquiry and remedial action are required.

The encouragement and development of every occupation in the national economy should be gauged by this measurement:— Can it accord to the experienced worker therein returns adequate to the reasonable discharge of the obligations which he may reasonably be assumed to have acquired at that stage in his working life? If not, it must be submitted to inquiry and remedial policy as that inquiry may suggest.

These processes, it is submitted, should be accepted as basic in exploring greater income security for the Canadian people,—the accurate assessment of the probable peak maximum national income and of the ways and means of influencing its capacity and its distribution to afford a standard of income for the average mature worker, reasonably adequate to the minimum living needs of a typical family, and then the adjustment of all minimum wage scales and fair prices for natural products, in relation thereto.

Such proposals admittedly involve broad problems of economic policy, and of the relation of supply and demand within Canada, and internationally—all of themselves of such extent as to lie outside the limits of a discussion, centring about the maintenance of income for the Canadian at a minimum level, effected by the gearing of production to that end. Moreover, they call for technical knowledge and competence within other fields than that of social administration. But granting all this, a warning at this point is not inappropriate that, no matter what the organization of Canada's own resources and services, her ability to attain and maintain an objective of happy work and reasonable well-being for all her citizens involves interest and responsibility outside their own geographic or political frontiers. The same dynamic objective is stimulating the life of all civilized peoples. It would be culpable folly for Canadians to ignore the fact that (even with the peak demand of war's daily destruction and a large part of the highly industrialized continent of Europe occupied and partially immobilized) the productive power of this country, put into mass production, has outraced anticipated demand for many lines of goods. The extension of the Dominion's two billion dollar non-repayable credits to Britain and the Allied Nations was not only an indication of a sense of war partnership but of this rate of production outstripping presumed demand in certain lines. Industrial lay-offs in various lines, even in wartime, similarly reinforce the need of realization of this relation between our power to produce and even a greatly heightened consumer demand within the country, which is to be discounted, too, by consideration of the comparative durability of heavy consumer goods for peacetime use. The hope of continuous gainful occupation, at a decent level of security for the Canadian people, therefore seems predicated upon the integration of our life in an international pattern and in a partnership in world production and trade.

With the reservation then that Canadians cannot hope to plan for their well-being and security within the vacuum of their own state alone, discussion can proceed to that part of the economic security for the state and the individual which rests upon welfare, as reinforcing economic, planning.

NOTES

1. Beveridge Report, p. 120.
2. For the standard budget suggested for Canada see Part II.

3. Report, L.C. Marsh, M.R. p. 26.

Historical Interpretations

3 From Alvin Finkel, *Social Policy and Practice in Canada: A History* (Waterloo: Wilfrid Laurier University Press, 2006), 169–92.

THE MEDICARE DEBATE, 1945–80

"The government sponsors the TB testing of cattle, pays for loss and has blood testing every year free of charge. What about humans? Let's take our hats off to Russia as far as health is concerned."[1] This was the conclusion of a group of farmers in Seaforth, Ontario, meeting in late 1943 to discuss the idea of a national universal medical care program. Sponsored by *Farm Radio Forum*, a CBC radio series, groups of farmers across the country responded to the proposals that were being mooted for state medical insurance. But the proposals being discussed were more radical than Canada's current medicare system. Medical care was to be removed from the private marketplace completely, and the costs of hospital care, doctors' visits, pharmaceutical costs, dental care, and eyecare were to be covered by a state-funded regime.

The farmers' groups revealed that conditions of health care in Canada, particularly in rural areas, were often grim. For example, a farmer in Elderbank, Nova Scotia, stated "Our doctor has 275 miles of highway to travel. Many do not consult him because of cost of services. Immediate federal action is needed." In Leader, Saskatchewan, another reported: "Our school is never visited by either doctor or nurse. This fall one family had a child with contagious disease . . . finally the school was closed up, as teacher and all pupils were sick. Mothers here, who never have a doctor at the birth of a child, least of all pre-natal care, most of them are wrecks and old long before their time."[2] Polls suggested that a national medicare scheme was the most popular reform discussed during the Second World War and its aftermath. In both 1944 and 1948, 80 per cent of Canadians expressed support, with the Québécois sharing this sentiment despite the claims of their provincial government and the Catholic Church that national medicare posed a threat to Quebec's traditions of individualism and Church control of social services.[3]

The dismal state of health services across the country fuelled the demand for state action. Canadians had reason to believe that they did not enjoy the full benefits of the medical knowledge of their time. While Sweden and New Zealand, both with universal state medical programs, had the world's lowest infant death rates in 1942—29 per 1000 live births—Canada's rate was 54. In all provinces, the infant mortality rate in rural areas was higher than the urban rate, usually quite significantly, for example 79 to 51 in Nova Scotia, 76 to 43 in Manitoba, and 63 to 30 in British Columbia. Significantly, Saskatchewan, where pressure from women's groups in the interwar period had led to the hiring of municipal doctors and the creation of "union" hospitals (hospitals operated by several municipalities uniting to pay for their construction and operation), had the country's lowest rural death rate for infants. In that province, 52 children per 1000 died in their first year of life compared with 43 in the province's cities.[4]

Still, the State Hospital and Medical League of Saskatchewan estimated that 34 per cent of all deaths were premature and that half of all provincial residents suffering disabling illnesses could have been free of disease if preventive care had been applied. As Tommy Douglas, soon-to-be premier of that province and generally regarded as the "father of Canadian medicare,"[5] noted in a broadcast in 1943, "If the average person were checked over by a clinic at stated intervals,

and treatment were available before the illness had reached a critical stage, not only would we live longer but the cost of health services in the aggregate would be less than it is now."[6] The National Committee for Mental Hygiene reported in 1939 that only 10 per cent of Canadians could comfortably pay for their medical services in a free-market system while 25 per cent were completely dependent on charity; the remaining 65 per cent could pay for normal services but were forced into debt or rejection of treatment if an operation or long-term care was required.[7]

Yet, despite popular support for medicare, it was not implemented in the early post-war period and, over the next two decades, pro- and anti-medicare forces were locked in constant battle. Advocates of medicare seemingly won, but the program that emerged disappointed them both in the limitations of its coverage and the structure of medical care that it embraced. This essay explores the structures of political decision-making, formal and informal, that resulted in the creation of a particular type of medicare in 1968.

FROM THE GREEN BOOK TO HOSPITAL INSURANCE

Though the federal government balked at the potential costs of national health insurance in 1945, it recognized that Canadians expected governments at all levels to invest in health care.[8] In 1948, it announced a program of conditional health grants to provinces to build and operate hospitals, train medical personnel, and carry out health research. The wealthier provinces, in turn, also provided funding to expand their network of hospitals and to increase the number of graduates from medical schools. From 1948 to 1953 alone, 46 000 hospital beds were added across Canada.[9]

Saskatchewan had elected a CCF government led by T.C. Douglas in 1944, and it had pledged to take steps toward the creation of a universal medicare scheme. Despite the un-availability of matching federal funds, Sas-katchewan forged ahead with plans to create universal hospital insurance in the province and end the distinction in hospitals between paying clients and charity cases. It immediately undertook a hospital construction project to en-sure that most residents lived close enough to a hospital to receive care close to home. Then it legislated tax-funded hospitalization insur-ance in 1947, becoming the first jurisdiction in North America to implement such a program. The province's general revenues as well as a prepaid monthly premium levied on families and singles would pay the costs of insuring that need, and not financial means, determined who used Saskatchewan hospitals. Saskatche-wan physicians largely supported this measure, while hospital administrators who opposed the legislation kept quiet after the premier threat-ened that the province could take control of the hospitals if the existing administrators no lon-ger wished to run them.[10]

British Columbia's Coalition govern-ment of Liberals and Conservatives faced se-rious competition from that province's CCF and also decided to implement a universal hospital insurance program, financed by premiums and a 3 per cent sales tax. Claim-ing that it wanted to blend the concepts of private and public responsibility, it included "co-insurance" (user fees) within its hospi-tal insurance program, despite protests from the CCF and the labour movement. Alberta presented yet a third model for paying hos-pital and other medical bills. Decrying both compulsory participation and centraliza-tion, the government established a series of health districts in 1946. District boards, which included both physician and con-sumer representatives, negotiated a health insurance scheme with municipalities, in-cluding the services to be covered for a max-imum payment of $10 per adult. While most costs were borne by the voluntary subscriber to the insurance scheme, hospital fees were

set at $1 per day, with the municipality and the province splitting the remaining operat-ing costs. Manitoba and Newfoundland also had voluntary programs, which had been established before Newfoundland joined Canada, enrolling about half the province's population.[11]

Louis St Laurent, like Mackenzie King, was less than enthusiastic about the federal gov-ernment creating a national health insurance scheme. But he was under tremendous pres-sure from the five provinces that were heavily subsidizing patients' costs to implement a na-tional program and lift at least half the burden of costs from the provinces.[12] Ontario weighed in on the provinces' side in 1955. About 70 per cent of Ontario residents enjoyed some form of hospital insurance coverage, but Premier Leslie Frost faced public pressure for the government to fund hospital insurance. This included pres-sure from hospital authorities. The community elites that ran the hospitals had been dealt a body blow by the Depression, as the number of paying customers dwindled while charity cases climbed. In the post-war period, they came to believe that their institutions needed the eco-nomic stability that public insurance alone could provide.[13]

Frost responded by insisting that fed-eral involvement was required, a viewpoint he stressed at a federal-provincial confer-ence in October 1955. St Laurent reluctantly agreed to federal-provincial discussions on hospital insurance. These discussions led to the *Hospital Insurance and Diagnostic Ser-vices Act* of April 1957, which established a formula for federal grants to provinces that implemented a provincial hospital insur-ance scheme. About half of all hospital costs would be borne by the federal government. The provinces chose the method of financing for their plans, but there were penalties for provinces that levied user fees. Passage of the legislation was eased by the lack of opposi-tion from the Canadian Medical Association (CMA), which, since 1949, had supported user-pay hospitals.[14] Their change of heart was dictated by the need to assuage public anger regarding high costs for hospital stays and to avoid more radical medicare programs that included costs of doctors' visits. The private insurance companies were the big losers in the debate, but were determined to fight to maintain the rest of their health insurance business by denouncing further state intervention in medical care.

TOWARD MEDICARE

If governments were to get involved in medical insurance, it was likely that they would require physicians to accept lower rates for various procedures as a means of reducing overall medical costs. In the United States, the growth of the private health insurance industry, also dominated by physicians, gave the American Medical Association (AMA) an incentive to spend lavishly to lobby politicians and propagandize Americans regarding the evils of a public health insurance program. Their efforts forestalled President Harry Truman's plans in the late 1940s to introduce a national universal medical insurance scheme despite widespread popular support for such a policy. In the context of the Cold War, the AMA painted state medicine as an exemplar of the programs that unfree Communist states imposed upon their hapless citizens, an image that was ironic in light of the introduction of state medicine in Britain and other European democracies. Supported by big business organizations, the AMA developed an impregnable opposition to state medicine in Congress that united northern Republicans with southern Democrats, the latter often wealthy conservatives elected from pro-medicare constituencies but able to avoid the issue by making the preservation of racial segregation the key to their election strategies.[15]

At the federal–provincial conference in 1955, St Laurent indicated that the federal government would only consider a national health insurance program when a majority of provinces representing a majority of citizens

were prepared to institute provincial programs. [. . .]

As with hospital insurance, it was the provinces that stepped up to the plate first to offer universal programs and then put the federal government on the hot seat for failure to make such provision a national responsibility. Once again, it was Saskatchewan's CCF government that led the way. Tommy Douglas, running for re-election in 1960, announced that with the federal government now paying half of Saskatchewan's hospital bills, his government could afford to implement universal medicare. Both the urban and rural poor, including most farmers, were unable to buy medical coverage, and the Saskatchewan government, like other provincial governments, was picking up the tab for medical bills for a growing section of the poor. It argued that this was unfair, first because it stigmatized those requited to rely on state aid and discouraged them from seeing doctors, and second because it placed heavy financial burdens on the state that a universal plan would offset with the tax or premium contributions of the better-off, which the private insurers claimed for themselves. But Saskatchewan faced a huge fight in implementing its program.

Saskatchewan had played a pioneering role in the provision of medical services in Canada. Its municipal doctor schemes and union hospitals of the interwar period, the result of the work of the farm women's movement, and particularly Violet McNaughton, challenged the notion of health as a commodity to be purchased by those with the wherewithal to do so. Nonetheless, such programs relied on voluntary participation by doctors rather than state coercion. The CCF's experiments with full-state operation of medical services before the 1960s were limited to a few areas of the province in which the government was able to enlist the support of progressive-minded physicians. However, after the government announced its intentions to have a province-wide medical insurance scheme, a community clinic movement

sprang up, a natural outgrowth of the populism that had produced both the major farm
movements in Saskatchewan and the CCF
itself. Health clinics with a holistic model
of health, in which nurses, social workers,
nutritionists, and dentists worked alongside
doctors, enrolled about 50 000 people in 35
regional associations in a province of less
than 1 million people.[16]

Most physicians had no intention of becoming salaried professionals working in
state-run clinics whose policies were determined by elected boards of non-physicians. In
line with the CMA, which aided them in carrying out an extensive propaganda campaign
against the government's plan, Saskatchewan
doctors insisted that individuals and families
should pay their medical bills via private insurance. If the province insisted that all citizens should be insured, it should direct them
to buy insurance from a private plan. Only
the poor should have their bills paid by the
state, with the state paying physician-dictated
rates for services that private plans paid. In
July 1962, when the government proved adamant that it would proceed with its plans, the
Saskatchewan branch of the CMA organized a
withdrawal of physician services.[17]

Upper- and middle-class supporters of
the physicians formed "Keep Our Doctors"
committees that accused the government of
imposing an unworkable policy for socialist ideological reasons. The corporate-owned
daily papers, always hostile to the CCF government, terrified people by suggesting that the
province might lose most of its doctors. With
both the CMA and national business organizations spending extravagantly to reinforce this
message through television and radio advertising, as well as by using the appearances of "expert" witnesses on news shows, Saskatchewan
residents were subjected to non-stop propaganda against state medicare. This was offset
by the support for medicare from the Saskatchewan Federation of Labour and the major farm organizations, though these groups
had limited access to the media.

The doctors' strike ended after 22 days as
a result of government negotiations with the
Saskatchewan branch of the CMA, in which the
doctors conceded a universal state program
and the government conceded many of the demands of the doctors. There would be no salaries for doctors or payments by the number of
patients that they served. Instead, fee for service, the principle that governed private insurance plans, would remain sacrosanct. Doctors
would continue to operate from their own private offices, and not only would doctors not be
forced to participate in a community clinic, but
those who chose to practise in a clinic would
receive direct funding from the state rather than
have to deal with the community clinic board.
Finally, doctors would have the choice of participating directly in the state plan either by requiring patients to pay bills and then bill the
plan or by staying out of the plan altogether and
billing patients with whatever fees they deemed
appropriate. This was simply a face-saving measure since both sides understood that most patients would choose to patronize doctors who
were in the prepaid medicare scheme.

[. . .]

MEDICARE'S OPPONENTS

Supporters of continued privatization and
voluntary participation in medical insurance
included the Canadian Medical Association,
the Canadian Dental Association, the Canadian Chamber of Commerce, the entire private insurance industry, the pharmaceutical
industry, and representatives of most other
industries. The premiers of British Columbia, Alberta, Manitoba, and Ontario opposed
medicare while Quebec's Premier Lesage was
opposed to federal legislation in a sphere of
provincial competence. The Atlantic premiers
generally supported medicare but wanted the
federal government to pay the lion's share of
the costs and to give them time to phase in any
universal program because they faced shortages of medical personnel. Only Woodrow

Lloyd in Saskatchewan was an unequivocal supporter of a fully state-operated scheme.[18]

The advocates of private insurance used a variety of arguments. For example, the British Columbia Medical Association, following the lead of the CMA,[19] argued that the monies that medicare would absorb could be better spent on "scholarships for medical students, to add rehabilitative and chronic care kids to our hospitals, to extend our mental health programme, and for many other important services." Directing taxes instead toward paying medical insurance was "foolhardy" because it meant "providing a service to those who are already providing it for themselves, as most British Columbians are doing through our system of voluntary health insurance."[20]

The CMA's brief added that the hospital insurance program, which the physicians regarded favourably, had expanded demand for hospital beds. The federal and provincial governments, it suggested, having created this demand by making hospitalization a free good, now had to cough up the money for more beds. Implicit, however, in this argument was that prior to the existence of a public program, the real health needs of the population, in the area of hospitalization, had been underserved despite the availability of private hospitalization insurance.[21] Nor did the physicians try to claim that private health insurance was meeting everyone's needs. They conceded that to achieve universal medical insurance coverage, about 3 million Canadians would have to have their bills paid by taxes collected from the rest of Canadians, who, in turn, would also have to pay for their own private insurance.

The CMA, while avoiding the Cold War rhetoric of its American counterpart in its opposition to state medicine, emphasized that doctors as a group would be hostile to state medical insurance and even more hostile to any efforts by the government to move them away from individual practice into group settings that might also include other types of medical practitioners. "Physicians by nature and by training are strongly individualistic

and it is not given to all doctors to function happily and efficiently as a member of a group." It could lead, in any case, to "assembly-line medicine."[22]

The Canadian Dental Association (CDA) also claimed that state monies could be better directed at other goals than a national insurance program. Admitting that most Canadians had little or no access to dentists, they pointed out that there was a dismal ratio of dentists to population—1 to 3000, compared with 1 to 1900 in the United States, with regional gaps that were best demonstrated by Newfoundland and Labrador's ratio of 1 dentist per 11 000 residents. If all Canadians suddenly had access to dental services, there would simply be too few dentists to accommodate them.

The dentists admitted that "education and income separately and together are strongly associated with going to the dentist." Yet the dentists largely ignored their own insight that money kept many Canadians from properly caring for their teeth, focusing instead on "people's lack of interest in preventative measures" as the way to improve dental health. They recommended that provinces make fluoridation of water supplies mandatory for municipalities, that Canadians consume less sugar, and that more government funds go to dental research. While cool to state involvement in dentistry, outside of dental education and research, the CDA did recognize some need for governments to fund potential consumers of dentists' services. Like the physicians, they supported state funding of necessary services for destitute Canadians. If governments were going to provide state dental service programs, they should restrict their programs to children.[23]

[. . .]

Both pharmacists and the pharmaceutical industry strongly opposed inclusion of prescription drugs in a state medical insurance plan, since it carried the implicit threat of state regulation of drug prices. The Canadian Pharmaceutical Manufacturers' Association (CPMA) reported soothingly that competition was lively at the manufacturing and retail levels of the industry: "The competitive aspect of research and development, combined with behaviour of prices and promotional activities, indicates that a satisfactory level of competition exists in the industry. Furthermore, this competition is directed in a manner which is socially desirable. Growth, product development and the general level of prices have been favourable rather than unfavourable to the consumer."[24] The pharmaceutical manufacturers assured the commissioners that after-tax profits of the industry were modest and the industry's expenditures on promotion were fairly restrained and served the purpose of informing physicians and others about useful pharmaceuticals.

In fact, the industry's profits, measured as a percentage of invested capital, were double the average for Canadian industries as a whole from 1953 to 1958. A study prepared in 1961 for the federal Department of Justice by the director of Investigation and Research, Combines Investigation Act, noted that apart from making large profits, the industry was absolutely profligate in its promotion expenditures, as it worked tirelessly to press physicians to use various new drugs. Patent laws protected drug companies that developed a new pharmaceutical product, and it was the knowledge that they had a monopoly for many years over a particular drug that caused pharmaceutical companies to spend millions trying to convince physicians to prescribe their product.

[. . .] Health care providers, such as doctors, dentists, and pharmacy owners, had a common interest in establishing a high price for their services, and happily confounded private provision with competition and efficient pricing.

Ultimately, the two arguments that were heard most frequently to discredit a compulsory public medical system were that it would deprive health practitioners of the freedoms that all business people ought legitimately to have in a democratic society, and that it would be so costly as to provoke crushing levels of taxation that would destroy Canada's

industrial competitiveness. The CMA stated starkly: "We consider government intervention into the field of prepaid medical care to the point of becoming a monopolistic purchaser of medical services, to be a measure of civil conscription. We would urge this Royal Commission to support our view that, exclusive of states of emergency, civil conscription of any segment of the Canadian population is contrary to our democratic philosophy."[25] Premier Leslie Frost of Ontario was prominent among anti-medicare politicians to invoke the industrial competitiveness argument. The country, he averred, "has already become a high cost economy. And that is affecting our trading and developmental position."[26]

MEDICARE'S SUPPORTERS

Medicare's supporters suggested that Canadians had collective rights to the best medical treatments that were available regardless of income, and that the right of individuals to receive affordable medical service outweighed the alleged rights of medical practitioners to price their services as they deemed best. Despite the crushing majority support for medicare evident in opinion polls, few Canadians were willing to come forward as individuals and suggest that they had received second-rate medical treatment because they were poor. A careful scouring of the thousands of briefs before the Hall Commission reveals only one case where an individual Canadian denounced her doctors for providing her family mediocre care because of their inability to pay. Her physician's scathing personal attack upon her in response demonstrated why few Canadians had the temerity to reveal personal cases of receiving poor treatment or being driven to bankruptcy to obtain necessary medical attention.[27] Instead, the horror stories that the commissioners heard as well as the main arguments countering the claims of private medicine came from organizations. Trade unions, social worker and welfare organizations, farmers' federations, and the United Church of Canada convinced the commissioners that they should adopt an ambitious national program.

The Canadian Association of Social Workers placed the case before the Hall Commission that many were deterred from seeking medical assistance at clinics because several hours might be required for them to fill out forms at the accounting department. Meanwhile, many people of middle means who did not qualify for the state care available to the indigent avoided seeking needed medical care because "it is going to come out of the food budget, or come out of the youngsters' clothing budget or something like this." The social workers observed that the stigma of receiving a charitable service discouraged usage of the service. It also created problems regarding the proper cut-off income for recipients. Better to have medicare available to all Canadians so that no one had to see it as either a special right or a special shame.[28]

The Canadian Federation of Agriculture (CFA) and several other major farm groups appeared before the commission and indicated that the majority of farmers could not afford private health insurance.[29] The United Church of Canada, whose General Council had called for a contributory national health plan since 1952, confirmed the CFA's impressions. The United Church brief added that urban immigrants, particularly unskilled workers from southern Italy, were perhaps even more vulnerable. These people were underpaid, ill-housed, insecure about their income, and prone as a result to both physical and mental illness. Yet they were too impoverished to be able to set aside the money for private health insurance.[30]

But the trade union movement probably proved the most effective in demolishing the arguments of industry and physicians that Canadians were gradually meeting their medical needs privately. In the post-war period, the trade union movement, which enrolled about a third of Canadian workers thanks to wartime and early post-war organizing successes, had succeeded in winning a variety of "fringe benefits" for their members in addition to wage increases and improvements in working conditions. A medical benefits package had become a common gain for trade unionists, and such prepaid medical insurance swelled the numbers of families whom the private insurance companies could claim as they pooh-poohed the need for a public program.

Unions' characterizations of the limitations of private coverage undermined such insurance industry boasting. National, provincial, and labour federations complained that the profit-driven insurance schemes that enrolled their members tended to severely restrict or deny coverage altogether in such areas as preventive health services, rehabilitation, mental health, dental services, and social services. Prescription drugs, nursing aid, appliances, eyeglasses, and hearing aids were rarely covered. Yet most of these plans had "costly deductible and co-insurance charges." As the Canadian Labour Congress (CLC) concluded, "It is too much to expect that a complete range of services can be made available on a universal basis to the Canadian people within the near future through the mere extension of the private pre-payment schemes. It is not physically, financially nor administratively possible."[31]

THE HALL REPORT AND THE IMPLEMENTATION OF MEDICINE

Emmett Hall and the majority of his fellow commissioners were won over, in large part, by the values and arguments of the supporters of a universal medicare program. Their 1964 report made some obeisance in the direction of business and physicians by recognizing that no doctor should be forced to join a national medicare program, and that doctors should remain in private practice even if they joined medicare rather than becoming civil servants working in government offices. Even more of a victory for the physicians was the commission's rejection of the National Health Service model of salaried physicians, which the labour movement had endorsed. Instead, the commissioners supported continuation of the fee-for-service model which was a hallmark of private insurance.[32]

However, the overall direction of the report reflected the persuasiveness of the opponents of the argument made by businesses and physicians. Wrote the commissioners: "The achievement of the highest possible health standards for all our people must become a primary objective of national policy and a cohesive factor contributing to national unity, involving individual and community responsibilities and actions. This objective can best be achieved through a comprehensive, universal Health Services Programme for the Canadian people." "Comprehensive," in Hall's view, included "all health services, preventive, diagnostic, curative and rehabilitative, that modern medical and other services can provide."[33] This meant that governments should not only provide universal coverage for physicians' services and for hospitalization but should also cover prescription drug payments for all Canadians, home care and prosthetic services as required, dental services for children, expectant mothers, and public assistance recipients, and eyecare for children and the poor. Most of these programs would exclude user fees, though each prescription would bear a dollar user fee and adults would be expected to pay one-third the cost of eyeglasses, which would however be free for children.[34] Taxation would pay for all Canadians to be covered by the national health program. In short, Hall had rejected the voluntary medical insurance schemes that Ontario, Alberta, and British Columbia had proposed as alternatives to the Saskatchewan plan because only the latter appeared to guarantee the potential of full coverage to all Canadians for all necessary medical services. [. . .]

The Hall Report put pressure on Lester Pearson's Liberal government, which had been elected in 1963, albeit without a parliamentary majority, to live up to its medicare promises. The Liberals had promised a national medicare program that would provide comprehensive services free of charge to children till they left school and to Canadians over 65 years of age. Everyone else would have services by general practitioners, specialists, and surgeons, along with diagnostic services, covered, except for the first $25. Even the left-wingers in the government were taken aback by the scope of services that Hall wanted a national program to cover. For a year the government waffled, and even in the throne speech of 1965, the government committed itself to medicare in only the vaguest terms. The NDP, which had endorsed the Hall Report *in toto*, demanded that the government implement its fullest set of recommendations immediately.[35]

The eventual compromise reached within the government called for medicare to be introduced in phases. The first phase would add physician and diagnostic services to the existing hospitalization coverage, while other components of the Hall vision would be introduced as fiscal means became available. In practice, though few Canadians could know it at the time, there would be no second phase for medicare, at least during the twentieth century.

The Liberals called a federal election in late 1965 but narrowly failed again to form a majority government. Their commitment to a modified version of the Hall recommendations during the election left them little alternative afterwards but to legislate a medicare bill. Initially, Pearson aimed for 1 July 1967, the one hundredth birthday of the country. However, continued provincial reluctance to accept the federal principles argued against such speed, as did the change in the balance of forces in the Liberal cabinet after the election.

Walter Gordon, the progressive finance minister, took responsibility for having advised Pearson to hold an early election, and resigned from cabinet. His replacement, Mitchell Sharp, held views similar to those of organized business and appeared in no hurry to implement medicare, which he claimed could have an undue impact on the federal treasury. Robert Stanfield, the new leader of the Conservative party, denounced "a vast new spending program."[36] But Sharp and his supporters were only able to delay medicare's implementation by one year.[37] On 1 July 1968, funds would be available to provinces with a medicare scheme that met the four principles of medicare. Still, the division within the Pearson cabinet encouraged provinces that opposed universality and public administration to move slowly. Only Saskatchewan and British Columbia presented plans in the month after the medicare deadline and began to receive federal funding in July.

By then, the dithering Pearson had been replaced as head of the government by the more decisive Pierre Elliott Trudeau. Trudeau scotched any further attempts from within the cabinet or the provinces to allow for either delays or modification of the medicare legislation. Within a year all provinces but Quebec had announced plans that met the criteria of the *Medical Services Act* of 1968. Quebec entered the plan in 1972.[38]

[. . .]

The creation of a national network of provincial medicare programs, all subscribing to the principles of comprehensiveness, universality, portability, and public administration, represented a major victory for progressive forces in Canada, backed by overwhelming public opinion. The combination of public campaigning by important social movements, including labour, farmers, and social workers, with support from key elements of the Liberal Party and the civil service, resulted in a Tory-appointed royal commission failing to suggest some sort of public–private mix that largely subordinated health service provision to profit-seeking health insurance companies and physicians. In turn, this led the Liberal government, divided for two decades on whether to implement its promises originally made in 1919 for a national public program, to finally deliver.

Canada's "first phase" of medicare provided far less comprehensive coverage for illness prevention and treatment than the National Health Service in Britain and similar programs in Scandinavia and Holland. The Soviet Union and its Cold War satellites in eastern Europe all provided sweeping free comprehensive medical care programs. The Hall Commission had looked to western European models rather than the United States in framing its recommendations, and the government rhetorically accepted the commission's conclusions. In practice, the desire to keep costs down resulted in a watering down of Hall's proposals that saw medicare's "first phase" limited to coverage of visits to hospitals and physicians, and diagnostic services. Further phases were not legislated. The late 1960s represented the high point of social reform rather than a first installment on social reforms that would fundamentally redistribute wealth in Canada.

NOTES

1. Health Study Bureau, *Review of Canada's Health Needs and Insurance Proposals* (Toronto, ON: Health Study Bureau, 1946), 41.

2. Ibid., 40–3.

3. Malcolm G. Taylor, *Health Insurance and Canadian Public Policy: The Seven Decisions that Created the Canadian Health Insurance System* (Montreal and Kingston: McGill-Queen's University Press, 1978), 166.

4. Health Study Bureau, *Review of Canada's Health Needs*, 3–4.

5. Georgina M. Taylor, "Ground for Common Action: Violet McNaughton's Agrarian Feminism and the Origins of the Farm Women's Movement in Canada" (PhD thesis, Carleton University, 1997).

6. "CCF Broadcast by T.C. Douglas, MP," William Lyon Mackenzie King Papers, MG 26, J1, Vol. 346, p. 297011, Library and Archives of Canada, (LAC).

7. Ibid., p. 297809.

8. "Resolutions, Annual Meeting, Held in Regina June 6–11, 1947," National Council of Women

of Canada (NCWC) Papers, MG 28 I 25, Vol. 90, File 1, LAC.

9. Malcolm G. Taylor, "The Canadian Health-Care System: After Medicare," in David Coburn, Carl D'Arcy, George M. Torrance, and Peter New, eds, *Health and Canadian Society: Sociological Perspectives*, 2nd edn (Toronto: Fitzhenry and Whiteside, 1987), 74.

10. Duane Mombourquette, "'An Inalienable Right': The, CCF and Rapid Health Care Reform, 1944–1948," in Raymond B. Blake and Jeff Keshen, eds, *Social Welfare Policy in Canada: Historical Readings* (Toronto: Copp Clark, 1995), 298–302.

11. Taylor, "The Canadian Health-Care System," 74, 84; Margaret A. Ormsby, *British Columbia: A History* (Vancouver: Macmillan, 1958), 487; Alvin Finkel, *The Social Credit Phenomenon in Alberta* (Toronto: University of Toronto Press, 1989), 123.

12. Eugene Vayda and Raisa B. Deber, "The Canadian Health-Care System: A Developmental Overview," in Blake and Keshen, *Social Welfare Policy*, 315.

13. David Gagan and Rosemary Gagan, *For Patients of Moderate Means: A Social History of the Voluntary Public General Hospital in Canada, 1890–1950* (Montreal and Kingston: McGill-Queen's University Press, 2002).

14. Brief of Canadian Medical Association, April 1962, Canada, Royal Commission on Health Services, RG 33, Series 78, Vol. 19, File 278, LAC.

15. Monte M. Poen, *Harry S. Truman Versus the Medical Lobby: The Genesis of Medicare* (Columbia, MS: University of Missouri Press, 1979); Lawrence R. Jacobs, *The Health of Nations: Public Opinion and the Making of American and British Health Policy* (Ithaca, NY: Cornell University Press, 1993).

16. Joan Feather, "From Concept to Reality: Formation of the Swift Current Health Region," *Prairie Forum* 16, 1 (Spring 1991): 59–80; Joan Feather, "Impact of the Swift Current Health Region: Experiment or Model," *Prairie Forum* 16, 2 (Fall 1991): 225–48; Stan Rands, "Recollections: The CCF in Saskatchewan," in Donald C. Kerr, ed., *Western Canadian Politics: The Radical Tradition* (Edmonton: NeWest, 1981), 58–64.

17. Robin F. Badgley and Samuel Wolfe, *Doctors' Strike: Medical Care and Conflict in Saskatchewan* (Toronto: Macmillan, 1967).

18. "Discussions with Provinces on Health Services Matters," Department of National Health and Welfare Papers, Vol. 45.

19. Evidence of Canadian Medical Association, April 1962, Royal Commission on Health Services.

20. Evidence of British Columbia Medical Association, February 1962, Royal Commission on Health Services, Vol. 12, File 150.

21. Evidence of Canadian Medical Association, April 1962, Royal Commission on Health Services.

22. Ibid.

23. Evidence of Canadian Dental Association, March 1962, Royal Commission on Health, Vol. 14, Exhibit 192, 1962.

24. Evidence of Canadian Pharmaceutical Manufacturers Association, May 1962, Royal Commission on Health Services, Vol. 20, File 291.

25. Evidence of Canadian Medical Association, 16 October 1962, Royal Commission on Health Services, Vol. 6, File 67.

26. Canadian Press Report of Leslie Frost Interview, 29 March 1961, Royal Commission on Health Services, Vol. 8.

27. Evidence of Mrs. Marguerite Miles, Toronto, n.d., File 355; Evidence of Dr. C. Collins-William, Toronto, n.d., File 375, Vol. 22, Royal Commission on Health Services.

28. Evidence of Canadian Association of Social Workers, 28 May 1962, Royal Commission on Health Services, Vol. 6, File 61.

29. Evidence of Canadian Federation of Agriculture, 27 March, 1962, Royal Commission on Health Services, Vol. 14, File 190.

30. Evidence of United Church of Canada, April 1962, Royal Commission on Health Services, Vol. 22, File 352.

31. Evidence of Canadian Labour Congress, 17 October, 1962, Royal Commission on Health Services, Vol. 6, File 68.

32. Royal Commission on Health Services, *Report*, vol. 1 (Ottawa: Queen's Printer, 1964), 29.

33. Ibid., 11.

34. Ibid., 19.

35. "Election 1963 Pamphlets," National Liberal Federation Papers, MG 28, IV-3, Vol. 1024, LAC; Bryden, *Planners and Politicians: Liberal Politics and Social Policy, 1957–1968* (Montreal and Kingston: McGill-Queen's University Press, 1997), 136.

36. The continued opposition of the premiers was clear in File 618.4, "Correspondence with Premiers," Lester B. Pearson Papers, MG 26, N-4, Vol. 199, LAC.

37. Ibid., 152–63.

38. Ibid., 164–7.

4 From Tina Loo, "Africville and the Dynamics of State Power in Postwar Canada," *Acadiensis* 39, 2 (2010): 23–47. Reprinted with permission.

Is there anything more to say about Africville? The very word resonates, suggesting the familiarity people have with the place and its history. As many Canadians know, Africville was an almost entirely black community located at the north end of Halifax fronting the Bedford Basin. Established in the 1840s, it was razed in the mid-1960s and its residents—then numbering about 400—were relocated by the city as part of a redevelopment plan designed by Gordon Stephenson (a student of the high modernist architect Le Corbusier). Perhaps stung by Stephenson's observation that Africville "stands as an indictment of society and not of its inhabitants," municipal authorities used relocation to rid Halifax of one of its "blighted" areas and to try to improve the lives of its residents.[1]

Like many post-war schemes to improve the human condition, urban renewal in Halifax fell short of delivering on its promises. The residents of Africville were certainly removed and the "slum" cleared, but the hoped-for integration and uplift were not entirely achieved. There were those who were glad to have left their old neighbourhood behind—Africvillers who believed their lives and their children's were much improved by the relocation. But others continued to suffer from insecure and inadequate housing. Moving from one marginal rental to another, they became urban nomads in an often unforgiving and unfamiliar environment. Some found themselves on welfare for the first time, unable to find a job that would pay the monthly rent—a new experience for those used to the more informal economies that governed life in Africville. Still others discovered the difference between good housing and a good life. For all its physical privations, life in Africville had afforded them privacy, freedom, and community.

[. . .]

My intervention does not so much take on the existing interpretations as it asks different questions. Mine is another story, both smaller and larger than the one that has been told. It is smaller in the sense that it is historical, attentive to the other contexts in which urban renewal occurred. As much as Africville and its relocation were the outcome of longstanding racism, the decision to raze the community was also a manifestation of a set of ideas characteristic of a particular historical moment. Relocation was an outcome of the progressive politics of the late 1950s and early 1960s and the solutions they offered to inequality.

[. . .]

The Africville relocation sheds light on some of the tensions inherent in the liberal welfare state, and it is in this regard that the story I tell is larger. While current scholarship frames Africville in terms of racism, for officials of the City of Halifax, and the liberal-minded more generally, Africville was a "welfare problem"—one that required them to figure out ways to meet the multiple and concrete needs of its residents. Racism might have been the reason Africvillers were disadvantaged and immobilized both socially and spatially, but the solutions liberals offered were aimed at meeting Africvillers' needs—for education, employment, adequate housing, and access to capital—rather than eliminating racial prejudice directly. The first step toward doing so was to move Africvillers out of their ghetto and physically integrate them into the city. As Africvillers discovered, however, integration was not belonging. In laying bare the gulf between the two, Africville shows us both the possibilities and the limits of the liberal welfare state to create the good life.

MAKING PROGRESS

To many people Africville was appalling not only because of its substandard housing, lack of sewers, and contaminated water, but also because it was a ghetto. The physical segregation and poverty of the black Haligonians who lived there were manifestations of the kind of deep-seated racism that was increasingly under attack in the North America of the late 1950s and the early to mid-1960s. As *Time* (Canadian edition) magazine put it in 1970: "The bulldozing of Africville exemplifies a determined, if belated, effort by the municipal and provincial government to right an historical injustice."[2]

Razing Africville and integrating the people who lived there defined progressive politics and social action at the time: it was a way to fight discrimination and to articulate and defend human rights; indeed, it *was* progress. But it was not the only manifestation of progressive politics and social action; the wave of urban renewal that swept Africville away was part of a larger one that hit North American cities in the post-war period, and part of a broader liberal moment in the province. Singled out for its racism by one social scientist in 1949, Nova Scotia took important legislative steps toward equality during the

1950s and early 1960s, dropping a clause in its education act that sanctioned segregated schools for blacks and passing laws regarding fair employment and accommodation practices as well as its first human rights act.[3] At the same time, the province also succeeded in modernizing its system of social welfare, finally replacing the poor law—which had not been significantly revised since 1879—with social assistance acts in 1956 and 1958.[4]

In this context of reform, the Stephenson plan enjoyed broad support. Not only did it appeal to those interested in racial equality, who saw it as the next logical step in improving the lives of the city's poorest residents, but it was also backed by the members of Halifax's financial and business communities who were keen to see it become a modern and prosperous port city.[5] Urban renewal and relocation would result in both better housing and an end to segregation. The alliance of progressives forged around Africville brought together blacks and whites; it included representatives from labour, business, and the churches; and it engaged politicians, planners, and social workers as well as some residents of the community itself.

At the same time the Stephenson report was issued, organized labour was at work in Nova Scotia to bring incidents of discrimination to light. In 1957, Sid Blum of the Jewish Labour Committee travelled to the province, interviewing blacks about their experience with discrimination and recording their views about what life in Nova Scotia's towns and cities was like.[6] There clearly was a problem with discrimination in the province; according to *Maclean's* magazine, Halifax was the eastern front of Canada's war for civil liberties—"the last frontier for the professional do-gooder."[7] [. . .]

So when Blum received a visit and letter from some Africville residents four years later in 1961 expressing frustration and concern about their housing situation and the possibility they would be forcibly relocated, he likely was not surprised and he certainly had a context in which to place their request for assistance.[8] In response, Blum told them he would send "our best man in this field" to help. Although he had no specific course of action to recommend, 30-year-old lawyer Alan Borovoy felt the residents had to make a deal with the city.[9] To put them "in a position where they had some strength and would not be screwed," he convened a meeting of civil rights organizations at the Nova Scotian Hotel in August 1962 as a first step toward building a broad-based progressive coalition that would fight the good fight, which in his view was one aimed at integrating Africville rather than continuing its segregation.[10]

The coalition that emerged from the meeting at the Nova Scotian would come to be known as the Halifax Human Rights Advisory Committee (HHRAC), a group that played a key role in the relocation process by overseeing the compensation agreements struck between Africville residents and the city. Although it had a membership of 31, its core consisted of ten people: three were Africville residents, who had organized themselves into a "Ratepayers Association" following the meeting with Borovoy, and the others—three blacks and four whites—were not. The latter were middle-class outsiders who came to civil liberties work through the faith communities they belonged to, their commitment to education or, in the case of some, a combination of both.

For instance, HHRAC members Charles Coleman and W.P. Oliver were both ministers at Cornwallis Street, the "mother church" of the African United Baptist Association. [. . .] Educator H.A.J. "Gus" Wedderburn served as the HHRAC's chair and recruited lawyer George Davis to the cause. At the time of Borovoy' s visit to Halifax, Wedderburn was involved with another civil rights organization, the Inter-racial Council, which was represented at the Nova Scotian Hotel by Fran Maclean. [. . .] Her husband, Donald, was the HHRAC's secretary. Like Fran, he was active in the Inter-racial Council, among many other organizations, and shared her commitment to education. Donald Maclean worked

for the province's Adult Education Division before taking a job as the assistant director of Dalhousie University's Institute of Public Affairs. [. . .]

The Macleans' interest in education, as well as Oliver's interest in an activist church, was shared by Lloyd R. Shaw, another key member of the HHRAC. A successful businessman and lifelong democratic socialist, Shaw encouraged such progressive practices as profit-sharing and employee ownership, promoted corporate responsibility, and was actively involved in a range of social issues (including housing, health care, and unemployment).[11] His interest in social reform generally and in Africville specifically grew from his Baptist faith. [. . .]

For these members of the HHRAC, integration and improved living conditions and opportunities were the prime motives for becoming involved with Africville. [. . .]

According to George Davis, the goal of the Halifax Human Rights Advisory Committee was integration. He and his colleagues felt "it would be an advantage to the coming generation to be placed in a position where they would not be a separate community but part of a larger community in which they would be competing as far as work, education, and housing were concerned." For Fran Maclean such opportunities constituted "having rights to be a full citizen," something necessary for "the development of the latent talents of all people."[12]

The involvement of people like Oliver, Coleman, Wedderburn, Davis, the Macleans, and Shaw connected Africville to different networks of power: to people in the municipal and provincial governments and in business, to the university, to the national community of planners, and the international world of human rights. These links raised the profile of Africville, and guaranteed the issues raised by members of the Halifax Human Rights Advisory Committee would get a hearing. [. . .] In 1963 the city retained Albert Rose, a professor of social work at the University of Toronto and architect of Canada's first and largest social housing project, Regent Park, which had been completed in 1957. Shaw and Rose were familiar with each other, both being members of the Community Planning Association of Canada.[13] Rose's philosophy of social housing likely resonated with the members of the Halifax Human Rights Advisory Committee as a whole: he believed the key to healthy housing lay in planned diversity. [. . .] [14]

While forming a coalition with civil liberties advocates strengthened the position of Africville's residents as Borovoy argued it would, doing so did not guarantee their wishes would be heeded. Both they and the members of the Halifax Human Rights Advisory Committee—some of whose members lived in Africville—agreed that there was a housing problem in Africville and that it would be useful for the city to have expert advice. But in recommending Albert Rose, a proponent of integration, the committee narrowed down the possible futures for Africville to one: relocation. Despite the fact that many residents had made it clear they did not want to leave Africville, Rose told them it was in society's (and their) best interests to do so and to integrate themselves with the rest of the city.[15] Overwhelmed and devastated by the conditions Africvillers lived in, he addressed a meeting of residents and the members of the Halifax Human Rights Advisory Committee: "Can a modern urban metropolis tolerate within its midst a community or grouping of dwellings that are physically and socially inadequate, not served with pure water and sewage disposal facilities?" he asked. "Can a minority group be permitted to reconstitute itself as a segregated community at a time in our history, at a time in the social history of western industrialized urban nations, when segregation either de jure (in law) or de facto (in fact) is almost everywhere condemned?"[16] For Rose, as for all the progressives involved with Africville, the answer was "no."

At a time when the civil rights movement in the United States was working to end segregation—particularly residential

segregation—as well as fighting for multiracial public housing, people like Rose and the members of the Halifax Human Rights Advisory Committee just could not understand the desire on the part of some of Africville's residents to rehabilitate their neighbourhood or to be moved to their own public housing facility. Nor could city officials. [. . .]

The extent to which both progressives and city officials were open to treating Africville differently was a direct result of their acknowledgement of its "unique" past: settled for over a century, Africville had endured a history of longstanding municipal neglect and poverty. Given these special circumstances, city officials were reluctant to simply impose the law. Although tearing down Africville's substandard buildings and expropriating the land was appealing in terms of economics and efficiency, and the fastest and cheapest way to initiate the redevelopment of the area, R.B. Grant, the director the Halifax's Development Department, advised against such an approach in 1962. While expenditures would be kept to the "absolute minimum," applying the letter of the law would be costly both to the city's reputation and the lives of the residents of Africville. Instead, the city needed to "temper justice with compassion in matters of compensation and assistance to families affected." Despite the risk of setting "unfortunate precedents," Grant insisted the course of action he outlined was justified in the "interests of history and fair treatment to [Africville's] residents."[17]

The Development Department's arguments for treating Africville differently were echoed by Albert Rose just over a year later. Although his report advised the city to act quickly to relocate and rehouse Africville's residents, Rose also urged municipal authorities to recognize the community's "unique" situation, one that required a comprehensive approach to resettlement. Africville was "far more than a housing problem": it was "a welfare problem . . . a multidimensional task" of a scale no government had dealt with before. There was a lot at stake in relocating the community's residents: for the first time in 25 years of slum clearance, public housing, and redevelopment activity, "the removal of a severely blighted area will take away from a large proportion of the residents, not merely their housing and their sense of community, but their employment and means of livelihood as well . . . "[18] City officials would have to plan carefully.

Rose's report was approved at a meeting of Africville residents in early January 1964, and by the city council shortly afterwards.[19] In deciding to negotiate rather than expropriate, and to treat relocation as a welfare issue rather than simply a housing issue, city officials acted in accordance with a notion of natural justice that stemmed from their recognition of Africville's history and the city's own role in creating the problems that plagued its residents. Formal expropriation proceedings worked against the interests of property holders: they were expensive, they put the onus on them to prove title, and they kept compensation within narrowly defined limits. Negotiations allowed for greater latitude. Acknowledging the welfare dimensions of relocation, city officials also agreed to assist with rehousing Africville residents and develop employment and education programs that would improve their economic and social prospects.

The decision to acknowledge and act on the community's differences in this way shaped the exercise of power and reveals much about the character of the welfare state and the character of Africville.

GROUNDWORK

Implementing the relocation fell to one man, 40-year-old Peter MacDonald, a provincial social worker seconded to the city to deal with the Africville file.[20] That a single individual was given the responsibility for relocating 400 people in just 20 months is indicative of the character of the welfare state at the municipal level: its power was neither anonymous nor,

it seems, particularly extensive. This was not simply a matter of economy, but also of humanity: relying on one individual to be the face of the relocation program reflected a belief held by city officials that "personal contact" was a key part of planned social change. [. . .] If we can refer at all to "technologies of oppression and regulation" operating in the Africville relocation, as Jennifer Nelson does, we need to bear in mind that they were a little like the Great and Powerful Oz, manipulated by a single, over-extended social worker working against an impossible deadline.[21]

If the machinery of power that characterized the welfare state in Halifax was not particularly robust, the context in which it worked made MacDonald's task all the more daunting. Like many of residents of Halifax, and like many of the members of the Halifax Human Rights Advisory Council, MacDonald was not especially familiar with Africville's residents or with how the place operated as a community before he was assigned the relocation file. Initially, his lack of knowledge was an obstacle to doing his job, but an even greater hurdle was the confusion surrounding land tenure.

Africville was almost completely illegible to the state. The city had agreed to compensate property holders at "full market value," but as it acknowledged, and as MacDonald soon learned, doing so was no easy task. It was difficult, if not impossible to ascertain from city records who owned the lands on which Africville residents lived. In planning for Africville's relocation, staff at the city's Development Department searched the original land grants back to 1750s. Unfortunately, after 1795 the records became "vague."[22] While an 1878 city atlas indicated that about 80 per cent of the land in Africville was owned by the city, the volume had no legal standing. Some clarification of title in the area came with the Canadian National Railway expropriations in the early twentieth century, and with the expropriations for Halifax's "Industrial Mile" in 1957.[23] With regard to the latter, however, it soon became apparent that the residents whose properties had been expropriated in 1957 had never been informed of that fact, probably because the "Industrial Mile" never materialized.[24] They had no idea they did not still possess the properties they lived on. Given its failure to inform them, the city agreed that it would proceed as if the 1957 expropriations had never taken place.[25]

City neglect also meant its tax rolls were no help in clarifying property ownership. Africville properties were not assessed regularly or at all until after 1956. [. . .]

Not being able to even locate a property might sound incredible, but a map and an understanding of how Africville's settlement evolved go a fair distance to explaining how and why this was the case. [. . .] The area, about 12 acres in size, was first settled in the 1840s by descendants of black refugees from the War of 1812–1814. Like much of Halifax's north end, Africville was rural in character and remained so into the twentieth century: people kept chickens, pigs, goats, and horses, supplementing their tables by fishing in the Bedford Basin. As Halifax grew in the second half of the nineteenth century Africville grew as well, expanding out from the initial 12-acre settlement. The municipal government allowed industry to encroach: railway tracks were laid through middle of community in the 1850s and expanded twice before the First World War, and a number of factories opened that manufactured bone meal fertilizer, cotton, and nails among other things. A coal handling facility on the waterfront and a stone crushing plant added to area's industrial character. As well, Africville was also the location of an abattoir, the city's sewage disposal pits (1858), the infectious diseases hospital (1870s), and a dump (1950). A residential population grew up amidst these developments, building houses and outbuildings in the spaces in between, giving the area its somewhat anarchic appearance.[26]

Africville's illegibility meant that Mac-Donald's job began with deciphering land tenure—determining what, literally, was to be negotiated. Ascertaining the boundaries of the properties in question and their genealogy was made even more complex by the fact many, if not most, of Africville's property holders died intestate.[27] In the absence of legal records, city officials realized they would have to investigate long-term occupation as well as registered deeds as legitimate sources of title in Africville.

To establish possessory title, Peter Mac-Donald had to rely on the local knowledge of neighbours and long-time residents.[28] Although it took some time for him to gain their trust to the extent they felt comfortable sharing what they knew, his patience was rewarded often with precise information.[29] [. . .]

In summarizing how he worked, Peter MacDonald emphasized how important community views were to ascertaining ownership. At first he "tried to get the story from the owner, and from there find out something at the records office, both at city hall and at the court house." But MacDonald also noted that "where there were no actual deeds . . . [we] pretty well went along with the story . . . the people would give. The property was handed down [from generation to generation], more or less by word of mouth. . . . So there was actually no written document for each particular property saying that one member of the family owned so many square feet and another owned another section or part of the property. So . . . [we] went along pretty well with the status quo as it was in the community."[30]

The information gathered in the process of establishing ownership and setting compensation was not confined to boundaries and buildings. As MacDonald observed, arriving at an amount was not a matter of applying a formula: "You couldn't go across the board and say this type of house, this type of property will pay X number of dollars." Instead, "a fair and equitable settlement" required considering whether the individuals involved were elderly or had dependent children, what their source of income was, and what debts they had—particularly for back taxes or hospital care. These would be cleared, and the amounts owing added to the compensation package.[31] As well, MacDonald made a determination about what in the way of appliances or furnishings people might need in their new lodgings, adding a "furniture allowance" to relocatees' financial settlements.

Property assessment and an assessment of character, as well as circumstance, could go hand-in-hand, as MacDonald's notations about who was "steadily employed," kept up their houses, or fostered children, suggest.[32] But the social worker was not alone in making judgments: Africville residents had opinions about each other that also influenced the settlements that were struck. [. . .]

The extent of local knowledge and the degree to which some of MacDonald's informants were able to comment on the circumstances of their neighbours speaks to the degree to which the relocation process was intertwined with community dynamics and could be incorporated into the local repertoire of welfare practices. [. . .]

If the illegibility of Africville made it impossible for MacDonald to simply impose settlements and forced him to consult with residents, then it also prevented residents from acting collectively. Just before the relocation, there was an effort to organize the people who lived in one area of the community to sell their land as a bloc. The attempt failed because some people had title to their land while others did not; in other words, efforts to organize came to naught because land title could not easily be clarified for the entire area, which put off potential buyers.[33]

While the uncertainty surrounding land ownership was an obstacle to collective bargaining, so too was the absence of a single leader or group of leaders in the community who could deal with the city. MacDonald came to his job in Africville thinking he would work with a handful of individuals who spoke for the community. [. . .] While Africville certainly had its leaders, in MacDonald's view none of them, either as individuals or together, commanded a following that was large enough to be considered a majority.[34]

In part, the absence of a leader or leadership group reflected the diversity of the community and the divisions within it. Africville may have been a single place, but it housed several distinct groups of people.[35] Noting that intermarriage linked Africvillers, and that the community was stable, Clairmont and Magill identified four different groups, each distinguished by their origins and kinship ties, their housing status, the part of Africville they lived in, and their involvement with the Baptist church—one of the anchors of the community.

The "marginals and transients" did not have any kinship ties to people in Africville, nor were they active in the church. The group included a handful of whites who, along with their black counterparts, lived in rented lodgings in an area known as "Around the Bend" in reference to the railway tracks that ran through the community. "Mainliners" had married into the community and had lived in Africville's main settlement area for a significant length of time. The community's elite had regular jobs and owned property; some were particularly active in the church. "Oldliners" were, as the name suggests, the people whose ties to the community went back to the mid-nineteenth century. They were the heart and soul of Seaview Baptist Church and usually owned homes, either in the main settlement or Around the Bend. Finally, there were the "residuals," a group whose kin ties went back no earlier than the last quarter of the nineteenth century. They were not involved in the church, had no legal claims to land or property, and rented or squatted in "Big Town"—ten houses that comprised what one resident called "the baddest part of Africville."[36]

Important itself to understanding the complex character of Africville, this pattern of social differentiation also manifested itself in different attitudes toward relocation. Not surprisingly, oldliners, who were the most deeply rooted in Africville, showed the most reluctance to leave, as did those Clairmont and Magill called residuals. In general, regardless of social group, the oldest Africvillers were the ones who opposed relocation the most. Mainliners comprised the handful of residents who did not like Africville and were most willing to move.[37] Interestingly, the three individuals whose names appear most often in the records as community leaders were mainliners: two were born in neighbouring communities, and the third was from the West Indies. Although Africville's leaders commanded a following of perhaps four or five families each, both they and their supporters were divided by different views on compensation.[38] The oldest among them argued that the city should give "a home for a home," while another pushed for financial compensation based on land value, reasoning that this would allow residents to purchase whatever kind of property they wished. The third, who removed himself from both a leadership role and the community early on, wanted something in between; indeed, he supported rehabilitation rather than relocation.[39]

[. . .]

Not being able to deal collectively with the residents, MacDonald was forced to negotiate with them family by family or one by one. This had a corrosive effect on what solidarity there was among Africville residents, as well as—occasionally—MacDonald's own legitimacy. In a small community, there were few secrets, least of all about who got what compensation. Sensitive to this, the city tried to control the flow of information: although it was required to publish settlements in the newspaper, it did so by property number, rather than the names of the owners. Jealousies were aroused nevertheless, and when rumours circulated about what their leaders had received, some Africville residents accused

them of being selfish and disingenuous—acting as community spokesmen in order to leverage their own position.[40]

Peter MacDonald also found himself caught in the cross-currents his decisions created: he was either the dupe of the cunning men and women of Africville or the nearest thing Halifax had to Niccolò Machiavelli, playing residents off each other. Dealing with people individually also undercut his authority: it made his decisions appear more arbitrary and perhaps less legitimate. While his job required him to deal with all of Africville's residents, it was clear to them that MacDonald spent more time with some people than with others. It could hardly have been otherwise. Those he got along with personally or who were supportive, received more attention; so, too, did the people he identified as possessing some influence, like the community's senior residents or those who had a position of authority in the church.[41] Those who rented or squatted got relatively little attention, in part because MacDonald's energies were focused on the all-consuming task of sorting out the ambiguities surrounding property ownership.

While it is hard to say whether more consideration meant better treatment, the time MacDonald spent with people created a space for some residents to shape the process of relocation. The three to four months it took on average to come up with a deal, and the time MacDonald spent with people during the follow-up after relocation, gave some Africvillers the room to wiggle a better deal for themselves.[42] [. . .]

REMEMBERING AFRICVILLE

Looking at how the relocation was accomplished on the ground reveals continuities in the delivery of welfare. The post-war state had some pre-modern qualities: welfare was still a face-to-face matter, characterized by a good deal of discretion and moral judgement.

Mapping the details of dispossession also divulges the complexities of Africville as a place. Its social differentiation as well as its illegibility meant that MacDonald's decisions were entangled with community dynamics, giving state power a hybrid quality and casting its oppression in a more multifarious light.

In the end, however, Africville was still destroyed, and its residents scattered throughout the city. So why does this story matter?

For one thing, it matters because it helps us understand the people who were involved as more than abstractions. They were not just "officials" or "authorities," "residents" or "relocatees," "whites" or "blacks," but imperfect people who acted, or tried to act, as thoughtfully as they could when they could. They did so within the context of profound racism, before a more militant language of rights had been articulated and before citizen participation was an accepted and financially supported part of urban planning.

Acknowledging this context does not mean individuals should not still be held to account for what they did—for exacting harm in the name of extending help—or that we ignore the structures of inequality that conferred power on some and took it away from others. Nor does it deny the possibility that the progressive politics of the members of the HHRAC as well as Robert Grant and Peter MacDonald might have masked a murkier and more longstanding agenda held by other city officials and supported by certain members of the public. It simply means that we also need to acknowledge who they thought they were and what they thought they were doing. Avoiding what E.P. Thompson called the "condescension of posterity" means taking everyone who was involved in the relocation on their own terms—as well as ours.[43]

Remembering Africville means acknowledging Robert Grant's insistence, as Halifax's director of development, that the city not expropriate—that its officials act with compassion. Remembering Africville means taking Peter MacDonald seriously when he said he tried to give Africville's residents choices where he could. For the Cape Breton social worker, "everyone had a right to a decent standard of living" and decency was determined by being able to choose—what your Africville property was worth, what sort of lodgings you wanted to house yourself in after you left that community, and what kind of furniture you had.[44] Because a decent life was also determined by how you were treated by others, MacDonald worked hard at establishing what he called a "meaningful relationship" with everyone he dealt with.[45] [. . .]

Perhaps this is just a story about how the road to Hell is paved with good intentions. I think it is more than that. Ultimately, the map of power that emerges from looking at the Africville relocation matters because it shows us people trying—at desks, over fences, around kitchen tables, and at community meetings. To a great extent, these are the spaces where we live our lives—where we become who we are. [. . .]

If Africville allows us to see who we are, it also gives us a standpoint from which to tell a larger story about why certain schemes to improve the human condition fail; it shows us the possibilities and limits of the liberal welfare state in meeting human needs.

[. . .]

The failure of this particular scheme to improve the human condition was rooted in how the state saw itself. To account for Africville we have to explore the contours of liberalism; we need to examine how liberals defined the role of the post-war state, drawing the line between legitimate and illegitimate intervention and how they conceived of human needs and how best to meet them. In other words, understanding the failure of forced relocation in post-war Canada requires understanding the ideology that structured the exercise of state power.

Albert Rose and the city conceived of Africville as a "welfare problem," a place whose residents had innumerable needs as a result of the racism that had shaped their lives. Meeting human needs is a challenging task for the state since needs vary both among people and over an individual's lifetime. Liberalism has met this challenge by drawing a distinction between public needs that the state has a responsibility to meet (for things like food, shelter, education, health care, and employment), and private needs that it does not and, liberals say, it should not meet because those needs are so varied, so individual, and so elusive. And if we do not always know what we need, then how can the state presume to know, much less impose, those needs on its citizens?[46]

Public needs are the ones that become entitlements; they become, for instance, the claims or rights we have to adequate housing, health care, or education. Private needs stay private. If the state meets our public needs adequately, then all of us as individuals will be in a better position to meet our private ones—or so the theory of liberalism goes.

[. . .]

For all of its gains, what is lost in our focus on rights is the need for community. This is why Africville is so important: in showing us the difference between integration and belonging it exposes the limits of the liberal welfare state. [. . .]

But giving Africvillers the entitlements that other people enjoyed—giving them equal rights and the opportunities that afforded—did not do anything to reconfigure relations in Halifax in a way that would create a different sense of belonging. Maybe it would have had there been more follow

through, had the programs for education and employment training been adequate, if the public needs of Africville residents had been met more fully. But that seems unlikely. What residents missed most after leaving Africville was something no program could have provided: friends and fellowship—the things that made home.

The failure of the Africville relocation did not lay primarily in inadequate programming. Instead, it was rooted in a fundamental difficulty the liberal state has in where and to what extent to intervene—in drawing the line between respecting individual choice and meeting needs. [. . .]

More broadly, the failure of the Africville relocation rested in the ideas that structured the liberal welfare state—in the balance liberals struck between freedom and solidarity. That balance could not incorporate fully the human need for belonging and the extent to which belonging was also a part of the good life—a powerful source of freedom. To liberals at the time, the desire on the part of Africville's residents to rehabilitate their community or to move as a group to another part of the city was anathema. In their view, this kind of belonging was segregation, it was exclusive, it was racist. But in place of this idea of community that seemed based on exclusion, liberals could offer only the most abstract sense of belonging—one that referenced a "universal brotherhood of man." Despite its legal power, the appeal to a common humanity and to our rights as human beings was not enough to nourish the need for community.

[. . .]

NOTES

1. Gordon Stephenson, *A Redevelopment Study of Halifax, Nova Scotia, 1957* (Halifax: Corporation of the City of Halifax, 1957), 28.

2. "In Search of a Sense of Community," *Time Canada* (6 April 1970), p. 10.

3. Ruth Danenhower Wilson, "Note on Negro–White Relations in Canada" *Social Forces* 28, 1 (1949): 77; Margaret Conrad, "The 1950s: The Decade of Development," in E.R. Forbes and D.A. Muise, eds, *The Atlantic Provinces in*

Confederation (Fredericton and Toronto: Aca-diensis Press and University of Toronto Press, 1993), 398; W.A. MacKay, "Equality of Op-portunity: Recent Developments in the Field of Human Rights in Nova Scotia," *University of Toronto Law Journal* 17, 1 (1967): 176.

4. Janet Guildford, "The End of the Poor Law: Public Welfare Reform before the Canada Assistance Act," in Judith Fingard and Janet Guildford, eds, *Mothers of the Municipality: Women, Work, and Social Policy in Post-1945 Halifax* (Toronto: University of Toronto Press, 2005), 49–75.

5. Richard Bobier, "Africville: The Test of Urban Renewal," *Past Imperfect* 4 (1995): 168–9; Den-nis W. Magill, "The Relocation of Africville: A Case Study of the Politics of Planned Social Change" (PhD diss., Washington University, 1974).

6. Jewish Labour Committee, Correspondence: Sid Blum's trip to the Maritimes to investigate discrimination against Negroes, MG 28, V75, vol. 40, file 8, LAC.

7. David Lewis Stein, "The Counter-Attack on Diehard Racism," *Maclean's*, 20 October 1962.

8. Donald H. Clairmont and Dennis W. Magill, *Africville: The Life and Death of a Canadian Black Community* (Toronto: Canadian Scholars' Press, 1974), 141.

9. Donald H. Clairmont and Dennis W. Magill, *Africville Relocation Report* (Halifax: Institute of Public Affairs, 1971), 121, 124.

10. "Interview with Mr. Borovoy, Director, Cana-dian Civil Liberties Assoc., Toronto, his office, Nov. 14, 2.30-4.30 PM," pp. 3–4, typescript, folder 85.11, Interview File – Al Borovoy, 1969, Institute of Public Affairs Fonds, Dal-housie University Archives.

11. "Lloyd Robert Shaw, 1914–1993," *New Mari-times* (November/December 1993).

12. Clairmont and Magill, *Africville Relocation Report* (electronic version), 136, 130.

13. Clairmont and Magill, *Africville Relocation Report* (electronic version), 152.

14. Albert J. Rose, *Regent Park: A Study in Slum Clearance* (Toronto: University of Toronto Press, 1958), 189.

15. See, for instance, "Residents want to keep homes in Africville," *Halifax Mail Star*, 9 August 1962.

16. On his sentiments after touring Africville, see Clairmont and Magill, *Africville Reloca-tion Report* (electronic version), 155. See also Albert J. Rose, "Report of a Visit to Halifax with Particular Respect to Africville, Novem-ber 24–26, 1963," in Clairmont and Magill, *Africville Relocation Report* (electronic version), Appendix F, p. A53.

17. "Africville, City of Halifax Development Re-port, July 23, 1962," in Clairmont and Magill, *Africville Relocation Report* (electronic version), Appendix A, pp. A4–A6.

18. Rose, "Report of a Visit to Halifax, with Particular Respect to Africville, November 24–26, 1963," in Clairmont and Magill, *Af-ricville Relocation Report* (electronic version), Appendix F, p. A54.

19. Only 41 Africville residents were at the meet-ing on 9 January 1964, when Rose's report was discussed, and 37 of them voted in favour Rose's recommendations. The city adopted Rose's report on 16 January 1964. See "37 Africville Residents Approve of Rose Report," *The Mail-Star* (Halifax, NS), 10 January 1964, as well as "City to Make Africville Move as Painless as Possible, Mayor Says," *The Mail-Star*, 17 January 1964.

20. Peter MacDonald had been working in his na-tive Cape Breton as a social worker before he was assigned to the Africville job. He was a graduate of St Francis Xavier University and the Maritime School of Social Work at Dal-housie. See "Named to shift Africville folk," *The Mail-Star*, 10 April 1964.

21. Jennifer J. Nelson, *Razing Africville: A Geogra-phy of Racism* (Toronto: University of Toronto Press, 2008), 5.

22. Clairmont and Magill, *Africville Relocation Re-port* (electronic version), 147 as well as Appen-dix A, p. A3.

23. "Africville: City of Halifax Development De-partment Report: Africville, 23 July 1962," in Clairmont and Magill, *Africville Relocation Report* (electronic version), Appendix A, p. A3.

24. Clairmont and Magill, *Africville Relocation Re-port*, 146.

25. "Memorandum re: Possible Acquisition of Prop-erty # 20 from P.F.C. Byars, City Manager, to Members of the Sub-Committee on Africville," 31 May 1965, p. 1, Africville Sub-Committee, 102- 42C, file 5, Halifax Regional Municipality

Archives (HRMA); "Memorandum re: Staff Report – Possible Acquisition of Property #12, #13, #15 owned by Mr -- , Africville, from P.F.C. Byars, City Manager, to Members of the Sub-Committee on Africville and the Representatives of the Human Rights Advisory Committee," 24 May 1967, p. 1, Africville Sub-Committee, 102-42C, file 17, HRMA.

26. Clairmont and Magill, *Africville: The Life and Death of a Canadian Black Community,* 93–7.

27. See Magill, "The Relocation of Africville," 36.

28. See Clairmont and Magill, *Africville: The Life and Death of a Canadian Black Community,* 60.

29. See "Interview with Peter MacDonald Concerning the Africville Relocation, July 4, 1969," p. 7, typescript, folder 85.12, Interview File – Peter MacDonald, 1969, Institute of Public Affairs Fonds, Dalhousie University Archives.

30. Clairmont and Magill, *Africville: The Life and Death of a Canadian Black Community,* 187.

31. Peter MacDonald interview, 9 July 1968, pp. 14–15.

32. Peter MacDonald interview, 9 July 1968, p. 15.

33. "Interview with Peter MacDonald re Africville Relocation, June 26, 1969" (John de Roche), p. 22, typescript, folder 85.13, Interview File – Peter MacDonald, 1965–1969, Institute of Public Affairs Fonds, Dalhousie University Archives.

34. "The History and Social Structure of Africville, an Interview with Peter MacDonald, Thursday, June 26, 1969" (John de Roche), pp. 10 and 12, folder 85.12, Interview File – Peter MacDonald, 1969, Institute of Public Affairs Fonds, Dalhousie University Archives.

35. Clairmont and Magill went so far as to argue that using "community" and "social structure" in reference to Africville was problematic because they "seem to imply greater system, stability, and homogeneity than Africville possessed." See Clairmont and Magill, *Africville: The Life and Death of a Canadian Black Community,* 62.

36. Clairmont and Magill, *Africville: The Life and Death of a Canadian Black Community,* 53–7.

37. Clairmont and Magill, *Africville: The Life and Death of a Canadian Black Community,* 57. See also Table 7.2, p. 209. While noting the relationship between social group and attitudes toward relocation, Clairmont and Magill note that 40 per cent of residents were "at least to some extent willing to be relocated when they became aware of the city's program" (208).

38. Peter MacDonald interview, 9 July 1968, p. 4.

39. Peter MacDonald interview, 26 June 1969 ("The History and Social Structure of Africville"), pp. 12–13.

40. Clairmont and Magill, *Africville: The Life and Death of a Canadian Black Community,* 183–4.

41. "Dennis W. Magill's Interview with Peter MacDonald, July 16, 1969," pp. 10–11, folder 85.13, Interview File – Peter MacDonald, Institute of Public Affairs Fonds, Dalhousie University Archives.

42. The process of negotiation took an average of three to four months for each settlement. After an agreement was reached, Peter MacDonald wrote it up and presented his recommendation to the city for approval. See Clairmont and Magill, *Africville Relocation Report* (electronic version), 186. Also see Clairmont and Magill, *Africville: The Life and Death of a Canadian Black Community,* 216.

43. E.P. Thompson, *The Making of the English Working Class* (New York: Pantheon, 1963), 12.

44. Peter MacDonald interview, 9 July 1968, p. 16; "Interview with Peter MacDonald re Africville Relocation, July 10, 1968" (Dennis W. Magill), p. 10, folder 85.14, Interview File – Peter MacDonald, 1968, Institute of Public Affairs Fonds, Dalhousie University Archives.

45. Peter MacDonald interview, 16 July 1968, p. 6.

46. My thoughts in this section are preliminary and are shaped by Michael Ignatieff, *The Needs of Strangers: An Essay on Privacy, Solidarity, and the Politics of Being Human* (New York: Penguin, 1984).

Chapter 10

Cold War Canada

READINGS

Primary Documents

1   From "Letter to My Son," Farley Mowat

2   Five caricatures related to Canada and the Cold War

Historical Interpretations

3   From "The Queer Career of Homosexual Security Vetting in Cold War Canada,"
    Daniel J. Robinson and David Kimmel

4   From "A 'Half-Hearted Response'? Canada and the Cuban Missile Crisis, 1962,"
    Asa McKercher

INTRODUCTION

Two superpowers emerged from the Second World War—the United States and the Soviet Union—and both sought to expand their influence and their respective political and economic systems in the new post-war world. The resulting confrontation would last from the mid-1940s until the collapse of the Soviet Union in late 1991. Initially, Canadians were largely unconcerned by the gathering storm. Rapid demobilization had reduced Canada's large wartime military to a small force, and many Canadians held reasonably favourable attitudes toward their erstwhile Soviet allies. But the rapid expansion of communism in both Europe and Asia, along with revelations that a major soviet spy ring had been operating in the Dominion, soon brought anti-communist sentiment to new heights. By the late 1940s, Canadian defence spending was rising again, and the RCMP's Special Branch, which was charged with counter-espionage, was actively investigating allegations of communist subversion. Canada played an important role in the early Cold War. The nation was a founding member of the North Atlantic Treaty Organization (NATO) in 1949, and Canadian troops were sent to Korean peninsula to help repel an attempted communist takeover of American-backed South Korea in 1950. By the 1960s, however, many Canadians were beginning to tire of anti-communist rhetoric. Left-wing ideas were popular among the country's youth, and Canada's role in containing "international communism" was being increasingly questioned. In fact, many Canadians regarded the growing American presence in Canada to be a greater threat to the nation than the distant spectre of Soviet communism. By the 1980s, as the Cold War entered its final phase, American officials sometimes openly despaired at Canada's growing indifference toward the conflict. Novelist Farley Mowat's letter to his son reflects the unease that many Canadians felt regarding America's role as a Cold War superpower. Along with philosopher George Grant, Mowat believed that the Canadian struggle against American domination was essentially a lost cause, but that it was nevertheless a cause worth championing. The caricatures that are reproduced in the following pages reflect the evolution of Cold War attitudes in Canada. The first piece, which was published by the Montreal *Gazette* during the Korean War, expresses Canadian anxieties regarding communist aggression. By the time the fifth cartoon was published, also by the *Gazette*, in the 1980s, Canadian attitudes had shifted considerably, and cartoonists regularly lampooned American defence initiatives, in this case the testing of US cruise missiles over Alberta. As our historical interpretations show, however, the Cold War was no laughing matter. In Daniel J. Robinson and David Kimmel's article, we see that Cold War anxieties over disloyalty intensified homophobia in Canadian society. Gay public servants were dismissed from their jobs over fears that their "immoral" nature made them security risks. Asa McKercher's article delves into Canada's role in the 1962 Cuban Missile Crisis, which brought the world to the brink of nuclear war. Unlike most historians of Canadian–American relations, who generally emphasize the tensions that arose during the crisis between President John F. Kennedy and Prime Minister John Diefenbaker, McKercher notes that Canada's diplomatic and military establishment sided with Washington in October 1962 and provided the United States with valuable assistance.

QUESTIONS FOR CONSIDERATION

1. What vision of the United States emerges from Farley Mowat's piece?
2. What Cold War anxieties are reflected in these cartoons?
3. Was Canada's involvement in the Cold War necessary?
4. What factors brought federal officials to launch a campaign to root homosexuals out of the public service?
5. What support did Canada's diplomatic and military establishment give to the United States during the Cuban Missile Crisis and how did it undermine the prime minister?

SUGGESTIONS FOR FURTHER READING

J.L. Black and Norman Hillmer, *Nearly Neighbours: Canada and the Soviet Union, From Cold War to Détente and Beyond* (Kingston: R.P. Frye, 1989).

Robert Bothwell, *Alliance and Illusion: Canada and the World, 1945–1984* (Vancouver: UBC Press, 2008).

Tarah Brookfield, *Cold War Comforts: Canadian Women, Child Safety, and Global Insecurity* (Waterloo: Wilfrid Laurier University Press, 2012).

Andrew P. Burtch, *Give Me Shelter: The Failure of Canada's Cold War Civil Defence* (Vancouver: UBC Press, 2012).

Andrew B. Godefroy, *In Peace Prepared: Innovation and Adaptation in Canada's Cold War Army* (Vancouver: UBC Press, 2014).

Joseph T. Jockel, *Canada in NORAD, 1957–2007: A History* (Montreal and Kingston: McGill-Queen's University Press, 2007).

Amy W. Knight, *How the Cold War Began: The Gouzenko Affair and the Hunt for Soviet Spies* (Toronto: McClelland & Stewart, 2005).

Edelgard Mahant and Graeme S. Mount, *Invisible and Inaudible in Washington: American Policies toward Canada* (Vancouver: UBC Press, 1999).

Sean M. Maloney, *Learning to Love the Bomb: Canada's Nuclear Weapons during the Cold War* (Washington: Potomac Books, 2007).

Robert Teigrob, *Warming Up to the Cold War: Canada and the United States' Coalition of the Willing, from Hiroshima to Korea* (Toronto: University of Toronto Press, 2009).

Reginald Whitaker, *Cold War Canada: The Making of the National Insecurity State, 1945–1957* (Toronto: University of Toronto Press, 1994).

——— and Steve Hewitt, *Canada and the Cold War* (Toronto: Lorimer, 2003).

Primary Documents

1 From Farley Mowat, "Letter to My Son," in A.W. Purdy, ed., *The New Romans: Candid Canadian Opinions of the U.S.* (Edmonton: M.G. Hurtig, 1968), 1–6.

My dear Sandy:

A couple of months ago you asked me whether I thought it had been worthwhile to have spent so much of my time and energy tilting against American windmills. Feeling that there was a certain measure of condescension in the question, I replied with one of my facile, TV-type answers: to wit, that there can be no other real choice open to a Canadian except to resist the Yanks and all their works so that we, as a people and a nation, may escape being ingested into the Eagle's gut, never to emerge again except—maybe—as a patch of excrement upon the pages of world history.

That should have disposed of your question—but it didn't, and the damned thing has been festering within me ever since. It has finally forced me, very reluctantly you can believe, to make a new evaluation of the belief which has sustained me through some twenty years of waging verbal warfare against the encroachments of Uncle Sam. Have I indeed been wasting my time? I'm afraid, God help me, that I have. I can no longer convince myself that we have even a snowball's chance in hell of escaping ultimate ravishment at the hands of the Yankee succubus. And what really hurts is the belated recognition on my part that there never *was* much chance; that Canadians have become so fatally infected with a compulsive desire to be screwed, blued, and tattooed as minions of the U.S.A.: that they not only do not wish to be saved— they are willing to fight against salvation with all the ferocity of cornered rats.

So wipe that smug smile off your face. You knew it all along, eh? Well, I should have known it too. God wot, enough people have tried to put me straight. There was Joey Smallwood for one (as smart a promoter as ever hustled a vote), who gave me a fatherly lecture about a year ago. "What the U.S. wants, it will get," he told me. "And if we don't *give* them what they want, they'll take it anyway. And what they want—is most of what we've got."

That was about as clear an expression of *Realpolitik* as one can expect from the political animal, even if it was primarily a rationalization intended to excuse our political masters for having *already* given the Yanks almost everything of any value in this country. Nevertheless, Joey's point was well taken since those who rule us (they do not "govern"—that word implies statesmanship combined with honourable intentions) have, for their own reasons, long since sold us out. Or maybe they just saw the light a long way back and, in keeping with their dubious professional practices, took the line of least resistance. Some of them, that is. Others sold out with deliberate intent. One day I must tell you the full and stirring story of one of the greatest of all such salesmen—C.D. Howe—and of how *he* put us on the block. Of course, Howe's plan was to sell us down the river on the national scale, and we've progressed since then. Now every single province is trying to conduct its own sellout, in direct competition with the Ottawa salesmen, and it wouldn't surprise me much to see the game, which is called "who'll sell out the mostest, the soonest," reach right down to the municipal level before too long. Hell, what am I saying? It is past that point already. Witness the almost frantic rush of businessmen and owners of Canadian resources to sell themselves and their holdings ("*their* holdings"? I mean *ours,* of course) for a quick handful of Yankee bucks.

Joey wasn't the only one to point me in the direction of acute awareness, and I must add, in my own defence, that I wasn't as stupid as you may think. I realized what the politicians, at least, were up to ages ago. My naivety—if such it was—lay in my continuing conviction that the *people* of this land would not forever continue to acquiesce in this piecemeal betrayal of themselves and of their country. I was much influenced by what took place in Cuba and, before that, in Mexico. I believed that if such small, relatively powerless serf states could muster the guts to really kick Big Uncle in the backside, the people of Canada might be goaded into an equivalent demonstration of courage. Alas, Canadians are not Mexicans or Cubans, and I realize now that I miscalculated on a horrendous scale in ever thinking that Canadians would risk cutting off rich Uncle's dole by assuming the posture of a Man.

This is a fact that I am going to have to learn to live with. We have become a prostrate people—by our own volition. Actually the only time Canadians even raise themselves on their elbows these days is to *defend* their chosen masters and to attack, with the bitter hostility only known to turncoats, those who dare reproach them for their spineless espousal of slave status. (If this letter to you should ever see publication, the response in the "Letters To The Editor" column will show you what I mean!)

But there is no point in running on about what's past. My concern is for the future, because the future contains the world in which you'll have to live. So I have a few words of wisdom for you. Here speaks the hoary elder, and if I belabour the obvious a bit, bear with me.

Despite poor old Lester Pearson's recent statement in *Maclean's* that "the Americans are the least imperialistic people in history" (honest to God—that's what he said!), the Yanks now control the largest empire the world has ever known. Its citizens have, as Henry R. Luce (founder of Canada's two favourite magazines—*Life* and *Time*) once put it, now risen to the challenge: "to accept wholeheartedly the duty and opportunity as the most powerful and vital nation in the world and in consequence to exert upon the world the full impact of our influence, *for such purposes as we see fit and by such means as we see fit*" (italics mine). In this delightfully frank statement, combined with one by John Foster Dulles—"There are two ways of conquering a foreign nation. One is to gain control of its people by force of arms. The other is to gain control of its economy by financial means."—you have the essential dogma subscribed to by the military-political-economic hegemony that runs the U.S.A. Once you understand this dogma you will have no difficulty understanding the true significance of current events in Spain, Korea, Greece, Formosa, the Philippines, Venezuela, Dominica, and all the rest of the sixty-odd serf states which are euphemistically referred to as U.S. "client" states. Note with particular attention that most of these U.S. "client" states are run by military, aristocratic, or political juntas of a totalitarian nature—juntas whose prime allegiance is to the hungry Eagle, rather than to their own peoples: juntas, many of which are maintained in power *by* the United States through classic applications of the principles of bribery, blackmail, subversion . . . and armed force.

Or, if you find such a mass of evidence too complex for easy assimilation, take a long look at Vietnam instead. Observe, if you dare, the fantastic and fearful similarities between the way the United States is behaving in that small and benighted country and the way Hitler behaved in *his* heyday.

Having done one or the other—preferably both—I ask you to consider the reality behind the American claims (ably supported by such pillars of righteousness as our own Paul Martin) to being the world's greatest defenders of democracy. Democracy? My God, it is to laugh . . . but bitter laughter it must be since demonstrably the United States is currently engaged in almost every form of domestic and external brutality, aggrandizement, degradation of the individual, and destruction of freedom which, so the U.S.A. maintains with a straight face, are the *singular* hallmarks of the beast called communism.

And what, you say, is this tirade in aid of? Well, it is intended to ensure that you

harbour no further illusions about living in a democracy or of being protected by one. You, my son, are a helot, born and bred under the aegis of the United States, and you had damned well better come to terms with this inescapable fact. The illusion of democracy is one that you and your generation can ill afford to nurture. You must recognize that hard reality which not all the cherry-flavoured words of all the hucksters in the world can adequately conceal—you are a serf, no more than that . . . and Massa lives away down south.

You must rid yourself of this delusion because, as I see things, there is no guarantee that the privileged position presently enjoyed by Canadians as "most-favoured serfs" will last. The day is near when the Yankees will see no further need to pamper us—they'll own us outright. And then we may expect to be subjected to the same forms of direct oppression that have been inflicted on most of the other peoples inhabiting the two American continents. The steady growth of overt totalitarianism within the Master State itself brings ominous intimations that the good, fat days for the people who sold themselves into bondage may even now be drawing to a close. And remember—a man who sells *himself* into slavery does not earn the gratitude of his master: instead he earns a deep contempt. We Canadians have well earned such contempt—and a wise slave knows that a contemptuous master is more to be feared, in the long run, than an angry one.

Which leads me to an aside I think worth making. Not *all* Canadians have sold themselves. As you are well aware, the French Canadians in Quebec don't share our desire for self-immolation. They are resisting and thereby rousing our particular hatred and resentment. Why so? It is not because we really fear the development of a true federation of two nations (many other countries live with such federations, and live well); it is because we are deathly afraid that the intransigence of Quebec will draw the cold and hooded stare of the

Eagle and thereby expose *us*, by implication, to the furies meted out to helots who revolt.

What I am trying to tell you is that nobody can, at this late stage, reverse the tide. Quebec, bravely as she may struggle, will fail. And so your own survival now depends on your becoming as selfishly inclined, as amoral as the men who have brought you and this country to its present sorry pass. You must needs become one of them, and you might as well become one of the overseer class, if you can make the grade. I recommend that you enter politics. Although you have not yet displayed the requisite capabilities for duplicity, cowardice, self-serving, and betrayal which pass for morality in high places, you might improve with practice. It is at least certain that a political career is one of the few available that will permit you to enjoy, with any security of tenure, the benefits accrued by renegades and sycophants.

You might conceivably consider entering the business world, as an alternative, but the opportunities it offers are strictly limited. This is the Holy of Holies, and since its true hierarchy is almost exclusively composed of citizens of the Master State (whether they are card-carrying citizens or only *de facto* citizens is of no import), the chances of a helot rising to those secure seats of power are almost non-existent. But as a politician you would be employed in the services of the Business God, and as a valuable and trusted slave, you would be deserving of good treatment and assured of a safe niche.

There is another course you might consider taking. You could follow the example of so many of your compatriots and anticipate events by journeying to Rome, before the Marines come north for you. As a beginning you could voluntarily enlist in the legions of the Eagle and thereby gain the jump on those of your generation who do not yet realize that the day approaches when the Ottawa satraps will join Australia, New Zealand, and other such in sending levies to fight America's wars for her. Since you have no Negro, Indian, Eskimo, or other dubious blood in your veins, you ought to be able to wangle a cushy job far from the sound of battle and from the stench of burning babies. Eventually you could hope to be rewarded with citizenship in the Master State, and although this would require that you reject all you have heretofore been taught to believe is good in man, it would at least provide you with something you never had before—a verifiable nationality.

I have only suggested a few of the possible funk holes, and you will easily think of many more. The point is that you *should* be thinking about them very seriously, and right now. Time is running out for your fellow slaves who, complacent and myopic as they are, believe they have made a splendid bargain with a kindly master. The cold and brutal hour when they learn the truth, and when they learn the price of their betrayal of themselves and of their land, lies close at hand. God help them then, for no one else will wish to, if they could.

2   Five Caricatures Related to Canada and the Cold War

Figure 10.1   *The World We Live In* by John Collins.

Figure 10.2   *RCMP Dilemma: Report to Ottawa or Washington?* by A.C. Kaufman

Figure 10.3   *Watch Dog* by Merle Tingley.

The Legionary, June 1959

Figure 10.4 *. . . And Now A Word From The Chopping Block* by Merle Tingley.

Figure 10.5 *Missile Cruise Tests over Alberta* by Aislin (alias Terry Mosher).

Historical Interpretations

3   Daniel J. Robinson and David Kimmel, "The Queer Career of Homosexual Security Vetting in Cold War Canada," *Canadian Historical Review* 75, 3 (1994): 319–45. Reprinted with permission from University of Toronto Press (www.utpjournals.com)

The Cold War is over but the historical assessment of its impact on post-war Canadian society has scarcely begun. Recent studies suggest that Canada's "homefront" was not entirely spared the ignominy of civil rights abuses commonly associated with Cold War America. Although in Canada no McCarthyesque figure or televised loyalty board hearings captured the public spotlight, there were many groups and individuals—among them Communists, labour leaders, academics, immigrants, and artists—whose varied left-wing political views or affiliations subjected them to state persecution and other organized forms of "red-baiting." Jobs were lost, careers ended, and lives ruined, the most notable example being Canadian diplomat Herbert Norman who committed suicide in 1957 when the United States Senate reopened an investigation of his political loyalty.[1] While scholarly work has elucidated Ottawa's handling of political and ideological threats during the Cold War, another important subject has received only passing notice: the federal government's security investigation and subsequent firing of homosexuals during the 1950s and 1960s. When the episode was recently brought to public attention, Prime Minister Brian Mulroney denounced it as "one of the greatest outrages and violations of human rights" which even "the passage of time . . . [has not made] any less odious."[2]

This "odious" event was a peculiar product of Cold War era "insecurities." Government officials maintained that homosexuals (almost exclusively males) fearing public exposure were security risks owing to their susceptibility to blackmail by hostile intelligence agencies. Along with political subversives and foreign spies, they were considered legitimate targets of investigation. The Royal Canadian Mounted Police (RCMP) took up the challenge wholeheartedly. A separate unit was formed to deal with the homosexual issue. And by the late 1960s the total number of RCMP files concerning homosexuals reached roughly 9000, only one-third of which involved government employees. In conjunction with this investigation, the federal government sponsored a research project that sought to "detect" homosexuality through the photographic measurement of eye movements of people shown hetero- and homoerotic pictures. The research was headed by Carleton University professor Robert Wake and was backed by officials from a number of federal departments. Dubbed the "fruit machine" by the Mounties, the project amounted to a four-year effort to enlist science in the cause of state security.

How this investigation and research project could reach such advanced and, to the modern reader, disturbing degrees is the result of many factors. The government's internal security system, soon after its founding in 1946, institutionalized procedures that provided both the security rationale and the investigative means for later anti-homosexual campaigns. These consisted of the government's early preoccupation with employee "character weaknesses" as a security concern, the predominant role of the RCMP in the security vetting process, and the importance of appeasing American security interests in Canada. As well, Canadian officials adopted some features of Washington's early 1950s efforts to root out homosexuals from federal offices, efforts that advanced far beyond a security rationale and into outright homophobia. Yet another example of US influence was the reliance of Dr Wake on the American psychiatric community for information concerning homosexual-detection methods. Throughout the period the most vehement opponents of the employment of homosexuals in any government capacity were the RCMP and the Department of National Defence (DND). Their common position derived in large measure from each organization's internal policy of automatically discharging all discovered homosexuals. Not all government officials, though, were as prejudiced as their police and military counterparts. As a result, the debate over the homosexual security issue was characterized by liberal-versus-hardliner disagreement.

The story is bitterly ironic. When the Canadian government earnestly turned its attention to the homosexual security question in 1958, it was to inquire whether security policies and procedures regarding "character weaknesses" might be moderated. The phenomenon that culminated in the RCMP's 9000-name homosexual index and the fruit machine was, in part, the unintended consequence of a liberal initiative.

While the Canadian government's investigation of homosexuals began in the late 1950s, the origins of this policy date back to an early Cold War development, the September 1945 defection of Igor Gouzenko. The ensuing royal commission, after concluding that a number of ideologically motivated public servants had passed on state secrets to Soviet agents, recommended the adoption of a more systematic and stringent approach to government security.[3] [. . .] A cabinet directive on security (CD no. 4) was issued in March 1948 stating that "maximum care" be used "to ensure that government employees are completely trustworthy."[4]

The investigative task outlined in CD no. 4 fell to the RCMP, which conducted two types of security probes. For government employees seeking the lower-level "confidential" or "restricted" security clearances, a simple record check was done. This process involved a criminal record check and a search of RCMP files for any links to "known subversive organizations." For "secret" and "top secret" clearances, along with the record check, a "field investigation" involving a "full enquiry into the antecedents of the employee" was conducted. Former employers and others "closely connected with the person" were contacted and interviewed.[5] While the Mounties conducted the investigations and compiled "adverse" reports on employees where evidence warranted, the authority to grant or deny a security clearance—in fact take any other course of action with respect to the employee—rested with the respective deputy minister.[6] The separation of fact-finding and decision-making functions was supposed to ensure that an overzealous RCMP did not unnecessarily deny security clearances. The most thorough study of the Security Panel's early years, however, suggests that this separation was more nominal than actual. Deputy ministers were largely unfamiliar with security issues and often deferred to the RCMP's more experienced judgment in these matters. The result, according to Reg Whitaker, was "a procedure by which the police would not only gather information, but would themselves evaluate it and in effect make recommendations on whether individuals were security risks."[7] [. . .] In the late 1940s the RCMP were conducting some 2000 security checks a month; by the mid-1950s this number had climbed to nearly 5000.[8]

Along with the RCMP's central role in the security vetting process, three other aspects of the Security Panel's operations are significant to the later targeting of homosexuals as risks. First, extreme secretiveness surrounded the security screening process. Second, the matter of "character weaknesses" was of increasing concern. The third aspect was Canada's sensitivity to American concerns when formulating its own security policy.

Unlike the United States, where government security systems were more open and allowed for appeals (albeit of a very limited nature), Canada's procedure was a closed-door affair without review provisions.[9] This undisclosed approach was viewed favourably by officials overseeing the system.[10] They argued that government employees secretly deemed security risks were spared the public humiliation and "black-listing" characteristic of American loyalty board hearings. In Canada, discreetly released public servants would not have their reputations smeared and their careers ruined. Thus they would be better placed to find other employment. Of course, this approach was something of a mixed blessing. Unlike the United States where the Attorney General's Office published a list of "subversive" organizations, in Canada the RCMP secretly dubbed many clubs and organizations "communist fronts," and suspicions were cast on members even if they had no way of knowing which associations were "acceptable" and which were not. Indeed, Canadian civil servants were most likely unaware that security reasons were to blame for a firing, transfer, or demotion. CD no. 4 stipulated that such matters be dealt with not on the basis of security, but rather "personal unsuitability."[11] [. . .]

This furtive and evasive approach becomes more troubling from a civil liberties perspective when viewed alongside the content of RCMP security reports. The first batch of RCMP security investigations, dated 1949, revealed that of 213 adverse reports, only 27 involved political subversion. The remaining 87 per cent comprised "character" or moral flaws such as gambling, adultery, drinking, or women having illegitimate children. No cases of homosexuality were cited. While Lucas was initially disturbed by these results, other civilian members of the panel soon accepted the Mounties' rationale for this comprehensive approach: individuals engaging in socially stigmatized behaviour were subject to blackmail because they had something to hide. In light of these developments a new classification category covering

"character weaknesses" was created. It entailed the following notice being placed in an individual's file: "information at hand, although not bearing directly on security, may be considered to affect the suitability of this person for employment in the public service." Thus the handling of character weakness became a routine feature of the internal security process. Though the frequency of "character weakness" entries declined in the early 1950s, they still comprised twice the number of "political" adverse reports.[12] It would seem, therefore, that Justice Minister J.L. Ilsley's assurances in the Commons on 22 June 1948 that government security screening would not devolve into "any irrelevant inquiry into the private lives of individuals" were in fact premature.[13]

The final significant feature of Ottawa's internal security system was its vulnerability to American pressure. When in 1920 the RCMP began collecting security intelligence, its covert operations were restricted to Canadian territory. This practice continued into the post-1945 period. Hence Canada, unlike Britain and the United States, lacked its own means of gathering foreign-based intelligence affecting the national interest.[14] Accordingly the RCMP depended on "friendly" security agencies like the Federal Bureau of Investigation (FBI) and, after 1947, the Central Intelligence Agency (CIA) for help in these areas. The FBI representative at the American Embassy in Ottawa actually worked out of RCMP headquarters until the mid-1950s. As well, the Mounties were in the habit of giving the FBI information on Canadian political subversives to which even federal cabinet ministers were denied access.[15] Compounding the asymmetrical relationship of the two countries' intelligence agencies was a larger structural dependence resulting from Canada's accelerating economic and defence integration with the United States after 1945.[16]

[. . .] This close interconnection between internal security and international intelligence links is underscored by the following excerpt from a government report on the topic:

> There is more than just an internal need for a security intelligence agency. Canada's international alliances require that it be able to assure its allies, with whom it participates in common defence arrangements, that it has a sound system of internal security. Allied countries will not entrust Canadian officials and political leaders with secret information unless Canada has in place effective structures and procedures for detecting and preventing foreign espionage.[17]

Logic indicates, therefore, that the security preoccupations of the senior partner were likely to become those of the junior partner seeking to preserve access to the former's intelligence secrets.

With these factors in mind we turn to the American government's security vetting of homosexual public servants in the early 1950s. "It is the opinion of this subcommittee," a December 1950 United States Senate report concluded, that homosexuals "are unsuitable for employment in the Federal Government" because their "degraded," "illegal," and "immoral" activities rendered them innately unreliable.[18] Since it was also an "accepted fact" that homosexuals were "prime targets" of blackmail by hostile foreign agents, such "sex perverts" constituted high-level security risks. Testimony from "eminent [though unnamed] psychiatrists" and an "abundance of [undocumented] evidence" confirmed the homosexual's depraved, pitiful, and socially abhorrent condition. Moreover, these persons were a physical threat to other employees: "[Homosexuals] will frequently attempt to entice normal individuals to engage in perverted practises. This is particularly true in the case of young and impressionable people who might come under the influence of a pervert . . . It is particularly important that the thousands of young men

and women who are brought into Federal jobs not be subjected to that type of influence while in the service of the Government. One homosexual can pollute a Government office." The report's recommendation that the government not "pussyfoot" about or adopt "half measures" regarding this issue was in fact preaching to the recently converted.[19] By early 1950 Washington had already stepped up its efforts to remove homosexuals from the federal payroll. While between 1947 and April 1950 an average of five homosexuals per month were dismissed from civilian positions, during the next year the total jumped to more than 60. The "lavender scare" became a frequent topic of concern for congressional leaders throughout 1950. The FBI took a prominent role in internal investigations, even opening a file on presidential candidate Adlai Stevenson's "alleged homosexuality." In March 1953 the State Department revealed that 425 of its employees had been released as a result of homosexual probes. The next month the Eisenhower administration issued Executive Order 10450 which specified that "sexual perversion" was definite grounds for dismissal from public positions. As a result, an average of 40 homosexuals per month were released in the following year.[20] At the same time Alfred Kinsey, whose widely read 1948 study on male sexuality argued that homosexual behaviour was more common than previously thought, was denounced as a communist by newspapers and the Catholic Church. By 1954 much of his private and federal research funding had been withdrawn.[21]

The influence of the American preoccupation with the homosexual security question manifested itself in amendments to Canada's immigration laws. A government committee overseeing revision of the Immigration Act met on 20 December 1950 and added "homosexuals, lesbians, and persons coming to Canada for any immoral purpose" to the list of prohibited classes. The proscription on homosexuals remained in the version that went before a Commons committee in June 1952 and which soon after became law. At no point during this committee or parliamentary debate did the subject elicit any comment. Thus the first time an Act of Parliament referred to "homosexual" as "a status or a type of person" (as opposed to specific "homosexual acts") passed unnoticed.[22] The law barred homosexuals from visiting Canada and applying as immigrants or permanent residents. As seen earlier in a different context, people denied entry to Canada on security grounds were also not informed of the actual reasons for this action.[23] Philip Girard argues that the principal backer of the homosexual exclusion was the RCMP, which oversaw the drafting of the new lists of prohibited categories. As well, Girard attributes the impetus for the homosexual ban to "American concern about the alleged laxity of Canada's security system," which was conveyed to Canadian officials via the RCMP and DND.[24]

Shortly after the passage of the Immigration Act, a new cabinet directive on security was issued. Among the October 1952 provisions was the recommendation that reliability from a security viewpoint take account of "defects of character" that might cause an employee to be "indiscreet, dishonest or vulnerable to blackmail."[25] Three years later a more detailed cabinet directive (CD no. 29) reaffirmed this policy position.

It also remains an essential of Canadian security policy that persons who are unreliable from a security standpoint, not because they are disloyal, but because of defects in their character which may lead to indiscretion or dishonesty, or may make them like subjects of blackmail, must not be employed in any position where they have access to classified information. Such defects of character may also make them unsuitable for employment on grounds other than security.[26]

"On grounds other than security" clearly echoed American policy in which the "general unsuitability" of homosexuals justified their exclusion from federal offices irrespective of security considerations. When cabinet met on 21 December 1955 to consider CD no. 29—which had been drafted by the Security Panel—it deemed the directive "eminently reasonable" and passed it without any discussion of the character weakness clause.[27]

While the character weakness provisions of internal security did not appear to concern the Liberal St Laurent government, such was not the case for its Tory successor. John Diefenbaker's twin election victories in 1957 and 1958 brought to the prime minister's office a man with a longstanding reputation as a civil rights advocate who had voiced concerns about government security screening as early as 1948.[28] In June 1958 Diefenbaker requested that security procedures affecting character weaknesses be re-examined with a mind to adopting a more liberal approach. G.F. Frazer of the Privy Council Office was charged with drafting a memo for consideration by the Security Sub-Panel, the interdepartmental body formed in 1953 to supervise much of the preparatory work for the Security Panels.[29] Frazer's memo noted that on only one occasion had a matter of character weakness "rendered an employee untrustworthy for access to classified information." That case involved a civilian employee of the Royal Canadian Air Force who in 1956 passed low-grade information to a Soviet official while inebriated. The incident was not thought serious and Frazer argued that character weaknesses as a whole were less sensitive than subversive threats. He therefore called for a "greater measure of fairness" when dealing with individuals whose loyalty was not in doubt. A more "sympathetic" handling of the matter was both possible and desirable.

[. . .]

This sympathetic impulse proved short-lived. Frazer's memo was not received enthusiastically when the Security Sub-Panel convened on 8 July (the first comprehensive discussion of character weakness in a security forum). DEA representative J. Timmerman described how on at least four occasions Soviet intelligence agents had (unsuccessfully) attempted to exploit character weaknesses by blackmailing Canadian personnel serving abroad. While he did not say specifically whether these cases involved homosexuality, he advocated the maintenance of current security regulations regarding "character weaknesses in general, and homosexuality in particular." F.H. Watkins, the DND representative, remarked that the military dismissed all discovered homosexuals as a matter of personnel policy regardless of security considerations. K.W.N. Hall of the RCMP emphasized the security aspect of the homosexual issue and noted the difficulties present in investigating such cases. In sum, rather than moderating the character weakness provisions of CD no. 29, the meeting endorsed actions to enhance counterintelligence measures: American and British governments' handling of the homosexual question would be consulted; departmental case histories of character-weakness blackmail attempts would be compiled and made available to the Security Panel; and the RCMP would contact the morality squad of the Ottawa Police Department to examine the latter's handling of related criminal cases. [. . .]

When completed nine months later, Wall's report confirmed the conservative position advocated by the Security Sub-Panel.[30] His paper discussed the 1955 Australian Royal Commission on Espionage and its conclusion that Soviet intelligence agencies were recruiting fewer ideological agents and instead targeting for blackmail government officials with character weaknesses. Furthermore, DEA had recently received a copy of a Soviet intelligence training manual describing techniques of blackmail to exploit the "human weakness[es]" of influential civil servants. Wall also compared British and American approaches to the subject, paying special attention to the conclusions of the 1950 Senate report described above. [. . .]

British practices, Wall noted, were decidedly more liberal. A 1956 Conference of the Privy Councillors on Security, while recognizing that homosexuals were potential subjects of blackmail, concluded that their employment posed "no greater threat than any other deviation from the straight and narrow path of virtue." Wall also mentioned the 1957 Wolfenden Report, which recommended the decriminalization of homosexual acts between consenting adults.

His conclusions, however, owed far more to Washington than London. The threat of blackmail, coupled with Hillenkoetter's assessment of homosexuals' natural propensity toward "instability, willing self-deceit, and defiance towards society," engendered both security and personnel-administrative reasons for their exclusion from public positions. In support of this view Wall referred to the DND submission to his study which advocated a ban on homosexuals from all government positions. It found that such persons were intrinsically "unreliable" and thus "unsuitable for employment from the point of view of good personnel management, quite apart from the security consideration."[31] Not surprisingly, Wall's final advice was against softening the character weakness provisions of CD no. 29.

When the Security Panel met on 6 October 1959 to discuss Wall's report, it became clear that a can of worms had been opened.[32] Within the panel, liberal-conservative divisions had begun to take shape. Among the liberals were Robert Bryce, secretary to the cabinet and panel chairman; Norman Robertson, undersecretary of state for external affairs; and Paul Pelletier of the Civil Service Commission. While Bryce acknowledged that the threat of blackmail would in most cases preclude homosexuals from gaining access to classified information, these persons could be transferred to "less sensitive departments." Robertson, claiming that Wall's report exaggerated the security risk presented by homosexuals, stressed that an individual's reliability involved a "mixture of considerations"; a homosexual's "great discretion" and "brilliant capacity for public service" might very well "neutralize" the security risks stemming from his sexual orientation. Like Robertson, Pelletier criticized Wall for overemphasizing the homosexual security danger and underscored the fact that never had a federally employed homosexual been successfully blackmailed into disclosing state secrets. Opposing these views were RCMP Commissioner Charles Rivett-Carnac and F.R. Miller, deputy minister of national defence. Rivett-Carnac reiterated the RCMP's position that homosexuals were a serious and widespread security threat. Miller sounded the familiar DND refrain that no homosexuals be allowed "in any capacity" within the public service. Split by such differences, the panel was unable to recommend to cabinet a course of action on the matter. Diefenbaker's original desire to reconfigure CD no. 29 appeared stymied.

National Defence's and the RCMP's extreme opposition to the employment of homosexuals was in fact a reflection of each organization's internal handling of the matter: all detected homosexuals, irrespective of security concerns, were discharged. This policy became a routine aspect of military operations during the Second World War, when enlistees and soldiers were given psychiatric examinations to determine their suitability for armed service. [. . .]

Similarly, the RCMP as a "quasi-military organization" had a hierarchical and rigid command structure. New recruits, usually straight out of high school, underwent a period of basic training. While in the force, Mounties' personal lives were subject to many controls. For example, recruits had to remain single during the first few years of service, and cohabitation with unmarried women was prohibited. Violators of the RCMP's internal discipline code were subject to harsh discipline, including what Mann and Lee record as "degradation rituals." [. . .]

The RCMP's direct involvement in investigating homosexuals in other government departments began in 1959. On 29 April 1960 J.M. Bella, director of the RCMP's security and Intelligence Branch, issued a report concerning the ongoing probe of federally employed homosexuals.[33] As a justification for the investigation, Bella referred to Wall's report, especially its conclusion that "homosexual characteristics" like "instability [and] willing self-deceit" constituted *prima facie* evidence of employee unreliability and of security risk. During the past year the force had uncovered 363 confirmed, alleged, and suspected homosexuals in 33 government departments and agencies.[34] These included such low-level security offices as the Central Mortgage & Housing Corporation, the Department of Public Works, and the Unemployment Insurance Commission. The largest totals were within the navy (199 of 363) and External Affairs (59 of 363).[35] Of the 363, 156 were classified as "confirmed" cases. Since 116 employees were listed as being either released or resigned, retired or deceased, it would seem that roughly 75 per cent of the "confirmed" group were no longer on the government payroll. But these numbers were only half the story. About 350 homosexuals outside the public service had also been investigated in order that, Bella wrote, "the most complete picture possible might be obtained." These persons warranted investigation because they might later seek government employment and, more importantly, because they were necessary sources of information for tracking down federally employed homosexuals. Record checks almost never uncovered "evidence of homosexuality," so to widen the security net the Mounties depended on the "opinions or knowledge expressed by friends and acquaintances, usually homosexual, of the person concerned." Homosexuals, while untrustworthy as government employees, were paradoxically considered reliable police informants.

Interviewing homosexual government workers, however, was problematic for the RCMP because, as noted above, official policy prohibited the disclosure of security grounds for any employee investigation. The RCMP was uncertain whether it had the proper terms of reference to interview homosexual civil servants. The force was also stymied by regulations that obligated it to disclose employee security information to the respective deputy minister. "We have already experienced difficulties arising from departments discharging homosexuals who have admitted their weakness," Bella lamented, and "we firmly believe that if it becomes a general practice to discharge homosexuals who co-operate with us these people will refuse to talk, and without their assistance this type of investigation cannot achieve complete success." To ensure the operation's viability, Bella recommended changes to CD no. 29 to facilitate the questioning of homosexuals and to restrict deputy ministers from launching disciplinary measures against employees until after the RCMP completed its investigations. Ironically, both liberals and conservatives were now seeking changes to CD no. 29.

When the Security Panel met again on 24 June 1960 to discuss the issue with specific reference to Bella's memo, there were more notable differences of opinion.[36] [. . .]

Over six months would elapse before a memo outlining the Security Panel's recent handling of the homosexual issue was sent to Diefenbaker and Fulton.[37] The brief, written by Bryce, raised a number of points suggestive of the panel's liberal spokesmen. Security investigations of homosexuals "should not be widespread" but restricted only to those employees susceptible to foreign intelligence blackmail. Cabinet approval for several courses of action was requested. Government departments with overseas missions were asked to compile a list of personnel with access to security-sensitive information. Afterwards, internal and RCMP investigations would determine if any of these employees

were vulnerable to blackmail. Lastly, all cases of discovered homosexuals would be referred to the Security Panel secretary before departmental actions were taken. Clearly, the narrow focus on the homosexual security implications centred mostly on employees subject to foreign posting ran counter to the RCMP's calls for a wider investigation. But not all was lost for the Mounties. The report also recommended that a research program to "devis[e] tests to identify persons with homosexual tendencies" be undertaken. In commenting on this development, Harrison noted that such tests could be used to disqualify homosexual candidates for public service positions on the grounds that they were "practising criminals" under sections 147 and 149 of the Criminal Code.[38]

This research project was that of Carleton University psychologist, Robert Wake, who with Don Wall's backing had written a preliminary report in June 1960 on the issue of homosexuality and government employment for the Security Panel. The paper outlined various approaches to managing the issue and recommended that a "fully considered research program" be established to "develop suitable methods of selecting personnel for sensitive positions.[39] Wake planned to spend his 1961–2 sabbatical year in the United States studying "sex deviates" and subsequently secured $5000—an appreciable sum in 1961—from the Department of National Health and Welfare to assist his research.[40]

[. . .]

On the surface, Ottawa's choice of Wake as a psychological expert of homosexuality would seem odd. He had no publication record on the subject. He had, however, become known to federal officials through his work as research consultant to a 1958 royal commission on criminal sexual psychopaths.[41] The brief reference to homosexuality in the commission's report was unflattering. While the commission did not recommend, as some witnesses advocated, that "all those convicted of homosexual offenses" be considered for indeterminate prison sentences, it did find that there were "profound problems raised by homosexuality."[42]

His sabbatical year in the United States complete, Wake submitted a report to the Privy Council Office in December 1962.[43] The paper begins with a discussion of the research of Evelyn Hooker and Alfred Kinsey, two dissenting voices within the psychiatric community who challenged orthodox views linking homosexuality with disturbed personalities.[44] The "abnormal" label affixed to homosexuals was a carry-over from earlier religious-moral condemnation of non-procreative sex practices. To comprehend homosexuality fully in its scientific setting it was necessary, Wake argued, to do away with crude stereotypes and "divest [one]self of prejudice." But Wake's initial progressive thrust gets lost in the remainder of the report. Kinsey's and Hooker's findings that male homosexuality was more common than previously thought meant, for Wake, that "the numbers are sufficiently large to be of concern to anyone interested in the problem of suitability." He then discussed homosexual "cure" methods (a concept anathematic to Hooker and Kinsey) such as anti-depressant drugs and aversion therapy. The latter technique, in which induced nausea coincided with a patient's viewing of homoerotic pictures, Wake concluded to be a "somewhat extreme" method, although "the fundamentals—a deconditioning-reconditioning approach—[were] sound."[45]

The bulk of the report, however, dealt with the "battery of tests" available to assess and detect homosexuality. Such methods included psychiatric interviews, medical exams, and projective, polygraph, plethysmograph (electronic or pneumatic measurement of blood volume in the finger), and palmar sweat tests. Examples of word association and masculinity-femininity tests were included in the annex of Wake's report. In the first set of tests, individuals linked to a polygraph or plethysmographic device heard a series of words, some of which contained double meanings known to homosexuals.[46] Nervous reactions to these words would, it was theorized, pinpoint gay subjects. In the masculinity–femininity tests people would respond affirmatively or negatively to such statements as "I like mechanics magazines," "I would like to be a nurse," or "I liked 'Alice in Wonderland' by Lewis Carroll." As Wake noted, an obvious methodological problem was the fact that the test's purpose was easily discernible and respondents could then lie to beat it.

The most promising method, however, was the Pupillary Response Test developed by E.H. Hess and J.M. Polt at the University of Chicago in 1960. While Wake had not seen the test in operation, he regarded it as a "relatively uncomplicated mechanism." Test subjects peered through an opening in a box and were shown pictures while a camera photographed pupil dilation and eye movement at half-second intervals. Allan Seltzer, one of Hess's graduate students, had successfully employed the test to differentiate between homosexual and heterosexual subjects based on their reactions to nude imagery. The merits of this method were that subjects remained unaware of the test's purpose, their reactions were involuntary, the results were available as soon as the film was developed, and the necessary equipment was relatively cheap and easy to assemble. Such a device, Wake argued, had research applications beyond homosexuality and could also be used "to detect alcoholism and other 'frailties'" among civil servants. Accordingly, Wake recommended that the federal government sponsor a research program to develop a Canadian version of the Pupillary Response Test. The project would require a part-time senior social scientist and a full-time masters-level clinical psychologist, and between $5000 and $10 000 of annual funding. A board of federal officials, including the RCMP, would oversee the project.[47] In early 1963 the Security Panel (with Minister of Justice Donald Fleming present) approved the project.[48]

What concerned panel members most during this 28 February meeting was the prospect of making changes to CD no. 29 in light of a report prepared by Wall examining security screening practices in the United States.[49] In October 1961 and June 1962 Wall had met with his government security counterparts in Washington and had come away impressed by the professionalism and thoroughness of the American system. Most security investigations there were done by university graduates (unlike in Canada where few Mounties had postsecondary training) who displayed balanced judgment and possessed a broad understanding of human behaviour. Significantly, Wall also noted that the Americans' approach to the "character weakness" question had changed substantially since the early 1950s:

> The [Civil Service Commission] indicated that it would be neither wise nor feasible to attempt to exclude all homosexuals from the public service . . . In addition there was general agreement that employees found to have some character defect should be treated fairly, objectively and privately, and to the greatest extent possible without jeopardy to their future careers elsewhere. Each case had to be considered on its own merits.[50]

In characteristic fashion Harrison expressed opposition to this "rather permissive attitude," while Robertson, Pelletier, and Bryce voiced varying degrees of support for a compassionate, case-by-case treatment of the subject. While homosexuals should be excluded from certain positions requiring Secret and Top Secret security clearances, they should wherever possible be transferred to "less sensitive positions." Paradox and irony were now aligned. The same meeting that approved the Orwellian-like Wake project also saw a majority of members express support

for a flexible and liberal approach to the homosexual question. None of the committee members appeared to realize that American security practices in the early 1960s were now charting a liberal course for Canadian policy makers.[51]

The influence of Wall's characterization of liberal American practices appeared in the new Cabinet Directive on Security issued in December 1963 (CD no. 35). For the first time "illicit sexual behaviour" was stated explicitly as an element of character weakness. Individuals demonstrating such behaviour would, under the new policy, normally be denied access to classified information "*unless* [original emphasis] after careful consideration of the circumstances, including the value of their services, it is judged that the risk involved appears to be justified."[52] This proviso allowed government officials to assess each situation on a case-by-case basis. Absent from CD no. 35 was any mention of character weaknesses to serve as a basis for denying employment "on grounds other than security," as was the case with CD no. 29. For Security Panel officials the matter now appeared settled; no subsequent meetings dealt with the homosexual issue.

But for the RCMP the issue was far from resolved. As noted earlier, in 1959 the Mounties launched an investigation of homosexuals both inside and outside the civil service. Annual reports of the Directorate of Security and Intelligence (DSI) reveal how quickly these investigations progressed. By 1960–1 some 560 federal employees had been identified, many of whom had "subsequently obtained employment elsewhere." This took place despite the fact that "owing to lack of evidence or corroboration" not all these 560 could be positively identified as homosexuals. The following year approximately 300 additional government employees were identified and, by this time, the "Directorate Index System" contained the names of some 2000 non-government homosexuals. In 1962–3 the RCMP complained that its investigators were "hindered by the lack of co-operation on the part of homosexuals" and, to compensate, the force was establishing contacts with the morality squads of urban police forces. By 1964–5 some 6000 homosexuals were on RCMP file. The next year this number climbed to 7500. And there were 97 homosexual adverse reports issued to government departments, a 117 per cent increase from the year before.

By 1967–8 continued interviewing and collaboration with other police agencies had brought the total number of files to some 9000, of which roughly only one-third were federal public servants.[53] Justice Minister Pierre Trudeau's proposed changes to the Criminal Code (1967) to legalize consensual gay sex did not worry Mountie investigators: "it would appear that as long as the social stigma of homosexuality remains, the element of its use for blackmail will exist and so, therefore, will the security risk factor." [. . .]

The Wake project, however, did not advance as far as the RCMP investigations. The DSI annual reports discuss briefly the ongoing difficulties it encountered. The Mounties were unable to recruit sufficient numbers of homosexuals as test subjects, and there was also reluctance among "normal males" within the force to volunteer. Research moved along fitfully; the annual report for 1964–5 recorded that tests on 51 subjects had proven "inconclusive." The following year the "lack of suitable subjects" again impaired the programs progress. The final reference to the study in 1966–7 noted that, while some headway had been made, conclusive means to identify homosexual subjects were still out of reach.[54] In the end, methodological obstacles shut down the fruit machine, concluding one of the most distasteful federal undertakings in recent history.

A number of domestic and external factors help explain the Canadian government's security investigation of homosexuals during the Cold War. Well before Ottawa turned its attention to the matter in the late 1950s, the Security Panel had adopted procedures which facilitated the later anti-homosexual campaigns. The *sub rosa* nature of the internal security system, in addition to removing any appeal possibilities for homosexuals, allowed the RCMP to widen its investigation without concern over public criticism. The panel's initial emphasis on character weaknesses like gambling and alcoholism established the precedent and investigative tactics for the homosexual purges. The RCMP's central role in the security vetting process, which exceeded its mandated fact-finding function, also expedited the process; the force, like DND, had strict anti-gay policies in its own department and sought to extend these to the wider public service. The panel was also highly sensitive to American security concerns. When in the early 1950s the United States stepped up its campaign to purge homosexuals from federal offices, Canada followed suit, first with changes to immigration legislation, and then a few years later with the RCMP investigation. The extent of American influence was ironically displayed in the early 1960s when Canada followed Washington's liberal lead and relaxed its own security provisions for character weaknesses.

As evidenced by this study, considerable differences of opinion characterized the Security Panel's handling of homosexual security vetting. The panel's liberal-minded representatives like Robertson and Pelletiers ought to restrict security probes only to those individuals privy to classified information. National Defence and RCMP officials, citing the "general unsuitability" of homosexuality within an organizational setting, lobbied to bar gays from all government positions irrespective of security considerations. Both moderates and hardliners, however, supported the Wake project and its promise of a scientific solution to this administrative and security problem. The tempering of the character weakness provisions of CD no. 35 (1963) indicates a policy triumph for the panel's liberal spokesmen. But the Mounties' continued and widespread investigation of homosexuals after 1963, largely beyond the purview of the Security Panel, suggests a practical victory of sorts for the panel's conservatives. Of course, for the many homosexuals affected by Ottawa's actions there was only defeat, accompanied, in all probability, by prolonged anguish.

NOTES

1. Roger W. Bowen, *Innocence Is Not Enough: The Life and Death of Herbert Norman* (Toronto: Douglas & McIntyre 1986).

2. Dean Beeby, "Mounties staged massive hunt for gay males in civil service," *Globe and Mail*, 24 April 1992; Beeby, "RCMP was ordered to identify gays," *Globe and Mail*, 25 April 1992. Earlier accounts appeared in two books by John Sawatsky, both based on unattributed sources: *Men in the Shadows: The RCMP Security Service* (Toronto: Doubleday 1980), 124–37; *For Services Rendered: Leslie James Bennett and the RCMP Security Service* (Toronto: Doubleday 1982), 171–84. The first official government acknowledgment of this event was reported by the Commission of Inquiry Concerning Certain Activities of the Royal Canadian Mounted Police [McDonald Commission], *Freedom and Security under the Law: Second Report* (Ottawa: The Commission 1981), vol. 2, 782. Also see Robert Winters, "Civil service homosexuals fired as 'security risks,'" *Montreal Gazette*, 23 Feb. 1985. On Mulroney, see "PM denounces 1960s purge of homosexual civil servants," *Globe and Mail*, 28 April 1992, and Bruce DeMara, "The persecution of the gays," *Toronto Star*, 9 Aug. 1992.

3. Canada, Royal Commission to Investigate the Facts Relating to and the Circumstances Surrounding the Communication by Public Officials and Other Persons in Positions of Trust of Secret and Confidential Information to Agents of a Foreign Power, *The Report of the Royal Commission* (Ottawa: King's Printer 1946).

4. See Reg Whitaker "Origins of the Canadian Government's Internal Security System, 1946–1952," *Canadian Historical Review* 65, 2 (1984), especially 157–8; J.L. Granatstein, *A Man of Influence: Norman A. Robertson and Canadian Statecraft 1929–1968* (Ottawa: Deneau Publishers 1981), 181–2, 272–6; McDonald Commission, vol. 1, 89; National Archives of Canada (NA), Privy Council Office (PCO), series 18, vol. 103, file S-100-D, Barclay to Cabinet Defence Committee 4, May 1946; file S-100, Heeney to Pearson, 2 June 1948.

5. PCO, series1 8, vol. 189, file S-100-I, Heeney to deputy ministers, 23 Feb. 1949.

6. McDonald Commission, vol. 1, 61.

7. Whitaker, "Origins," 159.

8. Reg Whitaker, "Left-Wing Dissent and the State: Canada in the Cold War Era," in C.E.S. Franks, ed., *Dissent and the State* (Toronto: Oxford University Press 1989), 196.

9. See Richard M. Freeland, *The Truman Doctrine and the Origins of McCarthyism: Foreign Policy, Domestic Politics, and Internal Security, 1946–1948* (New York: New York University Press 1985), sections 3, 5, and 7, and especially 117–34; Walter Goodman, *The Committee: The Extraordinary Career of the House Committee on Un-American Activities* (New York: Farrar, Straus, and Giroux 1968), chap. 5, especially 125ff, 135, 142; Alan D. Harper, *The Politics of Loyalty: The White House and the Communist Issue, 1946–1952* (Westport, CT: Greenwood 1969).

10. See Brooke Claxton's letter to Dean Acheson, 7 Dec. 1950, cited in Whitaker, "Origins,"180–1.

11. "Security Investigation of Government Employees," 5 March 1948, cited in Whitaker, "Origins," 162.

12. Whitaker, "Origins," 167–8, 176–7, and Granatstein, *Man of Influence*, 274.

13. Canada, House of Commons, Debates, 22 June 1948, 5630.

14. McDonald Commission, vol. 1, 60.

15. Sawatsky, *Men in the Shadows*, 14; C.W. Harrison, *The Horsemen* (Toronto: McClelland & Stewart 1967), 209; Whitaker, "Fighting the Cold War on the Home Front: America, Britain, Australia, and Canada," in Ralph Miliband et al., eds, *Socialist Register 1984* (London: Merlin Press 1984), 56.

16. Robert Cuff and J.L. Granatstein, *Ties That Bind: Canadian-American Relations in Wartime, from the Great War to the Cold War* (Toronto: Samuel Stevens Hakkert 1977), 113–29.

17. McDonald Commission, vol. 1, 41.

18. U.S. Congress, Senate, Committee on Expenditure in Executive Departments, *Employment of Homosexuals and Other Sex Perverts in Government* (Washington 1950), reprinted in Jonathan Katz, ed., *Government versus Homosexuals* (New York: Arno Press 1975).

19. *Employment of Homosexuals*, 4–5, 21.

20. John D'Emilio, *Sexual Politics, Sexual Communities: The Making of a Homosexual Minority in the United States, 1940–1970* (Chicago: University of Chicago Press 1983), 44.

21. Alfred C. Kinsey, *Sexual Behavior in the Human Male* (Philadelphia: W.B. Saunders 1948), chap. 21. See Ralph Slovenko, "The Homosexual and Society: A Historical Perspective," *University of Dayton Law Review* 10, 3 (spring 1985): 488. On Kinsey, see Cornelia V. Christenson, *Kinsey: A Biography* (Bloomington: Indiana University Press 1971), 163–6.

22. Philip Girard, "From Subversion to Liberation: Homosexuals and the Immigration Act 1952–1977," *Canadian Journal of Law and Society* 2 (1987): 7. See also Whitaker, *Double Standard: The Secret History of Canadian Immigration* (Toronto: Lester & Orpen Dennys 1987), 37–8.

23. Granatstein, *Man of Influence*, 273.

24. Girard, "From Subversion," 6.

25. Cabinet Directive no. 24, 16 Oct. 1952, cited in McDonald Commission, vol. 2, 782.

26. Department of External Affairs (DEA), file 50207-40, Cabinet Directive no. 29, "Security Screening of Government Employee," 21 Dec. 1955. We would like to thank Reg Whitaker for providing us with this document.

27. PCO, vol. 2659, Cabinet Conclusions, 21 Dec. 1955.

28. House of Commons, Debates, 19 June 1948, 5488. Diefenbaker also spoke out against the American government's handling of the Herbert Norman affair. See *Debates*, 15 March 1957, 2349; 10 April 1957, 3359; and 12 April 1957, 3493–9.

29. McDonald Commission, vol. 1, 89.

30. Canadian Security and Intelligence Service (CSIS), Access to Information Request (AIR) 91-088, Wall to Security Panel, 12 May 1959.

31. CSIS, AIR 91-088, Wall to Security Panel, 12 May 1959.

32. Ibid., Security Panel Meeting, 6 Oct. 1959.

33. CSIS, AIR 92-008, Bella to RCMP commissioner, 29 April 1960.

34. Confirmed cases were defined as "those who have been interviewed and admitted being homosexuals or who have been convicted in court on a charge of sexual deviation with another male." The "alleged" and "suspected" categories seem indistinguishable. The former were "those who have been named as homosexuals by a source or sources whose information is considered to be reliable." The latter were "those who [were] believed to be homosexuals by a source or sources who information is considered to be reliable." Ibid.

35. The documents give credence to John Sawatsky's account—based on unattributed interviews—of an RCMP investigation begun in late 1959 in which many homosexual employees of DEA were fired, including David Johnson, Canada's ambassador to Moscow (1956–1960). See *For Services Rendered*, 172–4. It was later revealed that John Holmes, another DEA senior official, also resigned in 1960 when his homosexuality was discovered. See Beeby, "RCMP was ordered." The case of John Watkins, who when ambassador to Moscow in 1955 was photographed by the KGB during a homosexual encounter, was not known to the RCMP until 1964. See *For Services Rendered*, 175–83, and Dean Beeby and William Kaplan, eds, *Moscow Dispatches: Inside Cold War Russia* (Toronto: James Lorimer 1987), xiii–xxxii.

36. CSIS, AIR 91-088, Security Panel Meeting, 24 June 1960.

37. Ibid., Bruce to Diefenbaker and Fulton, 26 Jan. 1961.

38. Ibid.

39. CSIS, AIR 92-008, Wake to Wall, n.d.

40. CSIS, AIR 91-088, W.H. Kelly, Directorate of Security and Intelligence internal memo, 8 June 1961; and Dean Beeby, "RCMP hoped 'fruit machine' would identify homosexuals," *Globe and Mail*, 24 April 1992.

41. *Report of the Royal Commission on the Criminal Law Relating to Criminal Sexual Psychopaths.*

42. The only cited testimony on the subject of homosexuality was that of John Chisholm,

chief constable of Metropolitan Toronto. Homosexuality, he said, "is a constant problem for the Police in large centres, and if the Police adopt a laissez-faire attitude toward such individuals, City parks, intended for the relaxation of women and children and youth recreation purposes, will become rendezvous (sic) for homosexuals . . . The saddest feature of all, however, is that homosexuals corrupt others and are constantly recruiting youths of previous good character in to their fraternity." *Report of the Royal Commission*, 27.

43. CSIS, AIR 91-088, "Report on Special Project by Dr. F.R. Wake," 12 Dec. 1962.

44. Hooker's studies, rather than being based on a clinical population, used the memberships list of the Mattachine Society, a US homophile organization founded in the early 1950s. Ronald Bayer, *Homosexuality and American Psychiatry: The Politics of Diagnosis* (Princeton: Princeton University Press 1987), 49–53; and Richard D. Mohr, *Gays/Justice: A Study of Ethics, Society, and Law* (New York: Columbia University Press 1988), 23.

45. CSIS, AIR 91-088, "Report on Special Project."

46. Such words included "queen," "circus," "gay," "bagpipe," "bull," "camp," "cruise," "blind," "drag," "fruit," and "trade."

47. CSIS, AIR 91-088, "Report on Special Project."

48. PCO, AIR 9293070, Security Panel Meeting, 28 Feb. 1963.

49. Ibid.

50. Wall also criticized RCMP investigators for overstepping their fact-finding function and advising on security risks. See CSIS, AIR 91-008, Harvison to DSI, Annex "A Summary of the Salient Points in United States Security Procedures," 4 March 1963.

51. PCO, AIR 9293070, Security Panel Meeting, 28 Feb. 1963.

52. Cabinet Directive no. 35, "Security in the Public Service of Canada," 18 Dec. 1963. From documents provided by Reg Whitaker.

53. CSIS, AIR 91-088, DSI Annual Reports, 1959–60 to 1967–8; Beeby, "Mounties staged massive hunt." After 1960 the DSI reports do not indicate how many government homosexuals were fired or resigned.

54. CSIS, AIR 91-088, Bordeleau to Wall, 25 Jan. 1963; and DSI Annual Reports, 1963–4 to 1966–7.

---

4   Asa McKercher, "A 'Half-Hearted Response'?: Canada and the Cuban Missile Crisis, 1962," *The International History Review* 33, 2 (2011): 335–52. Reprinted by permission of Taylor & Francis Ltd, www.tandfonline.com.

Summoned to meet with the Soviet Premier, Nikita Khrushchev, at the end of November 1962, the Canadian Ambassador at Moscow, Arnold Smith, readied himself for what he knew would be a vitriolic attack on Canada's actions during the Cuban Missile Crisis. Their lengthy discussion touched on a range of topics, from the status of Berlin, to disarmament negotiations, to the Soviet leader's domestic popularity. Then, Khrushchev launched into his expected attack, telling Smith that prior to the crisis Canadians "had taken a sober and just view of [the] Cuban situation," a position he had viewed as "sensible and admirable." Now that tensions had abated, Khrushchev urged Ottawa to revert to its former position on Cuba.[1] The Soviet leader's rebuke of Canada is surprising. It contradicts the commonly held view that Canada–US relations "reached their nadir" in October 1962 when the discovery of Soviet missiles in Cuba precipitated a standoff between the United States and Soviet Union during which Canada appeared to offer only hesitant support to its American ally.[2]

Hours after the President of the United States, John F. Kennedy, took to the airwaves on 22 October to disclose the presence of the weapons and to announce his response, Canada's Prime Minister, John Diefenbaker, rose in the House of Commons. In a poorly worded speech, Diefenbaker seemed to question Kennedy's actions as well as the president's claim that missiles were being deployed in

Cuba. Also, despite the highly integrated nature of the North American defence system, Diefenbaker demurred for several days over whether to put the Canadian military on the same level of readiness as US forces. Unbeknownst to Diefenbaker, who was unwilling to permit Canadian forces to go on alert until 24 October—two days after the US military had requested that this be done—Canadian Defence Minister Douglas Harkness had readied Canada's air force as well as its navy on 23 October.[3] As Canadian ships patrolled for Soviet submarines in the North Atlantic, Royal Canadian Air Force pilots readied themselves to defend North American airspace. Although Canada was the only US ally to take on an active military role during the October crisis, the prime minister's prevarications and the resulting confrontation between Canada and the United States are the main focus of the studies of Canadian reactions to the standoff between the superpowers.

The most prevalent view is that Canadian—or rather Diefenbaker's—inaction was inexcusable and greatly angered the United States. As Canada's foremost military historian has put it, the prime minister's "extraordinary immobility" during the crisis resulted from a "congenital inability to make difficult decisions," a profound distaste for Kennedy personally, and "resentment that, in his view, the United States had not met its obligation under the NORAD agreement to consult Canada."[4] NORAD, or the North American Air Defence Command, the joint command providing for the defence of North American airspace by both Canada and the United States, required mutual consultation in the event of a crisis. By October 1962, thanks to policy and personality differences, Kennedy and Diefenbaker loathed one another, and so during the crisis consultation did not take place. As a recent study has contended, the lack of consultation was the natural result of the disparate power relationship between Canada and the United States.[5] While Washington certainly failed to consult with any of

its allies throughout the crisis, Canada occupies a particularly important geographic position, a fact recognized by the distinct defence relationship enshrined by NORAD.[6] That the Canadian government did not receive special consideration has been a reason for some to decry US treatment of Canada throughout the crisis and to support Diefenbaker's hesitant actions.[7] Consultation and the issues arising from it have been the primary focus for historians, and they do show a rocky state of affairs between Ottawa and Washington.

Throughout the crisis Canada stood by the United States. While their prime minister bumbled about, Canadian officials from the Department of External Affairs played a helpful role by providing intelligence to the Americans, by using Canada's leverage with the Cuban government to seek a resolution to the crisis, and by acting as an intermediary between Cuba and the United States. Further, in analyzing the events of October and November, these officials took the view that Washington's actions were a justified response to dangerous provocations from Moscow and Havana. [. . .]

Since the success of the Cuban Revolution in 1959, Canada has maintained diplomatic ties with Cuba's government and has pursued a policy of trading with Cuba in all goods barring those possessing military or strategic value. This was different from the course that Washington embarked upon, particularly once a US embargo was put in place in October 1960, and US diplomats were withdrawn in January 1961. Occasionally, these differences resulted in open arguments as in May 1961, when the Canadian Minister of External Affairs, Howard Green, and the US Secretary of State, Dean Rusk, had a very tense exchange regarding Cuba. Spurred by the recent failure of the US-sponsored invasion of Cuba by Cuban exiles at the Bay of Pigs, Green emphasized to Rusk that US policy was severely mistaken. Prompted by this discussion, Rusk had cabled to Washington: "Believe it would be important for President to have frank talk with Prime Minister during Canadian visit about neutralist tendencies [in] Canadian policy especially as presented by . . . Green."[8] In contrast, the following year Green became quite concerned by the effect that Canadian policy toward Cuba was having on Canada–US relations.

Throughout 1962, a number of US officials had made their displeasure over the nature of the Ottawa–Havana relationship quite clear to their Canadian counterparts. The US Ambassador at Ottawa, Livingston Merchant, informed several Canadian cabinet ministers that Canada's influence in Washington had declined thanks in part to "ostentatious divergence" from the US position on Cuba.[9] [. . .]

Meanwhile, Canadian concern was growing over the state of another relationship, that between Havana and Moscow. From the Cuban capital, Canadian Ambassador George Kidd passed on a wealth of information on this subject to Ottawa. Many of these reports, sent also to the Americans and the British, dealt with Cuba's arms build-up over the summer of 1962. In mid-August, for example, Kidd sounded the tocsins over the increasing numbers of Soviet technicians, military personnel, and materiel arriving on the island.[10] The Soviets matched these provocative actions with dangerous rhetoric, a worrying mix. On 11 September, the TASS news agency released a statement from the Kremlin castigating US policy, and repeating Moscow's deep commitment to Cuba. Commenting on this declaration, Kidd observed that it marked a "new stage" in Cuban–Soviet relations for it constituted the "deepest Soviet commitment yet made to Castro." Wary because it seemed logical to expect that Moscow would henceforth demand a greater say over Cuban policy, Kidd also worried that Cuba was now on par with Berlin as a key centre of the cold war. Still, he felt that deepened Soviet involvement could also have the effect of moderating Cuban adventurism throughout Latin America. In this regard he reported

that the Soviets, in fact, seemed to be trying to reduce tensions. Thus, their guarantee that long-range missiles would not be installed in Cuba was heartening.[11] But Soviet arms shipments continued, and on the same day that Kidd sent this dispatch, the US president held a news conference to warn the Soviets against introducing offensive weapons into Cuba. Kennedy had made similar pronouncements the previous week and the growing tension in Washington was picked up by the Canadian Embassy in its reports back to Ottawa.[12]

Kennedy's warnings, combined with Kidd's worrying cables, worried members of External Affairs. Green, for one, was concerned by the frequent overflights of Canada by Soviet airplanes which often stopped to refuel at Canadian airports. There was a belief in External Affairs that these flights were being used to transfer military technicians and personnel to Cuba, and Green's specific worry was that Canadian acquiescence to these flights was making Canada complicit in the armament of the Cuban military. At his request, the Soviet chargé was called into the department to be told of Canadian concerns.[13] In regards to Cuba itself, Norman Robertson had a wide-ranging discussion in late September with Cuban Ambassador, Américo Cruz. [. . .] The following week, Robertson set down his thoughts on Cuba in a memorandum to Green. Hoping to offer his minister an assessment of the "situation behind the Sugarcane Curtain," he viewed the increasing Soviet military presence with anxiety. Nevertheless, Robertson felt that "there seems to be no substantial reason for terminating our present normal diplomatic relations with Cuba."[14]

A week later, 16 October, Kennedy received startling news that Soviet missiles were being deployed in Cuba; he and his key advisors then set about crafting a response. Over several days they debated a number of options, including bombarding the missile sites and invading the island. The course they set upon was to blockade Cuba—the term "quarantine" was used—and then demand that the missiles be removed. These measures would be announced by the president during a televised address, set for 7 PM on 22 October. During the first day of deliberations, in what appears to have been the only point at which Kennedy and his advisors considered Canada, Rusk had mulled over using the Canadian Ambassador at Havana as a go-between with Cuban leader Fidel Castro, but the idea was abandoned.[15] Ottawa was, however, amongst those governments that received a briefing from US officials prior to the President's address. [. . .]

Two hours before the presidential address, Merchant arrived at the prime minister's office, accompanied by Ivan White, the US Chargé, and two CIA officers. Waiting for them were Diefenbaker, Green, and Douglas Harkness. As the briefing began, Diefenbaker was confrontational, "brusquely" asking for an overview of Kennedy's speech and stating "let us face facts; an election is on in the United States." Merchant's insistence that the president would not play politics with such an important issue seemed to soothe the prime minister as did photographic evidence of the missile sites. At this point Diefenbaker "swung around from his original skepticism bordering on antagonism to a more considered friendly and co-operative manner." Green and Harkness also seemed convinced by the evidence; the former was "less shocked and less vocal than would be expected"; the latter was "cheered by the decisiveness of the President's course of action." As the meeting concluded, then, a pleased Merchant believed that the prime minister "was sobered and upset but . . . his earlier doubts had been dissipated and in the end he would give strong support to the United States." Merchant also observed, though, that "it was interesting . . . that at no point, despite pointed questions, did [Diefenbaker] make a commitment in this regards."[16] Importantly too, Merchant had made no mention of a NORAD alert, nor had the prime minister mentioned the idea

of UN inspections as he had been advised to do by External Affairs prior to the president's address.

[. . .]

Speaking in the Canadian House of Commons shortly after Kennedy's address, Diefenbaker echoed the president's "sombre and challenging" view, telling the gathered MPs that "the construction of bases for the launching of offensive weapons . . . constitutes a threat to most of the cities of North America including our major cities in Canada." Stating that "the determination of Canada will be that the United Nations should be charged at the earliest possible moment with this serious problem," he proposed that should there be "a desire on the part of the U.S.S.R. to have facts," a group of non-aligned nations could conduct "an on-site inspection in Cuba to ascertain what the facts are." This effort, an "independent inspection" made through the UN, would both "provide an objective answer to what is going on in Cuba" and constitute "the only sure way that the world can secure the facts."[17] Hardly a ringing endorsement of Kennedy's stance, Diefenbaker's statement did not go unnoticed. In Ottawa, the Cuban ambassador remarked to Alfred Pick, the head of External's Latin American Division, that "he had read and liked the Prime Minister's statement in the House" because the suggestion of an inspection "implied that Mr Diefenbaker himself doubted President Kennedy's assertions."[18] Pick was compelled to dissuade Cruz of this notion, but the damage was done. Speaking with David Ormsby-Gore, Britain's ambassador at Washington, Robert Kennedy, the US Attorney General, reported that "the only half-hearted response" to their actions that the White House had received was from the Canadian prime minister.[19]

Rather than being an assertion of doubt, the speech, or at least its phrasing, appears merely to have been a rather unfortunate gaffe, something that even Diefenbaker recognized immediately. In a cabinet meeting the following morning he told his colleagues that the press was pestering him over whether there were any doubts about the missile sites. Noting that there "were, of course, political overtones in the American attitude," Diefenbaker nevertheless averred that he, Green, and Harkness "had been convinced that there had been no exaggeration of the situation" by Kennedy.[20] That afternoon he told the House of Commons that "lest there be any doubt about my meaning," he had "not, of course, [been] casting any doubts on the facts of the situation as outlined by the president." Going on to explain that "there is ample evidence that bases and equipment for the launching of offensive weapons have been constructed in Cuba," Diefenbaker acknowledged that these "exist in sufficient quantities to threaten the security of this hemisphere." Importantly, he explained that Kennedy's plan involved using a UN Security Council resolution as a means to seek the missiles' removal, but he felt this effort would most likely fail due to the Soviet Union's veto. His purpose was not to compete with a US resolution; rather, it was to put forward a proposal which could be used in the event that the Soviet veto was used.[21] Thus, his proposal was meant to complement US initiatives, and given his claims that Kennedy had not exaggerated the evidence, one can conclude that Diefenbaker had initially blundered by emphasizing the role of the United Nations in the way that he had.

Prior to making this clarification, Diefenbaker had signed off on instructions to the embassy in Washington and to Canada's mission at the United Nations, telling these Canadian diplomats to seek out their US counterparts in order to discuss the inspection proposal. While doing so, they were to stress that the manoeuvre was not meant to cast doubt on the US claims; Ottawa's goal was simply to put in motion an initiative which could be used if and when the Soviet veto was employed.[22] [. . .]

As these talks were taking place, Robert Bryce, Clerk of the Privy Council and Canada's top civil servant, was carrying out prime ministerial instructions to determine the legality of the United States' quarantine. Bryce solicited the opinions of the Department of External Affairs and of the Chief of the Naval Staff. The latter's study of past naval blockades concluded that as the legality of the president's action was ill-defined and without precedent, Canada could accept the quarantine measure without acquiescing to anything illegal.[23] The DEA study, grounded in a discussion of international law, likewise noted the "*sui-generis*" nature of the US quarantine. As a result, there would be nothing wrong if Canada at least offered its tacit support.[24] To avoid a potential blunder, though, Norman Robertson advised Canadian officials to avoid discussing the legal merits of the quarantine in public.[25]

Canadian diplomats also moved quickly to respond to a request made by the US embassy on 22 October that Canada temporarily suspend overflight clearances for airplanes travelling to Cuba from the Soviet Union.[26] In a brief press conference following the prime minister's address to the House that evening, Howard Green announced that flights to Cuba from the Soviet bloc would no longer be permitted to land or refuel in Canada nor could they enter Canadian airspace.[27] Exceptions had to be made for both Czechoslovak Airlines and Cubana Airlines flights because both Cuba and Czechoslovakia belonged to the International Civil Aviation Organization (ICAO). However, as ICAO rules stated that civilian airlines could not be used to transport military equipment, Canadian officials could lawfully conduct searches of planes from these airlines to enforce this rule. [. . .]

Although Canada was co-operating with the United States by securing North American air space from civilian aircraft, there was far less official co-operation in terms of military security. As the US military went to Defense Condition (DEFCON) 3 alert on 22 October, US officials requested, via the Canadian element of NORAD, that Canada match this level of readiness.[28] As this request had come through military channels rather than a political one, Canada's military passed it on to the defence minister; Harkness in turn took it to the prime minister. Diefenbaker then referred the matter to the cabinet, where, during two meetings on 23 and 24 October, Canadian ministers fiercely debated whether or not to comply with the US request. At the conclusion of the first, and despite both Harkness's impassioned pleas and Diefenbaker's assertion that the facts presented by Kennedy in his address "were as cited," the cabinet resolved to delay.[29] This delay was spearheaded by the prime minister.[30] Harkness again pleaded his case the following day, and again, the ministers were deeply divided. Some offered the defence minister their support while others worried that a Canadian alert "might escalate the crisis." Thus, the only decision made was to delay once more.[31] Following this meeting Harkness presented Diefenbaker with a report showing that the United States military had moved to DEFCON 2, meaning the Americans were making immediate preparations for war. Galvanized by this news, the prime minister ordered that Canada's air forces be readied.[32] Unbeknownst to Diefenbaker, this was a mere rubber stamp. Harkness had already authorized an alert days before, and Canada's military commanders had immediately complied with this secret order. So although the prime minister had forced a delay, the Canadian military and the minister of defence, in fact, had ensured that Canadian forces were ready in case hostilities broke out.[33]

While Diefenbaker was fumbling about on defence issues, Green stumbled about on television. During an interview on 24 October, Canada's foreign minister made statements that "did little to convince his interviewers or anyone watching the program that the government was acting responsibly in concert with the United States and other allies to solve the crisis."[34] Indeed, he could cite no concrete examples of how Canada was co-operating with the US. Given the cabinet's indecision over NORAD, Green's misstep is not surprising, however. What is surprising is that so much has been made of Green's omissions and that little attention has been given to his statements in support of US policy. Asked if the Americans were being hypocritical in their reaction to the emplacement of missiles in Cuba given that they had placed missiles around the USSR, Green averred that the current situation was "very different." "It is obvious," he said, "that the Soviet Union has moved in secretly with these missiles, all the time proclaiming to the world that any missiles that the Cubans were getting were purely defensive . . . and now it turns out that that isn't the case." [. . .] At no point, though, did Green state what actions his government had taken to support the United States, an omission that has been criticized ever since.

Realizing that his interview had been insufficient, the following morning Green asked his Cabinet colleagues "whether Canada's position with respect to the U.S. action was clear to the public." Despite his comments the night before as well as Diefenbaker's statement in the House on 23 October, Green felt that the public unfortunately "did not appear to be sure whether Canada fully supported the U.S. action or whether it was neutral." Agreeing that "this situation should be corrected," the ministers advised the prime minister to make a further public statement "outlining what steps Canada had taken already and clarifying Canada's stand in support of the U.S. action."[35] In the House of Commons that afternoon Diefenbaker recounted the steps that Canada had taken to search Cuban-bound aircraft and revealed that Canadian NORAD units were on alert. He also attacked the Soviet Union, which "by its actions has reached out across the Atlantic to challenge the right of free men to live in peace in this hemisphere."[36] This strong rhetoric was matched by supportive actions by Canadian diplomats in Washington, Havana, and Ottawa.

In the US capital, on 26 October, Charles Ritchie and Basil Robinson called first on Robert Kennedy and then on the Secretary of State. Robert Kennedy was pleased to see Ritchie because he had just heard about Diefenbaker's statement to the House of Commons. Rusk read a copy of the same text and called it "very good." Ritchie also handed the Secretary of State a memorandum of conversation between Howard Green and Cuba's ambassador, Américo Cruz. The latter had asked the Canadians to carry a message to the Americans: while Cubans were willing to fight to the death, they were also willing to negotiate their differences with the United States. Thanking Ritchie for the information, Rusk suggested that Green might probe Cruz further. He also requested that the Canadian ambassador at Havana seek out Castro with the "aim of implanting the view that Cuba cannot possibly win." Ritchie was less than convinced that Rusk truly expected anything from this effort but he advised Ottawa of it nonetheless.[37] The Secretary of State likely put more stock in this channel than Ritchie thought as Rusk was already using Brazilian diplomats as a way to communicate with the Cuban government. Thus, he may sincerely have wished to use Canadian officials in this regard as well.[38]

Meanwhile, in both Havana and Ottawa, Canadians looked on with astonishment and worry at Cuban actions. Commenting on a fiery address that Fidel Castro had made as he had put Cuban soldiers and militia on alert, Kidd worried that the Cuban leader had failed to refute the US charges about the presence of the missiles and had neglected an opportunity to calm the situation. Instead, Castro had "reiterated his readiness to die with his people but seems rather less concerned about whether they or anyone else remains alive."[39] On 25 October, the Cuban ambassador called on Howard Green; a bitter discussion ensued, during which the Canadian foreign minister rebuked Cuban policy. [. . .]

Similarly, Ottawa was shocked by Soviet policy. In a memorandum to Green, Robertson felt that Moscow had "deliberately provoked a sharp United States reaction." Reviewing the US response, Robertson observed that in avoiding an immediate strike on Cuba and in "putting a squeeze" on the USSR, Washington's course was the "lesser of two evils." This was remarkable, he felt, because of the strong domestic pressure on the Kennedy administration to take a hard line, particularly with a mid-term election looming. Noting that there was some criticism of the US quarantine amongst Canadians, Robertson defended this measure as "a necessary response to clear provocation."[40] A detailed study of Soviet motivations, prepared in the European Division and funnelled up to the prime minister, also played up the provocative nature of Khrushchev's actions. Four goals of Soviet policy were highlighted: circumvention of North American air defences which were aimed northward; support for Castro's government and the defence of the "Cuban beachhead in Latin America"; improvement of the Soviet Union's bargaining position over Berlin; and creation of disunity amongst the Western allies. Moscow's actions therefore constituted a "serious threat" toward which Washington had shown considerable moderation. Highlighting the ongoing danger of the situation, the study noted, too, that following the imposition of the quarantine, the Soviets had also taken a moderate position and negotiations might therefore prove fruitful.[41]

Yet on 26 October there was only some vague possibility of a resolution, and so Charles Ritchie ominously counselled Ottawa that it appeared that a "second and more critical phase of the crisis" was about to begin.[42] The next day, Radio Moscow broadcasted a message from Khrushchev who offered to swap the missiles in Cuba for US missiles in Turkey. Ritchie rushed to the State Department to receive any information that William Tyler was willing to offer. Tyler, who warned that meeting Khrushchev's demand could seriously damage the NATO alliance, nevertheless felt that a potential schism was outweighed by the danger posed by the missiles. Despite this grim assessment, Ritchie was buoyed by a discussion with Ormsby-Gore, who confided that he had received word of secret and more constructive communications between the Soviet premier and the US president. After confirming this development with Tyler, Ritchie advised Ottawa that this news could herald a break in the crisis.[43] This was indeed the case and on 28 October Khrushchev announced that the missiles in Cuba would be dismantled. From the Canadian embassy in Moscow, Arnold Smith reacted to this news by exulting that the West appeared to have won the ball game, "though not yet [the] World Series." A firm US response, which had elicited "unexpected solidarity" from Canada and other governments, had forced the failure of a "calculated and dangerous Khrushchev gambit." This was a cause for cautious celebration. Still, Smith warned Ottawa that they all needed to keep their "eyes wide open for tricks."[44]

[. . .]

Castro's refusal to permit inspections briefly hampered a resolution of the crisis. The Americans therefore sought Canada's help to pressure the Cuban government. On the evening of 31 October, Ivan White approached Ross Campbell to ask whether Canada would be willing to "intervene strongly" with the Cubans by threatening to break off relations should Cuba refuse inspections. Failing that, would the Canadian government at least "protest Cuban intransigence" and stress to the Cubans that their obstinate position made it difficult to maintain normal relations? As White observed, Canada was "particularly well placed" to apply pressure because it held "some sort of influence with Castro." Campbell made no commitments but did reveal that Green had already underlined Canada's displeasure to Cruz. White's suggestion of using the severance of

Canada–Cuba relations as a bargaining tactic met with a decidedly negative reaction within External Affairs. Writing to Green, Robertson argued that such a move would be "self-defeating." The presence of the Canadian embassy in the Cuban capital had "frequently proved valuable" and to change Canada's policy at this point would imply that the maintenance of the relationship in the past had been a mistake. Furthermore, "even to hint at the possibility of breaking relations would be inadvisable." Despite this view, Robertson thought it was advisable that Kidd reiterate to Cuban officials that the UN should be brought in to oversee the dismantling of the missile sites.[45] In a cable to Kidd, Green therefore asked him to meet with the Cuban foreign minister, Raul Roa Garcia, to stress that "it was in Cuba's interest to co-operate" with the United Nations to resolve the crisis.[46]

Kidd had already had a number of run-ins with Roa. During a meeting on 30 October, he had listened to the Cuban foreign minister denounce the idea of UN inspections, but following through on his orders from Ottawa, Kidd spoke with Roa on 31 October to again urge Cuba's government to do its part to gain a resolution.[47] They met again the next day, this time to address Havana's mistaken belief that Canada was attempting to mediate the dispute between the United States and Cuba. Roa had mentioned this to Kidd during their discussion on 30 October; the Canadian ambassador, unaware that his government had made such an offer, cabled Ottawa to ask for clarification.[48] Officials in External Affairs greeted this news with disbelief for at no time had they offered to mediate anything. The conclusion they came to was that Cruz, lacking a firm grasp of English, had misconstrued Green's comments on the importance which Canada attached to inspections. Instructions to correct the misunderstanding were sent to Kidd, and Ross Campbell phoned the embassy in Washington. Speaking with Basil Robinson, Campbell asked that the State Department be informed of the situation lest the

Americans become worried that Canada was not on side.[49]

Kidd was busy not just in speaking with Cuban officials; he was also reporting on events on the island. Throughout the crisis, Kidd had commented on the positioning of the Soviet missiles and, once the crisis ended, the subsequent withdrawal of weaponry and personnel.[50] In addition, at the State Department's request, Ottawa had directed the Canadian embassy in Havana to send reports of the Cuban reaction to events and to report on whether Voice of America (VOA) broadcasts were having any influence.[51] In response, Kidd reported that despite Cuban attempts to jam the signals VOA broadcasts were being received, and many Cubans were tuning in. He noted that assessing the influence of the broadcasts was difficult, but that by making more information available, they were undoubtedly having some impact. Still, the "pervasiveness of Cuban propaganda and its reliant patriotic themes" was not easy to counter.[52] [. . .]

Reaction to the crisis in Ottawa was overwhelmingly concerned with the impact of the events on Canada–US relations. In an address to the Zionist Organization of Canada on 5 November, Diefenbaker underscored that there had never been "any question as to where Canada stood on the Cuban situation." While expressing his government's unequivocal support for the United States, he "made clear that consultation is a pre-requisite to joint and contemporaneous action being taken."[53] This speech was geared toward the prime minister's domestic critics who were clamouring for the government to explain why it has not stood more forthrightly beside the United States. As historians have noted, much of the criticism that Canada's government received for its actions or inactions during the missile crisis was from Canadians.[54] Basil Robinson addressed these concerns with State Department officials, telling them of his government's concern over public outrage. Diefenbaker, Robinson revealed,

was "quite surprised" that Canadians were upset with the apparent lack of "energetic and forthright steps in support of the U.S." Ottawa's position that the United States had had an obligation to consult with Canada was having little traction with the public; hence Canadian ministers might begin emphasizing what they had now come to privately realize: that "in case of self-preservation, the U.S. would if necessary act unilaterally."[55]

These concerns over US policy would have an impact over the following months regarding Canada's choice to equip Canadian forces with nuclear weapons, an ongoing issue since early 1959. The resulting political crisis over the nuclear weapons issue would bring down Diefenbaker's government in February 1963, and it has been argued at the time and since, that the Kennedy administration played a role in the prime minister's downfall. While the Americans certainly bear some blame for the collapse of Diefenbaker's government—a January 1963 State Department press release caused a stir by calling the prime minister a liar—it seems doubtful that the Americans "delight[ed] in scheming to obtain vengeance for Diefenbaker's diplomatic cold shoulder" during the missile crisis.[56]

There seems in fact to have been a general lack of criticism of the Canadians by US officials. Speaking with Basil Robinson in December 1962, Livingston Merchant did voice his disappointment over both the prime minister's statement in the House of Commons on 22 October and Green's television interview a few days later.[57] How much the opinion of the former US ambassador mattered is unclear, and Merchant may not have been aware of the amount of assistance that the Canadian government had given to the United States irrespective of Diefenbaker and Green's public blunders. Such assistance had pleased US officials and while the prime minister's statement of 22 October was noted, criticism did not come from the United States likely because little was expected of the

Canadians. The Cuban Missile Crisis was a contest largely between the USSR and the US, so much so that Cuba itself barely figured into the diplomatic picture.[58] As far as Washington was concerned, Canada, like most other countries, was largely irrelevant in the crisis. The transcripts of Kennedy's deliberations with his advisors attest that US officials gave little thought to a role for Canada's government, an omission also not surprising given the mutual hostility between the president and the prime minister. Still, Kennedy both sent Merchant to brief the Canadians and wrote a personal message to Diefenbaker, so there is something to be said for the relationship between Ottawa and Washington.

As the crisis then unfolded, and despite their prime minister's reluctance, Canadian officials, including Green, responded to the crisis by siding with Washington and by playing a helpful role in providing the Americans with intelligence, by monitoring flights heading toward Cuba, and by pressuring the Cuban government. In analyzing events, Canada's diplomats were sympathetic to their US ally and wary of Soviet and Cuban actions. Further, even though Diefenbaker did not order a military alert until 24 October, Canada's military, through the initiative of the Canadian defence minister, played its part in keeping North America secure. These efforts did not go unnoticed. In early November 1962, Rufus Smith, the political counsellor at the US embassy in Ottawa and one the officials who would draft the infamous State Department press release in January 1963, met with Canadian journalist Robert Reford to discuss Ottawa's response to the crisis. After Reford asked about reports of US unhappiness with Canadian actions or inactions, Smith stressed "the difference in assessing the value of specific actions and assessing the significance of tone, style, and timing of the public statements that accompany them." Referring to an incident in 1960 when the Canadian trade minister had called Cubans "fine businessmen," Smith said that "unfortunately" these types of statements tend "to be remembered by people, particularly editors, who may forget that in fact Canada has been more co-operative with [the US] trade embargo" than had other US allies.[59] Implicit, then, was that both the Prime Minister's 22 October statement and Green's television interview would be remembered more than Canadian efforts to support the United States throughout the October Crisis.

NOTES

1. Canadian Embassy, Moscow to External Affairs, tel. 661, 28 Nov. 1962, [Ottawa], L[ibrary and] A[rchives] C[anada], [Arnold Smith Papers], MG 31 E47, box 80, file 21.

2. G. Donaghy, *Tolerant Allies: Canada and the United States, 1963–1968* (Montreal, 2002), 7.

3. See P.T. Haydon, *The 1962 Cuban Missile Crisis: Canadian Involvement Reconsidered* (Toronto, 1993).

4. J.L. Granatstein, "When Push Came to Shove: Canada and the United States," in Thomas G. Paterson, ed., *Kennedy's Quest for Victory: American Foreign Policy, 1961–1963* (Oxford, 1989), 96–7. See also J. Glazov, *Canadian Policy toward Khrushchev's Soviet Union* (Montreal and Kingston, 2002) and P. Lyon, *Canada in World Affairs, vol. XII, 1961–1963* (Toronto, 1968).

5. P. Lennox, *At Home and Abroad: The Canada–US Relationship and Canada's Place in the World* (Vancouver, 2009), 39–55.

6. F. Costigliola, "Kennedy, the European Allies, and the Failure to Consult," *Political Science Quarterly* cx (1995), 105–23; and D. Munton and D.A. Welch, *The Cuban Missile Crisis* (Oxford, 2007), 65–6.

7. J.T. Jockel, *Canada in NORAD, 1957–2007: A History* (Montreal and Kingston, 2007), 54–60; and J. Maynard Ghent, "Canada, the United States, and the Cuban Missile

Crisis," *Pacific Historical Review* xlviii (1979), 159–84.

8. Rusk to Kennedy, 14 May 1961 [Boston, MA], J[ohn] F K[ennedy] L[ibrary], N[ational] S[ecurity] F[iles], series 1, box 18, file "Canada, General 5/15/61-5/30/61."

9. US Embassy, Ottawa to State, tel. A-291, 8 Feb. 1962, JFKL, NSF, Series 1, box 18, file "Canada, General, 2/62-3/62."

10. Embassy, Havana to External, Numbered Letter 401, 16 Aug. 1962, DEA, box 5352, file 10224-40 Part 12.2; an excellent overview of Canadian intelligence operations in Cuba is D. Munton, "Intelligence Cooperation Meets International Studies Theory: Explaining Canadian Operations in Castro's Cuba," *Intelligence and National Security* xxiv (2009), 119–38.

11. Embassy, Havana to External, tel. 172, 13 Sept. 1962, DEA, box 5352, file 10224-40 Part 12.2.

12. Embassy, Washington to External, tel. 2672, 14 Sept. 1962, box 5352, file 10224-40 Part 12.2.

13. Malcolm Bow to Robertson, memo, "Soviet Overflights," 3 Oct. 1962; and Robertson to Green, Memo, "Soviet Overflights of Canadian Territory," 4 Oct. 1962, DEA, box 5077, file 4568-40 Part 10.

14. Robertson to Green, memo, "Policy on Cuba," 5 Oct. 1962, DEA, box 5077, file 4568-40 Part 10.

15. "Transcript of a Meeting at the White House, Washington, 16 October, 1962, 11:50 AM," F[oreign] R[elations of the] U[nited] S[tates], *1961–1963* (Washington, 1996), xi. 32; and J. Hershberg, "The United States, Brazil, and the Cuban Missile Crisis (Part II)," *Journal of Cold War Studies* vi (2004), 9–10.

16. Memcon, "Meeting with Prime Minister Diefenbaker to Deliver Copy of President Kennedy's Letter of October 22 on Cuban Situation," 22 Oct. 1962 JFKL, NSF, Series 1, box 18, file "Canada, General 10/62-1/63." After hearing Merchant read the president's speech, the prime minister advised that a reference in the speech to the Soviet foreign minister as being a "dishonest and dishonourable" man be removed. Merchant relayed this to Dean Rusk and the advice was accepted.

17. Canada, House of Commons, *Debates* (22 Oct. 1962), 805–6.

18. Pick to Robertson, memo, "Views of the Cuban Ambassador on the Crisis," 23 Oct. 1962, DEA, box 4184, file 2444-40 Part 9.

19. UK Embassy, Washington to Foreign Office, tel. 2650, 23 Oct. 1962, [Kew], N[ational] A[rchives of the] U[nited] K[ingdom], PREM 11/3689. I am indebted to Galen Perras for providing me with this document.

20. Minutes, Mtg., C[abinet] C[onclusions], 23 Oct. 1962, 10:30 AM, [Library and Archives Canada, Record Group 2], P[rivy] C[ouncil] O[ffice], series A-5-a, box 6193.

21. Canada, House of Commons, *Debates* (23 Oct. 1962), 821.

22. External to Embassy, Washington and Permanent Mission, New York, outgoing messages V-104 and V-105, 23 Oct. 1962; see also: External to Embassy, Washington and Permanent Mission, New York, outgoing message V-478, 23 Oct. 1962; and M.N. Bow to A.E. Ritchie and Ross Campbell, memo, "Cuba," 23 Oct. 1962, DEA, box 4181, file 2444-40 Part 9.

23. Vice-Admiral Rayner to Bryce, memo, "Quarantine of Cuba and the Principles of Blockade," 23 Oct. 1962, DEA, box 5050, file 2444-B-40 Part 1.

24. Green to Diefenbaker, memo, "United States Quarantine against Cuba," 23 Oct. 1962, DEA, box 5050, file 2444-B-40 Part 1.

25. Robertson to Green, memo, "United States Quarantine against Cuba," 26 Oct. 1962, DEA, box 5050, file 2444-B-40 Part 1.

26. Ivan White to A.E. Ritchie, 23 Oct. 1962, DEA, box 4184, file 2444-40 Part 9.

27. External to Embassy, Havana, tel. XL90, 23 Oct. 1962, DEA, box 5077, file 4568-40 Part 10.

28. Jockel, *Canada in NORAD*, 57.

29. Minutes, mtg, CC, 23 Oct. 1962, 10:30 AM, PCO, series A-5-a, box 6193.

30. See Jockel, *Canada in NORAD*, 58, where he asserts that Diefenbaker was "firmly supported by Green." It is doubtful how much support Green may have given Diefenbaker, however. In his pseudo-memoir, Harkness recalled that Green in fact supported a military alert, and the Cabinet minutes contain no statement attributed to Green to challenge this argument; see Harkness's recollections in "The Nuclear Arms Question and the Political Crisis which Arose from it in January

and February 1963," LAC, [Douglas Harkness Papers] MG 32 B19, box 57.

31. Minutes, mtg., CC, 24 Oct. 1962, 9:30 AM, PCO, series A-5-a, box 6193.

32. D. Smith, *The Life and Legend of John G. Diefenbaker* (Toronto, 1995), 459.

33. Haydon, *The 1962 Cuban Missile Crisis*, 211; Ghent, "Canada, the United States, and the Cuban Missile Crisis," 180. The importance of Harkness's actions in terms of civil–military relations is covered in D.A. Welch, "Review of Peter T. Haydon's *The 1962 Cuban Missile Crisis: Canadian Involvement Reconsidered*," *Journal of Conflict Studies* xv (1995), 149–53.

34. Haydon, *The 1962 Cuban Missile Crisis*, 136; and H. Basil Robinson, *Diefenbaker's World: A Populist in Foreign Affairs* (Toronto, 1989), 289.

35. Minutes, mtg, CC, 25 Oct. 1962, 10:30 AM, PCO, series A-5-a, box 6193.

36. Canada, House of Commons, *Debates* (25 Oct. 1962), 911.

37. Memcon, "Cuban Situation," 26 Oct. 1962, EUR, CDC, POL, box 3, file "Cuba Quarantine, 1962"; Embassy, Washington to External, tel. 3166, 27 Oct. 1962, DEA, box 4184, file 2444-40 Part 11.

38. Hershberg, "The United States, Brazil, and the Cuban Missile Crisis (Part II)," 30–1.

39. Embassy, Havana to External, tel. 203, 24 Oct. 1962, DEA, box 5352, file 10224-40 Part 12.2.

40. Robertson to Green, memo, "Cuba at the United Nations," 26 Oct. 1962, DEA, box 4184, file 2444-40 Part 10.

41. Green to Diefenbaker, memo, "Soviet Intentions and Reaction in the Cuban Situation," 26 Oct. 1962, DEA, box 184, file 2444-40 Part 10.

42. Embassy, Washington to External, tel. 3163, 26 Oct. 1962, DEA, box 4184, file 2444-40 Part 10.

43. Embassy, Washington to External, tel. 3171, 27 Oct. 1962; Embassy, Washington to External, tel. 3173, 28 Oct. 1962, DEA, box 4184, file 2444-40 Part 11.

44. Embassy, Moscow to External, tel. 777, 28 Oct. 1962, DEA, box 4184, file 2444-40 Part 11.

45. Robertson to Green, memo, "Cuba," 1 Nov. 1962, DEA, box 4184, file 2444-40 Part 12.

46. External to Embassy, Havana, outgoing message M-102, 31 Oct. 1962, box 4184, file 2444-40 Part 11.

47. See Embassy, Havana to External, tel. 218, 31 Oct. 1962, DEA, box 4184, file 2444-40 Part 11; and George Kidd to Raul Roa, letter, 2 Nov. 1962, DEA, box 4184, file 2444-40 Part 12.

48. See Embassy, Havana to External, tel. 217, 30 Oct. 1962, DEA, box 4184, file 2444-40 Part 11; Embassy, Havana to External, tel. 222, 1 Nov. 1962, DEA, box 4184, file 2444-40 Part 12.

49. Robinson to Ritchie, memo, "Cuba," 1 Nov. 1962, DEA, box 3176, file "Cuba, 1960–1964."

50. See Embassy, Havana to External, tel. 211, 27 Oct. 1962, DEA, box 5352, file 10224-40 Part 12.2; and Embassy, Havana to External, tel. 229, 5 Nov. 1962, DEA, box 4184, file 2444-40 Part 12.

51. Embassy, Washington to External, tel. 3139, 26 Oct. 1962; Embassy, Washington to External, tel. 3175, 29 Oct. 1962; and External to Embassy, Havana, outgoing message G-162, 29 Oct. 1962, DEA, box 5352, file 10224-40 Part 12.2.

52. Embassy, Havana to Embassy, Washington, emergency tel. "Cuba Radio Broadcast," 30 Oct. 1962, DEA, box 5352, file 10224-40 Part 12.2.

53. Excerpt, "Address by the Prime Minister at the Diamond Jubilee Banquet of the Zionist Organization of Canada, Beth Tzedec Synagogue, Toronto, 5 Nov. 1962," DEA, box 4184, file 2444-40 Part 12.

54. Lyon, *Canada in World Affairs*, 54; Ghent, "Canada, the United States, and the Cuban Missile Crisis," 180.

55. Kriebel to Carlson, memo, "Luncheon Conversation with Basil Robinson, Deputy Chief of Mission, Canadian Embassy, 23 November 1962," 30 Nov. 1962; EUR, CDC, POL, box 3, file "Canadian Government, 1961–1962."

56. J. Kirk and P. McKenna, *Canada-Cuba Relations: The Other Good Neighbor Policy* (Gainesville, 1997), 62. On this debate, see J. Maynard Ghent, "Did He Fall or Was He Pushed? The Kennedy Administration and the Collapse of the Diefenbaker Government," *International History Review* i (1979), 246–70; Granatstein, "When Push Came to Shove"; P. McMahon, *Essence of Indecision: Diefenbaker's Nuclear Policy, 1957–1963* (Montreal, 2009).

57. Merchant to Rusk and Ball, letter, undated; attached to Brubeck to Ball, 10 Dec. 1962, JFKL, NSF, series 1, box 18, file "Canada, General, Rostow Memorandum and Related Materials, 5/61-5/63."

58. See J.I. Domínguez, "The @#$%& Missile Crisis: (Or What Was 'Cuban' about U.S. Decisions during the Cuban Missile Crisis?)," *Diplomatic History* xxiv (2000), 305–15.

59. Smith to file, memo, "Canadian Attitude Toward Cuban Crisis," 2 Nov. 1962, EUR, CDC, POL, file "Cuba Quarantine, 1962." Reford left this conversation out of his own account of Canada's role in the missile crisis; see Idem., *Canada and Three Crises* (Toronto, 1968), 149–217.

Chapter 11

The Quiet Revolution

READINGS

Primary Documents

Historical Interpretations

INTRODUCTION

When historians look at Quebec from 1960 onward, they often emphasize the speed with which things seemed to change there at that time. But there was no single, standard North American way of life that Quebec suddenly caught up to in the 1960s. Life was changing throughout Canada and the United States, and the profound changes in Quebec had been brewing for some time. In other words, looking for a definitive beginning or end to the "Quiet Revolution" is less important than acknowledging that the seeds of those changes had been sown long before Jean Lesage's Liberal party came to power in the provincial election of 1960, and that the push for change did not end with the Liberal defeat of 1966. It continued in the next decade with the October Crisis of 1970 and the 1976 election of the Parti Québécois, and beyond that with the failed sovereignty referendum campaigns of 1980 and 1995. In spite of the rapid shifts that occurred during the Quiet Revolution, many Quebecers were frustrated by the pace of change. Among these impatient radicals, the terrorists of the Front de libération du Québec (FLQ) were no doubt the most extreme. The FLQ issued its third and best-known manifesto after it kidnapped James Cross, the British Trade Representative in Montreal. The 1970 manifesto calls on ordinary Quebecers to rise up and overthrow capitalism and the federal state. The FLQ's actions did elicit some sympathy among the population, but the cause of Quebec independence was advanced far more successfully by moderates like René Lévesque. Lévesque played a key role in the formation of the Parti Québécois, and his 1968 work, *An Option for Quebec*, discussed the possibility of creating a new political relationship between Quebec and Canada. This would not be a radical solution, Lévesque argued, but the realization of Quebec's destiny as the homeland of a distinct people. The historical interpretations also examine crucial questions related to change. In his article, David Seljak chronicles the complex and sometimes contradictory thought of people who wanted to retain their religious ties to an institution, the Roman Catholic Church, which seemed to be both a force for change and a haven for reactionaries. The period between the late 1950s and the early 1980s brought profound shifts, but Seljak insists that the Church was able to handle these changes with relative calm. For his part, Sean Mills examines the relationship between feminism and nationalism during the Quiet Revolution. Initially, in the 1960s, leading figures in the women's liberation movement believed that their struggle was linked to the goal of creating an independent Quebec. By the 1970s, however, many feminists regarded the Parti Québécois with a measure of suspicion and began to reject nationalism as a vehicle for social change.

QUESTIONS FOR CONSIDERATION

1. What does the FLQ manifesto reveal about the goals and ideology of the Front de libération du Québec?
2. Who does Lévesque identify as "we," and how does he define this group?
3. Why do you think historians call this period the "Quiet Revolution" when it seems that plenty of people noticed what was occurring? Was there anything "quiet" about it?
4. Seljak paints the Catholic Church in Quebec during and after the Quiet Revolution as a dynamic institution, one that supported reform. How did an organization known for sticking to its traditions make such a transformation?
5. How did the Centre des femmes come to reject nationalism?

SUGGESTIONS FOR FURTHER READING

Michael D. Behiels, *Prelude to Quebec's Quiet Revolution: Liberalism versus Neo-nationalism, 1945–1960* (Montreal and Kingston: McGill-Queen's University Press, 2003).

Ramsay Cook, *Watching Quebec: Selected Essays* (Montreal and Kingston: McGill-Queen's University Press, 2005).

Graham Fraser, *René Lévesque and the Parti Québécois in Power* (Montreal and Kingston: McGill-Queen's University Press, 2001).

Michael Gauvreau, *The Catholic Origins of Quebec's Quiet Revolution, 1931–1970* (Montreal and Kingston: McGill-Queen's University Press, 2008).

José Igartua, *The Other Quiet Revolution: National Identities in English Canada, 1945–71* (Vancouver: UBC Press, 2007).

Kenneth McRoberts, *Misconceiving Canada: The Struggle for National Unity* (Don Mills: Oxford University Press, 1997).

David Meren, *With Friends Like These: Entangled Nationalisms and the Canada-Quebec-France Triangle, 1944–1970* (Vancouver: UBC Press, 2012)

Sean Mills, *The Empire Within: Postcolonial Thought and Political Activism in Sixties Montreal* (Montreal and Kingston: McGill-Queen's University Press, 2010).

Bryan Palmer, *Canada's 1960s: The Ironies of Identity in a Rebellious Era* (Toronto: University of Toronto Press, 2008).

William Tetley, *The October Crisis, 1970: An Insider's View* (Montreal and Kingston: McGill-Queen's University Press, 2006).

Primary Documents

1 From "FLQ Manifesto 1970," translated and edited by D.C. Bélanger, 2011.

EDITOR'S NOTE

The Front de libération du Québec (FLQ) was a terrorist organization founded in Montreal in early 1963. It conducted a decade-long campaign of terror in the hope of igniting a revolution that would lead to the establishment of an independent and socialist Quebec. On 5 October 1970, the FLQ's Libération cell kidnapped the British trade commissioner in Montreal, James Cross. This action triggered the October Crisis, an event that witnessed the suspension of civil liberties in Canada and the arrest of hundreds of individuals suspected of ties to the FLQ. The FLQ's use of the media was far more effective during the October Criseis than at any other point in its history. The Libération cell released the following manifesto shortly after kidnapping James Cross. Its broadcast was listed among the seven demands for Cross's release. Although the federal government initially attempted to suppress its circulation, Prime Minister Pierre Trudeau reluctantly allowed Radio-Canada to broadcast the manifesto on October 8. Designed to have broad appeal, the manifesto contained elements of joual (colloquial Canadian French). Its populism and irreverence struck a chord with many ordinary Quebecers.

FRONT DE LIBÉRATION DU QUÉBEC MANIFESTO

The Front de libération du Québec is neither the Messiah nor a modern-day Robin Hood. It is a group of Quebec workers who are determined to use every means possible to ensure that the people of Quebec take control of their own destiny.

The Front de libération du Québec wants total independence for Quebecers, united in a free society and purged for good of the clique of voracious sharks, the patronizing "big bosses"[1] and their henchmen who have made Quebec their private hunting ground for "cheap labour"[2] and unscrupulous exploitation.

The Front de libération du Québec is not an aggressive movement, but rather a response to the aggression perpetrated by high finance through the puppet governments in in Ottawa and Québec (the Brinks "show,"[3] Bill 63,[4] the electoral map,[5] the so-called "social progress" (sic) tax,[6] Power Corporation,[7] "Doctors' insurance,"[8] the Lapalme boys[9] . . .).

The Front de libération du Québec finances itself through voluntary taxes (sic)[10] levied on the establishments that exploit workers (banks, finance companies, etc.).

"The financially powerful, who uphold the status quo and who make up the majority of the traditional tutors of our people, have obtained the reaction they hoped for: a step backwards rather than the change for which we have worked harder than ever before, and for which we will continue to work" (René Lévesque, April 29, 1970).[11]

We briefly believed that it was worth channelling our energy and our impatience, as René Lévesque so aptly put it, into the Parti québécois,[12] but the Liberal victory[13] clearly demonstrates that what we call democracy in Quebec has always been, and still is, a "democracy"[14] of the rich. In this sense, the Liberal party's victory is a victory of the Simard-Cotroni[15] election riggers. Consequently, we have washed our hands clean of the British parliamentary system[16] and the Front de libération du Québec will never allow itself to be distracted by the electoral crumbs that the Anglo-Saxon capitalists toss Quebec's way every four years. Many Quebecers have realized the truth and are ready to take action. In the coming year Bourassa[17] will get what is coming to him: 100,000[18] revolutionary workers, armed and organized!

Yes, there are reasons for the Liberal victory. Yes, there are reasons for poverty, unemployment, slums, and for the fact that you, Mr. Bergeron of Visitation Street,[19] and also you, Mr. Legendre of Laval,[20] who earn $10,000 a year,[21] do not feel free in our country of Quebec.

Yes, there are reasons, and the guys at Lord know them, and the fishermen of the Gaspé, the workers of the North Shore, the miners of the Iron Ore, of Quebec Cartier Mining, and Noranda also know these reasons.[22] And the brave workers of Cabano[23] who "they" tried to screw again know many such reasons.

Yes, there are reasons why you, Mr. Tremblay of Panet Street[24] and you, Mr. Cloutier, who work in construction in St. Jérôme,[25] cannot pay for "vaisseaux d'or,"[26] replete with jazz and razzle-dazzle, like Drapeau[27] the aristocrat, who is so concerned about slums that he covers them up with coloured billboards to hide our misery from the wealthy tourists.[28]

Yes, there are reasons why you, Mrs. Lemay of St. Hyacinthe,[29] can't pay for little trips to Florida like the rotten judges and parliamentarians do with our money.

The brave workers for Vickers and Davie Ship,[30] who were sacked without notice, know these reasons. And the Murdochville men, who were crushed for the simple and sole reason that they wanted to organize a union and were forced to pay $2 million by the rotten judges simply because they tried to exercise this basic right[31]—they know justice and they know many such reasons.

Yes, there are reasons why you, Mr. Lachance of Sainte-Marguerite Street,[32] go and drown your despair, your bitterness, and your rage in a bottle of that dog's beer, Molson. And you, Lachance's son, with your marijuana cigarettes . . .

Yes, there are reasons why, generation after generation, you, the welfare recipients, are kept on social assistance. Yes, there are lots of reasons, and the Domtar workers in East Angus and Windsor[33] know them well. And the workers at Squibb and Ayers, and the men at the Liquor Board and those at Seven-Up and Victoria Precision,[34] and the blue collar workers in Laval and Montreal and the Lapalme boys know lots reasons.

The Dupont of Canada workers also know them, even if soon they will be able to express them only in English[35] (thus assimilated they will enlarge the number of New Quebecers, the immigrant darlings of Bill 63).[36]

And the Montreal policemen, those strong-arms of the system, should understand these reasons—they should have been able to see that we live in a terrorized society because, without their force, without their violence, everything fell apart on October 7![37]

We have had our fill of "Canadian"[38] federalism that penalizes the Quebec milk producers to satisfy the needs of the Anglo-Saxons of the Commonwealth;[39] the system which keeps the valiant Montreal taxi drivers in a state of semi-slavery to shamefully protect the exclusive monopoly of nauseating Murray Hill[40] and its proprietor—the murderer Charles Hershorn and his son Paul who, on the night of October 7, repeatedly tore the twelve-gauge shot gun from his employee's hands to fire at the taxi drivers, thereby mortally wounding Corporal Dumas, killed while undercover.[41]

We have had our fill of a federal system that exercises a senseless policy of importation[42] while the low wage-earners in the textile and shoe manufacturing trades,[43] who are the most ill-treated in Quebec, are thrown out into the street for the benefit of a clutch of damned "money-makers"[44] in their Cadillacs; we have had enough of a federal government which classes the Quebec nation among the ethnic minorities of Canada.

We have had our fill, as have more and more Quebecers, of a pathetic government that performs a thousand and one acrobatics to charm American millionaires into investing in Quebec,[45] la Belle Province, where thousands and thousands of square miles of forests, full of game and well-stocked lakes, are the exclusive preserve of these almighty twentieth century lords.[46]

We have had our fill of hypocrites like Bourassa who rely on Brinks armoured trucks,[47] the living symbol of the foreign occupation of Quebec, to keep the poor "natives"[48] of Quebec in fear of the misery and unemployment in which they are accustomed to living.

We have had our fill of the Ottawa representative to Quebec[49] who wants to give our tax money to the Anglophone bosses to "encourage" them to speak French, my dear, to negotiate in French.[50] Repeat after me: "Cheap labour is *main d'œuvre à bon marché* in French."[51]

We have had our fill of promises of work and prosperity, when in fact we will always be the diligent servants and boot-lickers of the "big shots,"[52] as long as there is a Westmount, a Town of Mount Royal, a Hampstead, an Outremont,[53] all the fortresses of high finance on St. James Street[54] and Wall Street; we will be slaves until all of us, the Québécois, have exhausted every means, including arms and dynamite, to rid ourselves of these economic and political "big bosses"[55] who are prepared to use every dirty trick in the book to better screw us.

We live in a society of terrorized slaves, terrorized by the big bosses like Steinberg, Clark, Bronfman, Smith, Neaple, Timmins, Geoffrion, J.L. Lévesque, Hershorn, Thompson, Nesbitt, Desmarais, Kierans.[56] Compared to them, Rémi Popol[57] the nightstick, Drapeau the "dog,"[58] Bourassa the twink of the Simards,[59] and Trudeau[60] the faggot[61] are peanut politicians!

We are terrorized by the capitalist Roman Church, even though this seems less and less obvious (who owns the property on which the stock exchange stands?);[62] by the payments to Household Finance; by the advertising of the grand masters of consumption: Eaton, Simpson, Morgan, Steinberg, General Motors . . . ; we are terrorized by the closed circles of science and culture which are the universities and by their "monkey see, monkey do" bosses like Gaudry[63] and Dorais[64] and by the assistant monkey Robert Shaw.[65]

There is an increasing number of us who know and suffer under this terrorist society, and the day is fast approaching when all the Westmounts of Quebec will disappear from the map.

Factory workers, miners, and loggers; service-industry workers, teachers, students, and the unemployed, take back what belongs to you, your jobs, your determination, and your liberty.

And you, workers at General Electric, you make your factories run; only you are capable of production; without you General Electric is nothing!

Workers of Quebec, take back today what is yours; take back what belongs to you. Only you know your factories, your machines, your hotels, your universities, your unions. Don't wait for some miracle organization.

Make your own revolution in your neighbourhoods, in your places of work. If you don't do it yourselves, other technocratic usurpers and so on will replace the handful of cigar smokers we now know, and everything will have to be done over again. Only you are able to build a free society.

We must struggle, not individually but together, until victory is ours, with every means at our disposal, like the Patriots of 1837–38 (those whom Our Holy Mother the Church hastily excommunicated to better sell out to British interests).[66]

In the four corners of Quebec, may those who have been contemptuously called "lousy French"[67] and alcoholics start fighting vigorously against the enemies of liberty and justice and put out of commission all the professional swindlers and robbers, the bankers, the businessmen, the judges, and the sold-out politicians!!!

We are the workers of Quebec and we will fight to the bitter end. With the help of the entire population, we want to replace this slave society with a free society, operating by itself and for itself, a society open to the world.

Our struggle can only be victorious. An awakening people cannot be kept in misery and contempt for long.

Long live free Quebec!

Long live our imprisoned political comrades!

Long live the Quebec revolution!

Long live the Front de libération du Québec!

NOTES

1. In English in the original text ("big boss"). The FLQ used English terminology as a form of derision and also as a means to highlight the dominant role of Anglophones in Quebec's economy.

2. In English in the original text.

3. In English in the original text. Shortly before the 1970 provincial election, the Royal Trust transferred thousands of financial certificates from Montreal to Toronto in a convoy of Brinks armoured trucks. The Royal Trust claimed that concerned clients had insisted that their investments and property be protected from a possible Parti québécois (PQ) victory. The well-publicized event was widely viewed as an attempt to dissuade Quebec voters from supporting the fledgling sovereignist party.

4. Enacted in 1969, Bill 63 was Quebec's first major language law. It guaranteed parents the right to choose the language of instruction for their children, but required that children who received their education in English acquire a working knowledge of French. Bill 63 also encouraged immigrants to learn French upon arrival in Quebec. The bill was viewed as a weak measure by many French-speaking Quebecers and contributed to the 1970 defeat of Jean-Jacques Bertrand's Union nationale government.

5. In 1970, Quebec's electoral map magnified the political power of rural ridings. This contributed to the Parti québécois' poor showing in the 1970 provincial election. The party drew the bulk of its support from urban areas in the early 1970s.

6. Federal tax designed to fund socialized healthcare. Quebec was denied its share of the funds until it implemented its own medicare program in late 1970.

7. Power Corporation is one of Canada's largest companies. Its chairman and chief executive officer, Paul Desmarais, is a media mogul and a long-time supporter of the Liberal party.

8. Early version of medicare.

9. The "Lapalme Boys" were a group of postal truck drivers who lost their jobs after the federal Post Office Department cancelled their company's contract. In 1970, they became something of a *cause célèbre* in Quebec. The FLQ listed their rehiring among its seven demands for the release of James Cross.

10. Allusion to Montreal Mayor Jean Drapeau's use of "voluntary taxes" (lotteries) to fund various city projects. The FLQ financed most of its terrorist activities through theft and bank robberies.

11. Statement made by René Lévesque (1922–1987), leader of the Parti québécois and later premier of Quebec (1976–1985), on the night of the 1970 provincial election. In 1970, the Parti québécois received 23 per cent of the popular vote, but only won 6.5 per cent of the seats in Quebec's National Assembly. This poor showing left many sovereignists disheartened and convinced radical fringe elements within the movement that violence was the only means to achieve independence and socialism.

12. Founded in 1968, the Parti québécois advocates sovereignty for Quebec, but wishes to maintain certain formal ties with the rest of Canada.

13. Led by Robert Bourassa, the Liberal party won a sweeping victory in the 1970 Quebec provincial election.

14. In English in the original text.

15. The Simard family were wealthy industrialists from Sorel, Québec. The head of the Simard family, Édouard Simard, was Robert Bourassa's father-in-law. The Cotroni family dominated Montreal's criminal underworld in the 1960s and 1970s. It is alleged that both families bankrolled the Quebec Liberal party.

16. The Parti québécois' poor showing in the 1970 provincial election can be attributed, in part, to the distortions of Quebec's electoral map (see note 5) and to the effects of Canada's British-style electoral system. Known as single-member district plurality, this system awards a parliamentary seat to any candidate who obtains the largest share of the vote in a particular riding, regardless of whether or not the candidate has received a majority of ballots cast. Single-member district plurality has traditionally hampered political parties whose support is significant but diffuse. This was the Parti québécois' case in the early 1970s.

17. Robert Bourassa (1933–1996), Liberal premier of Quebec (1970–1976, 1985–1994).

18. Allusion to Premier Bourassa's promise to create 100,000 jobs in 1971.

19. Visitation Street is located in a working-class and largely French-speaking area of Montreal.

20. Laval is a largely French-speaking suburb of Montreal.

21. A comfortable middle-class income in 1970 Quebec.

22. The Lord steelworks, Iron Ore of Canada, Quebec Cartier Mining, and Noranda Mines had poor records of labour relations in the 1960s. The Gaspé peninsula and the North Shore are resource-dependent regions in eastern Quebec.

23. Located in the Lower St. Lawrence, the town of Cabano was the centre of a major dispute in 1970 involving the Irving conglomerate of New Brunswick and the local population. Industrialist K.C. Irving had promised to build a mill in Cabano in exchange for logging rights in the region. Serious acts of vandalism occurred after Irving reneged on his promise.

24. Panet Street is located in a working-class and largely French-speaking area of Montreal.

25. Saint-Jérôme is at the foothills of the Laurentians, north of Montreal.

26. Allusion to Montreal Mayor Jean Drapeau's exclusive restaurant, le Vaisseau d'or. The restaurant featured a live classical orchestra.

27. Jean Drapeau (1916–1999), mayor of Montreal (1954–1957, 1960–1986). The FLQ bombed Drapeau's residence in 1969.

28. Allusion to Mayor Drapeau's various urban renewal programs.

29. St. Hyacinthe is in the Montérégie region, in southwestern Quebec.

30. The Vickers and Davie shipyards of Montreal and Lauzon were closed in 1969. Workers were only given two hours' notice of their termination.

31. Murdochville, a mining town in the Gaspé peninsula, was the site of a major strike in

1957. The dispute was centred on the workers' right to unionize and resulted in a significant defeat for organized labour. The courts would eventually order the United Steelworkers of America to compensate Gaspé Copper Mines for the strike.

32. Sainte-Marguerite Street is located in a working-class and largely French-speaking area of Montreal.

33. In 1968, a violent labour dispute took place in Domtar's pulp and paper plants in East Angus and Windsor, in Quebec's Eastern Townships.

34. Between 1966 and 1970, serious labour disputes occurred at Squibb Pharmaceuticals in Montreal, the Dominion Ayers in Lachute, the Quebec Liquor Board, Seven-Up's Montreal bottling plant, and Victoria Precision in Montreal. The FLQ bombed the residence of the Seven-Up plant's manager in 1967.

35. Dupont of Canada was known for its refusal to employ French Canadians in management positions and for its insistence that only English be used in its Quebec plants.

36. Under Bill 63, an overwhelming majority of immigrants chose to send their children to English school (see note 4).

37. On October 7, 1969, Montreal's police officers and firefighters staged an illegal strike. The city was rocked by several hours of violence and mayhem.

38. In English in the original text.

39. In mid-1970, federal civil servants had suggested that Quebec's milk production be curtailed.

40. In 1970, only the taxis and buses of the Murray Hill Company could carry passengers from downtown Montreal to Dorval (now Pierre Elliott Trudeau) Airport. This monopoly was contested by the militant Mouvement de libération du taxi, which had ties to the FLQ.

41. Taking advantage of the Montreal police and fire department strike of October 7, 1969, the Mouvement de libération du taxi attacked the garage of the Murray Hill Company. Several buses were burned and gunfire was exchanged. A number of people were injured, including FLQ members Jacques Lanctôt and Marc Carbonneau, and an undercover officer of Quebec's provincial police, Corporal Robert Dumas, was killed.

42. Since the 1940s, the Canadian government has tended to support multilateral tariff reduction.

43. The textile and shoe industries were the backbone of Quebec's manufacturing sector.

44. In English in the original text.

45. Like many Quebec premiers before him, Robert Bourassa was eager to encourage American capitalists to invest in Quebec. Premier Bourassa was in New York on a trade mission when the October Crisis began.

46. Until 1977, a good deal of Quebec's best hunting and fishing land was controlled by private clubs owned by wealthy Americans.

47. See note 3.

48. In English in the original text.

49. Probably an allusion to Premier Robert Bourassa.

50. Earlier in 1970, Premier Bourassa had discussed the possibility of provincial government action aimed at fostering the use of French in Quebec's business world.

51. The first part of this sentence is in English in the original text.

52. In English in the original text.

53. Westmount, Town of Mount Royal, and Hampstead are wealthy and largely English-speaking suburbs of Montreal; Outremont is a wealthy and largely French-speaking suburb.

54. St. James Street (rue Saint-Jacques) is the centre of Montreal's financial district.

55. In English in the original text ("big boss").

56. Many of the leading figures of Quebec's business establishment are listed in this sentence.

57. Rémi Paul (1921–1982), Union nationale minister of justice of Quebec (1968–1970).

58. In English in the original text.

59. Allusion to rumours regarding Premier Bourassa's sexual orientation and to his relationship with the wealthy Simard family. Bourassa married Andrée Simard in 1958.

60. Pierre Elliott Trudeau (1919–2000), Liberal minister of justice (1967–1968) and prime minister of Canada (1968–1979, 1980–1984).

61. In the 1960s, rumours regarding Trudeau's sexual orientation were fuelled by his 1967 Omnibus Bill, which decriminalized sodomy, and by his status as a bachelor.

62. The Sulpician Order owns extensive real estate on the island of Montreal.

63. Roger Gaudry (1913–2001), first lay rector of the Université de Montréal (1965–1975).
64. Léo Dorais (b. 1929), first rector of the Université du Québec à Montréal (1969–1974).
65. Robert Shaw (1910–2001), deputy commissioner-general of Expo '67 and vice-principal of administration at McGill University (1968–1971).
66. In 1837–1838, anti-colonial rebellions swept across southwestern Quebec. The Roman Catholic Church condemned the rebellions and refused to administer the sacraments to the rebels.
67. In English in the original text. Pierre Trudeau had used this expression to describe the French spoken by ordinary Quebecers.

2 From René Lévesque, *An Option for Québec* (Toronto: McClelland & Stewart, 1968), 14–30. © 1997 Éditions Typo et succession René Lévesque.

CHAPTER 1: "BELONGING"

We are *Québécois*.

What that means first and foremost—and if need be, all that it means—is that we are attached to this one corner of the earth where we can be completely ourselves: this Quebec, the only place where we have the unmistakable feeling that "here we can be really at home."

Being ourselves is essentially a matter of keeping and developing a personality that has survived for three and a half centuries.

At the core of this personality is the fact that we speak French. Everything else depends on this one essential element and follows from it or leads us infallibly back to it.

In our history, America began with a French look, briefly but gloriously given it by Champlain, Joliet, La Salle, La-Verendrye. . . . We learn our first lessons in progress and perseverance from Maisonneuve, Jeanne Mance, Jean Talon; and in daring or heroism from Lambert Closse, Brébeuf, Frontenac, d'Iberville. . . .

Then came the conquest. We were a conquered people, our hearts set on surviving in some small way on a continent that had become Anglo-Saxon.

Somehow or other, through countless changes and a variety of regimes, despite difficulties without number (our lack of awareness and even our ignorance serving all too often as our best protection), we succeeded.

Here again, when we recall the major historical landmarks, we come upon a profusion of names: Etienne Parent and Lafontaine and the Patriots of '37; Louis Riel and Honoré Mercier, Bourassa, Philippe Hamel; Garneau and Edouard Montpetit and Asselin and Lionel Groulx. . . . For each of them, the main driving force behind every action was the will to continue, and the tenacious hope that they could make it worth while.

Until recently in this difficult process of survival we enjoyed the protection of a certain degree of isolation. We lived a relatively sheltered life in a rural society in which a great measure of unanimity reigned, and in which poverty set its limits on change and aspiration alike.

We are children of that society, in which the *habitant*, our father or grandfather, was still the key citizen. We also are heirs to that fantastic adventure—that early America that was almost entirely French. We are, even more intimately, heirs to the group obstinacy which has kept alive that portion of French America we call *Québec*.

All these things lie at the core of this personality of ours. Anyone who does not feel it, at least occasionally, is not—is no longer—one of us.

But *we* know and feel that these are the things that make us what we are. They enable us to recognize each other wherever we may be. This is our own special wave-length on which, despite all interference, we can tune each other in loud and clear, with no one else listening.

This is how we differ from other men and especially from other North Americans, with whom in all other areas we have so much in common. This basic "difference" we cannot surrender. That became impossible a long time ago.

More is involved here than simple intellectual certainty. This is a physical fact. To be unable to live as ourselves, as we should live, in our own language and according to our own ways, would be like living without an arm or a leg—or perhaps a heart.

Unless, of course, we agreed to give in little by little, in a decline which, as in cases of pernicious anaemia, would cause life to slip slowly away from the patient.

Again, in order not to perceive this, one has to be among the *déracinés*, the uprooted and cut-off.

CHAPTER 2: THE ACCELERATION OF HISTORY

On the other hand, one would have to be blind not to see that the conditions under which this personality must assert itself have changed in our lifetime, at an extremely rapid and still accelerating rate.

Our traditional society, which gave our parents the security of an environment so ingrown as to be reassuring and in which many of us grew up in a way that we thought could, with care, be preserved indefinitely; that "quaint old" society has gone.

Today, most of us are city dwellers, wage-earners, tenants. The standards of parish, village, and farm have been splintered. The automobile and the airplane take us "outside" in a way we never could have imagined

thirty years ago, or even less. Radio and films, and now television, have opened for us a window onto everything that goes on throughout the world: the events—and the ideas too—of all humanity invade our homes day after day.

The age of automatic unanimity thus has come to an end. The old protective barriers are less and less able to mark safe pathways for our lives. The patience and resignation that were preached to us in the old days with such efficiency now produce no other reactions than scepticism or indifference, or even rebellion.

At our own level, we are going through a universal experience. In this sudden acceleration of history, whose main features are the unprecedented development of science, technology, and economic activity, there are potential promises and dangers immeasurably greater than any the world ever has known.

The promises—if man so desires—are those of abundance, of liberty, of fraternity; in short, of a civilization that could attain heights undreamed of by the most unrestrained Utopians.

The dangers—unless man can hold them in check—are those of insecurity and servitude, of inhuman governments, of conflicts among nations that could lead to extermination.

In this little corner of ours, we already are having a small taste of the dangers as well as the promises of this age.

A Balance Sheet of Vulnerability

The dangers are striking enough.

In a world where, in so many fields, the only stable law seems to have become that of perpetual change, where our old certainties are crumbling one after the other, we find ourselves swept along helplessly by irresistible currents. We are not at all sure that we can stay afloat, for the swift, confusing pace of events forces us to realize as never before our own weaknesses, our backwardness, our terrible collective vulnerability.

Endlessly, with a persistence almost masochistic, we draw up list after list of our inadequacies. For too long we despised education. We lack scientists, administrators, qualified technical people. Economically, we are colonials whose three meals a day depend far too much on the initiative and goodwill of foreign bosses. And we must admit as well that we are far from being the most advanced along the path of social progress, the yardstick by which the quality of a human community can best be measured. For a very long time we have allowed our public administration to stagnate in negligence and corruption, and left our political life in the hands of fast talkers and our own equivalent of those African kings who grew rich by selling their own tribesmen.

We must admit that our society has grave, dangerous, and deep-rooted illnesses which it is absolutely essential to cure if we want to survive.

Now, a human society that feels itself to be sick and inferior, and is unable to do anything about it, sooner or later reaches the point of being unacceptable even to itself.

For a small people such as we are, our minority position on an Anglo-Saxon continent creates from the very beginning a permanent temptation to such a self-rejection, which has all the attraction of a gentle downward slope ending in a comfortable submersion in the Great Whole.

There are enough sad cases, enough among us who have given up, to show us that this danger does exist.

It is, incidentally, the only danger that really can have a fatal effect upon us, because it exists within ourselves.

And if ever we should be so unfortunate as to abandon this individuality that makes us what we are, it is not "the others" we would have to blame, but only our own impotence and resulting discouragement.

The only way to overcome the danger is to face up to this trying and thoughtless age and make it accept us as we are, succeeding somehow in making a proper and appropriate place in it for ourselves, in our own language, so that we can feel we are equals and not inferiors. This means that in our homeland we must be able to earn our living and pursue our careers in French. It also means that we must build a society which, while it preserves an image that is our own, will be as progressive, as efficient, and as "civilized" as any in the world. (In fact, there are other small peoples who are showing us the way, demonstrating that maximum size is in no way synonymous with maximum progress among human societies.)

To speak plainly, we must give ourselves sufficient reason to be not only sure of ourselves but also, perhaps, a little proud.

CHAPTER 3: THE QUIET REVOLUTION

Now, in the last few years we have indeed made some progress along this difficult road of "catching up," the road which leads to the greater promise of our age.

At least enough progress to know that what comes next depends only on ourselves and on the choices that only we can make.

The enticements toward progress were phrases like "from now on," or "it's got to change," or "masters in our own house," etc.

The results can be seen on every side. Education, for us as for any people desirous of maintaining its place in the world, has finally become the top priority. With hospital insurance, family and school allowances, pension schemes, and the beginnings of medicare, our social welfare has made more progress in a few years than in the whole preceding century; and for the first time we find ourselves, in many of the most important areas, ahead of the rest of the country. In the economic field, by nationalizing electric power, by created the S.G.F., *Soquem*, and the *Caisse de Dépôts*[1] we have taken the first steps toward the kind of collective control of certain essential services without which no human community can feel secure. We also, at last, have begun to clean up our electoral practices, to modernize and strengthen our administrative structures, to give our land the roads that are indispensable to its future, and to study seriously the complex problems of our outmoded municipalities and underdeveloped regions.

To be sure, none of this has been brought to completion. What has been done is only a beginning, carried out in many cases without the co-ordination that should have been applied—and far too often in circumstances dictated by urgency or opportunity. All along the way there have been hesitations and, God knows, these still exist. In all these accomplishments mistakes have been made and gaps have been left—and whatever happens, even if we do a hundred times as much, this always will be so.

No One Will Do It for You

But in the process we have learned certain things, things which are both simple and revolutionary.

The first is that we have the capacity to do the job ourselves, and the more we take charge and accept our responsibilities, the more efficient we find we are; capable, all things considered, of succeeding just as well as anyone else.

Another is that there is no valid excuse, that it is up to us to find and apply to our problems the solutions that are right for us; for no one else can, much less wants to, solve them for us.

CHAPTER 4: THE BASIC MINIMUMS

On this road where there can be no more stopping are a number of necessary tasks which must be attended to without delay. Neglecting them would endanger the impetus we have acquired, perhaps would slow it down irreparably.

And here we encounter a basic difficulty which has become more and more acute in recent years. It is created by the political regime under which we have lived for over a century.

We are a nation within a country where there are two nations. For all the things we mentioned earlier, using words like "individuality," "history," "society," and "people," are also the things one includes under the word "nation." It means nothing more than the collective will to live that belongs to any national entity likely to survive.

Two nations in a single country: this means, as well, that in fact there are *two majorities*, two "complete societies" quite distinct from each other trying to get along within a common framework. That this number puts us in a minority position makes no difference: just as a civilized society will never condemn a little man to feel inferior beside a bigger man, civilized relations among nations demand that they treat each other as equals in law and in fact.

Now we believe it to be evident that the hundred-year-old framework of Canada can hardly have any effect other than to create increasing difficulties between the two parties insofar as their mutual respect and understanding are concerned, as well as impeding the changes and progress so essential to both.

It is useless to go back over the balance sheet of the century just past, listing the advantages it undoubtedly has brought us and the obstacles and injustices it even more unquestionably has set in our way.

The important thing for today and for tomorrow is that both sides realize that this regime has had its day, and that it is a matter of urgency either to modify it profoundly or to build a new one.

As we are the ones who have put up with its main disadvantages, it is natural that we also should be in the greatest hurry to be rid of it; the more so because it is we who are menaced most dangerously by its current paralysis.

Primo Vivere

Almost all the essential tasks facing us risk being jeopardized, blocked, or quietly undone by the sclerosis of Canadian institutions and the open or camouflaged resistance of the men who manipulate them.

First, we must secure once and for all, in accordance with the complex and urgent necessities of our time, the safety of our collective "personality." This is the distinctive feature of the nation, of this majority that we constitute in Quebec—the only true fatherland left us by events, by our own possibilities, and by the incomprehension and frequent hostility of others.

The prerequisite to this is, among other things, the power for unfettered action (which does not exclude co-operation) in fields as varied as those of citizenship, immigration, and employment; the great instruments of "mass culture"—films, radio, and television; and the kind of international relations that alone permit a people to breathe the air of a changing and stimulating world, and to learn to see beyond itself. Such relations are especially imperative for a group whose cultural connections in the world are as evident and important as ours.

Our collective security requires also that we settle a host of questions made so thorny by the present regime that each is more impossible than the next. Let us only mention as examples the integrity of Quebec's territory, off-shore rights, the evident in acceptability of an institution like the Supreme Court, and Quebec's need to be able to shape freely what we might term its internal constitution.

That collective personality which constitutes a nation also cannot tolerate that social security and welfare—which affect it daily in the most intimate ways—should be conceived and directed from outside. This relates to the oft-repeated demand for the repatriation of old-age pensions, family allowances, and, when it comes into being, medicare.

By the same token, and even more so, it relates to the most obvious needs of efficiency and administrative responsibility. In this whole vast area there are overlapping laws, regulations, and organizations whose main effect is to perpetuate confusion and, behind this screen, to paralyze change and progress.

The Madhouse

Mutatis mutandis, we find similar situations with equally disastrous results in a multitude of other areas: the administration of justice, jurisdiction in fields such as insurance, corporations, bankruptcies, financial institutions, and, in a general way, all economic activities which have become the most constant preoccupations of all men today and also the aspect of society in which modern states have seen their sphere of action grow most dramatically in the last couple of generations.

A Strong State

How can it be carried out? Let us mention only what is clearly obvious. Order must be re-established in the chaos of a governmental structure created at a time when it was impossible to foresee the scientific and technical revolution in which we now are caught up, the endless changes it demands, the infinite variety of things produced, the concentration of enterprises, the crushing weight that the greatest of these impose on individual and collective life, the absolute necessity of having a state able to direct, co-ordinate, and above all humanize this infernal rhythm.

In this up-dating of political structures that are completely overtaxed by an economic role they cannot refuse to play, the action demanded of the Quebec government, to be specific, would require at the very least new jurisdictions over industrial and commercial corporations, fiduciary and savings institutions, and all the internal agencies of development and industrialization, as well as the power to exercise a reasonable control over the movement and investment of our own capital.

So as not to belabour the obvious, we shall mention only for the record the massive transfer of fiscal resources that would be needed for all the tasks this State of Quebec should undertake in our name—not counting the tasks it already has, tasks that daily grow more out of proportion to its inadequate means: i.e., the insatiable needs of education, urban problems without number, and the meagreness or tragic non-existence of the tools of scientific and industrial research.

Very sketchily, this would seem to be the basic minimum of change that Quebec should force the present Canadian regime to accept in order to reach both the collective security and the opportunity for progress which its best minds consider indispensable.

We could certainly add to the list. But nothing could be struck from it easily.

For us, this is, in fact, a true minimum.

CHAPTER 5: THE BLIND ALLEY

But we would be dreaming if we believed that for the rest of the country our minimum can be anything but a frightening maximum, completely unacceptable even in the form of bare modifications or, for that matter, under the guise of the constitutional reform with which certain people say they are willing to proceed with.

Not only the present attitude of the federal government, but also the painful efforts at understanding made by the opposition parties and reactions in the most influential circles in English Canada all give us reason to expect that our confrontation will grow more and more unpleasant.

From a purely revisionist point of view, our demands would seem to surpass both the best intentions displayed by the "other majority" and the very capacity of the regime to make concessions without an explosion.

If we are talking only of revision, they will tell us, our demands would lead to excessive weakening of that centralized state which English Canada needs for its own security and progress as much as we need our own State of Quebec. And they would be right.

And further, they could ask us—with understandable insistence—what in the world our political representatives would be doing in Ottawa taking part in debates and administrative acts whose authority and effectiveness we intend so largely to eliminate within Quebec.

If Quebec were to begin negotiations to revise the present frame of reference, and persisted in this course, it would not be out of the woods in the next hundred years. But by that time it is most likely that there would be nothing left worth talking about of the nation that is now trying to build a homeland in Quebec.

During the long wait we would soon fall back on the old defensive struggle, the enfeebling skirmishes that make one forget where the real battle is, the half-victories that are celebrated between two defeats, the relapse in to divisive federal-provincial electoral folly, the sorry consolations of verbal nationalism and, above all, ABOVE ALL ELSE—this must be said, and repeated, and shouted if need be—above all the incredible "split-level" squandering of energy, which certainly is for us the most disastrous aspect of the present regime.

And as for this waste of energy, English Canada suffers from it, too. And there, too, the best minds have begun to realize this fact, let there be no doubt of that.

Two Paralyzed Majorities

For the present regime also prevents the English-speaking majority from simplifying, rationalizing, and centralizing as it would like to do certain institutions which it, too, realizes are obsolete. This is an ordeal which English Canada is finding more and more exhausting, and for which it blames to the exaggerated anxieties and the incorrigible intransigence of Quebec.

It is clear, we believe, that this frustration may easily become intolerable. And it is precisely among the most progressive and "nationalist" groups in English Canada, among those who are concerned about the economic, cultural, and political invasion from the United States, among those who are seeking the means to prevent the country from surrendering completely, that there is the greatest risk of a growing and explosive resentment toward Quebec for the reasons mentioned above.

And these are the very men among whom we should be able to find the best partners for our dialogue over the new order that must emerge.

We are seeking at last to carve out for ourselves a worthy and acceptable place in this Quebec which has never belonged to us as it should have. Facing us, however, a growing number of our fellow-citizens of the other majority are afraid of losing the homeland that Canada was for them in the good old days of the Empire, when they at least had the impression that they were helping to rule, and that it was all within the family. Today the centres of decision-making are shifting south of the border at a terrifying rate.

In this parallel search for two national securities, as long as the search is pursued within the present system or anything remotely resembling it, we can end up only with double paralysis. The two majorities, basically desiring the same thing—a chance to live their own lives, in their own way, according to their own needs and aspirations—will inevitably collide with one another repeatedly and with greater and greater force, causing hurts that finally would be irreparable.

As long as we persist so desperately in maintaining—with spit and chewing gum or whatever—the ancient hobble of a federalism suited to the last century, the two nations will go on creating an ever-growing jungle of compromises while disagreeing more and more strongly on essentials.

This would mean a perpetual atmosphere of instability, of wrangling over everything and over nothing. It would mean the sterilization of two collective "personalities" which, having squandered the most precious part of their potential, would weaken each other so completely that they would have no other choice but to drown themselves in the ample bosom of "America."

CHAPTER 6: THE WAY OF THE FUTURE

We think it is possible for both parties to avoid this blind alley. We must have the calm courage to see that the problem can't be solved either by maintaining or somehow adapting the status quo. One is always somewhat scared at the thought of leaving a home in which one has lived for a long time. It becomes almost "consecrated," and all the more so in this case, because what we call "Confederation" is one of the last remnants of those age-old safeguards of which modern times have robbed us. It is therefore quite normal that some people cling to it with a kind of desperation that arises far more from fear than from reasoned attachment.

But there are moments—and this is one of them—when courage and calm daring become the only proper form of prudence that a people can exercise in a crucial period of its existence. If it fails at these times to accept the calculated risk of the great leap, it may miss its vocation forever, just as does a man who is afraid of life.

What should be conclude from a cool look at the crucial crossroads that we now have reached? Clearly that we must rid ourselves completely of a completely obsolete federal regime.

And begin anew.

Begin how?

The answer, it seems to us, is as clearly written as the question, in the two great trends of our age: that of the freedom of peoples, and that of the formation by common consent of economic and political groupings.

A Sovereign Quebec

For our own good, we must dare to seize for ourselves complete liberty in Quebec, the right to all the essential components of independence, i.e., the complete mastery of every last area of basic collective decision-making.

This means that Quebec must become sovereign as soon as possible.

Thus we finally would have within our grasp the security of our collective "being" which is so vital to us, a security which otherwise must remain uncertain and incomplete.

Then it will be up to us, and us alone, to establish calmly, without recrimination or discrimination, the priority for which we are now struggling feverishly but blindly: that of our language and our culture.

Only then will we have the opportunity—and the obligation—to use our talents to the maximum in order to resolve without further excuses or evasions all the great problems that confront us, whether it be a negotiated protective system for our farmers, or decent treatment for our employees and workers in industry, or the form and evolution of the political structures we must create for ourselves.

In short, this is not for us simply the only solution to the present Canadian impasse; it also is the one and only common goal inspiring enough to bring us together with the kind of strength and unity we shall need to confront all possible futures—the supreme challenge of continuous progress within a society that has taken control of its own destiny.

As for the other Canadian majority, it will also find our solution to its advantage, for it will be set free at once from the constraints imposed on it by our presence; it will be at liberty in its own way to rebuild to its heart's desire the political institutions of English Canada and to prove to itself, whether or not it really wants to maintain and develop on this continent, an English-speaking society distinct from the United States.

—and a New Canadian Union

And if this is the case, there is no reason why we, as future neighbours, should not voluntarily remain associates and partners in a common enterprise; which would conform to the second great trend of our times: the new economic groups, customs unions, common markets, etc.

Here we are talking about something which already exists, for it is composed of the bonds, the complementary activities, the many forms of economic co-operation within which we have learned to live. Nothing says that we must throw these things away; on the contrary, there is every reason to maintain the framework. If we destroyed it, interdependent as we are, we would only be obliged sooner or later to build it up again, and then with doubtful success.

Now, it is precisely in the field of economics that we feel the pinch most painfully. In our outmoded constitutional texts and governmental structures, we flounder hopelessly over how to divided between our two states the powers, the agencies, and the means for action.

On this subject any expert with the slightest pretension to objectivity must certainly endorse the following statement by Otto Thur, Head of the Department of Economics at the University of Montreal (in a special edition of *Le Devoir*, June 30, 1967): "It is not the wording of a constitution that will solve problems [in the field of economics], but rather enlightened and consistent action, which brings about a progressive betterment of existing reality."

It seems to us, given a minimum of wisdom and, of course, self-interest—which should not be beyond the reach of our two majorities—that in the kind of association we are proposing we would have the greatest chance of pursuing jointly such a course of "enlightened and consistent action" worth more in economic affairs than all the pseudo-sacred documents with their ever-ambiguous inflexibility.

Such an association seems to us, in fact, made to measure for the purpose of allowing us, unfettered by obsolete constitutional forms, to pool our stakes with whatever permanent consultation and flexible adjustments would best serve our common economic interests: monetary union, common tariffs, postal union, administration of the national debt, co-ordination of policies, etc.

And nothing would prevent us from adding certain matters which under the present system have never had the advantage of frank discussion between equals: the question of minorities, for one; and also the questions of equal participation in a defence policy in proportion to our means, and a foreign policy that might, if conceived jointly, regain some of the dignity and dynamism that it has lost almost completely.[2]

We are not sailing off into uncharted seas. Leaving out the gigantic model furnished by the evolution of the Common Market, we can take our inspiration from countries comparable in size to our own—Benelux or Scandinavia—among whom co-operation is highly advanced, and where it has promoted unprecedented progress in the member states without preventing any of them from continuing to live according to their own tradition and preferences.

Making History Instead of Submitting to It

To sum up, we propose a system that would allow our two majorities to extricate themselves from an archaic federal framework in which our two very distinct "personalities" paralyze each other by dint of pretending to have a third personality common to both.

This new relationship of two nations, one with its homeland in Quebec and another free to rearrange the rest of the country at will, would be freely associated in a new adaptation of the current "common-market" formula, making up an entity which could perhaps—and if so very precisely—be called a Canadian Union.

The future of a people is never born without effort. It requires that a rather large number of "midwives" knowingly make the grave decision to work at it. For apart from other blind forces, and apart from all the imponderables, we must believe that basically it is still men who make man's history.

What we are suggesting to those who want to listen is that we devote our efforts, together, to shape the history of Quebec in the only fitting direction; and we are certain that at the same time we shall also be helping the rest of the country to find better future of its own.

NOTES

1. S.G.F. is *la Société Générale de Financement* (General Investment Corporation), an investment, holding, and management company designed to promote business and industry in the province, and financed by both public and private sectors. *Soquem* is *la Société Québécoise d'Exploration Minière* (Quebec Mining Exploration Co.), government-owned and the largest in the province. The *Caisse de Dépôts* is the investment arm of the Quebec Pension Plan.

2. In this paragraph some people have felt obliged—and others have hastened—to find a far-too-strict limitation imposed on Quebec's sovereignty. This would indeed be true if we proposed really to include Defence and External Affairs in the areas of actual association. These two are among the most important means through which a people can express its personality. But such is not our proposal.

Historical Interpretations

3 From David Seljak, "Why the Quiet Revolution Was 'Quiet': The Catholic Church's Reaction to the Secularization of Nationalism in Quebec After 1960," *CCHA Historical Studies* 62 (1996): 109–24.

Writing about the rapid secularization of Quebec society in the 1960s and 1970s, Hubert Guindon remarks: "In every respect except calendar time, centuries—not decades—separate the Quebec of the 1980s from the Quebec of the 1950s."[1] A similar observation might be made about the Church of Quebec and its development between 1960 and 1980. Before 1960, the Church exercised a virtual monopoly over education, health care, and the social services offered to French Quebecers who formed the majority of the population. During his years as premier from 1944 to 1959, Maurice Duplessis had declared Quebec a Catholic province and actively promoted the Church's welfare. In 1958, more than 85 per cent of the population identified themselves as Catholic and more than 88 per cent of those Catholics attended mass every Sunday.[2] A virtual army of nuns, priests, and brothers, which by 1962 numbered more than 50 000, oversaw the Church's massive bureaucracy.[3] This semi-established status and public presence was legitimated by the traditional religious nationalism, which united a conservative, clerical version of Catholicism and French-Canadian ethnic identity.

By 1980, the situation had changed dramatically. The Quebec state had taken over the Church's work in education, health care, and the social services. This "Quiet Revolution" meant that the state and not the Church was to be "the embodiment of the French nation in Canada."[4] While the roots of the Quiet Revolution could be seen in the rapid economic growth and the growth of state power of the 1920s,[5] the changes of the 1960s were experienced as a dramatic shift.

Thus the Church had to react both to its loss of real power and to its loss of control over the important symbols, stories, and values carried by traditional religious nationalism. By 1980 no nationalist group sought to promote a Catholic political culture or to remake Quebec's economy in conformity with the Church's social teaching. No one imagined that Quebec was a Catholic state. Like its control over schools, hospitals, and social services, the Church leadership saw its control over nationalist movements evaporate in two decades.

Remarkably, the Church reacted to the secularization of Quebec society with relative serenity. Certainly, the bishops and other religious leaders objected to the government's plans for the secularization of education and the religious communities opposed the reforms which turned their hospitals into public institutions.[6] But generally, Quebec society avoided the tragic cultural schism that marked the movement into secular modernity of Catholic countries like France and Italy. In Quebec, the Church did not withdraw into a "Catholic ghetto," anathematize the new society, and work toward a restoration of the old order.[7] Part of the reason for this was that many of the supporters of the reforms were members of the Church.

In Catholic societies, it is natural that opposition to the regime [has] its origins within the Church. The important question becomes how did Quebec avoid the history of schism experienced by France, Italy, Mexico, Spain, and other Catholic countries? For although the Quiet Revolution was inspired by and promoted some complaints against religion, even anti-clericalism, there was no massive rejection of religion on behalf of the modernizers. Even today [1996], while only 29 percent of Catholics attend mass on Sunday, most have retained their Catholic identity and insist on Catholic religious education for their children.[8]

The Quiet Revolution coincided with the reforms of the Second Vatican Council, which radically altered the Church's self-definition, and the emergence of a faith and justice movement in the late 1960s and 1970s. José Casanova has argued that the Council rejected any vision of religious establishment, that is, the use of state power to impose a Catholic religious monopoly on society.[9] Thus just as the Quebec state was declaring its autonomy from the Church, the Church was itself affirming the autonomy of political society, the freedom of individual consciences in political matters, and the need for citizens to involve themselves in the important debates and projects of their societies. Because of this coincidence, Gregory Baum has argued that Catholics in Quebec could be critical of the old Quebec and its religious nationalism, and still remain good Catholics. Despite misunderstandings, heated disagreements, and personal grievances, the Quebec Church and state learned to co-operate and compromise in a spirit of pluralism, reform, and tolerance.[10] This is not to say that the Second Vatican Council and the emergence of a faith and justice movement were the direct causes of the Church's acceptance of the new society and the new nationalism, but these developments allowed the Church to become more open to compromise and undermined the position of Catholic conservatives who dreamed of a restoration of the old society.

One of the most important issues was the Church's acceptance of the secularization of French-Canadian nationalism. If the Quebec state had the power to make the reforms of the 1960s "revolutionary," then the Church had the power to make the revolution "quiet"—or not. Its reconciliation to the

new nationalism has helped to determine the shape of Quebec culture and society after 1960.

While the British North America Act implicitly gave the Catholic Church a semi-established status in the province of Quebec, the two most important motors of modernization, democratic political structures and capitalist economic institutions, remained outside of its control.[11] Consequently, despite its important role in Quebec society, the Church was most often in the position of reacting to social change. From 1900 to 1930, the Church responded to industrialization and modernization with what Guindon has called an "administrative revolution," an unprecedented campaign to create new institutions and bureaucracies to meet the needs of French Catholics in every realm of modern urban life.[12] Besides multiplying its institutions which provided education, health care, and social services, the Church promoted the growth of Catholic labour unions, farmers' co-operatives, credit unions, pious leagues, newspapers, radio and television shows, films, and Catholic Action groups for workers, students, women, farmers, and nationalists. Conservative Catholics dreamed that these bodies would eventually reclaim all those functions in society that had been wrenched from the Church's control.[13]

While other peoples met the challenges of industrialization and modernization with programs of what sociologist Karl Deutsch has called "nation-building,"[14] French-Canadian nationalists embarked on an aggressive program of "church-building" with the goal of creating an "Église-nation" (nation-Church) rather than a nation-state. While they encouraged state intervention in specific projects (such as the colonization of the hinterlands of Quebec), French-Canadian nationalists usually preferred to resolve conflicts by creating religiously inspired social structures rather than appealing to state power. For example, in the Church's corporatist response to the Depression, the actions of the state were limited to those realms where the first agents of society (the family and the Church) were as yet incapable of fulfilling their responsibilities. Typically, French-Canadian nationalism was marked by a certain *anti-étatisme* and *apolitisme*.[15] Because it was rooted in a profoundly conservative, clerical, Catholic triumphalism, this nationalism could be xenophobic, intolerant, and repressive, as evidenced by its crusades against Jews, socialists, and Jehovah's Witnesses in the name of religious and national solidarity. Despite the anti-modern discourse that its authors employed, this bureaucratic revolution ironically promoted the modernization of French Quebec society including that of the Church itself and French-Canadian nationalism.[16] This modernization was certainly problematic. Critics drew attention to the gulf between the modern, multicultural, urban, industrial reality of Quebec society and a conservative Catholic ideology centred on rural values, ethnic solidarity, religion, and a rejection of politics and the state.[17] [. . .]

The rapid changes of the 1960s, known as the Quiet Revolution, grew directly out of the type of society that was formed in Quebec after 1867. After World War II, a "new middle class" of university-trained bureaucrats increasingly occupied important positions in the immense bureaucracy that the Church had created. While educated in Catholic culture and values, members of this clerically dominated bureaucracy were simultaneously socialized into modern, rational, and democratic values. Thus, they were uncomfortable with the conservative, undemocratic practices of the Duplessis regime and with the complicity of the Church in those practices.[18] They demanded the rationalization of the bureaucracy that oversaw education, health care, and social services. They also demanded its democratization and protested against its "clericalism," understood as the best positions being reserved for Church officials.[19] Consequently, the new nationalism was defined as much against the Catholic Church as the anglophone business elite.[20]

The ascent to power of these elites was assured when the Parti liberal du Québec (PLQ) took power in June of 1960. Inspired by a secular and modernizing nationalism, the Lesage government introduced a number of measures that radically redefined the role of the state. It took over the functions of the Church in education, health care, and social services. Through the nationalization of hydroelectric utilities and the creation of Crown corporations, the PLQ sought both to expand the influence of the government in the economy and to increase the presence of French Canadians in the upper levels of that economy.[21] The state bureaucracy increased at a tremendous rate, growing by 42.6 per cent between 1960 and 1965.[22] While the changes adopted by the Lesage government mostly satisfied the interests of the new middle class and francophone business people, some sought to promote a more democratic, humane, and participatory society. The Liberal government introduced more progressive labour legislation and important social welfare reforms. Supporters of the government's reforms attacked both traditional religious nationalism and laissez-faire liberalism. In doing so they created a new political nationalism that was adamantly secular, state-centred, and optimistically oriented to Keynesian liberalism or even social democracy.[23]

While accepting these reforms, Catholics attempted to find ways of adapting Church structures and Catholic thinking to the new context. Given the history and theology of the Catholic hierarchy in the 1950s, this reaction was by no means the obvious route to take. Even in the early 1960s, the bishops condemned the attack on traditional French-Canadian nationalism in the very popular book, *Les insolences du Frère Untel*.[24] Even though, led by Cardinal Paul-Émile Léger, they had accepted the urbanization of Quebec society and reluctantly had given up the strategies of colonization and corporatism, the bishops' traditional paternalistic attitude, obedience to Rome, moralizing spirit, and confusion between Catholicism and conservative ideology had remained intact.[25] Yet by 1970, the bishops had largely reconciled themselves to the autonomy of the state, the liberty of individual consciences in political questions, and the legitimacy of the new nationalism. The early opposition and later reconciliation of the bishops was paralleled in many sectors in the Church.

This reconciliation would have been impossible without the coincidence of the Quiet Revolution with the Second Vatican Council. In Quebec, the Church's redefinition of its relationship to modernity had three immediate consequences. First, it took the wind out of the sails of the conservative rejection of the new society. It made the project of the traditional nationalists impossible—since the Church hierarchy now refused its designated role as spiritual and cultural leaders of the attack on modernity. Second, it allowed Catholics—and even clergy and bishops—to support some projects of the Quiet Revolution in spite of their "laicizing" agenda. Finally, it inspired a new concern for development and social justice among Quebec Catholics. The Council affirmed the new direction of Catholic social teaching laid out by Pope John XXIII. Catholics sought to remain relevant to Quebec society and to participate, as Christians, in the important struggles of their society. This new social teaching, along with the reflections of the Catholic Church in Latin America, would lead to the emergence of a faith and justice movement in the 1970s. Influenced by this teaching, the Church in Quebec could develop a sustained ethical critique of the new society and the new nationalism while affirming their liberating aspects. Taken together these three developments meant that Quebec society avoided the painful cultural schism between Catholics and modernizers (both liberal and radical) that has marked other Catholic societies.

Within the Quebec Church, there were varying reactions to the new society and its new nationalism. Many Quebecers were no more interested in the religious reforms of Vatican II than they were in the political reforms of the Quiet Revolution.[26] For example, rural Catholics remained loyal to the traditional religious nationalism and continued to support the Union nationale. When that party adopted a political program similar to that of the PLQ, many of these voters shifted their support to the provincial wing of the Social Credit party, the Ralliement créditiste. The Ralliement wrestled with the question of independence and even absorbed two overtly independentist parties. While its conservative supporters were federalists, the party leaders pursued independence in order to protect the traditional social arrangement defined by religious nationalism from the incursions of the secular, modernizing, federal government.[27]

What was important about the Catholic nationalist groups and political parties which sought to redefine Quebec society along the lines of Catholic social teaching in the 1960s was that virtually all of them disappeared by 1970. Earlier in the twentieth century, nationalist movements had failed because they were politically irrelevant. In the 1960s, when the Catholic nationalist groups disintegrated, no new Catholic groups emerged to take their place, for they had become religiously as well as politically irrelevant. The Church no longer wanted to define its public presence in opposition to the new democratic society. Conservative Catholics who refused to adapt to the new society have limited their conceptualization of the public presence of the Church to its role in the school system, charity, community celebrations, pastoral services, and certain single-issue ethical debates such as abortion, pornography, and sexual morality. They have remained silent on the national question.

Not all those who rejected the new society and its new nationalism abandoned public life. After a long struggle, many conservatives came to accept the new state while maintaining their fidelity to the old nationalism. Particularly important voices were those of

François-Albert Angers and the Jesuit priest Jean Genest who attacked the supposed anti-clericalism of the Quiet Revolution in the pages of *l'Action nationale*. They argued that the growth of the state represented a new form of dictatorship and a violation of the rights of the Church. In 1965, Angers wrote:

> When the state is master in every domain, the people are masters in none. The phrase, "We are the state!," which we have not ceased repeating here, is the greatest load of rubbish ever proposed to put the people to sleep and to give the dictatorial green light to all [government] ministers who are, by definition, budding little dictators.[28]

Angers and Genest cast their arguments in nationalist terms: without the service of the Church, the nation was surely doomed to tyranny by the state on one hand and social and moral disintegration on the other. The sexual revolution, the feminist movement, and the youth culture of the 1960s, they thought, were surely signs of this degeneration.[29]

This position was also taken by the Jesuit journal *Relations*. Père Richard Arès railed against the reforms as a violation of the democratic rights of French Canadians. He found Bill 60, which promised to secularize and modernize the school system, especially threatening. In a 1964 editorial entitled "Le bill 60 et la democratie totalitaire," he argued that liberal democracy could become totalitarian because it sought to eliminate all intermediary bodies between the state and the individual. Naturally these bodies included the Church which, he argued, the Catholic families of Quebec had created and voluntarily put in charge of education, health care, and social services.[30] [. . .]

By the late 1960s, these conservatives were finally converted by the effectiveness of the new political nationalism. They translated their conservative values into a communitarian ethos that continued to inspire the Mouvement national des Québécois (formerly the Fédération des Sociétés-St-Jean-Baptiste), the journal *l'Action nationale*, and an important constituency within the Parti québécois (PQ). In the Church, they insisted that Catholicism maintain a public role and rejected the privatization of religion. They insisted that the Church be concerned with the national question and that it continue to contribute to Quebec culture. Conversely they also demanded that secular nationalist groups recognize the unique contribution that Catholicism had made to Quebec culture in the form of a communitarian ethos.

Conservative Catholics could not rally the rest of the Church behind their cause. On every important issue, from the debate on education reform to abortion, there was a Catholic presence on both sides of the issue. Consequently, it was impossible to identify Catholicism with the conservative rejection of the new society. For example, the contributors to the Dominican journal *Maintenant* consistently supported attempts to modernize Quebec society and reform the education system. [. . .]

In September 1967, *Maintenant* declared itself in favour of independence and socialism. Citing the domination of the economy by foreign capital and the low rate of participation of francophones in the upper echelons of the Quebec economy, the editorial team of *Maintenant* argued that only state intervention would allow French Quebecers to participate in the definition of their society. The editor, a Dominican priest named Vincent Harvey, argued that they were searching for "a democratic socialism of participation."[31] To use Fernand Dumont's term, they sought to define "*un socialisme d'ici*," that is, a socialism which would reflect the culture, values, and social reality of French Quebecers. While rooted in French-Canadian reality, this nationalism could not be isolationist; independence had to represent a first step in opening up Quebecers to a new participation in the modern world.[32]

[. . .]

The Jesuit journal *Relations* changed dramatically when most of the editorial team was replaced in 1969 and Père Irénée Desrochers became the editor. The new team rejected the conservatism of its predecessors and accepted the new society. It also became more sympathetic to the growing faith and justice movement within the Church. *Relations* dedicated itself to the theme of liberation, a term that had religious, social, and political meanings. Religiously, the Jesuits promoted the themes of democratization and reform within the Church, liberty of conscience, and new forms of Christian expression. Socially, the journal, an advocate of interventionist government and workers' rights since its inception in 1941, became more radical. Politically, *Relations* adopted a socialist position. Besides becoming a forum for the network of Christian Marxists known as the Reseau des politisés chrétiens, the Jesuits reported on and welcomed the development of liberation theology in Latin America and the ecclesial documents it inspired.

When they turned their socialist analysis to the situation of French Quebecers, the writers of *Relations* applied the insights of liberation theology and the Church's new social teaching. Of course, they did not consider French Quebecers to be colonized or oppressed to the same degree or in the same manner as Aboriginal peoples or poor nations. But the writers of *Relations* did judge that the teaching outlined in the 1971 World Synod of Bishops' document *Justice in the World* on the rights of peoples to development, self-determination, and social justice was relevant to the situation of French Quebecers.[33] In 1973 the editorial team of *Relations* declared its support for independence but only if it was tied to "the construction of a new type of society and to the blossoming of a real community."[34] Political independence was a first, necessary, but not sufficient, step toward the construction of a socialist society.

After a purge of the more radical element on the editorial board in 1976,

Relations adopted a more reform-oriented, social-democratic position. However, it never wavered in its support for the transformation of Quebec society and for the right of Quebecers to self-determination. The journal welcomed the 1980 referendum as a step toward a more participatory society; the democratic procedure in itself, they believed, served the common good. The staff supported a "yes" vote for several reasons. First they believed that sovereignty could be the first step toward building a more egalitarian and open society. Second, they wanted to lend their support to progressive groups in Quebec society— especially the labour unions and popular action groups—who saw the referendum as the best chance at democratizing Quebec's political institutions and transforming its socio-economic structures.[35] Finally, they wanted to send a message to English Canadians that Quebecers were not happy with the constitutional status quo. A yes vote would lead to more equal, just, and friendlier relations with the rest of Canada.[36]

The 1980 referendum was also the catalyst that induced the most important contributions by the Quebec bishops to the national question. The mood created by the Second Vatican Council had encouraged them to rethink the relationship of the Church to society and of the laity to the hierarchy. An important step in this evolution had been the creation of the Commission d'étude sur les laïcs et l'Église in 1968. The Dumont Commission, as it was known, firmly rejected the old Church and old Quebec and accepted the disestablishment of the Church in the Quiet Revolution as an irreversible development. It argued that the Church would have to become a "compagnon de route" with the people of Quebec.[37] This was a radical change from the ultramontanist view of the 1950s, which saw the institutional church as the framework of the *Église-nation*. According to the report, the Church would have to serve Quebec society while adopting a critical or prophetic stance toward its injustices. Influenced by liberation theology and the papal teaching on social justice, the bishops became critics of Quebec society, calling society and the state to task on such issues as unemployment, regional disparity, aboriginal rights, the plight of refugees and immigrants, the environment, and others.[38]

The bishops released two widely read and well-received letters during the referendum debate. In their first letter, they affirmed the right of the people of Quebec to determine their future collectively and the responsibility to decide important questions about their development democratically. They also insisted that nationalism had to be respectful of individual and community rights and defined "*le peuple québécois*" as all residents of Quebec, including French Quebecers, anglophones, immigrant minority groups, and the Aboriginal peoples. Furthermore, they hoped to foster an atmosphere of respect and tolerance and warned against the demonization of one's opponents, ethnic isolationism, prejudice and stereotyping, insulting rhetoric, and discriminatory practices.[39] Finally, they argued that the national question could not be abstracted from the search to create a more just social order in Quebec and the world.[40] [. . .]

The style of the bishops' teaching on nationalism was just as important as its content. The bishops stated that, while the Church affirmed Quebecers' right to self-determination, the hierarchy did not have the authority to tell them how to vote. Neither sovereignty-association nor federalism could be identified directly with the gospel message of liberty and responsibility. The role of the Church was to defend basic Christian values, which demanded that people decide their future in a mature, respectful, fraternal, and peaceful manner.[41] During the referendum campaign itself, the bishops ensured that the Church was not identified with either side. They warned the clergy to remain discrete; they could take sides but they had to present their opinions as their own and not as the Church's.[42]

While the principles laid out by the bishops may have been violated by individuals during the heat of the 1980 referendum debate, Catholic groups and institutions were remarkably disciplined during the campaign and consistent in emphasizing that their choices were based on political analyses that were open to democratic debate.[43] The style of their participation reflected a consensus on the Church's new attitude to secular Quebec and its new nationalism, which affirmed that the people of Quebec had the right to determine their own future through the democratic process and neither outsiders nor the Church itself could interfere. By taking this position, the Church affirmed the fact of its political and social "disestablishment" and accepted that the old Quebec had passed away. During the referendum, and perhaps for the first time in Quebec political history, no group sought to define Quebec as a Catholic society or proposed that Catholicism could provide a political culture or economic system for a pluralist, modern, industrial society. While this separation of Church and state was affirmed, no major Catholic groups supported the separation of the Church from Quebec society—either in the form of creating a Catholic ghetto (as in France after its secularizing revolution) or in allowing Catholicism to be defined as a purely private religion. Because of the Church's long history at the very centre of French-Canadian civil society, Catholics felt that the Church had to maintain a public presence.

In reaction to the new society and its nationalism, the Church maintained its moral authority and public presence by creating a sustained ethical critique that integrated its traditional commitment to Quebec society with the new social teaching coming from Rome, Europe, and Latin America. Nationalist claims had to be measured against two sets of criteria. The first was supplied by the Catholic teaching on the "common good." Did a nationalist movement promote the welfare of all citizens and not just one group? Was it democratic? Did it encourage mature, responsible citizenship and a balance between the rights and duties of individuals? Did it promote isolationism, racism, or xenophobia? The second was supplied by the new Catholic teaching on social justice. What was the "*projet de société*" attached to the nationalist movement? Did the nationalist project respect the rights of minorities and of the Aboriginal peoples? Did it seek to create a more just distribution of wealth? Was it open to participation by the poor and the marginalized? Would it promote a more just and open society? This position, while interpreted differently, was taken seriously by every Catholic group active in the nationalist debate after 1970.

The teaching carried an explicit limitation of the public role and authority of the Church itself. Even the Church could not define itself above the Christian values that it now recognized as inherent in the democratic process. The Church could, however, remind society of its commitment to democracy and denounce attitudes and practices that ignored the dignity and rights of individuals and communities. This teaching represented a dramatic turnabout of the Church's attitude to the democratic process. Catholics affirmed that even the heated and sometimes divisive debate around the 1980 referendum was a positive process in and of itself. The debate encouraged a "*prise de conscience*," an awakening to one's dignity, responsibility, and liberty as a citizen and person. In a society that Catholics had analyzed as encouraging people to become self-interested, depoliticized consumers, the nationalist debate came to be seen as encouraging serious reflection on issues of identity, common values, solidarity, and social justice.[44]

The Church's support for democratic participation, responsible citizenship, and individual liberty was remarkable when contrasted with its former opposition to those very features of modernity. It was the religious revolution inspired by Vatican II, the emergence of a faith and justice movement, and the struggles of Quebecers, that allowed the Church to adapt to the secular society created by the Quiet Revolution. This extraordinary shift leads to the conclusion that "centuries—not decades"—separate the Church of Quebec of the 1980s from that of the 1950s.

NOTES

1. Hubert Guindon, *Quebec Society: Tradition, Modernity, and Nationhood*, Roberta Hamilton and John L. McMullan, eds (Toronto: University of Toronto Press, 1988), 138.

2. Reginald Bibby, *Unknown Gods: The Ongoing Story of Religion in Canada* (Toronto: Stoddart, 1993), 6, table 1.1.

3. Jean Hamelin, "Société en mutation, église en redéfinition, le catholicisme québécois contemporain, de 1940 à nos jours," dans *La croix et le nouveau monde. Histoire religieuse des francophones d'Amérique du nord*, dir. Guy-Marie Oury (Montréal: Editions C.L.D./C.M.D., 1987), 224.

4. Guindon, *Quebec Society*, p. 104.

5. Jean Hamelin et Nicole Gagnon, *Histoire du catholicisme québécois. Le XXe siècle. Tome 1.*

1898–1940 (Montréal: Boréal Express, 1984), pp. 442–3.

6. Hamelin et Gagnon, *Histoire du catholicisme*, pp. 245–59.

7. Gregory Baum, *The Church in Quebec* (Ottawa: Novalis, 1991), pp. 15–47; David Martin, *A General Theory of Secularization* (New York: Harper and Row, 1978).

8. See Micheline Milot, "Le catholicisme au creuset de la culture," *Studies in Religion* 20, 1 (1991): 51–64.

9. José Casanova, *Public Religions in the Modern World* (Chicago: University of Chicago, 1994), 71–3.

10. Baum, *The Church in Quebec*, 38–47.

11. Guindon, *Quebec Society*, 103–4.

12. Ibid., 20–1.

13. Hamelin et Gagnon, *Histoire du catholicisme*, pp. 175–291; Nive Voisine, André Beaulieu, et Jean Hamelin, *Histoire de l'Église catholique au Québec (1608–1970)*, Première annexe au rapport de la Commission d'étude sur les laïcs et l'Église (Montréal: Fides, 1971), 55–72.

14. Karl W. Deutsch and William J. Foltz, eds, *Nation-building* (New York: Atherton Press, 1966).

15. See André-J. Bélanger, *L'Apolitisme des idéologies québécoises: le grand tournant de 1934–1936* (Québec: Presses de l'Université Laval, 1974), 3–5.

16. See William F. Ryan S.J., *The Clergy and Economic Growth in Quebec, 1896–1914* (Québec: Presses de l'Université Laval, 1966); Guindon, *Quebec Society*, pp. 107–9; and Hamelin et Gagnon, *Histoire du catholicisme*, 290.

17. Pierre Trudeau, "The province of Quebec at the time of the strike," in *The Asbestos Strike*, ed. Pierre Trudeau, trans. James Boake (Toronto: Lewis and Samuel, 1974), 1–81; Michael D. Behiels, *Prelude to Quebec's Quiet Revolution: Liberalism versus Neo-nationalism 1945–1960* (Kingston and Montreal: McGill-Queen's University Press, 1985), 98–9.

18. Guindon, *Quebec Society*, 21–4; Kenneth McRoberts, *Quebec: Social Change and Political Crisis*, 3rd edn (Toronto: McClelland & Stewart, 1988), 147–69.

19. Guindon, *Quebec Society,* 48–9; McRoberts, *Quebec*, 149–50.

20. McRoberts, *Quebec*, 148–51.

21. Ibid., 132–4.

22. Ibid., 136.

23. Guindon, *Quebec Society*, 40–3, 58; Léon Dion, *Nationalisme et politique au Québec* (Montréal: Hurtubise HMH, 1975), 54–119.

24. Hamelin, *Histoire du catholicisme*, 238–43.

25. Hamelin, "Société en mutation," 223.

26. McRoberts, *Quebec*, 169–72.

27. Paul-André Linteau, René Durocher, Jean-Claude Robert, et François Ricard, *Histoire du Québec contemporain. Tome 2. Le Québec depuis 1930* (Montréal: Boréal, 1989), 128.

28. "Hauteur et mauvaise foi envers nous de 'l'État c'est nous!,'" *L'Action nationale* 55, 3 (novembre 1965): 331. Translation by the author.

29. Jean Genest, "Jusqu'à la lie?," *L'Action nationale* 60, 3 (novembre 1970): 184.

30. Richard Arès S.J., "Le bill 60 et la démocratie totalitaire," *Relations* 279 (mars 1964): 65–6.

31. Vincent Harvey, O.P., Pierre Saucier, Hélène Pelletier-Baillargeon, André Charbonneau, Louis Racine, et Yves Gosselin, "To be or not to be," *Maintenant* 68–9 (août–septembre 1967): 236.

32. Ibid., 237.

33. Irénée Desrochers S.J., "Le principe du droit à l'autodétermination du Québec: amorce d'une réflexion pré-politique," *Relations* 366 (décembre 1971): 334–7; and "Le droit du Québec à l'autodétermination: les évêques se sont-ils prononcés?," *Relations* 372 (juin 1972): 163–8.

34. "Relations et l'avenir du Québec," *Relations* 386 (octobre 1973): 259; emphasis in the original.

35. Irénée Desrochers S.J., "La FTQ et le référendum," *Relations* 455 (janvier 1980): 11–14; "Le référendum et la question sociale," *Relations* 457 (mars 1980): 67, 93–5; "La CSN, la question nationale et le oui au référendum," *Relations* 459 (mai 1980): 155–7.

36. Albert Beaudry, "Le référendum: un pas dans la bonne direction," *Relations* 459 (mai 1980): 131–3.

37. Commission d'étude sur les laïcs et l'Église, *L'Eglise du Québec: un heritage, un projet* (Montréal: Fides, 1971).

38. Gérard Rochais, *La justice sociale comme bonne nouvelle: messages sociaux, économiques et politiques des évêques du Quebec 1972–1983* (Montréal: Bellarmin, 1984).

39. Baum, *The Church in Quebec*, 164.

40. "Le peuple québécois et son avenir politique: message de l'Assemblée des évêques du Québec, sur l'évolution de la société québécoise, le 15 août 1979," dans Rochais, *La justice sociale*, 137–44.

41. Assemblée des évêques du Québec, "Le peuple québécois," dans Rochais, *La justice sociale*, 137–44.

42. Jean Martel, "L'Église se fera discrète," *Le Soleil*, 26 avril 1980, B2; Jules Béliveau, "Mgr Gregoire est satisfait de la discrétion des prêtres," *La Presse*, 9 mai 1980, A12.

43. Dossiers "Vie ouvrière," "Oui à un projet de société," *Dossiers "Vie ouvrière"* 30, 141 (janvier 1980): 2–9; and Mouvement des travailleurs chrétiens, *La question nationale* (Montréal: Mouvement des travailleurs chrétiens, 1979).

44. Jacques Grand'Maison, *Nationalisme et religion. Tome 2. Religion et idéologies politiques* (Montréal: Beauchemin, 1970), 200–1.

4   Sean Mills, *"Québécoises deboutte!* Nationalism and Feminism in Quebec, 1969–75," in
    Michael D. Behiels and Matthew Hayday, eds, *Contemporary Quebec: Selected Readings
    and Commentaries* (Montreal and Kingston: McGill-Queen's University Press, 2011),
    319–37.

On the evening of 28 November 1969, two hundred women—many wearing chains to symbolize their oppression—charged out of their meeting place on Saint-Laurent boulevard into the middle of the street, where they sat down in a circle and waited to be arrested. The hundreds of riot police who were waiting outside proceeded to arrest 165 of the protesters, and, in less than an hour, Saint-Laurent was again open to its regular flow of traffic. The protest on Saint-Laurent, although small in size and relatively short in duration, was loaded with symbolic meaning. In the fall of 1969, as a spirit of revolt had been spreading throughout various sectors of Montreal society, the city's streets had become the primary space where dissident groups had gathered to make their voices heard. And in the tense atmosphere shaped by labour disputes, increasingly violent demonstrations, and the bombs of the FLQ, the Montreal administration passed Regulation 3926, effectively banning public protests in the streets of Montreal. Although many groups and individuals were quick to denounce the new regulation, the two hundred women protesters were the first to take to the streets and defy the law, loudly claiming their right to the city. Through their actions, the women protesters set the initial contours of a movement that would significantly challenge and ultimately transform Quebec's vocabularies of dissent, forever changing the political expressions of Quebec feminism, nationalism, and the left more generally.

The demonstration acted as a watershed in feminist mobilization. True, the women's liberation movement did not begin with the protest; throughout the fall of 1969, women on Montreal's English-speaking university campuses had been reading feminist literature, meeting together, and forming the Montreal Women's Liberation Movement (MWLM). But in the lead-up to the protest, and during the protest itself, many anglophone women close to the MWLM joined with francophone women from leftist groups, unions, and citizens' committees to create the Front commun des Québécoises, a group that had no leader, spokesperson, or official ties to any feminist organization.[1] In the aftermath of the protest, English- and French-speaking women, in roughly equal numbers, came together to form the Front de libération des femmes du Québec (FLF), a group that would become the most prominent public voice of women's liberation in Montreal.

Over the next two years, the FLF undertook many actions, organized and attended protests, and produced a series of important documents. Yet, due to factionalism and internal dissent, the group slowly came apart. When the group folded, the Centre des femmes, formed in part by ex-FLF members, was established. Its beliefs and goals were similar to those of the FLF. While the FLF and the Centre des femmes cannot be treated as a singular entity, the women who comprised the latter saw themselves as the logical continuation of the former. By giving their newspaper the same name as that of the FLF, and by maintaining many of the fundamental tenets of its ideology, the women of the Centre des femmes consciously sought to link the two groups.[2] Taken together, the two organizations represented the dawning of a new era in the history of Quebec feminism.

[. . .] For the FLF and, at the outset, the Centre des femmes, women's liberation was inextricably linked to the project of Quebec liberation, a project being advocated by a multidimensional mass movement seeking social transformation through a serious, if often contradictory, grappling with the meaning and legacy of empire in Quebec. Quebec's first women's liberation groups argued that Quebec women were marginalized both as women and as Quebeckers and that, as a result, their fight needed to be framed in the larger language of Quebec decolonization. But they saw their fight as being more than just about women or Quebeckers: what was at stake, as one group put it, was "not only our liberation, but also the liberation of all our people, and of all the peoples of the world."[3]

After its first year in existence, the FLF even went so far to expel its English-speaking members, claiming that their access to American feminist literature allowed them to control the group's ideology at the very moment that francophone women were attempting to develop their own autonomous voice of resistance. The link between feminism and national liberation, however, slowly unravelled at the Centre des femmes, and, by the early to mid-1970s, the goal of national liberation had given way to the struggle for women's liberation through working-class emancipation. The Centre des femmes' slow drift away from the politics of national liberation can be located, I argue, in the changes that were occurring in both the feminist and the nationalist movements in the 1970s as well as in the shifting parameters of the political left.

THE FLF, THE CENTRE DES FEMMES, AND NATIONAL LIBERATION

Women's lives were changing dramatically in the 1960s. Beginning in 1961, Quebec's birthrate dropped, births out of wedlock were increasing greatly, and married women came to occupy a greater role in the workforce.[4] In 1966, one-third of women aged 24 to 34 were in the paid workforce, and this number jumped to 39.9 per cent by 1971 and continued to climb.[5] Despite new-found economic independence, many opportunities for

individual self-development were blocked by the persistence of ingrained sexism. Although entering the workforce in record numbers, women, for the most part, were marginalized in "women's professions" and were often expected to work a double day, working in the paid labour force during the day while remaining responsible for housework in the evening.[6] Women did not sit idly by as society was changing around them. In the early 1960s, some Montreal women, like long-time labour activist Simone Monet-Chartrand, joined the Voice of Women, a women-based peace organization that denounced nuclear proliferation, advocated greater female participation in politics, and argued that it was up to women, in their role as mothers and educators, to defend the universal values of justice, love, and liberty.[7] In 1966 the long-time activist, suffragist, and social democrat Thérèse Casgrain founded the Fédération des femmes du Québec (FFQ), the first mass-based second-wave feminist organization in the province. And, only a few years later, a younger generation of women would begin claiming that women's liberation could only be achieved through transforming society's structures in their entirety.

In the fall of 1969, the ideas of women's liberation were making important inroads in Montreal, and, in October 1969, a group of English-speaking university students founded the Montreal Women's Liberation Movement.[8] Beginning in the early 1960s, a whole array of dissident and nationalist groups had been contesting the political and economic status quo, and, in the fall of 1969, the subordinate status of the French language had brought tens of thousands of people to the streets in protest. Given that the Montreal Women's Liberation Movement was founded at the exact moment that the province's political foundations were being rocked by explosive linguistic debates, it is no surprise that its role within Quebec society preoccupied the group from the very beginning. Deeply aware that it was an English-speaking group in the midst of a French-speaking society, and knowing that the English language was associated with social and cultural privilege, members of the group began establishing contact with women in the Quebec labour movement. In the meetings and contacts that ensued, anglophone women began talking with francophone women about the possibility of holding an all-women's protest to denounce the city's increasingly repressive political climate.[9] On 28 November, women from different backgrounds joined together to take to the streets to defend the right to protest in the city.

After the protest, a group of women decided to establish the FLF. It is of no small significance that the FLF was born in the streets of Montreal, amidst the atmosphere of generalized revolt that had engulfed the city in 1969. From its beginnings, the FLF was a hybrid movement, one that combined the insights of the nascent women's liberation movement in the United States (and, somewhat later, France) with conceptions of anti-colonialism that were being developed in Montreal. Its early members emerged from unions and citizens' committees, university campuses, and extra-parliamentary leftist organizations. By the late 1960s, the Quebec labour movement, and especially the Confédération des syndicats nationaux (CSN), had become a central element of the larger political upheaval, so it should be no surprise that the FLF's first meetings were held in the CSN's library.[10] After much discussion and negotiation, the FLF set its goal as the liberation of women through the creation of an independent and socialist Quebec.

While the anglophone women of the new group were influenced by the American women's liberation movement, the francophones, for the most part, broke away from the male-dominated labour movement, community organizations, and citizens' committees.[11] In mixed groups, the FLF maintained, women were relegated to subordinate and traditionally "feminine" roles, such as typing and making coffee. For "true revolutionaries," the FLF sarcastically remarked, there were "so many other things . . . to do besides worry about women." "Radicals have always had, and still have, the time to go out and get stoned on weekends," the FLF stated, "but not the time to create day nurseries [or] to organize domestic brigades, without which women cannot be expected to make the revolution."[12] In addition to being relegated to "feminine tasks" within the mixed groups, Stéphanie Lanthier demonstrates that women were also symbolically excluded from the larger movement. National liberation, she maintains, was built upon the subordination of women.[13] The creation of autonomous women's organizations, many activists increasingly believed, was a crucial step toward achieving a true "revolution in the revolution."

When women began accusing male theorists of not taking the specifics of gender oppression seriously, they were turning the language of emancipation back on the movement itself. They began arguing that, if women were to become free political subjects, they too would need to develop their own terms of reference and their own autonomous voice. Following the example of other marginalized groups, many women began arguing that they needed to break away, organize independently, and create political groupings and free social spaces of their own. By organizing autonomously, women began making their own independent analyses of their place in the larger struggle, of their own needs as women in the movement, and of the necessity of building a deeper and more inclusive understanding of the meaning of liberation.[14]

Throughout its turbulent two-year existence, the FLF fought to lay claim to the city and widen the sphere of female political participation. Members of the group plastered "Québécoises deboutte!" stickers around Montreal,[15] and they occupied taverns that did not permit the entry of women.[16] In one of its most daring activities, an FLF cell occupied the jury boxes of a Montreal courthouse during a hearing for Lise Balcer, one of the witnesses in the trial of FLQ member Paul Rose. Because women were not allowed to sit as jurors, Balcer refused to testify as a witness and was found in contempt of court. When she was in the witness box explaining the reasons for her refusal, seven FLF women from the audience charged to the front of the courtroom, took over the jury benches, and began yelling "discrimination!" and "la justice c'est de la merde!" They were sentenced to from one to two months in prison.[17]

In addition to trying to publicize these and other forms of discrimination, the FLF worked to develop a new interpretation of the world—one that sought to voice the concerns and desires of Quebec's oppressed and "colonized" women. It hoped to create new values and possibilities for the future.[18] In the summer of 1970, the FLF announced that some of its members were planning to found a newspaper—eventually entitled *Québécoisesdeboutte!*—that would be "exclusively devoted to women, and centred on the various aspects of their oppression." Finished were the days of having "feminine" pages in mainstream papers. From now on: "Quebec women will have an entire newspaper to themselves, where they can fully express the violence of their condition." It was up to women themselves to determine their own conditions of existence, to determine how to use their bodies and what to make of their lives. Women, the FLF argued, had never had a say in major decisions affecting their daily lives, and they were given "an education which prevented them from becoming full and equal human beings."[19] Through the dramatic actions, meetings, and publications of the FLF, the women's liberation movement became highly visible, ensuring that its analyses and critiques would have a significant effect on wider cultural structures.

In its first widely distributed text, the FLF outlined its goal of creating "*solidarity among all Quebec women* [emphasis in original]," which would, the group hoped, allow women "to articulate together the meaning of our liberation."[20] A first step in this liberation involved working to understand the world in their own terms. The women of the FLF stated that they were tired of being continually told that their liberation was implied by Quebec's national liberation. From its outset, the FLF saw its struggle as forming an essential element of Quebec's national liberation, which, it believed, also acted as the condition for women's emancipation. The FLF's slogan clearly reveals the primary tenets of its ideology: "No liberation of Quebec without the liberation of women, no liberation of women without the liberation of Quebec." The group therefore situated its struggle in the rhetoric of universal emancipation. "The liberation of women," an FLF bulletin declares, "will not be achieved by oppressing other groups or individuals, but forms part of a process of liberating all human beings. Roles must not be reversed; they must be transformed."[21]

Despite its heavy reliance on the rhetoric of national liberation, the FLF cannot be seen as merely derivative of the male-dominated movement. Women challenged the idea that Quebec liberation necessarily implied the liberation of women, arguing instead that women's liberation was one of the conditions for true liberation. "We believe that women will not be able to truly liberate themselves," the FLF declared, "unless their liberation forms part of a larger process of social liberation writ large, which will itself only be possible if it includes the participation of women at all levels."[22] By challenging gender relations from within the left, the members of the FLF hoped to deepen and broaden its humanistic claims. While it was imperative that feminists fight for women's emancipation, Quebec women could not forget that they also needed to join "the struggle for the national liberation of the Quebec people, without which their liberation would be illusory."[23]

By borrowing the language of national liberation, the members of the FLF placed their movement within a larger international context of anti-imperialism. From the beginning, Véronique O'Leary and Louise Toupin maintain, Quebec feminists "felt very close to women involved in Third World liberation movements."[24] Situating themselves internationally, the women of the FLF attempted to place their struggle on the same plane as other liberation movements, arguing that the situation was "the same for all exploited groups: Blacks, Quebeckers, and the colonized around the world."[25]

Drawing on analyses that dissident groups had been developing over the past decade, the FLF argued that the economic exploitation of Quebec women was deeply shaped by the interrelated forces of American imperialism, colonialism, and capitalism.[26] In its 1971 *Bulletin de liaison*, the FLF clearly outlined the interrelated nature of its program. According to its authors, the group was struggling: "For independence, because we are not only women, but *Québécoises* and as *Québécoises* we are colonized. For socialism because, even if the exploitation of women predates capitalism . . . we live today in a capitalist system which depends upon the exploitation of women."[27] To free themselves from national, sexual, and capitalist exploitation, the women of the FLF believed that it was necessary for feminists to struggle in independent women's organizations that advocated national liberation through socialist revolution. Building upon the analyses of both black activists and theorists of Quebec decolonization, many argued that the FLF needed to work toward "reconquering [women's] dignity as human beings."[28] And the group maintained that its focus and energy needed to be placed on the most marginalized, to reach "women from poor communities, as they have no material comforts to lessen their hardship, and because they have nothing to lose and everything to gain."[29]

By 1971, the FLF was divided into many "cells," each with its own unique take on effective political action, its own rationale for the necessity of women's liberation, and

its own understanding of the conditions of women's oppression. The two poles of the group, represented by "cellule II" and "cellule X," reflected many of the debates that were shaping the women's liberation movement across North America. Cellule II highlighted the ways in which the oppression of women was intimately related to capitalism and the family structure, and it argued for the close collaboration with mixed (male and female) groups. Cellule X, for its part, while recognizing the material nature of exploitation, pointed more directly to patriarchy as a system of oppression, insisted on complete autonomy from male groups, and oriented its activities around actions of cultural demystification.[30]

Despite the different ideological positions that prevailed within the groups, both maintained that the emancipation of women could only be achieved through a comprehensive program of national liberation. Cellule II argued that the "complete integration of women into the struggle for national liberation" was not only "an essential element of that liberation" but also crucial for "the abolition of [women's] own particular exploitation." Liberation would, after all, remain incomplete if it did not liberate "all Quebec men and women."[31] Another group argued that the FLF needed to be focused on one common objective: "the struggle for the sexual, social, political, and economic liberation of the Quebec woman in order to achieve her individual and collective self-determination."[32] And cellule X, the defender of an autonomous women's movement, and the group that went the furthest in identifying the common plight of all women under patriarchy, still maintained that the FLF "need[ed] to form part of the struggle for Quebec independence and social revolution."[33]

Seeing themselves as forming a part of a larger struggle for Quebec liberation, the women of the FLF looked to the ways in which a confluence of systems of oppression served to marginalize colonized women. Because of

their belief in the need for national liberation, they had a turbulent relationship with
English-speaking activist groups. The group
refused to participate in the anglophone-
organized abortion caravan to Ottawa, declaring that it would not "go and protest in front
of the Canadian Parliament when [it did] not
recognize the authority which it claims over
Quebec."[34] In addition to distancing itself from
English-Canadian feminist organizations, the
FLF's belief in the centrality of national liberation led it, in the fall of 1970, to exclude
anglophones from its ranks. O'Leary and
Toupin recount how the francophone women
of the FLF were worried about the imbalance
that existed between francophone and anglophone members of the group. It was during
a two-day meeting in the Laurentians, they
recall, that the francophone members decided
to exclude anglophones. "Among the reasons
put forward," O'Leary and Toupin state, "was
the argument that the anglophones, because
they had access to a wide array of American
and British documentation on 'Women's Lib.,'
exerted ideological control over the FLF, giving the group an American orientation which
had little regard for the specific realities of
Quebec." The foundational publication of
France's women's liberation movement, a special issue of *Partisans* entitled *Libération des
femmes, année zéro*, a collection of essays that
would have a deep influence on the women of
the FLF, was not available to Quebec women
until the spring of 1971.[35]

To the FLF's francophone members—
whose main theoretical influences remained
Simone de Beauvoir, Betty Friedan, and Frie-
drich Engels—the anglophones' imparting
of their knowledge and opinions seemed to
"reveal a thoroughly colonial attitude." Hoping to create a movement based on both an
international awareness of women's oppression and a firm understanding of specific issues relating to Quebec women, the FLF felt
that the movement must be composed only
of francophones. It was felt that francophone
women in Quebec, like black women in the
United States, needed to develop their own

autonomous voice. The anglophone members of the group, comprising about half of
the total membership, were shocked by their
exclusion from the organization that they had
helped to form. Many anglophones, "deeply
integrated into the francophone and separat-
ist community," were hurt and upset by their
exclusion and decided to stop feminist activity altogether.[36] In February 1971, the FLF also
decided that it would only conduct abortion
counselling in French, and the francophone
women moved out of the shared house on rue
Sainte-Famille.[37]

After two turbulent years of existence,
the FLF had staged many demonstrations,
opened a daycare, and published the first
edition of a newspaper. It experimented with
new non-hierarchical forms of organization,
and, although it had never attracted a large
membership, probably never surpassing 60
members organized in independent groups,
it had a large impact on Quebec's feminist
movement.[38] By 1971, however, internal divisions and a drastically reduced membership
discouraged the few remaining activists, and
they decided to dissolve the group. When
the FLF folded, the anti-colonial framework
for understanding the triple exploitation of
Quebec women was transported into the
Centre des femmes. When the Centre was established in January 1972, in part by ex-FLF
members, it intended to provide a forum for
consciousness-raising and studying the status
of women, and it decided to operate with an
organizational structure that differed greatly
from the decentralized model of the FLF.[39]
Unlike the FLF, which placed a great deal of
emphasis on spontaneous action, the women
of the Centre focused on analysis, attempting, in Heather Jon Maroney's words, "to
become a politically homogeneous nucleus
of revolutionary feminists." One of its most
important accomplishments was the publication of nine editions of *Québécoises deboutte!*
(with a circulation of roughly 1500 to 2000),
Quebec's first women's liberation newspaper
(with the exception of the one issue produced
by the FLF).[40]

In the Centre des femmes' first issue of *Québécoises deboutte!*, the group outlined its continued faith in the FLF's original principles. According to the paper, "the liberation of women is neither an individual nor a cultural liberation: the struggle for women's liberation needs to be waged within the framework of national, social, economic, political, and cultural liberation." It was therefore necessary to situate their "role as housewives, workers, and mothers in the context of Quebec society."[41] The Centre des femmes maintained a focus on Quebec workers and ensured that its social analysis was conducted within a Quebec framework. The FLF's slogan, highlighting the inextricable links between Quebec liberation and women's liberation, was printed on the cover of the first edition of the Centre des femmes' paper.

Because the struggle "necessarily implied the primary objective of radically changing society," the Centre des femmes sought not only to outline the terms of women's oppression but also to "clarify [its] objectives in the present conjuncture of the struggle of the Quebec people, choose [its] approaches, and work to draw Quebec women together into a revolutionary organization which [would] empower them."[42] One of its first initiatives was to use its newspaper as a forum to create a revisionist version of Quebec history. Offering a counter-narrative not only to dominant representations of the past but also to radical histories, which, like Léandre Bergeron's bestselling *Petit manuel d'histoire du Québec*, ignored the contributions of Quebec women, the Centre hoped to create a more inclusive history that could be used in contemporary political struggles. Because historians "are especially interested in the history of the White male dominant class,"[43] it was necessary to recover the voice of women in the past:

> For us Quebec women, history has not yet been written. Recent efforts to rewrite the history of the oppression of the Quebec people have again "neglected" to deal with our oppression. Even if the history

of Quebec women follows the main lines defined by a specific context shaped by our economy, politics, and identity, it still remains that we have lived a specific form of oppression due to the roles that we have been allotted by a patriarchal society.

The Centre therefore ventured, through a series of articles, to construct an alternative narrative of Quebec's past. With the goals of incorporating "the specific oppression of Quebec women" into the history of the province, the group reinterpreted prehistoric societies and re-examined events such as the Conquest and the Lower Canadian Rebellions from a women's perspective.[44]

THE END OF A "NATIONAL" DREAM

Although the Centre des femmes emerged out of the dissolution of the FLF and, at first, remained loyal to the FLF's nationalist principles, the group's nationalism slowly waned. The perspectives and possibilities opened by the dream of national liberation dimmed after the first few years of the 1970s, and national liberation no longer offered the promise of freedom that it once did. The Centre des femmes' abandonment of national liberation had many origins and must be located in the changing parameters of nationalism, feminism, and the left more generally. On the left, the increased ideological domination of Marxist-Leninism had an important impact on the group. The abandonment of the nation also occurred at the same time as did two other major changes—the group's decision to fully engage in the fight for legalized and state-funded abortion and its launching of an attack on the policies of the newly formed Parti Québécois (PQ).

[. . .]

In addition to advocating legalized and state-funded abortion, the Centre saw the criminalization of abortion as a corollary of capitalism. The question of abortion, the Centre argued, cannot be separated from a society's social, economic, and political structures. And in Quebec, the group maintained, the interests of the state and the church stood in direct opposition to those of working-class women.[45] Because capitalism relied upon the exploitation of women, the struggle for abortion "put into question the very foundations" of the economic system.[46]

In 1973, the Centre announced that the struggle to legalize abortion would become more central to its political program. Clearly establishing a link between capitalism and the nuclear family, the Centre declared that it was "taking a position" for the setting up of "free abortion on demand." Although the group had earlier considered abortion as "an important political problem," it had thus far refused "to enter the struggle." But now the Centre decided that it could no longer merely sit back and wait for a gift from the government.[47] A year later, in 1974, it would join with other like-minded groups and form the Comité pour l'avortement libre et gratuit.[48]

At the same time that the Centre des femmes was becoming heavily involved in the struggle to legalize abortion, the PQ, a party founded in 1968 out of a split in the provincial Liberal Party, was beginning to occupy an increasing amount of ideological space in the nationalist movement. At the beginning of the 1970s, the left had a complex relationship with the PQ. The party's rising fortunes and its position as a credible opposition to the governing Liberals attracted many who hoped that they could work within the party to bring it more to the left. While many decided to work within the PQ, others were attracted either to the flourishing world of Marxist-Leninism or to the politics of Quebec's major labour organizations. As the 1970s progressed, class politics began to assume priority over national liberation for many leftists, and this new conjuncture would have a significant impact on the Centre.

It is in the context of the changing ideological parameters of political dissent and the increased influence of Marxist-Leninism that the Centre's attack on the PQ needs to be situated. The language of national liberation had provided a set of resources that a nascent feminist movement was able to exploit, stretch, and extend to its own use. By challenging the left's language on its own terms, the women's liberation movement had significantly altered that very language. Yet the association of French-Canadian nationalism with pro-natalism had a long history in Quebec,[49] and the Centre des femmes believed that the policies of the PQ in the early 1970s were not those of an emancipatory movement of national liberation. The PQ did not envision an overturning of society's economic and social structures and, as far as the Centre was concerned, it made use of traditional nationalist tropes to restrict women to the roles of mothers and wives.

In 1973, the Centre des femmes launched a fierce attack against the PQ and, conflating the PQ with Quebec nationalism, it ultimately abandoned "the nation" altogether as its site of struggle. The immediate spark that set off the Centre's vehement reaction was, perhaps ironically, the PQ's adoption of "pro-women" resolutions at its February 1973 convention. The group outlined the PQ's six major resolutions that related to women: wages for a spouse (male or female) whose primary responsibility was housework, a substantial sum of money for women both before and after giving birth, paid maternity leave of six months, free daycare, services for parents with sick children, and a reform of marriage law to ensure that it would be egalitarian and that a woman would not be obliged to take her husband's name.

Although the PQ's resolutions seemed progressive, the Centre, drawing on Charles Gagnon's *Pour le parti prolétarien*, one of the founding documents of Quebec's Marxist-Leninist movement—argued that they were illusory remedies. The election of a few women to the executive and the passing of a few "pro-feminine" resolutions at its congress, the Centre argued, were deceiving. The party sought merely to institutionalize women's roles and to preserve the family, an institution that was both the bedrock of capitalism and responsible for the exploitation of women. The PQ, the Centre pointed out, did not resolve to provide free and legal access to abortions, nor did it advocate a socialization of housework. The party, which desired to see in power a nascent Quebec bourgeoisie allied to American imperialism, provided only false hope to workers and women, offering "crumbs to rally them around the idea of 'national unity.'"[50]

Even more worrisome than the PQ's insincere policies toward workers and women, the Centre believed, was the party's celebration of the nuclear family and (its inferred) female domestication. The idea of baby bonuses, while having the ostensible purpose of recognizing the role of mothers in society, the Centre argued, in reality institutionalized the "private work carried out within the family." Rather than "valuing the woman as an individual," moreover, "it [was] the woman-mother that [was] being glorified." The Centre des femmes also linked the PQ's desired preservation of the family with capitalism. Right-wing nationalist parties had always valued the family as the ideological basis for both capitalism and the authoritarian power of the state, and the PQ, the Centre argued, was no exception.[51] Because the Centre des femmes saw the nuclear family as an oppressive institution, the PQ's valorization of the family structure was seen as an impediment to the struggle for women's liberation. It was clear to the members of the Centre that, "behind the PQ's terminology of 'a partner at home' lurks the usual nationalist ideology of 'a return to the home,' with the ever-present glorification of the role of the wife and mother."[52]

At the same time that it vehemently opposed the PQ, the Centre began to distance itself from the national project in its entirety.

Quebec nationalism, it seemed, was no longer compatible either with the Centre's struggle for legalized and state-funded abortion or with its larger project of emancipation in general. In this, the women of the Centre followed a path similar to that of many other activists of the era who began situating themselves within a class-based movement and turning away from the language of national alienation. After the dissolution of the FLF, many of its former members re-entered leftist groups, and many turned to the increasingly class-oriented Saint-Jacques political action committee and the publication *Mobilisation*. The Quebec union movement and Marxist-Leninist groups, both of which were undergoing periods of mass expansion and militancy, were significantly affecting the intellectual climate of the city, and both began to integrate women's issues into their political programs.

As the rhetoric of national oppression slowly disappeared within Montreal's radical circles, the Centre increasingly focused on class exploitation, replacing its earlier slogan with a new formulation: "No liberation of housewives without the liberation of workers, no liberation of workers without the liberation of housewives!"[53] By shifting its focus toward class, the Centre began to see itself as forming a part of the international struggle of all women and workers. The Centre argued that it was by making women's liberation a "key demand of the working class that [women] will put an end to the present system of exploitation."[54] Women formed an essential, albeit unpaid and undervalued, element of the capitalist mode of production. By doing housework they reinforced the labour power of the husband, and their unpaid work in the home therefore acted as "the economic cement of the capitalist system." In a society in which human worth was determined by money, women were excluded from decision-making power.[55]

By the middle of the 1970s, women's liberation theory in Montreal had travelled a long way since it first made its appearance in 1969. But it was not just women's liberation theory that had changed. The transformations within the women's movement were part of a much larger transformation within the language and structures of the Quebec left. In the late 1960s and early 1970s, national liberation had opened up possibilities and fed the imaginations of radical activists. But by the early 1970s the Centre felt that its goals contrasted sharply with the PQ's desire to encourage the development of Quebec families. The PQ's program, it claimed, stood in direct opposition to its goal of eliminating gender discrimination. In addition to denouncing foreign exploiters, the Centre therefore began fighting against nationalism itself.

When the Centre conducted an internal evaluation of its activities in late 1974, it conceded that it considered itself to be "a core of avant-garde feminists with a 'leading' role to play in the feminist movement." The problem was that "the bases for the creation of this movement did not yet exist."[56] Plagued by internal division and conflict, the Centre des femmes dissolved just as the feminist movement was beginning a new chapter of thought and action. The founding of the FLF in 1969 marked the beginning of a new phase in the history of Quebec feminism, but by the mid-1970s, with the Centre des femmes itself disappearing, it was clear that this initial phase had come to an end. The United Nations declared 1975 International Women's Year, and the women's movement gained new momentum and assumed new forms, attracting an unprecedented number of participants.

In its first six years, the women's movement remained fluid, and it moved forward in an almost experimental fashion. Its members lived moments of intense creativity and extreme frustration. At least partly as a result of its example, feminist initiatives, including parent-run daycares, consciousness-raising groups, and creative feminist artistic productions, were flourishing by the mid-1970s. Yet while the movement expanded the possibilities of imagining a more just future, it was not without its own internal contradictions and shortcomings, and it produced its own dynamics of exclusion, remaining silent on many crucial questions, such as homosexuality and race.[57] [. . .] As future feminists sought to negotiate their own relationships with the other social movements of their times, the complicated legacies of the province's first advocates of women's liberation provided the contested ground upon which they would build.

NOTES

1. Solange Chalvin, "Le Front commun des Québécoises descendra dans la rue, ce soir," *Le Devoir*, 28 novembre 1969.
2. Véronique O'Leary et Louise Toupin, "Nous sommes le produit d'un contexte," dans *Québécoises deboutte! Tome I* (hereafter *QDI*) (Ville Saint-Laurent: Les Éditions du remue-ménage, 1982), 23. All translations from French are my own. The details from the opening paragraph are drawn from the documents collected in *QDI*.
3. Canadian Women's Movement Archives, University of Ottawa, box 31, "Revolution in the Revolution: Second manifesto by a collective of women in the Front de Liberation des Femmes Québécoises," Montreal, September 1971, 1.
4. Micheline de Sève, "Feminisme et nationalisme au Québec, une alliance inattendue," *Revue internationale d'études canadiennes*, 17 (1998): 159.
5. Violette Brodeur, Suzanne G. Chartrand, Louise Corriveau, and Béatrice Valay, *Le Mouvement des femmes au Québec: Étude des groupes montréalais et nationaux* (Montréal: Centre de formation populaire, 1982), 27.
6. Micheline Dumont, "The Origins of the Women's Movement in Québec," in Constance

Backhouse and David H. Flaherty, eds, *Challenging Times: The Women's Movement in Canada and the United States* (Montreal and Kingston: McGill-Queen's University Press, 1992), 86.

7. Judy Rebick, *Ten Thousand Roses: The Making of a Feminist Revolution* (Toronto: Penguin, 2005), 3–4. Quebec Voice of Women members, Brief to the Royal Commission on the Status of Women, May 1968, 1. See also Simone Monet-Chartrand, *Les Québécoises et le mouvement pacifiste, 1939–1967* (Montréal: Le Éditions Écosociété, 1993). For Monet-Chartrand's more general reflections on women's activism, see Simone Monet-Chartrand, *Pionnières québécoises et regroupements de femmes d'hier à aujourd'hui* (Montréal: Les Éditions du remue-ménage, 1990).

8. Martine Lanctôt, "La genèse et l'évolution du mouvement de libération des femmes à Montréal, 1969–1979" (MA thesis, Université du Québec à Montréal, 1980), 52.

9. Ibid., 58. See, also, "FLFQ Historique," été 1970, *QDI*, 65. See also Marjolaine Péloquin, *En prison pour la cause des femmes: La conquête du banc des jurés* (Montréal: Les Éditions du remue-ménage, 2007), 29.

10. Péloquin, *En prison*, 29, 34. In the testimonies reproduced in Péloquin's work, many ex-FLF members discuss the importance of the Quebec left of the 1960s, especially the journal *Parti Pris* and the labour movement, to their political awakening (204–28).

11. Ibid., 253.

12. "Revolution in the Revolution: Second Manifesto by a Collective of Women in the Front de Liberation des Femmes Québécoises," Canadian Women's Movement Archives, University of Ottawa, box 31, Montreal, September 1971.

13. Stéphanie Lanthier, "L'impossible réciprocité des rapports politique entre le nationalisme radical et le féminisme radical au Québec, 1961–1972" (MA thesis, Université de Sherbrooke, 1998), 117.

14. This ideology was most often articulated by the women who formed the FLF, although it was by no means confined to this organization. Another group of radical women in Montreal wrote the widely circulated *Manifeste des femmes québécoises* (Montréal: l'étincelle, 1971).

15. "Bulletin de liaison FLFQ," no. 1, juillet 1971, *QDI*, 102.

16. O'Leary et Toupin, "Des femmes de Longueuil," *QDI*, 98.

17. Guy Deshaies, "Un commando féminin prend d'assaut la tribune des jurés," *Le Devoir*, 2 mars 1971.

18. Péloquin, *En prison*, 27.

19. "FLFQ Fonctionnement," été 1970, *QDI*, 67.

20. Ibid.

21. FLF, "Bulletin de Liaison FLFQ – cellule journal," no. 2, août 1971, *QDI*, 117.

22. FLF, "FLFQ: Historique," été 1970, *QDI*, 66. See also Lanthier, "L'impossible réciprocité."

23. FLF, "Bulletin de Liaison FLFQ – cellule journal," no. 2, août 1971, *QDI*, 115.

24. O'Leary et Toupin, "Nous sommes le produit d'un contexte," *QDI*, 27.

25. FLF, "Bulletin de Liaison FLFQ – cellule journal," no. 2, août 1971, *QDI*, 116.

26. Ibid., 117.

27. FLF, "Bulletin de Liaison FLFQ – Ex-cellule 'X' et cellule 'O comme dans vulve,'" no. 2, août 1971, *QDI*, 119.

28. "Bulletin de liason FLFQ," no. 2, août 1971, *QDI*, 118. Cellule garderie.

29. "Bulletin de liason FLFQ," no. 2, août 1971, *QDI*, 120. Ex-cellule 'X' and Cellule "O comme dans vulve."

30. For a summary of the ideological differences within the different groups of the FLF, see "Bulletin de liaison FLFQ," no. 2, août 1971, *QDI*. Lanctôt, "La genèse," 77–81.

31. "Bulletin de liaison FLFQ," no. 2, août 1971, *QDI*, 111–12. Cellule II.

32. "Bulletin de liaison FLFQ," no. 2, août 1971, *QDI*, 114. Cellule cinéma-animation-formation.

33. "Bulletin de liaison FLFQ," no. 2, août 1971, *QDI*, 119. Cellule X and cellule O comme dans vulve.

34. FLF, Press Release, 8 mai 1970, Montreal, *QDI*, 71.

35. O'Leary et Toupin, "Un bilan de parcours," *QDI*, 76–7. See also Péloquin, *En prison*, 142.

36. O'Leary et Toupin, "Un bilan de parcours." For an important discussion of the separation of anglophone and francophone women, see Péloquin, *En prison*, 259–60. It should be noted that Péloquin recalls that, while the expelled anglophone members were both sad and hurt by the development, many nonetheless understood its necessity.

37. Heather Jon Maroney, "Contemporary Quebec Feminism: The Interrelation of Political and Ideological Development in Women's Organizations, Trade Unions, Political Parties and State Policy, 1960–1980" (PhD diss., McMaster University, 1988), 251.

38. Clio Collective, *Quebec Women: A History*, 360. Heather Jon Maroney estimates that a total of roughly two hundred women attended the FLF's meetings. See Maroney, "Contemporary Quebec Feminism," 249.

39. Péloquin, *En prison*, 203, 255–6.

40. Maroney, "Contemporary Quebec Feminism," 257–9.

41. "Lettre à nos camarades," *Québécoises deboutte!* novembre 1972, *Québécoises deboutte!* Tome II [hereafter *QDII*] (Ville Saint-Laurent: Les Éditions du remue-ménage, 1982), 18.

42. "Pour un féminisme révolutionnaire," *Québécoises deboutte!* décembre 1972, *QDII*, 50–1.

43. "Histoire d'une oppression," *Québécoises deboutte!* décembre 1972, *QDII*, 41.

44. "Histoire d'une oppression," *Québécoises deboutte!* vol. 1, no. 1, novembre 1972, *QDII*, 28.

45. "Les interêts en cause," *Québécoises deboutte!* juillet–août 1973, *QDII*, 220.

46. "Problème politique: Lutte politique," *Québécoises deboutte!* juillet–août 1973, *QDII*, 225. For an important history of the pro-choice movement in Quebec, see Louise Desmarais, *Mémoires d'une bataille inachevée: La lutte pour l'avortement au Québec, 1970–1992* (Montréal: Éditions Trait d'union, 1999).

47. Ibid., 225–6. It should be noted, however, that this decision was a subject of considerable debate and division among the women at the Centre des femmes. See "Bilan du Centre des Femmes à Montréal, Janvier 1972 à septembre 1974," novembre 1974, *QDI*.

48. Diane Lamoureux, "La lutte pour le droit à l'avortement (1969–1981)," *Revue d'histoire de l'Amérique française* 37, 1 (1983): 84.

49. See Roberta Hamilton, "Pro-Natalism, Feminism, and Nationalism," in François Pierre Gingras, ed., *Gender and Politics in Contemporary Canada* (Toronto: Oxford University Press, 1995), 135–52.

50. "Le P.Q. espoir ou illusion," *Québécoises deboutte!* avril 1973, *QDII*, 127–30.

51. Ibid.

52. "Sur notre condition: Un salaire à la ménagère?" *Québécoises deboutte!* avril 1973, *QDI*, 134.

53. "Pour une vrai fête des mères et ménagères," *Québécoises deboutte!* vol. 1, no. 6, juin 1973, *QDI*, 171.

54. "À la Regent Knitting . . . ," *Québécoises deboutte!* février 1973, *QDII*, 71.

55. "Sur notre condition: Les ménagères," *Québécoises deboutte!* mars 1973, *QDII*, 109, 113.

56. "Bilan du Centre des Femmes à Montréal, Janvier 1972 à septembre 1974," novembre 197 4, *QDI*, 157.

57. Even the editorial content of the *Birth Control Handbook* maintained a silence on homosexuality until 1973. See Christabelle Sethna, "The Evolution of the *Birth Control Handbook*: From Student Peer-Education Manual to Feminist Self-empowerment," *Canadian Bulletin of Medical History* 23, 1 (2006): 104.

Chapter 12

Immigration and Multiculturalism

READINGS

Primary Documents

1   From *Selling Illusions: The Cult of Multiculturalism in Canada*, Neil Bissoondath

2   From "Mapping Africadia's Imaginary Geography: An Interview with George Elliott Clarke,"
    Maureen Moynagh

Historical Interpretations

3   From "The Roots of Multiculturalism: Ukrainian-Canadian Involvement in the
    Multiculturalism Discussion of the 1960s as an Example of the Position of the 'Third Force,'"
    Julia Lalande

4   From "The Migration of African-Americans to the Canadian Football League during the
    1950s: An Escape from Racism?," Neil Longley, Todd Crosset, and Steve Jefferson

INTRODUCTION

While the end of the Second World War did not introduce Canada to immigration, it did mark
the beginning of a period in which a new and more diverse series of immigrant "waves" began
to arrive. Entrenched ideas and stereotypes about newcomers from various nations survived
the war, but it became more difficult for the Canadian government to enact laws restricting
immigration, to favour immigrants of certain racial and ethnic origins, and to uphold discriminatory or exclusionary policies. In the late 1940s, following a war fought to defeat the sort of
overt racism and ethnic biases that defined Nazi Germany, Canada portrayed itself as a welcoming place, especially to people fleeing countries that were behind the Iron Curtain. Even

though Canada's "founding peoples"—those of British and French origins—sought to retain their positions as social leaders, their respective shares of the population decreased when immigration laws changed in 1962 to end discrimination based on national origin, race, or religious allegiance, and changed again in 1976 to accommodate refugees and reunite families. As a result of these changes, the proportion of African and Asian immigrants increased significantly. In the midst of these developments, Canada adopted multiculturalism as an official policy in 1971. The policy explicitly stated that the Canadian government would acknowledge the contributions of all its various ethnic communities and, wherever possible, enact laws and policies that would respect the diversity of the Canadian population and the cultural differences among its various constituent groups. This amounted to a major reversal, considering that newcomers previously had been expected to conform to an essentially Anglo-Canadian set of norms. Official multiculturalism was reasonably well received in English-speaking Canada, however. It offered a contrast to America's "melting pot" and a rejoinder to French-Canadian appeals for the implementation of official biculturalism. Many in Quebec indeed regard official multiculturalism as a means to devalue the French fact, and the government of Quebec has long spurned multiculturalism in favour of a policy of integration. For their part, Canada's non-British immigrants embraced multiculturalism. They had long wished to see their contribution to Canadian society be formally recognized, though some discordant voices would eventually question the theory and practice of multiculturalism. One of these voices belongs to author Neil Bissoondath, a Canadian born in Trinidad, whose widely discussed 1994 book argued that multiculturalism hampers the integration of newcomers and contributes to the ghettoization of immigrant communities. Canadians often equate ethnic and racial diversity with immigration, but diversity in Canada pre-dates the immigration waves of the twentieth and twenty-first centuries. In a 1995 interview with Maureen Moynagh, writer George Elliott Clarke reflects on "Africadia," which is the term he uses to describe the community established by Black Loyalists and refugees in late-eighteenth-century Nova Scotia. Clarke's work bears witness to the presence of black people in Nova Scotia and to the vitality of their community, and it seeks to contest their erasure from the province's history and culture. The historical interpretations deal with two different issues: defining multiculturalism during the 1960s and early 1970s amid the worry over nationalism in Quebec and the latent racism that permeated post-war Canadian society. Julia Lalande looks at the role of Ukrainian community members as representatives of a "third force" influencing the Bilingualism and Biculturalism Commission during the 1960s. As a group whose roots in Canada pre-dated the First World War, Ukrainians saw themselves as having a claim, even a right, to speak along with or on behalf of other immigrants who did not want to see Canada defined rigidly as an Anglo-French state. Longley, Crosset, and Jefferson's piece examines the African-American athletes who migrated to post-war Canada to play in the Canadian Football League. Canadians often contrast racial segregation in the United States with the integration and harmony that is supposed to have existed in Canada, but the experience of African-American football players shows that patterns of prejudice were likely similar on both sides of the border.

QUESTIONS FOR CONSIDERATION

1. According to Bissoondath, what factors brought about the policy of multiculturalism?
2. How does George Elliott Clarke use history and literature to contest the erasure of black people from Nova Scotian history and culture?

3. Do you agree with the critiques of multiculturalism put forward by Bissoondath and Clarke?
4. What were some of the items that representatives of the Ukrainian-Canadian community wanted to see as part of Canada's multiculturalism policy? Why do you think some were not adopted?
5. Do you believe that post-war patterns of prejudice were similar in Canada and the United States? What factors might account for this?

SUGGESTIONS FOR FURTHER READING

Stephanie Bangarth, *Voices Raised in Protest: Defending North American Citizens of Japanese Ancestry, 1942–49* (Vancouver: UBC Press, 2008).

Richard J.F. Day, *Multiculturalism and the History of Canadian Diversity* (Toronto: University of Toronto Press, 2000).

Marlene Epp, Franca Iacovetta, and Frances Swyripa, eds, *Sisters or Strangers? Immigrant, Ethnic, and Racialized Women in Canadian History* (Toronto: University of Toronto Press, 2004).

Ninette Kelley and M. Trebilcock, *Making of a Mosaic: A History of Canadian Immigration Policy*, 2nd edn (Toronto: University of Toronto Press, 2010).

Patricia Roy, *The Triumph of Citizenship: The Japanese and Chinese in Canada, 1941–67* (Vancouver: UBC Press, 2007).

Triadafilos Triadafilopoulos, *Becoming Multicultural: Immigration and the Politics of Membership in Canada and Germany* (Vancouver: UBC Press, 2012).

Primary Documents

1   Excerpted from Neil Bissoondath, *Selling Illusions: The Cult of Multiculturalism in Canada*, 2nd edn (Toronto: Penguin Books, 2002), 26–40. Copyright © 1994 Neil Bissoondath. Reprinted by permission of Penguin Canada, a division of Penguin Random House Canada Limited.

Our memory of the past must be faithful to the future if it is to act as stimulus for the present.

—Naim Kattan, *Language & Society*, Fall 1987

Revolution drove them from their homeland, turning generations of achievement and service into history and family legend.

Splendid courtly uniforms gave way to more modest civilian dress, a certain wealth to a certain poverty. The excitements of imperial service were replaced by the uncertainties of a less structured existence. They ended up, after some meandering, in Montreal, stateless, penniless, admitted to Canada as agricultural labourers.

Count Paul Ignatieff and his wife, Natasha—he, once a reform-minded member of Tsar Nicholas II's cabinet; she, born a princess of the accomplished Mestchersky family—determined that there would be no surrender to straitened circumstances. They insisted to their sons—Nicholas, Vladimir, Alex, Lionel and George—that "the past was the past and that they must not end up like so many émigrés driving taxis and keeping their bags packed for the return journey to Petersburg." Neither did they try "to clamp their children within an émigré ghetto or to insist on Russian brides."

Paul and Natasha died before the end of the Second World War, she in August 1944, he a year later. They died in their modest cottage at Upper Melbourne, Quebec, far from the landscape and circumstances of their birth. But the attitudes they had inculcated in their sons were not without effect. Nicholas joined the University of Toronto as a Soviet expert intent on combatting anti-Soviet sentiment. Vladimir became a soils chemist, spending three decades with the Food and Agricultural Organization in Africa and Asia. Alec, a mining engineer, ended up running the Department of Mines in Canada's Ministry of Energy, while Lionel, in many ways the least reconciled to exile, obtained a doctorate and taught Russian literature at the University of Western Ontario. George, whose working life began at sixteen as an axeman in the forests of British Columbia, won a Rhodes Scholarship to Oxford and eventually developed into the consummate diplomat, his talents put to the service not of the Tsar, as they probably would have been had history been different, but to the government of Canada. The adjective "distinguished" is a word now almost synonymous with the man and his life.

The story of the Ignatieff family is not always a happy one—it includes its share of hardship, tensions and schism—but it is, in the romance of its details, extraordinary. It is not your typical refugee or émigré story; but, then, there may be no such thing except in a tale shorn, always unjustly, of its particularities, a human story without the humanity, a story disembodied. Nor is the story of the Ignatieff family particularly iconic: it has been repeated throughout the century, countless times and to varying degrees, in many countries.

Some may say that the Ignatieff boys were privileged. They benefitted from a superior education, their parents having scrimped and saved the tuition to Lower Canada College. It could be said that they benefitted from the efforts of Natasha who, in particular, provided an indispensable stability at home, a sense of a centre when all else had been lost. It could be said that they found strength in a knowledge of their past, a knowledge of their own worth unavailable to many.

It cannot be denied, though, that they were boys who grew into men who worked at their opportunities. If the Ignatieffs are seen, today, as part of the Canadian élite, it is not because of birthright or family fortune; it is because, through effect and achievement, they have made it so. All of these—the engagement of self with the ever-larger circles of family and society—are the imponderable particularities, the human details that make the story unique, that afford it notions of legend.

But there is, too, another aspect of the story, of every such story. For all of this—the uncertainties, the struggles, the failures and the successes—took place within a certain context, that of the country to which the family had come.

When Paul and Natasha arrived in Montreal, they were officially stateless, flotsam of history.

When they died, they died as official citizens of Canada.

When they were buried, they were places in a soil to which they belonged as much as it belonged to them.

Almost half a century after the death of grandparents he never knew in the flesh but whom, through history, through family memory, he may know with a greater intimacy than is ever granted to most of us, Michael Ignatieff ponders Paul and Natasha and the life that was theirs in a new country a world away from their own.

"How did my grandparents and their children, my father and mother, understand what was asked of them when they came to Canada in 1928 compared to what is asked and required of a Haitian arriving in Montreal in the 1980s?" he wonders aloud. "What has changed here? What are you allowed to assert of yourself that you weren't allowed to assert of yourself then?" They question is cast with a historian's eye—but a historian whose academic training has not robbed him of his sense of the blood and guts of history: people are central; they shape events and are in turn shaped by them. If journalism is the unconsidered reporting of raw history in the form of "facts," and if history is the considered ordering of "facts" into perceived truths, then Michael Ignatieff culls his perceptions from somewhere in the middle ground—after the passions have receded but before the dust has settled.

"I have some sense of a generational change here, that earlier waves of immigration understood integration here as We will learn the language, We will learn the values, We will learn the culture—and some of that had a semi-sacramental importance. My father could always tell you what it was like to stand in line in 1935 at City Hall in Toronto as a young university undergraduate and take the Canadian oath of citizenship: he had a feeling of a tremendously important rite of passage that left him incredibly patriotic as a Canadian to the end.

"I think some of it had to do with destitution. They had nothing when they came and they thought: We're not in a position to dictate the terms here, we're coming to a new, young country and we'll take what we can get. And if that meant being called a Bohunk and all the kinds of Slavic abuse [popular] in the twenties and thirties, well, so be it. They had the sense of this being a porous society, a society that wasn't defining the contract of integration in very demanding ways."

And yet, that contract of integration, while not demanding, had also established parameters of restriction defining the look of the society that immigration would create.

The Canada the Ignatieffs came to was one in transition. The country, with a population of just over 10 million, had emerged from the First World War bloodied but with a greater sense of itself. No longer content to be merely an adjunct to the British Empire, it began seeking ways to enlarge the colonial envelope, a process legitimized by the 1926 Balfour declaration that recognized "Britain and the dominions as equals in a Commonwealth partnership." It was the initiation in Canada of a slow process of decolonization.

Under the guidance of Mackenzie King in particular, Canada's acquiescence to British wishes was no longer automatic, the rush to arms to serve British interests no longer enthusiastic. The urge to greater independence culminated in the 1931 Statute of Westminster, which gave Canada full control over its foreign and domestic policy.

It was, on the whole, a country protective of its racial and cultural exclusivity. The native population was contained on reserves, the small black communities effectively isolated from mainstream life and entry to Canada by people deemed undesirable on racial and ethnic grounds severely restricted. American whites were encouraged, American blacks not. Landing fees of $25 or $50 were charged to all—except for Asians, who were levied $200. In 1923, this requirement was dropped—again except for Chinese, who were now required to pay a "head tax" of $250, a measure aimed exclusively at reducing the flow of their numbers.

Nor did East Indians, fellow loyalists to the British Crown, find favour. One of the more disgraceful incidents in Canadian history began on May 23, 1914, three months before the start of the war that would lead, among other consequences, to the overthrow of the Romanov dynasty in Russia and the uprooting of the Ignatieff family.

On that day, a freighter named the *Komagata Maru* dropped anchor off Vancouver. On board were 376 passengers, all from the Far East, many bearing the Sikh ceremonial name of Singh. The ship was quarantined, sealed off by armed guards, only an official government party allowed onboard or off. Official resistance to their admission to Canada centred on the existence of illness among the would-be migrants: twenty-two would be allowed to land, the others would have to sail on.

In the ensuing stalemate, immigration officials would not even let garbage off the ship. Food and water began running out. Many more fell ill. One died.

Then, in a move rigid with bureaucratic thinking, it was decided that the fate of the remaining 354 would binge on a test case of one of their number. A young Sikh farmer was chosen. He was tested, ruled inadmissible. Only a miracle would have led to a different conclusion. Deportation orders were issued, and on July 23, 1914, precisely two months after first dropping anchor, the *Komagata Maru* steamed away from Canadian shores.

As Glenda Simms, president of the Canadian Advisory Council on the Status of Women, has written, "This incident is cited in most discussions on state racism in Canada and serves as a reminder of the many past actions in which the country takes no pride."

But it must be borne in mind that Canadian suspicion of foreigners was not only, or purely, racial in character. The country was fine in its discriminations. As the historian Ramsay Cool points out, southern Italians, for instance, were viewed as irretrievably corrupt and so, unlike their northern brethren, were not welcome either.

In *None Is Too Many,* the chilling study of the effect of Canada's racial policies on the Jews of Europe, Irving Abella and Harold Troper write: "If Canada, unlike the United States, never legislated quotas against particular groups, Canada's government still enforced a restrictive immigration policy with unabashed racial and ethnic priorities. With public support, it knew what ethnic and racial groups it wanted and how to keep out those it did not . . . [T]hose groups that did not fit the national vision—especially Jew, Asians and blacks—were ever more often relegated by Canadian officials to the bottom of the list of those preferred."

On the whole, then, immigration at the beginning of the century was restricted to those who, at the end of the century, would be euphemistically referred to by some as "traditional immigrants," i.e., white and Christian. It was immigration defined by a sense of superiority based on race, ethnicity and class-consciousness—which evokes the persistent mystery of why a colonial people so readily adopts the word traits of the colonial master.

Even acceptance into Canada, though, did not guarantee fair treatment. As the late Ken Adachi points out in *The Enemy That Never Was,* naturalized citizens of Japanese origin and their Canadian-born children were routinely denied basic citizenship rights—the right to vote, the right to exercise certain professions such as law and pharmacy—but were not exempt from taxation or conscription. The distrust and fear of the "yellow peril" (a phrase coined by, of all people, Kaiser Wilhelm II) led to discriminations grand and petty: the 1907 riot in Vancouver when the Japanese district of "Little Tokyo" was attached by a mob out for blood; a policy throughout the twenties of reducing the number of fishing licences held by fishermen of Japanese descent, and even denying them the use of gas-powered boats; restrictions in theatre on where they could sit, in swimming pools on when they could swim—all of which culminated, of course, in the forces evacuations, internments and confiscations following the Japanese attack on Pearl Harbor in December 1941.

It is worth remembering, too, that despite the political successes of Sir Wilfrid Laurier, the mass of French Canadians lived with the knowledge that in the companies they worked for, they would always be the clerks and never the president—and advancement to head clerk required a measure of subservience and proficiency in a language not their own.

This, then, was one aspect of the country to which the Ignatieff family came in 1928, a country of easy social integration for those permissible under the unwritten racial and ethnic policies of the time. As people searching for a haven, for a life to replace the one they had lost, they could not be expected to have been concerned with the easy and ingrained injustices that did not directly affect them. As with all refugees, of far greater concern would have been the battle to secure a future.

Even their new land was not a place of vast promise. The economy was sliding into depression, the family's meagre savings vanishing in the economic withering. For the moment, it was survival that mattered, the questions of public policy that would concern the sons in later years intellectual luxury ill-afforded.

It would be decades and the tragedies of another world war before Canada would begin to grow out of its anaemic ethical adolescence and challenge itself to engage the complexities of a world in which the certainties and prejudices of empire had been forever shattered.

Most legislation follows the developing shape of society; it is a game of legislative catch-up. If hogs were once legally banned from running along the streets of Toronto, it was because they were doing just that— and causing what one imagines to be a fair amount of odorous chaos. The resulting legislation was an attempt to address a widely perceived social problem; it was based on a perception of consensus, and enjoyed legitimacy by offering a solution to citizens' anxieties. Legislatures, then, for the most part, follow in the choppy wake of society. Laws in a democratic society are engendered by event.

But activist governments, motivated by a vision not just of what society is but what it should be, are not content just to follow. They will seek, as much as possible, to engage a predetermined ideological agenda, establishing social and legislative programs designed to nudge (or shove) society in directions deems laudable. It is, to a certain extent, a Platonic approach to government, the construction of myth and structure aimed at the attainment of a reasonable Good. Such a government, philosophically opposed to, say, capital punishment, would initiate a program of persuasion to entice a populace philosophically committed to the death sentence away from it. Sometimes it works, sometimes it does not. Unless opposition is vigorous, though, the activist government will proceed with its agenda, leaving the game of catch-up to the people. How much to follow, how much to lead: it is the inevitable tension of democratic government.

Following, leading: each approach to government has its advantages and its disadvantages.

A government that simply follows the wishes of the electorate may appear more democratic but it also inevitably betrays a basic notion of democracy: if legislative decisions are to be made on the basis of consensus through referendum or poll, then debate, elections and parliaments become pointless. Better to established a civil service structure responsible for implementing the wishes of the majority as expressed through public opinion survey: the tyranny, then, of the majority.

An activist government, on that defines leadership in terms of (to use a military metaphor) "taking the point," also runs ricks. It can lead only so long as the people are willing to follow. Failure to engage the abilities or inclinations of the society will necessarily lead to resentment, resistance, loss of legitimacy—to, with perseverance, the tyranny of a minority. A government outdistances its electorate at its own peril.

Most governments attempt to mediate a line between the two approaches, a line that meanders along the graphs of its popularity.

The choice of the kind of government best suited to a country at any given time in its history is determined by the temper of the people it is meant serve. A people confident of itself and its future may be eager to be mobilized by visionary leadership, may be keen on the idea of being shown how to be better than it ever thought it could be.

In the 1960s, Canada became this kind of county. The land that had, early in the century, defined itself largely through notions of race was not immune to the powerful liberal ethic that the decade brought to North America. Canadians, like Americans, had been touched by the wave of inspiration unleashed by John and Robert Kennedy. They too had been inspired by Martin Luther King and had witnessed the at-times violent struggle for civil rights in the United States. They had made known their opposition to the war in Vietnam. And, at home, Quebec dramatically remade itself, almost willing into existence a new and vibrant society from a somnolent rural and religious past.

Out of such ferment, toward the end of the decade, emerged the vitality and apparent activism of Pierre Elliott Trudeau, the man who would remake Canada, a country prepared to follow him out of its traditional staidness into a more exciting version of itself. Trudeau, then, was invested by the Canadian public with a stylish Vision of the Good.

But an activist Vision of the Good, as already pointed out, rarely suffices on its own. For intellectual belief to be translated into public policy, it must encounter either a certain measure of public support based on ethical belief (such as in the abolition of the death penalty nationally or the establishment in Quebec of legal linguistic parameters, each of which is seen by its supporters as serving a greater good), or it must respond to the narrower demands of partisan political necessity. When these conditions coincide, the government enjoys what is known somewhat inelegantly as "a win-win situation."

Expectations of Trudeau were great. He would renew the country, he would unite it. He would gild us all in the sheen of his personality. The reality could never fit the fantasy. Big ideas came to Ottawa, ideas that prompted a snowstorm of studies and, by most accounting, the barest sprinkling of results. By the third year of his first prime ministerial mandate, the rose was wilting, Trudeaumania was transforming itself into Trudeauphobia, and concerns about the next campaign, the next mandate, began to make themselves felt. In 1971, with his government sliding steadily into unpopularity (thanks in large part to a policy of bilingualism that had been badly explained and insensitively implemented), Pierre Trudeau initiated a federal policy that would change the face of the nation forever, the official policy of multiculturalism.

> 3. (1) It is hereby declared to be the policy of the Government of Canada to (a) recognize and promote the understanding that multiculturalism reflects the cultural and racial diversity of Canadian society and acknowledges the freedom of all members of Canadian society to preserve, enhance and share their cultural heritage.
>
> —Canadian Multiculturalism Act

Retrospect does not always offer clarity; separating the social necessity from the political can be difficult, if not impossible. Politicians, in interview or in memoir, will always offer the most selfless of justifications—while their opponents will seek to highlight the selfish. It is curious, then, that while vigorously defending bilingualism in his memoirs, Pierre Trudeau never mentions multiculturalism. One cannot help wondering whether this omission can be taken as a measure of his intellectual commitment to the policy.

The view of journalist Richard Gwyn is uncompromising. "Trudeau's imperative, post-1972," he writes, "changed from doing what was right, rationally, to doing what was advantageous politically. So Trudeau had been criticised for ignoring the Queen; in 1973, the Queen came to Canada twice, a history-making precedent, with Trudeau at her side every step of the royal progress. So he had been accused of sloughing off the ethnics; up sprang a trebled multiculturalism program that functioned as a slush fund to buy ethnic votes."

It read like an indictment, multiculturalism boosted into the limelight not as a progressive social policy but as an opportunistic political one, not so much an answer to necessary social accommodation as a response to pressing political concern. If the emphasis on federal bilingualism had seemed to favour francophone Quebec at the expense of the rest of the country, enhanced multiculturalism could be served up as a way of equalizing the political balance sheet. The activist elected in 1968 became, four years later the opportunist fighting for his political life.

Former Quebec premier René Lévesque was frankly dismissive of the multicultural game. "Multiculturalism, really, is folklore," he once said. "It is a 'red herring.' The notion was devised to obscure 'the Quebec business,' to give an impression that we are all ethnics and do not have to worry about special status for Quebec."

This view is shared by the political scientist Christian Dufour who, in his book *Le Défi québécois*, offers two reasons for the advent of multiculturalism: "It was a matter of responding to the expectations of immigrants who arrived in Ontario after the Second World War and whose assimilation had not been completed. But it was also a way of refusing to recognize the bicultural nature of the country and the political consequences of Québécois specificity. Multiculturalism, in principle, reduces the Québécois fact to an ethnic phenomenon."

"A slush fund to buy ethnic votes"; reducing Quebec distinctiveness to "an ethnic phenomenon": immigrants, naturalized citizens, "ethnic" Canadians offered a hyphen (and government funds) in exchange for allowing themselves to be used as pawns in the old Canadian tug-of-war between anglophones and francophones. It is a sad and dispiriting view of a policy that, on the face of it, seems suffused with humanism. It is also a view that, in the atmosphere of suspicion that envelops the tug-of-war, bears the ring of truth.

But cynicism alone does not necessarily reign supreme; motives may not all be impure. Even a program aimed primarily at manipulation may benefit from a certain measure of heart and sincerity.

The Act for the Preservation and Enhancement of Multiculturalism in Canada, better known by its short title the Canadian Multiculturalism Act, is composed of phrases that bring to mind the Trinidadian expression "sweet talk." It is a document that, through the repetition of gentle and well-meaning generalizations, seeks to seduce.

The act recognizes "the existence of communities whose members share a common origin and their historic contribution to Canadian society" and promises to "enhance their development"; it aims to "promote the understanding and creativity that arise from the interaction between individuals and communities of different origins" and commits the federal government to the promotion of "policies and practices that enhance the understanding of and respect for the diversity of the members of Canadian society." It talks about being "sensitive and responsive to the multicultural reality of Canada."

Recognition, appreciation, understanding; sensitive, responsive, respectful; promote, foster, preserve: these words and others like them occur time and again in the Multiculturalism Act, repeated amid the thicket of legalistic phrasing like a mantra of goodwill.

Beyond this, the act goes from the general to the concrete by authorizing the minister responsible to "take such measures as the Minister considered appropriate to . . . (a) encourage and assist individuals, organizations and institutions to protect the multicultural reality of Canada in their activities in Canada and abroad; . . . (c) encourage and promote exchanges and cooperation among the divers communities of Canada; . . . (e) encourage the preservation, enhancement, sharing and evolving expression of the multicultural heritage of Canada; . . . (h) provide support to individuals, groups or organizations for the purpose of preserving, enhancing and promoting multiculturalism in Canada."

One feels like a bit of an ingrate in admitting that these words evoke less a sigh of reassurance than a shudder of suspicion. Questioning such sentiments is like doubting professions of motherly love: there is something slightly disreputable about it. And yet it is impossible to avoid a whiff of formaldehyde, a hint of the sterility of museum display cases. Impossible to ignore the image of colourful butterflies pinned to black velvet by careful and loving hands all for the greater glory of . . . the butterflies?

The Multiculturalism Act is in many ways a statement of activism. It is a vision of government, not content to let things be, determined to play a direct role in shaping not only the evolution of Canadian—mainly *English*-Canadian—society but the evolution of individuals within that society as well. As a political statement it is disarming, as a philosophical statement almost naïve with generosity. Attractive sentiments liberally dispensed—but where, in the end, do they lead?

The act, activist in spirit, magnanimous in accommodation, curiously excludes any ultimate vision of the kind of society it wishes to create. It never addresses the question of the nature of a multicultural society, what such a society is and—beyond a kind of vague notion of respect for human differences—what it means for the nation at large and the individuals who compose it. Definitions and implications are conspicuously absent, and this may be indicative of the political sentiments that prompted the adoption of the act in the first place. Even years later, the act—a cornerstone of bipartisan, federal social policy—shows signs of a certain haste. In its lack of long-term consideration, in its promise of action with no discussion of consequence, one can discern the opportunism that underlay it all. One senses the political hand, eager for an instrument to attract "ethnic" votes, urging along the drafting—and damn the consequences.

In its rush, the act appears to indulge in several unexamined assumptions: that people, coming here from elsewhere, wish to remain what they have been; that personalities and ways of doing things, ways of looking at the world, can be frozen in time; that Canadian cultural influences pale before the exoticism of the foreign. It views newcomers as exotics and pretends that this is both proper and sufficient.

Nor does the act address the question of limits: how far do we go as a country in encouraging and promoting cultural difference? How far is far enough, how far too far? Is there a point at which diversity begins to threaten social cohesion? The document is striking in its lack of any mention of unity or oneness of vision. Its provisions seem aimed instead at encouraging division, at ensuring that the various ethnic groups whose interests it espouses discover no compelling reason to blur the distinctions between them.

A cynic might be justified in saying that this is nothing more than a cleverly disguised blueprint for a policy of "keep divided and therefore conquered," a policy that seeks merely to keep a diverse populace amenable to political manipulation.

The Canadian Multiculturalism Act is in many senses an ill-considered document, focused so squarely on today that it ignores tomorrow. And it is short-sightedness that may account for the consequences it has brought about—for individuals, families, communities and the country as a whole.

It was a policy initiated by an activist government anxious about its future. The populace was willing to follow at the time—a happy conjunction of purpose for the Trudeau government—but, if the polls are correct, this may no longer be so thirty-odd years later. The temper of the country has altered, its circumstances changed. The same people who, in the sixties, were eager for leadership now seek a certain paternalism. Demoralized, enervated by social and economic adversity, they have turned resentful. They have grown conservative and self-protective, desirous not of the brave new world but of the safe old one. Times have changed, and a good idea

then may not be a good idea now—not only because the country is no longer what it once was but also because the policy itself has, in the eyes of many, frittered away into disillusionment and discredit.

Reality has a way of battering philosophy: it is reality's way of saying a new philosophy must be found. It may be time for the cow of multiculturalism to be stripped of its holiness.

---

2 From Maureen Moynagh, "Mapping Africadia's Imaginary Geography: An Interview with George Elliott Clarke," *ARIEL: A Review of International English Literature* 27, 4 (October 1996): 71–94. Reprinted with permission of Johns Hopkins University Press.

Africadian, the word George Elliott Clarke coined by fusing Africa with Acadia, is more than a convenient designation for Afro-Nova Scotians; it marks the conscious construction of an imagined community, and it is a project he engages in both through his poetry and his critical work on the Africadian cultural renaissance. Born in 1960, in Windsor Plains, Nova Scotia, Clarke is rooted in a cultural geography charted by the generations descended from Black Loyalists and refugees. The particular terrain inhabited by Afro-Nova Scotians is visited time and again in a variety of ways in his poetry, from the poems named for churches in black communities throughout the province in his first book, *Saltwater Spirituals and Deeper Blues* (Pottersfield Press, 1983), to the rebaptized Whylah Falls near the Sixhiboux River of Jarvis County in his novel in verse, *Whylah Falls* (Polestar Press, 1990), to the place names—Zarahemla, Gehenna, Axum-Saba, Africadia, Sierra Leonia—that "refer to states of mind, not actual geographies" in his most recent collection, *Lush Dreams, Blue Exile* (Pottersfield Press, 1994). In remapping the official geography of Nova Scotia, and in mapping places habitually ignored by the dominant culture, Clarke constructs a nation called Africadia in order to contest the ongoing erasure of the

historical presence and cultural distinctiveness of Afro-Nova Scotians. His two-volume anthology, *Fire on the Water: An Anthology of Black Nova Scotian Writing* (Pottersfield Press, 1991 and 1992) extends this project by assembling a cultural history comprised of autobiography, sermons, petitions, covenants, historical writing, songs, orature, essays, poetry, drama and short stories.

The re-writing of colonial history and the re-mapping of colonial terrain are two well-known postcolonial strategies, and Clarke deploys them self-consciously. Intent upon representing, both as spokesperson and as artist, the Afro-Nova Scotian community, Clarke writes from and to a particular locality, bringing to bear on that writing a nationalist vision that insists on tolerance, change, and adaptation as much as on the preservation and promotion of cultural difference and group identity. Keenly aware of the role language and print culture play in the scripting of a national narrative, Clarke writes his imaginary geography in order to claim ontological ground denied the black community in the larger Canadian narrative. Yet the community Clarke imagines is one that draws on diverse narratives from several places, including Nova Scotia, Canada, Africa, and Afro-America, even as it foregrounds

Africadia. This is not a contradiction; it is an integral part of the vision, one he elaborates in his current work, *Beatrice Chancy, A Passional*, which transplants to Africadia a twice-told-tale about the Cenci.

This interview took place in Halifax on 26 November 1995.

Who are you writing for?

I'm writing for anyone who reads English, although I do have certain audiences in mind. I am very interested in being read by my own fellow Black Nova Scotians, or to use my word, Africadians. I'm very interested in having some standing within my own community as a writer people know, and as a writer they may enjoy reading or hearing. I'm also interested in the larger community of people in Nova Scotia, and in the Maritimes in general, because part of my project is to make them more aware of our contributions and our historical presence in this part of Canada. Then there is the even larger audience of English Canadians, who often are unaware of our existence in this area. And then there is the United States, particularly African-Americans, who many of us are descended from and who represent our major "ethnic connection," and so I feel that we have a bond, or a potential bond with them that ought to be further developed.

Your work is peopled with real as well as fictive Afro-Nova Scotians—Portia White, Richard Preston, Lydia Jackson, Graham Jarvis. How do you view the commemorative dimension of your work? Do you see yourself doing the work of a historian, in some sense, through your poetry?

Yes, definitely. The need to commemorate has fuelled my writing since my youth. I try to struggle against the general absence and repression of the existence of Black Nova Scotians or Africadians in every major discourse in this province: in terms of economics, tourism, and social interactions of all sorts. In fact there's a book that just came out—I just bought a used copy yesterday—called *In the Annapolis Valley* [Halifax:

Nimbus, 1993], a collection of photographs published in 1993. Not one photograph, not one caption mentions anything at all about the presence of black people in the Annapolis Valley. I feel I am constantly writing against our erasure, and yet the erasure continues. If you read books that discuss the various ethnic groups that have contributed to Nova Scotia, the major ones that always are brought up are the Scots, the Acadians, and so on; my own group is often still overlooked. I remember deliberately writing way to receive the tourist brochures produced in 1993 and 1994 by Tourism Nova Scotia, and for two years I wrote letters, angry letters, to Tourism Nova Scotia protesting the fact that once again certain groups are mentioned and black people are not. Now, damn it, we have a history here, a history full of trials, triumphs, struggles, etc., and there is just no legitimate way that we can be excluded from the history of this place. And so this explains my commemorative efforts, and my general interest in involving history and photographs in my creative work, because it is a means of contesting that constant erasure, which has led ultimately I think to racism, to the idea that "you folks do not count; you're not even a fit subject for history." There's a whole side of Maritime/Canadian life that has been repressed, and it's the duty of all of us who are creating right now to address that fact.

I'd like you to address a slightly different dimension of this idea of commemoration. In talking about the NFB film "Remember Africville," you remarked that it uses memory to conjure both nostalgia and critical hindsight. Do you see yourself as engaged in a similar project? How do you understand the relationship between nostalgia and critical hindsight?

This is an important question. Nostalgia can be very dangerous, in that it *can* result in a kind of erasure as well, an erasure of the real conflicts, including intra-communal conflicts which did occur, particularly around questions of class, religion, gender, and so on, and so one has to be *nervous*, to be really critical about one's use of nostalgia. I often like to think of it in terms of the Italian meaning of the word which is to go back and recover memory. And so it can have strictly from that point of view a *degree* of critical consciousness, of critical hindsight. To deal with the notion of critical hindsight *is* necessary so that we *do not* forget the conflicts which exist and existed within a community. I don't think there any way that we can escape the pressure of history, the shaping forces of history, although different people can have different perspectives on how that history has been shaped and how it has been used. *But* we have to have our own sense of "*Je me souviens*," to use the *québécois* nationalist slogan. We do have to remember the legacies of slavery, segregation, and the pressures that these imposed on our community. In one sense that process can be nostalgic. On the other hand, we need to have that sharply critical stance.

I would like to talk about a specific use of history in one of your works. In "Whylah Falls," you suggest that the only way to tell the truth is "to disguise it" as fiction. Would you elaborate on that?

Yes. In some ways, that work did come out of my own personal experiences and also out of the stories that people told me that seemed to have some basis in reality, some basis in lived, biographical detail, and I wanted to be true to that, to bear witness to that. But, at the same time, I realized that for one thing I couldn't use real names, and that in some instances, perhaps, I would have to bend or alter some story lines in order to arrive at the particular truth of fiction. So there was a bit of a compromise. There was truth in what I wrote in terms of narrative, in terms of characters and events, but I did find it essential as well to alter things, so that in the end it is more a work of fiction.

I'm interested in this notion of "truth" as you present it here. In the same work, in fact on the same page, you also write "I know that this traitor language can turn / One truth into another or even / Against itself. Yet it is all we have." And I'm

reminded of the character Shelley's mistrust of language and, by extension, of Xavier Zachary, the poet figure. Could you talk about the power and limitations of language and the responsibility that places on the poet?*

Well, we know that reality is constructed to a large extent through language, or that our understandings of reality are dependent upon constructions rooted in language use. Being part of the population which has been at the receiving end of rather negative constructions, I think it is legitimate to have a distrust of how language gets used, in particular, how it gets used by those in power to disenfranchise others and to suggest that others deserve their disenfranchisement because they are poor, because they are ignorant, because they have a tendency toward crime, because their genes are defective, because they are of "naturally" lower intelligence, and so forth. All these various arguments which have been used, and are still used to support racism, are dependent upon certain constructions in language. For a long time these constructions were very potent and resulted in self-hatred within the black community itself, and were a denial of reality, as a matter of fact, because there were plenty of people who always went against these stereotypes and clichés and constructions. Particularly within the black community, I think one is writing against these received notions of blackness. And while at the same time one wants to create more realistic notions of blackness, one still has to be aware that one is working with a very defective device, or a device which can also be used against one. It's a two-edged sword, and we have to try to use it to defend and preserve our community on the one hand, and on the other hand it can also be used against us.

Given the focus on Africadia as a place in your poetry, I wonder if you might comment on what for you is the meaning of place?

I think for me this goes back to my answer to the first question which is, in a sense, the construction of an Africadian tradition within Nova Scotia. What I'm trying to do in my own work, and what I try to encourage others to do as well, is to be really *conscious* about it. For instance, I'm interested in re-writing the map of Nova Scotia. I mean, why should I call Hants County "Hants County?" I'll call it "States County," after a black family surname. Same thing with Digby County; that's Jarvis County for me. In the same way that the Mi'kmaq people have gone back to the original Mi'kmaq names for many of the places in this province in order to lay claim to it, we need to reclaim the province because we have been disenfranchised; we've been ignored, we've been erased in a sense from the map. In the case of Africville, we literally were bulldozed away and then just last year they changed the place-name Negro Point; they erased it from the map of Halifax. I think the black community should have been up in arms over that. I mean, we may not call ourselves Negro any more, but the fact that bit of land was called Negro Point represented our history. The city may have had good liberal reasons for wanting to get rid of it, thinking, "Oh, maybe this is an insult"; but in fact there was no community consultation, and it was just erased from the map. Tolerance means nothing if it doesn't mean the acceptance of difference and therefore the preservation and maintenance of difference. It's not good enough to say we'll accept you if you're like us. No. That's the liberal point of view. The conservative point of view, which is my point of view, is that "I accept you while you're different, and I value your difference. I'm not going to say that you have to be like me for me to accept you." *That* is intolerance of the grossest kind. And Africville was about that. Africville was about a liberal welfare state saying we cannot accept a black community; we have to destroy that community; we cannot accept its existence. It would have been far better to have said let us improve the housing; let us ensure that anyone who wants to live in Africville can—no matter who they are, no matter what their religious or racial background may be. I'm not in favour of segregation at all;

I'm totally opposed to it. But I do think that it's important that communities be able to exist so long as they do not keep other people from joining that community.

In terms of constructing this place of Africadia, what I'm attempting to do is to reassert difference and to look at Nova Scotia as an altered state. Of course, it wasn't originally Nova Scotia, anyway. It's a name that gets imposed, a Latin name, meaning New Scotland, so why can't we give it our own name? Let's call it Africadia. Let's make it an African place, since Africans live here. And let's re-orient our understanding of the province and its traditions and its history from our own unique vantage point, our own particularity. But to go further, for me as well, Africadia, since it isn't in a sense a real physical place, it becomes, therefore, very much a mythical notion, an intellectual construct, a soulful notion. And I've defined it as a place where the *free* self can live, a green space where the free self can live. As Frederick Ward says in his fine poem on Africville, "Africville ain't a place, it's us." It's in us, and that's my view of Africadia. It may not necessarily have to exist as a state with an anthem and standing army [laughs], but it is important that we understand that we have this unique vantage point which does exist within ourselves, and which is manifested in different ways at different times in different places with different groupings of people of African descent in this place that on paper we call Nova Scotia. But I don't think we have to accept these standard notions, and that it is important to claim the place for ourselves, and rename, reorder, rethink the whole thing.

Is this what you have in mind when, in the collection "Lush Dreams/Blue Exile," you suggest that the place names heading each section "refer to states of mind" rather than actual geographies? Among the place names are Africadia and Sierra Leonia, and I was wondering whether you would comment on what the imaginary geography of Africadia in particular means to you.

I think it's kind of an ideal place. It's a place of communion, and communion can take place around a kitchen table, with a bottle of rum, or something like that. It need not even be tied again to anything political or religious, but a place where people feel free to express themselves, to be themselves. I can think of the Baptismal ceremonies, with people wearing their white robes going down to the water, wading into the water and so on. It can be people singing, playing music of one sort or another. It can be all of that. And I suppose it also reflects a realization of the highest aspirations of the Canadian state in terms of notions of equality and liberty, and so it would also encapsulate these notions. And it's also a beleaguered state, a besieged state, a place that needs to be defended as well as explained, interpreted, in our own terms, and so it becomes an intellectual geography, a spiritual geography, for me.

[. . .]

I'd like to turn now to the work you've done representing the contemporary Afro-Nova Scotian, or as you've christened it, Africadian cultural renaissance, and I would like to begin by asking you to talk about the term itself.

The term seems to have arisen in 1983, which was an interesting year because a lot of things were coming about at that time. We had the play *Freedom* which was developed by students at Cole Harbour High, which was playing as part of the Nova Scotia Drama Festival, the scholastic drama festival, an annual event. Also my own first book of poetry came out that summer; David Woods produced a play that summer which was called "For Elsie Dorrington." *Four the Moment* was off the ground and running; they were beginning to perform across the country, and Walter Borden was developing his one-man show, *Tightrope Time*. Oh, and of course I can't neglect to mention Edith Clayton and her basket-weaving that was attracting attention. Maxine Tynes was also appearing on Arthur Black's show *Basic Black*, and doing broadcasts out of CBC Halifax. There seemed to

be, suddenly, this coalescence of people and forces that were interested in Africadian creative work of one sort or another coming out of our community at that time. It was Burnley "Rocky" Jones who first described this focus of interests as a renaissance . . . but four years later Rocky was against the idea of calling it a renaissance. He felt that there had been no break in the artistic and cultural development of the community. He's probably right about that. As he said, a lot of it took place within the church, and going back into the minutes I can see that, yes, people were putting on plays, people had been doing things. But I think what was different, beginning in the late 1970s and flowering into a more determined consciousness in the early 1980s, was that we did have a conscious group of people running around calling themselves artists—I mean people who were really serious, and who could afford to be really serious about it, since by that point we had developed a means to create art and survive, and not have to dedicate ourselves entirely to just making a living. Also, I think that since so much of this work does recall or build upon the Black Loyalist inheritance or experience, we can call it a renaissance, because there has been, to go back to the word nostalgia, a need for retrieving the memories and cultural traditions suggested by that experience. And so much of the "art" has been about going back to, or going through the historical record, and dramatizing certain incidents in the life of the community. To go back to the idea of spiritual geography, I can see this being manifested in the sense of renaming this place for ourselves. Also the idea of commemoration—recognizing our own heroes and their contributions to our community as well as to the larger Nova Scotian society—has been encapsulated in the idea of renaissance.

It is political as well as cultural. We see a real uprising in political organization and aspiration and intervention within various social arenas in the province, and that in turn helped to fuel or support some of the artistic endeavours. I know myself, with my involvement with the Weymouth Falls Justice Committee, and the whole fight around the Graham Jarvis killing, that this manifests itself at least in part in the desire to write about it, and to enlist the aid of other artists as well in discussing the situation. You can see this in the songs of *Four the Moment*, not only those that I've written, but those by Delvina [Bernard]. This is also true of Faith Nolan with her album *Africville*, in 1986, and that [Africville] has of course been a major theme for so many of us—Maxine Tynes, and Sylvia Hamilton as well with her movies, and investigation of women's history. There has been a strong connection between the need for political protest and intervention, and the desire to create artistic works of one sort of another. So, I do think that we can legitimately talk about a renaissance and that we also have to couch it in conscious political terms representing the need of a people to assert a presence. Maxine Tynes has a poem, "Black Song Nova Scotia," which ends simply with "We are here. We are here." In the context of our history in this place, that line is important, because we constantly have the feeling that "We aren't here. We aren't here" in terms of the larger society.

[. . .]

Do you see yourself and other Africadian writers functioning as a kind of vanguard for the black Nova Scotian community?

I don't know. At times I have; at times I've wanted to believe so, although there are elements of [W.E.B.] DuBois's talented tenth notion, of "We're the special ones, we get to lead everybody." There is a kind of bourgeois sensibility attached to that idea, but I don't know. It might even be better to think of it just in the sense of, well, some of us have to do some things. We just have to. I mean, that's just the way it is. Because not everyone is in a position to articulate certain problems, or to engage in certain struggles without incurring a tremendous cost. So those of us who can, do; many of us do. So, we may function as a

vanguard, but I don't know if it's conscious, and I'm not sure in the end that we can actually . . . I suppose we do, because there is leadership provided. Certainly when someone like Rocky [Jones] sets up the Dal[housie University] program for Mi'kmaqs and Blacks [Transition Year Program] that's a leadership role and it makes it possible for others to come behind. The same thing with the Black United Front, because you would find that almost everybody who has done anything in the black community, of whatever sort, has put in at least four months working at BUF. We can disparage it as much as we like, but Rocky [Jones] worked there, Walter [Borden] worked there, Sylvia [Hamilton] worked there, I worked there. David Woods worked there. I mean, almost everyone who's doing anything was on the BUF payroll. So even though most of us often found it quite regressive and not up to speed in terms of dealing with political problems, even though many of us got fired, or left in a huff from that organization, nevertheless, I think it did provide some training, and a place to air political disagreements with some of the leadership in the community and also it's a place to put certain ideas into action. "Vanguard" may be almost too grandiose a term, but certainly we have been involved in activities which have led to progressive development.

What about the dimension of your work as artists putting a Canadian and in fact specifically Nova Scotian spin on notions of blackness—I mean, to what extent is your poetry and the works of other artists read in the black community? Does your work put you in the position of vanguard in that respect?

Perhaps in some ways, because if we're marginalized within Nova Scotia and its history, we're even further marginalized within Canadian history and Canadian understandings of blackness, which are now invested much more with an understanding of blackness as related to the Caribbean and, although to a much much lesser extent, to Africa, and also to Black America. But there is a lack of understanding that Canada also practised slavery, that black people have been part of this country for a long, long, long time, and we have deep roots here. This position raises heckles with more recent arrivals, in some cases. I just attended a conference on black Canadian writing in Ottawa, in September, and there was a debate about this. I was on a panel with Adrienne Shadd who comes from the historic Ontario black community and we were both engaged in projects to go back, particularly to the nineteenth century and dig for whatever writers we can find, in order to construct this tradition of black Canadian writing, and at least two or three members of the audience who are first-generation West Indian Canadians objected to this, or at least didn't quite understand why the project was necessary. They said, you've got to confess that a lot of literature began with our arrival. That's absolutely right, but the problem with that is that it marginalizes—again—all those people who were struggling in obscurity, and who created whatever literature they did create against tremendous odds. This fact is important for us because we know that our history counts, and that it cannot be simply subsumed within the history that's being created by the more recent arrivals. There is a definite tension there.

Within the general construct of the African-Canadian community, there are all these further fissures, conflicts, or struggles within, over claims of identity and notions of blackness. My work is very much an effort as well not just to represent blackness in Nova Scotia and in Canada but also blackness within the black community, a particular Africadian blackness within the larger Canadian black community, and even the larger international black community because, as I was just saying, we are also erased within that context. Our blackness is not seen as being important. In fact, let me take as an example Paul Gilroy's book [*The Black Atlantic: Modernity and Double Consciousness*]. He hardly talks about Canada. It's not part of

the Black Atlantic! And that's a problem, even though he does mention the fact that Delaney wrote *Blake* while he was living in Canada, which, I would argue, makes it the first black Canadian novel—the fourth black American novel, but the *first* black Canadian novel. Now if we can claim Louis Hémon as a *québécois* writer, a Canadian writer, when he only lived here while he wrote *Maria Chapdelaine*, then I can't see why we can't do the same thing with martin Robinson Delaney. And I will, damn it! Why not? We have to claim all the writers and novelists we can from the nineteenth century.

I see our project as being part and parcel of what was necessary for mainstream Canadian culture in the 1960s: to do what Margaret Atwood described as search and rescue missions, to go back and reclaim people who'd been lost, and even those who could be claimed only tangentially as Canadian. In fact it might be helpful to read *Blake, or the Huts of America* from a Canadian perspective. You know, Delaney wrote it in Chatham, and so there are aspects of African-American culture which can probably only be understood from a Canadian perspective, which will be a difficult thing to sell to African-Americans! But our project is reflective of, and in fact influenced by, that effort, which is very consciously still being carried out, on the part of mainstream Canadians to construct a Canadian literary tradition. Canadian women writers have done the same thing, saying, "Who were our foremothers?" And by doing that, you reconstruct, you reconfigure the entire Canadian canon. It has to look different once you start to include all the people who have been left out, and the same thing will be true once we start to understand that Canadian literature also consists of African-Canadian writers who were writing a long time ago, and also the slave narratives out of the nineteenth century, which have never been accepted as part of Canadian literature. Why not? I think largely because of the mainstream Canadian need to distinguish ourselves positively from the United States. We've come up with this myth that there was no slavery here, or that if there was, that it wasn't as bad as the American slavery, as a means of saying, "See, we're better than them." While it's good that we remind ourselves of our difference, the myth is also dangerous in that it does cause us to repress elements of our history that ought to be confronted. In fact, the Canadian Civil Liberties Union recently published a poll which found that 83 per cent of Canadians were ignorant of that fact that slavery existed in this country. That's phenomenal. There's a reluctance on the part of the mainstream to embrace or understand the dimensions of black history within this country because we don't want to deal with racism, because that's meant to be an American problem, not a Canadian one.

[. . .]

You brought up Paul Gilroy, and one of the things for me that runs through "The Black Atlantic," which is also connected to the definition of modernity that he articulates, is the history of colonialism. How would you talk about the anti-modern impulse in Africadian culture in relation to colonialism or postcolonialism?

First of all, to go back to Gilroy, the colonialism that he's most concerned with is that of African-Americans, or what he calls "Americocentrism" at one point in the work; in fact, when I eventually write something on this in the next few weeks, the title of my piece is going to be "Must all Blackness be American?" His work did touch this off for me, as did Walter Borden's play, which I argue draws upon this African-American writer, Lorraine Hansberry, in order to decentre her, to pry her loose from an African-American context and in a sense Canadianize her, or Africadianize her, I suppose, which is part and parcel of the postcolonial project. This is what we have to do, in order to represent our own subjectivity. There's a little bit of Harold Bloom's notion of the anxiety of influence, too, embedded within this whole notion of needing to rewrite the imperial script, to go

back to the imperial influences and domesticate them, to make them our own.

This is where I part company with Gilroy really decisively, because he has disparaging comments to make about cultural nationalists whom he sees as being the root of all evil, and to a certain extent that's right—taken to an extreme, any nationalism is dangerous. On the other hand, I argue, you can never get rid of it. I suggest that even in Gilroy's own work, this is a huge contradiction. He's very conscious of what he calls Americocentrism and the need to contest this as someone writing form Britain, and someone wanting to accent the fact that not all blackness is American. Some ideas of blackness come from Africa, from the Caribbean, and even from Britain, and the idea of trying to create one standard blackness is very dangerous because we're all heterogeneous, and one cannot be essentialist or reductive about it. But at the same time, the very notion of a Black Atlantic reintroduces nationalism, because what it creates then is a different understanding of Pan-Africanism. This is what he ends up creating because even he cannot eliminate the idea of blackness, and it obviously must have some cogency; it must have some agency because it continues to persist. He didn't focus *enough* on what I think is an underlying theme, which is that black Americans really dominate the discourse about blackness. Instead of really contesting that, what he in fact did was write about African-American writers: DuBois, [Richard] Wright, [James] Baldwin, Delaney, and [Toni] Morrison. And I think he's right to emphasize the interconnectedness of so much of the thought and song, but nevertheless this thought gets promoted and gets produced and gets disseminated by African-Americans, and why is that? Or even if people come from elsewhere, it's Black America where they end up, really promoting their ideas or seeing them come to fruition there.

We are interested. I think like postcolonial writers elsewhere, in domesticating these so-called foreign or imperial influences. In fact, I think that Africadia is an interesting entity because we draw *so much* from African-American culture, *so much, it's amazing!* Well, I suppose it's not all that amazing since it's a natural culture for us to draw upon, given that the experience of being a minority is similar, and African-American culture is so widely disseminated. Even as a kid, growing up, it was not uncommon for me to see *Ebony* or *Jet* or *Essence*. From time to time, the church would deliberately go looking for more black-focused publications and so forth, coming out of the African-American experience. Our ministers would often come from the United States. So there's also been a constant injection of African-American influence into Africadia. But one of the things I want to do now, and I've just started this in terms of looking at Walter Borden's work, is to look at how the influence has been domesticated, how it's been rewritten and reinscribed so that it does suggest a more Nova Scotian or Africadian perspective, which goes back to what I was saying about cultural nationalism never disappearing. It's always there. One never does accept willy nilly cultural symbols, but I think, ultimately, in our own cultural productions that we end up making something Canadian. I think we do embrace the influence disseminating from that particular culture but we also change it.

You've contended that it is impossible to divorce the Africadian renaissance from nationalist thought. Why is that?

Well, again, this goes back to the question you raised about anti-modernism versus modernism, and again I'm going to go back to Grant. As Grant argues, any movement toward a nationalist vision has to be against modernity, it has to be anti-modern, so any art work which is going to talk about the experiences of Africadians as being a distinctive experience is engaging in a nationalist program. We are engaging in the construction of a particular vision, the construction of a particular identity which has to be to some extent "essentialist." Now essentialism

carries such negative connotations these days because so many people are opposed to nationalism, and I think this is a misunderstanding, because for one thing, nationalism will always be with us. It can never be totally obliterated and neither should it be, as far as I'm concerned, even though it must be kept in check. I think you need to have a certain amount of nationalism to exist as a distinctive group but at the same time, you have to have enough openness—liberalism, if you like—in order to get along with others. I think that what we should move toward is some universal understanding of human rights so that we do not have people being oppressed. At the same time, and it is going to require a fine balance, we also have to allow for the articulation and preservation of cultural difference, so long as it's non-violent, so long as it's not invested in coercions of others even within a group along the lines of gender and so forth. But that doesn't necessarily mean that we all have to follow the same things . . .

My argument is that society consists of this interconnecting but also contesting groups. If you accept this vision of reality, you understand that women will form groups to advance their rights; minorities will form groups, and do. Workers will form groups, and do, etc. Conservatism is about preserving notions of community and the social good, and the state as representing the people and so it appears to be unprogressive. But one can argue that a conservative vision does allow for progressiveness, and does allow for innovation, and in fact, I think that Africadian writers, when we look at it from a postcolonial point of view, can be seen as domesticating ideas of artistic development, and by domesticating, conserving them, nationalizing them. I think you've got to have cultural interchange and exchanges of ideas in order to grow, and in order to adapt as well, but the crucial point here is that this transformation take place on your own terms and not someone else's. That's when it becomes imperialistic. If we're going to value diversity, we have to value the preservation of diversity, which means that you adapt foreign influences on your own terms.

I want to ask you about the difficulties of producing as an artist in Canada, but particularly as a black artist in Canada, and I want to put that in the context once again of imperialism and multiculturalism. Peter Li has argued that Canada's multiculturalism policy has created a two-tiered, separate-but-not-equal funding system that continues to marginalize the work of ethnic minorities by creating a dichotomy between "Art," which is white and predominantly Anglo-Saxon, and "folklore," which is what everyone else does. I'd like to know what your thoughts are on this. I'd also like you to talk about the pressures created by the overwhelming economic influence of the US and the influence of US culture in Canada, and the kinds of difficulties that presents for a community of artists trying to get funding and being able to produce here, and particularly for black Canadian artists.

First of all, to deal with the second one, and this goes back to something I was saying earlier about the need for English Canada, but also Quebec, to define themselves vis-à-vis the US, and what this then often creates is a tendency to repress minority contributions to the state and to the culture and to the society. So that to oppose, say Norman Mailer, we have Margaret Atwood in English Canada, or Anne Hébert in Quebec, and through this tendency artists who come from minority communities are then further marginalized, or just kept marginalized, because they're not seen as contributing to the over-arching need, particularly among the cultural communities, to create a Canadian identity, or to maintain or foster a Canadian identity. They are seen as being preternaturally "other." They are seen as perhaps needing to combat the "local" problems of racism or linguistic annihilation, or perhaps as still being implicated in conflicts arising from their "homelands" and therefore not really having anything to contribute to the over-arching Canada-versus-the-US

mode that most of our cultural production takes place within. This has been true even in terms of the reception of my own work. There were a couple of reviews of *Whylah Falls* which basically suggested it wasn't Canadian. In fact, one writer said quite explicitly that the work didn't seem to be rooted in the Canada that "we" know, and that the writer (myself) seemed like a ghost among "us." It was a good review, but I wrote a letter to say, "I take umbrage with your use of these terms, suggesting that somehow I am not part of this 'we' and this 'us' that you mention"; and the reviewer was predictably "hurt" by this. . . . I remember sitting on a jury for the Ontario Arts Council in 1991. It was a blind competition, and we were looking at various manuscripts that had come in from artists looking for support and publishers looking for support for various projects, and one of the manuscripts, which I thought was really excellent, dealt with Arab-Canadian history; it was a magical realist thing and it dealt with the history of that community in Toronto around the First World War, and I thought it was just a beautifully written piece, so full of life and energy, and better than a lot of the other stuff that we'd seen, but the reaction of one of the very well-known Canadian writers who was on that jury was, "It's not Canadian." You know, the guy who wrote it, as it turns out, is a third-generation Canadian of Arab descent. So, I think these are all concrete examples of the kinds of constructions that take place among mainstream Canadian cultural industries and workers vis-à-vis artists coming from minority groups.

As a writer of African descent who's also Canadian, I have this need to continue to reach out to my fellow and sister Canadians and educate them at the same time that I also need to speak to members of my own racial and regional community or communities. So this is the same battle that all of us have—Dionne Brand, Austin Clarke, and many others. Actually, I came across a review of Dany Laferrière last year, in *Nuit*

Blanche by somebody, I forget his name. He was reviewing Laferrière's latest book, which is *Chroniques de la derive douce*, and he didn't like the book, but his attack was interesting because it did reveal a racist point of view. He talked about Laferrière "spitting in our white sauce." I don't think there was a single letter to the editor to protest that guy's review. Not one! And it's a mass market publication in Quebec. I'm sure that Haitian writers suffer the same marginalizations and disenfranchisements that writers of minority background in English Canada also face. So you have constantly to negotiate this Canadianness thing.

And now I'm getting it doubly, because a review of *Whylah Falls* just appeared in the *African American Review*, and they're claiming me as an African-American writer! So, you know, it's one damnation or another. In any event, my Canadianness is constantly being erased. Constantly! The question "Where are you from?"—which gets asked of writers of African descent, especially—raises hackles. There have been essays written about that question. Adrienne Shadd has one in the collection *Talking about Difference*, edited by Carl James and herself, and she talks about how this question is meant to ignore the possibility that people of colour are also Canadian, because there's just such a construction that whiteness is equal to Canadianness that we constantly have to negotiate and contest and quarrel with and change, and it doesn't even seem to matter how long you've been here. It still comes up and people from Nova Scotia and southern Ontario and New Brunswick are constantly being cast as American within the Canadian context, or if they're in Toronto they may be thought to be Caribbean. You know, they ask, "What island are you from?" And you say, "Cape Breton," or something like that. This tendency not to recognize the Canadianness comes in many different colours.

And in terms of multiculturalism, you're right, absolutely right. Particularly the way

it was envisioned and carried out under the Trudeau government, it did tend to emphasize the folkloric, the *supposedly* folkloric, and it has come in for attack because of that. But at the same time, we have to realize that a lot of those multiculturalism grants went to producing work which we are now studying and thinking about, and recognizing as being very significant Canadian work, and that many of those grants that may have been intended in a paternalistic way—simply to say to Italians in Toronto, "Well, continue to produce your newspaper"—may also have provided spaces for people to write. In the African-Canadian community, we took those grants and we used them. There was a conference held at McGill in 1980 on the role of the black artist in Canada, and it was funded by Multiculturalism, Secretary of State. The bureaucrats at the end of the chain might have thought, "Oh, we'll give black people something to do"; but, hey, we used that conference. That conference made it possible for us to meet from all across the country, for the first time. I went up there, David Woods went up there, Sylvia Hamilton was there, and I know that was a profound experience for all of us, coming out of Nova Scotia, to go there and meet black artists and writers and filmmakers and sculptors from Vancouver, and Montreal itself, and Toronto, and we were all there together discussing a black aesthetic and how does that work in the Canadian context, and deciding that it didn't work very well, particularly given the linguistic divide. In fact, the conference took place a week after the first Quebec referendum, and the Haitian artists basically walked out, and there was also a division between the Caribbean-born and native-born artists, and that took place on the last day of the conference. But still, it was a tremendous experience. I think multiculturalism has been taken and used by the ethnic cultural communities to benefit themselves, despite whatever paternalistic ideas the government had for promoting the programs. True, multiculturalism has created a second-tier kind of system in that works produced with a multiculturalism grant were not accorded the same kind of priority as works that came out with the Canada Council support. They were seen as perhaps coming from a ghettoized community, and there has been a problem along those lines, but at the same time, I don't think we could have avoided those problems anyway, even if everything had come out with Canada Council support as opposed to multiculturalism support, because there had been a reluctance to accept works by people from different ethnic backgrounds than either the prevailing Anglo or French backgrounds, and these works would have been marginalized or treated in a secondary way, anyway, no matter what.

What is your current project?

Well, as you know, I've got this *Beatrice Chancy* thing I'm working on. I hope it works out. I see it as being a postcolonial intervention once again in that I'm taking a story which began in late Renaissance Italy, and I'm transferring it to the Africadian context in the years 1801 and 1802. The original story has been done by everybody—Shelley, Artaud,

Dumas, Corrado Ricci, Moravia—and they've all been writing about this family called the Cenci, and particularly the female heroine in the story, Beatrice Cenci. Of course, I've anglicized the surname, and there've been changes in terms of plot and other characters, too, but essentially the story line is the same; I've just transferred it to this place and a different time. And racially it's different too, since it's not an all-white story in my case, but one in which the mixed-race daughter of a white master is raped by him and then kills him, and is hanged by the government of Nova Scotia at the end. It's set during the time of slavery and so there's also a kind of incipient slave revolt. I've been writing this work deliberately for the stage; and, actually, it started off as a libretto for an opera which is being written by James Rolfe, a Canadian composer from Ottawa/Toronto, now in residence at Princeton, where he's working on a PhD in music. We've been working together on this project for the last three years, and there will be the two versions: there'll be the libretto and there will be the verse play which I call a *Passional*.

Historical Interpretations

3 From Julia Lalande, "The Roots of Multiculturalism: Ukrainian-Canadian Involvement in the Multiculturalism Discussion of the 1960s as an Example of the Position of the 'Third Force,'" Originally published in *Canadian Ethnic Studies* 38, 1 (2006): 47–64.

INTRODUCTION

On 8 October 1971, Prime Minister Pierre Trudeau announced the first Canadian policy of multiculturalism to the House of Commons and only one day later addressed an audience of Ukrainian-Canadians at a Ukrainian Canadian Congress convention in Winnipeg.[1]

This public appearance is often interpreted as a sign that Trudeau acknowledged the strong contribution of Ukrainians during the multiculturalism discussions of the 1960s. Even today, Ukrainians are generally hailed as having been one of the most active participants in the entire debate on multiculturalism (Isajiw 1983, 113; Ferguson 1991, 307–8; Burnet and

Palmer 1988, 224). However, the specifics of their positions in the debate have not, thus far, been thoroughly studied.[2] As Marcel Martel points out, research in the area of politics usually focuses on politicians and largely ignores ethnic and other interest groups (2004, 1), but these groups are very important in the context of the multiculturalism debate. This article offers insight into Ukrainian-Canadians' position in the debate and thus an impression of the hopes and concerns of the third force. The third force consisted of the "other ethnic groups," because at the time of the debate, the Royal Commission on Bilingualism and Biculturalism (hereafter B&B Commission) divided Canadian society into three categories: the Founding Nations consisting of British and French Canadians, other ethnic groups, and First Nations. However, the B&B Commission only dealt with the first two categories (Government 1967, XXI–XXII).

Ukrainians are an interesting example of the position of the third force because they were (numerically) one of the largest of the other ethnic groups in Canada. According to the B&B Commission, they were also the best organized and most active group and could potentially lead the discussion.[3] Why were they so actively involved in the debate, and what did they hope to achieve? What kind of demands did they make, and how did they rationalize them? To what extent can we apply their position to the third force in general? How did the contribution of the other ethnic groups shape the discussion? [. . .]

DEFINITION OF MULTICULTURALISM

Multiculturalism is an important aspect of contemporary Canadian society, but it is often not quite clear what is meant by multiculturalism, and different authors have pointed out the ambiguity of the term. Will Kymlicka makes us aware that terms like multiculturalism, citizenship, federalism, or cosmopolitanism "are all normatively-laden, and while we often think we know what they mean, they are surprisingly ambiguous and vulnerable to misuse and inconsistent application" (Kymlicka 1998, 8). The ambiguity of the terminology is further influenced by the fact that the concept of multiculturalism can be divided into three components. On one hand, we have what Evelyn Kallen calls "social reality" (Kallen 1982, 51), meaning that people of different ethnic backgrounds live together in one society. Then there is the ideology of multiculturalism, the interpretation of which depends on the respective individual or institution. Finally, there is the policy of multiculturalism that depends on the respective government. Ideology and policy are not necessarily mutually exclusive. They can be intertwined, thereby influencing each other (Bociurkiw 1978; Kallen 1982). This article deals only with two of the three components of multiculturalism—the ideology and the policy, or rather, with their roots, which are embedded in the discussion of the 1960s. That was a time when multiculturalism was a very modern concept, and Canadians were searching for their meaning of multiculturalism, their ideology, and eventually, their policy. This process of developing an idea of a multicultural Canada started at a time of crisis and change in the country.

THE 1960S IN CANADA AND THE CREATION OF THE COMMISSION ON BILINGUALISM AND BICULTURALISM

Throughout the western hemisphere, the 1960s were a decade of revolution and change. In the United States, for example, the Vietnam War ignited protest movements that were further influenced by the civil rights and women's movements as well as a whole new youth culture. These developments swept across the border into Canada where they had a profound effect, especially on the younger generation (Owram 1996, 159–84; 216–47). However, the discussion on bilingualism and biculturalism (which later evolved into a debate on multiculturalism) was triggered by one of the major events of the 1960s specific to Canada—the Quiet Revolution in Quebec. During the 1960s, a new French-Canadian elite emerged that was no longer tied to the church, thereby developing a new kind of nationalism (Taylor 1993). The Quebec question gained especially strong attention from the media owing to the rise of violence, in particular in connection to the emergence of the Front de Libération du Quebec. In order to tackle the increasing problems affecting Canadian society—the threat of secession and the unrest in Quebec in general—the Royal Commission on Bilingualism and Biculturalism was established in 1963. Its task was to examine the state of bilingualism and (initially) biculturalism in Canada, focusing on the federal administration and on public and private organizations as well as opportunities for bilingualism in Canada (Government 1965, 143–44). Many groups that were part of the third force (the most vocal of which was the Ukrainian-Canadian community) were exasperated by the commission's focus on bilingualism, but talk of biculturalism frustrated them even more.

DEMANDS OF UKRAINIANS

For Ukrainian-Canadians, the early years of the discussion on multiculturalism coincided with the 75th anniversary of Ukrainian settlement in Canada in 1966.[4] By this time, Ukrainians had evolved into a strong community very much interested in the preservation of its language and traditions. In the 1960s, this concern with conserving their culture was expressed in their strenuous involvement in the multiculturalism debate. For example,

Ukrainians made the most submissions to the B&B Commission, and they actively discussed the issue in the community and in their newspapers (Bociurkiw 1978, 105).[5] Their submissions to the hearings of the B&B Commission, letters to politicians, speeches and addresses, as well as resolutions at community meetings offer insight into their position. The ideas—one could even call them demands—outlined in these sources can be classified into demands for participation, recognition, and equality.

Demands in the area of participation were often connected to the political sphere. At the end of the 1950s, the Diefenbaker government had already taken some steps to incorporate women or members of the third force into the administration. For example, the Minister of Labour Michael Starr was the first Ukrainian appointed to the federal cabinet (Momryk 1987). Encouraged by some preliminary successes, Ukrainians in Canada demanded more political representation for the "smaller ethno-cultural groups," often arguing that "only a person from a given cultural milieu can properly present his group's case, because of his total association and acquaintance with it."[6] In this context, they wanted the community's umbrella organizations—the Ukrainian Canadian Congress (UCC)—to be acknowledged as the official voice of the Ukrainian-Canadian community. As such, the UCC could advise the Canadian government and have more influence on day-to-day politics. As this proposal shows, the quest for more political influence was often connected to the achievement of greater recognition by the government.

Recognition was another catchphrase at the time, and this was a very broad term linked to several areas. Some proposals, such as the one made by Jaroslav Rudnyckyj, a prominent Ukrainian academic representative and a member of the B&B Commission, were rather far-reaching. He stated that Canada should be officially English/French bilingual at the federal level. However, he took into consideration so-called regional languages that also deserved protection, among them Ukrainian, German, and Italian. He proposed an amendment to the British North America Act stating that "notwithstanding anything in this section, any language other than English and French used by 10 per cent or more of the population of an appropriate administrative district of a province or territory shall have the status of a regional language; the legislation of the provision for regional languages shall be vested in the governments concerned" (Rudnyckyj 1967, 155–69). Other recommendations were often made in the sphere of education—one of the major foci of the discussion due to its connection to language development and preservation. Demands were made that Ukrainian (or the other ethnic groups' languages) should be offered as a credited subject in schools where demand existed and should receive matriculation status in universities.[7] The recognition of languages other than French and English was an important issue, because language itself was commonly regarded as the vehicle of culture, especially important for the preservation of religious identity.[8] Having Ukrainian recognized in schools was often seen as one way of ensuring the survival of the language as well as the survival of traditions.

Language was not the only factor considered important in education. School curricula and textbooks were criticized for their western European focus: it was argued that they should have a more international outlook.[9] Especially when it came to writing Canadian history, Ukrainians insisted that the contribution of the other ethnic groups should be taken into consideration. This would, of course, make more research necessary and go beyond the school's realm (Ukrainian National Youth Federation 1966, 14–22). Apart from educational issues, the media also played an important role. Groups recommended that the contribution of the third force should be more visible in the media,[10] such that the community could reach the wider Canadian public.[11] The media was a topic widely discussed in Canada, since the Canadian Broadcasting Corporation (hereafter the CBC) continually refused to broadcast in a language other than French or English (Ryan 1975, 151). All these demands in the sphere of language, education, and the media had one thing in common: they were directed toward a general recognition of the contribution of the other ethnic groups to Canada's development.

Another central aspect of such demands was the quest for equality. Ukrainians feared that they were not on quite the same footing as members of the Founding Nations. They were afraid that their aspirations were not accepted as equal to those of the British or the French Canadians. Walter Tarnopolsky, a writer on multiculturalism, law, and human rights and one of the many active Ukrainian-Canadian representatives, expressed this feeling of inequality and the hope that the new policy of multiculturalism might change the situation for Canadians of non-British, non-French origin. Referring to an editorial in the *Toronto Telegram* in which he was criticized for urging the ending of the monarchical tradition (as a Canadian of non-British descent), Tarnopolsky stated:

> The editorial in typical fashion said: "Why doesn't he go home where he came from?" Well home, of course, is Gronlid, Saskatchewan—and I do go home as frequently as I can. The point that I want to emphasize is that until the multiculturalism policy was adopted, and until this policy is effectuated, the fact that I was born in Canada would never put me on quite the same basis as someone who might have been born in the United Kingdom, and who had just immigrated to Canada.[12]

[. . .]

THE PIONEERING ARGUMENT

From the time of the first Indian-European contact in 1497 to Confederation in 1867, two groups determined Canadian history— the British and the French who explored and settled the country (Kelley and Trebilcock 1998, 21–60). Owing to this history, the B&B Commission saw the term "founding races" as "an allusion to the undisputed role played by Canadians of French and British origin in 1867 and long before Confederation" (Government 1967, XXII). During the 1960s, it became obvious that parts of the organized faction of the Ukrainian-Canadian community intended to jump on the bandwagon. They tried to make the case that they also had a special position in Canada owing to their experience as settlers. This argument— put forward by organizations encompassing members of all waves and generations—could only be made by linking the entire community to the first wave, whose many members had settled in dense compact blocks on the prairies and had a significant impact on the land and its surroundings (Darlington 1991; Lehr 1991; Martynowych 1991). During the debate on multiculturalism, the early settlement experience was used as an argument to support claims for recognition, participation, and equality. One could even say that the Ukrainian-Canadian community created a "pioneer myth" at this time.

THE PIONEER MYTH

The pioneer myth that dominated Ukrainian-Canadian literature after 1970 encompassed the initial hardships of settlement, the isolation of the early settlers, the discrimination they faced, as well as their constant efforts to succeed in the new country (Mycak 1996, 68ff).[13] The roots of this pioneer myth can be seen during the debate on multiculturalism. In the opinion of the Ukrainians of the 1960s, the early Ukrainian settlers were role models,

even heroes, and the allegory of Ukrainians as pioneers was evoked and perpetuated throughout the discussion.[14] Ukrainians were often referred to as having pioneered the prairies: they had turned wilderness into fertile land through hard physical work. Emphasis was given to the Ukrainian contribution in the area of agriculture, such as prize-winning wheat cultivation.[15] Characteristics attributed to Ukrainian pioneers— such as "a long and intimate contact with the soil" or the "love of freedom"—were often celebrated[16] and sometimes even transferred to the present community. For example, John Yaremko, a lawyer and politician of Ukrainian descent, stated that "if there is a single characteristic common to those of us of Slav descent in this country, it is a burning love of freedom and democracy."[17] In the eyes of many Ukrainians, the pioneering qualities and the hard work of the early settlers put Ukrainians on the same footing as the British or French Canadians.[18] Rudnyckyj went so far as to state that at least some Ukrainians saw themselves as the "founding races" of the prairies[19]—however, as Rudnyckyj himself pointed out this view could not be generalized for the entire community. Nonetheless, as Sonya Mycak states, "this national role— their ordination as a founding people of the Canadian nation—is the fourth motif which marks the prairie pioneer myth" (Mycak 1996, 68). In addition to the mostly agricultural work on the prairies, the Ukrainian involvement in the early Russian exploration missions was also cited in order to create a picture of "true pioneers."[20] As the historiography has shown, features of this myth, such as the hardship of settlement, the struggle to succeed in the country, and the discrimination that early settlers faced were rooted in the historical experience of Ukrainians in Canada (Martynowych 1991; Darlington 1991; Lehr 1991). However, it became a myth once it was generalized for all Ukrainians in Canada and once certain demands were connected to this pioneering experience (at least by part of the community). This implies an exclusive claim that does not take into consideration that Ukrainians were not the first, nor the only, ones to settle the prairies (Friesen 1987).

The 1960s also saw a spread of information on Ukrainians in Canada, further perpetuating the pioneer myth. Generally, publicizing these contributions was meant to celebrate Ukrainian cultural heritage, shed light on the historical roots of Ukrainian settlement in Canada, and reveal the Ukrainian contribution to the development of the country.[21] The third Ukrainian-Canadian senator Paul Yuzyk, for example, wrote *Ukrainian Canadians: Their Place and Role in Canadian Life* in order "to provide Canadians and visitors in Canada during the Centennial Year with all the important, authoritative information, in concise treatise form, about a leading dynamic Canadian ethnic group—the Ukrainian Canadians" (Yuzyk 1967, preface). Dr Vladimir Kaye[22] contributed a study on the early settlement period, thereby providing the first scholarly examination of Ukrainians in Canada (Kaye 1964). Publications such as booklets (often in the context of MA or PhD theses) came from Ukrainian Canadians in different corners of the country. They dealt with the contribution of Ukrainians to Canada and also with aspects of maintaining one's identity—and the corresponding struggle—(Gregorovich 1964; Darcovich 1967; Woycenko 1964). Furthermore, different aspects of Ukrainian-Canadian community life were brought to the attention of a wider audience; for example, the church (Trosky 1968), political life,[23] or the developments of particular communities.[24] In addition to publications focusing exclusively on Ukrainian Canadians, information about them could also be found in the general context of "the contributions of the other ethnic groups," for example, in publications by conferences such as the First National Conference on Canadian Slavs, where the Ukrainians also took a leading role (Slavutych et al. 1966). The 1960s

truly saw a very diverse range of publications concerning Ukrainian-Canadians. For the first time, the community researched and expressed its contributions to Canadian history on a larger scale. This literature was often seen as a tool "to fight for the truth about Ukraine and to take credit for our part in Canadian history."[25] The focus was generally on the contribution of Ukrainians to Canadian society and history, often specifically referring to Ukrainians as pioneers in this context.

Although government officials often referred to Ukrainians as pioneers, they rejected the idea of a special position for Ukrainians in Canada. Using the same argument, Canadian government officials could acknowledge the contribution of Ukrainian settlers and still argue against special rights for them. Additional arguments had to be found to underscore the demands made on behalf of the Ukrainian-Canadian community.

THE IMPORTANCE OF THE SITUATION IN THE HOMELAND

A frequent position taken to reinforce the desire to preserve their heritage was related to the situation in the homeland. Community leaders, especially, viewed activities in Canada in reference to what was going on in Ukraine. As Senator Paul Yuzyk said: "Ukrainians cherish Canadian freedom and democracy, as they are conscious of Ukraine's subjugation and bondage."[26] Indeed, Ukrainians in Canada, whether they were born in Canada or emigrated, had never been able to look back to a free homeland. Furthermore, all of Ukraine was part of the Soviet Union after 1945, and its inhabitants were subject to measures of Russification (Subtelny 2000, 521–6). Ukrainians in Canada, especially those who came as "Displaced Persons" after the Second World War, saw their role as preservers of Ukrainian culture, especially language, in the diaspora.[27] Members of the community felt they had to preserve what they had in Canada,[28] and it was often noted that this task was so much more important to Ukrainians than to other ethnic groups like the Italians or Germans because these groups had the opportunity "to go back" if they desired, an option that did not exist for Ukrainians in Canada.[29]

This "mission" to preserve Ukrainian culture in the diaspora was complicated by the fact that there had been no new wave of Ukrainian immigration since the late 1940s/ early 1950s, and Ukrainian language usage and community participation were declining in Canada (Reitz and Ashton 1980; Darcovich 1980). The preservation of language and heritage was only possible, it was argued, if there was enough money to fund organizations, language classes, and other activities. It was often assumed that the number of people speaking Ukrainian as their mother tongue, for example, would not decline further if there were more interest in minority languages in general and if greater encouragement were given (Woycencko 1964, 13f). In addition to language and culture preservation in Canada, Ukrainians also hoped to influence Canada's foreign policy regarding the Soviet Union, so that the country would "do everything to support and encourage the struggle of the captive nations for liberation."[30] This hope was almost realized when Prime Minister John Diefenbaker openly criticized the Soviet Union in his speech at the United Nations in 1960 (Palmer 1991, 20f; Hilliker 1986, 188f). Although there were other groups in Canada who had their homeland behind the Iron Curtain and who also fought for recognition and for their homeland's liberation, Ukrainians still saw their position as unique in Canada. Manoly Lupul, an education professor at the University of Alberta, made this clear when he stated: "In Canada the Baltic peoples are not numerous, and so it is to Canadians of Ukrainian descent that a phrase made popular by French Canadians in recent years best applies: 'We are not a people like the other(s).' For truly we are not."[31]

PARALLELS TO THE FRENCH CANADIANS

Parallels to the French-Canadian case become obvious upon comparative examination of both groups' position. Aspects like geographical density, the concept of French Canadians as a nation, coupled with the displayed desire and drive to survive were important for French Canadians throughout the multiculturalism discussion (Anderson 1981, 86–93). One argument Ukrainian-Canadians presented to have their group share this category was to indirectly compare their case to that of French Canadians. Ukrainians were presented as pioneers, and their strong bloc settlements in the prairies were offered as a reason for special language rights. Furthermore, it was stressed that they had a strong desire to survive (owing to the situation in the homeland), and maintaining their language was an important component. However, it must be stated that the comparison to the French was seldom directly made. Very few people openly asked that those "who have also concretely contributed to the building, development, and defence of Canada" should receive the same rights as the French Canadians,[32] or stated that the preservation of language was as important to Ukrainians as it was to the French Canadians.[33]

ARGUMENTS AGAINST A SPECIAL STATUS

A different, underlying rationale was put forth in direct co-operation with members of the other ethnic groups; that special status—for anybody—was unconstitutional and contrary to human rights. It was deemed unfair to select only two groups for survival, while the other groups were singled out for eventual assimilation. The case made was that "in democracy, one cannot apply one set of standards and moral principles to one group of citizens, and a different standard for another group of Canadians,"[34] because that would eventually lead to discrimination and devaluation. It was further argued that children would be discouraged from learning their mother tongue if they perceived it as unrecognized or devalued. Tarnopolsky, for example, stated that "a child who sees that the language of his ancestors is not important enough to be studied as a subject will inevitably feel that his forefathers were not quite equal."[35] Furthermore, the question of discrimination often came up in the context of civil service. Community activists feared that people of non-French, non-British background would be disadvantaged because they had to learn two additional languages.[36]

APPLICATION TO THE "THIRD FORCE"

These demands and arguments offer insight into the fears and hopes of the community. Ukrainians in Canada were afraid of being reduced to "second class citizens"[37] and demanded opportunities equal to those of the Anglo and French Canadians. Owing to the situation in the homeland, many Ukrainians in Canada were eager to preserve their heritage and culture, fearing that this might not be possible in the future without the implementation of multiculturalism. They also wanted their contribution to the building of Canada recognized and valued. Parallel to arguments for special status, it was alternately noted that there should be no special group rights because this might be considered unconstitutional. To what extent were these demands and arguments made on behalf of the Ukrainian-Canadian community representative of other groups of the third force?

Certainly, the Ukrainian-Canadian community was the most active participant in the discussion, and some arguments, for example, pioneering or the issue of the homeland, cannot be generalized to all groups, especially not in that combination.[38] Nonetheless, there are common aspects that hold true for many members of the third force. Many groups had an interest in preserving at least part of their heritage, whether it was just for personal reasons or in the context of a personal mission, as many Ukrainians saw it. In addition, many members of the third force feared being reduced to second-class citizens, thus facing discrimination in public life. An aspect that also interested many groups beyond the Ukrainians was the contribution made by other ethnic groups to the development of Canada as a country. Although most (including the majority of the Ukrainian-Canadian community) did not question the concept of two founding nations, they did know that they had made, and continued to make, an important contribution to the country, and they wanted this acknowledged through a multiculturalism policy.[39] Which demands made during the multiculturalism discussion were actually addressed in the policy? [. . .]

THE FOCUS OF THE MULTICULTURALISM POLICY OF THE 1970S

The language issue was high on the Ukrainian-Canadian agenda, and it was answered in 1969 with the Official Languages Act that made English and French the official languages in all federal institutions. The idea of regional languages, brought up by the Ukrainian community during that discussion, was not implemented by the Canadian government. However, the multiculturalism policy acknowledged in 1971 that Canada was a bilingual country with a multicultural character. The government saw its task as assisting all groups to overcome cultural barriers so that they would have the opportunity to "share their cultural expression and values with other Canadians." In order to reach this goal, the government would support the promotion of cultural encounters and help members of all cultural groups to acquire at least one official language. Furthermore, support would be given to research proposals, art displays, and projects that fought racism.[40] Comparing this policy and the first steps taken during the 1970s to appease the Ukrainian-Canadian community, it becomes obvious that the biggest changes and developments took place in the field of recognition. This is especially true for school curricula, textbooks, and the media, as well as general recognition of the contribution of the ethnic groups to the country through more research in this area.[41] However, the new multiculturalism policy confined the preservation of heritage to the private sector. Groups had the chance to preserve their heritage through government programs, but they had to apply for grants, and all efforts to mobilize their members had to come from within the community itself. The multiculturalism policy did not guarantee the ethnic groups' survival, instead focusing more on inter-group relationships.

Many Ukrainians were originally very content with, one could even say excited about, the multiculturalism policy.[42] Most importantly, something was finally implemented: it was officially stated that Canada was a multicultural country and the contribution of the other ethnic groups to Canada was officially recognized. Furthermore, the community now had the possibility of acquiring funds outside their own community, thereby widening their opportunities for survival. However, as the years went by and the make-up of Canadian society changed owing to a large influx of visible minorities, the focus of multiculturalism in Canada changed as well. Combating racism and helping people find their place in Canadian society (for example, through language courses) gained in importance, whereas cultural encounters were no longer a top priority (Burnet and Palmer 1988, 226–7; Avery 1995, 213–18). Many Ukrainians were dissatisfied with these changes, especially since they meant a shortage in budgets for cultural festivals and encounters (Bociurkiw 1978, 110–20). Ukrainians were more interested in preserving the status quo, whereas the multiculturalism policy adapted to changes in Canadian society and thus shifted its focus.

NOTES

1. Library and Archives Canada (hereafter LAC) MG31 D58 Vol. 8, File 27: Notes for the remarks by the Prime Minister to the Ukrainian Canadian Congress, Winnipeg, Manitoba, 9 October 1971.
2. Bociurkiw 1978, Jaworsky 1979.
3. LAC MG31 E55 Vol. 10, File Secretary of State, Resumé of the Report of the Royal Commission on Bilingualism and Biculturalism, Book Four; The Cultural Contribution of the Other Ethnic Groups, 8–15.
4. Martynowych 1991.
5. LAC RG26 Vol. 76, File 1-5-11, Part 4, *Ethnic Scene*, September 1964: A review of opinions, trends, and activities among the ethnic groups in Canada, 5–8; LAC MG31 E55 Vol. 10, File Multiculturalism 1971–1975: Notes for an address to be delivered by the Honourable John Munro, Minister Responsible for Multiculturalism, to the Ukrainian Canadian Committee Congress in Winnipeg, 12 October, n.d., 1.
6. LAC MG31 E55 Vol. 10, File Multiculturalism 1971–1975: Submission to the Joint Parliamentary Committee of the Senate and the House of Commons on the Constitution of Canada by the Ukrainian Alumni Association Toronto, 6ff.
7. LAC MG31 E55 Vol. 9, File Multiculturalism 1964–1971: Bohdan Bociurkiw, Bilingualism and Biculturalism as Seen by Western

Canadians of Other Ethnic Origins, an address presented at the Community Seminar on Bilingualism and Biculturalism at the University of Alberta in Edmonton, 23 April 1964, 5; LAC MG31 D58 Vol. 7, File 3: Submission to the Manitoba Advisory Committee for the Discussion of Bilingualism and Biculturalism, 30 January 1964, by the Ukrainian Catholic Brotherhood of Manitoba, 2f.

8. LAC MG31 E55 Vol. 9, File Multiculturalism 1964–1971: Bohdan Bociurkiw, Bilingualism and Biculturalism, 4; LAC MG31 D58 Vol. 7, File 3: Submission to the Manitoba Advisory Committee for the Discussion of Bilingualism and Biculturalism, 30 January 1964, by St. Andrew's College in Winnipeg, 2f.; LAC MG31 D58 Vol. 7, File 9: Bohdan Krawchenko, Toward a Development of Multiculturalism, an address presented at the Ukrainian Canadian University Students' Union, 8 August 1970, 4.

9. LAC MG31 E55 File Multiculturalism 1964–1971: Brief submitted to the attention of those assembled at the meeting held 19 March 1971, "YHO" Hall, Saskatoon, between representatives of the Saskatoon Ukrainian Community and Mr A. Lapchuk, Secretary of State's Office (brief prepared by the National Executive Canadian Ukrainian Youth Association), 8–9.

10. LAC MG31 E55 Vol. 9, File Multiculturalism 1964–1971: Bohdan Bociurkiw Bilingualism and Biculturalism, 5f; Ukrainian National Youth Federation of Canada 1966, 17f; LAC MG31 D58 Vol. 7, File 3: Submission to the Manitoba Advisory Committee for the Discussion of Bilingualism and Biculturalism, 30 January 1964, by the Markian Shashevich Society of Ukrainian Catholic Teachers, 5–7 (this brief also supported the abovementioned steps concerning language and history in schools).

11. LAC MG31 D58 Vol. 7, File 3: Submission to the Manitoba Advisory Committee for the Discussion of Bilingualism and Biculturalism, 30 January 1964, by the Ukrainian Catholic Women's League of Manitoba, 2.

12. LAC MG31 E55 Vol. 10, File Multiculturalism 1971–1975: The New Policy of Multiculturalism for Canada, an address delivered in Winnipeg at the Conference of Ukrainian Canadian Business and Professional Men's Clubs on Sunday, 10 October (n.d.), following the prime minister's elaboration of the Federal Government's Multiculturalism Policy given at the Congress of Ukrainian Canadians the evening before by W.S. Tarnopolsky, 2.

13. Sonia Mycak points out that the perpetuation of this myth was dependent on government funding through multicultural programs as well as the multicultural ethic in general.

14. Swyripa 1993, 225ff.

15. UNYFC, Canada's Culture, 11–14; LAC MG31 E55 Vol. 9, File Multiculturalism 1964–1971: Debates of the Senate. Maiden speech of the Honourable Paul Yuzyk, Senator, Canada: A Multicultural Nation, 3 March 1964, 6. Members of the first and second wave were also often labelled pioneers (see, for example, the obituary for John Swystun: LAC MG32 C67 Vol. 20, File 9: V. John Swystun, Q.C.).

16. LAC MG31 E55 Vol. 9, File Multiculturalism 1964–1971: An address by the Honourable John Yaremko to the Inter-University Committee on Canadian Slays Conference, 23 May 1971, 2; LAC MG32 C67 Vol. 20, File 10: Complete resolutions passed 14 October 1968, Ukrainian Canadian Congress, Winnipeg, 5f.

17. LAC MG31 E55 Vol. 9, File Multiculturalism 1964–1971: An address by the Honourable John Yaremko to the Inter-University Committee on Canadian Slays Conference, 23 May 1971, 1.

18. LAC MG31 D58, Vol. 9, File 12 (1): Paul Yuzyk, The Emerging New Force in the Emerging New Canada, at the Thinkers' Conference on Cultural Rights, 13–15 December 1968, 3–4.

19. LAC MG31 D58, Vol. 6, File 8: Rudnyckyj, Remarks regarding the texts of Dunton, Dion, and Hawkins—and additional comments regarding interim report, 19 September 1964, 1f.

20. LAC MG31 D58, Vol. 6, File 8: Rudnyckyj, Ethno-Lingual Groups in Canada, 30 January 1964, 3f; LAC MG31 D69, Vol. 6, File 14: Vancouver Sun, 6 December 1973, Ukrainians earned rights in Canada (letter to the editor by Michael Huculak); Subtelny 1988, 539.

21. Swyripa, 1978, 88–117.

22. LAC MG31 D69, Reel 2997, KAYE.

23. LAC MG32 C67 Vol. 18, File 4: Dr Kaye, Golden Jubilee of the Participation of Ukrainians in the Political Life of Canada, 1913–1963.

24. UCC Hamilton Branch, *Salute to Canada, 1867–1967*. Hamilton: UCC, 1967.

25. LAC MG31 D58 Vol. 6, File 7: Andrew Gregorovich, Ukrainian Canadian University Students, 2.

26. LAC MG31 E55 Vol. 9, File Multiculturalism 1964–1971: Maiden Speech of the Honourable Paul Yuzyk, Senator: Canada: A Multicultural Nation, 3 March 1964, 6f.

27. LAC MG31 D58, Vol. 6, File 7: Andrew Gregorovich, Ukrainian Canadian University Students, 2; LAC MG31 D58 Vol. 7, File 3: Submission to the Manitoba Advisory Committee for the Discussion of Bilingualism and Biculturalism, 30 January 1964, by the Ukrainian Catholic Women's League of Manitoba, 1. See also Lalande, 2006.

28. LAC MG31 D58 Vol. 8, File 10 (Multiculturalism): Panchuk on Multi-lingualism and Multiculturalism, no date given (Ukrainian Canadian Veterans Association), 4; LAC MG31 E55 Vol. 10, File Multiculturalism 1971–1975: The New Policy of Multiculturalism for Canada, an address delivered in Winnipeg at the Conference of Ukrainian-Canadian Business and Professional Men's Clubs on Sunday, 10 October, following the Prime Minister's elaboration of the Federal Government's Multiculturalism Policy given by W.S. Tarnopolsky at the Congress of Ukrainian Canadians the evening before, 3.

29. LAC MG31 D58 Vol. 8, File 17: Lupul, The Federal Government, Multiculturalism, and Education in Canada, 9.

30. LAC MG32 C67 Vol. 20, File 10: Complete Resolutions passed 14 October 1968, Ukrainian Canadian Congress, Winnipeg, 5–6.

31. LAC MG31 D58 Vol. 8, File 17: Lupul, The Federal Government, Multiculturalism, and Education in Canada, 7f.

32. LAC MG31 D58 Vol. 7, File 3: Mr V. Solman, Grand Knight, St Josephat Council 4138, Knights of Columbus, to the Manitoba Committee on Bilingualism and Biculturalism, 2.

33. LAC MG31 D58 Vol. 7, File 12: UNF, Montreal Branch, to the Commission of Inquiry on the Position of the French Language and on Language Rights in Quebec, September 1969, 3.

34. LAC MG31 D58 Vol. 7, File 12: UNF, Montreal Branch, to the Commission of Inquiry on the Position of the French Language and on Language Rights in Quebec, September 1969, 3; LAC MG31 E55 File Multiculturalism 1964–1971: Brief submitted to the attention of those assembled at the meeting held 19 March 1971, "YHO" Hall, Saskatoon, between representatives of the Saskatoon Ukrainian Community and Mr A. Lapchuk, Secretary of State's Office (Brief prepared by the National Executive of the Canadian Ukrainian Youth Association), 3.

35. LAC MG31 E55 Vol. 9, File Multiculturalism 1964–1971: *Saskatoon Star Phoenix*, 5 July 1971, Tarnopolsky sees multi-culture future for Canada.

36. LAC MG31 E55 Vol. 9, File Multiculturalism 1964–1971: Bociurkiw' speech at the Community Seminar on Bilingualism and Biculturalism at the University of Alberta in Edmonton, 23 April 1964; MG31 D58 Vol. 8, File 17: Lupul, The Federal Government, Multiculturalism, and Education in Canada, 6f.

37. This term often appears in the submission to the B&B Commission.

38. The Germans were numerically larger than the Ukrainians. However, owing to two world wars and other factors (e.g., a strong tendency for assimilation), interest in the preservation of heritage was not as strong (LAC MG31 E55 Vol. 10, File Secretary of State: Resumé of the Report of the Royal Commission on Bilingualism and Biculturalism, Book Four. The Cultural Contribution of the Other Ethnic Groups, 8).

39. Based on an evaluation of issues of the *Ethnic Scene*, a press organ of the Canadian government examining the ethnic press in Canada, and publications and correspondence by the Ethnic Press Federation.

40. LAC MG31 E55 Vol. 10, File Secretary of State: Statement by the Prime Minister, House of Commons, 8 October 1971, 1–6.

41. Findlay, Oliver, and Solberg 1974.

42. LAC MG31 D58 Vol. 8, File 17: Lupul, The Federal Government, Multiculturalism, and Education in Canada), 1f.

REFERENCES

Anderson, Alan. 1981. *Ethnicity in Canada: Theoretical Perspectives*. Toronto: Butterworths.

Avery, Donald. 1995. *Reluctant Host: Canada's Response to Immigrant Workers, 1896–1994*. Toronto: McClelland & Stewart.

Bociurkiw, Bohdan. 1978. Federal Policy of Multiculturalism and the Ukrainian-Canadian Community. In *Multiculturalism, Separatism, and Ukrainian Canadians: An Assessment*, ed. M. Lupul, 98–128. Edmonton: Canadian Institute of Ukrainian Studies Press.

Burnet, Jean R., and Howard Palmer. 1988. *"Coming Canadians": An Introduction to a History of Canada's Peoples*. Toronto: McClelland & Stewart.

Darcovich, William. 1967. *Ukrainians in Canada. The Struggle to Retain Their Identity*. Ottawa: Ukrainian Self-Reliance Association.

———. 1980. The "Statistical Compendium": An Overview of Trends. In *Changing Realities: Social Trends among Ukrainian Canadians*, ed. R. Petryshyn, 3–17. Edmonton: Canadian Institute of Ukrainian Studies Press.

Darlington, James. 1991. The Ukrainian Impress on the Canadian West. In *Canada's Ukrainians: Negotiating an Identity*, ed. L. Luciuk and S. Hryniuk, 53–80. Toronto: University of Toronto Press.

Ferguson, Barry. 1991. British-Canadian Intellectuals, Ukrainian Immigrants, and Canadian National Identity. In *Canada's Ukrainians: Negotiating an Identity*, ed. L. Luciuk and S. Hryniuk, 304–25. Toronto: University of Toronto Press.

Findlay, Peter, Michael Oliver, and Janet Solberg. 1974. "The Unpublished Research of the Royal Commission on Bilingualism and Biculturalism," *Canadian Journal of Political Science* 4, 7: 709–20.

Friesen, Gerald. 1987. *The Canadian Prairies: A History*. Toronto: University of Toronto Press.

Government of Canada. 1965. A Preliminary Report of the Commission on Bilingualism and Biculturalism. Ottawa: Queen's Printer.

———. 1967. Report of the Royal Commission on Bilingualism and Biculturalism. Book 1. *General Introduction. The Official Languages*. Ottawa: Queen's Printer.

Gregorovich, Andrew. 1964. *The Ukrainians in Canada*. Toronto: Ukrainian National Youth Federation of Canada.

———. 1991. Ukrainians in Metro Toronto. In *Narys istorii kongresu ukraintsiv Kanady v Toronto*, ed. W. Didiuk, 39–48. Toronto: Ukrainian Canadian Congress.

Hilliker, John F. 1986. Diefenbaker and Canadian External Relations. In *Canadian Foreign Policy. Historical Readings*, ed. J.L. Granatstein, 183–97. Toronto: Copp Clark Pitman.

Isajiw, Wsevolod. 1983. Multiculturalism and the Integration of the Canadian Community. *Canadian Ethnic Studies/Etudes ethniques au Canada 15*, 2: 107–17.

Jaworsky, John. 1979. A Case Study of the Canadian Federal Government's Multiculturalism Policy. MA thesis. Department of Political Science, Carleton University.

Kallen, Evelyn. 1982. "Multiculturalism: Ideology, Policy, and Reality," *Journal of Canadian Studies* 17, 1: 51–63.

Kaye, V.J. 1964. *Early Settlements in Canada, 1895–1900. Dr Josef Oleskow's Role in the Settlement of the Canadian Northwest*. Toronto: Ukrainian Canadian Research Foundation/University of Toronto Press.

Kelley, Ninette, and Michael Trebilcock. 1998. *The Making of the Mosaic. A History of Canadian Immigration Policy*. Toronto: University of Toronto Press.

Kymlicka, Will. 1998. *Finding Our Way. Rethinking Ethnocultural Relations in Canada*. Toronto: Oxford University Press.

Lalande, Julia. 2006. "Building a Home Abroad"—A Comparative Study of Ukrainian Migration, Immigration Policy and Diaspora Formation in Canada and Germany after the Second World War. PhD dissertation, University of Hamburg.

Lehr, John. 1991. Peopling the Prairies with Ukrainians. In *Canada's Ukrainians: Negotiating an Identity*, ed. L. Luciuk and S. Hryniuk, 30–52. Toronto: University of Toronto Press.

Luciuk, Lubomyr, and Stella Hryniuk, eds. 1991. *Canada's Ukrainians: Negotiating an Identity*. Toronto: University of Toronto Press.

Martel, Marcel. 2004. Managing Ethnic Pluralism: The Canadian Experience, 1860–1971. In *Meeting Global and Domestic Challenges*, eds T. Greven and H. Ickstadt (Berlin: Freie Universität Berlin), 110–24.

Martynowych, Orest. 1991. *Ukrainians in Canada: The Formative Period, 1891–1924*. Edmonton: Canadian Institute of Ukrainian Studies Press.

Momryk, Myron. 1987. "Mike Starr: From Mayor to Cabinet Minister," *Archivist* 14, 4: 10–12.

Mycak, Sonia. 1996. "'A Different Story' by Helen Potrebenko: The Prairie-Pioneer Myth Revisited," *Canadian Ethnic Studies/Etudes ethniques au Canada* 28, 1: 67–88.

Owram, Doug. 1996. *Born at the Right Time: A History of the Baby-boom Generation*. Toronto: University of Toronto Press.

Palmer, Howard. 1991. *Ethnicity and Politics in Canada since Confederation*. (Canada's Ethnic Groups, Booklet No. 17).

Petryshyn, Roman, ed. 1980. *Changing Realities: Social Trends among Ukrainian Canadians*. Edmonton: Canadian Institute of Ukrainian Studies Press.

Reitz, Jeffrey G., and Margaret A. Ashton. 1980. "Ukrainian Language and Identity Retention in Urban Canada," *Canadian Ethnic Studies/Études ethniques au Canada* 12, 2: 33–54.

Rudnyckyj, Jaroslav. 1967. Separate Statement. In Report of the Royal Commission on Bilingualism and Biculturalism. Book 1. *General Introduction. The Official Languages*, ed. Government of Canada. Ottawa: Queen's Printer.

Ryan, Claude. 1975. Canada: Bicultural or Multicultural? Speech given at the Heritage Ontario Congress, 2 June 1972. Reprinted in *Immigration and the Rise of Multiculturalism*, ed. H. Palmer, 147–51. Vancouver: Copp Clark.

Slavutych, Yaroslav, et al., eds. 1966. *Slavs in Canada*. Vol. 1, Proceedings of the First National Conference on Canadian Slavs, 9–12 June 1965, Banff, AB. Edmonton: Inter-University Committee on Canadian Slavs.

Subtelny, Orest. 2000. *Ukraine. A History,* 3rd edn. Toronto: University of Toronto Press.

Swyripa, Frances. 1978. *Ukrainian Canadians: A Survey of Their Portrayal in English-language Works*. Edmonton: University of Alberta Press.

———. 1993. *Wedded to the Cause: Ukrainian-Canadian Women and Ethnic Identity, 1891–1991*. Toronto: University of Toronto Press.

Taylor, Charles. 1993. Nationalism and the Political Intelligentsia: A Case Study. In *Reconciling the Solitudes*, ed. G. Laforest, 3–22. Montreal and Kingston: McGill-Queen's University Press.

Trosky, Odarka S. 1968. *The Ukrainian Greek Orthodox Church in Canada*. Winnipeg: Bulman Bros.

Ukrainian National Youth Federation of Canada. 1966. *Canada's Culture. Views of Canadian Youth of Ukrainian Origin*. A brief submitted to the Royal Commission on Bilingualism and Biculturalism, Toronto, June 1964. Toronto: UNYFC.

Woycenko, O. 1964. *Canada's Cultural Heritage: Ukrainian Contribution*. Winnipeg: n.p.

Yuzyk, Paul. 1967. *Ukrainian Canadians: Their Place and Role in Canadian Life*. Toronto: Ukrainian Canadian Business and Professional Federation.

4   From Neil Longley, Todd Crosset, and Steve Jefferson, "The Migration of African-Americans to the Canadian Football League during the 1950s: An Escape from Racism?," *The International Journal of Sport* 25, 10 (2008): 1374–97.

INTRODUCTION

This article focuses on a somewhat narrow aspect of this discourse on discrimination, and examines the notion of "quitting America" as a possible response to discrimination.

Quitting America is often a sub-theme of historical biographies on African-American athletes. Turn-of-the-century athletes such as Jack Johnson, Jimmy Winkfield, Marshall Taylor, and Moses Fleetwood Walker either quit or advocated quitting America. These biographies speak to the racial injustice of America, and by contrast, suggest the liberty that African-Americans could find elsewhere.

However, in the major team sports such as football, basketball, and baseball, African-American athletes have generally never had the opportunity to take their careers outside of America, largely because of the absence of professional leagues in other countries. These sports all originated in America, and their play at the major professional level has historically been restricted to America. Even now, with the existence of professional basketball leagues in Europe and professional baseball leagues in Asia, the representation of American players in these leagues is relatively small, and tends to be players not capable of playing in the major US leagues.[1]

There is, however, an important historical exception to these generalizations. During the mid-twentieth century, African-American football players had the opportunity to "quit" America and ply their trade in a relatively comparable professional league in Canada. Beginning in 1946, a steady, albeit relatively small, flow of African-Americans began to migrate to the Canadian Football League (CFL).[2] For some of these players, the decision to move north was simply a business or career decision—at the time, and unlike today, the CFL was a legitimate competitor to the NFL in the labour market, and it was not uncommon for the CFL to sign NFL-calibre players. For other African-Americans who went north, the move represented a hope that life would be better in Canada, and that opportunities would exist that were not possible in the US.

In this sense, Canada and the CFL have often been viewed in idyllic terms when it comes to their treatment of African-American football players. There is a perception held by some that, by migrating north to Canada, African-American football players were able to escape the racial injustices they often suffered in the US. This view appears to have its roots in the notion that Canada is a "gentler,"

more tolerant society, without the divisive socio-political history that characterizes much of the race relations in the US.

[. . .]

While there were certainly some exceptions, the 1950s generally predate any widespread concern for racial justice by whites in US society. Serious efforts to integrate US institutions were nascent at best. For these reasons, the 1950s give scholars a relatively clean period to explore the CFL as an alternative to the NFL for African-American football players.

BACKGROUND: THE CFL AND AFRICAN-AMERICAN FOOTBALL PLAYERS

The CFL

Professional football in Canada has roots that go back to the late nineteenth century. The game evolved out of the sport of rugby, but became a distinct game with the adoption of the forward pass in the 1920s. The game of Canadian football is very similar to American football. There are some rule differences— for example, Canadian football has 12 players per team on the field instead of 11, has three "downs" instead of four, and plays on a field that is 10 yards longer and 12 yards wider—but fundamentally the two games are the same, meaning that US players do not generally face prohibitive adjustments when they move north.

In its early days, the game was played at the amateur level, but it started to become "professionalized" during the 1930s. At about the same time, the first US players started arriving in the CFL. Prior to that point, teams in western Canada, where the population base was smaller, were at a distinct competitive disadvantage compared to their counterparts in eastern Canada, who had the benefit of a much larger talent pool to draw from. In 1935, the Winnipeg Blue Bombers, a team from western Canada, attempted to remedy this competitive imbalance by employing nine US players on their roster. With these players, Winnipeg won the Grey Cup that year—the first ever Grey Cup victory by a team from western Canada. With the success of Winnipeg, other teams also began to recruit from the US, and concern developed that US players would completely take over the Canadian game. These concerns prompted "import" restrictions on US players—by 1946 teams were prohibited from carrying more than five imports—i.e., Americans—on their roster.

As the Second World War ended, the CFL had stabilized at eight teams—four in the west and four in the east. These eight franchises, plus an additional team that was added in 1954, have provided the foundation for the league right up to the present. While today's CFL occupies very much of a second-tier status to the NFL, such was not the case during the CFL's "glory" days of the 1950s.[3] It was during that era that salaries in the CFL were generally comparable to NFL salaries—college football still dominated professional football in the US, and the NFL had not yet become the dominating commercial force that it is today.

[. . .]

African-Americans in the CFL

The CFL colour barrier was officially broken in 1946, when the Montreal Alouettes signed Herb Trawick and Virgil Wagner.[4] The Alouettes were a CFL expansion team in 1946, and their American general manager, Lew Hayman, no doubt used the signings as a means to gain an immediate competitive advantage over the existing teams in the league. These expectations were fulfilled as the Alouettes, led by Trawick and Wagner, won the 1949 Grey Cup in only their fourth year of existence.

Hayman's decision to sign Trawick and Wagner was apparently influenced by the positive reception that Jackie Robinson received while playing in Montreal. Robinson played

the 1946 season for the Montreal Royals, the Brooklyn Dodgers' top farm club, before making his historic major league debut with the Dodgers in 1947. Hayman felt that Montreal, which at the time was Canada's most cosmopolitan and diverse city, was ready for an African-American football player.[5]

[. . .]

Calgary brought Johnny Bright to the CFL. [. . .] Bright was already famous in the US for being the victim of one of the worst incidents of racist behaviour ever seen in US sports. In 1950, Bright, who was a star running back at Drake University in Iowa, travelled with his team to Stillwater, Oklahoma to play Oklahoma A&M (now Oklahoma State). What was significant was that Bright would be the first African-American college football player ever to play a game in the state of Oklahoma. In the days leading up to the game, some Oklahoma A&M players threatened Bright with physical harm. On the first play of the game, an Oklahoma A&M defender hit Bright with a forearm to the head, breaking Bright's jaw. The incident was captured by a *Life* magazine photographer, who went on to win a Pulitzer Prize for the photograph.

Bright was ultimately drafted in the first round of the 1951 NFL draft by the Philadelphia Eagles, but elected to sign with Calgary of the CFL. He played one year for Calgary, and then was traded to Edmonton for the 1954 season, where he went onto become the CFL's all-time leading rusher at the time of his retirement. Had Bright signed with Philadelphia, he would have become the first African-American player ever to play for the Eagles.

Winnipeg had Tom Casey from 1950–55, and he was joined in 1955 by Leo Lewis, who starred for nine years as a running back. Hamilton signed Bernie Custis in the early 1950s—in 1953, Custis became the first African-American to ever play quarterback in the CFL. In Toronto, both Ulysses Curtis and Bill Bass were signed in 1950. One team—the Saskatchewan

Roughriders—was slow to integrate. One African-American player, Gabe Paterson, appeared for the team during the 1948 season, but it was almost ten years before another African-American player would play regularly in Saskatchewan.[6]

A FRAMEWORK FOR ANALYSIS

Perspectives on Canadians and Race

[. . .] Humber's book on African-Canadian athletes is entitled "A Sporting Chance," and of mid-century Canadian football he writes: "The Canadian Football League survived the post-war popularity of the National Football League by providing opportunities for minorities to assume leadership positions. American Black George Reed, a great running back with the Saskatchewan Roughriders in the 1960s played an important role as a player representative and union organizer."[7]

This type of framing of Canadian sport, and Canadian football in particular, fits with a popular notion of Canada as a place of refuge for African-Americans. Beginning with the American Revolution, Canada has provided Africans with an alternative to the American slave system. The British provided safe and free passage to over 3000 escaped slaves and freedmen from New York to Nova Scotia at the end of the American Revolution in 1780.

After the War of 1812, the British again offered freedom to escaped slaves fighting on behalf of the English. About 2000 African-Americans crossed the border. In 1829, after three days of riots in Cincinnati, Canada offered resettlement into a community they called Wilberforce. US slaves and free blacks began to call Canada the "Promised Land," especially after slavery was banned in 1834 throughout the British colonies. By the mid-nineteenth century, Canada had about 40 black settlements.[8] Every American schoolchild is probably aware that the Underground Railroad led to the Canadian border, particularly after the passage of the Fugitive Slave Act.

However, what is often not emphasized in this framing of Canadian history is that, by and large, these migrations were temporary. Many of the Africans seeking refuge in Canada after the American Revolution opted to return to Africa with the British-sponsored Sierra Leone Company. It is estimated that the 30 years of black migration to Canada prior to the Civil War was reversed in less than a decade, as 30 000 black "Canadians" left during and after the Civil War to fight with the Union Army and be reunited with their families. Few, if any, of the black American immigrant communities in Canada, like Wilberforce, succeeded.

The next large migration of black Americans to Canada came after the First World War. Chaffing under Jim Crow and systemic racial intolerance, black Oklahoma farmers, encouraged by the Canadian government's promotion efforts to settle the western Canadian prairie provinces of Alberta and Saskatchewan, moved their operations north to Canada. When it became apparent that the immigrants from Oklahoma were not of European descent, protests and discontent quickly arose among the public. The Canadian government responded by blocking blacks from crossing the border—government officials even travelled to Oklahoma in an attempt to discourage, at the source, any further black farmers from making the trek north.[9]

By the 1950s, Canada was a very homogeneous society, with the great majority of its residents being of European descent. Blacks, or any other persons of colour, comprised an extremely small percentage of the population—according to the 1951 Canadian census, over 97 per cent of Canadians identified themselves as being of European origin, with the next largest group being those of Asian origin, who comprised about 1 per cent of the population. And while Canada does not share the long history of state-supported slavery with the US, Canada's mid-century immigration and segregation policies were not unlike that of the United States.[10]

[. . .]

Thus the cumulative evidence on the discriminatory tendencies of Canadians is mixed and often contradictory—on one hand, there is the somewhat idyllic view of Canada as a country largely free of such problems, while on the other hand there is considerable evidence that race and ethnicity issues have been significant factors in hockey. These mixed findings make it difficult to have conclusive and decisive a priori expectations about what the experiences may have been of those African-American football players who migrated to Canada in the 1950s, and suggest the need for empirical investigation.

An Economic Framework: Sources of Discrimination

An additional framework in which to analyze the experiences of African-Americans in the CFL is to employ Becker's[11] seminal work on the economics of discrimination. Becker identifies three possible sources of labour market discrimination—employers, co-workers, and customers. With the former, it is the employer himself/herself who holds the discriminatory preferences toward a certain group, whereas with the latter two it is the firm's employees and customers, respectively, who hold the discriminatory views, with the employer simply being forced to respond to these views for fear of alienating the firm's other employees or its customers.

In the context of this paper, Becker's categorizations can provide insight into the type and extent of discrimination that African-Americans may have been expected to find in the CFL, relative to their experiences in the US. In this regard, a key question is this: how did the composition of these three groups—customers, co-workers, and employers—differ in Canada relative to the US, and to what extent would these differences have resulted in Canada providing a more favourable playing environment for African-Americans?

With the customer group, the differences are most clear—the fans of the CFL were predominantly white Canadians, while fans of the NFL were predominantly white Americans. To what extent, then, could these two groups of fans be expected to have different attitudes toward African-Americans? Perhaps most importantly, the histories of the two countries with respect to racial issues are very different. The US legacy of slavery, systemic racial terror, and government-supported segregation undoubtedly impacted the beliefs and values of white Americans in ways not generally seen in Canada, and could be hypothesized to lead to African-Americans experiencing more racist behaviour in the US compared to Canada. In other words, white Canadians could be expected to exhibit less racial hostility toward African-American players on their favourite team, compared to those fans in the US.

However, this is certainly not meant to imply that one would expect African-American players to be free of racism in Canada. White supremacy is pervasive across countries, cultures, and races, and one would not expect Canada to be any exception. Further, during the 1950s, Canada was a very homogeneous, white European society, and could not generally be considered either multicultural or multiracial. To the extent that racism is based, in part, on a fear of "differences," Canada during the 1950s and 1960s would seem to have been ripe for racist behaviour. The very fact that African-American players in Canada were so identifiably different from the population as a whole made them "stand out," and no doubt made them potential targets of discriminatory behaviour.

Turning to co-worker discrimination, for African-Americans playing in Canada during the 1950s, their "co-workers," i.e., teammates, included two groups: white Canadians and white US players. A league rule enacted in 1946 limited teams to only five imports on their roster at any one time; this number was subsequently increased to seven in 1950. This meant that most of the teammates of African-American players during this era were actually Canadian. Almost invariably, and unlike today, these Canadian players were white, reflecting Canada's homogeneous population at the time. The issues here, then, are relatively the same as they were for fan discrimination: in particular, to what extent do white Canadians—in this case football players and not fans—hold prejudicial views against African-Americans? As was hypothesized in the previous section, while there may be reason to believe that African-Americans would still face some level of racist behaviour from white Canadian players, this may, in general, be less than what they would have faced from white American teammates if they had played in the NFL.

This leads to the next complicating issue—some of the teammates of African-American players in Canada were, in fact, white Americans from the US. Thus, to the extent that African-American players would face discriminatory treatment from white teammates if they played in the NFL, they would presumably also face such treatment from their white US teammates in the CFL. The only situation where this would not be the case is if the white US players in the CFL had fundamentally different racial views than the white US players in the NFL, something for which there is no a priori reason to believe.

A similar issue arises when one considers the possibility of employer discrimination. While CFL teams were generally owned by Canadians—either as community-owned entities, or by private businesspeople—the coaching staffs of these teams were almost always white Americans. In fact, some CFL head coaches came to the league after having been head coaches in the NFL. [. . .]

What this means is that, while African-American players who came to Canada may have been distancing themselves from white US *fans*, they were certainly not distancing themselves from white US coaches. To a lesser extent, they were not completely distancing themselves from white US teammates. In this regard, then, one might expect some of the barriers African-Americans faced in the NFL to also be present in the CFL.

[. . .]

QUALITATIVE EVIDENCE

[. . .]

Off-Field Experiences in the Broader Community

Perhaps the best place to begin the discussion is with George Reed, an African-American running back who played from the early 1960s to the mid-1970s with Saskatchewan. Reed is noteworthy for being vocal about the racism he faced in Canada. He rejected the idyllic view that Canadians often have of themselves, and noted that "a lot of people in Canada kind of shut their eyes and think discrimination doesn't exist."[12] Reed's views on racism are particularly influential because he was not just any ordinary player—a 2006 survey by the Canadian TV network TSN voted Reed as the second greatest player in the entire history of Canadian football (after white American Doug Flutie).[13]

In a 1967 interview with the *Toronto Telegram* newspaper, Reed spoke out about the off-field problems he faced:

> There is flagrant discrimination against Negroes in Regina. I have come face-to-face with more racial problems in my five years in Regina than I ever had living in a suburb of Seattle. In the beginning I couldn't find anyone who would rent me

an apartment. . . . My five-year-old son, who never knew what discrimination was, is suddenly called names he doesn't understand. My wife has become so defensive that when she leaves the house she's like a coiled Cobra that's ready to strike at anybody. Regina is like living in the heart of Alabama as far as I'm concerned.[14]

The *Telegram* article was seeking Reed's reaction to comments made earlier that year by Ted Watkins. Watkins, who had played for the Ottawa Rough Riders since 1963, had told a CBC-TV interview that "I have had many problems in Ottawa which made me feel like I was in Mississippi somewhere."

Years later, Reed said he wouldn't retract a word, and didn't regret his comments, even though they drew a strong backlash at the time.

The Regina media were all over me. Reginans who thought their city was just fine were outraged that I had said otherwise. Molson [the major Canadian brewer that was his off-season employer] demoted me and almost fired me. . . . I have never said I hate Canada. I've never said I dislike Canada. What I have said is, don't say those problems don't exist.[15]

As high-profile athletes, many African-American players often faced an uncertain and unpredictable social world outside of football. Reed once commented:

There would be occasions when racial slurs were said on the field or sometimes even from the stands. . . . What bothered me more than anything was dealing with situations away from the job. On Sunday afternoons and at practice I knew where I was supposed to be, what my responsibilities were, how I was expected to act before, during and after the game or the practice. The rest of the time, though,

I didn't know where I fit in or what I was supposed to do. Like, you're not allowed to go and have a beer in this spot. Okay, I understand; am I allowed to go and say hello to this person or not? I felt sometimes that I could unwittingly get into trouble just for being in the wrong place or talking to the wrong person.[16]

Reed, like many other African-American players in the CFL noticed a double standard: African-American football players were treated differently from other blacks. He elaborates:

Another thing that was really hard to take after I became well-known . . . is how people started to change towards me. They didn't change towards the problem, they changed towards me. It actually became harder for me after I was accepted for membership at the Wascana Country Club, after I was welcomed into this place and that place, but another black person, whether he was an athlete or not, was not accorded the same privilege. . . . If I wasn't George Reed, football player, most of the people who glad-hand and welcome me wouldn't give me the time of day.[17]

Calgary's Ezzert "Sugarfoot" Anderson voiced comments similar to Reed regarding the double standards that often existed in Canada.

Our country club here in Calgary didn't allow Jewish people or black people, but they said Woody [Strode] and myself could come. That kind of struck me as a little odd and I never did go. If I hadn't been a Stampeder, they wouldn't have let me in, so I just didn't go up. Coming from Arkansas, nothing that happened to me in Calgary was anything to write home about.[18]

These comments of Reed and Anderson regarding invitations to join country clubs raise a further issue. In cities such as Regina and Calgary, where there were almost no other blacks other than the African-American football players, and where football players were revered, the potential "costs" of being black in Canada could be (at least partially) mitigated by the potential benefits of "tokenism" and athletic privilege.[19]

Racism was sometimes very overt. On a road trip to Winnipeg, Calgary coach Les Lear (one of the few Canadian coaches in the league since the Second World War) threatened to pull his entire team out of a hotel when he was told that Anderson and Woody Strode, Calgary's other African-American player at the time, couldn't stay at the hotel. Winnipeg coach George Trafton reportedly acted similarly in an incident involving Tom Casey.[20]

There were also complaints from some African-American players about discrimination in securing off-field jobs. Willie Fleming, a star running back for British Columbia in the late 1950s and early 1960s, stated in 1967 that "the Negro is a hero on the field, and a bum off it, when it comes to getting work."[21] Winnipeg's Leo Lewis, who played during the same era as Fleming, said "In all my years in Winnipeg I was never offered a job that was worthwhile. It would have been different if I were white."[22]

La Verne Barnes, whose husband Emery Barnes played for the BC Lions during the 1960s, wrote a book[23] that could be viewed as a strong indictment of the way in which African-American football players were treated in Canada. Barnes claimed that not only were African-American players of that era often lured to Canada without realizing how few blacks actually lived in Canada, but that they were frequent targets of racist discrimination once they arrived. According to Barnes,

racism in the CFL is very real. All kinds of injustices and little humiliations happen to black ball players. The media know it,

the management knows it, and the ball players themselves are keenly aware of it. But it is something that isn't talked about. In public. It is very unchic to rap about racism in the CFL out loud. About the way black ball players are traded and put on waivers for socializing with white girls. . . . About the cities of Vancouver, Regina, and Winnipeg that are well-known in the league as being less likely to have many black ball players.[24]

Conversely, however, some African-Americans were adamant that conditions for blacks were much better in Canada than the US. George Dixon, who played with Montreal from 1959 to 1965, felt that he enjoyed a lifestyle in Canada that was not available in the US. He commented in 1967: "I go to the best country clubs . . . the plushest restaurants, and I live in a fine neighborhood. . . . My wife and I have the kind of social relationships we couldn't have in Connecticut."[25]

Similar sentiments were expressed by Edmonton star Johnny Bright. While he endured many racist incidents in Canada, these incidents were often relatively covert, as opposed to the more overt racism of the Deep South. In this regard, Bright stated: "I never felt in the northern states or in Canada that my life was in danger, but that wasn't the case down south. There they'd kill you and throw your body in the swamp for being a different color."[26]

There were also considerable differences across teams in attitudes toward African-Americans. For example, Edmonton and Montreal were considered the most welcoming.[27] At the other end of the spectrum was Regina, home of the Saskatchewan Roughriders.

Football-Related Experiences

A persistent theme of African-American players from that era was the view that CFL teams had unofficial quotas limiting the number of

African-American players per team. Ralph Goldston, who played for Hamilton in the 1950s and was later an assistant coach for Montreal, said in a 1967 interview "some cities, some coaches are afraid to play too many Negros."[28] Emery Barnes of BC noted that "it looks strange when players change from year to year, but the number of non-whites remains constant."[29] Such a notion was even indirectly supported from the management side, when Ottawa general manager Red O'Quinn once noted "you might have a clique develop, say, if you have more than five coloured players."[30]

Beyond these unofficial quotas, the attitudes of team management and coaches also often manifested themselves much more directly and overtly. Saskatchewan's first African-American player was Gabe Patterson in 1947 and 1948. He had a brief, and apparently unhappy and lonely, stay with Saskatchewan, and Saskatchewan would not employ another African-American for almost ten years. There were rumours that Patterson met hostility from the southern US players on the team and from the team's coach, Alabama native Fred Grant. There were also rumours that, at the team's wind-up party following the 1948 season, Grant walked out of the room when he saw Patterson walk in.[31] Herb Trawick, discussed earlier as the first African-American to play in the CFL, apparently met with similar hostility when Douglas Walker took over the Montreal coaching duties in 1952. Walker, who was a southerner, and a long-time coach at Wake Forest University in North Carolina before coming to Montreal, was reported to have been contemptuous toward Trawick.[32]

[. . .]

Rollie Miles, who would later star for Edmonton, actually came to Canada to play baseball in Regina, Saskatchewan, in 1950. Kelly[33] contends that, while the Saskatchewan Roughriders were aware of Miles's ability as a football player, they were not interested in him because he was black. The Edmonton

Eskimos, whose management had a more tolerant attitude, soon discovered Miles and quickly signed him to a contract.

By many accounts, Miles was the best player in Canada in 1953, but did not win the award because of racism.[34] The football reporters of Canada, perhaps influenced by Miles's outspoken views on race, voted his Edmonton teammate Billy Vessels as the league's MVP. Another of Bright's teammates at the time—a star Asian-Canadian player named Normie Kwong—later commented that "conditions in the country then weren't conducive to a person of color winning awards."[35]

Ron Atchison, a Canadian who played from 1952 to 1968 for Saskatchewan, recalls Edmonton's on-field power, led by Bright and Miles, and, in the process, notes Saskatchewan's lack of African-American players, and the racial stereotypes that often prevailed:

They had Bright, Kwong, and Miles. They were the scourge of the league. That goes back to before the Riders had any black ballplayers. We were just starting to get black men on our team. We were the last to do so. I remember trying to find out why there were no blacks on our team because we had had one black ballplayer here before my time. People said the women chased him so damn much the executive said they'd never have another one.[36]

African-American players also had to deal with teammates. When Leo Lewis came to Winnipeg in 1955, the beginning of a ten-year CFL career, there was only one other black player (Tom Casey) on the team. Lewis recalls: "There were some negative experiences. I think any racial problems we had with Canadian ballplayers were brought about because of Americans from the southern states. I do believe that. Generally speaking Winnipeg was a good town. There wasn't much racism that I could see. Canada was a great place."[37]

It was reported that Herb Trawick often faced hostility from his teammates—in fact, one report claimed that Trawick actually faced more racial slurs from his Canadian teammates than from his American teammates.[38]

Awkward situations would often develop when there were an odd number of African-American players on the team. In Ottawa during the mid-1960s, the team had only three African-American players, so one of them—Bo Scott—roomed alone when the team travelled, despite the fact that there was one "leftover" white player as well, who also roomed alone. Scott said: "Nobody ever asked me if I prefer to live alone."[39]

In Calgary during the mid-1960s, African-American Lovell Coleman claimed that "there were . . . white players . . . who made sure black players didn't hear about their parties."[40] Also on that Calgary team was Eagle Day, a white US quarterback from Ole Miss, who, unlike his white teammates, was quite willing to express his views on race. Day reportedly told a magazine writer of the day that he (Day) believed segregation was the only successful racial policy.[41]

The experiences of Cookie Gilchrest, an all-pro running back in the AFL and the CFL, also challenged the notion that Canada was a racially tolerant place for African-Americans. Gilchrest was an outspoken running back with a keen sense of justice. In 1957, he led the Hamilton Tiger-Cats to a Grey Cup victory. Following the win, Gilchrest asked management for a $500 dollar bonus to pay rent for his new family. Not only did the football star not get the bonus, but he was traded to Regina for being so bold as to request one. He later returned to Toronto with the Argonauts, but after the 1961 season, as he puts it, he was "sold" against his wishes to the fledgling Buffalo Bills. Years later, when he was elected to the CFL Hall of Fame he refused the invitation because of what he claimed were the racist practices of league officials.

Gilchrest's experience with CFL ownership stands in contrast to his US experience. As in Canada, Gilchrest enjoyed an All-Star career in the AFL, making the league's All-Star team from 1962 to 1965. In 1965 Gilchrest led a player boycott against the city of New Orleans in response to the treatment the black players received from white service workers at the AFL All Star Game. AFL owners supported Gilchrest and the black players, and the 1965 All Star Game was moved to Houston.

SOME QUANTITATIVE TESTS

Given these observations from former players that indicate that race did matter in the mid-century CFL, further empirical testing is warranted. In economics, a variety of quantitative tests can be employed to test for the various types and forms of discrimination. These tests rely on data, rather than personal reflection and observation, to make assessments about the prevalence of discrimination.

[. . .]

Overall Representation Compared to the NLF

As a first test, the overall representation of African-Americans in the CFL can be compared with their representation in the NFL. While such a comparison doesn't directly speak to whether African-Americans experienced any discriminatory treatment in the CFL, it does provide insights into whether they were treated differently in Canada compared to the US.

Starting with the US, in 1950, only 14 blacks were employed in the NFL—an average of about one per team in the 13-team league. Furthermore, they were concentrated on just a few teams—not surprisingly, some of the most successful teams. Nine of the 14 African-Americans playing in the NFL in 1950 were on the playing field for the championship game between the Browns and the Rams.[42] These 14 African-Americans comprised only about 3 per cent of the players in the league that year. Compare this to the CFL, where, by our research, there were about seven African-Americans in the league in 1950, also an average of about one per team. However, because of the roster limitations on imports, African-Americans represented about 13 per cent of the US players in the CFL, as opposed to the NFL's comparable figure of 3 per cent.

By the late 1950s, approximately 40 African-Americans were playing in the NFL annually,[43] representing about 10 per cent of the league's players. In contrast, our research reveals that the CFL averaged about 14 African-Americans per year, or about 25 per cent of the slots allocated to Americans. Even as late as 1967, African-Americans occupied only about 20 per cent of the roster spots in the NFL, compared with about 35 per cent of the spots allocated to US players in the CFL.[44]

Entry Discrimination

Economists define entry discrimination in sport as a situation where the non-preferred group of players is less likely to be hired, relative to counterparts of equal talent in the preferred group, thus resulting in the non-preferred group being "underrepresented" in the workplace. Thus, to gain entry into the league, the non-preferred players must, on average, actually be superior performers to those in the preferred group. How much superior the average non-preferred player must be depends on the magnitude of the discrimination.

Table 1 compares the average performance levels of African-American players with white US players for the same three years examined above: 1953, 1959, and 1968.[45] Two performance measures are employed: whether the player was ultimately elected to the CFL Hall of Fame, and the number of times a player was voted a divisional All-Star during his career.

The table shows that African-American players were consistently better performers than their white US counterparts: African-Americans were more likely to be selected as All-Stars, and (with the exception of the 1959 players) were much more likely to be voted to the Hall of Fame. This implies that CFL teams failed to employ sufficient numbers of African-Americans—in other words, by replacing some white Americans with African-Americans, teams could have increased their overall talent level. Failing to do so implies that teams valued white US players over African-Americans for reasons other than their on-field talent—presumably indicating some type of racial discrimination at work.[46]

Finally, if entry discrimination was, present, then those teams that integrated more quickly should have had a competitive advantage on the field. In this regard, Table 2 shows, for the CFL's West Division, each team's winning percentage over the 1950–61 time period, along with the total number of All-Star selections from that team.

Table 1 Average Performance Levels of African-American players and White US Players in CFL, Selected Years

	1954		1959		1968	
	White	Black	White	Black	White	Black
Career All-Star selections per player	2.06	3.63	1.81	3.11	2.50	3.24
Proportion voted to Hall of Fame	0.14	0.63	0.21	0.22	0.15	0.29
N	49	8	52	9	60	21

Table 2 CLF West Division teams' Winning Percentages and All-Star Selections, 1950–61

	Win %	All-Stars: Black	All-Stars: White	All-Stars: Total
BC	29	2 (5.1%)	15 (7.6%)	17 (7.2%)
Calgary	37	6 (15.4%)	33 (16.7%)	39 (16.5%)
Edmonton	67	16 (41.0%)	49 (24.7%)	65 (27.4%)
Saskatchewan	42	2 (5.1%)	47 (23.7%)	49 (20.7%)
Winnipeg	68	13 (33.3%)	54 (27.3%)	67 (28.3%)
TOTAL		39 (100%)	198 (100%)	237 (100%)

Most importantly, these All-Star selections are subdivided into African-American and white US players.

The table shows, not surprisingly, the teams with the most total All-Star selections—Winnipeg and Edmonton—had the highest win percentage during the time period. However, these two teams were the only teams that captured a greater proportion of the division's African-American All-Stars (33.3 per cent and 41.0 per cent) than of the white US All-Stars. Further, if one looks specifically at Edmonton and Saskatchewan, while both teams captured an almost equal proportion of the white US All-Stars (24.7 per cent vs. 23.7 per cent), Edmonton captured a much greater proportion of the African-American All-Stars than did Saskatchewan (41.0 per cent vs. 5.1 per cent). This may lend empirical support to the notion discussed earlier that Edmonton was a more welcoming place for African-Americans than was Regina. One could hypothesize that the slow rate at which Saskatchewan integrated African-American players was at least partially responsible for its relatively poor on-field performance during the 1950s.[47]

Fan Discrimination and Player Card Prices

One source of data that has frequently been employed by economists to test for customer/fan discrimination is to use player card prices.[48] The theory is that card prices are a relatively pure measure of fan preferences toward players. If, holding performance constant, players from the non-preferred group have, on average, lower card prices, this may be a reflection of fan-based discrimination. Card prices, unlike for example, a player's salary, are impacted only by fan preferences, and not by the preferences of team owners, coaches, GMs, or teammates.

In this regard, CFL player card prices are examined for three distinct seasons: 1954, 1959, and 1968. Card prices are taken from the 1998 *Charlton Canadian Football Card Price Guide*, and these prices are then regressed on a series of independent variables intended to reflect a player's performance (HALL, STAR), position (QB, RB-RC), nationality (IMPORT), and race (AA).

The results of the regression are reported in Table 3. Interpretation of the independent variables is as follows:

- HALL is a dummy variable equalling 1 if the player is a member of the CFL Hall of Fame, 0 otherwise;
- STAR is the number of times the player was a divisional All-Star during his career;
- QB is a dummy variable equalling 1 if the player was a quarterback, 0 otherwise;
- RB-RC is a dummy variable equalling 1 if the player was a running back or receiver, 0 otherwise;

Table 3 Regression results: player card prices (t-statistics in parenthesis)

Variable	1954	1959	1968
Constant	19.18 (5.37)	3.12 (5.01)	3.56 (10.61)
HALL	36.71 (6.80)	4.13 (3.35)	4.76 (7.11)
STAR	1.81 (2.25)	0.33 (1.73)	0.16 (1.73)
QB	16.61 (3.07)	5.29 (4.32)	3.09 (4.63)
RB-RC	8.87 (1.84)	−0.18 (−0.19)	0.56 (1.11)
IMPORT	5.31 (1.36)	0.24 (0.33)	−0.11 (−0.27)
AA	−19.00 (−2.83)	−0.53 (−0.43)	−0.15 (−0.25)
R^2	0.65	0.49	0.58
N	80	88	131

- IMPORT is a dummy variable equalling 1 if the player was an import (i.e., American), 0 otherwise;
- AA is a dummy variable equalling 1 if the player is African-American, 0 otherwise.

All variables except AA are control variables.
[. . .]

The results indicate that, for all three seasons examined, the coefficient on AA is negative, indicating that, *ceteris paribus*, the card prices of African-American players are lower than the corresponding card prices of other players. Statistically, the results are strongest for the 1954 season—for that season, the coefficient on AA is not only significant at the 1 per cent level, but the coefficient is of a relatively large magnitude. It indicates that, all else equal, the card prices of African-American players from that year are $19.00 lower that other players of equal ability. To put this in perspective, the average overall card price for that year was $38, meaning African-American players had card prices that were about 50 per cent below what would be expected.

While these card prices reflect current valuations by fans of past players, the card prices do not have any direct impact on these former players themselves, either now or during the players' playing career. However, any fan biases against African-American players would not only manifest themselves in current card prices but would have probably manifested themselves in other ways during the player's career. To the extent these fan biases existed at the time, these biases would render African-American players economically less valuable to their teams than their white counterparts—i.e., if fans prefer, all else equal, white players to black players, teams will find it financially advantageous to respond to these preferences. This response may have taken the form of teams paying African-American players less than white players, for a given level of talent (i.e., salary discrimination), or African-American players being underrepresented on teams, given their talent level (i.e., entry discrimination).

[. . .] In general, this analysis of player card prices should be viewed as simply one of many alternative means to test for the presence of discrimination. The results should not be viewed in isolation, but rather as a complement to the larger body of other evidence, both quantitative and qualitative, that is uncovered on the issue.

CONCLUSIONS

The research presented here complicates our understanding of African-American football players and their quest to play the game in Canada. Canadian professional football represented a viable alternative for highly skilled African-American players who faced racial discrimination in the United States. Further, the fact that African-Americans were much better represented, in a relative sense, in the CFL compared to the NFL suggests that the league was more tolerant toward blacks than its American competitor. But the research also suggests that these players faced discrimination in Canada and in the CFL. The economic tests support anecdotal data that suggest players faced racial discrimination in the hiring practices of the CFL and in the community at large.

This research also suggests that the mid-century racial dynamics of the sport systems of Canada and the United States may have been more similar than they were different. The colour barriers in sport that existed in the United States were also practised in Canada.

Indeed, the colour barrier in hockey remained in place until 1958. Further, the racial politics of the northern US and Canada were also similar. During the mid-century, provinces were just beginning to pass anti-discrimination laws. Immigration laws and practices that barred or severely limited people of colour entering Canada had not yet been challenged. For all these reasons, we contend the mid-century Canadian sports system was less a refuge for African-American athletes, as it is so often presented in the academic literature, and more simply another employment opportunity within a North American system of white supremacy. This is not to suggest that there were no differences between the leagues or the countries, but rather that those difference have been overstated. And, as a result, the racial discrimination experienced by black American athletes working in Canada has not been fully explored.

[. . .]

NOTES

1. For example, a perusal of the 2007 rosters of professional basketball teams in Italy (found at www.eurobasket.com) shows the typical team having two to three African-Americans on the squad, most of whom with little or no previous NBA experience. To our knowledge, there have not been any academic studies that have chronicled the experiences of African-Americans playing in overseas basketball or baseball leagues.

2. Technically, the name "Canadian Football League" was not officially adopted until 1958, but for convenience the term is used here to describe professional football in Canada even before 1958.

3. See Boyd and Scrivener, *Legends of Autumn*, for a history of the CFL's "glory" years of the 1950s and 1960s.

4. Trawick and Wagner were the first "official" African-Americans in the CFL, although a team picture of the 1930 Regina Roughriders (forerunner to the Saskatchewan Roughriders) includes an African-American player by the name of Stonewall Jackson. It was rumoured that Jackson was a US porter working on the Canadian railway system and would occasionally play football as he travelled across the country.

5. Josh Bell-Webster, "Herb Trawick," available online at www.cfl.ca, accessed 29 Jan. 2007.

6. That one team in the league, the Saskatchewan Roughriders, was slow to integrate, is similar to the situations found in baseball and the NFL, where the Boston Red Sox and the Washington Redskins lagged well behind their respective league brethren when it came to integration. In both of these latter cases, the attitudes of the team owner—Tom Yawkey in the case of the Red Sox and George Marshall in the case of the Redskins—have often been cited as the reason for this unwillingness to integrate (for a comprehensive discussion of

the Red Sox situation, see Bryant, *Shut Out*). In the case of the Roughriders, it is not readily apparent why the team was particularly slow to integrate. The team was community-owned and thus was governed by a group of individuals from the community, rather than one sole individual. One hypothesis is that the collective attitudes of this management group were such that African-American players were not welcome in the organization.

7. Humber, *A Sporting Chance*.
8. Winks, *The Blacks in Canada*.
9. See ibid.
10. Ibid.
11. See Becker, *The Economics of Discrimination*. Becker won the 1992 Nobel Prize in Economics, in part for his path-breaking work on the economics of discrimination. For an overview of the current state of the economics literature on discrimination in sport see Kahn, "The Sports Business as a Labor Market Laboratory," and Longley, "Racial Discrimination."
12. Proudfoot, "The Negro in the CFL," 5.
13. See http://www.tsn.ca/cf1/feature/?/fid=10867.
14. Chaput, *Saskatchewan Sports Legends*, 213–14.
15. Ibid., 214–15.
16. Ibid., 213–14.
17. Ibid., 215.
18. Kelly, *Green Grit*, 122.
19. One measure of discrimination, or lack thereof, might be the extent to which black American CFL players resettled in Canada. While it is beyond the limits of this project to do a systematic analysis of the lives of individual black CFL players from this era, we did come across some anecdotal evidence. While some clearly made a life for themselves beyond football in Canada, we were nonetheless struck by how many CFL stars returned to the US—including Tom Casey, Woody Strode, Kenny Washington, and Cookie Gilchrist. The tension between the opportunity that the CFL represented and the dream of a racially just United States is captured in the personal history of the Bright family. Johnny Bright, a symbol for Canadian racial harmony and US racial hostility, made a life for himself and his family in Canada, but his wife and children never became Canadian citizens. In this way, the journey of African-Americans to the CFL resembles other

African-American migrations to Canada following the revolutionary war and prior to the civil war—Canada proved to be a temporary refuge. The desire to immigrate was driven by conditions in America, with blacks in Canada often playing the role of longing exiles in a foreign land.

20. Kelly, *Green Grit*, 123.
21. Proudfoot, "The Negro in the CFL," 5.
22. Ibid., 5.
23. Barnes, *The Plastic Orgasm*.
24. Ibid., 142.
25. Proudfoot, "The Negro in the CFL," 5.
26. Kelly, *The Grey Cup*, 22.
27. Kelly, *Green Grit*, 123.
28. Proudfoot, "The Negro in the CFL," 5.
29. Ibid.
30. Ibid.
31. Kelly, *Green Grit*, 123.
32. Bell-Webster, "Herb Trawick."
33. Kelly, *The Grey Cup*, 22.
34. Ibid., 22.
35. Ibid.
36. Ibid., 324.
37. Ibid., 22.
38. Bell-Webster, "Herb Trawick."
39. Proudfoot, "The Negro in the CFL," 5.
40. Ibid.
41. Ibid.
42. MacCambridge, *America's Game*.
43. Ross, *Outside the Lines*.
44. Proudfoot, "The Negro in the CFL."
45. Players included in this analysis are only those that had a player card issued for them in the year in question. Constantly changing rosters and imprecise and inconsistent historical record-keeping for rosters make it extremely difficult to identify all players in a given year. However, by using player cards, one can be reasonably assured that most of the prominent players are being identified.
46. This argument presumes that there was a sufficient supply of quality African-American players that could have moved into these positions.
47. This issue highlights the trade-off involved for teams such as Saskatchewan. To the extent fans may have had preferences against seeing African-American players on the team, the cost of indulging such preferences was that the

team performed more poorly on the field. In other words, fewer African-American players led to fewer wins. One interesting extension to this discussion would be to examine attendance data across the league during this era to determine which two competing factors—the desire to have fewer African-Americans on a team, versus the desire to win—were the strongest. Unfortunately, consistent and reliable attendance data from this era is not generally available.

48. See, for example, Scahill, "A Reinvestigation of Racial Discrimination and Baseball Cards."

REFERENCES

Barnes, LaVerne. 1971. *The Plastic Orgasm*. Toronto: McClelland and Stewart.

Becker, Gary. 1957. *The Economics of Discrimination*. Chicago: University of Chicago Press.

Boyd, Denny, and Brian Scrivener. 1997. *Legends of Autumn: The Glory Years of Canadian Football*. Vancouver: Greystone.

Bryant, Howard. 2002. *Shut Out: A Story of Race and Baseball in Boston*. New York: Routledge.

Chaput, John. 2005. *Saskatchewan Sports Legends*. Calgary: Johnson Gorman.

Humber, W. 2004. *A Sporting Chance: Achievements of African-Canadian Athletes*. Toronto: Natural Heritage Books.

Kahn, Lawrence. 2000. "The Sports Business as a Labor Market Laboratory," *Journal of Economic Perspectives* 14, 3: 75–94.

Kelly, Graham. 1999. *The Grey Cup*. Calgary: Johnson Gorman.

———. 2001. *Green Grit*. Toronto: Harper Collins.

Kidd, B. 1996. *The Struggle for Canadian Sport*. Toronto: University of Toronto Press.

Longley, N. 2006. "Racial Discrimination," in Wladimir Andreff and Stefan Szymanski, eds, *Handbook on the Economics of Sport*. Cheltenham: Edward Elgar.

MacCambridge, M. 2005. *America's Game: The Epic Story of How Pro Football Captured a Nation*. New York: Anchor Books.

Proudfoot, Dan. "The Negro in the CFL," *Canadian Magazine*, 18 November, 1967.

Robinson, Randall. 2004. *Quitting America: The Departure of a Black Man from His Native Land*. New York: Penguin Group.

Ross, Charles K. 1999. *Outside the Lines: African Americans and the Integration of the National Football League*. New York: New York University Press.

Scahill, Edward. 2005. "A Reinvestigation of Racial Discrimination and Baseball Cards," *Eastern Economic Journal* 31, 4: 537–50.

Winks, R. 1997. *The Blacks in Canada: A History*. Montreal: McGill-Queen's University Press.

Chapter 13

First Nations: Contemporary Issues

READINGS

Primary Documents

1   From *Statement of the Government of Canada on Indian Policy, 1969* [the White Paper], Jean Chrétien

2   From *Citizens Plus* [the Red Paper], the Indian Chiefs of Alberta

Historical Interpretations

3   From "Women's Class Strategies as Activism in Native Community Building in Toronto, 1950–1975," Heather A. Howard

4   From "Canada's Other Red Scare: The Anicinabe Park Occupation and Indigenous Decolonization," Scott Rutherford

INTRODUCTION

The historical episodes highlighted in this section were chosen to illustrate some of the ways in which First Nations and others have interacted in the "contemporary" era. We recognize some of the challenges referred to in both the primary and secondary readings because today many band members live off-reserve in cities like Toronto, or because the 1969 plan of Pierre Trudeau's government to dismantle the Department of Indian Affairs might gather both sympathy and opposition if proposed again. The current relationship between Indigenous and non-Indigenous people in Canada is affected by many of the same concerns that have troubled leaders in both communities for about 60 years. In particular, the need for Canada's various levels of government to fulfill longstanding promises to Indigenous Canadians ties the past to the present. It is important to see the 1950s through to the 1970s as an era in which both groups acknowledged the needs of *modern* Indigenous people, even though distrust and discomfort remained. The primary sources here are a matched set. In the "White Paper" (a name given in Canada and Great Britain to formal statements of government policy), the Canadian government suggested the eventual end of the bureaucracy that administrated several aspects of life for Indigenous people. Prime Minister Pierre Trudeau wanted them to adopt a standard kind of citizenship, rather than being afforded special rights. He told Indigenous people he wanted to give them the "power to change your own condition" by conferring individual rights in place of the collective rights negotiated in treaties. In their response, the "Red Paper," the Indian Chiefs of Alberta contended that Indigenous people should be "citizens plus." They feared that Trudeau's set of suggestions would wipe away the obligations that the government had undertaken in the past but never quite fulfilled. They wanted First Nations to remain distinct from the multicultural consensus that was gaining momentum during the 1960s. Our historical interpretations investigate two forms of activism among Indigenous people in Canada during the same period. Heather A. Howard focuses on the experience of successful young Aboriginal women who moved to Toronto from 1950 to 1975. She discusses the participation of these women in the emergence of an urban Aboriginal "middle class" and explains how these women used their social mobility to support the development of Indigenous community organizations and to foster pride among Aboriginal women in Toronto. Scott Rutherford explores a more dramatic kind of activism. He analyzes the Indigenous occupation of Anicinabe Park in 1974. He summarizes the local grievances and shows how Aboriginal activists related their struggle to the global struggles against colonialism. The integration of Indigenous people in Canadian society, the rise of limited forms of self-government, and the ongoing question of land claims are but a few examples of the contemporary developments that are connected to the complex historical relationship between Indigenous people and other Canadians. This relationship still remains in need of improvement today.

QUESTIONS FOR CONSIDERATION

1. What did the 1969 proposals from the federal government recommend regarding land claims? Citizen status?
2. What does "citizens plus" mean?
3. Is there an issue that has been more important to the recent history of Canada's Indigenous people than assimilation and resistance to it?
4. How were Indigenous women living in Toronto able to resist assimilation?
5. What were the objectives of the Ojibway Warriors Society (OWS) in Kenora in the 1970s? How did Aboriginal activists in Ontario inscribe their movement within a global framework of resistance?

SUGGESTIONS FOR FURTHER READING

Christopher Alcantar, *Negotiating the Deal: Comprehensive Land Claims Agreements in Canada* (Toronto: University of Toronto Press, 2013).
John Borrows, *Canada's Indigenous Constitution* (Toronto: University of Toronto Press, 2010).
Alan C. Cairns, *Citizens Plus: Aboriginal Peoples and the Canadian State* (Vancouver: UBC Press, 2000).

Canada, Royal Commission on Aboriginal Peoples, *Report of the Royal Commission on Aboriginal Peoples*, 5 vols (Ottawa: The Commission, 1996).

Canada, Truth and Reconciliation Commission of Canada, *Canada's Residential Schools*, 6 vols (Montreal: McGill-Queen's University Press, 2016).

———, *Final Report of the Truth and Reconciliation Commission of Canada* (Toronto: Lorimer, 2015).

Jean Chrétien, *Statement of the Government of Canada on Indian Policy, 1969* (Ottawa: Queen's Printer, Cat. No. R32-2469, 1969).

Ken Coates, *The Marshall Decision and Native Rights: The Marshall Decision and Mi'kmaq Rights in the Maritimes* (Montreal and Kingston: McGill-Queen's University Press, 2000).

Tom Flanagan, *First Nations? Second Thoughts*, 2nd edn (Montreal and Kingston: McGill-Queen's University Press, 2008).

Greg Poelzer and Ken S. Coates, *From Treaty Peoples to Treaty Nation: A Road Map for All Canadians* (Vancouver: UBC Press, 2016).

Janet Silman, *Enough Is Enough: Aboriginal Women Speak Out* (Toronto: Women's Press, 1987).

Annis May Timpson, *First Nations, First Thoughts: The Impact of Indigenous Thought in Canada* (Vancouver: UBC Press, 2010).

Primary Documents

1   From Jean Chrétien, *Statement of the Government of Canada on Indian Policy, 1969* [the White Paper], 3, 6–11. http://www.ainc-inac.gc.ca/ai/arp/ls/pubs/cp1969/cp1969-eng.pdf. p. 1. Reproduced with the permission of the Minister of Public Works and Government Services Canada, 2011.

To be an Indian is to be a man, with all a man's needs and abilities. To be an Indian is also to be different. It is to speak different languages, draw different pictures, tell different tales and to rely on a set of values developed in a different world.

Canada is richer for its Indian component, although there have been times when diversity seemed of little value to many Canadians.

But to be a Canadian Indian today is to be someone different in another way. It is to be someone apart—apart in law, apart in the provision of government services and, too often, apart in social contacts.

To be an Indian is to lack power—the power to act as owner of your lands, the power to spend your own money and, too often, the power to change your own condition.

Not always, but too often, to be an Indian is to be without—without a job, a good house, or running water; without knowledge, training or technical skill and, above all, without those feelings of dignity and self-confidence that a man must have if he is to walk with his head held high.

All these conditions of the Indians are the product of history and have nothing to do with their abilities and capacities. Indian relations with other Canadians began with special treatment by government and society, and special treatment has been the rule since Europeans first settled in Canada. Special treatment has made of the Indians a community disadvantaged and apart.

Obviously, the course of history must be changed.

To be an Indian must be to be free—free to develop Indian cultures in an environment of legal, social and economic equality with other Canadians.

SUMMARY

1 Background

The Government has reviewed its programs for Indians and has considered the effects of them on the present situation of the Indian people. The review has drawn on extensive consultations with the Indian people, and on the knowledge and experience of many people both in and out of government.

This review was a response to things said by the Indian people at the consultation meetings which began a year ago and culminated in a meeting in Ottawa in April.

This review has shown that this is the right time to change long-standing policies. The Indian people have shown their determination that present conditions shall not persist.

Opportunities are present today in Canadian society and new directions are open. The Government believes that Indian people must not be shut out of Canadian life and must share equally in these opportunities.

The Government could press on with the policy of fostering further education; could go ahead with physical improvement programs now operating in reserve communities; could press forward in the directions of recent years, and eventually many of the problems would be solved. But progress would be too slow. The change in Canadian society in recent years has been too great and continues too rapidly for this to be the answer. Something more is needed. We can no longer perpetuate the separation of Canadians. Now is the time to change.

This Government believes in equality. It believes that all men and women have equal rights. It is determined that all shall be treated fairly and that no one shall be shut out of Canadian life, and especially that no one shall be shut out because of his race.

This belief is the basis for the Government's determination to open the doors of opportunity to *all* Canadians, to remove the barriers which impede the development of people, of regions and of the country.

Only a policy based on this belief can enable the Indian people to realize their needs and aspirations.

The Indian people are entitled to such a policy. They are entitled to an equality which preserves and enriches Indian identity and distinction; an equality which stresses Indian participation in its creation and which manifests itself in all aspects of Indian life.

The goals of the Indian people cannot be set by others; they must spring from the Indian community itself—but government can create a framework within which all persons and groups can seek their own goals.

2 The New Policy

True equality presupposes that the Indian people have the right to full and equal participation in the cultural, social, economic and political life of Canada.

The government believes that the framework within which individual Indians and bands could achieve full participation requires:

1. that the legislative and constitutional bases of discrimination be removed;
2. that there be positive recognition by everyone of the unique contribution of Indian culture to Canadian life;
3. that services come through the same channels and from the same government agencies for all Canadians;
4. that those who are furthest behind be helped most;

5. that lawful obligations be recognized;
6. that control of Indian lands be transferred to the Indian people.

The Government would be prepared to take the following steps to create this framework:

1. Propose to Parliament that the Indian Act be repealed and take such legislative steps as may be necessary to enable Indians to control Indian lands and to acquire title to them.
2. Propose to the governments of the provinces that they take over the same responsibility for Indians that they have for other citizens in their provinces. The take-over would be accompanied by the transfer to the provinces of federal funds normally provided for Indian programs, augmented as may be necessary.
3. Make substantial funds available for Indian economic development as an interim measure.
4. Wind up that part of the Department of Indian Affairs and Northern Development which deals with Indian Affairs. The residual responsibilities of the Federal Government for programs in the field of Indian affairs would be transferred to other appropriate federal departments.

In addition, the Government will appoint a Commissioner to consult with the Indians and to study and recommend acceptable procedures for the adjudication of claims.

The new policy looks to a better future for all Indian people wherever they may be. The measures for implementation are straightforward. They require discussion, consultation and negotiation with the Indian people—individuals, bands and associations—and with provincial governments.

Success will depend upon the co-operation and assistance of the Indians and the provinces. The Government seeks this co-operation and will respond when it is offered.

3 The Immediate Steps

Some changes could take place quickly. Others would take longer. It is expected that within five years the Department of Indian Affairs and Northern Development would cease to operate in the field of Indian affairs; the new laws would be in effect and existing programs would have been devolved. The Indian lands would require special attention for some time. The process of transferring control to the Indian people would be under continuous review.

The Government believes this is a policy which is just and necessary. It can only be successful if it has the support of the Indian people, the provinces, and all Canadians.

The policy promises all Indian people a new opportunity to expand and develop their identity within the framework of a Canadian society which offers them the rewards and responsibilities of participation, the benefits of involvement and the pride of belonging.

HISTORICAL BACKGROUND

The weight of history affects us all, but it presses most heavily on the Indian people. Because of history, Indians today are the subject of legal discrimination; they have grievances because of past undertakings that have been broken or misunderstood; they do not have full control of their lands; and a higher proportion of Indians than other Canadians suffer poverty in all its debilitating forms. Because of history too, Indians look to a special department of the Federal Government for many of the services that other Canadians get from provincial or local governments.

This burden of separation has its origin deep in Canada's past and in early French and British colonial policy. The elements which grew to weigh so heavily were deeply entrenched at the time of Confederation.

Before that time there had evolved a policy of entering into agreements with the

Indians, of encouraging them to settle on reserves held by the Crown for their use and benefit, and of dealing with Indian lands through a separate organization—a policy of treating Indian people as a race apart.

After Confederation, these well-established precedents were followed and expanded. Exclusive legislative authority was given the Parliament of Canada in relation to "Indians, and Lands reserved for the Indians" under Head 24 of Section 91 of the British North America Act. Special legislation—an Indian Act—was passed, new treaties were entered into, and a network of administrative offices spread across the country either in advance of or along with the tide of settlement.

This system—special legislation, a special land system and separate administration for the Indian people—continues to be the basis of present Indian policy. It has saved for the Indian people places they can call home, but has carried with it serious human and physical as well as administrative disabilities.

Because the system was in the hands of the Federal Government, the Indians did not participate in the growth of provincial and local services. They were not required to participate in the development of their own communities which were tax exempt. The result was that the Indians, persuaded that property taxes were an unnecessary element in their lives, did not develop services for themselves. For many years such simple and limited services as were required to sustain life were provided through a network of Indian agencies reflecting the authoritarian tradition of a colonial administration, and until recently these agencies had staff funds to do little more than meet the most severe cases of hardship and distress.

The tradition of federal responsibility for Indian matters inhibited the development of a proper relationship between the provinces and the Indian people as citizens. Most provinces, faced with their own problems of growth and change, left responsibility for their Indian residents to the Federal Government. Indeed, successive Federal Governments did little to change the pattern. The result was that Indians were the almost exclusive concern of one agency of the Federal Government for nearly a century.

For a long time the problems of physical, legal and administrative separation attracted little attention. The Indian people were scattered in small groups across the country, often in remote areas. When they were in contact with the new settlers, there was little difference between the living standard of the two groups.

Initially, settlers as well as Indians depended on game, fish and fur. The settlers, however, were more concerned with clearing land and establishing themselves and differences soon began to appear.

With the technological change of the twentieth century, society became increasingly industrial and complex, and the separateness of the Indian people became more evident. Most Canadians moved to the growing cities, but the Indians remained largely a rural people, lacking both education and opportunity. The land was being developed rapidly, but many reserves were located in places where little development was possible. Reserves were usually excluded from development and many began to stand out as islands of poverty. The policy of separation had become a burden.

The legal and administrative discrimination in the treatment of Indian people has not given them an equal chance of success. It has exposed them to discrimination in the broadest and worst sense of the term—a discrimination that has profoundly affected their confidence that success can be theirs. Discrimination breeds discrimination by example, and the separateness of Indian people has affected the attitudes of other Canadians towards them.

The system of separate legislation and administration has also separated people of Indian ancestry into three groups—registered Indians, who are further divided into those who are under treaty and those who are not; enfranchised Indians who lost, or voluntarily relinquished, their legal status as Indians; and the Métis, who are of Indian ancestry but never had the status of registered Indians.

THE CASE FOR THE NEW POLICY

In the past ten years or so, there have been important improvements in education, health, housing, welfare, and community development. Developments in leadership among the Indian communities have become increasingly evident. Indian people have begun to forge a new unity. The Government believes progress can come from these developments but only if they are met by new responses. The proposed policy is a new response.

The policy rests upon the fundamental right of Indian people to full and equal participation in the cultural, social, economic, and political life of Canada.

To argue against this right is to argue *for* discrimination, isolation and separation. No Canadian should be excluded from participation in community life, and none should expect to withdraw and still enjoy the benefits that flow to those who participate.

1 The Legal Structure

Legislative and constitutional bases of discrimination must be removed.

Canada cannot seek the just society and keep discriminatory legislation on its statute books. The Government believes this to be self-evident. The ultimate aim of removing the specific references to Indians from the constitution may take some time, but it is a goal to be kept constantly in view. In the meantime, barriers created by special legislation can generally be struck down.

Under the authority of Head 24, Section 91 of the British North America Act, the Parliament of Canada has enacted the Indian Act. Various federal-provincial agreements and some other statutes also affect Indian policies.

In the long term, removal of the reference in the constitution would be necessary to end the legal distinction between Indians and other Canadians. In the short term, repeal of the Indian Act and enactment of transitional legislation to ensure the orderly management of Indian land would do much to mitigate the problem.

The ultimate goal could not be achieved quickly, for it requires a change in the economic circumstances of the Indian people and much preliminary adjustment with provincial authorities. Until the Indian people are satisfied that their land holdings are solely within their control, there may have to be some special legislation for Indian lands.

2 The Indian Cultural Heritage

There must be positive recognition by everyone of the unique contribution of Indian culture to Canadian society.

It is important that Canadians recognize and give credit to the Indian contribution. It manifests itself in many ways; yet it goes largely unrecognized and unacknowledged. Without recognition by others it is not easy to be proud.

All of us seek a basis for pride in our own lives, in those of our families and of our ancestors. Man needs such pride to sustain him in the inevitable hour of discouragement, in the moment when he faces obstacles, whenever life seems turned against him. Everyone has such moments. We manifest our pride in many ways, but always it supports and sustains us. The legitimate pride of the Indian people has been crushed too many times by too many of their fellow Canadians.

The principle of equality and all that goes with it demands that all of us recognize each other's cultural heritage as a source of personal strength.

Canada has changed greatly since the first Indian Act was passed. Today it is made up of many people with many cultures. Each has its own manner of relating to the other; each makes its own adjustments to the larger society.

Successful adjustment requires that the larger groups accept every group with its distinctive traits without prejudice, and that all groups share equitably in the material and non-material wealth of the country.

For many years Canadians believed the Indian people had but two choices: they could live in a reserve community, or they could be assimilated and lose their Indian identity. Today Canada has more to offer. There is a third choice—a full role in Canadian society and in the economy while retaining, strengthening and developing an Indian identity which preserves the good things of the past and helps Indian people to prosper and thrive.

This choice offers great hope for the Indian people. It offers great opportunity for Canadians to demonstrate that in our open society there is room for the development of people who preserve their different cultures and take pride in their diversity.

This new opportunity to enrich Canadian life is central to the Government's new policy. If the policy is to be successful, the Indian people must be in a position to play a full role in Canada's diversified society, a role which stresses the value of their experience and the possibilities of the future.

The Indian contribution to North American society is often overlooked, even by the Indian people themselves. Their history and tradition can be a rich source of pride, but are not sufficiently known and recognized. Too often, the art forms which express the past are preserved, but are inaccessible to most Indian people. This richness can be shared by all Canadians. Indian people must be helped to become aware of their history and heritage in all its forms, and this heritage must be brought before *all* Canadians in all its rich diversity.

Indian culture also lives through Indian speech and thought. The Indian languages are unique and valuable assets. Recognizing their value is not a matter of preserving ancient ways as fossils, but of ensuring the continuity of a people by encouraging and assisting them to work at the continuing development of their inheritance in the context of the present-day world. Culture lives and develops in the daily life of people, in their communities and in their other associations, and the Indian culture can be preserved, perpetuated and developed only by the Indian people themselves.

The Indian people have often been made to feel that their culture and history are not worthwhile. To lose a sense of worthiness is damaging. Success in life, in adapting to change, and in developing appropriate relations within the community as well as in relation to a wider world, requires a strong sense of personal worth—a real sense of identity.

Rich in folklore, in art forms and in concepts of community life, the Indian cultural heritage can grow and expand further to enrich the general society. Such a development is essential if the Indian people are again to establish a meaningful sense of identity and purpose and if Canada is to realize its maximum potential.

The Government recognizes that people of Indian ancestry must be helped in new ways in this task. It proposes, through the Secretary of State, to support associations and groups in developing a greater appreciation of their cultural heritage. It wants to foster adequate communication among all people of Indian descent and between them and the Canadian community as a whole.

Steps will be taken to enlist the support of Canadians generally. The provincial governments will be approached to support this goal through their many agencies operating in the field. Provincial educational authorities will be urged to intensify their review of school curriculae and course content with a view to ensuring that they adequately reflect Indian culture and Indian contributions to Canadian development.

3 Programs and Services

Services must come through the same channels and from the same government agencies for all Canadians.

This is an undeniable part of equality. It has been shown many times that separation of people follows from separate services. There can be no argument about the principle of common services. It is right.

It cannot be accepted now that Indians should be constitutionally excluded from the right to be treated within their province as full and equal citizens, with all the responsibilities and all the privileges that this might entail. It is in the provincial sphere where social remedies are structured and applied, and the Indian people, by and large, have been non-participating members of provincial society.

Canadians receive a wide range of services through provincial and local governments, but the Indian people and their communities are mostly outside that framework. It is no longer acceptable that the Indian people should be outside and apart. The Government believes that services should be available on an equitable basis, except for temporary differentiation based on need. Services ought not to flow from separate agencies established to serve particular groups, especially not to groups that are identified ethnically.

Separate but equal services do not provide truly equal treatment. Treatment has not been equal in the case of Indians and their communities. Many services require a wide range of facilities which cannot be duplicated by separate agencies. Others must be integral to the complex systems of community and regional life and cannot be matched on a small scale.

The Government is therefore convinced that the traditional method of providing separate services to Indians must be ended. All Indians should have access to all programs and services of all levels of government equally with other Canadians.

The Government proposes to negotiate with the provinces and conclude agreements under which Indian people would participate in and be served by the full programs of the provincial and local systems. Equitable financial arrangements would be sought to ensure that services could be provided in full measure commensurate with the needs. The negotiations must seek agreements to end discrimination while ensuring that no harm is inadvertently done to Indian interests. The Government further proposes that federal disbursements for Indian programs in each province be transferred to that province. Subject to negotiations with the provinces, such provisions would as a matter of principle eventually decline, the provinces ultimately assuming the same responsibility for services to Indian residents as they do for services to others.

At the same time, the Government proposes to transfer all remaining federal responsibilities for Indians from the Department of Indian Affairs and Northern Development to other departments, including the Departments of Regional Economic Expansion, Secretary of State, and Manpower and Immigration.

It is important that such transfers take place without disrupting services and that special arrangements not be compromised while they are subject to consultation and negotiation. The Government will pay particular attention to this.

4 Enriched Services

Those who are furthest behind must be helped most.

There can be little argument that conditions for many Indian people are not satisfactory to them and are not acceptable to others. There can be little question that special services, and especially enriched services, will be needed for some time.

Equality before the law and in programs and services does not necessarily result in equality in social and economic conditions.

For that reason, existing programs will be reviewed. The Department of Regional Economic Expansion, the Department of Manpower and Immigration, and other federal departments involved would be prepared to evolve programs that would help break past patterns of deprivation.

Additional funds would be available from a number of different sources. In an atmosphere of greater freedom, those who are able to do so would be expected to help themselves, so more funds would be available to help those who really need it. The transfer of Indian lands to Indian control should enable many individuals and groups to move ahead on their own initiative. This in turn would free funds for further enrichment of programs to help those who are furthest behind. By ending some programs and replacing them with others evolved within the community, a more effective use of funds would be achieved. Administrative savings would result from the elimination of separate agencies as various levels of government bring general programs and resources to bear. By broadening the base of service agencies, this enrichment could be extended to all who need it. By involving more agencies working at different levels, and by providing those agencies with the means to make them more effective, the Government believes that root problems could be attacked, that solutions could be found that hitherto evaded the best efforts and best-directed of programs.

The economic base for many Indians is their reserve land, but the development of reserves has lagged.

Among the many factors that determine economic growth of reserves, their location and size are particularly important. There are a number of reserves located within or near growing industrial areas which could provide substantial employment and income to their owners if they were properly developed. There are other reserves in agricultural areas which could provide a livelihood for a larger number of family units than is presently the case. The majority of the reserves, however, are located in the boreal or wooded regions of Canada, most of them geographically isolated and many having little economic potential. In these areas, low income, unemployment and under-employment are characteristic of Indians and non-Indians alike.

Even where reserves have economic potential, the Indians have been handicapped. Private investors have been reluctant to supply capital for projects on land which cannot be pledged as security. Adequate social and risk capital has not been available from public sources. Most Indians have not had the opportunity to acquire managerial experience, nor have they been offered sufficient technical assistance.

The Government believes that the Indian people should have the opportunity to develop the resources of their reserves so they may contribute to their own well-being and the economy of the nation. To develop Indian reserves to the level of the regions in which they are located will require considerable capital over a period of some years, as well as the provision of managerial and technical advice. Thus the Government believes that all programs and advisory services of the federal and provincial governments should be made readily available to Indians.

[. . .]

In many situations, the problems of Indians are similar to those faced by their non-Indian neighbours. Solutions to their problems cannot be found in isolation but must be sought within the context of regional development plans involving all the people. The consequence of an integrated regional approach is that all levels of government—federal, provincial and local—and the people themselves are involved. Helping overcome regional disparities in the economic well-being of Canadians is the main task assigned to the Department of Regional Economic Expansion. The Government believes that the needs of Indian communities should be met within this framework.

2 From The Indian Chiefs of Alberta, *Citizens Plus* [the Red Paper], 1–9.

A. THE PREAMBLE

To us who are Treaty Indians there is nothing more important than our Treaties, our lands and the well being of our future generation. We have studied carefully the contents of the Government White Paper on Indians and we have concluded that it offers despair instead of hope. Under the guise of land ownership, the government has devised a scheme whereby within a generation or shortly after the proposed Indian Lands Act expires our people would be left with no land and consequently the future generation would be condemned to the despair and ugly spectre of urban poverty in ghettos.

In Alberta, we have told the Federal Minister of Indian Affairs that we do not wish to discuss his White Paper with him until we reach a position where we can bring forth viable alternatives because we know that his paper is wrong and that it will harm our people. We refused to meet him on his White Paper because we have been stung and hurt by his concept of consultation.

In his White Paper, the Minister said, "This review was a response to things said by Indian people at the consultation meetings which began a year ago and culminated in a meeting in Ottawa in April." Yet, what Indians asked for land ownership that would result in Provincial taxation of our reserves? What Indians asked that the Canadian Constitution be changed to remove any reference to Indians or Indian lands? What Indians asked that Treaties be brought to an end? What group of Indians asked that aboriginal rights not be recognized? What group of Indians asked for a Commissioner whose purview would exclude half of the Indian population in Canada? The answer is no Treaty Indians asked for any of these things and yet through his concept of "consultation," the Minister said that his White Paper was in response to things said by Indians.

We felt that with this concept of consultation held by the Minister and his department, that if we met with them to discuss the contents of his White Paper without being fully prepared, that even if we just talked about the weather, he would turn around and tell Parliament and the Canadian public that we accepted his White Paper.

We asked for time to prepare a counter proposal. We have received assurances that the implementation process would not take place. However, the Federal rhetoric has not been substantiated by action. In fact, there is every indication that the implementation process is being carried as fast and as fully as possible. For example, the Departmental officials have prepared their budgets so as to make implementation possible. They rationalize this action by saying that if the White Paper on Indians is implemented their programs must be set whereby they can achieve the implementation within five years or if it does not come about that they can have better programs. Where is the moratorium that we have asked for on activities on the implementation on [sic] the White Paper?

The Minister of Indian Affairs has stated publically [sic] that he is not attempting to throw the Indians over to the provinces in spite of what is contained in writing in his White Paper. Yet, while maintaining this contradictory position he writes a letter to the Premier of Alberta dated February 20, 1970 stating that the Federal Government would transfer funds to the Province for the extension of provincial services to reserves; but these funds would be gradually phased out with the assumption that at this point the Provincial Government would bear full financial responsibility for the provision of these services.

Where is the consistency of the Minister's position when he tells Indians verbally that their reserves will not come under the Provincial tax system but his White Paper and his letter of the Premier say otherwise.

The Indian Chiefs of Alberta meeting in Calgary addressed a letter to the Honorable Pierre E. Trudeau dated January 22, 1970. That letter said:

"This assembly of all the Indian Chiefs of Alberta is deeply concerned with the action taken by the Minister of Indian Affairs and Northern Development, the Honorable Jean Chrétien, regarding the implementation of the Indian policy.

Time and time again, on the one hand, the Minister has declared publically [sic] to the Canadian people that the Indian Policy contained proposals to be discussed with the Indian people. On the other hand, Indian Affairs officials have been recruited for implementation teams to go ahead with the implementation of the policy paper.

We find this double-headed approach contradictory. A glaring example is the appointment of the Claims Commissioner.

Another example is the concentrated public relations program being conducted to impose the White Paper on the Canadian public. We find this incompatible with the Just Society. Discussions between the Federal Department of Indian Affairs and provincial governments have also been initiated.

This assembly of all the Indian Chiefs of Alberta reaffirms its position of unity and recognizes the Indian Association of Alberta as the voice of all the Treaty Indian people of this province. As representatives of our people we are pledged to continue our earnest efforts to preserve the hereditary and legal privileges of our people. At this meeting of Alberta Indian Chiefs, we have reviewed the first draft of our Counter Policy to the Chrétien paper. We plan to complete our final draft in the near future, for presentation to the Federal Government.

We request that no further process of implementation takes place and that action already taken be reviewed to minimize suspicions and to make possible a positive and constructive dialogue between your government and our people."

In his reply, dated February 19, 1970, to telegrams sent by the Chiefs' Conference of January 22nd, the Minister states that "the policy proposals, which were put forward in quite general terms will require modification and refinement before they can be put into effect." In a preceding sentence attempting to explain his Consultation and Negotiation Group which we know as the implementation team, he says, "I believe that the policy that has been proposed is a correct one, I expect that my Consultation and Negotiations officers will also try to persuade the Indian people, and Canadians generally, that the direction of the policy proposals is indeed in the best interest of all concerned."

If this is his belief, where is his so called flexibility, especially, when Indian people disagree with his mythical concepts of him leading the Indians to the promised land?

B. THE COUNTER POLICY

B.1. Indian Status

The White Paper Policy said "that the legislative and constitutional bases of discrimination should be removed."

We reject this policy. We say that the recognition of Indian status is essential for justice.

Retaining the legal status of Indians is necessary to be treated justly. Justice requires that the special history, rights and circumstances of Indian People be recognized.

The Chrétien Policy says, "Canada cannot seek the just society and keep discriminatory legislation on its statute books." That statement covers a faulty understanding of fairness. Professor L.C. Green found that in other countries minorities were given special status. Professor Green has concluded:

"The 1969 Statement of the Government of Canada on Indian Policy is based on the assumption that any legislation which sets a particular segment of the population apart from the main stream of the citizenry is ipso facto conducive to a denial of equality and therefore discriminatory and to be deplored. Such an attitude indicates a complete lack of understanding of the significance of the concept of equality, particularly in so far as the law concerning the protection of minorities is concerned.

" . . . It is perhaps not easy to define the distinction between the notions of equality in fact and equality in law; nevertheless, it may be said that the former notion excludes the idea of a merely formal equality . . .

"Equality in law precludes discrimination of any kind; whereas equality in fact may involve the necessity of different treatment in order to obtain a result which establishes an equilibrium between different situations . . .

"To attempt to maintain that the rights of the Indians result in discrimination against them or are evidence of a denial of their equality in the sense that their status is reduced thereby, is to indulge in an excessively narrow view of the meaning of words, of the purpose of equality and of the nature of discrimination."[1]

The legal definition of registered Indians must remain. If one of our registered brothers chooses, he may renounce his Indian status, become "enfranchised," receive his share of the funds of the tribe, and seek admission to ordinary Canadian society. But most Indians prefer to remain Indians. We believe that to be a good useful Canadian we must first be a good, happy and productive Indian.

B.2. The Unique Indian Culture and Contribution

The White Paper Policy said "that there should be positive recognition by everyone of the unique contribution of Indian culture to Canadian life.["]

We say that these are nice sounding words which are intended to mislead everybody. The only way to maintain our culture is for us to remain as Indians. To preserve our culture it is necessary to preserve our status, rights, lands and traditions. Our treaties are the bases of our rights.

There is room in Canada for diversity. Our leaders say that Canada should preserve her "pluralism," and encourage the culture of all her peoples. The culture[s] of the Indian peoples are old and colorful strands in that Canadian fabric of diversity. We want our children to learn our ways, our history, our customs, and our traditions.

Everyone should recognize that Indians have contributed much to the Canadian community. When we signed the treaties we promised to be good and loyal subjects of the Queen. The record is clear—we kept our promises. We were assured we would not be required to serve in foreign wars; nevertheless many Indians volunteered in greater proportion than non-Indian Canadians for service in two world wars. We live and are agreeable to live within the framework of Canadian civil and criminal law. We pay the same indirect and sales taxes that other Canadians pay. Our treaty rights cost Canada very little in relation to the Gross National Product or to the value of the lands ceded, but they are essential to us.

B.3. Channels for Services

The White Paper Policy says "that services should come through the same channels and from the same government agencies for all Canadians."

We say that the Federal Government is bound by the British North America Act, Section 9k, Head 24, to accept legislative responsibility for "Indians and Indian lands." Moreover in exchange for the lands which the Indian people surrendered to the Crown the treaties ensure the following benefits:

(a) To have and to hold certain lands called "reserves" for the sole use and benefit of the Indian people forever and assistance in the social[,] economic, and cultural development of the reserves.
(b) The provision of health services to the Indian people on the reserve or off the reserve at the expense of the Federal government anywhere in Canada.
(c) The provision of education of all types and levels to all Indian people at the expense of the Federal government.
(d) The right of the Indian people to hunt, trap and fish for their livelihood free of governmental interference and regulation and subject only to the proviso that the exercise of this right must not interfere with the use and enjoyment of private property.

These benefits are not "handouts" because the Indian people paid for them by surrendering their lands. The Federal Government is bound to provide the actual services relating to education, welfare, health and economic development.

B.4. Enriched Services

The White Paper policy says "that those who are furthest behind should be helped most." The policy also promises "enriched services."

We do not want different treatment for different tribes. These promises of enriched services are bribes to get us to accept the rest of the Policy. The Federal Government is trying to divide us Indian people so it can conquer us by saying that poorer reserves will be helped most.

All reserves and tribes need help in the economic, social, recreational and cultural development.

B.5. Lawful Obligations

The White Paper Policy says "that lawful obligations should be recognized." If the Government meant what it said we would be happy. But it is obvious that the Government has never bothered to learn what the treaties are and has a distorted picture of them.

The Government shows that it is willfully ignorant of the bargains that were made between the Indians and the Queen's Commissioners.

The Government must admit its mistakes and recognize that the treaties are historic, moral and legal obligations. The redmen signed them in good faith, and lived up to the treaties. The treaties were solemn agreements. Indian lands were exchanged for the promises of the Indian Commissioners who represented the Queen. Many missionaries of many faiths brought the authority and prestige of whiteman's religion in encouraging Indians to sign.

In our treaties of 1876, 1877, 1899 certain promises were made to our people; some of these are contained in the text of the treaties, some in the negotiations, and some in the memories of our people. Our basic view is that all these promises are part of the treaties and must be honored.

Modernize the Treaties

The intent and spirit of the treaties must be our guide, not the precise letter of a foreign language. Treaties that run forever must have room for the changes in the conditions of life. The undertaking of the Government to provide teachers was a commitment to provide Indian children the educational opportunity equal to their white neighbors. The machinery and livestock symbolized economic development.

The White Paper Policy says "a plain reading of the words used in the treaties reveals the limited and minimal promises which were included in them . . . and in one treaty only a medicine chest." But we know from the Commissioners' Reports that they told the Indians that medicine chests were included in all three.

Indians have the right to receive, without payment, all healthcare services without exception and paid by the Government of Canada.

The medicine chests that we know were mentioned in the negotiations for Treaties Six, Seven and Eight mean that Indians should now receive free medical, hospital and dental care—the same high quality services available to other Canadians.

[. . .]

The Indian people see the treaties as the basis of all their rights and status. If the Government expects the co-operation of Indians in any new policy, it must accept the Indian viewpoint on treaties. This would require the Government to start all over on its new policy.

[. . .]

NOTE

1. L.C. Green, *Canada's Indians—Federal Policy* (Edmonton: Government of Alberta, 1969).

Historical Interpretations

3 From Heather A. Howard, "Women's Class Strategies as Activism in Native Community Building in Toronto, 1950–1975," in Susan Applegate Krouse and Heather A. Howard, eds, *Keeping the Campfires Going: Native Women's Activism in Urban Communities* (Lincoln, NE: University of Nebraska Press, 2009). Reprinted with permission from the University of Nebraska Press.

Another important decision was to come to Toronto and live with my grand-daughters. I was very concerned for them. They had finished High School and wanted to go to Business College. So I decided to come with them just for a year. That's all I intended. But then I became involved in the Indian community here in Toronto, and realized the bad image Indians have . . . and so I felt I just couldn't leave. . . . It never occurred to me that I would run a boarding house for other students. I was only thinking of my relatives.

Rosamund Vanderburgh, *I Am Nokomis, Too: The Biography of Verna Patronella Johnston*

This was the response Verna Patronella Johnston (Anishinaabe, 1910–1995) gave anthropologist Rosamund Vanderburgh when asked why she came to Toronto in the 1960s from her home on the Cape Croker reserve located about one hundred miles northwest of the city. Vanderburgh documented Johnston's life in the book *I Am Nokomis, Too*, published in 1977. Her words "I was only thinking of my relatives" embody a common transition for Native women in rural–urban migration, from their roles as providers of shelter, food, and cultural knowledge transmission to kin to new roles as activists and strategists for building community for Native people in the city.

Like Johnston's granddaughters, between the end of World War II and the early 1970s, many Native women in Ontario came to Toronto in the hopes of accessing higher education, jobs, and freedom denied them on reserves under the oppression of federal government tutelage. However, much of the literature on Native rural–urban migration in Canada concentrates on an association between urbanization and social problems, or on Native peoples' "failure" to assimilate into urban society.[1] Conversely, I contend that attention to women's experiences in the history of Native community building in Toronto illustrates diversity and complexity in the socio-economic life of Native urban migrants. For some, their personal journeys to Toronto positioned them as members of an emergent Native "middle class," itself characterized by the particularities of Native historical and cultural experiences, which I discuss in the first section of this article.

In particular, many Native women in this position did not equate their relative economic success with assimilation. Rather, they utilized their class mobility to support the structural development of Native community organizations and promote positive pride in Native cultural identity in the city. In the second section, I sketch some of the intersections between Native women's lives and the development of community for thousands of Native people in Toronto between 1950 and 1975. I describe the involvement of Native women in the North American Indian

Club (1950–78), from which emerged the Native Canadian Centre of Toronto (founded 1962), the city's oldest Native community centre, and the women's participation in the Native Centre's Ladies' Auxiliary. Their experiences also highlight the specificity of emerging Native "middle-class" identity in Toronto. This is further explored in the third part of this article, examining the engagement of Native women in socio-economic class mobility, Native image making, and networking with women members of the Toronto white elite. Their work here served as a means to generate positive forms of Native identity grounded in notions of cultural pride and authenticity, while also securing resources to empower Native community self-determination.

WORK IN THE CITY AND THE EMERGENCE OF URBAN NATIVE "MIDDLE CLASS"

"So You Are Coming to Toronto" was the title of a pamphlet issued by the Canadian government for Native people who, by the late 1930s, had begun migrating in large numbers to the city. The pamphlet (circa 1957) featured on the cover three attractive young Native women in nurses' uniforms. Inside, practical paternalistic suggestions were given, such as "pay your rent, be on time for work, and spend your money wisely." In a further attempt to de-emphasize stereotypical "Indianness," it also warned young Native people that "consumption of alcoholic beverages has led to the ruin of many people," and they should "follow all the rules of personal hygiene, cut your hair, and refrain from questionable entertainment." On the other hand, the pamphlet also advised that Native people should not be "alarmed if many foolish questions are asked of you. Many people have not had the benefit of your experience and who is better prepared to advise them about Indians than yourself?

Always be courteous in your reply, even if the question appears silly."[2]

This pamphlet was addressed specifically to young Native people attending a particular technical school in Toronto, but it is a rare concrete example of federal attempts to control the behaviour of urbanizing Native people in Canada. Unlike in the United States, Native urban migration in Canada in the last century was in many instances more a form of resistance to the assimilative oppression of government control and surveillance on reserves than it was a strategically implemented plan concocted by federal authorities to assimilate Native people into mainstream.[3] It was responded and reacted to, more than it was instigated. [. . .] Native people also utilized and maximized the "tools of the oppressors" to resist assimilation and to organize their struggles to strengthen and assert Native cultural identity, self-determination, and inherent rights within the urban context.[4]

Various pathways led individual Native women to come together as "middle-class" activists. Some found their way to the city and to higher education through work as nannies in the homes of wealthy Toronto families. In interviews I conducted for the Toronto Native Community History Project in connection with my dissertation research, a number of women told me how working as nannies opened new doors for them. Many had good domestic skills, but little English language competency. Time spent with a white elite family gave them the chance to improve their English, and some were allowed to attend classes in secretarial school, nursing, or teaching in their time off. Several also strategically engaged the "benevolence" of their wealthy white employers and other new contacts in mobilizing the funds and political will necessary to establish and develop Native-based community organizations and services, beginning with the North American Indian Club in 1950, and the Native Canadian Centre of Toronto, incorporated in 1962.

These Native women, along with men who gained skills in the armed forces or trained as teachers and in technical trades, began to form a professional middle class in the burgeoning Native community in the city. They actively sought to integrate into the cosmopolitan and consumer lifestyle of mainstream society in the city, while valuing and promoting their Native heritage. They also tended to hold relatively conservative political views, in contrast to their peers who were involved in the Red Power movement, one of whom described the Toronto Native community in 1974 as "the biggest number of middle-class Native people in Canada [who] liked the benefits they were receiving from the system, or were afraid of the system. They wanted to prove they were not trouble-makers."[5]

This urban Native middle class needs to be understood within the parameters of specific historical, cultural, and socio-economic contexts for Native and non-Native relations in Canada. [. . .]

The legacy of imperialism and colonialism, the specific and enduring nature of Native poverty, and practical and symbolic gendered divisions of labour are also contributing factors to understanding how class is conceptualized from a Native perspective. Socio-economic relations emerging from imperialism and colonialism contributed a particular blend of occupational, ethnic, and gendered characteristics of Native Canadian identity. There is an association between Native identity and particular rural, "bush," and reserve occupations, such as fur trade, guiding, and lumber work. These "traditional" jobs correspond to the symbolic opposition between Native and urban identities. They likewise contribute to a gender division in urban Native identity. "Traditional" jobs are mostly associated with men, and this has perhaps added to the limitations on the types (general labour) and duration of work (short-term and transient) for Native men during the early days of mass urban migration in the post–World War II period. Native women, on the other hand, had come to occupy jobs in the colonial economy that were relatively transferable to the urban context, such as working in domestic jobs. Women also accessed opportunities made available to them through Christian conversion efforts, becoming involved in church activities and organizing. Canadian Indian policy since the mid-1800s also actively instituted a virtually irreversible state of extreme poverty among Native people. Just as *urban* and *Native* have been constructed as impossible contradictions, *poor* and *Native* have correlated as an inseparable basis of Native identity.[6]

[. . .]

Mark Nagler's 1970 ethnography of Native urbanization in Toronto did not offer an analysis of occupational differences between the 85 men and 65 women he interviewed. However, scrutiny of the jobs he listed as "Characteristics of Indians Interviewed" reveals that Native women in the study could be categorized in higher numbers in occupations considered professional, middle class, or "white collar," as Nagler terms them, and men were statistically more present among working-class or blue-collar sectors. Forty-five per cent of the women were found to be in "professional" or "middle-class" occupations, such as health professions, office work, and teaching, compared with 19 per cent of the men.[7]

Native middle class is thus constituted from particular historical, gendered, and cultural contexts and is therefore distinctive from the notion of class for the general Canadian population. Class is not merely determined by salary, but by the perceived prestige associated with jobs such as secretarial or office work. Sherry Ortner provides a model for how classes are relationally constituted, in that "they define themselves always in implicit reference to the other(s)." She further argues that "it appears overwhelmingly

the case in working-class culture that women are symbolically aligned, from both the male point of view and, apparently, their own, with the 'respectable,' 'middle class' side of those oppositions and choices."[8] When this approach is applied to understanding the urban Native middle class, it is clear that some Native people moving to the city are not simply becoming assimilated because they adopt the wider North American cultural goals of aspiring to middle-class lifestyles. Rather than a linear movement toward assimilation, there is a processual production of urban Native culture that is relational to "class." For Native people the definitions of lower-, middle-, working-, or professional class categories are constructed through the ongoing interactions within and between Native and non-Native communities.

WOMEN'S LIVES AND ORGANIZATIONAL DEVELOPMENT: THE NORTH AMERICAN INDIAN CLUB, THE NATIVE CANADIAN CENTRE OF TORONTO, AND THE LADIES' AUXILIARY

I found the "So You Are Coming to Toronto" pamphlet among the personal papers donated to the Toronto Native Community History Project by a founding member of the Native Canadian Centre of Toronto, Ella Rush. She had attached a note to the back of it that read, "Rules the Indian Affairs gave to all the newcomers (mostly girls) who came down to Toronto." Rush came from the nearby Six Nations of the Grand River reserve in the 1930s to train to be a nurse. Through school and work, she came to meet many other young Native people who, like herself, were in the city to make better lives for themselves than could be had on the increasingly economically and culturally depressed reserves. They formed a social network, which quickly came to include people from a wide diversity of Native cultures. Many pursued higher education (which meant beyond the limit of grade eight available on reserves) through military training and in technical schools, where they became nurses, teachers, and secretaries.

[. . .]

The first known gathering place for the burgeoning Toronto Native community in the twentieth century was at the house of a family named Jamieson who were from the Six Nations of the Grand River reserve. As early as the mid-1920s, they welcomed all young Native people into their home, primarily to provide an opportunity for them to meet and socialize with each other. After World War II, Ella Rush and several others (mostly women) who had met regularly at the Jamiesons' home felt they should try to form a club. They approached the YMCA and founded the North American Indian Club there in 1950. Under the auspices of the YMCA a minimum number of members were required to form a new club. Patricia Turner, also of Six Nations, who was a founding member along with her mother, remembered that a few Native men took out several memberships to meet the male numbers requirement.

At that time it was estimated that only two or three hundred Native people lived in the city. In retrospect the numbers may have been much higher. In light of the racism Native people faced in the city, the tendency of many was to respond with invisibility, attempting to pass for white if possible. Many were made to feel ashamed of their heritage or were cut off from their roots through removal to residential schools, like Hettie Sylvester, an Anishnaabekwe from the Beausoleil First Nation who stated: "Being at residential school for 12 years took away a lot of my culture. I thought I was like everyone else. It wasn't until I left that I realized I was Indian. And it wasn't until the last few years that I began to understand what being Indian means."[9]

Sylvester came to Toronto in 1940, when she was 19. She got her first job housekeeping and working as a nanny through the YWCA and was an early member of the Indian Club. She was later a founder of the Native Canadian Centre's craft shop, which still provides an important source of income for the Centre. She was president of the Centre's Ladies' Auxiliary for 15 years. Her residential school experience highlighted her inequality in racial terms when she came to the city, not realizing she was Indian until she left. However, the city was also a place where she could meet other Native people and utilize resources to organize a cultural community, in which her own identity as an Aboriginal person could be cultivated.

Another early member of the Indian Club, Lillian McGregor, came to the city as a teenager during World War II and worked as a nanny. McGregor pursued her education to become a nurse. She was born on Whitefish reserve on Birch Island in 1924 and spent her childhood there. During the summers in 1938 and 1939 she worked at a tourist lodge in the area. In 1939, when she had completed the eighth grade, she worked as a waitress at the lodge. This, she says, helped her to learn more English and to gain more confidence in herself. This was also where McGregor had the opportunity to become the nanny for a family from Toronto. Not wanting to jeopardize her chance of getting a higher education, she, her family, and the Toronto family worked it out so she could complete high school while looking after the children and doing her housework duties in the evenings and on weekends. McGregor is still very active in the community, serving until 2008 as elder in residence at the University of Toronto, where she received an honorary doctorate in 2002, and on the Native Canadian Centre's Taam Kadinikiijiik (Elders Council). Her opportunities in the city rested upon her own ambitions, but they were fostered also within a context of cross-cultural class negotiations between her own family, who were prominent on the reserve, and the Toronto elite family, who had the power to assist her.[10]

[. . .] In addition to their involvement in establishing the North American Indian Club and the Native Canadian Centre of Toronto, Native women formed the Native Centre's Ladies' Auxiliary in 1963. These women were particularly instrumental in the continuity and development of Native cultural pride, through education, social support, and the institution of an urban market for Native art and crafts, which supplied both financial and cultural support to the Native Centre and the community in Toronto.

Native women who organized community activity also shared the experience of being on the front line of the immediate social, health, employment, and educational needs of Native people in the city. Therefore, in addition to social events, early North American Indian Club activities also included hospital visiting and clothing and food drives. Later, the Ladies' Auxiliary provided counselling and inmate visiting at the Kingston Prison for Women. The *Toronto Native Times* reported several times on the Ladies' Auxiliary's trips to Kingston, and the social conditions that put the women in jail in the first place became a central concern for the Auxiliary.[11] The Auxiliary's first president, Millie Redmond, a Potawatomi from Walpole Island First Nation, became interested in trying to help women in penal institutions set up their own clubs, on one occasion saying: "Perhaps a club could be formed to coordinate programs which would help the women's stay behind bars be a more pleasant and meaningful experience. Perhaps our visit will help create the kind of interest necessary for such a club to be formed."[12]

Redmond, who passed away in the early 1990s, is often credited in the Native community with being the main founder of the North American Indian Club. She was also behind numerous other Native programs and organizations in the city. In the 1930s she was a frequent visitor to the home of the Jamieson family mentioned earlier, who welcomed young Native people into their home.

She reflected on how that experience led her to think about forming a community organization for Native people in the city:

> I wanted to do something—meet other Native people. And that's how I got the Native Indian Club started in my home, where I'd start to meet Native people. We wanted to get a club going, just like the Scottish and the Irish, and the German clubs. And we didn't have any so we called the Y and asked them to help— and sure enough they did. I helped form the Ladies' Auxiliary with Ella Rush. . . . Helping to form the Indian Club was one of the real good things because we got to know each other.[13]

Other Ladies' Auxiliary women like Josephine Beaucage also made the trips to Kingston penitentiary to demonstrate and teach craft making. She saw teaching as part of her mission to bring traditional practices and elements of Native culture to spaces where they might re-affirm Native identity and forge links of cultural solidarity, whether in the city or the penitentiary.[14] Beaucage was born on the Nipissing reserve in 1904. She worked for Northland Boatlines as well as in tourist camps during the summer; in the winter she and her husband worked on their traplines. In 1960 her husband suffered brain damage from nearly drowning in a boating accident, and their daughter, who lived in Toronto, convinced Beaucage to bring him to the city, where he might receive better health care. Unfortunately, he never recovered, and he died in 1970.

Beaucage pursued higher education in secretarial school and then taught herself how to do beadwork, a craft for which she soon learned she had a natural talent. She was responsible for starting beadwork classes at the Native Centre and in a number of other locations, many of them sponsored by the Toronto Board of Education. Eventually she was busy teaching traditional crafts throughout the province of Ontario. Beaucage's work life and her commitment to sharing her bead-work skills with others illustrate not only the contributions of women to cultural continuity and community, but also to the wider economy. About her career as a beadworker and Native crafts instructor, she recalled:

> I started to go out teaching in different places. I went to reserves [all] around. And when I used to go to these reserves, I ordered all my leather through B.B. Smith here in Toronto. I used to order by thousands, hundreds and thousands of square feet of leather for each course that I give. And the same with the bead company. I got my beads from a big bead company here in Toronto and that was the only bead company I would deal with. When [the owner] saw me he would say, "Boy, thank you for your advertisement—for advertising us."[15]

These women were particularly instrumental in the development of the urban market for Native arts and crafts, which supplied structural, financial, and cultural support to the Native Canadian Centre and to the wider Native community in Toronto. For example, between 1963 and 1968 Ladies' Auxiliary member Dorothy Jones of Six Nations was responsible for obtaining crafts from local reserves to sell to raise money for the Centre. An outspoken advocate for Native people representing themselves, Jones placed a high emphasis on the authenticity of the crafts. In1966 in the first edition of Centre's newsletter, later called *Beaver Tales*, it was reported:

> Mrs Dorothy Jones personally selects all the articles in the display in an effort to be sure that the handicraft is a true representation of high quality Indian handicraft, indicative of the ability of the old-time craft workers. . . . Here you may find lovely hand-loomed necklaces of beads (made by Indians long before

the Japanese made replicas for the tourist trade), fur-trimmed moccasins, beautiful woven baskets for various purposes, birchbark and horn rattles, drums and quill boxes. . . . At the present time, Mrs Jones could use more birchbark and sweetgrass items, but remember—of careful workmanship![16]

Hettie Sylvester's recollections of how the Native Centre's craft shop was started during her service as president of the Ladies' Auxiliary illustrates how the Ladies' Auxiliary's work combined cultural, social, and economic concerns in their volunteer service to community development. They were not only generating economic development through the organization of craft production and sales, but they also emphasized and articulated the value of positive Native identity, pride, and strength within the urban context. They also ensured the availability of some form of traditional social structures, particularly in terms of the roles of women as advisers and cultural transmitters.[17] Sylvester recalled fondly:

> I said, "Let's get Indian Crafts." I always had in my mind that I was an organizer. When I got to be president I was the busiest person, there was a project going on every month, fundraising or something. I enjoy working there, and not only as a salesperson. A lot of people come in and talk to me as their mother, I think. They come talk to me and tell me their problems. It is really interesting to listen to them and what they go through. I don't know why, there was a counselling room back there, but maybe they see me as motherly, I don't know. I liked it. I enjoy talking to these people.[18]

The variety of experiences of these Native women are departures from the stereotypical moulds to which Native people are generally expected to conform, grounded in the deeply entrenched view that there is some fundamental contradiction between Native identity and the cosmopolitanism of the city. [. . .] However, Native people in Toronto challenge the urban-Indian oxymoron, not by assimilating but by generating a rich and diverse Native community. The achievement of this richness and diversity has been the result of a range of dynamic struggles mediated by race, gender, and class relations with both non-Natives and within the Native community.

NATIVE URBAN CLASS MOBILITY, COMMUNITY BUILDING, AND NETWORKING WITH ELITES

As part of the emergent Native middle class, many of the Ladies' Auxiliary women were also key in a strategic collaboration with wealthy white women, which helped to provide much of the funding needed to establish the Centre. In particular they nurtured relationships between the Native Canadian Centre and the Imperial Order of the Daughters of the Empire (IODE). The IODE, founded in 1900, is an international organization devoted to Commonwealth citizenship. It was made up primarily of women from the urban industrial upper class, who engaged in a variety of benevolent works. In the 1960s IODE women turned their attention to concerns of Canadian national identity and citizenship. They focused their energies and resources on the integration of immigrants and Native people into Canadian society. IODE members were mobilized by a combination of ideological, gender, and class motivations that included their sense of duty to act benevolently and charitably toward the less fortunate in society and to contribute to the project of nation-building, patriotism, and citizenship. In the 1960s they were instrumental in establishment of at least five urban Native Friendship Centres across Canada, including the Toronto Centre.

[. . .]

The middle-class status of some of the Native women involved in the Indian Club and the Ladies' Auxiliary afforded them a degree of "leisure," which allowed them to commit time and effort to community service. They pursued the dual goals of ensuring and the integrity of Native cultural identity in the city and building financial support for the establishment and delivery of services to Native people. This initially captured the attention of organizations like the IODE. The women of the Native Centre's Ladies' Auxiliary and the IODE held in common a rejection of mainstream feminist perspectives that were perceived to present the home and family as oppressive institutions that imprisoned women. They also shared a desire to see improvements in the social conditions and recognition of Native people in Canada. Where they differed was in the underlying culturally based motivations behind these perspectives. The culture of the dominant class deployed an ideology that constructed gender roles in terms of a "calling" to carry out the bidding of the empire and citizenship. Native women's actions were based in their common experiences of politicized identity, cultural appropriation and devaluation, and their sense of duty to affirm Native cultural identity and build strong self-determined communities.

CONCLUSION

Native women's volunteer work in the early years of community building in Toronto did not represent a uniform platform for action, but rather was composed of diverse perspectives that changed over time and depended much on the concerns and directions taken by those in leadership positions. Under the guidance of Millie Redmond, for instance, the activities of the North American Indian Club and the Ladies' Auxiliary led to the establishment of social services for Native people in the city. Dorothy Jones and Ella Rush were significant in affirming a positive image for Native people in the urban environment, as well as the development of a discourse around the authenticity of Native identity emergent from the common experiences of people from diverse Native cultural backgrounds. Women like Hettie Sylvester and Josephine Beaucage were instrumental in the development of the urban market for Native art and crafts and also contributed to the transference and adaptation of traditional Native women's roles of leadership and cultural transmission in the urban context. The types of Native women's activism described in this article highlight the links between gender and class mobility

for urban Native people and the shaping of identity and community. They illustrate the dynamics of Native urbanization in the post–World War II era, particularly in terms of the gendered character of volunteer service and of educational and employment opportunities in the city for Native people. Native women's work and volunteer service has impacted the struggle for social equality and community development. Native women have also rejected the restrictions of reserve life, maximized opportunities in the urban context, and cultivated a space for the revitalization and growth of Native culture and identity, while striving for social justice.

NOTES

1. For example, Hugh Brody, *Indians on Skid Row* (Ottawa: Northern Science Research Group, Dept of Indian Affairs and Northern Development, 1971); Trevor Denton, "Strangers in Their Land: A Study of Migration from a Canadian Indian Reserve" (PhD thesis, University of Toronto, 1970); Edgar Dosman, *Indians: The Urban Dilemma* (Toronto: McClelland & Stewart, 1972); Larry Krotz, *Urban Indians: The Strangers in Canada's Cities* (Edmonton, AB: Hurtig, 1980); Mark Nagler, *Indians in the City: A Study of the Urbanization of Indians in Toronto* (Ottawa: Canadian Research Centre for Anthropology, Saint Paul University, 1970); Joan Ryan, *Wall of Words: The Betrayal of the Urban Indian* (Toronto: PMA Books, 1978); William Stanbury, *Success and Failure: Indians in Urban Society* (Vancouver: University of British Columbia Press, 1975).

2. Canadian Indian Affairs Branch, "So You Are Coming to Toronto," circa 1957, Ella Rush Collection (pamphlets, flyers, and posters), Toronto Native Community History Project, Native Canadian Centre of Toronto.

3. For an overview of US urban relocation policy, see Donald L. Fixico, *Termination and Relocation: Federal Indian Policy, 1945–1960* (Albuquerque: University of New Mexico Press, 1986).

4. Heather Howard-Bobiwash, "Dreamcatchers in the City: An Ethnohistory of Social Action,

Gender and Class in Native Community Production in Toronto" (PhD dissertation, Dept of Anthropology, University of Toronto, 2005).

5. Vern Harper, *Following the Red Path, the Native People's Caravan, 1974* (Toronto: NC Press, 1974), 44.

6. Evelyn Peters, "'Urban and Aboriginal': An Impossible Contradiction?" in Jon Caulfield and Linda Peake, eds, *City Lives and City Forms: Critical Research and Canadian Urbanism* (Toronto: University of Toronto Press, 1996).

7. Nagler, *Indians in the City*, 95–103.

8. Sherry Ortner, "Reading America: Preliminary Notes on Class and Culture," in Richard G. Fox, ed., *Recapturing Anthropology: Working in the Present* (Santa Fe, NM: School of American Research Press, 1991), 172.

9. Edna Manitowabi, "Hedy Sylvester: The Founder of the Centre's Craft Shop," *Boozhoo, Newsmagazine of the Native Canadian Centre of Toronto* 1, 4 (1987): 35–7.

10. "'There's So Much to Learn Each Day': A Profile of Lillian McGregor," *Native Canadian Newsletter* (Native Canadian Centre of Toronto) 10, 1 (October 1996): 1, 3.

11. The *Toronto Native Times* was a community-based monthly newspaper published by the Native Canadian Centre of Toronto between 1968 and 1981. Including this publication, the Centre has always produced some form of

regularly appearing serial during its 40-plus year history.

12. Irene Lee, "Ladies' Auxiliary Visits KP," *Toronto Native Times* (Native Canadian Centre of Toronto) 2, 4 (April 1971): 8.

13. Millie Redmond, interview by Evelyn Sit, Toronto Public Library Indian History Project, OHT 83030, 1983, 27–9.

14. Josephine Beaucage, interview by Cyndy Baskin, Toronto Public Library Indian History Project, OHT 83037, 1983.

15. Beaucage, interview by Cyndy Baskin, 13.

16. *Canadian Indian Centre of Toronto Newsletter*, February–March 1966, 4.

17. See Susan Lobo, "Urban Clan Mothers: Key Households in Cities," in Susan Applegate Krouse and Heather A. Howard, eds, *Keeping the Campfires Going: Native Women's Activism in Urban Communities* (Lincoln, NE: University of Nebraska Press, 2009), 1–21.

18. Hettie Sylvester, interview by Jaime Lee, Toronto Public Library Indian History Project, OHT 82020, 1982, 9–10.

4   Scott Rutherford, "Canada's Other Red Scare: The Anicinabe Park Occupation and Indigenous Decolonization," in Dan Berger, ed., *The Hidden 1970s: Histories of Radicalism* (New Brunswick, NJ: Rutgers University Press, 2010). Reprinted by permission of the author.

In October 1967, the Parliament of Canada came alive after Robert Thompson, a representative of the right-wing Social Credit Party, accused Cuba of sending revolutionary messages to First Nations people[1] in western Canada by way of Radio Havana.[2] The governing Liberal Party took the accusation seriously by promising to investigate the charge; the country's media intelligentsia, however, could not contain its sarcasm. Though the government's official investigation was just beginning, readers in western Canada were assured that "the White man doesn't have anything to worry about."[3] As the nationally read *Globe and Mail* put it: "There is no Ché in Canada: there is just an alleged Indian in Havana. . . . If Cuban based insurrection comes it will play for only a summer season: the Cubans will prefer the heat and sultry eyes of the Latin quarter to the cold reality of our northern winter."[4]

Neither Ché nor Fidel rode across the chilly western plains to lead a First Nations "Red Power" rebellion in 1967. Despite this, we should avoid quickly dismissing how local actions in opposition to colonialism and racism in Canada during the late 1960s and 1970s related to similar global movements. Montrealers, for example, rang in the 1970s by wrestling through the question of their own unique relationship with colonialism and the many different paths toward decolonization.[5] Meanwhile, new immigrants to Canada, including many young Caribbean and West Indian students, envisioned "the Great White North," especially Montreal and Toronto, as centres of imperial power. Accordingly, they developed their own form of Black Power to undo racism and capitalism in Canada while simultaneously shaping the politics of liberation in their homelands of Jamaica, Martinique, and Haiti.[6] Debates raged among "Old" and "New" leftists and a smattering of New Democrats, liberals, and conservatives as to how American economic and cultural imperialism interfered with Canadian sovereignty.[7]

The sociologist Howard Ramos argues that in Canada, during the period between 1973 and 1976, twice as many Indigenous protest actions and legal challenges took place per year as compared to any year between 1960 and 1969.[8] Yet, perhaps because Red Power in Canada reached its zenith some time after 1968, the global imagination of Indigenous activists is often forgotten. Historian Ken Coates suggests that this internationalism resulted in the emergence of "a dramatic new rhetoric . . . immersed in the language of decolonization and antiracism."[9] The 40-day armed occupation of Anicinabe Park in Kenora, Ontario, during the summer of 1974 by the Ojibway Warriors Society was one such moment, demonstrating intersections between the global and the local. In this event, we can observe links between Indigenous engagement with colonialism and capitalism in Canada and the global forces of international decolonization that were dominant in the post–World War II period. The nearly six-week occupation illuminates the intersections of identity politics and the culture of anti-colonialism in the 1970s. Commentators on all sides of the conflict explained the drama in a language that extended beyond the nation.

FROM MARCHES TO OCCUPATIONS

The Anicinabe Park occupation in 1974 was not the first sign of public resistance in Kenora during the 1960s and 1970s. In the summer of 1965, a widely read magazine article exposed Canadians to the poor living conditions, lack of economic opportunities, and racism faced by First Nations men and women in the Kenora area. Journalist Ian Adams described the world of First Nations people in Kenora as reminiscent of the injustices endured by African-American men and women in the southern United States.[10] That November, Kenora became the site of what was described at the time as Canada's first "civil rights" march. Five hundred people, from seven different reserves, marched hand-in-hand down Main Street, only stopping upon arrival at a meeting of town council to have a list of grievances read aloud by those leading the procession.[11] Town council members attempted to downplay the situation. Media from all over Canada, though, immediately jumped to claim Kenora as the country's own Little Rock or Selma.[12]

Beyond sensational headlines, the march generated responses from a variety of reform-minded organizations. The Ontario Human Rights Commission, in conjunction with local Indigenous leaders and a hesitant town council, formed a committee to oversee the implementation of programs and the documentation of further abuses.[13] The human rights workers assigned to Kenora remained busy throughout the period, documenting the everyday discrimination endured by First Nations members. Other well-meaning people, including student and church-based activists, converged to conduct studies and carry out various projects that they hoped would improve the lives of First Nations in the Kenora area. These efforts, in addition to the increased media attention, helped keep racism and segregation exposed. However, as the 1960s gave way to the 1970s, Indigenous people saw little improvement. Across the country, on rural reserves and in urban ghettos, First Nations and Métis continued to face debilitating effects of social and cultural oppression. Yet, like so many other marginalized people did during this time, young Indigenous women and men publicly challenged the powers they believed impeded their opportunity to live freely. They did so by developing new languages to theorize their oppression and new methods by which to reshape their daily lives. In the words of Howard Adams, a radical Métis intellectual, they replaced "the civil rights movements of the 1960s" with movements for liberation and self-determination. The era of Red Power had arrived.[14]

This is the climate within which the Ojibway Warriors Society (OWS) emerged. Formed in 1972 by a group of Ojibway men and women from northwestern Ontario, the group first drew significant attention in November 1973, with a 36-hour occupation of a federal Department of Indian Affairs office in Kenora. Once inside the offices, they told those who would listen that the "powwow at Indian Affairs" was to bring attention to a number of grievances, including greater economic autonomy for First Nations, compensation for the mercury contamination of a river near the Grassy Narrows reserve, and an end to the overtly racist actions and physical brutality against First Nations in Kenora.[15] Officials agreed to consider the grievances and did not charge the OWS for the occupation. Though this moment of rebellion passed somewhat unnoticed outside of Kenora, the ground had been broken for a new type of resistance to take shape the following year.

1974: ANICINABE PARK

The OWS helped organize a major gathering in Kenora in late July 1974, in an effort to bring together Indigenous people from across North America. They promoted the conference as an opportunity to "unify our Indian people" for "drastic changes," and plans were made to accommodate close to five thousand people at Anicinabe Park, a 14-acre parcel of land on the southeast edge of Kenora.[16] While not declaring so publicly, town officials were worried "that the rally was going to be a mere cloak for subversive activities."[17] The presence of Dennis Banks and other members of the American Indian Movement (AIM), the memory of the Warriors' occupation of Kenora's Department of Indian Affairs office less than a year earlier, and rumours that white vigilantes were prowling the area had the town officials questioning whether they could effectively police such an event. In response to the privately expressed concerns of Mayor Jim Davidson, Grand Council Treaty #3 President Peter Kelly wrote that the OWS would conduct their own security patrol.[18] He recommended, however, that the town would be wise to "police their own people, particularly their own police," some of whom were known for their "hostile and prejudicial attitudes."[19]

As the weekend conference got underway, hundreds of people drummed, danced, and talked with each other. While attendance was lower than expected, the estimated five hundred who came to the park finished the weekend by listening to the conference's keynote speaker, Dennis Banks, the national director of AIM. On trial that summer along with Russell Means for their roles in the Wounded Knee standoff, Banks was given special permission to cross the US–Canadian border to speak in Kenora.[20] Banks argued that colonial oppression had inflicted shame on Indigenous people across North America. Yet he did not limit his remarks to simply providing examples of oppression, because, in his opinion, the colonized did not need much evidence that they were colonized. Instead, Banks argued that First Nations people could work together for their own protection. "When society initiates and creates laws detrimental to our members, then we must disobey those laws. We must disobey the laws of the crooks. We must disobey the laws of people who have forgotten about mother earth and human rights."[21] The time to resist, according to Banks, was now [. . .]. Once he finished, those who remained watched a taekwondo exhibition—martial arts for self-protection.[22]

On the morning of July 23, a day after the conference ended, news spread that the 150 members of the OWS would not vacate the park until the land was "liberated Indian territory."[23] Town officials quickly tried to downplay the development, suggesting that those left in the park were staging "nothing more than a sit-in."[24] "Let them have the park," Mayor Jim Davidson told the *Toronto Star*, "After a week or so they will drift away and there will be no problem."[25] Louis Cameron, the OWS's 24-year-old spokesperson, from Whitedog reserve, who would become the focus of much media attention, responded to the prognosis of a short-lived sit-in with his own forecast: "We'll live here . . . we may even get married here."[26]

The OWS listed 25 points of contention that were organized as local, provincial, and national concerns. At the top of the list was a demand that propelled the early days of negotiations: a claim to Anicinabe Park, a parcel of land with disputed legal entitlement.[27] Yet there were 24 other issues, many of which received scant media attention. Most expanded on the grievances first laid out during the 1973 Indian Affairs office sit-in and again in press releases prior to the Ojibway Nation Conference. The OWS requested attention in the form of an "investigation into the violent deaths of Indian people in the Kenora area," increased availability of jobs, more co-operation from town police, and "better and fairer coverage of Indian issues in the local press." Most of the provincial and national issues demanded reforms to the justice system in order to better reflect First Nations values, as well as a "speedy and just settlement of land claims,"[28] and compensation for the people devastated by mercury pollution, an act that the OWS called "an outright crime against two communities."[29]

Away from Kenora, AIM organized solidarity rallies in Toronto toward the end of the occupation's first week, with Vernon Bellecourt speaking to an audience of between 50 and 100 people.[30] By the second week, the first signs of serious negotiations appeared, as did media reports of a tentative deal. Such reports, however, were premature.[31] In fact, the OWS believed that negotiations were bypassing or not taking seriously most of their demands. In part, this frustration resulted from the Department of Indian Affairs sending an official who, admittedly, had little power to make decisions for the federal government.[32] "We came honestly to talk," Cameron exclaimed, "but we have to return to the park and tell our people there is no hope in these talks."[33] Furthermore, some in the OWS were growing skeptical of their own negotiating committee (made up of representatives from Grand Council Treaty #3), so much so that the militants took negotiations with government and municipal officials into their own hands. Some townspeople and media outlets portrayed this split as evidence that the park occupiers had lost support of First Nations

around the Kenora area. A press release from Treaty #3 refuted this argument: "The Grand Council Treaty #3, the organization of Chiefs in the Kenora–Fort Frances area, wish to reiterate their solidarity with the desire for immediate changes as expressed by the Ojibway Warrior Society now occupying Anicinabe Park. The fact that some Indian people are turning away from peaceful approaches to change is a direct result of years of exploitation and persecution of Indian people by those with power."[34] Internal disagreements clearly existed, as did distrust among some militants toward the chiefs, but the message to the public remained clear: the divide and conquer tactics of colonialism were not going to work this time.

With the OWS members representing themselves at the bargaining table, talks continued to focus mainly on the land question and on getting the park occupiers to relinquish their weapons. While government negotiators focused on the peaceful resolution of the occupation, a different form of militancy began to rise outside of the park. Some white citizens began to advocate a new, more aggressive, strategy to end the standoff, one that abandoned negotiation.[35] [. . .] The first meeting of the Committee of Concerned Citizens (CCC) reportedly drew seven hundred residents. They discussed a number of strategies for ending the occupation. These included storming the park to "evict" the OWS if a ten-day truce, established in early August, passed without a resolution.[36] One person in attendance, reflecting the concern that the CCC would be perceived by non-Kenorans as a white vigilante group, told reporters that "they don't want to act like a bunch of red necks or the Ku Klux Klan, *but it will be necessary* if something doesn't happen soon" (emphasis added).[37]

Amid rumours that some police were eager to storm the park, and in the face of growing militancy from white townspeople, negotiations took on a more desperate tone. Various attempts at having human rights committees and government arbitrators oversee the talks could not break the impasse. Finally, an unlikely arbitrator arrived on the scene. After much consternation from elected officials, all sides agreed to let Dennis Banks take on the role of mediator.[38] Shortly thereafter, the OWS agreed to lay down their weapons on August 19 as an act of "good faith"—not, however, as an act of surrender. "The Ojibwa Warriors Society has spoken," Cameron announced. "We will now see if the government listened."[39] Ten days later, on August 29, 1974, the OWS, in conjunction with Dennis Banks and representatives from Grand Council Treaty #3, agreed to a tentative deal with the town, the provincial government, and the federal government, with further promises to study and implement several of the OWS recommendations. Grand Council Treaty #3 would file a land claim on behalf of the OWS for Anicinabe Park, which, in the meantime, would reopen and remain a free camping and recreation space for all visitors. Town council noted that if the land claim was not settled by May 1, 1975, "the matter of charges for use of Park facilities will be reviewed."[40] As well, it was agreed that, for the most part, the park occupiers would be granted amnesty, save for a variety of minor theft- and vandalism-related charges. Moreover, no trials would "take place until the land claim concerning Anicinabe Park" was resolved.[41]

UNDERSTANDING THE PARK OCCUPATION AND RED POWER IN THE 1970S

The six-week occupation brought Indigenous protest, armed struggle, and the town of Kenora back into the national and international spotlight. One might call it a moment of struggle between the colonized and the colonizer. In the broadest sense, this is true. The Anicinabe Park occupation pitted colonized First Nations against white settlers who had actively oppressed First Nations for centuries.

While these binaries make the occupation understandable, unquestioned adherence to them is problematic. Media coverage, public protests, and the state response show that in an increasingly globalized world, Indigenous militancy could elicit a wide spectrum of meaning.

Throughout the 1960s and 1970s, Indigenous critiques of Canada were shaped by a worldview that integrated their actions within a wider sphere of global rebellion. One of the enduring legacies of Red Power is that it attempted to stretch the definition of who was colonized, seeking links among Indigenous peoples, other racialized minorities, and the working poor. In doing so, groups such as the OWS demonstrated a social imaginary that simultaneously looked to the global, national, and local as sources of knowledge and as spaces in which their political activism could have importance. Such recognition is important because, in the words of historian Ken Coates, a global view "provided broad explanations which helped make sense of the nuances and complexities of local historical circumstances."[42] Yet helping make sense of one's circumstances should not be confused with providing a recipe for change. The historian Anthony Hall illustrates this point through his work on George Manuel, a Shuswap activist whose book *The Fourth World: An Indian Reality* became an influential text for the growth of pan-indigeniety in the 1970s. Before becoming the first president of the National Indian Brotherhood, Manuel travelled extensively outside of Canada, attending, for example, Tanzanian independence celebrations. Though he drew inspiration from such liberation struggles, Manuel's work also critiques Third World decolonization for, in the words of Hall, leaving "little room for the recognition of the value, worth, and contemporary applicability of Indigenous knowledge and philosophy."[43] Howard Adams, a Métis activist and intellectual from Saskatchewan, approached Third World decolonization in a similar fashion. In *Prisons of Grass*, published at the height of Red Power in Canada, Adams wrote at length about how Malcolm X and Frantz Fanon shaped his approach to decolonization, especially the need to liberate the mind and body from the effects of racism and colonization. Yet when it came time to discuss tactics for decolonization, Adams advocated abandoning the idea of "revolutionary nationalism" exemplified by "Cuba and Vietnam" for an approach he termed "radical nationalism"—essentially meaning local struggles for Indigenous sovereignty.[44]

The OWS spoke of locating Red Power within a global moment, but one that was contextualized within an Indigenous historical framework. [. . .]

Organizing under the title of "Ojibway Warriors Society" also used the past to move forward. OWS literature, along with articles published by the Toronto Warrior Society, informed readers that the Warriors Society was a response "to the specific conditions and needs of the people," that sought "justice and the return of the rights of our people." The Toronto Warriors Society implicitly created a sense of global consciousness by including a wide variety of international stories in its newspaper, *Native Peoples Struggle*. This included a story that documented a trip to China made by a group of Indigenous men and women, "a message from an Amazon Indian to his North American relatives," and a comparative study of the health of Indigenous children in Canada with that of children in Vietnam. The newspaper also published the stirring "Apolitical Intellectuals," a poem by Guatemalan poet Otto Rene Castillo and noted that "Castillo was one of the leading poets of Guatemala. In the year 1967, in a show of guerrilla strength, he died fighting for his people."[45] In pamphlets and interviews, the OWS portrayed itself as not simply an incarnation of the 1960s and 1970s, but as a contemporary materialization of a long-standing Ojibway tradition. As a result, besides being in solidarity with contemporary global struggles, the warriors who fought in

Kenora were the heirs of warriors who "fought the invaders, the British troops, the French troops and the Spanish troops throughout North America."[46] Such a narrative located the Anicinabe Park occupation within a pan-Indigenous anti-colonial struggle. Moreover, it explicitly depicted the summer of 1974 as one moment in a centuries-long resistance.

Indigenous anticolonial movements attempted to use representations of the past as ways to move forward in the 1970s. Yet the present provided a variety of political challenges. As within many movements, gender was a site of struggle within Red Power. One way to understand this is to situate Red Power within a global framework. Kristin Ross is one of many to argue that the recovery of manhood shaped Fanon's anti-colonial philosophies, an insight Laura Pulido argues was "one of the main impulses" of "Third World left" activism of the 1960s and 1970s in Los Angeles.[47] According to historian John Sayer, AIM leader Russell Means used similar language at the Wounded Knee trials in 1974, characterizing activism as an avenue to reclaim and express "Indian manhood."[48] Similar themes emerged in the Anicinabe Park occupation. Louis Cameron spoke often about the role of Ojibway men as the protector of Indigenous communities, an analysis seemingly echoed by some women, as well. OWS activist Lyle Ironstand recalled how his wife spurred him into action by challenging him to act like the men who took over Wounded Knee.[49] Accounts from various Red Power activists however demonstrate that attempts to recover manhood often failed to challenge contemporary forms of patriarchy and consequentially blunted political success. [. . .]

Women from diverse Indigenous nations responded in various ways to the masculinity of anticolonial struggle in the late 1960s and early 1970s. I have found only a small number of public commentaries from Indigenous women located in Canada, none of which came directly from the Anicinabe

Park occupation. In an account of her years spent as a Red Power activist, Lee Maracle relates the difficulty faced by women who wanted to be involved in radical anti-colonial activism while at the same time having to attend—usually without help—to the needs of young children. Vern Harper suggests that Indigenous men involved in the Native Peoples' Caravan took seriously the challenges by women to deal with sexist, and sometimes homophobic, behaviours. In his words, "a lot of us were just opening our eyes and ears for the first time."[50] However, for Indigenous women, the patriarchy and sexism they encountered in everyday life, and for some, in radical political movements, were deeply connected to their tenuous racial and national status, as defined by the Indian Act. Challenges to the most significant clauses, those that at their essence stripped Indigenous women—but not men—of their "Indian" identity if they chose to marry non-Indigenous Canadians, were the most public anti-colonial (and feminist) struggles led by Indigenous women in the 1970s. Ironically, though the challenge to the Indian Act can be thought of as an act of anti-colonial persuasion, in the mid-1970s, at the time of the Anicinabe Park occupation, prominent Indigenous nationalists vehemently rallied against such measures. Bonita Lawrence suggests that since 1968, when the federal government attempted to replace the entire Indian Act in favour of assimilation, many official Indigenous leaders and representatives viewed changing any part of the Indian Act as way for the federal government to erode Indigenous nationhood through step-by-step assimilation.[51]

Anti-colonial actions in the 1970s, such as the Anicinabe Park occupation, need to be understood through both culture and politics. The same holds true for how the public made sense of dramatic moments such as that in Kenora. Throughout the six weeks, the occupation drew intense interest from local, national, international, and alternative media. In the mainstream, the tone of the coverage varied, from condemnation and cynicism to sympathy and pity for Indigenous people in the Kenora area. The narrative told to readers was one that undoubtedly represented men as the central actors in the drama. Though the mainstream press noted the presence of "mothers and children" in the park, the views of Indigenous women, either as militants or otherwise, remained unknown to those following the occupation. Stereotypes that conceived Indigenous women as either "squaws" or "princesses" pervaded media representations. Even the new stereotype of the revolutionary woman—baby in one hand, rifle in the other—did not appear in the media coverage of the occupation, save a single photograph in one radical leftist publication in Canada.

Representations of Indigenous men, however, were far more present. [. . .] The widely circulating photographs and television images of brown-skinned men holding guns in Anicinabe Park portrayed the militants as a late-twentieth-century return of the romantic warrior figure that had simultaneously fascinated and scared white people for centuries. During the occupation, the press seemed to stretch the binary of warrior versus elder to mean male militant versus male elected official. Though, as noted earlier, Grand Council Treaty #3 publicly attempted to create distance from this divisive discourse, I suggest that much of negative characterization of the OWS was a way to control who was allowed to speak, and in what form. This is made clear in a lengthy editorial in northern Ontario's largest newspaper, the *Chronicle Journal* of Thunder Bay. Instead of issues, the editorial suggested, the OWS were simply publicity seekers, martyrs, and naïve "young Indians" believing that they could change the world "with a wave of the magic wand."[52] Recalling his night in the park, *Globe and Mail* reporter Derik Hodgson characterized the militants as "thugs," "madmen," and "crazies" who "talked tough" and giggled when pointing guns at people's faces. He described a park inhabited by giddy revolutionaries who spent the night "serenading policemen" with beating drums and talking revolution, which, reportedly, was a philosophy adopted from Algerians and Angolans.[53] [. . .] Nationally, as commentators demonstrated, such characterizations, based in colonial-racist stereotypes, were a political tool that could discredit the voice of Ojibway militants. Such representations suggested that Indigenous people were expected to have only one voice—and one that required the legitimation of white people.

Alongside reports that Third World philosophies inspired the OWS, AIM became a target for commentators who tried to characterize the six-week occupation as the work of foreign agents. AIM's presence at, or at least inspiration to, the Anicinabe Park occupation cannot be denied. [. . .] Yet blaming outsiders was another strategy to delegitimize the voice and claims made by the OWS. The discourse of "bad Indians" storming across the 49th parallel to corrupt and destroy the harmonious relations that docile "good Indians" had with their white Canadian neighbours is not unique to Canada, or the 1970s, as several historians have demonstrated.[54] This dichotomy of good or bad Indians in the 1970s, coded through references to AIM and outside interference, can also be seen as a commentary on the symbolic status of race and nation in Canada. AIM was not only provoking otherwise "good Indians" but also in the words of one journalist they were doing so with American methods rather than Canadian.[55] Not only could the OWS be ridiculed for fitting the stereotype of the "bad Indian," they were also betraying the code of peaceful co-existence that supposedly characterized Indigenous-white relations in Canada. This alleged racial harmony was a marker of Canadianness itself. The OWS acknowledged its intellectual and political debts to AIM as well as other decolonization struggles, as indicated by Cameron's references to Algeria and Angola. [. . .]

The meanings of transnational associations, however, were not uncontested. Indigenous militants used their global language to foster a sense of power and history that located struggle outside local boundaries. During the mid-1970s, imagining intersections between Indigenous resistance in Canada and global consciousness was a way for sympathetic journalists and allies to positively portray the occupation. During the occupation, author and journalist Les Whittington suggested, in an article sympathetic to the Indigenous militants, that the stance of the OWS "echoes the posture of their ancestors who fought the white man." Moreover, returning to armed resistance was "nothing less than the renewal of the wars of the last century."[56] [. . .] A smattering of radical leftist groups in Canada were not shy in making sense of local Indigenous movements through a transnational framework. Through public protests and literature, Maoists—whose involvement in Red Power activism sparked controversy[57]—along with various Trotskyist groups, supported and helped shape the idea that actions such as the park occupation were not unlike anti-colonial uprisings in Africa, the Caribbean, and Latin America. Other leftists, such as those involved with the social democratic publication *Canadian Dimension*, tended to make more subtle reference to the transnational aspect of Red Power. In a multi-article feature that appeared in the fall of 1974, the authors argued that the occupation grew out of problems "inherited" from nineteenth-century colonial polices. Moreover, the OWS were "good leaders" who "seized the initiative in Kenora, took risks they felt necessary and demonstrated themselves to be skilled tacticians during the negotiations."[58] The significance of Kenora for activists, however, was that it served as an example of "the ones who will get fed up enough to trade in their copies of Robert's Rules of Order for a volume of Frantz Fanon."[59] They had turned away from North American parliamentary procedure for Third World–inspired armed resistance.

CONCLUSION

During the late 1960s, some commentators scoffed at the idea that national liberation movements would find a home among First Nations in Canada. Rumours of Cuban-inspired insurrection, for example, were imagined as the paranoid fantasies of the far Right or the deluded Left. Yet by the mid-1970s, ignoring the influence of global decolonization on local struggles proved impossible. During the Anicinabe Park occupation, the OWS partially attributed the spirit and substance of their actions to movements outside of Canada. Such statements of global solidarity were not simply superficial bravado. While the occupation faded into memory in the last months of 1974, the connections—either imagined or real—between Red Power activists and other radicalized minorities grew stronger. [. . .]

The Anicinabe Park occupation represented many different things to many different people. This article has tried to make sense of some of those narratives, most notably those that tie the occupation into broader global histories of radical politics and culture of the 1970s. As Indigenous movements inch closer to the centre of our understanding of the 1960s and 1970s, many questions need to be considered. Of great importance is a better understanding of the relationship between global and local interactions. It is not enough to demonstrate how anti-colonial and anti-racist movements in Canada adapted a global political imaginary to local campaigns for justice. We should also move to understand how the spirit and substance of these movements across Canada shaped the actions of others who imagined the possibility of new worlds in the 1970s. Doing so promises not only to open up new windows to our understanding of the past, but also, perhaps, to help create new spaces to imagine future movements for justice and dignity that reach across personal, local, national, and international borders.

NOTES

1. A note on terminology: I use *First Nations* to refer to the Aboriginal peoples of Canada. *Indigenous* is used here to refer collectively to First Nations, Inuit, and Métis peoples.

2. "Seditious Cuban Broadcasts Charged," *Montreal Gazette*, 18 October 1967, 1; Lewis Seale, "SC Charge: Cubans Inciting Quebec," *Globe and Mail*, 18 October 1967, 1; Tom Hazlitt, "Is Cuban Radio Inciting Separatists, Indians? MP asks," *Toronto Star*, 18 October 1967, 4; Robert Wright, *Three Nights in Havana: Pierre Trudeau, Fidel Castro and the Cold War World* (Toronto: Harper Collins Publishers, 2007), 106. The numerous biographies, memoirs, and autobiographies of both Lester Pearson (Canada's prime minister in October 1967) and Fidel Castro do not mention this incident.

3. Gary Lautens, "Fidel! Our Indians Are Pretty with It—I Mean, Those Beads," *Toronto Star*, 1 November 1967, 4.

4. "New Empires," *Winnipeg Free Press*, 19 October 1967, 33.

5. On Quebec and decolonization in the 1960s and 1970s, see Sean Mills, "The Empire Within: Montreal, the Sixties, and the Forging of a Radical Imagination" (PhD diss., Queen's University, 2007).

6. See David Austin, "All Roads Lead to Montreal: Black Power, the Caribbean, and the Black Radical Tradition in Canada," *Journal of African-American History* 92, 4 (Fall 2007): 513–36.

7. For a broad overview of the Left in Canada during the 1960s and 1970s, see Ian McKay, *Rebels, Reds, Radicals: Rethinking Canada's Left History* (Toronto: Between the Lines, 2005), 183–210.

8. Howard Ramos, "Divergent Paths: Aboriginal Mobilization in Canada, 1951–2000" (PhD diss., McGill University, 2004), 53.

9. Ken Coates, *A Global History of Indigenous Peoples: Struggle and Survival* (New York: Palgrave Macmillan, 2004), 239.

10. Ian Adams, "The Indians: An Abandoned and Dispossessed People," *Weekend Magazine*, 31 July 1965, 2–6.

11. A. Alan Borovoy, *Uncivil Obedience: The Tactics and Tales of a Democratic Agitator* (Toronto: Lester Publishing Ltd., 1991), 33.

12. Ian Adams, "The Indians: An Abandoned and Dispossessed People," *Weekend Magazine*, 31 July 1965, 2–6; Perry Anglin, "100 Kenora Indians Plan 'Selma' March," *Toronto Star*, 17 November 1965, 1, 4; "The Shame of Our 'Mississippi' Indians," *Toronto Star*, 22 November 1965, 6; Tim Traynor, "Kenora: Racial Hotspot That Rivals Little Rock," *Winnipeg Free Press*, 27 November 1965, 10.

13. The Ontario Human Rights Commission maintained extensive documentation of the day-to-day discrimination and racism endured by First Nations people in the Kenora area.

14. Howard Adams, *Tortured People: The Politics of Colonization,* rev. edn (Penticton, BC: Theytus Books, 1999).

15. Ojibway Warriors Society, "Statement to Indian Affairs," 27 November 1973. Ojibway Warriors Society, "Statement to the Press," 27 November 1973.

16. Ojibway Nation Conference, promotional poster, July 1974.

17. E.C. Burton, *Journal of a Country Lawyer: Crime, Sin and Damn Good Fun* (Blaine, WA: Hancock House Publishers, 1995), 199.

18. In 1873, the Canadian government and First Nations (mainly Ojibwa) people around the Lake of the Woods (Kenora) area entered into Treaty #3. Significant debate continues over the treaty's terms. Grand Council Treaty #3 is the official territorial political organization for the 28 nations (26 in Ontario, 2 in Manitoba) that are represented by Treaty #3.

19. Peter Kelly, correspondence to Jim Davidson, 16 July 1974.

20. See Burton, *Journal of a Country Lawyer,* 215–17.

21. Dennis Banks quoted in April Holland, "Native People Urged to Work Together," *Kenora Daily Miner and News*, 22 July 1974, 1.

22. "Conference Orderly on the Weekend," *Kenora Daily Miner and News*, 22 July 1974, 14.

23. David Lee, "100 Armed Indians Seize Kenora Park," *Winnipeg Free Press*, 23 July 1974, 1.

24. Clarence Dusang, "Sessions Held over Protest," *Kenora Daily Miner and News*, 24 July 1974, 1; David Lee, "Little Reaction to Takeover; Park Indians More Militant," *Winnipeg Free Press*, 24 July 1974, 1.

25. Pat Brennan, "'Let Indians Have the Park,' Kenora Mayor Opposes Force," *Toronto Star*, 24 July 1974, 2.

26. Ken Nelson, "Leader Vows He Won't Leave the Park," *Kenora Daily Miner and News*, 25 July 1974, 1.

27. At issue was the legality of the town's 1959 purchase of the land from the federal government, who had held it as "Indian land" since the signing of Treaty #3. The state claimed that the purchase was legal; the OWS, with the support of Grand Council Treaty #3, argued that not only was it illegal for the federal government to sell the land in 1959, but that the land should not have been the federal government's to sell in the first place.

28. Louis Cameron interviewed in James Burke, *Paper Tomahawks: From Red Tape to Red Power* (Winnipeg: Queenston House Publishing, 1976), 378–96.

29. Louis Cameron, *Ojibway Warriors Society in Occupied Anicinabe Park, Kenora, Ontario, August, 1974* (Toronto: Better Read Graphics, 1974), 9.

30. The rally took place at Queen's Park in Toronto on Friday, 26 July 1974.

31. "Agreement Likely on Indian Dispute: Mayor to Release Details Later Today," *Kenora Daily Miner and News*, 2 August 1974, 1. David Lee, "Mayor Is Contradicted: No Pact, Say Kenora Indians," *Winnipeg Free Press*, 3 August 1974, 1.

32. "Little Progress Seen at Joint Meeting," *Kenora Daily Miner and News*, 1 August 1974, 1; "Only Limited Success in Kenora Discussions," *Chronicle-Journal*, 1 August 1974, 17.

33. Louis Cameron quoted in "Little Progress Seen at Joint Meeting," 1, and "Only Limited Success in Kenora Discussion," 17.

34. Grand Council Treaty #3, "Press Release," 4 August 1974, 2.

35. "500 Kenora Citizens Hold Meeting, Demand Indians Drop Weapons," *Chronicle-Journal*, 7 August 1974, 3.

36. David Lee, "Kenora Residents Ask End to Park Takeover," *Winnipeg Free Press*, 7 August 1974, 1, 5; Bruce Kirkland, "The Indian Occupation: Backlash Brewing by Kenora's Whites," *Toronto Star*, 24 August 1974, B7; "Citizens' Committee Outlines Meeting," *Kenora Daily Miner and News*, 26 August 1974, 1; and Ross Porter, "Group Says No Law and Order Exists," *Kenora Daily Miner and News*, 26 August 1974, 1.

37. Marion Fawcett quoted in David Lee, "Kenora Residents Ask End to Park Takeover," *Winnipeg Free Press*, 7 August 1974, 5; Dennis Braithwaite, "Obey the Law? Who's Going to Make Us?" *Toronto Star*, 4 September 1974, B6.

38. "Local Crown Attorney Wants Banks on Scene," *Kenora Daily Miner and News*, 15 August 1974, 1.

39. Louis Cameron quoted in "Militants Lay Down Arms," *Kenora Daily Miner and News*, 19 August 1974, 1; "Indians Lay Down Their Arms as Talks Resolve Park Siege," *Montreal Gazette*, 19 August 1974, 1.

40. James N. Davidson, mayor's office, 28 August 1974.

41. Letter co-signed by Douglas T. Wright, deputy provincial secretary for social development, and E.C. Burton, crown attorney, Ministry of the Attorney General, 29 August 1974, 2.

42. Coates, *A Global History of Indigenous Peoples*, 243.

43. Anthony J. Hall, *The American Empire and the Fourth World: The Bowl with One Spoon* (Montreal and Kingston: McGill-Queen's University Press, 2003), 240.

44. Howard Adams, *Prison of Grass: Canada from a Native Point of View* (1975; rpt. Calgary: Fifth House Publishers, 1989), 167–70.

45. *Native Peoples Struggle: An Organ of the Toronto Warrior Society* 1, 1 (July 1975), McMaster University Archives, Canadian Liberation Movement fonds, Box 19, File 23.

46. "Caravan 1974: Correspondence re Caravan from West to Ottawa, 1974," Trent University, CASNP, Box 2, File 16.

47. Kristin Ross, *Fast Cars, Clean Bodies: Decolonization and the Reordering of French Culture* (Cambridge, MA: The MIT Press, 1996), 158–9; Laura Pulido, *Black, Brown, Yellow, and Left: Radical Activism in Los Angeles* (Berkeley: University of California Press, 2006), 184.

48. John William Sayer, *Ghost Dancing the Law: The Wounded Knee Trials* (Cambridge, MA: Harvard University Press, 1997), 91.

49. Lyle Ironstand in Burke, *Paper Tomahawks*, 365–6.

50. Vern Harper, *Following the Red Path: The Native Peoples Caravan 1974* (Toronto: NC Press Limited, 1979), 27.

51. See Colleen Glenn with Joyce Green, "Colleen Glenn: A Métis Feminist in Indian Rights for Indian Women, 1973–1979," in Joyce Green, ed., *Making Space for Indigenous Feminism* (Centralia, WA: Fernwood Press, 2007), 235; for the most comprehensive examination of Indian Act regulations on gender and its centrality to colonialism in Canada, see Bonita Lawrence, *"Real" Indians and Others: Mixed Blood Urban Native Peoples and Indigenous Nationhood* (Vancouver: UBC Press, 2004).

52. "An Unnecessary Occupation," *Chronicle Journal*, 16 August 1974, 4.

53. Derik Hodgson, "Revolutionary Rhetoric, Indian Phrases Mix Tom-Toms and Tough Talk at Kenora Campsite," *Globe and Mail*, 6 August 1974, 2.

54. Daniel Francis, *The Imaginary Indian: The Image of the Indian in Canadian Culture* (Vancouver: Arsenal Pulp Press, 1992), 167; Ward Churchill, *The Ward Churchill Reader* (New York: Routledge, 2003), 194–8.

55. "Trouble at Anicinabe," *Chronicle-Journal*, 25 July 1974, 4.

56. Les Whittington, "Ojibway Nation Rebelled against Injustices Steeped in Time," *Gazette*, 20 August 1974, 7.

57. See David Ticoll and Stan Persky, "Welcome to Ottawa: the Native People's Caravan," *Canadian Dimension* 10, 6 (1975): 14–31.

58. John Gallagher and Cy Gonick, "The Occupation of Anicinabe Park," *Canadian Dimension* 10, 5 (1974): 22, 35.

59. Wayne Edmonstone, "A Cure for which There Is No Disease," *Canadian Dimension* 10, 5 (1974): 33. Edmonstone originally wrote his comments for the *Toronto Sun*, after which they were reprinted in *Canadian Dimension*'s feature on Anicinabe Park.

Chapter 14

Canada in a Globalizing World

READINGS

Primary Documents

Historical Interpretations

INTRODUCTION

With our ability to access goods, services, and especially cultural products across borders and oceans more quickly and conveniently than ever, the world may not actually be smaller, but it certainly seems that way. Canadians consume foreign-made goods like never before, and—thanks to satellite and web services—we are able to access international news and culture in a way that would have been unimaginable just a generation ago. Economic and cultural globalization are now a fact of life, but they did not emerge out of nowhere. For Canada, an important step toward this new global order was the Canada–US Free Trade Agreement, which came into effect in the late 1980s. To the extent that they were aware of the agreement, Americans regarded it as essentially economic in nature, while Canadians, who were keenly aware of free trade negotiations from the onset, viewed it as almost existential in its ramification. Supporters of free trade believed that the agreement would save Canada from economic ramifications and decline, whereas opponents warned that free trade would destroy Canadian culture and threaten the nation's social programs. Free trade prevailed after a lengthy and divisive debate, and Mexico joined the North American free trade club in the early 1990s.

The trend since then has been toward the opening up of international markets, most notably through the World Trade Organization. Resistance to these changes has tended to come from citizens' groups and non-governmental organizations, and it is the voice of one of these groups that provides our first primary source. Maude Barlow's Council of Canadians wanted to demonstrate the varied ways in which the free trade deal of the late 1980s would alter the lives of Canadian workers and consumers. The picture she paints here combines statistical evidence that free trade had already significantly affected Canada with the suggestion that there are more profound economic and social changes to come. Canada's cultural establishment was overwhelmingly opposed to free trade, and most of the political cartoons that we have included in this chapter express anxiety at the prospect of further continental integration. The obvious power discrepancy between Canada and the United States is frequently highlighted, and the architect of free trade, Conservative Prime Minister Brian Mulroney, is satirized as a lackey of the United States. One cartoonist, from the Regina *Leader Post*, chose however to lampoon Canadian anxieties over Americanization, noting humorously that the process had long passed the point of no return. Our historical interpretations examine globalization and international affairs at the provincial level. Dimitry Anastakis tells the story of Volvo's venture into Canadian manufacturing, showing us that globalization has a history before the free trade era. The company's Nova Scotian plant failed to give the automaker a strong presence in the North American market, but it shows us how interconnected and complex global trade had become by the 1960s. Shifting the focus to international relations, Louis Bélanger examines the Quebec government's paradiplomatic efforts. He notes that both the Liberal Party and the Parti Québécois have sought to increase Quebec's international presence, but that the province's paradiplomacy at times has been hindered by the federal government.

QUESTIONS FOR CONSIDERATION

1. According to Barlow, what are some of the downsides of the Canada–US free trade deal, and how would these be worsened under a free trade agreement that embraces Mexico as well?
2. What images of Canada and the United States are present in these cartoons?
3. Has the process of globalization ended, or will we see greater levels of economic and cultural exchange than we see today?
4. What were some of the problems that plagued Volvo's plant in Nova Scotia? Were all of these problems the result of globalized industry?
5. What forms has Quebec paradiplomacy taken since the 1960s and what goals has it sought?

SUGGESTIONS FOR FURTHER READING

Dimitry Anastakis, *Autonomous State: The Struggle for a Canadian Car Industry from OPEC to Free Trade* (Toronto: University of Toronto Press, 2013).
Dimitry Anastakis and Andrew Smith, eds, *Smart Globalization: The Canadian Business and Economic History Experience* (Toronto: University of Toronto Press, 2014).

Abigail B. Bakan and Daiva K. Stasiulis, *Negotiating Citizenship: Migrant Women in Canada and the Global System* (London: Palgrave Macmillan, 2003).

Maude Barlow, *Too Close for Comfort: Canada's Future within Fortress North America* (Toronto: McClelland & Stewart, 2005).

Stephen Clarkson, *Uncle Sam and Us: Globalization, Neoconservatism, and the Canadian State* (Toronto: University of Toronto Press, 2002).

Murray Dobbin, *The Myth of the Good Corporate Citizen: Canada and Democracy in the Age of Globalization*, 2nd edn (Toronto: Lorimer, 2003).

L. Ian Macdonald, ed., *Free Trade: Risks and Rewards* (Montreal and Kingston: McGill-Queen's University Press, 2000).

Gillian Roberts and David Stirrup, *Parallel Encounters: Culture at the Canada–US Border* (Waterloo, ON: Wilfrid Laurier University Press, 2012).

Winfried Siemerling and Sarah Phillips Casteel, *Canada and Its Americas: Transnational Navigations* (Montreal and Kingston: McGill-Queen's University Press, 2010).

Thom Workman, *Social Torment: Globalization in Atlantic Canada* (Black Point, NS: Fernwood Books Ltd, 2003).

Primary Documents

1 From Maude Barlow, "The Free Trade Agreement Fails Canada," *American Review of Canadian Studies* 21, 2/3 (Summer–Autumn 1991): 163–9. Copyright © ACSUS. Reprinted by permission of Taylor & Francis Ltd, www.tandfonline.com on behalf of ACSUS.

The Canada–US Free Trade Agreement has been a failure in Canada. While some argue that three years is too short a time in which to judge a trade deal of this magnitude, most Canadians remember the extravagant promises of immediate rewards made by the Mulroney government—rewards of jobs, savings, and prosperity—and rightly hold their government accountable for the massive deterioration of the Canadian economy.

Free trade is a misnomer. It implies simply a trade deal in which both sides agree to liberalize trade between them by bringing down barriers to that trade. But this deal did far, far more. It is a sweeping economic harmonization agreement that covers resource sharing, services, standards, and the movement of people and capital. So far, Canada is doing all the harmonizing. The free trade agreement is, in fact, the foremost tool used by the governments of the two countries to realign the historic balance in Canada between public and private enterprise. It has shifted economic power from elected governments to the private sector and locks future Canadian governments into this model. For Canada the issue goes beyond the traditional public versus private debate. For Canada the issue goes to the heart of our identity, our culture, and our very existence.

The histories of Canada and the United States are very different. Because our country is so vast and geographically harsh, and because we had and have such a sparse population, mostly strung along the US border, we had to develop a distinct economic model of sharing for survival. We entrusted our government to develop a mix of public and private enterprise to provide services in areas business alone would not have been able to enter or maintain profitably. This distinct economy not only served to foster a different way of life in Canada but also prevented us from being absorbed into the United States. To have permitted the marketplace to dictate all economic decisions would have doomed the young country.

So we developed a railway, an airline, a national broadcasting system, and some of the finest national social programs in the world. We also developed mechanisms to maintain some measure of economic control in the face of massive foreign (mostly American) domination of our industry and resources. We implemented protections for our cultural industries to ensure that we would have Canadian perspectives on the world and to make room for the work of Canadian artists and writers. Without such protections, Canada is overwhelmed by the dominant, mass entertainment industry of a neighbour ten times our size.

The free trade agreement, in effect, challenges every single part of this distinct Canadian system and, in so doing, threatens the very survival of our country. In leaving undefined for future talks what the United States considers to be unfair subsidies, the deal has exposed every Canadian government practice that helps foster our economic independence. Our constitutional requirement to provide equal opportunities and services to all regions of Canada is being challenged. Our marketing system to regulate farm supplies in order to give some measure of security to our farmers is under the axe. It is not that Canadian farmers are not as smart or resourceful as American farmers. But they operate in different conditions. As one Manitoba farmer explains, "My 'level playing field' is under snow for eight months of the year."

Now battered by a recession that increasingly resembles the depression of the thirties, Canada has been stripped by the free trade agreement of its ability to respond with programs that would kick-start the economy and protect those sectors most hurt. For a branch-plant economy like Canada, this reality is devastating. Big transnationals, who now make all the financial choices for the

country, are "rationalizing" their production out of Canada, and government is powerless to stop them. Canada is losing its manufacturing base and, with it, its ability to continue providing universal social programs.

The numbers are wrenching. Flooded by cheaper American imports, hundreds of Canadian companies have shut down. With no reason to stay, many hundreds of others have moved to the United States. In the first year of free trade, 92 per cent of all new businesses set up in Buffalo, New York, were Canadian. US corporate parents, no longer required to create employment in Canada, converted Canadian plants to warehouses. By the spring of 1991, there were at least 350 000 manufacturing jobs lost in Canada. (The equivalent in the United States would be 3 500 000 jobs.) This is just the tip of the iceberg. In 1990, Canada's manufacturing output decreased by 10 per cent—depression-level statistics. In the same year, the manufacturing workforce shrank 11 per cent. Everyone agrees now that many of these jobs will never return. In Ontario, the industrial heartland of the country, well over half of the layoffs of the last two years have been due to plant closures. This contrasts to the recession of 1982 when less than one-quarter of the layoffs were related to plant closures.

Free trade is not the sole reason for this disaster. Linked is the relatively high price of the Canadian dollar against the American, a situation many Canadians believe was an unwritten part of the free trade deal. Our former low dollar would have helped offset the manufacturing losses of free trade, but it was clearly an important irritant to American industry, who made it plain that a higher Canadian dollar was prerequisite to a deal. Free trade, cheaper goods, and a tough new consumer tax [are] driving millions of Canadians south of the border to shop, placing hundreds of retailers in peril.

But free trade has failed to secure Canadian producers market access to US consumers, and US industry interests continue to punish Canadian products with quotas and countervailing duties. As well, Canada did not gain exemption from US trade law. Since the free trade deal was signed, US harassment of Canadian exporters has increased. Canada has won only one of the sixteen cases that have come before the binational dispute panels set up under the deal—a dispute over pork—and the US trade negotiator, Carla Hills, refused to abide by it, thus politicizing what was supposed to be a non-political way for the partners in the free trade agreement to come to the resolution of trade disputes between them. Canadians were sold the free trade deal on the basis that we needed it to secure a dispute settlement mechanism. We can be forgiven for asking if it was worth destroying our manufacturing base to create what is arguably a more vulnerable situation for Canada. After all, the United States implementing legislation (Section 409) created a new weapon to assist producers to harass Canadian exporters suspected of using unfair subsidies.

The free trade–driven corporate restructuring has been a one-sided affair. Record mergers, takeovers, closures, downsizing, and rationalizations have destroyed thousands of jobs, and the promised high-value jobs have not materialized. And the takeover of the Canadian economy continues unabated. The Mulroney government scrapped Pierre Trudeau's Foreign Investment Review Agency in 1985 and replaced it with an agency that has not turned down one single application for a takeover in the six years of its existence. In the two years ending in the spring of 1990, a record 1403 Canadian companies were taken over, at a price of over $35.5 billion. Only 8 per cent of this is new investment in Canada. These takeovers are directly connected to job loss. For every billion dollars of profit made by a Canadian firm in Canada, 765 jobs are created. For every billion dollars of profit made by a US firm in Canada, 17 jobs are created.

Now, the free trade agreement is about to be extended to Mexico, and eventually to all of Latin America, creating the greatest military and economic trade block the world has ever known. Dependent on American capital and technology, Canadian resources (secured in the Canada–US Free Trade Agreement) and the cheap labour of Mexico and points south, this block is intended to balance the growing economic clout of Europe and Japan. The model, however, is very different. Free trade, North American style, is based on cheap, plentiful labour and the willingness of Latin American countries to look the other way when Fortune 500 companies abuse the environment, which they do often. Mexico and Canada will be required to enrich the core economy of the United States and their continued political acquiescence will be expected.

Canadians are very wary of the next round of free trade talks, and the polls show it. At the heart of this fear is our perception that, as a model for international economic agreements, it is fundamentally incompatible with Canadian interests. To support the extension of free trade would be to legitimize the Canada–US deal, and its critics seek its abrogation, not its enlargement. Canadians are also wondering what promises our government gave to the United States to be included in this round. It is apparent that the United States preferred to negotiate separate bilateral agreements with a number of countries but reluctantly allowed Canada to sit at the table, so long as we didn't become a "spoiler" at the talks.

Already, US negotiators have declared that Canada cannot maintain the protections for its cultural industries that it managed to safeguard in the Canada–US deal. A standstill clause (which many criticized as giving Canada no future power to bring in any new measures as needed to sustain Canadian cultural integrity), it nevertheless protected current Canadian content regulations, which, for instance, are the underpinnings of our national public broadcasting system, the Canadian Broadcasting Corporation. This exemption will be doomed, however, in the trilateral negotiations, leaving Canada totally vulnerable to bullying by American entertainment giants, such as Jack Valenti, who wants to crush any obstacles in his bid for international free trade in the film business. "The prospect of pain must be inserted into the equation, else the solution will never be suitable," he once said.

Quite simply, US corporate interests want to make the hemisphere safe for business. They want uniform rules for investment and services, an end to any screening of foreign investment by member countries of this trade block, and restrictions on their ability to set any rules governing the behaviour of American transnationals. Such agreements rob a country of economic sovereignty. Most transnational companies located in the United States now view Canada as just another domestic market, one about the size of California. Rendered the political equivalent of a regional interest, Canadian branch plants have neither autonomy nor clout: what is good for them, or Canada, is irrelevant. The few rights that Canada maintained to regulate foreign investment in the Canada–US Free Trade Agreement are slated for elimination in the trilateral talks.

And the job losses that started in 1988, when Canada signed the free trade agreement with the United States, will accelerate under hemispheric free trade. Canada's manufacturing industries are now adding Mexico to their choices of relocation, and the process is well under way. Forty-five companies, which collectively shed some 15 000 jobs in Canada in 1989–90 (well before the trend was really started) were active in the *maquiladora* of Mexico. Whole sectors of our economy are vulnerable. Our workers simply cannot compete with the wages paid to the workers of Mexico. Auto parts, plastics, furniture, food processing, appliances, chemicals, and textiles—all will likely be wiped out.

Most disturbing, our automotive sector will not survive. Governed by the Canada–US Auto Pact, this key sector was threatened by a weakening of its enforcement measures by the first free trade deal. Under a trilateral deal, the remaining enforcement measures will be erased, and Canadian auto makers will be in a head-to-head battle for survival against massive, cheap production of the *maquiladoras*. The argument that Canada will lose the low-end jobs, and that we will keep the high-technology jobs does not hold water. It is cheaper by far for a company to locate its high-skilled labour in an American plant bordering Mexico, and ship the components a short distance across that border for assembly, than to develop the products in Canada and ship them all the way to Mexico. Besides, business leaders admit that a well-run *maquiladora* can attain the productivity of a "first-world" plant in several years.

The options for Canadians will be to accept a dramatic lowering of standards, wages, and working conditions to keep businesses here. The threat of Mexico is already a silent partner at every employee–employer negotiation. Because no protections—social, environmental, or wage—are being established, it will be as if someone placed a huge funnel on the North American continent. Not only will the jobs slide relentlessly south, there will be enormous pressure to downgrade standards, laws, and working conditions to the lowest common denominator.

Canadians are rightly angry and frightened by this process. We have been told that we have to become more competitive, and we accept that. There are, however, different ways to become competitive. A country can slash spending, taxes, wages, social programs, communication and transportation infrastructures—in fact, government itself—in the hopes of attracting foreign investment because it is cheap to do business in such a system. Or, it can invest—in people, in education, in research and development, in communications—in short, in all of the areas that require an active nation-state and strong government–business co-operation.

Mexico has done the former, destroying its agricultural industry and driving wages to historically low levels. Canada has chosen this route as well, and the downward spiral has no bottom. As a result, we are beginning to resemble our American neighbours: deep divisions between rich and poor, food banks, inner-city violence, and a weakest-to-the-wall, survival-of-the-fittest mentality that is not only destroying our culture but threatening to destroy our actual existence.

This should matter to American friends for several reasons. A destabilized, impoverished northern neighbour would serve no American interest. If Canada's economy is converted to a third-world status, we will lose much of our value as a trading partner.

For American environmentalists, it is essential to understand that the concern is not only the fact that Mexico is a haven for acts of corporate environmental crime. Extensive job losses to Mexico in the manufacturing sector will force Canada to turn increasingly to the production of raw resources, deepening our dependence on their exploitation. Canada is now losing its resource policy on massive, guaranteed exports of fossil fuels, foreign ownership and the destruction of our forests, and deregulation of our energy production. The whole continent will suffer as a result.

Finally, for many Americans, Canadian social programs have been held up as a model. Our medical system, for instance, is not only universal, it is delivered more cheaply than health care in the United States. Surely the pursuit of prosperity must be linked to a rise in the standard of living for all, or we must ask what such a search is for. And surely it must place value on the unique contributions and characteristics of the different players. Canada is an exceptional friend and neighbour to the United States. It would be to no one's advantage to go any further with a trade arrangement that aims for the lowest common set of standards and in the bargain may destroy at least one of the participants.

2 Five Caricatures Related to the 1988 Free Trade Agreement and Subsequent Federal Election

Provincial Archives of Saskatchewan, Brian Gable fonds, Accession # 2015-056

Figure 14.1 *What's Really Scary Is . . .* by Brian Gable

AGAINST FREE TRADE	FOR FREE TRADE
- RAY.	- ANDREW.
- LIBERAL-LEFT.	- TORY.
- PROFESSIONAL.	- BUSINESSMAN.
- ETHNIC BACKGROUND.	- WASP.
- MASTERCARD.	- AMERICAN EXPRESS.
- MAZDA.	- BUICK.
- C.B.C.	- C.T.V.
- MACLEAN'S.	- FINANCIAL POST.
- EXPOS.	- BLUE JAYS.
- SCOTCH or WINE (WHITE).	- RYE AND DIET PEPSI.
- JANE FONDA.	- DOLLY PARTON.
- PASTA.	- BEEF.
- WORRIED THAT FREE TRADE MIGHT ELIMINATE HIS JOB.	- ISN'T WORRIED ABOUT FREE TRADE ELIMINAT-ING RAY'S JOB.

Figure 14.2 *Against Free Trade, For Free Trade* by Aislin (alias Terry Mosher)

Figure 14.3 *Free Trade* by Aislin (alias Terry Mosher)

Figure 14.4 *Free Trade* by Serge Chapleau

Figure 14.5 *Free Trade* by Aislin (alias Terry Mosher)

Historical Interpretations

3 From Dimitry Anastakis, "Building a 'New Nova Scotia': State Intervention, the Auto Industry and the Case of Volvo in Halifax, 1963–98," *Acadiensis* 34, 1 (Autumn 2004): 3–30. Reprinted with permission.

When the first Volvo "Canadians" rolled out of the company's new assembly facility in Dartmouth, Nova Scotia in the summer of 1963, the event was heralded by Premier Robert Stanfield as the harbinger of a "New Nova Scotia," which would quickly vault the province to the forefront of the manufacturing age. This sentiment was echoed by Volvo officials as well, who saw the plant as a crucial beachhead into an important foreign market. As the earliest non-North American–owned automotive facility built on this continent (Honda opened its first American facility in 1982), the plant emerged as a result of the federal and Nova Scotia governments' efforts to actively encourage industrial development. Yet Volvo's experiment in North America fell far short of the governments' lofty goals: operated as a simple assembly venture, the facility reached a maximum production of never more than a few thousand vehicles and employed only hundreds of workers in the province. After its initial burst of enthusiasm, the Volvo Corporation itself exhibited a lukewarm attitude toward the plant, providing only limited investment and support for its Canadian offspring. By the late 1990s, overcapacity in the auto industry in Europe and North America, reorganization of Volvo and the new realities of the quickly changing global auto industry resulted in the parent company's decision to close the plant. In 1999 Volvo was purchased by Ford of the United States, allowing the company to import the cars directly from Sweden duty-free under the 1965 Canada-United States Automotive Products Trade Agreement (Auto Pact). A

year later in 2000, this arrangement ended with the demise of the Auto Pact at the World Trade Organization.[1]

The story of the Nova Scotia Volvo plant is part of the end of "national" auto strategies and auto companies and the emergence of a world industry. The Volvo experiment is also the story of state intervention in the Canadian auto industry from a regional perspective. Provincial and federal government industrial policies provided incentives to the company to locate in Nova Scotia during a particularly activist period of state initiatives in industrial development. The federal government's auto policy was shaped by determined civil servants in Ottawa who were keen to generate as much economic activity as possible in this important sector of the Canadian economy. Interventionist industrial policy was central to the new Liberal government of Lester Pearson, and the creation of the 1965 Auto Pact, a key driver in encouraging automotive production, reflected this new approach. In Halifax, provincial politicians and policy makers were also keen to develop Nova Scotia's industry beyond traditional resource extraction, and utilized the newly created Industrial Estates Limited (IEL) to foster their activist bent. This new attitude was epitomized by the provincial government of Robert Stanfield. Volvo's experience in Nova Scotia points to some obvious questions: How did Volvo fare at the hands of the federal government in comparison with the rest of the automotive industry, which was overwhelmingly located in central Canada—principally Ontario? On balance, given that the venture lasted for nearly four decades, could the Volvo plant be considered a successful venture? Why did Ontario plants thrive under the Canadian state's central automotive policy—the Auto Pact—but the Volvo plant did not? How did the Halifax plant fit into Volvo's corporate strategy? In the final analysis, were the policies implemented by the two governments to persuade Volvo to locate and remain in Nova Scotia a success?

[. . .]

In a period characterized by the federal government's efforts to improve Canadian industry and the economic status of the Atlantic provinces through the creation of the departments of Industry and Regional Economic Expansion—and similar efforts by the Nova Scotia government such as IEL and the Voluntary Economic Planning Board—the establishment of Volvo in Dartmouth-Halifax stands out as a fascinating case in the industrial evolution of both Canada and the Maritimes. Although both the federal and provincial governments were instrumental in facilitating the establishment of Volvo in Nova Scotia, the operation was beset by numerous difficulties, including issues surrounding the plant location and operation of the facility, a changing market that put Volvo products at a disadvantage and the failure to achieve new or a broader range of production in the facility. In the end, however, these problems only partially contributed to the demise of the plant. The story of Volvo Halifax is a unique tale that illustrates the limits of 1960s-era federal and provincial industrial development initiatives in the rapidly changing and highly competitive global auto sector. Although instrumental in luring the plant to Nova Scotia, limited tariff reduction measures, small-scale direct infrastructure concessions and local boosterism could not sustain Volvo's small Halifax operation, a reflection of changing trade regimes, the large economies of scale required by the evolving automobile industry, and the shifting worldwide strategy pursued by Volvo by the 1990s.

FEDERAL AND PROVINCIAL INTERVENTION IN THE CANADIAN AUTO INDUSTRY: 1958–65

Between 1962 and 1965, Canadian policy makers sought new methods to encourage industrial development in the automotive sector, primarily through the use of duty-remission schemes that were export incentives.[2] Responding to demands for change in the industry from workers, firms and academics, the governments of Progressive Conservative John Diefenbaker and Liberal Lester Pearson created these programs in an effort to spur auto industry production and solve an increasingly difficult balance-of-payments problem. In October 1962, the Diefenbaker Conservative government created a special "remission plan" for automatic transmissions, an item which had been predominantly imported by Canadian industry until that time. Manufacturers were now forced to pay the 25 per cent duty on automatic transmissions (a measure that had not been enforced previously), but received a 100 per cent rebate (and a 100 per cent rebate on up to 10 000 imported engine blocks as well) for every dollar increase in the amount of Canadian goods they exported over and above a 12-month base period. The plan worked well, and by the time the Liberals came to power in 1963, the rebate scheme was having a positive impact on the industry.[3]

The newly elected minority Liberal government, also searching for ways by which to reduce the massive deficit on current account goods, took aim directly at the auto industry. In October 1963, C.M. "Bud" Drury, the minister of the newly created Department of Industry, introduced a plan that was intended to both alleviate the balance-of-payments burden and boost production even more than the Conservative plan had. The Liberals' new plan was a drastic expansion of the Conservatives' rebate scheme. Now, for every dollar of exported goods over and above the base year, manufacturers would be allowed to remit an equal amount on dutiable exports; the plan was also extended to all automotive exports. It was expected to run for three years and could, according to Drury, lead to an increase of between $150 and $200 million dollars in exports, a substantial chunk of the expected $500 million deficit for 1963–4.[4]

While the Conservative plan had raised few American eyebrows, the Liberals' broad, far-reaching scheme provoked an immediate response. The Americans were dismayed at the Canadian unilateral action, and chided the Canadian government that "any measures adopted to deal with Canada's balance-of-payments problems should not artificially distort the pattern of trade or interfere with the normal exercise of business judgement." The US State Department warned that American trade laws left open the possibility that a private interest might take exception to the plan, which could force the American government to take retaliatory measures.[5] By April of 1964, the American predictions were realized. That month, the Modine Manufacturing Company of Racine, Wisconsin initiated a complaint with the US Treasury Department that, under US trade law, the Canadian program constituted an unfair trade advantage. With a private corporation forcing the US government's hand because of Canadian unilateral actions (while the Canadian government steadfastly defended the program), relations between the two governments became strained. Both governments quickly realized that unless they resolved the issue, a trade war in the important automotive sector would be unavoidable.[6] As a result, the two sides negotiated the far-reaching and innovative Auto Pact, which erased tariffs for automotive trade between the two countries as long as each side achieved certain requirements.

Volvo's interaction with the Canadian state emerged parallel to and as a part of the federal government's automotive policy. As we shall see, Volvo asked for and achieved special status within the Canadian government's automotive policy and then continued to receive special treatment under the new automotive regime that governed automotive-state relations after 1965. Canadian state planners were willing to "bend the rules" to ensure that Volvo could operate in this country; in exchange, the presence of the company provided jobs and investment and promised to be a catalyst for further industrial development.[7]

While this explains the federal government's interventionist role in the auto industry, it does not explain the efforts of Nova Scotia's government to play a role in luring Volvo to Nova Scotia nor the motives and policies of the Nova Scotia government concerning provincial intervention in the auto industry. [. . .]

In 1956 Conservative Robert Stanfield won the Nova Scotia provincial election on a platform that espoused industrial renewal based on effective state intervention in a number of sectors in the Nova Scotia economy. Stanfield was determined to diversify the province's economy, which had suffered the collapse of traditional Nova Scotia industries—especially coal. Since the end of the Second World War, Nova Scotia had faced increasing unemployment and slowly declining economic prospects. As part of its platform, Stanfield's new government implemented a host of economic policies designed to assert government planning more forcefully in directing the provincial economy. These policies began to take a clear shape after 1960, and chief among them were the Voluntary Planning Act of 1963, which was intended to improve business-government communication, and IEL, the provincial development Crown corporation.[8]

IEL's first president was Frank Sobey, the scion of the supermarket chain, who was appointed in 1957. Considered a titan amongst Nova Scotia's business elite, Sobey worked at the unsalaried position until 1969, during which IEL attracted numerous businesses to the province, including textile, rubber, food processing and, of course, automotive companies.[9] [. . .] By 1968, more than 60 firms had been supported by IEL initiatives, and Sobey boasted that nearly 10 000 jobs had resulted from IEL agreements and projects, adding $40 million to the province's revenue.[10]

In the case of Volvo, both provincial policies (IEL's direct support for plant and investment) and federal policies (tariff concessions) were key to attracting it to the Dartmouth-Halifax region in the early 1960s. Yet Volvo's decision to come to Nova Scotia stemmed from more than just the incentives offered by the two governments.

VOLVO ARRIVES IN CANADA: 1962–65

Volvo, which means "I go" in Latin, was founded in 1924 by Assar Gabrielsson and Gustaf Larson, two employees of ball-bearings maker SKF, and it became an independent company in 1935. From the first hand-built model in the 1920s, the company grew impressively. By 1962 Volvo production reached over 100 000 cars, buses, and trucks at 13 facilities in Sweden employing 18 000 workers. The company's ethos was very conservative and focused on quality: there were only 15 different vehicle designs in Volvo's history, the vehicles were offered in only seven different colour choices and 11 per cent of its employees were involved with product inspection. As one excited Volvo Canada employee later reported, "Volvo rejects more component parts than any other car maker in the world."[11]

Volvo Canada was incorporated on 21 July 1958, a year after the first importation of Volvos to Canada by a British Columbia firm which arranged to distribute the cars nationwide. After 1959 Volvo sales increased dramatically, and the company responded by setting up its Canadian administrative headquarters in Toronto, which

established a dealer network. With the nationwide growth in Canadian sales, in early 1962 the company began to consider setting up a plant in Canada. The company's president of Canadian operations, D.W. (Pat) Samuel, a New Zealander, was key to hatching the agreement that saw Volvo arrive in Canada.[12] Samuel was dispatched by the parent company to negotiate with the federal and provincial governments toward gaining better terms for the company to facilitate the establishment of a plant and ease its initial production.

Samuel arrived in Ottawa in October of 1962 to begin discussions with Diefenbaker's Minister of Finance George Nowlan. Volvo had decided upon setting up their operation in Nova Scotia, Samuel told Nowlan, due to the province's relative proximity to Sweden and its year-round ice-free ports, a prerequisite for a venture which was to be heavily dependent on imports from the home country. The company was keen to begin production as soon as possible, Samuel argued, but the current content regulations for automotive production were unrealistic for an operation as small as Volvo. Under the 1936 Tariff Act, which still governed the auto trade in 1962, the most-favoured-nation (MFN) tariff rate was 17.5 per cent for all autos and most parts. In order to gain duty-free access for imported parts, a company was required to achieve 40 per cent Commonwealth (essentially Canadian) content for companies producing 10 000 units, 50 per cent for companies producing between 10 000 and 20 000 units and 60 per cent for companies producing over 20 000 vehicles.[13] In Ontario, the tariff schedule had the effect of facilitating much Canadian production by the established US-owned manufacturers, but would be punitive for any other company in its initial production stages. For a company like Volvo, which had the added cost of importing from the distant locale of Sweden, it was impossible to reach the 10 000 vehicle mark in the first period of production. In other words, without some special dispensation, Samuel argued, Volvo could not make a go of it.

Moreover, Samuel informed the minister that Volvo's initial plan was to be a bare-bones operation, one in which the company simply reassembled partially knocked-down (PKD) vehicles. There would be few Canadian parts added to the major vehicle components shipped from Sweden and bolted together in Nova Scotia. The Canadian plant would not even paint the vehicles, as the parts would arrive already coloured in Volvo's famous seven-colour range of choices. The operation was to employ Canadian labour and include some Canadian parts (headlights, bumpers, and perhaps tires) but, again, the scale and size of the operation made it difficult to reach even basic Canadian content levels. While the facility would be an important step in Nova Scotia industrial development, Volvo in Nova Scotia was not going to be the next Windsor, Oshawa, or Oakville—at least not yet.[14]

Nowlan was sympathetic. As a native Nova Scotian and a "red tory," he believed in the utility of interventionist programs that could help areas such as his home province.[15] The Volvo idea also fit well within federal plans for the entire Canadian auto sector. A 1961 Royal Commission on the Automotive Industry chaired by University of Toronto economist Vincent Bladen pointed to the need for exports in the industry, which was hampered by short production runs designed for a small market and a dependence on US parts imports.[16] This dependence on US parts imports stemmed from Canadian tariff law, which allowed duty-free imports for any parts of "a class or kind" not made in Canada. The almost entirely US-owned Canadian assembly industry took advantage of this situation to import massive amounts of vehicles and parts. As a result, the Canadian industry faced a difficult situation: If the market for autos in Canada performed poorly, employment and production declined. If the market performed well, massive US parts and vehicle imports would send the Canadian

trade balance spiralling downward. By 1962, auto imports accounted for 90 per cent of Canada's nearly $500 million trade deficit. In response, the government had created the duty-remission scheme that allowed companies to increase their imports of transmissions and engines duty-free if they increased their exports of other parts from Canada.[17]

While Volvo could not take advantage of the transmission/engine program (the company did not yet have facilities in Canada), Nowlan was eager to find some relief for Volvo so that it could begin production in Canada. Thus, the company was granted a number of tariff concessions from the Diefenbaker government to ease their way into production, as Volvo represented a "special case" that involved the establishment of new enterprise in Canada. In return for assurances that Volvo train 500 Canadians as mechanics and hire at least 400 workers at their new plant, the company received remission of duties on bodies, engines, and parts through a process similar to the transmission/engine program. The company's Canadian content requirements were to be slowly increased as Volvo adapted to the Canadian market.[18] In Nowlan's view, Volvo gained the benefit of "temporary tariff arrangements," and would be "increasing their purchases in Canada quite quickly once they become well established." Initially, Volvo was allowed to begin production with virtually no Canadian content while importing their parts duty-free.[19]

[. . .]

The site for a plant was also to be supported by Nova Scotia tax dollars through the granting of loans to the company to secure a facility. Samuel and company representatives investigated a number of sites in late 1962, and decided that Halifax-Dartmouth was the best location: since the company was dependent on shipments from Sweden, and Halifax was the closest major North American port to Sweden, it made sense to locate there.[20] The city's good road and port infrastructure also helped to convince Volvo. In January 1963

Samuel informed IEL that the company had leased a 55 000 sq. ft. dockside former sugar refinery owned by Acadia Sugar Refineries Co. in Dartmouth for $2 million for three years. For its part, IEL loaned the company funds for the lease at very favourable terms (8 per cent) until a plant could be built "to order" by the Crown corporation.[21] The new Volvo facility was little more than a converted warehouse. With the rail transportation issue and lease with IEL worked out, Volvo began working closely with Nova Scotia trade minister Manson to identify Nova Scotia companies as potential suppliers.[22]

Halifax was also ideal because of its lower labour costs, especially in comparison to those in the traditional Canadian automotive-producing communities in Ontario. Volvo officials were well aware that the average hourly industrial wage in Halifax in 1963 was $1.86 while the average hourly wage of a GM worker in Oshawa was between $2.16 and $2.29.[23] Thus, Nova Scotia's proximity to Sweden was not the only locational benefit bestowed upon the company as the Halifax location would produce a significant labour cost advantage. By February 1963, Canadians were being trained in Sweden in anticipation of the plant's opening.[24]

On 21 February 1963, the announcement of Volvo's Nova Scotia plant was made simultaneously in Halifax and Ottawa. Publicly, Samuel and the company enunciated a number of reasons for Volvo's decision to locate in Nova Scotia. In interviews with the financial press, Samuel stated that Volvo's move was because of the potential for both the market in Canada and production in Nova Scotia: "The main one is that we think we have a car that is suitable for the Canadian market and Canadian conditions. . . . I also believe that to sell a car in volume in Canada you must build it in Canada." He also saw a "growing nationalistic spirit" among Canadians, and that the plan was an "experiment" for the parent company.[25] Samuel boldly predicted that the plant would produce 5000

vehicles in its first year and 7500 in its second. Dartmouth Mayor I.W. Akerley's efforts in the final negotiations was also pointed out by Samuel as being pivotal to Volvo's decision to locate in the area as was the help of the provincial government—especially IEL.[26] While he did not mention IEL's role in facilitating the export of Volvo cars to central Canada, Samuel did state that Halifax's excellent rail connections to central Canada and the eastern United States had played a role in the company's decision.[27]

[. . .]

The Volvo announcement sparked a burst of Nova Scotia pride. Volvo's arrival was likened to an "economic miracle" by Stanfield in the legislature, an event he "could hardly believe. . . . For years we have all dreamed of something like this, and now the dream has become a reality."[28] The Halifax *Chronicle-Herald* also captured the spirit unleashed by the announcement: "All Nova Scotians should rejoice in the good fortune of Dartmouth, chosen yesterday as the location for a branch assembly plant of the giant Swedish car manufacturer, Volvo."[29] Volvo's Samuel heralded the choice of Nova Scotia as a testament to the "inherent traditions of quality of workmanship dating back to Nova Scotia's period of eminence as one of the world's biggest builders of wooden ships." Nova Scotia was, according to Samuel, "The cradle of Canadian craftsmanship."[30] Samuel himself was feted by the *Chronicle-Herald* as a man of "confidence" who helped embody the spirit that Volvo was bringing to Nova Scotia.[31]

[. . .]

The arrival of Volvo prompted an economic mini-boom in the region. Within weeks of Volvo's start-up, a number of other automotive and automotive-related companies announced their intentions to establish operations in Halifax, including Continental Can Co. and Surrette Battery.[32] Within months, William Docsteader, sales manager for the company, stated publicly that he expected many different firms to follow Volvo to

Dartmouth. The company's move to the area was, in his opinion, not only big news in Canada, but "big news all over the world."[33] In an effort to spur such growth, Volvo worked with Nova Scotia trade minister Manson to organize a Volvo-oriented trade show for prospective firms to understand the company's supplier needs.[34]

Volvo's arrival also generated interest from other non-North American auto companies about the possibility of setting up facilities in the province. In March 1963, IEL General Manager R.W. Manuge quietly held talks with Reneault and Peugot, and the province was actively recruiting Toyota through Canadian Motor Industries Limited, an outfit fronted by Toronto entrepreneur Peter Munk, which was also trying to establish auto assembly in the province.[35] In April it was reported that the United Kingdom's main auto association, the Society of Manufacturers and Traders Limited (SMMTL), was canvassing Nova Scotia locations for potential future sites. While the Volvo move had turned some heads in Europe, a 10 per cent surcharge on European imports by the Diefenbaker government had also generated newfound interest by British companies in Volvo-like knock-down operations in Canada.[36]

Notwithstanding the initial enthusiasm for the prospects of the Volvo plant and the development it might generate, the plant's beginnings were humble. The first crew of Volvo Nova Scotians received 12 weeks training. None had any experience in automotive assembly, yet many had backgrounds as mechanics. Assembly operated on a one-station system as opposed to a fully automated assembly line.[37] Only 5 of the first 100 employees were from Sweden. Initially, the company produced 15 to 20 vehicles a day. The company assembled imported body shells from Sweden, which were matched with Canadian-assembled Swedish engines and mechanical parts plus some parts supplied by Canadian manufacturers.[38]

[. . .]

The company quickly took advantage of the US market under the scheme as well. Gunnar Engellau, president of parent company AB Volvo, who appeared at the Dartmouth grand opening, stated that the company was "definitely interested in the export market." He was hopeful that the company could develop a market for its Canadian-built cars among Commonwealth countries, and that the Nova Scotia plant would produce for the US market.[39] In December 1963 Volvo Canada announced that 75 Volvos would be sold in New England. Although Volvo already sold 18 000 vehicles in the US, Canadian sourcing was seen as a way to boost production in Canada and a way to save on tariffs by taking advantage of the export-incentive nature of the duty-remission scheme. Moreover, Volvo had faced continuous product shortages in the United States.[40]

Notwithstanding the initial production increases and potential for the export market in the US, Volvo's output in Canada fell far from the company's early, optimistic predictions of Volvo Canada President D.W. Samuel. Instead of 5000 vehicles in 1963 and 7500 in 1964, Dartmouth had not even broken the 4000 vehicle mark by 1965. By June 1965, Canadian content was up to approximately 40 per cent and Volvo was producing 75 cars per week, boosting its annual production to 3500 cars.[41] Employment, which had originally been targeted at 300–400, had stalled at 101 employees. Faced with the difficulties of slow production and disappointed expectations, the company also faced the uncertainty created by a significantly altered automotive trade and regulatory regime after 1965.

VOLVO UNDER THE AUTO PACT, 1965–95

On 16 January 1965 Prime Minister Lester Pearson and President Lyndon Johnson signed the Canada-United States Automotive Products Trade Agreement at Johnson's "L.B.J.

Ranch" in Texas.[42] The agreement aimed to rationalize the North American industry for the benefit of producers and consumers alike, cement the strong continental ties and spirit of co-operation between the two countries and resolve a difficult issue in the US–Canadian trade relationship. The creation of the Auto Pact was precipitated by the unilateral Canadian efforts in 1962–4 to boost Canada's flagging auto industry and redress its rapidly deteriorating current account balance, a deficit that was largely the result of massive auto and parts imports from the United States. When the US and Canadian governments realized that the issue might deteriorate into a full-fledged trade war between the two countries, negotiations began in earnest.[43]

By the fall of 1964, the two sides came to an agreement. Duty-free trade in autos and parts was to be limited only by the different provisions governing each country. The agreement stipulated that imports to the US could come only from Canada and required 50 per cent North American content. In Canada, only certain *bona fide* manufacturers that maintained a ratio of production to sales and a base Canadian value-added rate were allowed to import from any country, though the US was the most likely country of origin. This intergovernmental agreement was complemented by a series of agreements between the Canadian government and the US-owned Canadian subsidiaries of the major auto producers referred to as "letters of undertaking." The companies promised to boost their investments in Canada over the next three years and to increase the Canadian content of their production by 60 per cent of whatever increase might occur in their sales in a given year. Instead of unrestricted free trade, the Auto Pact provided for a tightly managed limited sectoral trade area in autos and parts.

As the two governments and the American Big Three auto makers had been the instigators of the new agreement, it was primarily designed to benefit the US-based companies, largely to the exclusion of offshore manufacturers. While the Canadian government consulted extensively with the Canadian Big Three presidents, Volvo's representatives did not participate in the Auto Pact discussions. But with Volvo in mind, the Auto Pact did include a part which stipulated that the government of Canada could designate a manufacturer "not falling within the categories" in the Annex as being entitled to duty-free treatment. This allowed the government to designate Volvo under the agreement at a 40 per cent Canadian value-added (CVA) rate (being the dollar amount of Canadian labour or parts added to a vehicle), which was in keeping with the company's previous content commitments and did not preclude the company's participation in the new regime.[44]

Although the new agreement provided immense benefits for GM, Ford, and Chrysler, as they could now import and export across the border tariff free as long as they maintained their commitments in Canada and content requirements in the US, Volvo would benefit as well. The company could now import duty-free from Sweden, as the Canadian negotiators had ensured that the Canadian aspects of the agreement applied to third countries. In other words, Volvo could import parts from Sweden duty-free if they continued to maintain their Auto Pact commitments. This meant massive savings, and provided an opportunity for further growth as long as Volvo increased its Canadian presence.[45]

In its first years of operation, the Auto Pact proved to be immensely successful as expansion in the auto sector was impressive. The main players in the industry, the American Big Three, expanded their facilities greatly in the period immediately following the agreement's signing. One Department of Industry official estimated that of the over 50 major automotive-related projects announced by October of 1965, nearly half were by subsidiaries of US companies. The official noted that in many instances, the companies specifically declared that the reason for the growth was the automotive agreement, though many had been planned before 1965 because of growing Canadian demand.[46] During the first two years of the Auto Pact, every major manufacturer, including Volvo, opened or expanded at least one major facility in Canada, which accounted for much of the $260 million target in the letters of undertaking.[47] By the late 1960s, the Big Three had all boosted production and increased their investments. In 1969, the Canadian auto industry produced over one million vehicles for the first time, a massive increase over the 325 000 total vehicles produced in 1960.

[. . .]

While the tariff relief was welcomed by the company, continued disappointing production figures sparked stories that Volvo intended to flee to greener pastures. Compounding these rumours was the fact the company's lease at the Atlantic Sugar Refineries Plant was expiring in 1967 and that the company did not wish to renew the lease with Volvo.[48] Moving the company's head office to Toronto in 1966, and setting up a major parts depot at a new $1.2 million facility in Toronto, did not help matters. In early 1966 Volvo Canada President Kohler was forced to quell rumours that the company was moving to Quebec; he publicly stated the company was eager to remain in Nova Scotia.[49]

Volvo did move, but only to a new facility across the harbour from Dartmouth. After difficult deliberations over choosing a new site and a host of false starts, in 1966 Volvo took possession of a new and larger plant on Halifax's Pier 9. Built by IEL and leased to Volvo, the facility was a 190 000 sq. ft., $1 million investment by the Crown corporation.[50] Incentive was further provided by the Halifax City Council, which offered a 10-year tax-benefit package. The plant's location allowed Volvo to load shipments directly into the facility.[51] Again, this move by Volvo was heralded as a signal that the company was in Nova Scotia to stay, although the company did not own the building outright.

By 1968 Volvo, like the rest of the industry in Canada, had improved its position. That year, the new plant produced nearly 5000 Volvo 140 Series vehicles and had increased turnout from 360 cars a month to over 420; in November, in fact, the company boosted production at the Halifax facility from 120 to 130 cars a week. However, this optimism for Volvo's prospects did not stop company president Kohler from reminding Nova Scotia Premier G.I. Smith that the plant required provincial assistance "to further strengthen our position in Canada, and thereby create more jobs and opportunities for your area."[52]

[. . .]

Nonetheless, rumours continued to persist that the plant's position was precarious, a situation which was exacerbated by labour difficulties. In 1974 UAW Local 720, in a strike position following the end of their contract, were locked out by the company after negotiations broke off over the issue of overtime rates. Volvo representatives made it clear to Nova Scotia officials that they could not operate the facility under the overtime provisions being demanded by the union; Volvo executives were, in the view of IEL President Dean Salsman, "very disturbed and concerned about the negotiations."[53]

[. . .]

A number of other problems beyond the plant's control hindered its operation during the early 1970s. A 1971 report from the Centre for Automobile Safety in Washington, DC claiming that Volvo's cars were not as safe as advertised was widely publicized, and prompted the Halifax *Mail-Star* to question the reliability of Volvo Canada vehicles.[54] In its critique of Volvo safety, the paper also erroneously stated that the company was receiving "advances" from IEL. In response, Volvo Canada strenuously defended the quality of its cars and the integrity of its workforce, and vehemently repudiated the assertion that it had received any inappropriate "advances."[55] In the fall of 1973 a strike that closed the Port of Halifax led to production delays and the eventual closure of the Volvo plant for two weeks in November.[56] Both incidents added to the difficulties the company faced during that period.

Notwithstanding these setbacks, in 1975 the company reached its peak production and assembled more than 13 000 units. For the remainder of the decade, the plant produced between 7000 and 12 500 vehicles every year.[57] By 1980, while the rest of the automotive industry was in the depths of a severe recession, Volvo representatives were cautiously optimistic of the plant's long-term prospects. Although output usually remained less than 10 000 vehicles per year, Volvo's sales in Canada were increasing, which led to further production increases and underlined the importance of consistent output to meet that domestic demand.[58]

By the mid-1980s, however, Volvo Canada was producing only a fraction of what had been expected in 1963. In-vehicle Canadian content was barely 5 per cent and the vast majority of the Canadian value added at the Halifax plant resulted from labour costs. Ironically, tires from Michelin, which had been the other significant provincial effort to attract new industry to the province, were used on Nova Scotia Volvos—but they were imported from Germany rather than being delivered from the province's own plants in Pictou County and Bridgewater.[59]

This lack of content curtailed Volvo exports from Halifax to the United States. While Canadian officials gave the company preferential treatment to import from Sweden without achieving its content requirements, it was prohibited from exporting to the US if it did not achieve a 50 per cent "North American Content" threshold, which it never attained. As a result, the company was unable to use Halifax as a source for exports to the US which, by the mid-1970s, had become its largest market.

A new Halifax plant did not really provide the production that was necessary for the Canadian market either. In 1987 Volvo and IEL announced that the company would leave the Halifax plant at Pier 9 to move to an entirely new facility constructed at a cost of $13.5 million by Volvo at Bayer Lake Industrial Park. Volvo's move was sweetened by further tax breaks given by the municipal government, which required the company to pay only a fraction of its municipal tax bill for the next ten years. While some municipal councillors voiced concern about the continuing breaks for the company, especially after it was reported that Volvo Canada had been increasingly profitable during the 1980s, the municipal measures passed with little dissent.[60] During the move to the new facility, Volvo planned to reduce its workforce, which led to further labour difficulties at the plant as a wildcat strike ensued. Production reached near-record lows, and Volvo workers recall the move with bitterness.[61] Their bitterness would reach a breaking point only a few years later. By the mid-1990s, the company faced new challenges in its North American strategy—one which required drastic changes to its Halifax plant.

THE END OF VOLVO'S CANADIAN ADVENTURE, 1995–98

On 8 September 1998, Volvo announced that it was closing the Bayer Lake assembly plant, stating that it was no longer "economically viable" to produce cars in Halifax for the Canadian market. Volvo Canada President Gord Sonnenberg stated that the facility was simply too small for the long-term plans of the company. A plant that produced less than 10 000 vehicles was no match for one that produced over 100 000. Moreover, the company argued that economies of scale were key to their tariff concerns. Even with the 6.1 per cent Canadian tariff for complete vehicles, it was still more efficient to build the cars in Sweden at the large-scale plants and ship them to Canada. This was particularly true for the US export market. The closure also provoked rumours that Volvo was in greater financial trouble than the company was letting on and that the Halifax facility was being shuttered in part to address its over-capacity problems in Europe.[62] There was also speculation that the company was being pursued as a takeover target.

On 11 December 1998, the last Volvo assembled in Canada, a four-door S70 sedan, quietly rolled out of the facility and was donated to the IWK Grace Health Centre by the company and the workers.

Why did the Volvo venture in Canada, which had begun with such optimism and enthusiasm, end so sadly? The project, which was heralded as representing the start of a "New Nova Scotia" in 1963, ended with an unhappy and very public labour dispute and plant takeover. How did a venture which had the benefit of federal and provincial programs to spur industrial development come to such an ignominious end? Notwithstanding the plant's uneven existence, on balance can Volvo's Canadian venture be considered a success?

Some have viewed the story of Volvo in Canada as an example of corporate exploitation. Critics of the company argue that "Volvo did not 'bring a little bit of Sweden' to Nova Scotia; instead the company quickly adapted to and exploited the peripheral conditions of its new location."[63] The company took advantage of a weakened economic jurisdiction and lower labour costs, and gained the benefit of preferential treatment in tariff, capital, and infrastructure policies from federal and provincial governments—all in exchange for the promise of booming employment and increased industrial development. But that promise never materialized. Volvo never employed more than 200 people directly in the plant; its partial-knock-down system resulted in few secondary jobs in either parts or assembly; the plant produced barely 10 000 vehicles in an average year, a shadow of the over 100 000 vehicles produced at Volvo's European operations.

Others might compare the shortcomings at Volvo in Nova Scotia with the success of other assembly facilities in Ontario, and place the blame at the feet of a central Canadian-oriented federal government. After all, provincial representatives often felt slighted at the hands of the federal government when it came to government contracts—such as the military truck order—or felt that Ontario conditions were dictating the terms of Nova Scotia labour. When Volvo announced the Halifax closure, local reporters noted that the executives came to the press conference "with their Ontario public relations experts in tow."[64] Criticism toward the federal government, however, or its automotive policy could not be too harsh. After all, Volvo had been included in the Auto Pact, something not even the Honda and Toyota facilities in Ontario could boast.[65] Furthermore, Volvo had been given preferential tariff treatment by the federal government from the outset and had even gained further concessions under the Auto Pact. Instead, when it came to federal automotive policy, Volvo's status as a "regional" producer actually resulted in beneficial treatment. Volvo's demise was not a result of regional discrimination in favour of Ontario.

The end of Volvo's Canadian venture can also be seen as a failure in corporate strategy. Although Volvo was keen to exploit a new market, it never committed adequate resources to the plant or made a concerted financial investment in the Halifax operation. Such an effort may have paid off in far greater sales in Canada and a significant growth in Volvo's overseas market, but the company's managers were unwilling to commit wholeheartedly to their Canadian facility. Volvo's reluctance to boost its facility in Canada contrasted sharply with the Canadian Big Three plants in Ontario and Quebec, particularly after 1965: the GM, Ford, and Chrysler facilities received billions of dollars in new investment, not only in response to the companies' requirements under the Auto Pact but because these firms understood the benefits of sourcing production in Canada.[66]

Volvo faced constraints, of course, that largely precluded it from taking more advantage of its Canadian facility. First, Volvo did not have the benefits of proximity that the Big Three boasted. Windsor, where much of the Canadian auto industry was located, was only across the river from Detroit, America's "Motor City." Halifax, on the other hand, was thousands of miles from Sweden—there was no chance of developing "just-in-time" production techniques or of merging production schedules and operational plans of Volvo's Canadian and Swedish facilities, as happened with the Big Three after 1965. By the 1990s, the Halifax operation remained a far-flung outpost of the company, a remnant of a bygone era where a niche independent auto company such as Volvo had attempted to build its own multinational presence.[67] While Volvo's other "foreign" plants established during this period—Ghent, Belgium in 1965 and Kuala Lumpur, Malaysia in 1967—continued to function, their survival reflected local considerations (European integration and tariff requirements to be in Southeast Asia) rather than any coherent international policy.

Second, Volvo's Halifax plant was caught in a proverbial catch-22. The plant originated under tariff rules designed for small-scale production for the Canadian market. It lacked the economies of scale necessary to take full advantage of its Auto Pact status to export into the US market; doing so required hitting the necessary 50 per cent North American regional content guarantees under the agreement, a prohibitively expensive undertaking for a company of Volvo's size at a plant of Halifax's stature. Volvo's corporate managers likely saw little benefit in boosting investment or production in a facility that was originally intended as a beachhead into the Canadian market and which remained as such for all of its existence. With the concessions and incentives provided by the federal, provincial, and municipal governments, it

cost the company little to maintain the facility. In return for these generous inducements, Volvo provided nominal employment and minimal Canadian value added while gaining a measure of good corporate citizenship.

Indeed, in providing continued preferential treatment, both the federal and provincial governments showed that they could only do so much in an automotive industry that experienced so much change during the period under examination. Tariff concessions and plants built for Volvo did provide an incentive for the company to set up operations in Nova Scotia but governments could not control the market or the management decisions of the company. In this case, state intervention was beneficial in attracting the firm to Nova Scotia but could do little after the plant was established in the face of the vagaries of the marketplace or the quickly changing world auto industry. State intervention can be successful, but it can only be as successful as the partners with which it is dealing.

At its core, the departure of Volvo from Halifax did not happen because Nova Scotia was a poor choice for an auto plant or because Nova Scotia auto workers were not capable or effective. Nor did Volvo's departure hinge upon unrealistic tariff rules or overly demanding content regulations by the federal government. While many of the location and labour difficulties the plant faced certainly curtailed the growth of its production, Volvo left Halifax because of a rapidly changing world automotive industry, because it could not take advantage of new trade regimes to exploit its largest market, and because the economies of scale, which were realistic in 1963, were utterly unrealistic in 1998.

In the end, the plant itself may not have been a success, but it did provide employment for hundreds of workers in the Halifax area for over three decades. The plant takeover illustrates how valued those jobs were by the employees. As Anders Sandberg noted before the closure of the facility, "There are several reasons why Volvo workers stay in what appear to be less than satisfying jobs. The wages are high by Nova Scotia standards. There is little else to do. The workers are relatively old and know few other skills; in 1994, the average age was close to 50 years. These are facts of which the workers are critically aware and constantly reminded by management."[68] For these people, Volvo's Halifax venture had nothing to do with corporate exploitation: the company provided jobs where none had existed before, and the governments' willingness to use taxpayer funds to provide incentives was not a case of Volvo "taking advantage" of Canadian largesse but a genuine effort at economic development that did not, in the end, have a lasting effect.

In the long run, the battle over the closure of Volvo Halifax may have been moot. In 1998 the Ford Motor Company purchased the auto assembly operations of Volvo of Sweden. With the new arrangement, it is highly unlikely that Ford would have continued to operate the facility, given that they could import Volvo cars directly from Sweden into the United States duty-free under the Auto Pact because of the change of ownership. Even the demise of the Auto Pact, following the 2000 World Trade Organization ruling that the agreement was contrary to international trade laws, would have likely led to the end of the plant. Without the preferential tariff treatment afforded by the agreement, Volvo would not have continued to build cars at its tiny Canadian operation. Corporate consolidation and the globalization of the automotive industry would have quickly shuttered the plant, something that sporadic production and uncertain facilities had not managed to do in nearly four decades.

NOTES

1. Dimitry Anastakis, "Requiem for a Trade Agreement: The Auto Pact at the WTO, 1999–2000," *Canadian Business Law Journal*, 34, 3 (February 2001): 313–35.
2. Dimitry Anastakis, "Auto Pact: Business and Diplomacy in the Creation of a Borderless North American Auto Industry, 1945–1971," PhD thesis, York University, 2001.
3. John Holmes, "From Three Industries to One: Towards an Integrated North American Automobile Industry," in Maureen Molot, ed., *Driving Continentally: National Policies and the North American Auto Industry* (Ottawa, 1993), p. 27.
4. Simon S. Reisman to Walter Gordon, "Proposals to Reduce Trade Deficit in Automobile Industry," 28 August 1963, RG 19 (Department of Finance), vol. 3946, file 8705-1-1, National Archives of Canada [NA] and Canada, *Debates of the House of Commons*, 25 October 1963, pp. 3999–4000.
5. "United States Aide Memoire: Confidential," 24 October 1963, RG 19, vol. 3946, file 8705-1-1, NA.
6. "Time Bomb May Lie Under Exports; Opposition Intensifies," *Globe and Mail*, 31 July 1964; "U.S.–Canada Trade War Feared in Wake of Auto Export Row," *Globe and Mail*, 4 August 1964; Charlotte Yates, *From Plants to Politics: The Autoworkers Union in Postwar Canada* (Philadelphia, 1993), p. 118.
7. Canada, Cabinet Conclusions, 27 December 1962, RG 2, vol. 6193, 1962, NA; *Ward's Automotive Reports*, 12 November 1962 and 4 March 1963.
8. James Bickerton, *Nova Scotia, Ottawa and the Politics of Regional Development* (Toronto, 1990), pp. 142–3.
9. Bickerton, *Politics of Regional Development*, pp. 236–7.
10. Frank Sobey, "Industrial Estates 'prepared for risks,'" *Financial Times*, 15 October 1968.
11. "Volvo a 'Go' Company Similar to GM in U.S.," *Financial Post*, 23 February 1963; Eric Dennis, "Volvo Expanded Rapidly," *Chronicle-Herald* (Halifax), 22 February 1963. Lindholm and Norstedt, *The Volvo Report*, pp. 5–13.
12. "D.W. Samuel—A Man of Confidence," *Chronicle-Herald*, 12 June 1963; D.W. Samuel, interview by author, telephone and letter, Toronto, 20 May 2002.
13. In August 1945, Order-in-Council P.C. 5623 modified the 40 per cent content bracket

by raising the level to 15 000 units. This was intended to ease the way for Nash (later American) Motors, which planned to begin production in Canada. The order remained in effect until the 1965 tariff changes.

14. Samuel, interview by author, 20 May 2002.
15. Bickerton, *Politics of Regional Development*, pp. 140–1.
16. Bladen, *Royal Commission on the Automotive Industry*.
17. Anastakis, "Auto Pact," ch. 2.
18. Canada, Cabinet Conclusions, 27 December 1962, RG 2, vol. 6193, NA; *Ward's Automotive Reports*, 12 November 1962 and 4 March 1963.
19. "First Plant in Canada," *Chronicle-Herald*, 21 February 1963; "Changes in Tariff aid to company," *Chronicle-Herald*, 22 February 1963; Samuel, interview by author, 20 May 2002.
20. "Will Provide Building," *Chronicle-Herald*, 21 February 1963; Lauchie Chisholm, "Maritimes' 'New Sweden' Gulps its 'Second Wind,'" *Financial Post*, 15 June 1963.
21. Minutes of the IEL Executive Committee, 5 December 1962, 18 December 1962, 23 January 1963 and 11 February 1963, RG 55, Trade and Commerce, vol. 11, file 7, Nova Scotia Archives and Record Management [NSARM].
22. Minutes of the IEL Executive Committee, 18 December 1962 and 1 February 1963, RG 55, Trade and Commerce, vol. 11, file 7, NSARM; "Canadian Volvo Month Away, Green Workers Being Trained," *Financial Post*, 11 May 1963.
23. "Canadian Volvo Month Away," *Financial Post*, 11 May 1963.
24. "First in Dominion," *Chronicle-Herald*, 21 February 1963.
25. "200–300 Workers, Mostly Canadian, Will be Employed," *Chronicle-Herald*, 21 February 1963; Carlyle Dunbar, "What Volvo Bid Means to Maritimes," *Financial Post*, 23 February 1963.
26. "Mayor's Efforts in Getting Plant Are Praised," *Chronicle-Herald*, 11 April 1963.
27. "Why Volvo Went to Dartmouth," *Chronicle-Herald*, 11 June 1963.
28. Nova Scotia, Debates of the Legislative Assembly, 25 February 1963, pp. 174–5.
29. Editorial, "Surest Way," *Chronicle-Herald*, 22 February 1963.
30. "Why Volvo Went to Dartmouth," *Chronicle-Herald*, 11 June 1963.

31. "D.W. Samuel—A Man of Confidence," *Chronicle-Herald*, 11 June 1963.
32. "Volvo Has Broken the Trail," *Financial Post*, 29 June 1963; "N.S. firms to be offered Volvo parts production," *Chronicle-Herald*, 4 April 1963.
33. "Volvo Sales Manager Outlines Company Plans," *Chronicle-Herald*, 11 April 1963.
34. "N.S. firms to be offered Volvo Parts Production," *Chronicle-Herald*, 4 April 1963; "Volvo opens 'opportunity show' for N.S. producers," *Chronicle-Herald*, 11 April 1963.
35. Minutes of the IEL Executive Committee, 12 March 1963, RG 55, Trade and Commerce, vol. 11, file 7, NSARM.
36. Eric Dennis, "U.K. auto firms taking second look at Maritimes," *Chronicle-Herald*, 4 April 1963; Eric Dennis, "Volvo's Lead May Induce More Firms to Come to Canada," *Chronicle-Herald*, 22 February 1963.
37. "Canadian Volvo Month Away," *Financial Post*, 11 May 1963.
38. "Swedish Industrial Giant Gets Beachhead in Canada," *Financial Post*, 23 February 1963.
39. Chisholm, "Maritimes' 'New Sweden,'" *Financial Post*, 15 June 1963.
40. After 1965, however, Volvo was unable to ship cars from its Halifax plant due to tariff rules under the Auto Pact. See "Volvo, too, plan export of Canadian cars to U.S.," *Financial Post*, 21 December 1963.
41. "Second Company to Assemble Cars," *Financial Post*, 26 June 1965.
42. Lester Pearson, *Memoirs, Volume 3, 1957–1968* (Toronto, 1975); Lawrence Martin, *The Presidents and the Prime Ministers, Washington and Ottawa Face to Face: The Myth of Bilateral Bliss, 1867–1982* (Toronto, 1982) and J.L.G. Granatstein and Norman Hillmer, *For Better or For Worse: Canada and the United States to the 1990s* (Toronto, 1991).
43. Greg Donaghy, "A Continental Philosophy: Canada, the United States and the Negotiation of the Auto Pact, 1963–1965," *International Journal*, 52, 3 (Summer 1998); James F. Keeley, "Cast in Concrete for all Time? The Negotiation of the Auto Pact," *The Canadian Journal of Political Science* XVI, 2 (June 1983); and Anastakis, "Auto Pact."
44. Lyndon Watkins, "Monday Make or Break for Canadian Volvo," *Chronicle-Herald*, 15 January

1965; "Puts Volvo 'Fully in Trade Plan,'" *Chronicle-Herald*, 12 February 1965.

45. Dimitry Anastakis, "The Advent of an International Agreement: The Auto Pact at the GATT, 1964–1965," *International Journal* 55, 4 (Autumn 2000): 583–602.

46. K.W. Burke (Officer, Mechanical Transportation Branch) to C.D. Arthur, 18 August 1965, K.W. Burke to File, 19 August 1965 and K.W. Burke to File, 20 August 1965, all in RG 20, vol. 1826, 1022–17, part 3, Automotive Agreement Enquiries, August–December 1965, NA; "Facts Relating to Expansion of Automotive Industry in 1964 and 1965," Department of Industry, 8 October 1965, RG 20, vol. 1793, file Automotive Correspondence, NA; K.W. Burke, "Quarterly Report on the Auto Industry," 19 November 1965, RG 20, vol. 1775, file V.8001-260/A4, part 2, MTB, Auto Industry, 1965–1968, NA.

47. The exact nature of Big Three spending on plant and parts has never been disclosed by the corporations.

48. Minutes of IEL Executive Committee, 17 November 1965, RG 55, Trade and Commerce, vol. 12, file 6, NSARM.

49. "Volvo Disappointed, May Pull Out of Here," *Chronicle-Herald*, 17 January 1966; David Crane, "Kohler Kills Rumours about Volvo Pull-out," *Financial Post*, 22 January 1966; "Chances of Volvo Staying Brighten," "Volvo President, Mayor of Quebec Meet in Hotel" and "Nova Scotia Has Good Chance to Keep Volvo," *Chronicle-Herald*, 19 January 1966.

50. K. Kohler to G.I. Smith, 19 January 1968, RG 100, vol. 41, file 14.1, Trade and Industry, NSARM.

51. "Volvo Considers Shift to Halifax," *Chronicle-Herald*, 25 May 1966; Lyndon Watkins, "New 10 Year Agreement Signed by Volvo Plant," *Chronicle-Herald*, 1 June 1966; "Volvo Looks for Space," *Chronicle-Herald*, 15 April 1967; "Volvo plant nears single shift capacity," *Financial Post*, 5 October 1968.

52. K. Kohler to G.I. Smith, 19 January 1968, RG 100, vol. 41, file 14.1, Trade and Industry, NSARM; "Volvo boosts production in Nova Scotia," *Financial Post*, 2 November 1968.

53. Dean Salsman to George Mitchell, 9 July 1974, RG 55, Trade and Commerce, vol. 5, file Volvo, NSARM.

54. "Check-Up for Volvo," *Mail-Star* (Halifax), 9 September 1971.

55. Ove P.F. Lindblad (Volvo Canada) to Finlay MacDonald (IEL), 15 September 1971, RG 55, Trade and Commerce, vol. 5, file Volvo, NSARM.

56. Gunnar K.G. Jennegren (Volvo Canada) to George M. Mitchell, 13 December 1973, RG 55, Trade and Commerce, vol. 5, file Volvo, NSARM.

57. Anders Sandberg, "Missing the Road: Working Life at Volvo Nova Scotia," in Ake Sandberg, ed., *Enriching Production: Perspectives on Volvo's Uddevalla Plant as an Alternative to Lean Production* (Brookfield, US, 1995), p. 270.

58. Patricia Best, "Volvo Canada: Making it in Halifax," *Financial Post*, 2 August 1980.

59. Volvo Research Group, "The Volvo Story in Nova Scotia," *New Maritimes: A Regional Magazine of Culture and Politics*, VII, 5 (May/June 1989): 16–17.

60. At the Pier 9 site, Volvo was paying only 27 per cent of its annual municipal tax bill of $130 000. The new Bayer's Lake deal was similar. Sandberg reports that the company made profits of between $8–$12 million between 1984 and 1989. See Volvo Research Group, "The Volvo Story," p. 18 and Sandberg, "Missing the Road," p. 277.

61. Sandberg, "Missing the Road," p. 275.

62. Roger Taylor, "Volvo plant closure shocking but not unexpected," *Chronicle-Herald*, 15 September 1998.

63. Sandberg, "Missing the Road," p. 278.

64. Roger Taylor, "Volvo plant closure shocking but not unexpected," *Chronicle-Herald*, 15 September 1998.

65. By the early 1990s, Toyota and Honda were producing over 200 000 vehicles annually at their Ontario plants and employing over 3 000 workers yet did not have official Auto Pact status. Volvo, with less than 10 000 vehicles produced yearly and barely 200 workers, had Auto Pact status.

66. One Department of Industry official estimated that Auto Pact investment in the 1965–70 period was over $1 billion.

67. Kenneth Good and Skye Hughes, "Globalization and Diversification: Two Cases in Southern Africa," *African Affairs* 101, 402 (2002): 39–59.

68. Sandberg, "Missing the Road," p. 277.

4   From Louis Bélanger, "The Domestic Politics of Quebec's Quest for External Distinctiveness," in *Contemporary Quebec: Selected Readings and Commentaries,* eds. Michael D. Behiels and Matthew Hayday (Montréal: McGill-Queen's University Press, 2011) 761–77.

For more than 40 years now, the Quebec government has conducted a distinct diplomatic activity, taking advantage of all the room for manoeuvre given by the Canadian Constitution and using its political leverage inside the federation. The goal of this article is to examine the internal motivating factors for Quebec's international actions and, as it does, it attempts to respond to the following questions: To what can we attribute the specific character of Quebec's case with respect to other manifestations of international involvement by non-central governments? What are the most important international objectives pursued by Quebec? What methods and strategies are used in order to attain these objectives? Are these strategies proving to be effective; that is, are these objectives being attained?

Such an exercise could not be accomplished without taking into consideration the highly intersubjective nature of Quebec's international presence and status. In the first place, there would obviously be no call for truly international dealings on the part of Quebec if there were no foreign partners available to undertake such relations with its official representatives, sometimes at the highest levels. More importantly perhaps, Quebec's foreign policy makers, who are well aware of the situation, are primordially concerned by the interpretation that will be made outside Quebec of the ultimate purpose of this policy, and they integrate this information into their strategies. Therefore, Quebec's objectives of international assertion are adapted to different registers of meaning from which foreign actors would interpret its foreign policy behaviour. Thus, from the decolonization era of the 1960s to our current post-modern period, and depending on the sensitivity of their interlocutors, Quebec officials have tried to craft their interventions in order to be considered as representatives of a nation, a province,

a homeland, an economy, a people, a state. Similarly, Quebec's identity itself, on whose behalf this autonomous foreign policy is pursued, is the object of constant negotiation between the way in which Quebeckers perceive themselves and how this corresponds to the types of legitimate expression of identity emerging within the world order.[1]

AN IDENTITY-BASED PARADIPLOMACY

Recent works on the international involvement of non-central governments (NCGs) have shown the importance of distinguishing between two manifestations of this phenomenon, widely referred to as paradiplomacy.[2] On the one hand paradiplomacy is triggered by functional interests—that is, interests of local governments as agents of economic development and managers of the human and environmental resources of a given territory. In such cases, the development of paradiplomatic activities will generally be decentralized, strongly associated with specific transnational issues, and erratic.

On the other hand, some NCGs are pursuing a paradiplomacy in the name of identity-based interests. In those cases, the existence of a common identity and of a certain kind of "national interest" gives coherence and continuity to the involvement in international affairs, while subjecting it to the politics of identity and nation-building. [. . .]

A little comparative analysis will immediately highlight the fact that Quebec's paradiplomatic activity belongs to this second category. As a federated state, or simply as a member of the very large family of NCGs, Quebec seeks, by projecting its domestic jurisdictions onto the international scene, to defend its economic, environmental, and even social interests. But these functional imperatives explain only a small part of the Quebec government's international interventionism. And they certainly do not explain the political scope and significance acquired by Quebec paradiplomacy. As several authors have pointed out, Quebec's international action, in terms of its scope and continuity, is clearly distinct from that of other NCGs. Earl Fry notes:

> Quebec is the world's foremost proponent of subnational government activity in the international sphere. Until 1996 the government of Quebec had more offices opened overseas, more staff devoted to international activities, and more money appropriated for international pursuits than the nine other provinces combined. Even more surprisingly, Quebec spends more and has a larger international staff than all 50 US states *combined*.[3]

This situation was threatened in 1996 by reductions in the international affairs budget and the network of foreign diplomatic representation, but has since been partly re-established. Today, the Quebec government still maintains a network of 25 offices abroad, covering 20 countries and employing 239 people. The Ministry of International Relations budget is $98 million, to which should be added the portion of activities in the Departments of Immigration and of Industry and Commerce devoted to international programs.[4] In addition to this immediate measure of Quebec's international activity, its remarkable continuity must also be highlighted. In spite of certain fluctuations in its priorities, Quebec's paradiplomacy has been sustained for 40 years by an institutionalized and coherent policy that contrasts sharply with the instability and contingency that generally characterize similar experiments carried out elsewhere in the world.[5]

The two cases most similar to Quebec's from this viewpoint are those of Catalonia and Wallonia. Along with them Quebec belongs to a specific class of NCG, corresponding to what could be called, although rather clumsily, "stateless nations." Michael Keating notes this radical difference that the motivation for nation-building gives rise to in the area of paradiplomacy:

> In those cases where regions encapsulate a sense of distinct national identity and nation-building project, external projection is qualitatively different from those cases where it is motivated only by functional considerations. In the former, paradiplomacy is used in a highly political manner, either to prepare the ground for eventual independence, or as an element in stateless nation-building, a strategy to acquire as much as possible of the substance of national independence, without worrying too much about the formal status.[6]

DOCTRINE AND OBJECTIVES

In its 2001–2004 strategic plan, the Quebec Department of International Relations clearly states what are, in its view, the interests the government is pursuing on the international scene:

> The two major axes on which Quebec's international interventions are articulated since the early days of the Quiet Revolution are the continuous search for socio-economic progress as well as an always renewed will of affirmation of the Quebec culture and identity.[7]

First and foremost, this affirmation requires that the government's mere capacity to act at the international level be maintained and developed.[8] This linkage between international access and recognition and identity affirmation is key to the understanding of Quebec's paradiplomatic activity. Hence, we can say that Quebec's international politics consists of an effort to define the external contours of a distinct Quebec national identity. By distinct national identity, I do not mean only distinct from Canada as a whole. I am referring to the concept of "external distinctiveness" defined by Paul Kowert as the aspect of political identity that establishes how a political entity distinguishes itself from others, not only by its relative independence but also by the way in which it expresses its preferences, interests, goals, and so on by its external behaviour.[9]

Insofar as it is implicated, the government of Quebec is not only the vehicle for expression of a given Quebec identity, but one of the principal agents of the development of a very specific conception of what is or should be this identity. In return, it draws from this external recognition and identity its legitimacy as State as well as the legitimacy of its role in Quebec society. For this reason, the history of the development of Quebec international politics over the last 40 years cannot be disassociated from that of the consolidation of, broadly speaking, a "stateful," modern, secularized, and open Quebec identity, built in opposition to a stateless French-Canadian ethnicism, traditionalism, and Catholicism.

To illustrate this point, it may be useful to go back to the birth of Quebec paradiplomacy in the early 1960s. In fact, this period represents the birth of modern Quebec foreign policy, since the provincial government had few and scattered undertakings abroad before this date.[10] When Georges-Émile Lapalme, minister in the new government of Jean Lesage, went to Paris in 1960, his main objective was not primarily to obtain recognition from France of an international political or legal status for Quebec. Rather, this was suggested by his French counterparts. For him, it was more important to break with the traditional national identity of French Canada and entrench the Quebec identity in the universalist and modernist cultural shift—also

reflective of a vigorous nation-state—which André Malraux, De Gaulle's minister for Cultural Affairs, was advocating in France at the time.[11] Explaining his ambition succinctly, Lapalme stated that "the time has come to view the provincial state as a cultural phenomenon."[12] In this way, an initiative grew out of the desire to associate Quebec's national identity with the French cultural model, a desire that led to the establishment of a Quebec Delegation in Paris and to the signing of the first international agreements of co-operation with France. These were the acts on which Quebec's paradiplomacy was founded. Thus, France was not only, as a sovereign state, willing to establish high-level contacts in the interest of the Quebec government, but that action furthered France's own politics of identity-building, politics defended by Malraux to re-legitimize the role of the state in the early fifth Republic. We can also see that this initiative was not triggered by cultural functional interests: Lapalme was not interested in France's culture as such; he was interested in the cultural mission of an interventionist state.

Another founding moment of Quebec's quest for international recognition was the enunciation of the Gérin-Lajoie doctrine, named after the Lesage education minister who, in 1965, defined the principles on which the Quebec government's international policy was based. The doctrine founded the rationale, based on identity and not just constitutionality, for autonomous international action for Quebec. The legal argument, affirming the capacity of the Quebec government to manage its own foreign policy in fields relevant to its constitutional powers, has been re-affirmed recently under Chapter 11 of Bill 99, the current government's response to the Federal "clarity bill":

> The Quebec State is free to consent to be bound by any treaty, convention or international agreement in matters under its constitutional jurisdiction.

No treaty, convention or agreement in the areas under its Jurisdiction may be binding on the Quebec State unless the consent of the Quebec State to be bound has been formally expressed by the National Assembly or the Government, subject to the applicable legislative provisions.

The Quebec State may, in the areas under its jurisdiction, establish and maintain relations with foreign States and international organizations and ensure its representation outside Quebec.[13]

In the Gérin-Lajoie statement, this legal argument was juxtaposed with another—that is, the necessity for Quebec to be able to express itself on the international scene on any matter concerning its identity. In his famous 1965 speech before the consular corps, Gérin-Lajoie stated explicitly: "Quebec is more than just one federated state among others. It is the political instrument of a cultural group, distinct and unique in greater North America."[14] The relative consistency with which this dimension of the doctrine has been repeated by successive governments in Quebec is remarkable. Beyond some significant divergences in their constitutional programs, the main political parties in Quebec City have never really reconsidered the Quiet Revolution's reformulation of Quebec identity, but have rather worked to strengthen it. Of course, fluctuations have been observed in partisan orientations. As such, Parti Québécois (PQ) governments have tended to present their international action as the means for Quebec to have direct access to the international community, and they did so first as a "people" in the 1980s, then as a "modern nation" in the 1990s.[15] As for the Quebec Liberal Party governments, they have tended to include foreign policy in the more functional and transnational area of NCG foreign relations.[16]

However, differences between the two major parties are diminishing, especially due to the Liberal Party's increasing support for the Gérin-Lajoie doctrine. This evolution initially manifested itself in the form of electoral promises; for example, the 1998 Liberal election platform contained specific proposals with respect to international politics, whereas there were none in the 1994 platform. It then took a significant turn during recent reform of the party position on the political and constitutional future of Quebec. Indeed, the Quebec Liberal Party today demands, among other things, official recognition by Canada of Quebec's international personality, Quebec's right to speak for itself among international organizations in its fields of jurisdiction or areas related to its cultural uniqueness, and an increase in its relations with states and governments, sovereign or otherwise. It must be noted that it is primarily in the name of the full expression by Quebec of its identity that the Quebec Liberal Party puts forward these demands.[17]

Faced with these demands, the Canadian government has always refused to consider the possibility of recognizing Quebec as having an international personality. It has agreed to certain arrangements, but has refused to embark on a course of formalizing and institutionalizing a general framework governing Quebec's international action. The official position of the federal government when the Gérin-Lajoie doctrine emerged, and during Quebec's first steps on the international scene, is revealed in two ministerial statements.[18] In them, Ottawa expressed the opinion that the federal government is the only one constitutionally empowered to represent the federation in matters of foreign policy—that is, the only government with the authority to undertake international commitments, appoint ambassadors, and express itself during international conferences. On the latter point, which will be an important issue for decades to come, the federal government admitted the possibility of provincial participation at certain conferences related to their fields of jurisdiction, but only as members of the Canadian delegation, and according to the model adopted for Canada's participation in the UNESCO conferences. This interpretation of the Constitution, conferring a monopoly to the central government for conducting foreign affairs, was evidently contested by the Quebec government on the ground that nothing in the Constitution supports the federal interpretation.[19] It argues that the treaty-making power delegated by the Crown in 1947 was transferred to the executive power, which, in Canada, is exercised by federal and provincial governments, each sovereign in their area of competence.[20] As for the model provided by the mode of participation in the UNESCO conferences, it did not satisfy Quebec's demand to be able to express itself with a distinct voice.

Ever since, within this climate of legal ambiguity, the Quebec government has been seeking to make the most of any room to manoeuvre that its political weight gives it to build and reify the external distinctiveness of Quebec as state and nation. This places Quebec's international relations at the heart of a permanent strategic triangle. The government will seek to establish its foreign relations so as to satisfy both the requirements of its quest for recognition of identity and the expectations of its foreign partners, while fitting into the flexible, but nonetheless constraining, terms in which the Canadian government wishes to conduct its relations.

FORMS OF QUEBEC PARADIPLOMACY

International Conferences: From Francophonie to the Network on Cultural Diversity

If there is any means for Quebec to demonstrate its external distinctiveness, it is through participation in international conferences. Politically, Quebec benefitted greatly from its inclusion by France in the co-operation

networks that followed decolonization, where diplomatic patronage was a common practice. Thus, in 1968, at Gabon's invitation but France's suggestion, Quebec attended the meeting of the Conference of National Education Ministers (CONFÉMEN) in Libreville on its own behalf. Since then, la Francophonie has been the preferred battleground for the Quebec-Canada conflict over Quebec's international personality.

In 1971, a first compromise between Quebec and Ottawa enabled Quebec to get membership within the Agency for Cultural and Technical Cooperation (ACCT) as a "participating government," after this status became part of the Agency's charter. A second compromise was worked out in 1985, when the governments of Canada and Quebec agreed on a formula allowing Quebec to participate in the new Summits of Francophone Heads of State and Government. The 1985 agreement gave Quebec the same status as it had within the ACCT when co-operation and development issues were being examined during summits. In return, Quebec agreed to recognize the federal government's authority in international political and economic issues.[21] The result is a hybrid form of international participation for the Quebec government, which finds itself part of the Canadian delegations to the Organisation de la Francophonie, but able to speak for itself in many areas and to benefit from distinct identification. This is a formula resembling that adopted by some federal states and one that Quebec would like to see extended to other fora.

This compromise was negotiated at a time when the area of cultural and technical co-operation held a dominant place in the deliberations of the Francophone organization. However, already in the first few summits, the question of high politics became increasingly predominant, often bordering on official discussions. Quebec's initial reaction was to fear this trend, for it constituted a threat to become a marginal actor in the discussion and even a potential ground for the federal government to repudiate its initial commitment. Thus, the Liberal government was at the beginning of the 1990s openly opposed to both the creation of new permanent institutions by the Conference of Heads of States and Government as well as the extension of co-operative activities beyond sectors traditionally covered by the Agency.[22] Then, prior to the Cotonou Summit, during negotiations between Paris, Ottawa, Quebec, and Brussels over the reform of institutions, Quebec requested that the changes in structures not weaken Quebec's status, and publicly expressed its fears on the eve of the Ministerial Conference in Marrakech in December 1996.

It is interesting to note that not only did this evolution not bring about a calling into question of Quebec's participation in la Francophonie,[23] as may have been feared, but the 1999 Moncton Summit established that the status accorded to Quebec during summits would be expanded in order to cover all the ministerial meetings placed under the auspices of the Organisation de la Francophonie, which Ottawa had tried to challenge the year before.

Just as the Moncton Summit was being prepared, a new front opened up for Quebec—international conferences on cultural diversity. Canada is one of the major leaders of the international mobilization to encourage embedding the rights and obligations of states to protect national and minority cultures in international conventions, but has first objected to the Quebec government speaking on its own behalf in international forums on this question. The Canadian position was that on such questions the Quebec government should be content to participate in the Canadian delegation without being allowed to speak on its own behalf. Since this is a direct issue of Quebec identity, the present PQ government not only refused to participate in an international conference convened by the Canadian government in June 1998, but decided this was a matter for extending the

rights and status that it already enjoys in la Francophonie. The Quebec government thus adopted, in March 1999, an official statement demanding the federal government allow them to participate, within Canadian delegations but with freedom of speech, in the work of international organizations dealing with education, language, culture, and identity.[24] Although it refused to negotiate such a general framework, the federal government afterwards allowed the Quebec Minister of Culture and Communication to join, with freedom of expressing Quebec's own view, the Canadian delegation during annual meetings of the Network of Ministers of Culture, in which states that support defending the principle of cultural diversity participate.

Quebec's participation in international conferences clearly demonstrates the determining influence the identity factor exercises on the way Quebec conducts its international affairs. Indeed, it can be noted that when acting on behalf of Quebec culture—the least problematic element in defining a distinct Quebec identity—the government is better able to mobilize the political resources it needs to legitimize its international action and obtain concessions from the federal government. Furthermore, what is sought is clearly recognition of distinctiveness rather than defence of functional interests since, basically, Canada's and Quebec's positions on most of the issues involved, as in the case of cultural protectionism, are similar.

International Agreements: Legal Expression of a Distinct Identity

With the signing of the first co-operation agreements with France, the necessary governmental resources were mobilized to create an organization within the Quebec governmental apparatus responsible for its international policy. Ottawa's reaction to this process was very strong. When it learned in 1965 that the French and Quebec governments had negotiated an agreement on education whose scope extended well beyond this area since it was instituting a permanent Commission of Cooperation between the two states, the federal government hastened to insist that the document to be signed be covered by an official exchange of letters between Canada and France. This is in fact what occurred, but there was no mention of the France–Canada instrument in the France–Quebec agreement. The Quebec government quickly realized that this type of agreement would, in and of itself, allow it to assert its international personality. It was therefore decided to institutionalize the practice by designating the documents pertaining to an exchange of signatures between the Quebec government and a foreign public authority as "ententes," thereby instituting a practice of ratification and presenting these agreements as having autonomous legal value. This despite the fact that the federal government considers "ententes" to be synonymous with "understanding"—that is an instrument by which no legal obligations are created. And so, between 1964 and 2000, the Quebec government signed 497 of these ententes, of which 287 are still in force. Over half of these ententes signed by the Quebec government involve a government or governmental agency representing a sovereign state as a foreign partner.[25]

By involving itself in sectors of international co-operation such as social security or civil law where there is no doubt as to its domestic jurisdiction, the Quebec government seeks to negotiate ententes with sovereign governments signing co-operation agreements with Canada, to allow implementation of these agreements in Quebec. Thus, an important proportion of ententes signed with sovereign partners are in fact instruments extending treaties signed by Ottawa. But the Quebec government is cautious to undertake this type of action only if the partners respect its own rules of the game, which aim to conceal the Quebec instrument's relation of dependence with respect to the Canadian instrument.[26] For example, Quebec did not proceed with an entente on social security matters negotiated with Belgium due to the introduction of a clause into the treaty signed by the Canadian and Belgian parties qualifying the future entente with Quebec as an "administrative agreement" appended to the treaty.[27]

More recently, former Canadian Foreign Affairs Minister Axworthy intervened with France in 1997, calling for certain provisions in the Agreement on Judicial, Civil, and Commercial Cooperation negotiated by Paris and Quebec, which gave Quebec the status of "contracting party" and protesting the fact that the entente did not mention the 1996 judicial co-operation agreement in force between Ottawa and Paris. It should be noted, returning to the topic of bipartisan convergence, that on this occasion the National Assembly of Quebec unanimously adopted a motion calling for the federal government to end its objection to the implementation of this entente. The central argument developed by Quebec in this case was based on the uniqueness of the tradition of Quebec's civil law with respect to the rest of Canada, which gives it its own judicial personality. Due to this dispute over status, Quebec and France had not yet signed their negotiated entente.

The Paradiplomatic Apparatus

The existence inside the Quebec State of an actual "paradiplomatic service," complete with its own minister, a corps of officials specializing in international affairs, and a network of foreign representatives, undoubtedly constitutes an expression of Quebec's external identity. As Hocking has noted, the mostly fragmented nature of the international activity of NCGs clearly demonstrates that they are responding to functional interests and denotes the absence of a coherently articulated national interest.[28] However, in Quebec's case, the existence of a doctrine is accompanied by the institutionalization of a true "microdiplomacy," which not only goes hand in hand with Quebec's distinctive international identity, but also participates in its reification.

Free from the traditional French-Canadian identity, but not yet completely in line with the modern version of Quebec identity, the bureaucratic structure administering Quebec's external relations in the early 1960s actually defined its area of intervention as indistinctly Canadian and international. For example, the mandate of the Department of Cultural Affairs' early "Service du Canada français d'outre-frontières" was to build bridges with Francophones throughout North America. This corresponded to a conception of Quebec identity as the fatherland of all North Americans of French-Canadian descent. The creation in 1967 of the new Department of Intergovernmental Affairs signalled a desire to coordinate this type of sectorial activity, but based on a conception of the external that included both government foreign relations and federal-provincial affairs. The external distinctiveness was still very "provincial." It was not until 1974 that a real foreign policy structure, the one of a state, took shape within this department, owing to the repatriation of the Department of Education and the Department of Cultural Affairs' services of external co-operation. In addition to creating the "Direction générale de la coopération internationale" (International Cooperation Branch) responsible for sector programs, the "Direction générale des relations internationales" (International Relations Branch) was also created and organized into directorates, each one responsible for a region of the world. It is also the 1974 Law on the Ministry of Intergovernmental Affairs that centralized the authority to coordinate the foreign relations of the government.

However, it took until 1985 for the PQ government to create a bona fide Department of International Relations, which would undergo various transformations in subsequent years under the Liberals and the PQ, first adding external commerce and immigration to its responsibilities and then withdrawing them. Nevertheless, from this point forward, the Quebec government clearly assumed that international affairs constituted one of its legitimate fields of intervention and that its foreign policy should be conducted in a structured manner. To fulfill this task, and to communicate the national interest that would guide its activity, Minister Bernard Landry invited Quebec civil society to a "Sommet du Québec dans le monde" (Quebec in the World Summit). This led to the writing of an initial statement of international policy, a long document of 204 pages in which is stated in detail, region by region, sector by sector, the desire to make the state of Quebec, together with the people, into a vehicle of privileged access for Quebeckers to the concert of nations: "An actor on the international scene, Quebec wishes to assume its role as a reputable interlocutor with regards to the international community and promote the interests of its citizens as well as those of the community according to the established rules."[29]

Far from calling into question the necessity of a coherent international policy for Quebec, the federalist Liberals consolidated this approach during their last sojourn in office (1985–1994). They did this by concentrating even more responsibilities within the department and giving them an even longer foreign policy statement than the previous one, which differentiated itself in terms of the priority given to questions of low politics, but maintained an integrated governmental approach. In fact, it is under the Liberals that the department has reached a historical peak in allowed budget, with more than $126 million in 1992–1993. This number has to be compared to the meagre $80 million that was budgeted by the sovereignist PQ government for 1997–1998, after the implementation of the drastic cuts decided in 1996.[30]

Obviously, the Quebec diplomatic apparatus would be quite incomplete without its network of foreign representatives. The establishment of this network also goes hand in hand with the strengthening of modern Quebec identity. When Lesage took power in 1960, the Quebec government had only one office in New York. However, the General Delegations in Paris and London opened in 1961 and 1962, and by 1993 the government was maintaining 28 General Delegations, Delegations, and offices, employing over 430 people all over the world. Since then, budget reductions have severely reduced Quebec's foreign outreach capacity. However, here again, the most important partners from the perspective of the reification of Quebec's international personality would be saved. For example, the delegation-general in Paris, the only one in the network with special quasi-ambassadorial status, has roughly maintained its staff at 72 employees. Similarly, the government maintains the bureau of tourism that it opened in Washington, DC, in 1978, which it uses to circumvent federal government rules aiming to prevent its provincial government representatives from residing permanently or regularly in the US capital.[31] Moreover, new representations were recently created in Barcelona and Munich, close to the governments of the non-sovereign states of Catalonia and Bavaria, which are very active in matters of identity-based paradiplomacy and with whom, for this reason, the Quebec government shares a community of interests and views.

QUEBEC IDENTITY AND CANADIAN FOREIGN POLICY

Despite the important variations in resources it has devoted to it, the Quebec government maintained over the past 40 years a paradiplomatic activity that remains remarkable by its scope and continuity. It did so in the name of the promotion of a distinct political identity and on the basis of a legal doctrine that is opposed by the Canadian central government.

If Quebecers have tended to support the initiatives of their provincial government on the international scene and have come to see Quebec as a legitimate representative of their external identity, it is in good part because Canada has increasingly resisted recognition of this identity as politically legitimate and has conducted its foreign policy accordingly. Things could have evolved differently. At the same time as the Gérin-Lajoie doctrine was being developed, then–Prime Minister Lester B. Pearson accepted the idea that Quebec was, within Canada, the possessor of a distinct identity: "Even though Quebec is a province within the national Confederation, it is more than a province, in the sense that it is the homeland of a people: it clearly constitutes a nation within a nation."[32] In fact, not only did the federal government at the time recognize to a greater extent the existence of a collective Quebec identity than those who would follow them, but as Louis Balthazar explains, Canadian foreign policy at the time was itself quite fragile, still searching for its own basis of identity, and first reacted toward the Quebec issue according to "the Canadian tradition of conciliation, compromise and internationalism."[33] And, as showed by some significant experiences like Quebec's participation in the Francophonie Summit and organizations, there are practicable solutions to integrate in Canadian foreign policy an external expression of Quebec identity.

However, with the arrival in 1968 of Pierre Trudeau at the head of government, any possibility of making room for Quebec's identity in Canadian foreign policy was excluded. Indeed, for Trudeau, the necessary response in the face of Quebec's demands was not to allow Quebec's identity to be expressed within Canada, but to couch it in a new bilingual and multicultural national concept that would lead to a negation of Quebec's uniqueness. Moreover, Trudeau's Canadian vision was centralist while, at the same time, insisting on the principle of the equality of provinces. This approach is known to have profoundly marked Canadian identity. It became a huge obstacle to the incorporation of Quebec in Canadian foreign policy, at least in a manner that would allow Quebec to express its identity. Moreover, it is significant that Quebec obtained the federal consent that allows it to participate today in the Francophone Summit, thanks to the arrival in power of Brian Mulroney in 1984, but before the collapse of Meech, when it still seemed possible to test Trudeau's heritage—which is, it seems, no longer the case today.

Even as a province like any other, Quebec is kept at a distance from the processes of formulating or managing Canadian foreign policy, except for a few isolated cases such as the implementation of treaties with respect to human rights or ad hoc consultation mechanisms during negotiation of commercial agreements.[34] In general, Canadian foreign policy is formulated and conducted as if Canada were not a federation. In the present context of globalization, and while the Canadian government prides itself on having democratized its foreign policy, this way of doing things makes less and less sense. And it risks appearing more and more anachronistic, since other industrialized countries with federal or quasi-federal systems, like Belgium, Germany, Spain, and even the very conservative Switzerland, have recently adapted their institutions in order to give their respective NCGs rights to participate in foreign-policy making.[35]

The consolidation of a coherent paradiplomacy in Quebec thus accompanies an increase in the practical incompatibility of finding ways to express Canadian and Quebec identities within the same foreign policy. This is particularly evident in the above-mentioned case of the emergence of a new international agenda surrounding the notion of cultural diversity. Although the federal government wishes to champion this cause, it will never be able to appear as a legitimate defender of Quebec's interests as long as its official foreign policy, under its chapter entitled "Canadian values and culture," ignores the existence of a Quebec culture.[36] Moreover, it cannot efficiently articulate a discourse in favour of cultural diversity within the international community while at the same time refusing Quebec the right to become a partner in the process.

* * *

I have tried here to describe how Quebec paradiplomatic activity obeys motives that are firmly rooted in the province's politics of identity. This does not mean that the Quebec government's involvement on the international scene is simply an expression of a fixed national identity. Paradiplomacy, in the Quebec case, has been both an external reflection of the evolution of Québécois identity and a means for the government to defend its own version of what this identity should be. Over the past 40 years, though, the view that Quebec should benefit from a distinct international presence has become consensual in Quebec society. This has provided the government with the political support it needed to confront its federal counterpart's principle of the indivisibility of foreign policy.

Domestic politics, however, covers only one side of the equation. As the other contributions to this issue serve to highlight, Quebec's quest for external distinctiveness and Ottawa's efforts to contain it are highly dependent on the international environment. From one region or period to the other, the sensitivity of foreign interlocutors to paradiplomacy will vary enormously.[37] In this respect, the last decade of the post–Cold War climate of suspicion against any claims of identity, which were readily associated with violent demonstrations of nationalism, was not a favourable one for the conduct of identity-based paradiplomacy. Today the tide may be changing. In a context where new virtues are being found in diversity and the external and internal autonomy of national minorities in countries close to Canada like Belgium, Spain, and the United Kingdom, Ottawa's resistance to recognizing the international role Quebec already plays risks appearing increasingly anachronistic. This would only serve to further justify the pursuit of an autonomous foreign policy for Quebec.

NOTES

1. Louis Bélanger, "L'espace international de l'Etat québécois dans l'après-guerre froide: vers une compression?," in Alain G. Gagnon and Alain Noël, eds, *L'espace québécois* (Montréal: Québec/Amérique, 1995), 90–2.

2. See Francisco Aldecoa and Michael Keating, eds, *Paradiplomacy in Action: The Foreign Relations of Subnational Governments* (Portland, OR: Frank Cass Publishers, 1999) and the special issue, "Les relations internationales des régions en Europe," *Études internationales* 30 (December 1999), edited by Jacques Palard. The concept of *paradiplomacy* was forged by Ivo D. Duchacek in *The Territorial Dimension of Politics: Within, Among, and Across Nations* (Boulder, CO: Westview Press, 1986).

3. Earl H. Fry, *The Expanding Role of State and Local Governments in U.S. Foreign Affairs* (New York: Council on Foreign Relations Press, 1998), 77.

4. Ministère des Relations internationales, *Rapport annuel 1999–2000* (Québec: Ministère des Relations internationales, 2000), 57, 61.

5. Brian Hocking, "Patrolling the 'Frontier': Globalization, Localization and the 'Actorness' of Non-central Governments," in Aldecoa and Keating, 32–5.

6. Michael Keating, "Regions and International Affairs: Motives, Opportunities and Strategies," in Aldecoa and Keating, 13.

7. Ministère des Relations internationales, *Le Québec dans un ensemble international en mutation: Plan stratégique 2001–2004* (Québec: Ministère des Relations internationales, 2001), 27. My translation.

8. See ibid., 30–1.

9. Paul Kowert, "The Three Faces of Identity," in Glenn Chafetz, Michael Spirtas, and Benjamin Frankel, eds, *The Origins of National Interests*, (Portland, OR: Frank Cass Publishers, 1999), 1–34.

10. See Louise Beaudoin, "Origines et développement du rôle international du gouvernement du Québec," in Paul Painchaud, ed., *Le Canada et le Quebec sur la scene internationale* (Québec/Montréal: Centre québécois de relations internationales/les Presses de l'Université du Québec, 1977), 441–70.

11. Maurice Riel, "Témoignage de Maurice Riel," in Jean-François Léonard, ed., *Georges-Émile Lapalme* (Sillery: Presses de l'Université du Québec, 1988), 205–9.

12. Marcel Fournier, "G.-É. Lapalme: culture et politique," in *Georges-Émile Lapalme*, 164.

13. National Assembly, *Bill 99. An Act respecting the exercise of the fundamental rights and prerogatives of the Québec people and the Québec State* (Québec: Québec Official Publisher, 2000), 5.

14. Paul-Gérin Lajoie, "Allocution prononcée devant les membres du corps consulaire de Montréal le 12 avril 1965," in *Le Québec duns le monde: Textes et documents I* (Sainte-Foy: Association Québec dans le monde, 1990), 101–6.

15. Gouvernement du Québec, *Le Quebec dans le monde ou le défi de l'interdépendance: Énoncé de politique de relations internationales* (Québec: Ministère des Relations internationales, 1985). Bernard Landry, *Les relations internationales du Québec: Refléter notre réalité. Notes for an address by Bernard Landry, Deputy Premier, Minister of International Affairs, Immigration and Cultural Communities, Minister responsible for la Francophonie,* Montreal, 14 December 1994, 4. See also Ministère des Relations internationales, *Le Québec dans un ensemble international en mutation. Plan stratégique 2001–2004* (Québec: Ministère des Relations internationales, 2001), 28–9.

16. Gouvernement du Québec, *Le monde pour horizon. Le Québec et l'interdépendance: éléments d'une politique d'affaires internationales* (Québec: Ministère des Affaires internationales, 1991), 11.

17. Comité spécial du Parti Libéral du Quebec sur l'avenir politique et constitutionnel de la société québécoise, *Le choix du Québec: Affirmation, autonomie et leadership. Rapport préliminaire* (Québec: Parti libéral du Quebec, 2001), 25–30.

18. Paul Martin, *Fédéralisme et relations internationales* (Ottawa: Imprimeur de la Reine, 1968). Mitchell Sharp, *Fédéralisme et conférences internationales sur l'éducation* (Ottawa: Imprimeur de la Reine, 1968).

19. Ministère des Affaires intergouvernementales, *Document de travail sur les relations avec l'étranger.* Notes préparées par la délégation du Québec au Comité permanent des fonctionnaires sur la constitution, Québec, 5 February 1969.

20. See Ivan Bernier, *International Legal Aspects of Federalism* (London: Longman, 1973), 55–57.

21. Jacques-Yvan Morin, Francis Rigaldies, and Daniel Turp, *Droit international public: Notes et documents. Tome II: Documents d'intérêt canadien et québécois* (Montréal: Éditions Thémis, 1992), 519.

22. Gouvernement du Québec, *Le monde pour horizon. Le Québec et l'interdépendance: éléments d'une politique d'affaires internationales* (Québec: Ministère des Affaires internationales, 1991).

23. Louis Bélanger, "Les enjeux actuels de la participation du Québec a la francophonie multilatérale: de la paradiplomatie à la protodiplomatie," *Politique et société* 16 (1997): 39–59.

24. Gouvernement du Quebec, *Déclaration du gouvernement du Québec concernant la participation aux forums internationaux trairant d'éducation, de langue, de culture et d'identité* (Québec: Ministère des Relations internationales, 24 March 1999).

25. André Samson, "La pratique et les revendications québécoises en matière de conclusion d'ententes internationales," communication présentée devant le 1er congrès de la Société québécoise de droit international, Québec, Université Laval, 17 May 1984, 10–11; Anne-Marie Jacomy-Millette, "Rapport canadien," *Revue belge de droit international* 17 (1983): 79. Ministère des Relations internationales, Guide de la pratique des relations internationales du Québec (Québec: Ministère des Relations internationales, 2000), 82. Data transmitted by the Ministry of International Relations Director of Legal Affairs, 12 February 2001. Louis Bélanger, "L'espace international de l'État québécois dans l'après-guerre froide: vers une compression?," in Alain G. Gagnon and Alain Noël, eds, *L'espace québécois* (Montréal: Québec/Amérique, 1995), 92–5.

26. There are few exceptions to this practice. Two notable cases are social security ententes signed with the United States and Italy.

27. Francois Crépeau, "Les obligations internationales d'un Québec souverain en matière d'immigration," in *Exposés et études. Volume 1: Les attributs d'un Québec souverain* (Québec: Assemblée nationale du Québec, Commission d'Étude des questions afférentes à l'accession à la souveraineté, 1992), 120.

28. Brian Hocking, "Patrolling the 'Frontier,'" in Aldecoa and Keating, 33.

29. Gouvernement du Québec, *Le Québec dans le monde ou le défi de l'interdépendance. Énoncé de politique de relations internationales* (Québec: Ministère des Relations internationales, 1985), 43. Our translation.

30. Gouvernement du Québec, *Le monde pour horizon. Le Québec et l'interdépendance: éléments d'une politique d'affaires internationales* (Québec: Ministère des Affaires internationales, 1991), 17–21. For FY 1992–1993. Data provided by the Department of International Relations.

31. External Affairs Canada, *Federal–Provincial Relations: Operational Framework* (Ottawa: External Affairs Canada, January 1989), 26–9; Jean-François Lisée, *Dans l'oeil de l'aigle: Washington face au Québec* (Montréal: Boréal, 1990), 307–12.

32. Kenneth McRoberts, "Les perceptions canadiennes-anglaises du Québec," in Alain-G. Gagnon, ed., *Québec: État et Société* (Montréal: Québec/Amérique, 1994), 112.

33. Louis Balthazar, "The Quebec Experience: Success or Failure?," in Aldecoa and Keating.

34. Daniel Turp, "Le comité permanent fédéral-provincial-territorial des fonctionnaires chargés des droits de la personne et sa participation à la mise en oeuvre des traités," *Annuaire canadien des droits de la personne* (1984–1985): 77–136. Douglas M. Brown, "The Evolving Role of the Provinces in Canada-U.S. Trade Relations," in Douglas M. Brown and Earl H. Fry, eds, *States and Provinces in the International Economy* (Berkeley, CA: Institute of Governmental Studies Press, 1993), 93–144.

35. Réjean Pelletier, "Le Québec au niveau international: l'exemple suisse," *Le Devoir,* 6 July 2001, A6.

36. Government of Canada, *Canada in the World. Government Statement* (Ottawa: Public Works and Government Services Canada, 1995), 34–9.

37. Louis Bélanger, "The Changing World Order and Quebec's International Relations: An Analysis of Two Salient Environments," in Michael J. Tucker, Raymond B. Blake, and P.E. Bryden, eds, *Canada and the New World Order: Facing the New Millennium* (Toronto: Irwin Publishing, 2000), 163–84.